The Urban Impacts of Federal Policies

JOHNS HOPKINS STUDIES IN URBAN AFFAIRS

CENTER FOR METROPOLITAN PLANNING AND RESEARCH
THE JOHNS HOPKINS UNIVERSITY

David Harvey, *Social Justice and the City*
Ann L. Strong, *Private Property and the Public Interest: The Brandywine Experience*
Alan D. Anderson, *The Origin and Resolution of an Urban Crisis: Baltimore, 1890–1930*
James M. Rubenstein, *The French New Towns*
Malcolm Getz, *The Economics of the Urban Fire Department*
Ann L. Strong, *Land Banking: European Reality, American Prospect*
Jon C. Teaford, *City and Suburb: The Political Fragmentation of Metropolitan America, 1850–1970*
Norman J. Glickman, ed., *The Urban Impacts of Federal Policies*

THE
URBAN IMPACTS
OF
FEDERAL POLICIES

Edited by

NORMAN J. GLICKMAN

for the U.S. Department of Housing and Urban Development

THE JOHNS HOPKINS UNIVERSITY PRESS

BALTIMORE AND LONDON

Manufactured in the United States of America

The Johns Hopkins University Press, Baltimore, Maryland 21218
The Johns Hopkins Press Ltd., London

Library of Congress Catalog Number 79-2368

ISBN 0-8018-2292-0 hardcover
ISBN 0-8018-2299-8 paperback

Library of Congress Cataloging in Publication data
will be found on the last printed page of this book.

The views expressed in these papers are those of the authors and do not represent official views of the agencies for which they work.

Contents

Foreword

Would we have built the interstate highway system had we known about the additional costs—the costs of providing schools, streets, parks, and sewers—the newly reachable areas, and the loss of tax base to central cities? Surely, yes. But we would have designed the system so as to reduce the negative urban impacts. Unfortunately, negative urban impacts were not explicitly and carefully considered during the decision-making process.

Now, for the first time, using a predictor called urban impact analysis, we can begin to anticipate the total impact of federal programs on cities. In what I believe may be the decade's most important contribution to urban research and planning, the President now requires that an urban impact analysis be done on each major policy initiative.

Urban impact analysis is not additional theory. Instead, it applies existing tools and developing methodologies to predict the direction of impacts on cities, suburbs, and nonmetropolitan units. Using it, policy-makers will be able to consider the effects of a program before deciding on its desirability. It may be that some programs will be rejected because the analysis indicates that the costs are too high. In cases in which other considerations outweigh the negative impacts, it will be possible to plan for and minimize the resulting problems.

Urban impact analysis is to be applied to *all* major initiatives, not just those with an urban focus. Clearly, welfare and energy programs, along with many others, must be included because they all have differential effects on cities, suburbs, and nonmetropolitan areas. Clearly, too, we must look not just at new programs but at programs already in place. The reasons are obvious: we must ensure that federal policy does what it is intended to do and that negative side effects are lessened.

I would like to applaud the foresight and good sense of Katharine Lyall, Deputy Assistant Secretary for Economic Affairs in the Office of Policy Development and Research, for initiating urban impact analysis within the U.S. Department of Housing and Urban Development and developing a unit with the capacity to do high quality work. David Puryear, Director of the

Economic Development and Public Finance Division within her office, has had direct supervisory responsibility for the unit; he too deserves praise for the fine work produced by his staff.

DONNA E. SHALALA
Assistant Secretary for Policy Development and Research

Acknowledgments

The Urban Impacts of Federal Policies, a conference held in Washington, D.C., on February 8 and 9, 1979, and this volume, which evolved from it, required the skill and hard work of several people. The conference was jointly sponsored by the U.S. Department of Housing and Urban Development's Office of Policy Development and Research (HUD/PD&R) and The Johns Hopkins University's Metropolitan Center for Planning and Research. The Metro Center staff, under the direction of Dr. Jack Fisher, provided an ideal institutional arrangement and made the conference run efficiently. In particular, I thank Dolores Sullivan for her hard work in making the preparations that resulted in a smoothly flowing two days. Following the conference, Diane Richey made an enormous contribution toward putting this book in order through her liaison work among the thirty-six authors, The Johns Hopkins University Press, and myself.

At HUD, several colleagues were crucial to this endeavor. Assistant Secretary Donna E. Shalala gave encouragement and support for all of PD&R's efforts in urban impact analysis, participated in two of the conference sessions, and kindly wrote the Foreword to this volume. Her enthusiasm for urban impact analysis research and her overall leadership at PD&R created a first-rate intellectual environment in which to organize this project.

David L. Puryear, then Director of the Division of Economic Development and Public Finance, provided early guidance on the parameters of the conference, suggested potential participants, and in addition, co-authored Chapter 19. His support was a crucial element in the success of the conference.

Elizabeth Dahl, James Greenfield, Mark Miller, and Dan Robinson aided me with editing and proofreading efforts in the spring and summer of 1979. Without their help, the task of publishing this volume so quickly would not have been possible.

Finally, I would like to thank Katharine C. Lyall, who served as Deputy Assistant Secretary for Economic Affairs at the time of the conference.

Katharine Lyall possesses intellectual strength, quickly grasps the general nature and specific aspects of a research problem, and is able to write and speak with great clarity and vision. Her stewardship of the Office of Economic Affairs from 1977 to 1979 and her solid support for this conference volume were extremely important.

NORMAN J. GLICKMAN
Washington, D.C.
August, 1979

Editor's Introduction

WHY URBAN IMPACT ANALYSIS?

This volume contains twenty-five papers concerning impacts of federal policies on urban areas, a subject that is important in terms of both the analysis of public policy as it relates to cities and the study of urban change itself. The substantial growth of Federal and other government activity in the past four decades makes the study and full understanding of the spatial effects of federal programs more appropriate than ever. Little previous research has touched on this subject in any depth.

Collectively, the chapters in this book make important contributions to discussions of urban public policy in several ways. First, as noted, they focus on the impacts of federal policy in an explicitly spatial framework. Understanding the effects of federal policies on cities thus provides a better understanding of the urban development process.

Second, each chapter helps build a methodological framework for urban impact analysis (UIA), a new initiative under President Carter's National Urban Policy that requires federal executive agencies to estimate in advance the absolute and differential effects of some of their new programs (including expenditures and regulations) on various types of jurisdictions. Since this is a new government undertaking, few guides for carrying out UIAs exist. Therefore, both government and academic analysts should benefit from the insights collected here.

Third, this volume discusses a wide variety of federal policies, including defense spending, tax and transfer policy, housing and transportation programs, health care, energy and the environment, and intergovernmental relations. Readers will find the individual chapters on specific policies—with their unique urban focus—of interest in supplementing more traditional views of those subjects.

Fourth, the papers are written from a variety of disciplines. Although many of the authors are economists, the volume contains contributions from analysts with backgrounds in political science, architecture, city planning, regional science, sociology, engineering, social work, and social psychology. In addition, the authors come from universities, private firms, nonprofit research institutes, and Federal and local governments. Therefore, a diverse mix of talents is represented here. It is clear that UIAs require a multidisciplinary approach.

THE PAPERS

Overviews of urban impact analysis

The volume is organized in six parts. Part 1 provides the reader with an overview of some of the basic issues underlying urban impact analysis. Norman Glickman's opening chapter provides a review of several methodological and policy issues in this emerging area of inquiry and makes a set of recommendations for future development of the field. Among the issues that he discusses are (1) the time frame and timing of UIAs, (2) impact types (direct vs. indirect, absolute vs. differential, quantitative vs. qualitative, etc.), (3) spatial units and variables to be used, (4) the role of interpersonal equity considerations, (5) evaluation criteria, (6) the use of analytic models, (7) data problems, and (8) substitution (i.e., whether federal expenditures merely replace local or private funds that would have been spent anyway). Glickman notes some of the problems inherent in extending traditionally aspatial social science methodologies to UIAs and suggests ways of overcoming them. He further argues that present governmental UIA efforts are misdirected and that greater resources, a broadening of the types of programs to be studied, and public scrutiny are needed.

The second chapter, by Lester Salamon and John Helmer, provides an "insiders" view of the UIA process from the perspective of the Office of Management and Budget, the agency that has had primary responsibility for formulating guidelines for the UIA progress within the federal executive branch. The authors provide important insights into the political and institutional aspects of the Federal government's attempt to undertake UIAs and compare UIA efforts to previous "impact statement" exercises, such as environmental impact statements (EIS).

Georges Vernez's paper (Chapter 3) employs data on federal expenditures collected by the Community Services Administration (CSA) to give an overview of the spatial distribution of the federal budget. (Later, in Chapter 5, Thomas Anton uses the same data set for further analysis.) Vernez examines the distribution of federal outlays among cities with a population of 50,000 or more and shows how this distribution varied among programs in 1970 and 1976. He also observes the destination of outlays among Census regions and to cities of various types. Vernez shows that the distribution of federal outlays, in aggregate, is responsive to the spatial distribution of the population and economic activity; that is, federal outlays to cities are concentrated in the fast-growing Southern and West Coast regions and interregional disparities of federal outlays have increased between 1970 and 1976, primarily because of shifts in defense spending. He also demonstrates that the federal budget is "slightly 'pro-city' " in that a larger percentage of the budget goes to cities than their percentage of the population warrants.

Ann Markusen begins her critique of UIA in Chapter 4 by tracing the important differences between UIA and EIS with respect to scope, structure, authorship, and accountability. Fundamentally, her view is that UIAs subtly shift the object of research from private sector behavior and outcomes to the public sector since the focus of urban impact analysis is often the unintended consequence of government actions alone. She argues that the impacts of private actions on cities should be analyzed in addition to those of the Federal government. Markusen suggests several alternatives to the present policy structure, some of which coincide with those proposed by Glickman in Chapter 1.

Data and methodological issues

Part 2 (Chapters 5 through 8) considers some data and methodological issues in urban impact analysis in greater detail. Thomas Anton (Chapter 5) and Roger Bolton (Chapter 6) deal primarily with the data problems noted by some of the authors in Part 1. Anton digs deeply into federal outlays data (introduced by Vernez in Chapter 3), traces the spatial distribution of large portions of federal budget outlays from 1971 to 1977, and outlines methods for making the CSA data set more useful to analysts. He shows that for certain federal programs and functions, county-level analysis can now be undertaken. For other programs, however, city-specific data are not yet available in an accurate and usable form; this is particularly true of defense Department data.

Roger Bolton's essay (Chapter 6) on defense spending deepens Anton's discussion of DOD-related data problems. Bolton argues that defense procurement data (especially on subcontracts) are relatively weak in their spatial detail, although a new DOD data series will reduce this problem in the future. However, Bolton's paper goes far beyond data problems, speaking to issues involving worker vulnerability to base closings; the temporal pattern of demand in a region resulting from a change in defense spending; direct, indirect, and supply effects; the use of regional models (such as input-output and econometric models) in examining defense policy; and the possibility of reusing the physical capital of abandoned bases. In doing so, he employs some of the categories of urban impact "issues" defined in Chapter 1.

Matthew Edel's main focus (Chapter 7) is on the conceptual problem of distinguishing impacts of federal policy on "places" from those on "people." Concerned that UIAs will mean that jurisdictional or spatial emphases will replace, rather than supplement, attention to disadvantaged population groups, Edel examines the results of using population groups instead of places as the object of policy. In this regard, he discusses two important issues. First, the "ecological fallacy" (the attribution of the average characteristics of a place to its individuals) is shown to result in misleading policy prescriptions. Edel gives an example from poverty policy: since not all residents of poverty areas are poor, and since not all poor people live in poverty areas, targeting a poverty program to areas rather than to individuals will not efficiently target funds.

Second, Edel considers the problem of "capitalization" with regard to UIAs. That is, the benefit of programs designed by area may be captured by landowners or those who control other immobile resources, rather than other residents. A program that makes a neighborhood more attractive will attract mobile resources (such as households and labor), drive up land prices, and thus benefit landowners. This is an important consideration in neighborhood-oriented programs that may lead to the displacement of existing residents (an issue also discussed by Greenberg, Leven, and Little in Chapter 13). After viewing some of the advantages of a spatial focus, Edel concludes that such attention is too restrictive, and he proposes that UIAs be required to consider both spatial and population-group definitions of costs and benefits.

Part 2 concludes with another methodological exercise: the use of an empirical model in urban impact studies. Kenneth Ballard, Norman Glickman, and Robert Wendling employ an 11,000-equation multiregion econometric model of the United States to measure the impacts of the U.S. Department of Housing and Urban Development (HUD) budget and a (hypothetical) redistribution of Federal government grants-in-aid on regions. This model, based upon regression analysis, shows considerable flexibility in analyzing the macroeconomic spatial effects of federal programs.

Income transfer programs
    Part 3 is the first of four parts of the book that look at the direct and indirect urban impacts of federal policies in detail. Here, the focus in on income transfer programs: welfare reform (Chapter 9), Section 8 rental assistance (Chapter 10), national health insurance (Chapter 11), and wage subsidies and other manpower policies (Chapter 12).

Sheldon Danziger, Robert Haveman, Eugene Smolensky, and Karl Taeuber examine President Carter's 1977 welfare reform proposal (called the Program for Better Jobs and Income [PBJI]) in terms of its impact on both people and places. The authors find that the PBJI would not have had large urban impacts but would, overall, have had a small, ameliorative effect on some urban problems. Had PBJI been enacted, it would have reduced the incidence of poverty and concentrated this reduction in areas with low per capita income and high preprogram incidence of poverty; reduced income disparities among persons within and among urban areas; reinforced current trends in relative regional growth and, hence, favored the fast-growing, relatively poor Sunbelt region over the high income but relatively slow-growing Snowbelt region. It would have distributed Public Service Employment jobs toward urban areas with low per capital income and high levels of poverty but would have failed to target these jobs in high unemployment areas. Finally it would have concentrated fiscal relief on those states now making relatively high welfare payments to relatively large numbers of recipients. The authors employ a large-scale microsimulation model to derive these results.

Chapter 10 concerns HUD's Section 8 Housing Assistance program, which provides rental supplements to low income families. In this chapter, David Rasmussen employs Section 8 program information as well as experimental data from the Experimental Housing Alliance Program (a large-scale housing allowance experiment involving both supply and demand side components) administered by HUD beginning in 1970. Rasmussen notes two general impacts of Section 8. First, he considers the effect on the housing stock from the building of new units and the upgrading of older ones; in turn, neighborhood quality and fiscal condition of local governments are also affected. Second, there are (more important) effects stemming from the financial assistance provided to households through Section 8. Given these general impacts, Rasmussen indicates some of the problems (such as substitution) inherent in estimating program impacts on variables such as housing units affected, neighborhood quality, employment, income, fiscal condition, and population.

Chapter 11, by Charles Anderson, contains an analysis of the urban impacts of three national health care proposals. After comparing the programs with regard to range and levels of benefits, financing mechanisms, and cost and efficiency guidelines, Anderson assesses the urban impacts with particular respect to metropolitan fiscal condition and other variables. He concludes that there will be a demand-created increase in medical care services due to lower out-of-pocket costs for services and that there will be a concomitant expansion of employment and capital in the health care industry. In addition, the cost of health services to local governments will decrease owing to the transfer of some financial responsibilities to the Federal government. Finally, the equity aspects of the three proposals are considered, with the Kennedy-Corman Bill being the most progressively financed and most generous with respect to benefit levels.

Wage subsidies are the principal subject of Chapter 12 by George Tolley and Ronald Krumm. The authors develop a framework for estimating the short- and long-run effects of manpower policies (manpower training, unemployment insurance, public employment, and wage subsidies) and give detailed attention to the spatial effects of a fifty-cent-per-hour wage subsidy targeted on unemployed workers. Their empirical results show that the over half-million-worker increase in employment would be concentrated in the Northeast.

Urban-related programs

Part 4 (Chapters 13–18) contains six urban impact analyses of urban-related programs. Edward Greenberg, Charles L. Leven, and James Little consider a hypothetical increase in federal spending on neighborhood self-help programs. They find that the urban impacts would be positive in terms of the improvement of housing units and neighborhood condition. The authors also indicate that in order for neighborhood self-help programs to be fully successful, they must be coordinated with other social programs and be set within an overall strategy of urban development.

Susan Jacobs and Elizabeth Roistacher analyze one of the Carter administration's major urban economic development initiatives, the Urban Development Action Grants (UDAG) program, in Chapter 14. Funded at a level of $400 million per year, this HUD-administered discretionary program attempts to target its limited resources on "distressed" cities and urban counties. The objective of UDAG is to stimulate the private sector to create employment in and to improve the fiscal viability of local economies. The Jacobs and Roistacher chapter outlines the brief history of economic development programs and explores the rationale for a targeted economic development effort with its reliance on a "one-shot" capital subsidy that characterizes the Action Grant program.

The urban impact analysis itself focuses on commitments made to cities, suburbs, and nonmetropolitan areas by HUD, private firms, and other federal and local sources. Within this spatial scheme, projects are further disaggregated by type (e.g., industrial, residential, commercial, and hotel). The capability of the Action Grants to "leverage" private funds is also discussed, and comparisons are made of the leveraging ratios by jurisdiction and project type.

Chapter 15 considers the regulation of air pollution in urban areas, primarily by the Environmental Protection Agency. Edwin Mills and Hyun-Sik Kim summarize much of the previous research on air pollution damages, particularly studies of property values, wage rates, and health. Mills and Kim argue that the 1970 amendments to the Clean Air Act rely basically on a system of discharge permits that involve poor economic incentives and stress inputs rather than outputs. They indicate that the most important set of impacts involve damage to health and property amounting to about $30 billion annually; on the other hand, the cost of achieving legislatively mandated standards are about 50 percent of that figure. The authors conclude that it is unlikely that an abatement program will have substantial effects on urban size or form, although such a program would tend to make cities more compact than otherwise.

In Chapter 16 Stephen Putman analyzes the intraregional effects of highway construction. He uses a group of land use simulation models to show the shifts in the inter- and intraurban location of employment and population.

The first set of simulations illustrates the regionwide consequences of local zoning policy decisions, the relationships between a change in the highway system and consequent regionwide changes in the spatial distribution of households, and the regionwide consequences of local land use control policies and their relationship to transportation systems. A second group of analyses, conducted with a more sophisticated form of the models than that used for the first set, begins with an investigation of the effects of a metropolitan area's existing highway system on the ability of subareas in that region to respond to regionwide increases or decreases in growth rates. A second simulation examines the regionwide spatial patterns of location of households that result from overall regional changes in the cost of transportation and shows how increased transportation costs lead to subnucleation in the region while decreased transportation costs lead to further suburbanization and sprawl. A last test examines small-scale changes in the highway system, such as "downtown" parking charges and changes in bridge tolls.

Putman's general conclusions concern both substance and method. Regarding substance, Putman shows that highway systems have a variety of impacts in metropolitan areas, some of which are not usually considered in preparing standard urban impact analyses. The traditional examination of highway impacts simply considers the results of constructing new facilities. An impact that is perhaps equal, or even greater, in importance is the long-range effect of an existing highway facility on the speed and nature of a region's ability to respond to exogenous changes. Concerning methodology, Putman suggests that integrated transportation and activity location analyses are essential if the wide range of potential urban impacts of highway systems are to be usefully and thoroughly examined. Finally, he suggests that, at certain levels of detail, regionwide analyses are necessary, while neighborhood analyses can be carried on by different methods as long as they are undertaken within the context of the knowledge of regionwide phenomena.

David Boyce (Chapter 17) also discusses the impacts of transportation on urban areas but, unlike Putman, focuses upon rail transit. In particular, Boyce examines the $6 billion federal investment in the rail transit programs in eleven large metropolitan areas since the mid-1960s. His contribution centers on the intrametropolitan and long-term impacts of transit systems. First, he finds that the impact on overall land development is modest, with specific sites attracted to the Central Business District and to specific station areas. Second, there has been some effect on residential and employment location. Although rail transit is not an important industrial location determinant compared to many other factors, household location decisions are influenced by station locations. Third, most of the impact of rail transit occurs within a region: total population or employment in regions with rail systems do not appear to be greater or lesser than in other (non-rail) regions. In addition, as with the highways discussed in Chapter 16, most of the important effects of rail rapid transit take place in the long run. Physical changes occur gradually unless they are highly planned. This is true, of course, of all infrastructure programs.

Susan Wachter explores some of the neighborhood effects of Federal Housing Administration (FHA) insurance programs in Chapter 18. Specifically, she examines the 1968 Congressional amendments to the National Housing Act that attempted to increase the amount of mortgage insurance flowing to low income urban areas. The urban components of a national program are discussed, and the often ambiguous and conflicting set of impacts that result from the 1968 amendments is highlighted in this chapter.

For instance, the provisions of the legislation that increase urban neighborhood property values include the increased demand for urban homeownership that results from the increased availability and lower costs of mortgage financing, the increased maintenance of the urban housing stock that results from increased homeownership, and the positive neighborhood effects that result from increased property maintenance. On the other hand, portions of the 1968 Act create negative neighborhood effects, by raising default, foreclosure, and abandonment rates and by lowering property maintenance. When neither mortgagor nor mortgagee bears the financial consequences of property abandonment, each lacks the incentive to prevent it. The low down payment provisions and near-zero equity loans provided by the programs limit the borrower's loss and the 100-percent insurance limits the lenders' loss from undermaintenance and abandonment.

Federal tax system

Part 5 contains three chapters about the federal tax system. In Chapter 19, Kathy Hayes and David Puryear investigate the urban effects of the Revenue Act of 1978. The law, which reduced personal and business taxes by nearly $35 billion in 1979, is shown to have wide-ranging and unintended spatial effects. In general, the personal income tax revisions work in favor of central cities, while the business tax revisions stimulate the shift of economic activity out of central cities.

According to Hayes and Puryear, personal income tax rate reductions and an increase in personal exemptions and standard deductions lower the subsidy to homeownership and thus reduce the incentive for leaving the central city, where rental units are the predominant form of housing. But, the increase in the capital gains exclusion moderates the favorable central city impact of the personal income tax package because suburban areas receive a disproportionately large share of capital gains income. Also, there is an allowance in the legislation for a one-time exclusion of capital gains on the sale of one's residence for taxpayers fifty-five years old and older. Since a disproportionately larger percentage of recent movers who are fifty-five and over live in the suburbs, this exclusion favors suburban areas. Overall, however, the tax rate changes outweigh the effects of the special exclusion and the increase in capital gain exclusions; thus, the personal income tax cuts are, on balance, "pro-central city."

The corporate income tax rate reduction will have a significant differential central city–suburban impact if there are systematic differences in the size of firms located in cities relative to suburbs. Data limitations make the measurement of the impact of this provision indeterminate. However, the liberalization of the Investment Tax Credit (ITC) reinforces its existing spatial bias in favor of new activity in suburban or nonmetropolitan areas. Older central cities are at a comparative disadvantage in attracting new investment. Stimulating investment through the ITC accelerates the decentralization of economic activity. Except for services, which are highly concentrated in central cities, usage of the ITC varies inversely with employment concentration in central cities. One liberalization, however, the eligibility for the ITC of expenditures for the rehabilitation of structures in use for at least twenty years, has potential for a positive central city impact.

Roger Vaughan (Chapter 20) discusses the effects of Federal government tax policies on fiscally distressed State and local governments. He examines three mechanisms by which federal policies could be modified to improve local fiscal condition without significant costs to the U.S. Treasury. First, State and local governments could be allowed to offer taxable bonds with interest cost subsidies provided by the Treasury. Second, the state portion of General Revenue Sharing could be used to subsidize state property tax "circuit breakers" (state-imposed limits on property tax liabilities based upon the income or age of the property owner) in the form of a matching grant. And third, federal incentives could be offered to reduce interstate tax competition to attract business.

Vaughan believes that the three initiatives could lead to greater fiscal strength for the state and local sector in general, particularly for those jurisdictions that are laboring under fiscal strains. He says that there are sufficient data available to predict that the first two initiatives are likely to provide fiscal assistance to State and local governments at negligible cost to the Federal government. There are insufficient data to analyze the spatial impacts of the third initiative, although there are some a priori reasons for believing that the initiative may help states and jurisdictions and may encourage more efficient local development efforts.

Martin Holmer's contribution in Chapter 21 involves the use of a microsimulation model (Holmer uses an extended version of the model employed by Danziger et al. in Chapter 9) to analyze the effects of a reduction of federal income tax rates on individuals. Specifically, Holmer examines the proposed Kemp-Roth Bill, legislation that would reduce personal income tax rates by one-third, the federal income tax analogue to California's Proposition 13. After describing the model in detail, including the recent improvement in its components, the effects of Kemp-Roth on labor supply, earnings, federal income taxes, and disposable income by income class and region are discussed. Holmer also reports the effects of Kemp-Roth on consumption, production, and labor demand. Some of the significant data and other methodological problems involved in using such a model for policy analysis are also discussed in this chapter.

Intergovernmental relations

The final set of essays, contained in Part 6, involves the complex set of intergovernmental relations in our federal system. Harold Bunce and Norman Glickman (Chapter 22) and Paul Dommel (Chapter 23) analyze portions of the so-called New Federalism, the Community Development Block Grant (CDBG) and General Revenue Sharing (GRS) programs, respectively.

CDBG is HUD's program for community development in which funds are distributed to localities in a formula basis. The funds are then spent on a variety of activities (formerly undertaken by the categorical programs that CDBG replaced), such as urban renewal, model cities, housing rehabilitation, neighborhood improvements, and others.

Bunce and Glickman pay close attention to the determination of the formulas that could be used to allocate CBDG funds. Currently, a dual formula is in effect. Under it, cities choose between the original 1974 formula in which a city's property is weighted 50 percent, its population 25 percent, and overcrowded housing 25 percent, and a 1977 formula based upon poverty (weighted 30 percent), old housing (50 percent), and population growth lag (20 percent). The 1974 formula reduced funding for larger and older central cities, especially those in the North, compared to the displaced categorical programs. The 1977 formula restored some of the lost money to those areas.

Using factor analysis, the authors utilize a "needs index" for cities based on twenty socioeconomic variable, and they discuss alternative formulas' targeting efficiency based on cities' needs. They also view the kinds of redistribution of Block Grant funds that would take place under different formula specifications. They find that little interregional redistribution must necessarily take place under the formulas tested but that reallocations could occur from less needy suburbs to more needy central cities, given a fixed amount of CDBG funds.

The focus of Chapter 23 by Paul Dommel is on the targeting capability of General Revenue Sharing: how well does this nearly $7 billion Treasury Department program target aid to the neediest areas? Targeting analysis of revenue sharing is made difficult by the complex allocation system that gives separate entitlements to layered governments—state, county, and townships and municipalities within a county. Dommel presents the analysis in two parts, a spatial analysis (states and municipalities) and a needs analysis. The needs analysis measures revenue sharing allocations against population change, poverty, and an "urban conditions index" composed of the factors of community age, poverty, and population change, similar to the index used by Bunce and Glickman in Chapter 22.

The spatial analysis shows that, on a per capita allocation basis, the GRS formula generally favors the Middle Atlantic, New England, Pacific, and East South Central Census regions. If, however, the analysis is based on the increase and decrease of shares over time, with the exception of New England, the formula tends to favor the Southern and Western regions.

Among the types of municipalities in Dommel's sample, central cities do significantly better on a per capita basis than other types of communities, although there has been a very slight decline in the central cities' share over time. Among the central cities, the allocation system tends to favor most the large central cities of the Northeast on a per capita basis, although central cities in the South Atlantic and East South Central regions also do well relative to the mean.

Dommel concludes that the political history of GRS offers little hope that the allocation system can be altered to change the targeting impact of the program. However, the findings on the targeting impacts among large cities suggest that the revenue sharing formula may be a useful instrument for any supplemental fiscal assistance program to assist the neediest cities.

Supplemental fiscal assistance is the subject of Chapter 24, where John Ross discusses the Anti-Recession Fiscal Assistance (ARFA) program, a program that sought a countercyclical stimulus for the national economy and fiscal support for local governments. ARFA was implemented between mid-1976 and mid-1978 to distribute $3.5 billion of federal funds to State and local governments. As with CDBG and GRS, a formula was used to allocate funds: the GRS allocation was multiplied by the "excess" local unemployment rate.

Ross cites three issues that make it particularly difficult to judge the impacts of ARFA on urban areas. The first issue concerns targeting. While it is known in part where the money went, given the varied nature of the goals of this program, it is difficult to develop a standard against which to measure that distribution. Second, because of the problem associated with substitution, it is very difficult to determine *how* or even *if* the money was spent by the recipient governments. Finally, even if the expenditures could be traced, we do not yet have the analytical capacity to follow the direct and indirect impacts of those expenditures on particular groups living in particular areas. Given these caveats, Ross finds that ARFA did provide aid to the most distressed governments; also, central cities received more in per capita allocations than their suburbs received.

The final chapter, by Robert Yin, discusses an interesting facet of urban impact analysis: the effect of federal programs on the structure and functioning of local governments, which occurs because many federal programs (such as CDBG or CETA) require local governments' participation in implementation. The implementation process itself may thus have an impact that is independent of the substance of the program being administered: new jobs may be created within local government, new agencies may be established, and local administration may have to become increasingly tuned to federal requirements.

As evidence of these impacts, this chapter cites the increasing proportion of local government revenues that come from federal funds as well as various structural changes that have occurred in five case-study cities. In general, the cities that Yin examined established new local agencies that acted as bureaucratic counterparts (e.g., prime sponsors) to federal programs. The cities had also established intergovernmental offices, often with representatives in Washington, D.C., to deal with federal-local relationships.

The evidence indicates, according to Yin, that subtle changes may have occurred in local governments in a manner suggesting that they have become "victims" of "creeping federalism." Furthermore, these changes can be directly related to the areas of concern of urban impact statements. Thus, the implementation impacts may affect all the UIA target variables, may have significant distributional effects geographically, and may be directly related to major urban policy goals (e.g., the focus on distressed cities or the desire to promote greater public-private cooperation in urban economic development). However, Chapter 25 concludes that most of these effects, though potentially significant, will nevertheless often go undetected because the existing methodology for conducting urban impact analyses is flawed. It ignores cross-program effects (impact analyses are to be conducted on a program-by-program basis only), and it provides no clear opportunity for assessing such qualitative changes as shifts in power relationships, for instance, between city and county government. Yet these impacts may, in the long run, be more important than the program-specific impacts that are presently the focus of analytic attention.

CONCLUSIONS

What have we learned from this selection of papers? Several themes and issues seem to run through the volume. Most involve methodology (not surprisingly, since explorations of methodological issues was a major object of inquiry for the papers), although others raise substantive and political concerns. It appears that the following issues are central, and they appear to form an agenda for future research.

First, *several methodological approaches were followed in viewing the many kinds of programs*. For instance, several authors used formal empirical models for analyses of programs (Ballard et al.; Danziger et al.; Putman; Holmer); some policies were evaluated by nonmodel statistical techniques (Tolley and Krumm; Bunce and Glickman); and still others used a variety of other methods. It is clear there is no "one" methodology adaptable to UIAs of different policies.

Second, *data problems abound in urban impact analysis*. The discussions by Anton, Bolton, Rasmussen, Hayes and Puryear, and Ross certainly demonstrate how better urban or program data could make analytic efforts more manageable.

Third, *many conceptual problems confront practitioners in this field.* For instance, the measurement of policy effects is influenced significantly by the level of substitution assumed (Rasmussen; Jacobs and Roistacher; Ross). Other conceptual issues raised include the capitalization of benefits, the ecological fallacy, "people" versus "places," the proper time frames for analysis, impact types, and the criteria for judging impacts.

Fourth, *the role of equity and race in UIAs has not gotten full attention.* Both issues, clearly intertwined with the "people" versus "place" controversy, are brought forward (Edel; Ballard, et al.; Rasmussen; Wachter; Greenberg et al.; Dommel).

Fifth, *ambiguity often characterizes urban impact analysis.* Single programs may have elements that have conflicting spatial emphasis; this has been shown clearly in the work of Wachter and Jacobs and Roistacher. More importantly, policies (often operated by different agencies) may work at cross-purposes—one oriented to (say) central cities and the other to the suburbs. Yin indicates this in his essay.

Sixth, *urban impact analysis needs a broader scope.* For instance, the present governmental focus on new initiatives of single agencies does not allow for consideration of broad-based, multiagency efforts such as energy development or welfare reform. Moreover, the range of base programs of agencies should be scrutinized; Glickman briefly summarizes an effort to analyze HUD's budget in Chapter 1. Yin shows the need to look at the impacts of many programs on single cities. Another shortcoming of current research, as Markusen argues, is the effect of private activities on cities. Many observers agree that the actions of firms and households have at least as much effect on urban development as do federal policies. Also, the research is dominated by consideration of economic variables (such as income and employment), when many noneconomic variables ought to be more fully considered. Attempts to quantify results (even when data bases are demonstratively weak) are given much more importance than qualitative analysis; perhaps less attention should be paid to quantitative efforts.

To conclude, it appears that these first attempts to develop urban impact analyses are interesting and important. They further policy analysis and the study of urban development in significant ways. However, much future research is needed if the urban impact analysis process is to become an important factor in government and academic activity.

PART I

Overview of Urban Impact Analysis

CHAPTER ONE

Methodological Issues and Prospects for Urban Impact Analyses

NORMAN J. GLICKMAN

INTRODUCTION

This paper serves as an overview of some of the methodological and policy issues surrounding *urban impact analysis* (UIA) of federal programs. This relatively new direction in policy study (which is required by the President's National Urban Policy) seeks greater detail on the *spatial* dimensions of federal government policies,[1] including expenditures, regulations, and taxation. UIAs thus extend traditional views of the efficiency and distributional aspects of policy study, adding a spatial dimension often previously ignored.

This is no easy task as policies influence urban development in complicated and often not well-understood ways. There are policies that have direct effects on cities while others influence them quite indirectly. Short-term and long-term impacts may also differ greatly. To illustrate, federal policies may be divided into four categories with respect to their direct impacts. First, there are *general* policies that have national orientations but that have indirect effects on urban life. Within this category would be defense spending and youth employment programs. Second are the programs that are *targeted* on localities (such as Urban Mass Transit Administration [UMTA] programs and Community Development Block Grants [CDBG]) that have more direct

The author would like to thank Kenneth P. Ballard, Joseph Daleiden, Stephen Gale, William Grigsby, Bennett Harrison, John Helmer, Susan S. Jacobs, Charles L. Leven, Katharine C. Lyall, Seymour Mandelbaum, Mark D. Menchik, David Rasmussen, Andrew Reschovsky, Benjamin H. Stevens, Seymour Stotland, George S. Tolley, Georges Vernez, and Susan M. Wachter for their helpful comments on earlier drafts of this paper.

[1] UIAs are not generally done on individual projects, as in the case of Environmental Impact Statements. They are meant to view broader programs and policies.

expenditure effects on cities. Third, there is a class of programs that affect cities indirectly by *changing relative prices* generally in the economy; wage subsidies, air pollution regulations, gas price deregulation, and minimum wage laws fit into this grouping. Fourth, there are programs that influence *relative prices in localities* directly. One would include assisted housing programs such as U.S. Department of Housing and Urban Development's (HUD) Section 8 or UMTA operating subsidies here.

Each type of program might require different analytic, data, and institutional considerations. Therefore, the problem of understanding the spatial ramifications of federal (or other governmental) policies is a difficult one.

Since the process of undertaking UIAs is so new, many methodological issues face analysts. In order to better understand the methodological bases for UIAs, HUD's Office of Policy Development and Research brought together in a conference some leading academic and government analysts to discuss the nature and consequences of federal policies on urban areas. Their views are the basis of this volume. This topic is now relevant and important within Washington's "policy community" because of the introduction to the budgetary process of UIAs. It is also becoming significant in academic circles because of a set of interesting methodological issues which surround UIA research.

Beginning with the formulation of the Fiscal 1980 budget, federal agencies must prepare a UIA for each *significant new initiative* as part of its budget submissions to the U.S. Office of Management and Budget (OMB). These UIAs must include analysis of the new initiative with regard to its impact on cities and communities in terms of several key socioeconomic variables. Urban impact analyses thus consist of attempts to gauge the *spatial dimensions* of public policies. That is, how do policies affect central cities, suburbs, non-metropolitan, and other spatial units, absolutely or relatively?

How might UIAs aid in the policy process? A prime example of where a UIA might have been useful is in the planning for the interstate highway system which, when conceived two decades ago, took no account of the potential interregional and intraregional impacts of this massive public works program. Of course, *ex post*, some have come to understand, and often rue, the consequences of this program. The building of this system may have accelerated metropolitan decentralization and the outmigration from the Northeastern states and destroyed neighborhoods. I do not argue that the interstate system should not have been built; only that had there been a UIA done on the highway program in 1956 and its spatial implications thus better understood, it might have been built somewhat differently.[2] More importantly, other compensatory programs might have been devised to lessen some of the interstate system's negative impacts.

---

[2] See Putman's paper on highway systems in this volume. Henceforth, articles cited by author's name but with no date or other additional reference are in this volume.

Some history

In 1977, President Carter convened the Urban and Regional Policy Group (URPG), chaired by HUD Secretary Patricia Roberts Harris, to draft an urban policy statement. The URPG made its recommendations on March 23, 1978 (URPG, 1978). On' March 27, 1978, the President issued his National Urban Policy message (HUD, 1978) which included requests for a broad range of urban initiatives, among them a National Development Bank, neighborhood self-help programs, labor-intensive public works, spatially targeted employment and differential investment tax credits, targeted federal procurement and facilities location, and improvements in existing programs. The President also adopted the URPG request that "all government actions must be evaluated ahead of time with respect to possible urban impacts and, to the extent possible, be shaped and carried out in a manner consistent with our overall urban policy." (URPG, 1978, p. III-5)

The URPG report, therefore, provided the genesis for UIAs and the Office of Management and Budget was asked to provide leadership in the process of using urban impact analyses in future policy review, and to supply formal documentation for UIAs. On August 16, 1978, the President signed Executive Order 12074 calling for "Urban and Community Impact Analysis" of major initiatives proposed by each agency. That is, federal agencies are now responsible for the preparation of a UIA and its submission to OMB along with other documentation as part of the budget process (and, as such, UIAs are for the sole use of OMB officials and are not available to the public). Circular A-116, which accompanied the Executive Order and which gives OMB's guidelines, is discussed in detail by Salamon and Helmer in the next chapter. Since this is a new governmental activity which will not be familiar to many, some of the elements of UIAs are outlined below.

The importance of UIAs

As noted in the next two sections of this paper, there are a great number of difficult problems inherent in analyzing the urban and community impacts of federal policies. The methodological, data, and institutional constraints underlying UIAs are inherently "messy" and inexact when compared to some other kinds of policy analysis. However, there is an importance to UIAs that transcends these problems as we face the 1980s. The National Urban Policy as defined by the URPG consists of the summation of the pieces of legislation, regulatory changes, and other actions which are its components. As of this writing, few of the President's urban policy recommendations have been implemented and, given the austere nature of the Fiscal 1980 budget towards urban-related spending, it is not likely that many will be enacted in the near future.[3] Therefore, the relative importance of UIAs has increased, in part,

---

[3] For instance, federal grants-in-aid to cities will decrease by 5.3 percent in real terms between the Fiscal 1979 and Fiscal 1980 budgets, despite a nominal increase (from $82.1 to $82.9 billion). Funds for community and regional development will decline

by default. But there are more positive reasons for pursuing UIAs. Through these analyses, the Federal government has the opportunity to influence the structure of its policies in such a way that urban areas will not be adversely affected in an era where social spending appears to be losing its relative share of the federal dollar. If, as argued below, UIAs only serve to "raise the consciousness" of decision-makers in the different executive agencies and elsewhere in the Federal government with respect to urban issues, then progress, however slight, will have been made. And useful work can be done if the present UIA framework is broadened, if resources are provided to carry out these efforts, and if institutional barriers can be overcome. There are some unique opportunities to advance both policy analysis and urban development study through UIAs at relatively low research costs.

The remainder of this paper consists of a discussion of some of the major methodological issues encountered in urban impact analyses and criticisms of the present methodologies, suggestions for possible extensions of this analytic mode, and recommendations for future work in this field.

ISSUES IN URBAN IMPACT ANALYSIS

There are several elements that are critical in urban impact analyses, as we shall see throughout this volume. This section denotes some of the items that have been considered in formulating a UIA. Some of them may be obvious, some not. A few of the issues can be easily resolved, whereas others need additional study. However, the experience to date with UIAs indicates that these issues arise fairly often.

Time and timing

Obvious consideration should be given to *short-term* and *long-term* impacts of programs, although a precise delineation of the time frame may be difficult. An initial impact may have a long-term effect on a city or region that is quantitatively or qualitatively different from its short-term impacts. For instance, in housing and transportation infrastructure programs, long-term impacts will often swamp short-run effects in importance. Short-term consequences of such programs are primarily through direct construction activity (and related multiplier effects), whereas the long-term ramifications may be on the nature and fabric of the city or community. If neighborhood effects, scale or agglomeration economies, or other factors come into play in the long term, the differences brought about by time may be very crucial. Also, the timing of impacts of policies may differ among cities, affecting some before others. Therefore, *time* is an extremely important issue to be considered.

---

by 26.8 percent, and education, training, employment, and social service spending will drop by 7.8 percent. The number of low income families receiving rental housing assistance will be reduced by 10 percent in 1980. Such real cuts in social- and urban-related spending will likely have significant impacts on the cities and the poor.

A related consideration has to do with the *timing* of the analysis with respect to program implementation. For instance, UIAs were done in 1978 (based, in general, on 1976 or 1977 data) for Fiscal 1980; however, implementation of such policies will not take place until 1981 or later. Since economic and social conditions can change significantly over this long time period, the UIA (and other program analysis) may be badly outdated by the time that the policy is carried out. This is particularly important with regard to changes in macroeconomic conditions (as discussed later in this paper) that may occur in the future, resulting in reconsideration of program options.

Types of impacts

Several kinds of impacts are involved. The most obvious are *direct* and *indirect*. In many cases a policy's goal may not relate directly to urban areas, but many of its indirect effects will, in fact, affect cities. For example, the U.S. Environmental Protection Agency's (EPA) water and sewer grants seem to have promoted urban sprawl, although their legislated purpose was quite aspatial. The 1978 energy program is another example where indirect effects may be important, as Markusen shows. Additionally, the initial impact of a policy should be followed through its multiplier and other effects on variables which will be influenced indirectly. In this regard, the question of relative impacts of different kinds of government spending (for example, defense versus health care) could be measured if the analytic framework is broadened. For the present discussion, it is important to understand the relationship between the spending of an additional federal dollar and its ultimate impact on the private economy.

We are also interested in the difference between *absolute* and *differential* effects. That is, the extent to which a policy influences cities in an absolute way (in terms of dollars spent, income created, and so forth) as opposed to how it affects central cities relative to the suburbs and nonmetropolitan areas. The OMB guidelines require consideration of both absolute and differential effects.

A third way of looking at impacts has to do with the size of the impacts *relative to the size of the programs*. Some programs that are relatively small in size are not likely to have very large absolute impacts. However, their effects may be large relative to program size and we should indicate this when it is so. The basis for the Urban Development Action Grants (UDAG) program, for instance, is the leveraging of relatively large amounts of private funds with small HUD grants. In theory, the impact ought to be large relative to program size. Jacobs and Roistacher examine this below.

Finally, and perhaps most importantly, *qualitative* as well as *quantitative* impacts must be considered. In many cases there will be little or no data and quantitative impacts may not be feasible to estimate. In such cases the probable direction and likely magnitude of impacts will be discussed, without making precise empirical estimates at all.

Spatial units

Several spatial dimensions are important, such as *interregional* (North versus South, New England versus South Atlantic), *intraregional* (metropolitan versus nonmetropolitan within a federal or Census region), *intrametropolitan* (central city versus suburb or suburb versus suburb within a Standard Metropolitan Statistical Area [SMSA]), and *intraurban* (the effects on one neighborhood versus another within a jurisdiction).[4] These elements may be considered in urban impact analysis, although with varying degrees of importance. Some programs will have important interneighborhood effects (HUD's Section 312 housing rehabilitation loan program, UDAG, and the CDBG program), while others either will not have important neighborhood effects, or the effects will be difficult to measure or to anticipate. The OMB guidelines specifically call for the differentiation among central cities, suburbs, and nonmetropolitan entities. At minimum, one should look at those spatial dimensions, but the intraurban and interregional effects should also be considered when important.

Furthermore, attention should be given to *distressed cities* (those with high unemployment rates, low real incomes, or other indicators of decline) whose aid is one of the objects of the President's urban policy. HUD, the Brookings Institution, and others have developed distress measures for cities which could be used here; such measures have been used in some detail by Bunce and Glickman, and Jacobs and Roistacher in this volume.

Finally, impacts may differ according to *city size*. This may be true if policies systematically try to help, for example, large cities or because secondary (multiplier) effects differ according to city size (that is, larger cities, *ceteris paribus*, will have larger multipliers because of larger internal markets).

Variables to be analyzed

It is difficult to select the proper variables to be analyzed. Data availability is certainly one consideration, but consistency with the goals of the President's urban policy is also important. The variables selected by OMB reflect a combination of the two because some reflect the socioeconomic impact on *places* (such as local fiscal condition) and *people* (such as migration, and the incomes of the low income population) as well as data which are often available on a small area basis. Variables studied should include: (a) *Population*. The influence of a policy on population and the demographic and social mix of an area. That is, will the program lead to inmigration or outmigration of the population, particularly the minority population? The effects on mobility are considered in an interregional framework in the welfare reform paper by Danziger et al. in this volume. Additionally, the effects on suburbanization and migration within a jurisdiction should be considered. Greenberg, Leven, and

---

[4] OMB guidelines do not require interregional, intraregional, or intraurban analysis, despite the importance of understanding such differences.

Little indicate the potential effects of neighborhood self-help programs in one neighborhood on the population of nearby areas. (b) *Employment*. The impact of the program on employment levels, with particular respect to minorities. Consideration should be also given to the type of employment generated with regard to skill, occupation, job stability, wage levels, mobility, and other categories. Furthermore, the effects of policies on industrial location factors is important. (c) *Income*. The impact of a program on per capita or total income levels of an area, with particular respect to low income individuals, should be ascertained. (d) *Fiscal Condition of Local Governments*. The consequences for tax and spending elements of local government activity related to the policy under study should be estimated. For instance, what level of matching funds are required by federal legislation or what kinds of future operating costs will be required by the infusion of federal funds for a piece of infrastructure? (e) *Other Variables*. When relevant, the impact on other variables should be viewed. For instance, in analyzing many HUD programs it has been found that analyzing "housing units affected" and "neighborhood conditions" is important and relevant. Other variables may be useful for other programs.

Equity

Although equity issues are not adequately addressed in A-116 at present, consideration should be given to *intraarea, interarea*, and *interpersonal* income differentials. That is, to what extent will a given policy increase or decrease income equality within an area (within a central city or within a suburban ring), between areas (between a central city and the suburbs), and among people? Obviously, a given program will affect equity in the various spatial dimensions in different ways. For instance, a policy which reduces income disparities within a jurisdiction may not narrow income disparities between jurisdictions.

Also, there may be conflicts between "place" and "people" equity, which are addressed in detail in Edel's paper and which have been the focus of many policy discussions. The "people" versus "place" equity issue has several aspects (Glickman, 1979, chapter 7) and has been widely debated. Of interest here is the fact that some federal funds are distributed to *places*, in part according to measures of the distress of its *people* (unemployment rates, poverty rates); this is true for general revenue sharing and CDBG, for instance. Yet the ultimate beneficiaries of these funds are sometimes the nonpoor who live in "distressed" cities. Therefore, allocations to a *place* do not guarantee that the "right" people will be served. So, although a "place" orientation is useful, and is clearly the major thrust of both the National Urban Policy and A-116, many argue that a "people" focus is ultimately more important. Additionally, it should be understood that some programs that have urban impacts in terms of population, employment, and so forth, may not affect interpersonal, intraarea, or interarea income distribution significantly.

Criteria

A vexing problem concerns analytic criteria. What constitutes a "positive" or "negative" urban impact? Should a program which has 45 percent of its employment impact in central cities be considered "positive"? What if only 23 percent of the impact was there; is this "negative"? Furthermore, there are questions about potential trade-offs among variables (such as increased employment versus a deteriorating neighborhood condition) which are affected by programs. No guidance on criteria has been given by OMB, nor are any plausible on a simple *a priori* basis. Particularly, for agencies with no direct urban mission, the evaluation of the spatial impacts of their programs is quite difficult to establish. Criteria need to be developed in order for the UIA process to move forward.

Analytic models

Several kinds of empirical models could be employed in these studies. In this volume, for instance, authors have used input-output, microsimulation models (Danziger et al. and Holmer), econometric techniques (Ballard, Glickman, and Wendling), and intraurban land use models (Putman) in analyzing the urban impacts of federal policy. Regression and factor analysis are employed by Bunce and Glickman. Using models, however, may not always be the primary analytic framework for this book or in UIA analysis in general (none were used by agencies in the first round of UIAs), but models might be utilized when relevant and available. Models need to be existing or easily adaptable to the specific needs of this kind of analysis, and this may not always be the case. As noted below, few good small area models exist in any event and further research in this area should be supported.

Program context

In some cases, consideration could be given to the relationship between the program (or set of programs) being analyzed and related programs. To what extent do the urban impacts of a given policy depend upon its interactions with other, related policies? This consideration has been shown to be important in the study by Greenberg, Leven, and Little, which indicates that the relationship between the neighborhood self-help program under study and the Section 8 housing assistance program of HUD was crucial. Similarly, HUD's Section 312 is tied to CDBG, as Glickman and Jacobs (1978) show. Additionally, one may want to indicate whether or not the *scale* of the program matters. That is, would a program of $400 million per year have a qualitatively different set of urban impacts from one of twice that size? The answer would depend, in part, on the *targeting* of the funds. A concentrated expenditure pattern might make a spatially intense, smaller program more efficient than a more widely dispersed, larger one. However, this is a subject which needs considerably more research.

Alternatives

Consideration should be given to alternative specifications of a given program which may mitigate some of its "negative" urban impacts, however defined, although such is not presently required by OMB. For instance, might a different spatial targeting scheme be beneficial to those cities in most need of federal help? Both Dommel (general revenue sharing) and Bunce and Glickman (CDBG) explicitly discuss the impacts of alternative formulas on distressed cities.

Ambiguity

Analysts will often find that a policy's impact will not be consistent with respect to cities of the same type, for example in size or income level. Also, some parts of a program may imply increased employment in central cities, while another part may "tilt" towards the suburbs. As an example, Wachter shows the different directions that a change in FHA lending rules can take with respect to neighborhood condition. For UDAG, a strategy of investing in centrally located shopping malls might, on the one hand, adversely affect neighborhood shopping centers or, on the other hand, increase the influx of suburban shoppers to central cities, thus increasing the latter's economic base. Therefore, spatial policy impacts are complex and hard to track, not unlike other policy results.

Data

A major problem which affects both governmental and academic researchers alike is the often critical lack of data. This is true in at least four ways. First, the program under study may lack a history from which data could be obtained for analyzing its prospective consequences; this is, of course, true for completely new programs, but also for substantial changes in existing ones. Therefore, the analyst cannot measure impacts in such cases but must make projections by reference to similar programs or to experimental data. Rasmussen gives an example of this. Second, urban data sources in general are often inadequate. Quality small area data are sparse and/or nonexistent for important socioeconomic variables such as migration, production, housing stock, and others. There are often considerable time lags between the activity (for example, a new job created) and the reporting of this event by government sources. Furthermore, local data are often estimated (or constructed) from national baselines rather than directly measured. Moreover, government data are generally collected for administrative rather than research purposes and are not, therefore, available in proper form for analytic purposes. Often, too, access to data is impossible because of governmental confidentiality rules. Anton, Bolton, and Vernez make particular note of data problems in their papers. This is true for urban analysis in general, but is often critical in UIA work. Third, there are gaps in small area multipliers and other necessary data-based analytic mechanisms.[5] These data problems relate to a fourth problem: the lack of good small area empirical models. Few input-output, econometric or other models have been built for small areas (Glickman, 1977), and this leaves a serious analytic gap to UIA researchers. Other data problems abound in these analytic exercises.

The revenue side: closing the accounts

Another factor has often been missed in previous UIA work: federal spending is treated as exogenous to localities—as "new money" or "manna from Heaven"—not properly as *net* of taxes collected from the same jurisdictions. The result is a large overstatement of the urban impacts of federal spending programs. This, of course, is a conceptual error, but one that is understandable from certain perspectives. First, when treating individual programs it is difficult to consider the totality of federal activity (expenditures and revenues) in a jurisdiction. (However, when treating broad-based programs or the entire federal budget, as discussed in the next section of this paper, the revenue side must be considered.) Second, data on revenue collections for small areas are often not available although total expenditures (as Anton discusses) frequently are. At any rate, the revenue side of federal activity needs more conceptual and data development.

Substitution

When making estimates of urban impacts on such variables as expenditures or employment, it is important to understand the extent to which a given program merely replaces private market or local government activity. This is known as the "substitution effect" in the case of public-private situations; when federal activity replaces local activity, this is known as "fungibility" (*see* Ross and Tolley and Krumm on this issue).

These factors often arise. For instance, can one judge whether a Section 8 unit would have been built by private developers in the absence of the program? Would local governments have undertaken local job training without the Comprehensive Employment and Training Act (CETA)? Obviously, the size of the resulting impacts will differ according to judgments about the degree of substitution. If one assumes that *none* of the activity would have occurred without a program (0 percent substitution), then the resulting impacts will be large. Alternatively, if there is an assumption of close to 100 percent substitutability, then the urban impacts will be smaller.

The issue is a complicated one for several reasons. First, there have been

---

[5] The U.S. Commerce Department's Bureau of Economic Analysis, for instance, has produced its "RIMS" (Regional Industrial Multiplier System) system of interindustry multipliers for 173 BEA economic areas (Water Resources Council, 1977). Although some of the methods used to arrive at the RIMS multipliers have been criticized, they represent a good first basis for estimating secondary effects of spending programs. However, one cannot use the RIMS system for central cities or suburban subregions without significant adjustments of the BEA area multipliers.

few studies of this issue which result in more than rough guesses of the degree of substitution. Second, there are cases in which one cannot make judgments about the substitution effects at the national level, but estimates of those at the local level are more feasible. Third, the degree of substitution will clearly vary over the business cycle; when there is a recession, there is less substitution than when there is an upswing, since there is relatively less private activity during downturns. Fourth, there is a timing issue involved, especially in the case of programs such as UDAG: the flow of HUD funds may speed up the completion of a project which might be completed by a private firm anyway. This complicates the measurement of substitution.

It can be argued, though, that the degree of substitution in central cities is probably less than in the suburbs since private firms may perceive more risk to investments in such locales. This is probably true for lending and insurance institutions and construction firms, for instance. This means that urban impacts for central cities may tend to be *understated* and suburban impacts *overstated* (since there is more substitution there) in some impact studies.

Analytical capability and institutional response

There appears to exist a certain "human capital" problem with respect to UIAs within the Federal government. That is, few federal agencies have the relevant personnel schooled in urban economics and related fields who are capable of undertaking such studies. Because no additional resources have been provided to agencies to complete these studies using nongovernmental analysts, this has often resulted in inadequate UIAs. Furthermore, the capacity of the small OMB staff involved in the UIA process to thoroughly review agency UIAs is questionable. Although this staff is highly qualified, it is minuscule relative to the potential flow of reports from the other executive departments. These problems may be reduced as the agencies adjust to this new analytic endeavor, but at present there are potential problems.[6] The situation, therefore, is akin to that in the 1960s when the Planning, Programming, Budgeting System (PPBS) was introduced to the Federal government. The bureaucracy never fully adapted to the demands of the system, contributing to its inability to take hold and significantly influence policy.

There are other serious questions of an institutional nature that must be answered before UIA can proceed very far, even if the data and methodological issues are adequately settled. (1) Who is to do future UIAs? One problem—the lack of adequate manpower within most agencies—has just been mentioned. However, is it reasonable for OMB and the White House Domestic Policy Staff to expect agencies to do unbiased analyses of their *own* programs? Clearly, the positive aspects of urban impacts will be emphasized in an agency's own review. (2) Why should agencies endeavor to improve their

---

[6] This subject is discussed in the last section of this paper.

skills in UIAs? To insure this, it must be shown by OMB that UIAs *count* in the decision-making process. That is, agencies must understand that OMB budget examiners and the OMB-UIA staff not only evaluate agency UIAs, but also *use them* in making budgetary decisions. To date, it is not clear that this has been forcefully done (and it may not be true that UIAs are really important in budget decisions), although subsequent budget discussions may persuade agencies to try harder. This may be difficult for several reasons. Among them: (a) the fact that a UIA is but one of several pieces of information considered by the budget examiners in the budget process and programs can be approved (or disapproved) on many other grounds; (b) the lack of resources to staff UIA efforts may be interpreted by agencies to mean that OMB is not as interested in spatial issues as in other questions; and (c) the hope among some bureaucrats that "this UIA thing" will just go away and leave them alone if properly ignored; remember the fate of PPBS!

To conclude, there are a wide range of methodological, conceptual, data, institutional, and other issues which surround urban impact analysis. The process is inherently inexact, ambiguous, and subject to many problems which have been noted above. Furthermore, the UIA process, as it now stands, is quite limited and in need of both greater depth and breadth.

SOME ADDITIONAL DIRECTIONS
FOR URBAN IMPACT ANALYSES

There are several directions which urban impact analyses could take in the future. Reference here is not only to a narrowly governmental view (amended future OMB guidelines, for example), but for scholarly analysis as well. Some of these possibilities are discussed in the remainder of this section.

Broad-based new initiatives

Thus far, individual agencies have been responsible for writing UIAs for individual new programs.[7] However, there are often new federal initiatives

---

[7] For instance, HUD was required to analyze the spatial impacts of programs it proposed to initiate in Fiscal 1980, such as a new multifamily housing assistance program, expansion of Section 108 (part of CDBG), changes in Section 701, and an extension of FHA insurance to commercial and industrial properties. Since these programs were rejected by OMB budget examiners on other grounds, the UIA exercise, which generally showed large positive impacts on distressed central cities and the poor, was of little ultimate value. This leads to a related question: What were the urban impacts of budget *cuts* (or on proposed programs not approved) imposed by OMB on agency budgets for Fiscal 1980? No analysis has been done on the kinds of programs eliminated or reduced by the budget examiners in their attempt to achieve a $29 million budget deficit, although it appears that many social programs were sacrificed to finance expanded defense expenditures. These decisions are likely to have some substantial differential spatial effects. Should OMB be required to do UIAs on *its* decisions?

that are much broader and cut across departments. The new energy legislation is a good example. As Markusen and others note, the energy bill will clearly have differential effects among our regions and cities. Yet, little, if any, consideration of the energy bill's urban impacts has been taken into account by the U.S. Department of Energy, the White House, or the Congress. That is why we have broadened the definition of "UIA" for this volume. It is wide-ranging programs such as energy and welfare reform that tend to provide the most interesting avenues of research and analysis, precisely because they have such potentially broad and significant impacts, urban and otherwise. The discussion below provides another example of a broad-based initiative with interesting potential urban impacts: solar energy development.

An example: solar energy's potential urban impacts. As with energy in general, some "urban time bombs" might be present in solar energy development. During 1978, there was an interagency Domestic Policy Review (DPR), centered in the U.S. Department of Energy, which recently made recommendations to President Carter on future solar options (U.S. Department of Energy, 1978). The solar example encompasses some of the problems inherent in the current "one-program-at-a-time" approach.[8]

Although the contribution of solar energy to the Nation's energy needs is currently small and may not grow immensely in the near- or mid-term, the potential impact of solar development on cities must be examined. No attention is given to the spatial impacts of solar development within the DPR; the word "city" does not appear in the text. However, the implications of solar energy for different kinds of cities and their people might, over long periods, have differential and, perhaps, serious consequences.

The technological bases which have developed within the solar energy effort favor low-density, single-family home development at the expense of high-density, multifamily buildings. Solar also favors new buildings relative to existing ones, since "retrofitting" old homes is prohibitively expensive at this time. Therefore, the benefits of solar development in general would mean that suburban areas, where there is a higher proportion of new, single-family homes in low-density patterns, would probably gain solar technology's benefits at the expense of central cities where there are greater concentrations of multifamily and old buildings. Any solar energy option with emphasis on new,

---

[8] In this section and in the discussion on solar energy alternatives, I assume essentially what the DPR assumed in its analysis. For instance, that there is wide public demand for solar development, that all segments of the population (e.g., rich and poor) should benefit from solar energy, and that conventional fuel costs affect the viability of solar but that solar only weakly affects conventional energy markets. Not all of these assumptions, or others of the DPR, are necessarily true. For example, there is little evidence that much solar development is cost-effective for many households (e.g., the poor) at this time (or in the foreseeable future), even though the DPR assumes in most cases that it is. In this analysis of the DPR, I take the DPR group at its word and work through the ramifications of its analysis and recommendations.

often expensive homes, also benefits upper income people at the expense of the poor. The latter are also primary central city dwellers, so that the overall impact for central cities of solar may be doubly bad.

Although this is partly inevitable due to current technological and economic factors, the DPR does very little to suggest ways of mitigating this situation. In fact, the incentives in the program options tend to reinforce central city suburban quality-of-life differentials rather than reduce them; also, it may further suburban sprawl. This is true for the reasons delineated below.

TECHNOLOGICAL OPTIONS. The increased use of passive solar design[9] is given great emphasis throughout the DPR report. Passive construction favors areas where there is new, low-density development and where buildings can be planned to face south (to maximize exposure to sunlight) and can be separated; the tendency thus far has been for such development to take place in suburban areas and generally in higher-priced single-family dwellings. Furthermore, in the street grid patterns so common to central cities, the passive option is not physically possible for the great majority of homes, single-family or otherwise. Also, few technological options are given that aid multifamily, high-density dwellers. It is clear that under present conditions most of the benefits of solar will go to new, single-family homes. Probably these will be built in the suburbs and inhabited by upper income people.

FINANCING MECHANISMS. The use of tax credits as the primary financing mechanisms in the DPR list of options has perverse consequences for central cities and the poor in at least two ways. First, tax credits effectively by-pass a large majority of poor families who pay little or no federal income taxes. The poor cannot, therefore, take advantage of this incentive. Second, industrial tax credits (also part of the solar package) in general tend to favor new construction over existing buildings as Hayes and Puryear show later in this volume. This means that industries that take advantage of the credits probably will be the ones which build new structures. These, as previous industrial location studies have shown, will primarily be suburban and in the southern tier region. Therefore, the already-significant anticity employment shifts inherent in the suburbanization process will be reinforced in tax credits for industries. Thus, the tax credit notion has a double impact on the poor and the distressed cities in which they often reside; it does not allow them to benefit from tax reductions to employ solar energy in their homes and may help continue the suburban shifts of population and jobs. About two-thirds of all federal expenditures under the DPR's Option 2 are for residential or industrial tax credits. The DPR (U.S. Department of Energy, 1978 *Attachment*, p. 15) indicates a $1000 credit per dwelling unit to the builder.

LOW INCOME HOUSEHOLDS. The effects of the DPR recommendations for the poor have already been discussed in part in connection with the nature

---

[9] Passive solar design means that structural elements of the building are used for heating and cooling.

of current technology and the primary financing mechanism. The DPR's specific recommendations regarding the poor are extremely weak and disappointing. The DPR's Option 1 provides low income households only with existing DOE weatherization programs to increase energy conservation, but does not adequately deal with the introduction of solar energy to poor households. It is a "do nothing new" option. DPR's Option 2 provides a $40 million pilot program of grants aimed at low income families over a four-year period and for $10 million/year for solar use in subsidized housing programs. Even Option 3 calls only for pilot projects to "retrofit" public housing units. Thus, roughly $500 million will be spent directly on low income groups over five years, compared to an anticipated total incremental federal solar expenditure of $44.3 billion under this most ambitious of the three options. Furthermore, many of these relatively small expenditures targeted on the poor (except for those for public housing) are for *poor homeowners*. Renters, often at the very bottom of the income scale and more often living in central cities, are not fully discussed by the DPR.

Solar energy: some alternatives. There are a number of ways in which the anticentral city impacts of the DPR's solar energy recommendations might be lessened. Although it is recognized that current technology makes it difficult to use solar energy in such areas, there are some technological, financial, and institutional changes that might make the solar option more useful to central cities and to the poor.

TECHNOLOGY. The solar industry has developed around the concept that solar technology should be primarily adapted to single-family homes. This is partly a result of technical factors (such as the ratio of roof space to living space is greater in single-family homes than in multifamily dwellings), but also by marketing considerations. Several possibilities should be further considered: First, alternative technologies could be developed which make solar technology more adaptable to multifamily dwellings. Federal Research, Development and Demonstration (RD&D) efforts should place more emphasis on such technologies and on the technical problems that have made retrofitting existing dwellings so difficult.[10] Second, the technology for large-scale collectors outside cities could be given research and subsidy priority. Third, neighborhood-scale collectors (with larger storage capacity than for single-family homes) have been developed which could be used for one-thousand-unit areas and which could take advantage of scale economies not available in single-family home collectors. Further development of neighborhood-scale technologies should be encouraged by federal initiatives.

FINANCING MECHANISMS. Less emphasis should be placed on tax credits (even tax rebates are more economically progressive) and more emphasis on

---

[10] As noted in footnote 8, if solar energy prices, via technological breakthroughs or some other mechanism, are able to hold down conventional energy prices, nonsolar users will benefit. This will be an unlikely occurrence, especially in the short run.

subsidies to homeowners. Moreover, whatever financial mechanism is used, it should be *targeted* to people and cities who are in the most need of energy savings.

Several possibilities exist with regard to this issue. First, direct solar subsidy programs could be targeted in a more concentrated way to low and moderate income families than under current legislation. Second, tax credits, if they are to remain part of the federal strategy, should be *spatially* targeted. For instance, a *differential* investment tax credit which gives higher tax subsidies could be directed at the poorer cities, especially the central ones.[11] This would reduce employment loss through normal tax credit-induced industrial investments. For residential units, poor families could be helped by tax credits only if, when the tax credit is larger than their tax bill, they would get a *rebate* from the U.S. Treasury to cover the difference. Third, the loan program currently available under the National Energy Act (NEA) to finance lower income people in both solar and conservation efforts could be used. Fourth, financial mechanisms should be devised to aid renters. For example, inducements to landlords to convert to solar and to encourage weatherization by allowing a more rapid write-off of such investments in multifamily buildings could be employed. Additionally, conditions for eligibility for meter conservation loans under the NEA for landlords might be predicated upon meeting certain thermal performance standards (which could include weatherization or solar additions). Also, public housing and other subsidized housing programs, such as HUD's Section 8, could receive more federal subsidies for solar energy than proposed under any of the options in the DPR. Finally, if suburban solar users withdraw in part from using utility-generated power, mechanisms must be found so that the fixed costs of operating utilities should not be borne by the nonsolar, central city energy users.

INSTITUTIONAL. Some institutional changes would help make solar energy more "urban" in its orientation. Neighborhood groups, cooperatives, nonprofit corporations, and other units should be encouraged by legislation and financial incentives to engage in the ownership, leasing, installation, and servicing of solar technology. Again, nonprofit groups and cooperatives would, like the poor, benefit only if tax credits could be turned into tax rebates for such organizations because tax credits do not provide incentives for these sorts of institutions. For example, cooperatives and nonprofit corporations could be helped to organize neighborhood-scale projects. Tenants in multifamily buildings and owners of townhouses could be encouraged to collectively develop off-site solar installations. Second, there should be considerable technical assistance to neighborhood groups for installation, servicing, and so forth, of neighborhood-based solar technologies, although this might be done more

---

[11] At present, many of the poor reside in central cities. Should there be substantial inmigration of middle income families and the concurrent displacement of the poor from the core (as is taking place now, at least on a limited basis), then the tax credits should be targeted to jurisdictions that are in financial distress in the future.

efficiently through utilities. Finally, long-term local level land planning should be supported by federal funds (perhaps through HUD's 701 program) to limit the amount of suburban sprawl which might be further encouraged by wide-scale solar, especially passive solar, use. Such planning efforts must be undertaken in order to conserve and use most efficiently the scarce and valuable urban landscape.

In conclusion, solar development is useful in its own right and should be encouraged as a means of providing the Nation with a renewable source of energy. However, underlying technology, financial mechanisms, and institutional constraints give solar development a suburban and upper income bias which could be mitigated by some of the suggestions noted above without hurting overall solar development. More concern for our cities by the DPR—or an explicit urban impact analysis which points out these potentially negative urban impacts of such a broad set of policies—would make solar power a more useful future energy source for our cities.

The solar example is but one of several new, broad-based, multiagency initiatives which might be analyzed through an expanded conceptualization of urban impact analysis. Danziger et al. provide another in their paper on welfare reform, and Anderson does likewise with respect to National Health Insurance. Important to this paper's discussion is: this analysis must be done *before* an initiative is in place and the analysis must be done carefully and comprehensively.

Analyzing the urban impacts of base programs

Taking the above analysis a step further, researchers should look at the *base portions of existing programs* more intensively. That is, if the focus is merely on new initiatives, policy-makers will not understand the impact of an agency's (or set of agencies') overall budget(s), which constitutes perhaps 95 percent of its activity. Therefore, OMB's guidelines might be amended to include the major programs and regulations of a given agency.

A relatively straightforward methodology has been applied to the major components of HUD's budget in recent months as a prototype of such a UIA extension. First, a set of *case studies* of HUD's major programs was designed.[12] These case studies analyzed a common set of variables in a common analytic and data framework and consisted of detailed examinations of the incentives put in force by the programs. Qualitative judgments were made when data were not available.

The results of these integrated case studies were aggregated by two methods. First, variables common to all studies (such as income, expenditures, employment, and housing units affected) were compared for central cities,

---

[12] These programs were: Community Development Block Grants, Public Housing and Section 23 Leased Housing, Section 8 (new, existing, and substantial rehabilitation), Federal Housing Administration, Government National Mortgage Association (targeted tandem), Section 312, and Urban Development Action Grants.

FIGURE 1: Organization of Research to Analyze the HUD Budget

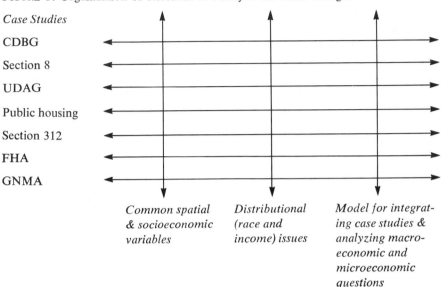

Case Studies

CDBG

Section 8

UDAG

Public housing

Section 312

FHA

GNMA

Common spatial   *Distributional*   *Model for integrat-*
& socioeconomic   *(race and*   *ing case studies &*
variables   *income) issues*   *analyzing macro-*
                                                economic and
                                                microeconomic
                                                questions

suburbs, and nonmetropolitan areas when data permitted; also data were tabulated to contrast interregional differences in program impacts. Equity issues were analyzed as well. Second, the Commerce Department's multi-region econometric model called "NRIES,"[13] developed by Ballard and Wendling (1978), was used. HUD budget data were applied to NRIES in order to calculate the state-by-state direct and indirect impacts of HUD's programs.[14] The HUD protoype UIA research design is depicted in Figure 1.

A summary of some of the HUD Budget Urban Impact Analysis (HBUIA) quantitative results are given in Table 1. There, the percentage of direct expenditures and commitments by HUD for Fiscal 1977 for city types and major regions is given. Overall, 57.6 percent of such funds went to central cities, 25.1 percent to suburban portions of SMSAs, and 17.3 percent to nonmetropolitan areas. Among the programs studied, however, there was a wide variation in spatial spending patterns. GNMA-Targeted Tandem (89.9 percent), UDAG (70.9 percent), and existing Public Housing (67.6 percent) had particularly high concentrations in central cities; on the other hand, Section 8-New (39.9 percent) and FHA-Insured Single Family New Construction (38.6 percent) had much lower-than-average central city allocations.

Table 1 also indicates some socioeconomic variables that can be compared to the HUD spending patterns: personal income, population, number of peo-

---

[13] For 'National-Regional Impact Evaluation System."

[14] For a detailed account of this research, *see* Glickman and Jacobs (1979), and Ballard, Glickman, and Wendling in this volume.

ple in poverty, and the amount of deficient housing. What emerges from a comparison of HUD expenditures/commitments and personal income, for example, is that central cities are net beneficiaries (that is, they received 57.6 percent of the HUD activity though they have only 45.7 percent of the Nation's income); some redistribution can be said to be taking place from the suburbs and nonmetropolitan areas towards central cities as the last group gets more than its "share" of HUD funds. Central cities also receive nearly twice the funds than they would if funds were allocated on the basis of population.

Table 1 shows a similar set of figures for the four major regions. Section 8-Substantial Rehabilitation and UDAG funds are concentrated in the Northeast, whereas nearly 90 percent of the FHA-Insured Single Family New Construction activity is in the South and West. Looking at the comparison between total HUD activity and personal income, one does not see as much redistributions as in the city-type portion of Table 1. The South and West are slight "gainers" over the Northeast and North Central regions.

The HBUIA quantitatively and qualitatively estimated total gross expenditures (direct plus multiplier-induced indirect spending), neighborhood condition, employment, earnings, and housing units affected. Combining the detailed case studies and the NRIES model-based analysis, the HBUIA gives a clearer picture of the urban impacts of HUD's major activity than previously available. Although there are difficult data, conceptual, and other problems in doing such analysis, HUD's prototype might be a good model for other agencies' efforts.

Analyzing the major components of the federal budget

A further development might involve looking at the major components of the federal budget in a manner similar to the HUD prototype study discussed above. Again, the combination of case studies and models could be used to analyze *clusters of base programs* (Figure 2). These base program clusters could include: (1) *social welfare transfers*, including Aid to Families with Dependent Children, Social Security, Supplemental Social Insurance, Section 8, and Medicare; (2) *defense expenditures*, including procurement, personnel and non-Department of Defense spending on aerospace and other items; (3) *intergovernmental transfers*, such as general revenue sharing and other grant programs; (4) *energy and environment*, including the 1978 energy package, existing environmental regulations, and land use laws; (5) *resource development*, such as agriculture and other nonenergy-related resources; (6) *urban and economic development*, such as housing, manpower, and other economic development programs. Such clusters of programs make up most of the federal budget, although they do not exhaust it.

Each case study, as with individual UIAs, would analyze the major direct and indirect impacts of the clusters using a common set of variables (such as employment or income) and the principal incentives put in motion by the

TABLE 1: Percent Distribution of Gross Activity and Impacts, by City Type and Region of Selected HUD Programs, 1977

	City Type				Region				
	Central Cities	Suburbs	Non-metro-politan Areas	Total	North-east	North Central	South	West	Total
ASSISTED HOUSING									
Completed and existing housing									
Section 8 assistance payments									
New construction	39.9	34.9	25.2	100.0	40.2	33.0	15.3	11.5	100.0
Substantial rehabilitation	62.6	28.6	8.8	100.0	67.7	13.4	10.6	8.3	100.0
Existing housing	45.7	34.8	19.5	100.0	28.2	20.4	27.8	23.6	100.0
Total	45.5	34.7	19.7	100.0	30.0	21.4	26.3	22.2	100.0
Public housing	67.6	13.7	18.7	100.0	41.4	19.9	26.3	12.4	100.0
Total	63.0	17.6	18.9	100.0	39.3	20.2	26.3	14.2	100.0
New projects									
Section 8 assistance payments									
New construction	39.9	34.9	25.2	100.0	40.2	33.0	15.3	11.5	100.0
Substantial rehabilitation	62.6	28.6	8.8	100.0	67.7	13.4	10.6	8.3	100.0
Total	42.5	34.2	23.3	100.0	43.4	30.7	14.8	11.1	100.0
Public housing	57.6	11.7	30.7	100.0	29.3	14.7	30.1	25.9	100.0

Total	45.4	30.0	24.7	100.0	40.8	27.7	17.6	13.9	100.0
Total assisted housing	51.8	25.6	22.6	100.0	40.3	25.1	20.7	14.0	100.0
OTHER PROGRAMS									
Section 312 rehabilitation	61.0	26.0	13.0	100.0	34.0	23.0	19.0	24.0	100.0
CDBG[a]	56.0	25.4	18.6	100.0	25.9	23.2	33.7	17.2	100.0
GNMA-targeted tandem	89.9	5.3	4.7	100.0	36.5	21.1	29.9	12.6	100.0
FHA-insured multifamily	86.9[b]	86.9[b]	13.1[b]	100.0	33.4	26.1	20.4	20.2	100.0
FHA-insured single family	38.6	60.1	1.4	100.0	6.9	5.4	34.6	53.2	100.0
UDAG[a]	70.9	13.2	15.9	100.0	35.9	34.0	16.4	13.6	100.0
Total other programs	61.3	24.9	13.9	100.0	28.6	25.0	25.2	21.2	100.0
GRAND TOTAL	57.6	25.1	17.0	100.0	32.8	25.0	23.5	18.6	100.0
Socioeconomic variables									
Personal income (1975)	45.7	34.8	19.5	100.0	29.6	27.3	23.4	19.7	100.0
Population (1976)	28.9	38.9	32.2	100.0	28.9	26.4	26.3	17.9	100.0
Number in poverty (1976)	38.0	23.0	30.0	100.0	23.2	21.6	39.2	16.0	100.0
Deficient housing (1976)	43.1	18.9	37.9	100.0	27.2	22.1	39.0	11.7	100.0

Notes: For further information on gross activity, *see* Glickman and Jacobs (1979), Chapters 2–9.

[a] GNMA Targeted Tandem data are for FY 1978; UDAG data represent commitments from FY 1978 through October 1979.
[b] FHA-insured multifamily data are available in metropolitan-nonmetropolitan form and are not included in city-type totals.

FIGURE 2. Organization of Research to Analyze the Federal Budget

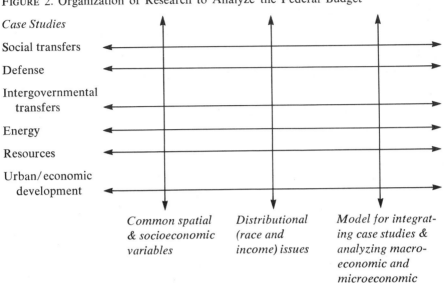

Case Studies

Social transfers

Defense

Intergovernmental
    transfers

Energy

Resources

Urban/economic
    development

*Common spatial
& socioeconomic
variables*

*Distributional
(race and
income) issues*

*Model for integrat-
ing case studies &
analyzing macro-
economic and
microeconomic
questions*

programs (such as migration or industrial location changes) under study.

The effects of individual programs could be aggregated by two methods. First, the common variables could be simply "summed" across programs. This has been done in the HUD prototype study. However, additionally, empirical models could be used to capture the total effects of a set of programs. Such is the case in the welfare reform paper by Danziger et al., where the authors use the Poverty Institute–HEW microsimulation model[15] to simulate the interregional and intraregional impacts of the 1977 Carter administration welfare reform proposal; Holmer's paper in this volume on the effects of federal tax limitation proposals uses the same model. Holmer (forthcoming) has also analyzed major components of the federal budget with this model, at least for 23 large regions.

A research effort, involving HUD, HEW, and the U.S. Department of Commerce's Bureau of Economic Analysis (BEA), is underway that is of potentially great importance in furthering this type of study. First, extensions of the Poverty Institute–HEW model will be made to include a more detailed analysis on labor supply responses in the social transfers area as well as the addition of a large-scale federal expenditures module. Finer areal breakdowns will be made via new Regional Industrial Multiplier System (RIMS) data from BEA to give central city and suburban multipliers for selected SMSAs and industries. Also, adjustments of the Community Services Administration data on federal expenditures will be used for the analysis (*see* Anton's paper on

[15] For a detailed description of the model, *see* Golliday and Haveman (1977).

these data). These and other adjustments will provide a good *microeconomic* approach to analyzing the spatial effects of federal expenditures and revenues.

Second, a *macroeconomic* view will be gained with an expansion of BEA's NRIES model. As Ballard, Glickman, and Wendling show in their paper in this book, this multiregional, econometric model is useful in examining the regional impacts of the federal budget. Furthermore, with appropriate modifications, NRIES can evaluate some of the macroeconomic issues that are raised below: the relationship between national macropolicy and urban development. NRIES will be extended in several respects in later HUD-BEA research to take better account of macropolicy variables, substate economic activity (via the new RIMS data), and in other ways.

Together with the work on the microsimulation model, this will provide a better basis for understanding the major spatial effects of the federal budgetary process. Within such a framework, some of the questions raised above may be answered, such as comparisons of different kinds of spending and the "net" effects of policies after tax collections are subtracted from federal expenditures in a locality. Moreover, especially through the microsimulation model, it may be possible to examine the contribution of the federal budget simultaneously with respect to *changes in interspatial* (such as North versus South) *and interpersonal* (such as reduction in poverty) *inequality,* an important and difficult policy question.

A combination of these two approaches (case studies and models) would generate a meaningful approximation of the "tilt" of a set of programs. Figure 2 summarizes the basic proposed approach. In this manner, the federal budget could be *monitored* on a regular basis with respect to its spatial impacts. The Federal government would, therefore, have a better sense of where its funds were being spent—directly and indirectly—than it does at the present time.[16] This would allow constituent demands to be viewed much more explicitly than currently. With the analytic tools at hand, and improved urban data systems, this could be accomplished.

Other issues to be addressed by urban impact analyses

Thus far, in this section of this paper, I have shown a progression of urban impact analysis from the current single new initiatives studies to broadbased initiatives to base programs to the bulk of the federal budget. There are several other issues of great importance that involve the federal role in urban development, although many of these items are not always budget items. The following section briefly catalogs some of them.

Macroeconomic forces and urban development. One interesting issue involves the relationship between individual government policies (and all of them taken as a whole) and their impacts on cities, as opposed to the impact

---

[16] For interesting analyses of the federal budget, *see* Raskin (1978) and Pechman (1978).

of the workings of the macroeconomy. For instance, we would like to know whether business cycle activity has more or less effect on cities and regions than do all government programs. In this regard, we will want to fully understand the relationship between the business cycle and urban development. We should be in a position to comment on macropolicy (monetary and fiscal) decisions, including stabilization policies, in terms of their effects on urban development. For instance, what happens to cities during fast (slow) growth and/or high (low) interest rate periods? What are the effects of inflation on urban development? Few good studies of these issues exist and we must have answers to these questions. Milne, Glickman, and Adams (1978), for instance, using a multiregion econometric model, show that the northern tier regions do better relative to the "Sunbelt" under conditions of expansionary monetary and fiscal policy (and rapid growth of gross national product [GNP]) than they do under slow-growth conditions. Ballard and Wendling (1978) report similar findings. More research should be done on the urban impacts of the business cycle; *see also* Vernez et al. (1977) on this subject.

The international division of labor and urban areas. Extremely little attention has been paid to the changing balance of economic power within the developed world and between developed and less developed countries, and the effects of this situation on American cities. Internally, we have seen the flow of capital from the older (northern) industrial belt towards (southern) regions with lower labor costs, "better" business climates, and growing markets. Now, increasingly, with the growth of multinational corporations, shifts in plant location are being made to Third World countries (such as Korea and Taiwan) coupled with increases in the relative prices of primary products, especially oil. What are the likely impacts of such important (largely exogenous) changes on the American system of cities? What will happen to different types of cities (for example, old and declining, new and growing) under various scenarios about the future world economic order? Future research should be devoted to this important factor in the growth of American cities (Sarbib, 1978).

Demographic shifts. Another broad set of issues that may have powerful influences on cities concerns demographic shifts in the United States population. During the past 20 years there have been great changes in fertility and migration patterns. As many have pointed out, in the 1960s the then-high birth rate and the rural-to-urban migration pattern favored metropolitan areas and big central cities. The 1970s, however, have brought a sharp reversal of both trends and, with them, a decline in the fortunes of central cities. Between 1970 and 1977 more than twice as many people left central cities than migrated to them. Despite discussions of "gentrification" there continues to be a general pattern of urban deconcentration (movement away from central cities and, to a lesser extent, from SMSAs) coupled with the fact that this deconcentration is dominated by the middle and upper income people. This has meant increasing economic, social, and racial segregation. The poor, aged, and nonwhite populations have been increasingly concentrated in large, industrial centers that have declining economic bases. A third trend, that may be considered "pro-urban," involves changing demographic structure with respect to household formation and size. The average family size has fallen significantly as young couples have fewer children; increasingly such (often middle income) families have found central city living attractive. They look for smaller dwellings, often near their central city workplaces, and are less concerned with school quality than families with children.[17]

The implications of these trends on cities are already proving to be significant. We must forecast where decline will occur and learn to *plan for decline* in cities and regions where population levels are falling; moreover, we must devise social policy to cope with the dependent population often left behind. Alternatively, we will have to devise policies to reverse the decline of those cities. The implications of fertility, migration, and household formation trends for policy mean different emphasis in the output mix of local governments and the housing industry. At the national level, the implications of demographic change on tax and transfer policy should be better studied. Again, this area is not well understood, and future urban impact analysis must consider demographic shifts to be helpful to policy-makers at the national or local level.

Regulatory activity. There is a wide range of regulatory activity with direct and indirect urban impacts. Only major regulations are covered by OMB Circular A-116, and only those of operating agencies; Mills and Kim address a set of these, air pollution control regulations, in this volume. However, there are many other regulatory functions carried out within *independent regulatory agencies*, such as the FAA, ICC, and others, that may be relevant for UIAs and that are currently exempt from A-116. For instance, the Civil Aeronautics Board's recent partial deregulation of air fares may have long-term impacts on smaller, less profitable, route cities. The possible deregulation of interstate trucking rates is another example: a potential ramification of this is a further change in industrial location patterns. It is argued by some that trucking rate deregulation by the Interstate Commerce Commission would hurt small towns because any deregulation-induced price cutting would make such places unprofitable for many trucking firms. Others, however, believe that deregulation could lead to lower freight rates, greater efficiency, and better service to customers in communities of all sizes. Given this debate and the potentially significant spatial effects of this policy change, it is important to study trucking deregulation. Not only should we look at the base spending programs of operating agencies, we should examine the functions of regulatory agencies as well.

Impacts on individual cities. The thrust of UIAs to date has been on single

---

[17] Sometimes, however, the urban poor are displaced and have worse housing as a result.

programs which affect city types differentially. An interesting and useful exercise would be to examine the converse: what are the impacts of *all* federal policies taken together on *one* city? Research should be mounted to understand the full effects of spending, regulatory, tax, and other policies, for example, on Mobile or Boston.[18] Yin's paper looks at the administrative and bureaucratic responses of local governments, but more must be done.

Extensions of UIAs: a summary

This last section has shown some directions which UIAs might take in the future, and has suggested that we must broaden the definition of these analyses to include broad-based new initiatives, agency base programs, clusters of interagency programs (such as social transfers), and the entire federal budget. Additionally, I have suggested a range of issues, such as business cycle developments, international trade, regulatory activities, and demographic shifts, that should be studied with regard to their urban impacts (*see* Figure 3 for the sequence of research indicated). Finally, I have suggested that the effects of all federal activity on a city be examined. In short, I argue that the current institutional arrangement is seeking answers to questions (that is, about new initiatives) that are less important than those discussed in this section of the paper, and is doing so on a weak analytic, conceptual, and resource base. If we are truly interested in the spatial impacts of federal policies, the directions outlined in this section should be given serious attention. The next section sets out some recommendations concerning the future of urban impact analysis.

CONCLUSIONS AND RECOMMENDATIONS

Several points have been raised in the preceding sections which will be briefly summarized here. The set of conclusions given are in the form of recommendations for further development of urban impact analyses.

(1) There has been a modest but worthy start at understanding some of the spatial impacts of federal policies through current OMB procedures. However, given the relatively small number of new initiatives approved by OMB in Fiscal 1980 and the generally minuscule nature of new initiatives vis-à-vis base programs, *a significant expansion and reorientation of the UIA process should be undertaken* if this exercise is to be meaningful. As noted above, clusters of new initiatives, base programs, regulatory activity, macroeconomic

---

[18] Additionally, given the rapid growth of nonfederal government activity in the past 20 years, state and local activity should be analyzed by UIAs. The problems in doing so are large, given the sparse analytic capacity of most local governments. However, the Federal government, consistent with the National Urban Policy, should encourage states to formulate their own urban strategies and to evaluate the impacts of their own programs on jurisdictions within their borders. HUD is now considering a demonstration program on UIAs for localities which hopefully will provide a first step in this direction.

FIGURE 3: Directions of Impact Analysis Research Urban

INDIVIDUAL NEW INITIATIVES (e.g., new man-power training program)

BROAD-BASED NEW INITIATIVES (e.g., welfare reform, solar energy)

AGENCY BASED PROGRAMS (e.g., HUD, DOD)

FEDERAL BUDGET (e.g., clusters of base programs)

NONBUDGET ITEMS (e.g., regulatory activity, inter-national trade)

policy, and other important federal policies, should be explored more carefully. We should concentrate on a few major initiatives and agency base
programs each year, rather than spending resources on minuscule and less
important new initiatives. The solar energy and HUD budget analyses noted
above are good examples. Furthermore, the present OMB guidelines should
be broadened to include interregional and intraurban activity and equity questions in order to be more complete. Finally, some notion of criteria should
be established so that UIAs have more meaning.

(2) There should be an *ongoing monitoring of the federal budget* in order
to understand the full spatial effects of federal spending and tax policy. A
methodology for doing so has been indicated above. We should have a better
understanding of where federal policies operate, and the kinds of effects that
they have on our cities.

These reforms and extensions will require several items if they are to be
successful.

(3) There must be substantially more *resources* devoted to the training of
personnel who undertake UIAs.

(4) An *impartial advisory panel* should be appointed as an arm of OMB
(or as an independent information-gathering agency such as the U.S. Department of Labor's National Manpower Commission or it should be like the
policy-oriented Council of Economic Advisers) to review agency UIAs and
perhaps do some research itself. The panel would consist of experts both in
and out of government. The appointment of a panel speaks to three problems
inherent in the current system: the possibly biased nature of UIAs done by
agencies on their own programs, the limited capacity of OMB's staff to review
UIAs, and the inability to get quick, expert advice on UIAs and to guide the
ongoing development of UIA methodologies.

(5) *Better program and urban data*[19] need to be collected in a standardized, centralized form in order to make UIA efforts—so often done in a short
time period—capable of being done more efficiently.

(6) Investment should be made to support the development of *impact
models* and other analytical techniques such as those used elsewhere in this
volume, and also noted in this section.

(7) Finally, *public interest and other groups should be allowed access to
the UIAs* once they are completed. This would open up governmental processes and make the consequences of policies to regions and people more
explicit.

I have attempted to set forth some major elements of urban impact analysis
and some suggestions for further implementation of this potentially important
new policy instrument. Probably little in the way of major urban initiatives
will be forthcoming in the next few years; therefore, we must be sure that

[19] The interagency Urban Data Task Force has been working on the problem of urban
data needs.

existing and future nonurban programs are reasonably balanced with regard to cities. UIAs, if they do little more than "raise the consciousness" of decision-makers in the federal bureaucracy towards the concerns of cities and the poor, will constitute a small step forward in the implementation of the President's urban policy.[20] Perhaps urban consciousness-raising is all we can realistically hope for in the age of Proposition 13, the Kemp-Roth Bill, and general austerity towards social spending. UIAs will not "save the cities," but might help reduce some of the unintended negative effects that some federal policies may have on urban areas. UIAs exist as the only "teeth" in the President's urban policy and should not be allowed to go the way of Environmental Impact Statements or PPBS.

REFERENCES

Ballard, K., and Wendling, R. "The National-Regional Impact Evaluation System: A Spatial Model of U.S. Economic and Demographic Activity." Paper read at the Twenty-fifth North American Meetings of the Regional Science Association, 1978. *Journal of Regional Science*, forthcoming.

Glickman, Norman J. *Econometric Analysis of Regional Systems: Explorations in Model Building and Policy Analysis*. New York: Academic Press, 1977.

———. *The Growth and Management of the Japanese Urban System*. New York: Academic Press, 1979.

———, and Jacobs, S. S. "The Urban Impacts of HUD's Section 312 Program." In *Urban Impacts Analysis No. 4*. Washington, D.C.: U.S. Department of Housing and Urban Development, 1978.

———. *The Urban Impacts of the Budget of the Department of Housing and Urban Development*. Washington, D.C.: U.S. Department of Housing and Urban Development, 1979.

Golladay, F. L., and Haveman, R. H. *The Economic Impacts of Tax-Transfer Policy: Regional and Distributional Effects*. New York: Academic Press, 1977.

Holmer, M. "Regional Economic Effects of the Federal Budget." In *Proceedings of the COUPE Conference on Interregional Growth in the American Economy*, edited by W. Wheaton. Washington, D.C.: Urban Institute, forthcoming. Article written in 1978.

Milne, W. J.; Glickman, N. J.; and Adams, F. G. "A Framework for Analyzing Regional Decline: A Multiregion Econometric Model of the United States." Paper read at the Twenty-fifth North American Meetings of the Regional Science Association, 1978. *Journal of Regional Science*, forthcoming.

Pechman, J., ed. *Setting National Priorities: The 1979 Budget*. Washington, D.C.: Brookings Institution, 1978.

[20] Several items proposed in the initial urban policy statement have been withdrawn by the White House or defeated by Congress. For instance, the *New York Times* (January 4, 1979) reported $3.4 billion in cutbacks (mostly in the elimination of labor intensive public works). Severe reductions in CETA (from 725,000 jobs to 540,000 jobs) and countercyclical revenue sharing (from $500 million to $150 million) are also anticipated for Fiscal 1980.

Raskin, M. G. *The Federal Budget and Social Reconstruction: The People and the State*. New Brunswick: Transaction Books, 1978.

Sarbib, J-L. "Preliminary Notes on the Future of American Cities in an Internationalized Economy." Mimeographed.

U.S. Department of Energy. *A Domestic Policy Review of Solar Energy*. Response memorandum. Washington, D.C.: U.S. Department of Energy, 1978.

U.S. Department of Housing and Urban Development. *The President's National Urban Policy Report*. Washington, D.C.: U.S. Department of Housing and Urban Development, 1978.

Urban and Regional Policy Group. *New Partnership to Conserve America's Communities*. Washington, D.C.: U.S. Department of Housing and Urban Development, 1978.

Vernez, Georges, et al. *Regional Cycles and Employment Effects of Public Works Investment*. Santa Monica: Rand Corporation, 1977.

Water Resources Council. *Guideline 5: Regional Multipliers; Industry-Specific Gross Output Multipliers*. Washington, D.C.: U.S. Government Printing Office, 1977.

CHAPTER TWO

Urban and Community Impact Analysis: From Promise to Implementation

LESTER M. SALAMON AND JOHN HELMER

In his urban message of March 27, 1978, President Jimmy Carter promised to establish a new procedure to identify the potential urban or community impacts of major federal initiatives in advance of decisions. The promise reflected the first official response to a longstanding concern of students of federal urban policy—a concern that the positive impacts of federal programs aimed at helping the nation's cities or other troubled areas are regularly swamped by other federal actions whose effects may be just the opposite. This concern found especially persuasive expression in 1977 with the publication by the Rand Corporation of a major analysis of the urban impacts of federal policies. While this study made clear that the exact extent of the federal impacts on urban areas is difficult to determine, it left no doubt that these impacts are pervasive, stretching well beyond the narrow confines of what is traditionally considered federal urban policy (Barro and Vaughan, 1977). In a sense, this work suggested that the Federal government not only has had an *explicit* urban policy for decades, but an *implicit* urban policy as well, resulting from the frequently inadvertent urban impacts of other federal programs.

For a President committed to a comprehensive urban policy but inclined to pursue it through the redesign and reorganization of existing programs rather than the addition of new ones, the concept of a systematic analysis of the urban impacts of nonurban policies seemed irresistible. Through such a process, the inadvertent urban impacts of the full range of federal policy could be surfaced and addressed. In this way the Federal government could aid the cities without having to spend additional funds: it would simply avoid hurting them.

The views expressed here are those of the authors and do not necessarily represent those of the Office of Management and Budget.

33

Because it seemed so irresistible, however, the urban impact concept underwent little critical analysis during the deliberations over urban policy. Originally proposed by various officials at the U.S. Department of Housing and Urban Development (HUD), it was carried along in successive drafts with little effort to spell out the nature of the commitment it might require, either in terms of analytical resources or in terms of policy. Like so many good ideas that find their way into policy, little attention was focused prior to the decision on how this one would be implemented, or what it would entail.

The purpose of this paper is to explain how the urban impact system outlined in the President's urban message was translated from a vague promise into an operating process, and how it functioned in its first trial run. After a brief review of the background from which the urban and community impact analysis concept emerged, the major decisions made in the implementation of this new tool of policy management, and the reasons for them, are identified. The paper then outlines the experience with this process during its first months of operation and concludes with a discussion of a number of lessons to which this experience gives rise.

Since the authors were involved in the detailed design and early operation of the urban and community impact analysis (UCIA) process, the discussion here may not be entirely free of bias. Nevertheless, it is our hope that readers will find in this account an accurate explanation of these decisions and a clearer understanding of the process that has resulted.

BACKGROUND

The problem: regional tilts in federal policy

The basic rationale for a process that takes regular account of the unintended geographical impacts of federal policies is simple and straightforward. The Federal government now spends at least $30 billion a year on programs to relieve economic distress and inadequate living conditions in various parts of the country. These expenditures reflect a growing awareness that pockets of economic stagnation and rapidly changing demographic patterns can be serious obstacles to the achievement of national economic and social goals. Yet while these expenditures are rising, the Federal government is also pursuing other policies that accentuate rather than relieve regional disparities. Oftentimes the effects of these other policies are unintended or undesired. They result from the fact that some national policies have different consequences for different types of places, and also that without analytical foresight and effective coordination, there is no way that policy-makers operating within organizationally narrow terms of reference can avoid them.

Recent Rand studies illustrate how widely varied the impacts of federal programs are between regions, within regions, and between different types of urban areas (Vaughan, 1977; Vernez and Vaughan, 1978). Table 1 provides some examples. It also shows the limitations of our present analytical capability to assess the often conflicting effects of policies in specific areas, as indicated below:

Tax incentives for new plant investment encourage plant construction in suburban or nonmetropolitan areas rather than rehabilitation of existing inner city firms;

Regulatory decisions affect the regional distribution of investment, although impacts here are difficult to pinpoint with accuracy; and

Minimum wage regulation works against economic growth in labor surplus areas, while the effects on regional employment distribution are unknown.

Taken together these unintended consequences can swamp the impacts of the explicit programs designed to relieve regional distress. To the extent that this happens, precious budget resources are wasted.

What has given this realization special force is the combined weight of two political realities: the prevailing climate of fiscal austerity and a growing regional sensitivity in the Congress and elsewhere. The first of these, reflecting a preoccupation with the inflation problem, has undermined support for new programs to carry out goals like the improvement of our cities, and has focused attention instead on how to improve existing efforts or minimize existing impediments. The second, reflecting the changing balance of economic fortunes among regions of the country and the redirection of federal grant dollars as a consequence of increased reliance on formula distribution systems, has created a political clientele demanding closer attention to the regional tilts of federal policies (*see*, for example, Moynihan, 1977; and Rothenberg, 1977).

Past efforts at regional analysis and policy coordination

This concern about the potentially conflicting geographical impact of federal programs had fortunately already found some expression in existing policies and procedures by the time of President Carter's urban message in 1978. While the previous efforts tended to focus on the more explicit and visible urban and regional programs, they constituted a body of experience and institutional processes that significantly influenced the design of the system that resulted from the President's 1978 directive. Most importantly, they constituted the context into which the new process had to fit.

One of the earliest such expressions of concern about the need to coordinate urban and regional policies was Section 204 of the 1966 Model Cities Act. It required that applications for federal loans or grants for major construction and infrastructural development be "submitted for review" to area-wide planning agencies, and include indications that local government planners had had an opportunity to assess proposals and ensure that they complied with existing development plans. Both this, and the requirements for review and coordination of federal, state, and local planning laid down in the Intergovernmental Cooperation Act of 1968, focused on the impacts of Federal government projects at the local level. At the federal level, the U.S. Office

TABLE 1: Federal Policies and the Demand for Goods and Services

Federal Policy	Interregional Effects	Intraregional Effects	Effects by Type of Urban Area
Macroeconomic policies			
Aggregate monetary and fiscal policies	Northeast conforms more closely to national cycles, grows more slowly, and responds more volatilely than other regions to aggregate national changes	Central cities appear to be more cyclically volatile than suburbs and suffer recessions more deeply	Urban areas with high employment concentration in durable goods industries experience volatile employment fluctuations Large urban areas conform more closely to the nation than small ones Large cities tend to experience more rapid inflation than small ones
Automatic fiscal stabilizers	Unknown	Unknown	Unknown
Personal income tax changes	Favor high income regions	Favor high income suburbs	Unknown
Corporation income tax changes	Slight favor to growth regions	Unknown	Unknown
Investment tax credits	Favor growth regions	Favor growth suburbs	Unknown
Public works programs	Favor growth regions	Favor suburbs	Unknown
Public employment programs	Unknown	Favor central cities	Program grants tend to be concentrated in large cities
Federal spending and purchasing			

Aggregate tax and expenditure patterns	Favor low income regions at the expense of the Northeast; tax receipts fall short of expenditures in growth regions	Expenditures tend to be concentrated in central cities	Unknown
Defense contracts	New England and Pacific areas have benefited from high federal expenditures	Unknown	Unknown
Defense salaries	Concentrated in the South and West	Unknown	Unknown
Sewage and water treatment facilities	Unknown	Have aided suburban development	Favor rapidly growing urban areas
Federal transfer payments	Stimulate redistribution from rich to poor regions; Northeast receives higher per capita welfare payments than elsewhere Retirement payments have benefited the Sunbelt	May have aided in the concentration of poor households in central cities	Unknown
Labor			
Income redistribution and taxes	Relatively high unemployment and welfare payments in the Northeast may have led to a relative reduction in labor force participation and higher unemployment in that region	Unknown	Unknown

TABLE 1 (continued)

Federal Policy	Interregional Effects	Intraregional Effects	Effects by Type of Urban Area
Minimum wage	Unknown	May have led to increased unemployment in central cities in which affected labor is concentrated	Unknown
Unionization	High membership rate in Northeast has resulted in higher wages which may have slowed growth	Unknown	Unknown
Occupational Safety and Health Administration	Affects regions according to industrial structure. Results unknown	Unknown	May affect older cities more severely
Manpower programs	Unknown	Tend to benefit central city labor force	Unknown
Transportation			
Regulation	Increase in freight rates has encouraged decentralization Rail-based industries in Northeast have suffered with the rise of trucking	Rail-based central city industries have suffered with the increase in trucking, which encourages suburbanization	Cross subsidy from large to small towns
Subsidies Highways	Have favored growth regions at the expense of Northeast Subsidy in construction from North to South and Mountain area	Favor suburbs	Favor poorer, smaller towns at the expense of large towns

Waterways	Cities served by waterway systems have benefited at the expense of railroad-based cities	Unknown	Recent developments may have favored the South Have diverted trade-offs from rail
Mass transit	Small cities receive higher per rider subsidy	May encourage suburbanization of population	Unknown
Rail	May favor large cities	May favor central cities	May favor Northeast in the future
Air	Cross subsidy from large to small cities	May favor central cities Airports usually constructed in suburbs	Unknown
Energy			
Regulation	Unknown	Unknown	Natural gas regulation has deprived the Northeast of gas supplies
Subsidies	Subsidies for rural electrification may encourage decentralization	Unknown	Unknown
Capital			
Tax structure	Unknown	Tax structure may have encouraged decentralization	Unknown
Regulation	Pollution control may affect older cities more severely	Pollution control may affect central cities more severely	Unknown
Subsidies Business loans	Unknown	May encourage central city investment	Unknown

Source: Vaughan (1977).

of Management and Budget (OMB) has had responsibility for monitoring compliance with both pieces of legislation, and in 1969 drew up OMB Circular A-95 to set out the rules and procedures which the legislation had called for.

This Circular has undergone periodic revisions since then, but its principal weaknesses remain. The requirements for review and coordination are not mandatory, and at the local and areawide planning levels, they are not easily accomplished by authorities whose jurisdictions are highly fragmented, and who are themselves subject to conflicting and contradictory federal agency rules. An OMB assessment of the A-95 process reported that it "cannot assure coordination, but it is designed to create a climate for intergovernmental cooperation in which coordination is more likely to come about" (U.S. Office of Management and Budget, 1976, p. 4).

Also in 1969, Congress wrote into the provisions of the National Environmental Policy Act the requirement that federal agencies analyze their proposed projects to identify a wide range of environmental impacts, and also to weigh the environmental benefits and costs of alternative proposals. This analytical procedure was also an attempt to coordinate federal government action with the environmental policy objectives enunciated in the Act. For the most part, the reporting requirement, known as an Environmental Impact State (EIS), has been applied to agency projects whose impacts are again limited to specific geographic localities. In 1975 alone, for example, federal agencies assessed more than 30,000 different projects for their environmental impacts, and although most of these assessments fell far short of a full-scale EIS, between 1970 and 1976 about 6,000 EISs were prepared. Substantial litigation has tested the analytical and procedural adequacies of these statements and a little less than 5 percent have been ruled inadequate and ordered to be repeated.

In a review of the EIS process, the Council on Environmental Quality (CEQ) has urged agencies to focus their analysis more on program than project decisions. "The realization is growing," CEQ reported in 1976, "that many federal actions can be grouped under program statements for more useful and systematic analysis. Repetitive actions or actions that affect a clearly delineated, meaningful geographic area are often defined as programs and are grouped into program EISs" (U.S. Council on Environmental Quality, 1976, p. 12). In 1975, 38 analyses were submitted to CEQ covering program proposals.

While the EIS procedure remains one instrument for both analytical review and policy coordination, its scope is widely perceived as limited. Although, in fact, the wording of the statute defines environmental impacts very broadly, administratively speaking the EIS procedure has not resulted in the wide coverage of urban and regional policy-making which its framers perhaps intended. Instead, the focus as well as the impact of the statements has largely been at the level of individual projects and specific localities.

Other procedural approaches have also been tried, and although their purpose was not originally to focus on urban and regional policy, in time they have come to represent significant new tools for the President and the Executive Office to apply in that direction. For instance, in November 1974, President Ford issued Executive Order 11821 with the objective of improving agency decision-making and coordinating agency initiatives with the President's concern for limiting the cost of government and the rate of inflation. The method adopted was called, somewhat inappropriately, the Inflation Impact Statement (IIS).

The Executive Order, along with OMB Circular A-107 which implemented it, required federal agencies to identify those legislative and regulatory proposals which were major by prevailing standards. Before these were sent to the Congress or (if regulations) published in the *Federal Register*, agencies were to prepare analyses of the proposal's costs and benefits, as well as the costs and benefits of alternatives. Two Executive Office units monitored compliance. OMB oversaw the analytical process as a whole, and also evaluated IISs prepared for proposed legislation. The Council on Wage and Price Stability (COWPS) was responsible for evaluating IISs of proposed rules and regulations.

The emphasis in this effort was on traditional economic cost-benefit analysis. According to one staff evaluation:

The principal objective of the IIS program was to induce agency decision-makers to be more sensitive to the whole range of effects—particularly the hidden and often very costly consequences to the consumer—of prospective government actions. More specifically, the aim is to: (a) make agencies in their rulemaking processes and in developing legislative proposals more accountable for their actions' economic effects; (b) provide a management tool of use primarily to the agency and secondarily to COWPS/OMB, in considering how the expected costs to society from a proposed action compare with its expected benefits, and how these benefits compare with the costs and benefits of possible alternative government actions... (Hopkins, 1976, p. 4).

The IIS procedure marked a significant shift in analytical focus from the localized impacts identified in the A-95 and EIS procedures. Threshold criteria for identifying proposals to be analyzed were $100 million in increased costs for the national economy as a whole in one year, or $50 million in one year for a single economic sector, industry or level of government. In most cases, IIS analyses did not draw attention to the urban or regional dimensions of cost-benefit ratios. But, by focusing on particular sectorial or industrial costs, it was possible to identify how regulatory or legislative proposals developed by agencies might strike hard, often unintentionally, at the economic health of particular cities, groups of urban areas, states, or regions.

The weakness of the IIS process was largely the result of its relatively short life; it expired on December 31, 1976, at the close of the Ford administration, after less than two years of operation. In so short a time, agencies were not able to regularize the role which IISs could play in the formulation of policy proposals. Rather, as the same staff evaluation explained:

Typically an agency uses the IIS more as an input to the decisions that are made *after* the proposal is published than to those made *before* such publication. To the extent that the analysis is performed outside the office which develops the proposal (which is especially likely where an office has very limited analytical capability), the analysis is not apt to be an important input in the proposal's development. Furthermore, much of the work on an IIS is completed just prior to the proposal's publication, which limits the effect of the analysis in molding the initial proposal (Hopkins, 1976, p. iv).

Notwithstanding, the Executive Office had established a precedent for using agency analytical staffwork, directed to cover particular kinds of policy impacts, as a method for executive decision-making, review, and coordination. To be sure, OMB and the President's Domestic Policy Staff have traditionally had the potential for undertaking this type of review, but conventional budget review and legislative clearance processes at OMB have not attempted to do this regularly for all major policy decisions. What was novel about the IIS process was that it provided Executive Office policy-makers with an overall perspective on agency initiatives, and by identifying conflicting goals, hidden costs, and inadvertent impacts, it enhanced the central capability for coordination.

Although Executive Order 11821 expired and the IIS process ceased formally at the end of 1976, the Carter administration decided to revive the regulatory analyses which the IISs had begun. Executive Order 12044, issued on March 23, 1978, provided, among other things, for a similar process of agency identification of major regulations, and the completion of regulatory analyses for those regulations that "may have major economic consequences for the general economy, for individual industries, geographical regions, or levels of government." The addition of a geographic or regional focus to the analyses was a notable, if not widely appreciated, expansion of coverage. In addition, the wording clearly indicates that both OMB and COWPS, which resumed responsibility for the new regulatory analyses as they had done with IISs, were to try to institutionalize the analytical process in time to have a real influence over policy decisions themselves. The organizational network was also expanded for review of the regulatory analyses. A Regulatory Analysis Review Group (RARG) was established to comment on, evaluate, and if necessary reject, agency submissions, and this group included several additional agencies and Executive Office units, including, in addition to the OMB, COWPS, the Council of Economic Advisers (CEA), the Domestic Policy Staff (DPS), the Office of Science and Technology Policy, CEQ, and 11 cabinet level agencies.

As with the IIS process, the emphasis of RARG review has been on assessing the costs and benefits of regulatory proposals in a conventional macroeconomic or sectorial framework. By and large, despite the language of

Executive Order 12044, quoted before, the tendency has not been to focus on the regional or urban area effects of primary concern to the Carter urban policy.

Beyond the special coordinating devices just described, the regular budget and legislative clearance processes provide additional mechanisms through which to achieve greater coordination of federal program activities. While these established processes provide an effective tool for evaluating the explicit and overt impacts of policies, however, they are far less effective in evaluating inadvertent or implicit impacts, including those related to geographical concerns. In addition, the organization of the budget and legislative review processes tends to emphasize program-by-program analysis rather than cross-cutting policy concerns.

In short, while a number of efforts have been made to build greater sensitivity to the potentially conflicting geographic impacts of programs into the policy process, these efforts left significant gaps and did not provide the kind of systematic assessment of both explicit and implicit regional tilts that was increasingly called for. It was to fill these gaps that President Carter, on March 27, 1978, promised to create "a continuing mechanism" that would make the "analysis of the urban and regional impact of new programs . . . an integral and permanent part of all policy development throughout our government."[1]

DESIGNING THE PROCESS

While the President's urban message outlined the basic contours of the new urban and community impact analysis system, however, it left open many of the crucial characteristics that would determine how this system would operate. These were resolved in the course of preparing two further documents, both of which were ultimately issued on August 16, 1978: first, Executive Order 12074; and second, OMB Circular A-116 (see Appendix). Prepared under the auspices of OMB, but with the assistance of the Domestic Policy Staff and an informal working group of agency and outside experts, these documents formally mandated the UCIA system and established its basic structure and operations.[2]

In the course of preparing these implementing documents, five major issues had to be resolved. The purpose of this section is to outline these issues, and then to identify the key considerations that affected their resolution.

[1] Statement of President Jimmy Carter, March 27, 1978, on the occasion of the signing of the Urban Message to Congress.

[2] Involved in preparing Executive Order 12074 and OMB Circular A-116, in addition to the authors, were Janet McNair of OMB; Marshall Kaplan, Franklin James, Katharine Lyall, and David Puryear of HUD; Ralph Schlosstein of the Domestic Policy Staff; as well as an informal advisory group composed of Leo Penne, Harvey S. Garn, Thomas Mueller, Roger Vaughan, Georges Vernez, James Sundquist, and Francis Viscount.

Major issues

The first major issue that had to be resolved in designing the UCIA system involved the question of *which initiatives* to subject to the process. Since the purpose of the urban impact process was to examine the geographical consequences of policies not commonly thought of as "urban" policies, it was clear from the outset that coverage would have to be broad, embracing such areas as tax policy and regulatory actions, as well as the major spending programs of the government. But questions arose about whether all such actions should be examined, or only major ones; and, if the latter, how "major" initiatives were to be identified. In addition, since the impact of some programs differ from application to application (e.g., major construction projects), the question of whether to apply the process to project-by-project decisions had to be resolved.

A second major issue concerned the *types of impacts* to examine. Theoretically, any aspect of urban life—from air quality to the availability of cultural resources—could qualify as an urban impact to be examined by urban and community impact analysis. So cast, however, the task would be clearly unmanageable. Nevertheless, the President's urban policy gave only slight hints about which impacts were most important. According to the President's message to Congress of March 27, 1978, the goal of the urban policy was to "make America's cities better places in which to live and work." The policy sought improvements in urban employment opportunities, fiscal conditions, social and health services, physical environment, cultural and aesthetic life, neighborhood involvement, and mobility. Translating such a policy into a measurable set of goals against which other program initiatives could be judged posed a difficult philosophical and analytical challenge.

The third issue involved in designing the urban impact process concerned the *type of analysis* that would be required. To be credible in the policy process, urban and community impact analyses had to be more than subjective "guesstimates." Given the state of the art, however, it seemed unlikely that detailed quantitative assessments could be made with any confidence. In fact, in its survey of the intraregional effects of federal policy, the Rand Corporation was able to claim reliable knowledge of the impacts of only 10 of the 28 policies examined, and only for the direction of impact. In eight other cases, even the direction of impact could only be guessed at, while for the remaining 10 (including such areas as energy regulation and welfare) it was unknown (Vaughan, 1977, pp. x–xi).

A fourth issue had to do with the *locus of responsibility* for the urban impact process. Involved here were two types of questions: first, whether to centralize or decentralize responsibility for the actual analytical work; and second, what sort of monitoring or review mechanism to put in place to ensure the quality of the analysis and to feed its results into the decision-making process.

A fifth major design issue that had to be resolved concerned the nature, timing, and procedures for *outside review* of the urban impact process, both by Congress and by other interested publics. At issue here was the question of whether to treat the urban impact analyses as public documents or as internal advisory materials.

Major considerations in resolving the design issues

Three major considerations shaped the ultimate resolution of these basic design issues and hence the structure and content of the urban impact analysis process during its start-up phase. These considerations emerged in part from the political and institutional circumstances that prevailed when the process was launched, and in part from the designers' analysis of what was necessary to make the process as effective as possible under the circumstances.

Integration into the policy process. The fundamental consideration in the design of the urban and community impact analysis process was to create a mechanism that was built squarely into the ongoing policy processes of the government, and not set far off in splendid isolation. This consideration reflected the judgment that the whole point of the impact analysis process was to influence decisions, not just to produce scintillating analyses, and that if trade-offs had to be made between the character and quality of the analysis and its usefulness for decision purposes, they should favor the latter. Because there are only three processes—the budget process, the legislative clearance process, and the new regulatory analysis process referred to above—that provide any regularized, general overview of agency policy and program initiatives, much of the implementation effort, therefore, focused on designing a system that could mesh with the rhythms and requirements of these three processes. This, in turn, shaped the decisions on three major design issues: the *assignment of responsibility* for the process; the *timetable* and, by implication, the *nature of the analysis* that could be expected; and the *degree of public scrutiny* possible.

LOCUS OF RESPONSIBILITY. Because the responsibility for managing each of the three major processes available in the Federal government to coordinate and monitor policy and program changes is vested in OMB, OMB was the logical home for the urban and community impact system. It was not, however, likely to be a very hospitable home. For one thing, the agency lacked the kind of expertise in regional analysis that the UCIA process required. Budget examiners are trained as program specialists, not regional or urban analysts. Their ability to assess the potential geographic impacts of the programs they monitor is therefore limited. More importantly, the OMB professional staff was likely to view the UCIA process as a diversion from OMB's major responsibility, which is to review programs and judge their effectiveness and operational efficiency. Most budget examiners feel they lack the time and resources to carry out even this basic function adequately, especially given the increased pressures on them to find ways to reduce spending, limit agency personnel increases, and reduce inflation. In addition, the brief experience with the Ford administration's inflation impact process left a residue of doubt about the utility of the UCIA exercise. What evidence was there, examiners asked, that anyone, including the President, would take this process seriously when our national priorities competed with it for attention?

Because of the likelihood of a cool reception in OMB, alternative locations for the UCIA process were considered. These ranged from new Executive Office or White House units (recommended variously by the League of Cities, Senator Muskie, and the Advisory Committee on National Growth Processes in a 1976 report), to the DPS or the CEA, to a line department.

Each of these alternatives had drawbacks, however. Creation of a new Executive Office or White House unit, for example, ran directly counter to the President's commitment to reduce the size of the Executive Office of the President, a commitment that had just been implemented in Reorganization Plan No. 1 of 1977. In addition, such units have grown so numerous that some end up with marginal participation in major policy decisions. Both CEA and DPS, by contrast, have ready access to key decisions, but they have other problems. CEA focuses primarily on macroeconomic issues and has historically shied away from the kind of regional and geographic preoccupation that had to be the major concern of the UCIA process. DPS had greater interest, but lacked the staff resources or the institutional processes to manage such a system of review on a regular basis itself. Finally, the idea of placing responsibility for the UCIA process in a line department would have meant placing one Cabinet officer in a position to review budget requests and program initiatives of the others, an arrangement certain to produce antagonisms and, therefore, unlikely to work.

In view of these competing concerns, the decision was made to assign to OMB the primary responsibility for managing the UCIA process, but to involve the DPS formally in the designation of the initiatives subjected to analysis and in the decisions about how to treat the results of urban and community impact analysis in the deliberations leading to presidential decisions on major policy issues.

Within OMB, responsibility for the new UCIA process was located on the management side. This was partly by happenstance: the staff of the President's Reorganization Project in OMB had earlier identified the need for such a process in the course of an examination of the Federal government's economic analysis and policy machinery and, therefore, was in the best position to design the new process and get it working. This assignment made sense organizationally as well; however, since the UCIA process called for a crosscutting view of the budget and legislative program that no individual budget division is in a position to undertake, and that neither the Budget Review Division—which oversees the preparation of the budget—nor the Legislative Review Division—which oversees the clearance of legislation—was inclined to take on.

Under the terms of Circular A-116, OMB's role in the process is fourfold:

(1) to make sure that all relevant initiatives are identified and subjected to analysis in a timely fashion; (2) to provide guidance on the content of the analysis; (3) to review and certify the completeness and technical competence of the analysis; and (4) to transmit the results of the analysis to the relevant policy-makers. Two major functions are assigned to the agencies however: the initial identification of the initiatives that are candidates for UCIAs; and the actual preparation of the analyses. While this has a "fox-guarding-the-chicken-coop" quality to it, it was a necessary concomitant of the decision to build the process into the policy decision stream and to place major responsibility for it in the Executive Office of the President, where staff resources are limited. Fortunately, a survey conducted by the Reorganization Project revealed that virtually every Cabinet department and many of the independent regulatory agencies have some capability to perform such regional analysis, although less than four percent out of a total of 130 agency units surveyed reported assigning a priority to regional economic analysis, and even those units with significant expertise in this area were not often called upon to apply it to the preparation of options papers for senior decision-makers (Table 2). What this suggested is not only that the departments could handle the UCIA analytical burden, but also that the new requirement could have the desirable side effect of giving greater prominence to the regional analysis staffs within the agencies by tying them into a formal process similar to that in the Executive Office of the President. Coupled with a system for OMB technical review of the impact analyses, this arrangement of responsibilities seemed a reasonable way to meet the UCIA commitment within the prevailing resource constraints.

TIMING AND CHARACTER OF ANALYSIS. In addition to influencing decisions about the allocation of responsibilities for the UCIA process, the decision to integrate it as closely as possible into the ongoing budget, legislative review, and regulatory analysis processes also determined the schedule that would apply and, through it, the type of analysis that could be expected. Under OMB procedures, the budget process each year spans a period of 18 months, beginning with the issuance of planning letters to the agencies in the spring of one year, and concluding with congressional approval of appropriations and the official start of a new fiscal year on October 1 of the following year. In practice, however, the active period of Executive Office budget and legislative review is far more limited. According to OMB procedures, agency budget requests are due at OMB on or around September 15 each year. Not until late July, however, do internal agency processes begin to determine the major initiatives that will be candidates for inclusion in the agency's budget, and not until mid- to late August do agency heads make final decisions about the nature and scope of the initiatives they will transmit to OMB as part of their budget submissions. OMB review then spans a six- to seven-week period between the middle of September and early November. What this means in practice, therefore, is that the time actually available to analyze the potential

TABLE 2: Regional Economic Analysis Units in the Federal Government

	Types of Regional Analysis Activity							
	Info. Collection	Models Forecasts	Rpts. for Officials	Legis. Support	Public Info.	Staff Support	Inter-Agency Coord.	Options Preparation
Department of Agriculture								
Agric. Stab. & Conserv. Serv.	X		X	X	X	X		
Econ. Stat. & Coop. Serv.	X	X	X	X	X	X	X	X
Forest Service	X	X	X	X	X	X	X	X
Department of Commerce								
Off. of Chief Economist			X	X	X			
Bureau of Econ. Analysis		X	X	X	X	X		
Off. of Asst. Sec. for Policy	X		X	X			X	X
Industry & Trade Admin.	X	X	X	X	X	X	X	X
Department of Defense								
Off. of Econ. Adjustment		X	X	X	X	X	X	X
Federal Communications Commission								
Common Carrier Bureau		X						
General Services Administration								
Emergency Econ. Stab. Div.	X	X	X	X	X	X	X	
Resources Management Div.	X		X	X	X	X	X	X
Econ. Preparedness Div.						X		
Applied Economic Div.		X	X		X			
Housing and Urban Development								
Off. of Policy Dev. & Research	X	X				X	X	
Interstate Commerce Commission								
Bureau of Economics	X					X	X	

Department / Agency									
Department of Interior									
Bureau of Mines	X		X	X	X	X	X	X	X
Bureau of Reclamation	X	X	X	X	X	X	X		X
Off. of Minerals Policy & Res. Analy.	X	X	X	X	X	X	X	X	X
Bureau of Land Management	X	X	X	X	X		X	X	X
Department of Labor									
Off. of Trade Adjust. Assist.	X	X	X	X	X	X	X	X	X
Bureau of Lab. Stat. (Off. of Wages & Indust. Rel.)			X	X	X	X	X		
Bureau of Lab. Stat. (Off. of Price & Living Cond.)	X	X	X	X	X	X	X	X	
Bureau of Lab. Stat. (Off. of Prod. & Technology)	X		X	X	X	X	X	X	
Bureau of Lab. Stat. (Off. of Employ. Struct. & Trends)	X	X		X	X	X	X	X	
Employ. & Training Admin. (Unemploy. Insurance Services)	X	X	X	X		X	X	X	X
Department of Transportation									
Off. of Sys. & Econ. Dev.	X	X	X	X	X	X	X	X	X
Research & Spec. Prog. Direc. (Materials Transp. Bureau)	X	X	X		X	X		X	
Fed. Highway Admin.	X								
Off. of Environ. Quality	X			X					
Asst. Sec. for Policy & Internat. Aff.	X	X	X	X					
Department of Treasury									
Off. of State & Local Finance	X	X	X	X	X	X	X		X
U.S. International Trade Commission	X	X	X	X					

Source: President's Reorganization Project, Economic Analysis and Policymaking Project, Survey I.
Note: Based on incomplete tabulation as of February 28, 1978.

geographical impacts of major budget or program initiatives is typically no more than 12 weeks—from mid-July (when the structure of the agency budget first becomes clear) to mid-October (when OMB analysis of the budget begins drawing to a close).

Similar time constraints apply to legislative proposals. Although such initiatives are supposed to be included in the budget submissions, they are rarely spelled out in sufficient detail by budget time to permit serious analysis. Not until the period between January and April do agencies finalize such proposals and submit them for OMB clearance in bill form. Because the new congressional budget procedures require that such new initiatives be reported out of committee by May 15, however, the legislative clearance process within OMB is typically rushed, so that proposals can get to the Congress in time for committee hearings, markups, and votes.

Reflecting this timetable, OMB Circular A-116 specifies that the UCIA process should commence each year with the submission by agencies of a list of their anticipated major initiatives by August 15. UCIAs on these initiatives are then to be submitted along with the rest of the agency's budget package on September 15, and by no means later than the OMB hearings on the agency's budget, typically within two to three weeks of submission. In the case of new legislation, A-116 specifies that UCIAs must be prepared by the time legislation is submitted for OMB clearance. Finally, with respect to regulations, A-116 adopts the timetable established under Executive Order 12044 on regulatory analysis. Under this timetable, agencies must list their anticipated regulatory actions twice yearly. For each major regulation, an "economic analysis" must be completed and made available for public review at least 60 days prior to the promulgation of the regulation.

With time so short, the opportunity to generate new data or undertake sophisticated quantitative assessments of impacts is rather limited. Under the circumstances, much of the analysis must be qualitative, specifying expected directions and general magnitudes of impacts, but not precise amounts of impact. In the implementing circular, therefore agencies were instructed to quantify impacts "to the extent possible," but were assured that "where reliable quantification is not possible, qualitative assessments are acceptable" (A-116, Sec. 5).

PUBLIC REVIEW. Building the UCIA system into the budget and legislative review processes also affected the degree of public scrutiny that would be possible. This is so because agency budget submissions are treated as internal advisory documents not available for public release. Such treatment is essential to the executive budget process in order to ensure that the only budget documents reaching the Congress are the ones officially transmitted and approved by the President.

In return for providing the UCIA system ready access to perhaps the most important decision process in the government, the UCIA system had to accept the same prohibitions on outside scrutiny that apply to the rest of the budget.

While this eliminated a potentially important check and balance on the results, however, it also promised to guarantee greater candor on the part of the agencies preparing the analyses. This was consistent with the purpose of the UCIA process: to alert key decision-makers of potential negative geographic impacts of the policies they are considering, and to do so prior to decisions. Since presidents will inevitably find it necessary on occasion to take actions that have such negative impacts, keeping such analyses under wraps is probably crucial to the integrity of the process itself. Otherwise the incentives will be strong either to shade the outcomes or neglect the requirement because of possible political embarrassment. At any rate, forced to choose between a public process and one that was built into the formal Executive Office decision-making mechanisms, the designers of the UCIA system chose the latter.

Keeping the process manageable. The second major consideration that shaped the design of the urban and community impact process was a determination to keep the process simple and manageable to avoid a massive paperwork burden. This consideration reflected a desire to deflect the general hostility that existed toward government regulation and delay in general, and toward the perceived analytical burdens imposed by the EIS requirement in particular. In fact, what limited press criticism there was of the UCIA process dwelled heavily on this point. One wag went so far as to note that impact statements had become so numerous in government (environmental, urban, inflation, export, regulatory, and others) that an Impact Statement Impact Statement was sure to be next, and that the acronym for this—ISIS—was the Egyptian goddess of reproduction. In this climate, a process that tried to do too much was clearly doomed to failure.

Given this sentiment, the challenge for those designing the UCIA process was to create a meaningful mechanism that nevertheless avoided the perceived paperwork and analytical excesses of its predecessors. In practice, this dictated a policy of *restraint* with respect to both the scope and content of the new system. Decisions on the range of initiatives to be subjected to UCIAs, the types of impacts to examine, and the agencies to be covered all reflected this basic approach.

WHICH INITIATIVES? During the deliberations over the President's urban policy, three basic conclusions emerged regarding the scope of the new impact requirements: first, that it would apply to all types of federal actions (expenditures, tax policy, and regulations), and not just to new spending programs or to programs explicitly aimed at urban areas or development purposes; second, that it would apply prospectively to new initiatives, not retrospectively to existing programs; and third, that it would apply to decisions on programs and policies, but not to individual decisions on particular projects. The first of these conclusions grew out of the basic research that gave rise to the UCIA concept, much of which emphasized the role of tax and regulatory policies, as opposed to federal spending programs, on urban and regional development patterns. In fact, since the regular budget and legislative review processes were available to analyze the urban and community impacts of the explicit urban and regional programs, the focus of the UCIA process had to be on those programs whose urban and community impacts were more subtle and inadvertent. The second conclusion reflected the fact that the urban policy itself involved a major review and redirection of base programs, so that further analysis of these programs was considered redundant. The third reflected anxieties about creating another project review mechanism like the EIS which would largely duplicate what exists.

Even within these parameters, however, important decisions remained on the scope of UCIA coverage. Most importantly, some way had to be found to differentiate the significant initiatives from the less significant and thereby keep the new requirement manageable. Otherwise, the UCIA process would be throughly swamped, because the number of new budgetary, legislative, and regulatory changes generated by the federal departments and agencies in any one year reaches well into the thousands.

Early in the process, therefore, a decision was made to restrict the coverage to "major" initiatives. The problem, then, was to define "major." This could be done in any of three ways: first, in terms of the size or scope of the initiative; second, in terms of the potential consequences of the initiative on cities or other geographic areas; or third, in terms of a procedure by which one or more informed actors would make judgments using whatever standards they considered appropriate.

While each of these approaches had unique strengths, each also had important weaknesses. A quantitative standard would be the most reliable and the easiest to administer, but could miss a number of important initiatives whose dollar cost was slight but whose urban and community impact was potentially substantial (such as deregulation of the airlines). Defining "major" proposals as those with potentially substantial urban and community impacts would avoid this latter problem, but involved a tautology since it would basically require an urban and community impact analysis to determine whether such an analysis was necessary. And such an approach would likely miss the initiatives of greatest interest to the process, those whose potential urban and community impacts are not obvious or inadvertent. The procedural approach offered greater flexibility but, because of this, greater opportunity for important initiatives to fall through the cracks.

The approach ultimately adopted in OMB Circular A-116 was a combination of these three approaches, with emphasis on the third. Under it, sponsoring agencies were given primary responsibility for identifying their major initiatives each year. To do so, they are requested to provide to OMB and DPS brief summaries of *all* their anticipated initiatives by August 31 of each year, and to indicate which of these they consider "major" and therefore subject to the UCIA requirement. These agency nominations are then reviewed by both OMB and DPS to make sure no significant issues are missed. As guidance to agencies in making their selections, moreover, the A-116 provides a list of suggestive criteria for determining which proposals are "major," including such factors as: direct budget cost, costs for entities other than the Federal government, centrality to the agency's or the administration's mission or purposes, visibility, likely urban or community impact, or any other factors the agency considers appropriate (Sec. 3[b]). The intent, clearly, is to include *all* the really important agency proposals whether or not someone thought *a priori* that they would have a negative impact on cities or other areas.

In the case of regulations, OMB Circular A-116 defines a "major" regulation as any one for which a "regulatory analysis" must be completed under the terms of Executive Order 12044 on regulations. Under these terms, a major regulation is one that will result in "(a) an annual effect on the economy of $100 million or more; or (b) a major increase in costs or prices for individual industries, levels of government, or geographic regions" (Executive Order 12044, Sec. 3[a][1]).

WHICH AGENCIES? Since even the major initiatives of some agencies are so small or so irrelevant to the purposes of the UCIA process that it makes no sense to subject them to the process, provision had to be made for some form of exemption process. This was done by allowing agencies to petition the OMB director for specific release from the process's requirements.

In addition to this, however, a mandatory exemption had to be provided for the independent regulatory commissions, which by virtue of their legal status as independent agencies reporting directly to Congress, rather than to the President, are legally exempt from presidential executive orders and OMB circulars. Although they can comply with such directives, the compliance is voluntary. This point was vigorously reaffirmed during the discussions preceding promulgation of Executive Order 12044 on regulations in March 1978, and could therefore hardly be reversed in Executive Order 12074 on urban and community impact analysis only five months later. Since regulatory actions by these independent commissions can have significant geographic consequences, this exemption has serious implications for the UCIA process. Fortunately, however, these consequences have been minimized by the willingness of several of these agencies to comply with the requirements of Circular A-116 voluntarily.

WHICH IMPACTS? Perhaps the most difficult issue in the design of the UCIA process concerned the designation of the actual impacts to assess. Each actor in the urban policy process began with a different notion about what constituted the most important indicators of negative urban or community impact —the quality of housing, the availability of jobs, the degree of racial segregation in housing, the quality of the air, the poverty rate, the soundness of land use patterns, the loss of population, the "quality of life," and so on. Not surprisingly, agencies sought to include as core indicators impacts that reflected basic agency missions in the expectation that the impact analysis process would then provide further justification for the agency's programs.

The pressures were, therefore, great to expand the list of potential impacts in terms of which initiatives would be judged, so that it would be possible for every agency to say something positive about the urban and community impact of virtually every program.

Such an approach was clearly inconsistent with both the analytical and management requirements of the UCIA process, however. It was, therefore, decided to identify a core set of indicators in terms of which all initiatives would have to be analyzed, but to leave agencies the option to analyze as well "such other factors as the agency may consider appropriate and feasible." This approach provided a reasonable compromise between the need for some common ground for comparing and contrasting initiatives and the fact of program diversity; and it did so without subjecting agencies to an excessive analytical burden.

In selecting the core set of indicators, three criteria were used. First, the impact had to be linked in an understandable way to the goals of the urban policy. Second, it had to be theoretically quantifiable, or at least not unduly nebulous, so that serious analysis would be possible. Finally, there had to be readily available data on the impact, organized in a way that made the analysis called for in the UCIA process feasible (that is, data had to be organized along geographical lines).

Ultimately, four impact indicators were found to meet these criteria, and were therefore the ones mandated in OMB Circular A-116: employment, especially minority employment; population size and distribution; income, especially that of low income households; and the fiscal condition of State and local governments. Under the terms of the A-116, all major initiatives must be subjected to analysis in terms of these impacts. Together with the invitation to analyze other impacts as well, at the discretion of the agency, the result was a system that promised to be at once limited and flexible.

Geographical breadth. Although the original conception that led to the UCIA system anticipated assessing only the *urban* impacts of federal actions, the deliberations on the urban policy quickly demonstrated that the impact process, like the urban policy as a whole, could not afford to be too narrowly focused in geographical terms and hope to survive politically. A formal process of "urban impact analysis" could be expected to prompt immediate calls for a counterpart "rural impact analysis" process. Early in the discussions, therefore, a decision was made to broaden the original concept so that the same analytical process would accommodate the analysis of a variety of geographical consequences.[3]

Not only did this make political sense, however, it also made analytical sense. This was so because what is of concern in the UCIA process are not

---

[3] Reflecting this, the name of the process was changed from "urban impact analysis" to "geographical impact analysis" in early drafts to convey this broader scope. This was then changed to "urban and community impact analysis" largely for stylistic reasons.

just the absolute impacts of initiatives on particular types of places (e.g., does the initiative increase or decrease investment in cities?), but also the relative impacts *among* types of places (e.g., does the initiative boost investment more in suburbs than in central cities?). In fact, the relative impacts may be more important because an initiative can adversely affect a certain type of place even while delivering absolute benefits to it if it provides even greater benefits to other types of places that are in competition with it. To capture these relative impacts, it is not sufficient to examine how an initiative affects one type of place. Rather, the impacts on a variety of types of places must be examined and then compared.

In deciding which types of places should be the geographical focus of urban and community impact analysis, three considerations were important. The first was the special interest the urban policy statement reflected in central cities, as opposed to suburban areas or rural areas. The second was the urban policy's emphasis on "distressed communities," that is, communities with extensive poverty or unemployment. The third was the need to restrict the analysis to types of places for which data were readily available. This meant utilizing standard Census classifications whenever possible.

Consistent with these considerations, OMB Circular A-116 specified five types of places for which the impacts of initiatives should be analyzed: central cities, suburban communities, nonmetropolitan communities, communities with above-average unemployment, and communities with below-average per capita income. According to the Circular, UCIAs must examine not only the absolute impact an initiative has on each of these places, but also the differential impact it has on each compared to what it has on the others. In this way, the process provides not just an urban impact analysis, but also a rural impact analysis.

THE EARLY RECORD

With the issuance of OMB Circular A-116 in mid-August 1978, the urban and community impact process promised in the President's urban policy went into effect for the Fiscal 1980 budget. How well did the process work during this first trial run, and what lessons does the limited experience to date suggest about the structure and efficacy of the process?

In answering these questions, it is important to bear in mind that a process like the UCIAs requires more than a single budget round to become institutionalized. Indeed, the budget process itself took time to develop. This is especially true in view of the fact that the UCIA process was not formally launched until well into the Fiscal 1980 budget season. As a result, the time available for submission of lists of initiatives; selection of candidates for UCIAs; preparation of analyses, review and certification of analyses; and redesign of initiatives was more telescoped than it would normally have been. Finally, because of budget stringency, the Fiscal 1980 budget contained fewer new initiatives than earlier budgets, so that the UCIA process had fewer occasions to demonstrate its effectiveness.

Despite these constraints, the indications are that the UCIA process worked surprisingly well in its first trial run. Most major agencies have taken the requirement seriously and are doing competent work. An informal network of specialists has taken shape throughout the government to carry out the UCIA mandate, creating an institutional capacity and sensitivity for analysis of the geographic implications of policies.

Altogether, 12 agencies prepared 24 UCIAs for the fall review of the Fiscal 1980 budget. Each agency submitting a UCIA received a written evaluation of the analysis, and, where necessary, staff of the urban impact office in OMB met with agency analysts to discuss redrafting and improvements in the materials submitted. Lengthy discussions were also held between the UCIA staff and the appropriate budget examiners prior to the preparation of director's review books, and subsequent to the reviews themselves, in order to clarify the implications that the UCIA process had brought to the surface. In a number of cases, the director and deputy director of OMB requested that proposals be reexamined in light of the evidence brought out in the UCIAs.

As noted in Table 3, 13 agencies indicated no major initiatives for the Fiscal 1980 budget and therefore submitted no UCIAs. In some cases, the important decisions were made prior to the Fiscal 1980 budget review; for example, the Civil Aeronautics Board's deregulation policy and the related development of policy for air service to small and medium-sized communities. In other cases, such as the Department of Defense, many policy and program decisions represented commitments to design or planning, which were not

TABLE 3: Agencies Indicating No Major Initiatives for Urban and Community Impact Analysis in Fiscal 1980 Budget

- Community Services Administration
- Civil Aeronautics Board
- Federal Trade Commission
- National Endowment for the Arts
- National Credit Union Administration
- U.S. Civil Service Commission
- Overseas Private Investment Corporation
- General Services Administration
- Justice
- National Aeronautics and Space Administration
- Equal Employment Opportunity Commission
- Department of Defense
- Tennessee Valley Authority

TABLE 4: Agencies Receiving an Exemption in Fiscal 1980

Agency	Reason for Exemption
• Agency for International Development	No domestic programs
• National Science Foundation	No relevant impacts identifiable
• U.S. Arms Control and Disarmament Agency	No relevant impacts identifiable
• U.S. Commission on Civil Rights	Study group only
• National Labor Relations Board	No relevant impacts identifiable
• Committee for Purchase from Blind and Handicapped	Too small
• Pennsylvania Avenue Development Corporation	Area-specific
• National Mediation Board	No relevant impacts identifiable
• Federal Maritime Commission	No relevant impacts identifiable
• Railroad Retirement Board	No relevant impacts identifiable
• International Communication Agency	No domestic programs
• Smithsonian Institution	No relevant impacts identifiable
• Export-Import Bank	No relevant impacts identifiable
• Farm Credit Administration	No relevant impacts identifiable
• Commission of Fine Arts	Too small
• Renegotiation Board	Too small
• State Department	No domestic programs
• Federal Energy Regulatory Commission	Independent regulatory agency
• National Capital Development Commission	Area-specific

initiatives as such, or which could not be assessed in UCIA terms so early in the planning cycle.

In addition to these 13 agencies, 19 others were granted exemptions under the terms of Section 6(b)(i) of the A-116 (Table 4). Such exemptions were restricted to agencies that fell into one of three categories: they were extremely small; their programs were such that urban and community impact analysis would be clearly inappropriate and unnecessary; or they were independent regulatory agencies that exercised their legal right to indicate an intention not to comply with the requirements of Circular A-116.

Because UCIAs are treated as internal OMB staff documents as discussed above, it is not possible to release detailed information about the analyses or provide full substantiation of their impact on budget decision-making at this time. A few general observations can be made, however:

- *Impacts* identified in most analyses were usually *small and positive* in a direct or absolute sense. Relative impacts—that is, the difference spread between central city, suburban, or nonmetropolitan areas by an identifiable impact—were estimated infrequently.
- *Inadvertent impacts* were identified as a result of this process in several cases. (In one instance, detailed analyses were ordered for the Fiscal 1979 spring re-

view.) Two other initiatives had the potential for shifting benefits and program resources from one type of urban area to another, but the available data did not allow certain analysis.

* *Quality control.* The quality of UCIAs submitted varied widely among agencies. In some instances, the report was little more than a project justification and failed to conform to A-116's format (these were sent back for revision). In most of the remaining cases, analysis was of good quality, limited only by data problems or difficulties in the targeting of the initiatives themselves.

* *Agency burden.* The heaviest burden fell on the Departments of Housing and Urban Development; Interior; Transportation; Health, Education, and Welfare; and Labor. Even so, the burden was not excessive. On average, UCIAs from these agencies were 25 pages long. None of the staffs involved reported difficulty in completing the assignments within the four to five weeks allowed, and the quality of the work submitted was high.

The ultimate question about the UCIA process, of course, is not how good the analyses are, but what effect they have on actual decisions. Given the nature of the process, however, this will always be a difficult judgment. UCIAs can hardly be expected to replace all the other pressures that come to bear in the formation of policy. Moreover, the real impact of the process may be as a deterrent inducing agencies to build a greater urban and community sensitivity into their proposals from the outset, so that the changes will be incorporated into the proposals prior to preparation of the UCIAs. Finally, since the ultimate consumers of the UCIAs are the President and his top advisors, the success of the process depends critically on the priority these officials attach to it. If they fail to ask for UCIA assessments, or if they regularly disregard the results, the process will fail no matter the quality of the analysis or the seriousness of the implementation.

All of these elements have found some reflection in the first half year of experience under the UCIA process. Of the new initiatives submitted and subjected to UCIAs, few survived the budget review process, but there is little evidence that the UCIAs were responsible for the decisions. In at least two cases, however, UCIAs surfaced issues that would otherwise have been overlooked, and that prompted top policy-makers to reassess, though not ultimately to change, policy directions.

Far more difficult to assess is the UCIA role in the legislative review process that follows the preparation of the budget, since this process is still underway at this writing. Compared to the budget process, legislative review is far less structured, which means that it poses far greater challenges for urban and community impact analysis: schedules are more flexible, priorities less clear, and responsibilities more nebulous. In this situation, end-runs of established procedures are standard fare, as Cabinet secretaries and White House staffers seek to bypass their opponents on the way to obtaining presidential commitments.

While a number of legislative initiatives have evaded the UCIA requirement as a consequence of this greater fluidity, the overall record seems credible, especially given the relative novelty of the UCIA requirement and the need to educate participants about its operations. At this writing, UCIAs are either completed or underway for most major initiatives—welfare reform, transportation deregulation, and multinational trade. Even in areas where tight time constraints and bureaucratic gamesmanship permitted some evasion of the process, political pressures are at work to correct this. In short, though the operation of the UCIA process has been far from perfect, it certainly compares favorably with the experiences under comparable processes during their first months of operation.

LESSONS AND CONCLUSIONS

While it is clearly too soon to draw any firm lessons from the operation of the UCIA process to date, several tentative lessons do seem worth noting. The first is that the benefits of locating the UCIA process in OMB seem clearly to outweigh the costs. The policy development process is simply too amorphous and unstructured, too given to last-minute changes and subtle redirections, to monitor effectively from any single agency base. The vantage point of the Executive Office of the President, and the clout of OMB, are crucial.

At the same time, however, this location has its costs. As we have seen, it determines key elements of the structure of the process: the reliance on agency analytical capabilities, the schedule, the treatment of the products as internal advisory documents, and the resulting absence of detailed public scrutiny. It can also affect the attention devoted to the process, since OMB will always have other, frequently more pressing, priorities competing for agency attention. The UCIA process will therefore always be in danger of being neglected at OMB, though this would be the case to some extent no matter where the process is located, since those charged with responsibility would have to bring their case to OMB or some other Executive Office unit eventually anyway. Despite the drawbacks, however, regular access to the central executive branch policy processes seems worth the costs.

The second general lesson that emerges from the experience to date with urban and community impact analysis concerns the analytical underpinnings of the process. Ultimately, the effectiveness of the UCIA process will be shaped by the reliability of the analytical base on which it rests. Unfortunately, however, that base is rather weak. Except in rare cases, it is not possible to demonstrate with any real confidence that a causal link exists between particular federal actions, or even collections of actions, and particular indicators of geographical change (such as population or tax base). Perhaps even more distressingly, one cannot draw a reliable link between particular operational indicators of urban and community change and the underlying concepts of real interest to policy-makers (such as the health and welfare of urban residents). Is it possible, for example, that the vitality of some cities might be enhanced if they lost population, or if they underwent economic transformations that showed up temporarily as net job reductions? What set of changes should federal action seek to encourage if it wants to contribute to fiscally sound, socially viable communities? Will structural unemployment be addressed best by encouraging the mobility of labor or the movement of job opportunities? These and other questions must have better answers than are now available before the UCIA process can become a really effective tool of policy, instead of merely a source of descriptive information.

Finally, it is clear that the UCIA process is no substitute for the regular political processes through which governmental policies are set. At best, the UCIAs can provide a tool of policy analysis that raises issues for policy determination. But to preserve its access and its credibility, the process itself cannot afford to become identified with any particular policy position, including the position that regional concerns should take precedence over other concerns. Even if it took a position, moreover, the existence of the UCIA process is no guarantee that "good" urban or regional policies will emerge. Ultimately, that will depend not on the process itself, but on what the process is connected to, both in terms of administration goals and policies and in terms of external political forces. Indeed, even the existence of the process is dependent on outside support and interest because UCIAs are designed to surface matters that some would prefer to have downplayed or ignored. Whether the process survives and prospers, therefore, will depend as much on the nature of the political support for raising these issues as on the technical merits of the analyses. If those concerned with the spatial impact of federal policies have sufficient clout and can make their concerns felt, then the UCIA process can be effective. If they do not, it will fail.

What exists now, in short, is a still-fragile experiment in policy coordination. As with other such experiments, this one faces an uphill struggle to establish its credibility and effectiveness. Perfecting the internal processes for this type of analysis is only one part—and perhaps not the most crucial part—of what is needed to make the mechanism work. As important over the long run is the emergence of a constituency for the process, and the insistence by this constituency that the interesting experiment that has started be continued.

APPENDIX
EXECUTIVE OFFICE OF THE PRESIDENT
OFFICE OF MANAGEMENT AND BUDGET
Washington, D.C. 20503

August 16, 1978   Circular No. A-116

To the Heads of Executive Departments and Establishments

SUBJECT: Agency Preparation of Urban and Community Impact Analyses

1. *Purpose.* This Circular provides instructions for the preparation and submission of urban and community impact analyses by executive branch agencies. These analyses are to identify the likely effects of proposed major program and policy initiatives on cities, counties, and other communities as defined below and to inform decisionmakers of proposed agency actions that may run counter to the goals of the President's urban policy.

2. *Background.* The President, in his March 27, 1978, urban policy message to the Congress, announced that executive agencies would be required to prepare urban and community impact analyses for major policy and program initiatives which they propose. He determined that such analyses are necessary in order to ensure that potentially adverse impacts of proposed Federal policies on cities, counties, or other communities be identified during the decisionmaking process.

3. *Proposals to be Assessed.* Urban and community impact analyses are to be prepared on proposed major policy and program initiatives identified by each agency. All types of initiatives should be considered candidates for this type of analysis, including new programs, expansions in budget outlays, program changes leading to shifts of resources among recipients, program changes affecting State and local governments, changes in tax provisions, new regulations, new regulatory authorities, and other changes in policy or program direction. This Circular is not intended to require urban and community impact analyses of individual projects, however.

Of the types of initiatives identified above, agencies are to subject only their major initiatives to urban and community impact analysis. It is recognized, however, that there is no simple, uniform rule that can be applied to all agencies to identify the initiatives that are major. The following general criteria are therefore intended to provide agencies some guidance in making these selections.

    a. In the case of *regulations*, major initiatives are those that will be the subject of economic analyses under Executive Order 12044; and

    b. In the case of all other initiatives, major initiatives are those that are clearly the most important agency proposals in terms of any of the following:

        i. direct budget cost, either immediately or over time;

        ii. costs for entities other than the Federal Government;

        iii. centrality to the agency's or Administration's mission or purposes;

        iv. visibility;

v. likely impact on cities or other types of communities, either in absolute terms or in terms of giving advantages to one type of city or community over other types; or

vi. such other factors as the agency considers necessary or appropriate to identify its major initiatives.

As specified more fully in the procedures section below, agencies will indicate in advance which of their initiatives they consider major and therefore subject to the requirements of this Circular. The Office of Management and Budget (OMB), in consultation with the Domestic Policy Staff, will review these agency designations and make any necessary modifications.

4. *Impacts to be Analyzed.* In order to guarantee uniformity and focus in agency efforts, Sections (a), (b), and (c) below outline the general guidelines agencies should follow in conducting urban and community impact analyses. Not every category or locus of impact will be appropriate in each agency's analyses, however, and some agencies may anticipate urban or community impacts not identified in the guidelines. Therefore, agencies may, with OMB's concurrence, add to or amend the guidelines in order to report the urban and community impacts that are most relevant and useful.

a. *Types of Impacts.* To the extent analytically feasible, analyses should identify the impact a proposed major initiative is anticipated to have with respect to:

i. employment, especially minority employment;

ii. population size and composition, including the degree of racial concentration or deconcentration;

iii. income, especially that of low-income households;

iv. the fiscal condition of State and local governments; and

v. such other factors as the agency may consider appropriate and feasible to analyze, such as neighborhood stability, housing availability, availability and quality of public services, degree of urban sprawl, environmental quality, cost of living, or others.

b. *Locus of Impacts.* For each of the foregoing types of impact, the analysis should seek to identify:

i. absolute impacts, including direct or indirect benefits or costs, on the following types of places:
   • central cities
   • suburban communities
   • nonmetropolitan communities
   • communities with higher than average rates of unemployment
   • communities with per capita income lower than the U.S. average, taking account, where possible, of differences in tax rates and cost of living
   • such other categories of places as the agency considers appropriate and necessary;

ii. relative impacts, that is, any differential effects that an initiative is likely to have on one type of place as compared to other types, with special attention to the types of places noted in b(i) above.

c. *Time Period.* Analyses should clearly identify the time period over which the indicated impacts are anticipated. Where appropriate, impacts that are short term (under 3 years) should be differentiated from those that are long term (3 or more years).

5. *Types of Analysis.* Projected urban and community impacts should be quantified to the extent possible. However, where reliable quantification is not possible, qualitative assessments are acceptable. Urban and community impact analyses are to be brief (about 15–20 pages) and should contain a 2–3 page summary of impacts accompanied by explanatory material indicating the basis for the judgments in the summary. Attachment A provides a suggested format for the summary of impacts, but agencies may alter this format if necessary.

To the extent possible, agencies should utilize the regulatory analyses required under Executive Order 12044 and the assessments of impacts on the "quality of the human environment" required under Executive Order 11514 in completing their urban and community impact analyses.

6. *Procedures.* The procedures to be used for different types of major initiatives are as follows:

a. Regulations. The procedures outlined in Executive Order 12044 will apply. Urban and community impact analyses should be incorporated into the economic analyses of significant regulations required in Executive Order 12044.

b. Legislative and Budgetary Proposals.

i. By August 31 of each year, each executive department or agency, unless specially exempted by the Director of OMB, shall submit to the Director of OMB, with a copy to the Assistant to the President for Domestic Affairs and Policy, brief summaries of all the initiatives it tentatively expects to include in its legislative program or budget submission, and nominate those it will subject to urban and community impact analysis. OMB, in consultation with the Domestic Policy Staff, will review these agency nominations and request additions or deletions as appropriate. When proposals are advanced at other times of the year, a similar procedure will apply to determine which should be subjected to urban and community impact analysis, and this procedure should be activated as far in advance of the final Executive Office decision as possible.

ii. For the initiatives so identified, agencies shall submit urban and community impact analyses as part of their regular legislative and budget submissions, according to the procedures outlined in OMB Circular A-19 for legislation and OMB Circular A-11 for budget proposals. OMB, in consultation with the Domestic Policy Staff, will review the resulting analyses to determine their compliance with the requirements of this Circular and may request revisions by either the submitting agency or any other agency with expertise in the area.

   iii. For the Fiscal Year 1980 budget season, the procedures outlined in 6(b)(ii) above will apply, except that agency designation of which initiatives to subject to urban and community impact analysis will be due on September 15, 1978, and the analyses themselves will be due one day prior to the agency's budget hearing at OMB.

  c. Other Major Initiatives. For other proposed major policy or program changes, agencies should submit urban and community impact analyses to OMB and the Domestic Policy Staff as far in advance of decisions as possible. Such analyses will form part of the material required for final action.

7. *Definitions.* For purposes of this Circular, the following definitions apply:

  a. Central city—a city of 50,000 population or more forming the central core of a Standard Metropolitan Statistical Area, as defined and designated by OMB Circular A-46, as revised.

  b. Suburban community—any place, other than a central city, within a Standard Metropolitan Statistical Area.

  c. Nonmetropolitan community—any place located outside a Standard Metropolitan Statistical Area.

  d. Fiscal condition—the relationship between the resources available to units of general government and the expenditures committed and other financial obligations undertaken by such governments.

  e. Direct costs—those costs experienced by the Federal Government, either in the form of budget outlays or in the form of revenue losses.

  f. Indirect costs—costs resulting from Federal Government action but borne by others (e.g., business cost increases due to pollution control requirements or increases in the cost of delivering State and local government services). Included here are reallocations of benefits among geographic areas, types of recipients, etc., due to changes in eligibility, distribution formulae, and the like.

  g. Minorities—Hispanic; Black, not of Hispanic origin; Asian or Pacific Islanders; American Indian or Alaskan Native.

  h. Low income—households with low income as defined in the Comprehensive Employment and Training Act.

8. *Effective Date.* This Circular is effective immediately and will remain in effect until rescinded.

9. *Inquiries.* All questions or inquiries should be directed to the Office of Management and Budget, Deputy Associate Director for Organization Studies, Economic Development Division. Telephone number (202) 395-5017.

James T. McIntyre, Jr.
Director

ATTACHMENT A

Proposed Format for Summary of Urban and Community Impacts

The attached is intended to provide a suggested format for summarizing the results of urban and community impact analyses. The summaries are not intended to substitute for the impact analyses themselves, but rather to supplement them by providing a succinct overview of the basic conclusions. The summaries should be attached to the complete analyses when they are submitted to OMB.

The impacts to be summarized in the summary sheets are those identified in Section 4(a) of the Circular plus such others as the agency considers necessary and appropriate. As indicated, both absolute and relative impacts are to be noted. Relative impacts are those that affect different places disproportionately—for example, an investment tax credit may benefit both central cities and suburbs absolutely, but may provide special advantages to suburbs compared to central cities because new plant investment may tend to concentrate in non-central city locales.

Each conclusion noted on the summary should be supported and explained in the body of the impact analysis. Where quantitative assessments and empirical proof are lacking, qualitative judgments supported by expert opinion, simulations, or state-of-the-art judgments will be acceptable.

Agency: _____

URBAN AND COMMUNITY IMPACT ANALYSIS

Summary

A. *Background*
  1. Initiative:
  2. Brief Description of Initiative (including extent of Federal control over uses of funds):
  3. Overall Objectives and Likely Benefits:
  4. Costs:
B. *Impacts*
  1. *Impacts on central cities*, including those with high unemployment rates and those with low per capita incomes.
    a. *Absolute Impacts*
    b. *Relative Impacts*
  2. *Impacts on suburban communities*, including those with high unemployment rates and low per capita incomes.

     a. *Absolute Impacts*
     b. *Relative Impacts*
3. *Impacts on nonmetropolitan communities*, including those with high unemployment rates and those with low per capita incomes.
     a. *Absolute Impacts*
     b. *Relative Impacts*
4. Other (please specify):
     a. *Absolute Impacts*
     b. *Relative Impacts*

Prepared By:

Telephone Number:

Approved By:

Date Prepared:

REFERENCES

Barro, Stephen M., and Vaughan, Roger J. *The Urban Impacts of Federal Policies*, vol. 1, *Overview*. Santa Monica: Rand Corporation, 1977.

Hopkins, Thomas D. *An Evaluation of the Inflation Impact Statement Program Prepared for the Economic Policy Board*. Washington, D.C.: Council on Wage and Price Stability, 1976.

Moynihan, Daniel Patrick. *The Federal Government and the Economy of New York State*. Washington, D.C.: U.S. Senate, July 1977.

Rothenberg, Jerome. *New England Regional Impact of Federal Policies. Report to the Federal Regional Council*. Cambridge: Massachusetts Institute of Technology, November 1977.

U.S. Council on Environmental Quality. *Environmental Impact Statements: An Analysis of Six Years' Experience by Seventy Agencies*. Washington, D.C.: U.S. Council on Environmental Quality, 1976.

U.S. Office of Management and Budget. *A-95: What It Is—How It Works*. Washington, D.C.: U.S. Office of Management and Budget, 1976.

Vaughan, Roger J. *The Urban Impacts of Federal Policies*, vol. 2, *Economic Development*. Washington, D.C.: Rand Corporation, June 1977.

Vernez, Georges, and Vaughan, Roger J. "Countercyclical Public Works Programs." Paper read at Economic Development Administration conference, U.S. Department of Commerce, Washington, D.C., 1978. Mimeographed.

CHAPTER THREE

Overview of the Spatial Dimensions of the Federal Budget

GEORGES VERNEZ

INTRODUCTION

Effective analysis of the impacts that federal programs have on urban areas requires detailed and accurate knowledge about where federal funds are allocated, what services are delivered, who delivers these services, and who receives the benefits or pays the costs. Knowledge of these implementation patterns is a necessary input to any analysis of urban impacts, and thus precedes it.

This paper focuses on one specific implementation issue: where federal outlays are distributed.[1] The analysis is for Fiscal 1976, but wherever possible shifting trends since 1970 are noted. It also examines how two major program characteristics—formula versus project grant programs and jurisdictional eligibility—affect the distribution of federal program outlays. Finally, it discusses a number of issues bearing on the policy interpretation of the observed distribution of federal outlays: reliability of the available data, spillovers of program outlays, substitution of local or private outlays by federal outlays, and assessment of the desirability of the observed distribution.

The purpose of this paper is not to argue for changes in the spatial distribution of federal outlays, but to highlight the nature of this distribution and indicate the complexity in interpreting the meaning of its pattern.

This paper draws in part upon research conducted by the Rand Corporation for the Economic Development Administration. *See* Vernez, Vaughan, and Yin, 1979.

[1] Recently a number of studies have focused on the geographical distribution of the federal budget. For a review *see* Rafuse, 1978, pp. 127–39. Most of these studies focused on broad regional disparities or on one component of the federal budget. This study, in contrast, focuses on the distribution of all federal outlays, major functional outlays, and outlays of selected individual programs to cities.

AREA DEFINITIONS

"Urban and community impact" analysis, mandated by executive order since August 1978, requires a definition of the geographical unit or units of interest. In discussion of the spatial impacts of federal policies, concerns most often focus on disparities between regions, between metropolitan and non-metropolitan areas, between urban and nonurban areas, between central cities and suburbs, and between cities of different characteristics. In past analysis, however, even the definitions used for these terms varied, making cross-studies comparisons difficult and possibly affecting the conclusions drawn. In the future, commonality of geographical unit definitions should be sought to facilitate comparisons by the U.S. Office of Management and Budget (OMB) and other policy-makers of urban and community impact analyses among different programs. Ability to compare relative performance among programs is an important aid to budgetary decisions.

Region

The term "region" can be used in ways that cause confusion. Most recently, the focus has been on disparities between the "Sunbelt" vis-à-vis the "Frost-belt" or "Snowbelt" regions. But there is an astonishing lack of consensus regarding the precise set of states classified in each of these two regions.[2]

There are also the two sets of regional definitions used by the U.S. Bureau of the Census. The first set divides the nation into four Census regions: North-east, North Central, South, and West Coast. The second set subdivides these four regions into nine Census divisions each containing from three to nine states. These divisions are most convenient for analysts making extensive use of Census data.

But other data assembling federal agencies define regions differently. For instance, the Bureau of Economic Analysis (BEA) in the U.S. Department of Commerce divides the country into eight regions that do not coincide with the Census regions or divisions.

Finally, the federal agencies define the regional boundaries for their pro-grammatic and administrative purposes in an overlapping manner; the regions of one agency do not always coincide with the regions of others. Although OMB Circular A-105 of 1969 established a uniform set of ten regions to which federal agencies have to conform, not all federal agencies do so. The Economic Development Administration (EDA), for instance, is still or-ganized according to six economic development regions. Overlapping on these disparate set of regions are the nine multistate regional commissions, such as the Apparachian Regional Commission, which overlie yet another set of varying regional breakdowns on our national landscape.

This regional balkanization does not facilitate consistency of regional anal-

---

[2] For a description of the many definitions that have been used in various studies, *see* Rafuse, 1977.

yses, and in some cases, impairs their feasibility or increases their cost. It is not rare to have programmatic data available by agency-defined regions and relevant regional characteristics data available under varying regional definitions depending on whether Census, Bureau of Labor Statistics (BLS), or BEA data are used. While consistent aggregation from states data is often possible, it is also costly. That may be one reason why OMB's guidelines (OMB Circular A-116) for urban impact analysis does not contemplate analysis by regions.[3]

Urban and metropolitan[4]

The Census Bureau defines an "urban place" as a community of 2,500 or more population. Douglas, Wyoming (pop. 2,677), for example, is an urban place. According to this definition, about 70 percent of the national population lives in urban places, but many of these are rural in character.

There is also what the Census Bureau calls an "urbanized area," that includes at least one central city inhabited by a population of over 25,000 and a surrounding closely settled territory. About 60 percent of the national population live in these areas, which more closely fit our perception of what urban means.

Most frequently, however, "urban" refers to the Census Bureau's Standard Metropolitan Statistical Area (SMSA). It includes an "urbanized area" plus, in many cases, some immediately surrounding territory that is more rural than urban but within commuting distance of the central city. About two-thirds of the national population live in metropolitan areas. In most cases, SMSAs coincide with the Labor Market Areas (LMAs) used by the Bureau of Labor Statistics in reporting its area employment, unemployment, and other economic characteristics data. But there are more SMSAs (279) than LMAs (224). Also 12 LMAs are not designated as SMSAs and 17 LMAs do not coincide with SMSAs. The latter are located mostly in the Northeast.

Either of the latter two definitions is useful to perform one-point-in-time analyses. However, frequent changes in the areas included in LMAs and SMSAs definitions create problems of consistency in analyses performed over time.

City

City-suburb disparities will be a major concern in the preparation of urban impact analyses of federal programs. Yet confusion about the meaning of those terms can easily arise.

The recent debate on "distressed cities" tended to focus on the central cities. Currently there are 375 central cities ranging in size from 20,000 to nearly 8 million and housing about 31 percent of the Nation's population. This focus

---

[3] Political considerations, however, were probably more important in that decision.

[4] Portions of the remainder of this section rely on Nathan and Dommel, 1977, pp. 284–85.

on central cities, however, has excluded suburban cities which may well be the next "distressed" areas. Throughout the 1950s and 1960s, employment and population grew more rapidly in suburban than in central cities. However, during the 1970s, a reversal of this trend is emerging.[5] For instance, in the "Old Manufacturing Belt," employment in the average central city grew as much between 1970 and 1975 as it had during the entire previous decade, while it fell to one-third of its previous level in the average suburban city. In the "Sunbelt" and Mountain and Western regions, employment is growing more slowly in the average suburban city than in the average central city. The problem of slow growth and even decline is no longer limited to central cities and, in some places, has shifted from central to suburban cities.[6]

Thus, a second and perhaps more meaningful way of defining cities is to include both central and suburban cities. An important issue, though, concerns the population cutoff size for inclusion in this definition. It may be placed at 500,000, 50,000, 20,000, or less. If placed at 500,000, there are just 27 cities housing 15 percent of the population. If 50,000 is chosen, there are 397 cities, including both central and suburban cities, housing 31 percent of the population. A lower population cutoff would further increase the number of areas defined as cities.

The above range of optional geographical definitions is not exhaustive. It serves to highlight the need for some degree of geographical standardization in the preparation by the various federal agencies of the now-mandated urban and community impact analyses. Nonstandardization runs the risk of producing analyses that are not readily comparable and may even result in urban impact conclusions conflicting with one another. However, while some definitional standardization is desirable, it should not be carried too far. Federal programs differ in objectives, targeting, and intended area impacts to which the geographic unit of analysis selected must be sensitive. Also, as suggested earlier, the focus on central cities and on North-South disparities is likely to change as spatial changes in the distribution of the Nation's population and economic activities occur.

CITY BIAS OF FEDERAL OUTLAYS

The focus of this overview of the distribution of federal outlays is on cities—including central and suburban cities—of 50,000 inhabitants or more. In 1975, about 31 percent of the United States population resided in them. The following three major questions are addressed:

[5] This refers exclusively to suburban cities of 50,000 or more, not suburban areas in general.

[6] These trends are reflected in the increased number of metropolitan areas experiencing population decline. Since 1970, 10 of the 25 largest SMSAs have failed to register any significant population growth. Although only about one-sixth of all SMSAs no longer grow, one in three metropolitan residents lives in one of these "no growth" areas.

- To what extent are federal outlays concentrated in cities of 50,000 or more inhabitants? And how does this concentration vary among programs?
- How are outlays going to cities distributed among Census divisions?
- How are outlays going to cities distributed among types of cities distinguished by income level, population size and growth, unemployment level, and geographical location within SMSAs (central cities versus suburban cities)?

These questions are examined for all federal expenditures (including federal procurements and grants programs); major functional areas of the federal budget; and selected large federal grants-in-aid programs to State and local governments. The latter include the six largest intergovernmental grants-in-aid federal programs: General Revenue Sharing ($6.2 billion obligated in Fiscal 1976); the Department of Labor's (DOL) Community Employment and Training Assistance (CETA) ($5.8 billion); Highway Research, Planning and Construction ($4.5 billion); Wastewater Treatment Construction ($4.3 billion); Community Development Block Grants (CDBG) ($2.4 billion); and Urban Mass Transportation ($1.5 billion). Also included are a number of smaller programs selected for their special significance to the development of cities: from the Law Enforcement Assistance Administration's (LEAA) ($.6 billion); U.S. Department of Health, Education, and Welfare's (HEW) vocational education ($.45 billion) and work incentive programs ($.34 billion); Community Action ($.3 billion); EDA's Grants and Loans for Public Works and Development ($.16 billion); Small Business Administration's (SBA) loans ($.1 billion);[7] and Business Development Assistance Grants ($.05 billion). Together, they distribute about 45 percent of about $60 billion (Fiscal 1976) in federal grants-in-aid to State and local governments.

To describe the spatial distribution of the federal budget, we used the federal outlays data compiled by the Community Services Administration to compute concentration ratios of federal outlays (for each program and the major functions of the federal budget) in cities, for all cities of 50,000 or more, and for cities grouped by Census divisions and by types in both 1970 and 1976. The concentration ratios measure the percentage share of federal outlays spent in specific cities divided by the percentage share of the national population residing in these cities. A value greater than one indicates that the specified cities receive a share more than proportional to their population. A few words of caution about this measure are warranted. First, another measure of concentration could have been used, such as federal outlays per $1,000 of personal income or per dollar of state-local revenues.[8] It was decided to standardize relative to population on the ground that people rather than places are the eventual target of federal outlays. Second, there is no

---

[7] In addition to direct grants, this program provided $1.5 billion of indirect federal support in the form of loan guarantees.

[8] These measures, as well as the one adopted here, were used in a study of the regional distribution of federal grants-in-aid by Vehorn, 1977.

a priori reason why federal outlays ought to be equally distributed (on a per capita basis) among areas of the country. Indeed, most federal programs are deliberately targeted to address problems of places or people that appear with different intensity in different areas. Furthermore, many federal programs provide support for one-shot capital investments or procurement contracts in a specific area one year and in another area in the following year. Thus, any concentration of federal spending in a given year, in one type of city or another, does not imply this concentration is "unfair" or "inequitable."

Federal outlays to cities

In aggregate, federal outlays—excluding national debt interest—are slightly "pro-city" (*see* Table 1). Approximately 35.8 percent of these outlays were allocated to cities of 50,000 inhabitants or more, although only 30.9 percent of the national population reside in cities that size. With the exception of transportation infrastructure, every major functional area of the federal budget distributes proportionately more funds to cities than to other areas of the country—including rural areas and suburban areas.

Most concentrated in cities are outlays for development and defense. The first, because more development funds are obligated for the urban-oriented community development programs than for the more broadly targeted area and regional development programs. And the second, because defense suppliers continue to be more concentrated in cities than in suburban or rural areas, even though some decentralization has been taking place.

Least concentrated in cities are outlays for transportation infrastructure, human capital development, and relief. Highway construction outlays dominate funding for transportation infrastructure, and they are predominantly made outside of cities where growth is taking place, as discussed below. However, other transportation infrastructure outlays for airports and water channelization and ports are, as expected, concentrated in cities. Outlays for human capital and relief are directed to people, and are distributed among cities and other rural and suburban areas of the country roughly proportionately to population. *What these data suggest is that the spatial distribution of the federal budget in aggregate is responsive to the spatial distribution of the population and of economic activities, rather than leading or running counter to the predominant trends in the geography of population and business location.*

Table 2 shows wide variations among specific programs in their distribution of outlays between cities and other areas of the country. The outlays by four of the six largest federal grants-in-aid programs to State and local governments are heavily concentrated in cities: Urban Mass Transportation Administration (UMTA); CDBGs; and wastewater treatment work construction grants. The size of these programs combined with their targeting "favoring" cities underline their importance to city officials and these officials' resistance to any retargeting that might result in aid reduction.

Among the largest grants-in-aid programs, the highway and revenue sharing programs are two notable exceptions. In Fiscal 1976, cities received practically no outlays for highways. As the interstate highway system nears completion, more federal highway funds could be redirected to urban areas. However, a number of barriers may impede the use of federal highway funds to solve the problems in urban areas. First, many proposed radial highways have been withdrawn from the interstate system in response to the growing opposition of threatened residential neighborhoods and of environmentalists despite a preponderance of evidence that without radial highways, central city locations are less attractive to business.[9] Second, arterials and other major road systems are excluded from the federal highway system even though in developed urban areas they are the predominant movers of goods and people. Third, federal highway funds are distributed to states which in turn allocate those funds (in part at their discretion) among jurisdictions of the state. Some states may favor rural over urban areas. And fourth, the program is one of the few remaining federal programs requiring state/local matching funds. Some urban areas may lack sufficient funds to match their full allocation of highway construction funds.

Revenue sharing outlays are evenly distributed between cities and other areas of the country. Universal eligibility for all local jurisdictions and inclusion of population in the allocation formula of revenue sharing has a spreading effect on the distribution of these funds.

Like their larger counterparts, the smaller programs selected for their importance for local development are also generally "pro-city." Outlays for vocational education, law enforcement, and community action are the most concentrated in cities where the problems they are intended to address are typically concentrated. The three smallest programs examined—grants and loans for public works and development facilities (EDA), small business loans (SBA), and business development loans (EDA) are least concentrated in cities. EDA programs past mandate was to target primarily on rural areas, and the distributions of its outlays reflects that objective.

Computation of the percentage of all cities having received outlays from any one of the programs examined reveal a point of considerable interest for urban impact analysis: In a given year, not all cities receive funds from a specific program. In 1976, from 2 to 99 percent of all cities received funds depending on the programs (Table 2). Generally, the smaller the program, the lower the proportion of cities that receive funds from that program. The combination of eligibility requirements and funding availability means that some cities may receive funds in one year, while others may benefit in another year. Thus, limiting the analysis of urban impacts to one specific year will be too short to capture the distributional breadth of these impacts. Time-series analysis is necessary to determine whether a constant "subset" of cities or all cities eventually benefit from a specified federal program.

[9] Environmental Impact Center, 1975.

TABLE 1: City Concentration Ratios of Federal Outlays by Budget Function, by Regional Location of Cities, Fiscal 1976

| Functions | Outlays, FY 1976 (millions) | All Cities | Northeast | |
			New England	Middle Atlantic
Development				
Area & regional dev.	$1,492.9	0.62	0.57	0.98
Community dev.	3,001.0	1.79	1.82	0.81
Other advancement & reg. of commerce	986.7	0.92	1.11	0.52
Total 1976	*5,480.6*	*1.32*	*1.57*	*0.86*
(1970)	(4,765.4)	—	(1.43)	(1.10)
Access infrastructure				
Air transportation	1,670.4	1.83	0.54	0.34
Water transportation	1,498.0	1.38	0.97	1.62
Ground transportation	7,340.8	0.63	1.33	2.41
Other transportation	101.9	1.19	11.97	0.30
Total 1976	*10,613.1*	*0.93*	*1.14*	*1.58*
(1970)	(8,031.5)	—	(0.92)	(0.97)
Human capital				
Manpower training	6,992.9	2.16	1.19	0.89
Education & social serv.	25.4	1.24	0.87	0.65
Vocational education	4,392.3	1.16	0.81	1.08
Higher ed., research, & general ed. aid	3,721.9	1.57	1.25	0.94
Health	31,652.8	0.70	0.79	1.79
Total 1976	*46,785.3*	*1.03*	*0.97*	*1.33*
(1970)	(26,030.9)	—	(1.31)	(0.96)
Relief				
Social services	2,897.4	0.96	0.68	1.40
Retirement & disability ins.	87,725.7	1.21	1.12	1.10
Unemployment ins.	2,162.0	1.02	1.29	1.48
Pub. assist. & other income sups.	18,194.5	0.69	0.71	1.69
Gen. rev. sharing & fiscal assist.	6,700.5	0.61	1.29	1.43
Disaster relief & ins.	170.2	1.00	1.20	2.17
Total 1976	*117,850.3*	*1.09*	*1.08*	*1.18*
(1970)	(59,421.2)	—	(1.42)	(0.91)
Defense				
Construction	1,630.5	0.58	0.12	0.13
Supply price contracts	42,415.2	—	0.96	0.57
Payrolls	38,331.2	—	0.42	0.48
Total 1976	*82,376.9*	*1.22*	*0.76*	*0.53*
(1970)	(59,375.4)	—	(0.72)	(0.71)

Northeast			South		West Coast	
East North Central	West North Central	South Atlantic	East South Central	West South Central	Mountain	Pacific
0.38	1.01	2.32	1.83	0.75	5.17	0.14
0.81	1.41	1.18	1.10	1.00	1.23	0.30
0.76	0.97	1.22	0.66	1.17	1.71	1.07
0.75	*1.30*	*1.33*	*1.14*	*0.99*	*1.80*	*0.86*
(0.71)	(1.36)	(1.46)	(0.94)	(0.78)	(1.31)	(0.86)
0.70	1.43	1.48	1.04	2.39	2.35	0.76
0.20	0.15	0.77	0.60	1.47	0.06	1.61
0.66	0.41	0.49	0.47	0.24	0.79	0.64
0.41	0.17	0.22	0.33	0.13	0.85	0.34
0.57	*0.67*	*0.85*	*0.67*	*1.16*	*1.12*	*0.58*
(0.50)	(0.74)	(0.79)	(0.54)	(1.63)	(0.90)	(1.53)
0.92	0.76	1.80	1.30	0.75	1.10	0.99
0.21	0.58	0.19	0.55	0.17	12.64	0.79
0.76	0.86	1.80	1.36	1.06	1.39	0.78
0.78	0.99	1.61	1.63	0.92	1.11	0.90
1.35	0.55	0.71	0.58	0.40	0.50	0.49
1.09	*0.70*	*1.30*	*1.01*	*0.64*	*0.86*	*0.73*
(0.85)	(1.03)	(1.65)	(1.27)	(0.82)	(1.25)	(0.84)
0.68	0.86	2.02	1.46	1.04	0.98	0.56
0.96	1.00	1.46	1.04	0.77	0.83	0.89
0.80	0.84	0.76	1.01	0.56	0.81	1.01
0.73	0.56	1.33	1.01	0.84	0.76	0.76
0.69	0.78	1.05	1.25	0.94	1.04	0.77
0.17	2.45	0.99	0.39	0.54	0.52	0.45
0.92	*0.95*	*1.43*	*1.05*	*0.78*	*0.43*	*0.46*
(1.04)	(1.04)	(1.44)	(0.82)	(0.75)	(0.85)	(0.96)
0.34	0.38	1.02	0.58	1.18	1.53	3.13
0.57	0.89	0.67	0.44	0.98	1.23	2.27
0.39	0.80	2.47	1.43	1.21	1.93	1.60
0.50	*0.86*	*1.31*	*0.78*	*1.06*	*1.48*	*2.04*
(0.60)	(0.77)	(1.11)	(0.76)	(1.44)	(1.09)	(1.66)

TABLE 1 (continued)

Functions	Outlays, FY 1976 (millions)	All Cities	Northeast	
			New England	Middle Atlantic
Other				
Atomic energy defense	1,236.5	1.24	0	1.25
General science, space, & tech.	3,583.6	—	2.86	0.87
Water resources & power	3,686.7	1.60	0.05	1.16
Pollution control & abatement	4,903.1	1.30	0.56	0.82
Energy	2,704.5	—	0.38	0.63
Recreation	807.6	0.90	1.27	0.57
Law enforcement & justice	2,202.4	1.25	0.90	1.12
Postal service	12,577.7	1.66	1.21	1.12
Veterans benefits	19,217.6	1.23	1.03	0.77
Other	17,564.8	—		
All federal expenditures (excluding national debt interest)				
1976	331,690.7	1.16	0.93	0.99
(1970)	(194,121.5)	—	(0.94)	(1.09)

In summary, this examination of the distribution of federal outlays between cities and other areas (rural and suburban) suggests that:

- The distribution of federal outlays in the aggregate is slightly "pro-city." Most concentrated in cities are outlays for defense and development; and least concentrated in cities are outlays for transportation infrastructure, human capital development, and relief.
- Outlays of the largest federal grants-in-aid programs for State and local governments are more concentrated in cities than aggregate federal outlays. Notable exceptions are outlays under the revenue sharing and highway programs.
- Because of limits on individual program funding, not all cities benefit from a given federal program in a given year. To ascertain whether a constant set of cities or all cities eventually benefit from a specified federal program, urban impact analyses should trace the distribution of outlays over a multiyear period.

Distribution among cities, by region

This and the next subsection consider how federal outlays going to cities are distributed among cities first by Census divisions,[10] and second, by type.

---

[10] The classification of states by the nine Census divisions is as follows: *New England:* Connecticut, Maine, Massachusetts, New Hampshire, Rhode Island, Vermont; *Middle*

| Northeast | | | South | | West Coast | |
East North Central	West North Central	South Atlantic	East South Central	West South Central	Mountain	Pacific
0	3.76	0.85	0	0.47	9.50	0.01
0.48	0.44	0.69	0.27	0.32	1.67	1.92
0.84	0.23	0.97	8.07	0.52	0.70	0.25
0.93	2.12	1.57	0.53	0.78	0.87	1.13
0.47	0.84	0.93	0.42	0.41	5.85	1.72
0.38	1.40	2.30	0.66	0.54	5.17	0.97
0.59	0.78	1.79	1.06	1.14	0.95	1.06
0.98	1.05	1.25	0.84	0.76	0.94	0.88
0.71	1.06	1.44	1.40	1.25	1.52	1.04
0.77	0.92	1.30	1.11	0.88	1.15	1.22
(0.75)	(0.98)	(1.06)	(0.96)	(1.02)	(1.03)	(1.56)

Source: Compiled from data on federal outlays by geographical location provided by the Community Services Administration.

Note: Concentration ratio is the percentage share of each type of outlay divided by the percentage share of population in each type of area. Dashes mean not available.

Aggregate federal outlays going to cities are most concentrated in cities of the southern and West Coast regions, and least concentrated in cities of the northern regions. The differential has slightly increased since 1970 and is large enough to underscore the debate between northern and southern mayors and governors on issues concerning the retargeting of federal outlays (see Table 1). Also, variations *within* these broad regions are large enough to deserve attention. In the South, per capita concentration in cities of the South Atlantic division was the highest (1.30) of all Census divisions, while per capita concentration (.88) in cities of the West South Central was typically lower than in cities of the northern region. In the latter region, per capita federal outlays were lowest in cities of the East North Central division in

Atlantic: New Jersey, New York, Pennsylvania; *East-North Central:* Illinois, Indiana, Michigan, Ohio, Wisconsin; *West North Central:* Iowa, Kansas, Minnesota, Missouri, Nebraska, North Dakota, South Dakota; *South Atlantic:* Delaware, District of Columbia, Florida, Georgia, Maryland, North Carolina, South Carolina, Virginia, West Virginia; *East South Central:* Alabama, Kentucky, Mississippi, Tennessee; *West South Central:* Arkansas, Louisiana, Oklahoma, Texas; *Mountain:* Arizona, Colorado, Idaho, Montana, Nevada, New Mexico, Utah, Wyoming; *Pacific:* Alaska, California, Hawaii, Oregon, Washington.

TABLE 2: City Concentration Ratios for Selected Program Outlays, by Regional
          Location of Cities, Fiscal 1976

Program	Agency	Problems	All Cities	% Cities Pop. 50,000 or More with Outlays in 1976
State & local govt. fiscal assist.	Treas.	Jurisdiction	1.00	99
Community dev. & training assist. (CETA)	DOL	Juris./ People	2.41	61
Highway research, planning, & construction	DOT	Place	a	a
Construction grants for waste-water treatment works	EPA	Juris./ Activities	1.34	56
Community dev. block grants	HUD	Place/Juris.	1.91	80
Urban mass trans. assist.	DOT	Place	2.24	51
Improving & strengthening law enforcement	LEAA	Place	2.54	10
Vocational ed.	HEW	People	2.39	9
Work incentive program	HEW/ DOL	People	1.82	12
Community action	CSA	Place/Juris. People	1.82	62
Grants & loans for pub. works & dev. facilities	EDA	Place/Juris.	0.45	9
Small business loans	SBA	Place		
Direct outlays			1.50	65
Indirect fed. outlays			1.12	93
Business dev. assist.	EDA	Place		
Grants			0.54	3
Indirect fed. support			1.58	2

1976. This pattern is generally consistent with those found in other studies:
Variations *within* broad regional definitions are at least as large as variations
among regions, suggesting that regional analysis is no substitute for disaggregated analysis by smaller geographic areas.[11]

   Relief and defense expenditures, as the largest budget items, are the prin-

[11] *See* Vehorn, 1977.

Northeast and Central				South			West Coast	
New Eng-land	Mid-dle Atlan-tic	East North Cen-tral	West North Cen-tral	South Atlan-tic	East South Cen-tral	West South Cen-tral	Moun-tain	Pacific
1.29	1.43	0.69	0.78	1.05	1.25	0.94	1.03	0.77
1.23	0.76	0.94	0.81	1.96	1.51	0.80	0.91	1.00
—	—	—	—	—	—	—	—	—
0.52	0.84	0.92	2.18	1.38	0.53	0.83	0.69	1.19
2.13	0.78	0.81	1.56	0.98	1.05	0.99	1.17	0.89
1.52	2.43	0.70	0.35	0.42	0.39	0.20	0.57	0.66
0.74	0.67	1.09	1.09	2.03	1.46	1.05	1.01	0.80
0.87	0.85	1.02	1.12	1.76	1.66	1.03	1.01	0.68
0.83	1.03	1.15	0.77	1.34	0.82	0.48	1.57	1.00
1.23	1.01	0.99	0.77	1.41	0.79	0.95	0.97	0.91
0.19	1.15	0.31	2.54	1.21	3.19	1.20	0.89	0.71
0.72	0.95	0.98	0.70	1.45	0.98	1.19	1.21	0.91
1.09	0.55	0.51	1.47	0.80	0.85	1.91	2.45	1.13
—	2.23	1.01	4.21	—	—	0.41	0.03	
—	1.17	—	8.06	—	—	—	—	1.56

Source: Compiled from data on federal outlays by geographical location provided by the Community Services Administration.

Note: Concentration ratio is the percentage share of each type of outlay divided by the percentage share of population in each type of area. Dashes mean not available.

[a] Less than one percent.

cipal determinants of the distribution of aggregate federal outlays among cities by region. Relief outlays are concentrated in cities of the South Atlantic division, possibly reflecting the higher concentration of elderly people there. Defense outlays are also concentrated in cities of the South Atlantic division; less so than in cities of the Mountain and Pacific divisions. This concentration has increased since 1970, reflecting the continuing spatial shift of defense suppliers to climatically favorable areas. Per capita outlays for defense are among the lowest cities of the East and West North Central subdivisions, but more surprisingly, relief per capita outlays are also among the lowest in these cities.

For other functional areas of the federal budget, there are no evident broad regional patterns. Within regions disparities are larger. Per capita development outlays are highest in cities of New England and lowest in cities of the adjacent East North Central division in 1970 as in 1976; per capita outlays for transportation are highest in the Middle Atlantic division and lowest again in the adjacent East North Central division; and finally, per capita outlays for human capital are highest also in cities of the Middle Atlantic division and lowest in cities of the West North Central division.

For federal outlays in aggregate, interdivisional city disparities increased between 1970 and 1976. Defense outlays are the primary cause for this increase. For all other major functions of the federal budget, interdivisional disparities either remained constant (development and transportation infrastructure) or decreased (human capital development and relief).[12] Finally, interdivisional disparities are lower for federal outlays in aggregate than for any individual major function of the federal budget.

Cities in no one single Census division are systematically "favored" by all major federal grants-in-aid programs. Cities located in the New England, Middle Atlantic, and East South Central divisions received the highest concentration of revenue sharing outlays. There is, however, no systematic bias between southern and northern cities. CETA outlays have a somewhat different regional targeting pattern. They concentrate in cities located in the South Atlantic and East South Central divisions. Cities in the Middle Atlantic and West South Central divisions were least "favored."

Construction grants for wastewater treatment work tend to be concentrated in cities of the West-North Central and South Atlantic divisions. Cities located in New England were least "favored." And CDBGs were most concentrated in cities of the New England and West North Central divisions, while those located in the Middle Atlantic and East North Central divisions were least "favored."[13]

The other programs considered display similar variations in their targeting on cities of different regions. For instance, small business loans (SBA) tend to be concentrated in cities of the southern region, while EDA's business development assistance tends to be concentrated in cities of the northern region.

---

[12] Standard deviations for interdivisional per capita federal outlays increased from .11 in 1970 to .16 in 1976 for aggregate federal outlays, from .34 to .48 for defense outlays, and from .27 to .29 for development outlays. They remained constant at .30 for transportation infrastructure outlays and decreased from .26 to .20 for human capital development, from .23 to .19 for relief outlays.

[13] Post-1976 changes in the CDBG allocation formulas are expected to redistribute proportionately more funds to cities in those divisions.

In summary, distribution of the federal budget in cities, by Census regions and divisions suggests that:

- Cities in no one single Census division are systematically "favored" by all federal grants-in-aid programs.
- Aggregate federal outlays going to cities are most concentrated in cities of the southern and West Coast regions. Relief and defense outlays, as the largest budget items, are the principal factors determining this distribution.
- For federal outlays in aggregate, interdivisional disparities among cities located in different regions have increased between 1970 and 1976. Increased regional disparities in the distribution of defense outlays are the primary cause of this increase. Interdivisional disparities for other major functions of the federal budget have either remained constant or decreased.
- Cities located in the East North Central region received the lowest per capita aggregate federal outlays in 1976 as in 1970.
- Relief and human capital development outlays were distributed least unequally in 1976 as in 1970.
- Disparities observed between northern and southern cities mask even larger disparities among cities within divisions of these two regions.

Distribution among type of cities

Federal policy is concerned with a number of city problems: population decline, low income, and unemployment. Because the intensity of each of these problems may vary in a given city, all three of these indicators are used separately in this analysis of the distribution of federal outlays among types of cities. In addition we distinguish among low and high hardship cities as defined by a composite index of urban conditions combining three indicators—population decline, old age, and economic conditions.[14] Also we distinguish between cities of different size and location within a metropolitan area (for example, central versus suburban cities). Tables 3 and 4 display the city concentration ratios by types of cities for federal outlays in aggregate and by function, and for selected individual grants-in-aid programs, respectively.

In 1976, federal outlays in aggregate were distributed fairly evenly among all types of cities. For instance, declining cities received proportionately the same as fast-growing cities, high unemployment cities the same as low unemployment cities, and low income cities the same as high income cities. The only exception was a slightly higher concentration of total federal outlays in medium-sized cities, relative to small and large cities and, in central cities, relative to suburban cities. There is no noticeable change in this pattern between 1970 and 1976, except for a slight increase in concentration of total federal outlays in growing cities relative to declining cities.

Targeting on cities of different types varied by major functional areas of the federal budget and among individual grants-in-aid programs.

---

[14] For details on the construction of this index, *see* Nathan et al., 1977.

TABLE 3: City Concentration Ratios of Federal Outlays by Budget Function, by Type of City, Fiscal 1976

| Function | Per Capita Income, 1970 | | Population Growth, 1970–75 | | | Unemployment Rate, 1976 |
	Low Income Cities (≤$3304)	High Income Cities (>$3304)	Declining Cities (≤0)	Slow Growth Cities (0–15.0)	Rapid Growth Cities (>15.0)	Low Unemployment Cities (<8.9)
Development						
Area & regional dev.	1.32	0.68	1.00	1.01	0.90	1.52
Community dev.	1.30	0.70	1.05	0.89	0.87	1.03
Other advancement & reg. of commerce	0.94	1.05	1.10	0.75	0.89	0.92
Total 1976	*1.26*	*0.75*	*1.05*	*0.89*	*0.87*	*1.08*
(1970)	(1.19)	(0.80)	(1.08)	(0.82)	(0.77)	(0.98)
Access infrastructure						
Air transport	1.20	0.80	0.96	1.14	0.82	1.49
Water transport	0.70	1.28	1.24	0.46	0.56	0.75
Ground transport	0.85	1.14	1.31	0.38	0.27	0.40
Other transport	0.39	1.57	0.49	2.58	0.03	0.31
Total 1976	*0.92*	*1.07*	*1.17*	*0.66*	*0.50*	*0.81*
(1970)	(0.93)	(1.05)	(1.17)	(0.62)	(0.64)	(0.90)
Human capital						
Manpower training	1.20	0.80	0.98	0.97	1.17	1.13
Education & social serv.	0.30	1.66	1.29	0.42	0.23	1.90
Vocational ed.	1.08	0.91	0.88	0.99	2.14	1.47
Higher ed., research, & gen. ed. aid	1.14	0.86	0.96	0.99	1.34	1.19
Health	0.48	1.49	1.30	0.36	0.37	0.51
Total 1976	*0.85*	*1.14*	*1.12*	*0.70*	*0.92*	*0.89*
(1970)	(1.08)	(0.91)	(1.03)	(0.87)	(1.13)	(1.20)
Relief						
Social services	1.03	0.96	0.97	0.84	1.85	1.49
Retirement & disability ins.	1.10	0.89	1.03	0.97	0.76	0.89
Unemployment ins.	1.00	1.00	1.13	0.74	0.57	0.69
Pub. assist. & other inc. sup.	0.87	1.12	1.05	0.81	1.10	0.79

Unem-ployment Rate, 1976	Hardship Index		Size (thousands)				
High Unem-ploy-ment Cities (≧8.9)	Low Hard-ship Cities (<100)	High Hard-ship Cities (≧100)	Small Sized Cities (<100)	Medium Sized Cities (100–300)	Large Sized Cities (>300)	Central Cities	Sub-urban Cities
0.69	0.86	1.03	0.83	1.67	0.77	1.18	0.18
0.98	0.81	1.15	0.75	1.33	0.95	1.08	0.63
1.04	0.75	1.20	0.44	0.79	1.30	1.13	0.38
0.95	*0.81*	*1.14*	*0.72*	*1.31*	*0.97*	*1.10*	*0.54*
(1.00)	(0.74)	(1.20)	(0.73)	(1.32)	(0.95)	(1.10)	(0.49)
0.71	1.22	0.81	0.54	0.74	1.28	1.14	0.35
1.14	0.32	1.57	0.31	0.29	1.56	1.14	0.37
1.34	0.32	1.49	0.17	0.74	1.42	1.18	0.18
1.39	0.20	1.66	0.18	2.94	0.48	0.40	3.62
1.10	*0.60*	*1.30*	*0.31*	*0.67*	*1.39*	*1.15*	*0.32*
(1.05)	(0.66)	(1.26)	(0.41)	(0.50)	(1.43)	(1.14)	(0.34)
0.92	0.95	1.02	0.72	1.62	0.83	1.13	0.38
0.47	0.38	1.50	0.38	0.61	1.39	1.14	0.37
0.72	1.14	0.82	0.81	1.78	0.73	1.16	0.25
0.88	0.91	1.05	0.82	1.38	0.90	1.12	0.45
1.27	0.36	1.52	0.19	0.58	1.48	1.17	0.23
1.06	*0.69*	*1.23*	*0.50*	*1.13*	*1.13*	*1.15*	*0.31*
(0.87)	(0.88)	(1.05)	(0.66)	(1.39)	(0.95)	(1.09)	(0.55)
0.71	1.03	0.95	0.73	1.67	0.81	1.19	0.12
1.06	0.84	1.12	0.99	1.12	0.95	1.02	0.88
1.17	0.70	1.24	0.79	0.93	1.10	1.06	0.71
1.11	0.75	1.20	0.69	0.82	1.19	1.10	0.51

TABLE 3 (continued)

| Function | Per Capita Income, 1970 | | Population Growth, 1970–75 | | | Unemployment Rate, 1976 |
	Low Income Cities (≤$3304)	High Income Cities (>$3304)	Declining Cities (≤0)	Slow Growth Cities (0–15.0)	Rapid Growth Cities (>15.0)	Low Unemployment Cities (<8.9)
Gen. rev. sharing & fiscal assist.	1.08	0.92	1.04	0.87	0.99	0.90
Disaster relief& ins.	0.90	1.09	1.03	1.09	0.25	0.94
Total 1976	*1.07*	*0.92*	*1.03*	*0.95*	*0.82*	*0.89*
(1970)	(1.16)	(0.83)	(1.02)	(0.98)	(0.75)	(0.88)
Defense						
Construction	0.61	1.62	0.38	1.42	5.44	1.96
Supply price contracts	0.80	1.19	0.86	1.32	1.05	1.06
Payrolls	1.23	0.78	0.63	1.68	1.98	1.39
Total 1976	*0.95*	*1.04*	*0.78*	*1.45*	*1.42*	*1.18*
(1970)	(1.03)	(0.96)	(0.89)	(1.17)	(1.34)	(1.28)
Other						
Atomic energy defense	1.48	0.54	0.72	1.76	0.81	0.89
Gen science, space, & tech.	0.68	1.30	0.96	1.17	0.70	0.81
Water resources & power	1.20	0.80	0.88	1.25	1.16	1.33
Pollution control & abatement	0.99	1.00	1.03	0.81	1.30	1.05
Energy	0.93	1.06	0.82	1.37	1.30	1.06
Recreation	1.00	0.99	0.90	0.80	2.70	1.24
Law enforcement & justice	1.03	0.96	1.04	0.83	1.14	0.83
Postal service	1.03	0.96	1.10	0.81	0.68	0.84
Veterans benefits	1.09	0.91	0.92	1.20	0.98	1.15
All fed. exp. (exc. national debt interest)						
1976	0.98	1.01	0.98	1.04	0.99	1.01
(1970)	(0.98)	(1.01)	(1.02)	(0.95)	(0.87)	(1.03)

Unemployment Rate, 1976	Hardship Index		Size (thousands)				
High Unemployment Cities (≥8.9)	Low Hardship Cities (<100)	High Hardship Cities (≥100)	Small Sized Cities (<100)	Medium Sized Cities (100–300)	Large Sized Cities (>300)	Central Cities	Suburban Cities
1.05	0.79	1.17	0.76	0.96	1.10	1.08	0.63
1.03	0.82	1.05	0.54	1.00	1.17	1.11	0.47
1.06	*0.83*	*1.13*	*0.94*	*1.09*	*0.98*	*1.04*	*0.81*
(1.06)	(0.85)	(1.11)	(1.02)	(1.22)	(0.89)	(1.01)	(0.93)
0.44	1.72	0.40	0.78	0.70	1.21	1.15	0.33
0.96	1.34	0.71	1.26	1.26	0.78	0.78	1.93
0.77	1.31	0.73	0.87	1.31	0.91	1.06	0.70
0.89	*1.33*	*0.72*	*1.12*	*1.27*	*0.83*	*0.88*	*1.48*
(0.83)	(1.24)	(0.80)	(0.91)	(1.28)	(0.90)	(0.94)	(1.24)
1.06	1.12	0.89	1.53	1.93	0.39	0.82	1.76
1.10	0.86	0.90	0.62	1.95	0.73	0.79	1.90
0.80	0.78	1.18	0.12	1.35	1.18	1.21	0.07
0.96	0.76	1.19	0.92	1.41	0.85	1.03	0.84
0.96	1.14	0.81	0.52	1.80	0.83	1.02	0.88
0.85	0.92	1.06	0.56	1.45	0.97	1.02	0.86
1.09	0.76	1.20	0.41	0.62	1.38	1.20	0.11
1.09	0.75	1.20	0.67	0.96	1.13	1.08	0.61
0.91	1.05	0.95	0.92	1.04	1.00	1.03	0.85
0.98	0.96	1.03	0.86	1.12	0.99	1.01	0.91
(0.97)	(0.93)	(1.04)	(0.83)	(1.13)	(1.00)	(1.01)	(0.92)

Source: Compiled from data on federal outlays by geographical location provided by the Community Services Administration.

Note: Concentration ratio is the percentage share of each type of outlay divided by the percentage share of population in each type of area. Dashes mean not available.

TABLE 4: City Concentration Ratios of Selected Program Outlays, by Type of City, Fiscal 1976

Program	Agency	Problems	Low Income Cities	High Income Cities	Declining Cities	Slow Growth Cities	Rapid Growth Cities	Low Unemployment Cities	High Unemployment Cities
State & local govt. fiscal assist.	Treas.	Jurisdiction	1.08	0.92	1.04	0.87	0.99	0.90	1.05
Community dev. & training assist. (CETA)	DOL	Juris./ People	1.22	0.78	0.99	0.94	1.18	1.10	0.93
Highway research, planning, & construction	DOT	Place	—	—	—	—	—	—	—
Construction grants for waste-water treatment works	EPA	Juris./ Activities	0.98	1.01	1.04	0.79	1.30	1.04	0.97
Community dev. block grants	HUD	Place/ Juris.	1.41	0.60	1.03	0.92	0.94	1.01	0.99
Urban mass trans. assist.	DOT	Place	0.75	1.23	1.35	0.31	0.13	0.28	1.41
Improving & strengthening law enforcement	LEAA	Place	1.05	0.95	0.87	1.02	2.16	1.38	0.77
Vocational ed.	HED	People	1.19	0.81	0.84	1.04	2.32	1.76	0.56
Work incentive program	HEW/ DOL	People	1.08	0.91	0.98	1.01	1.04	1.51	0.70
Community action	CSA	Place/ Juris./ People	1.12	0.88	1.10	0.80	0.73	0.78	1.12
Grants & loans for pub. works & dev. facilities	EDA	Place/ Juris.	1.45	0.57	1.03	1.18	—	0.98	1.00
Small business loans	SBA	Place	1.06	0.93	0.96	1.04	1.18	1.02	0.98
Direct outlays			1.11	0.89	0.78	1.36	1.75	1.42	0.75
Indirect federal outlays			1.83	0.20	1.48	—	—	0.79	1.11
Business dev. assistance	EDA	Place							
Grants									
Indirect federal support			2.04	—	0.55	2.43	—	1.61	0.75

State & local gov. fiscal assist.	Treas.	Jurisdiction	0.79	1.17	0.76	0.96	1.10	1.08	0.63
Community dev. & training assist. (CETA)	DOL	Juris./People	0.97	1.01	0.65	1.59	0.87	1.13	0.42
Highway research, planning, & construction	DOT	Place	—	—	—	—	—	—	—
Construction grants for waste-water treatment works	EPA	Juris./Activities	0.78	1.17	0.97	1.40	0.83	1.04	0.81
Community dev. block grants	HUD	Place/Juris.	0.81	1.14	0.89	1.45	0.84	1.04	0.80
Urban mass trans. assist.	DOT	Place	0.26	1.53	0.09	0.60	1.51	1.18	0.17
Improving & strengthening law enforcement	LEAA	Place	1.31	0.66	0.41	1.85	0.86	1.19	0.13
Vocational ed.	HEW	People	1.26	0.72	0.87	2.19	0.54	1.19	0.13
Work incentive program	HEW/DOL	People	0.99	0.94	0.68	2.07	0.66	1.19	0.13
Community action	CSA	Place/Juris./People	0.73	1.21	0.58	1.02	1.14	1.10	0.52
Grants & loans for pub. works & dev. facilities	EDA	Place/Juris.	0.82	1.15	0.97	1.26	0.89	1.10	0.53
Small business loans	SBA	Place	0.91	1.07	0.69	1.11	1.06	1.07	0.67
Direct outlays									
Indirect federal outlays			1.25	0.79	1.02	1.11	0.85	1.05	0.77
Business dev. assistance Grants	EDA	Place	0.23	1.65	3.40	0.44	0.31	1.08	0.62
Indirect federal support			0.62	1.32	3.49	0.97	0.05	1.20	0.10

Source: Compiled from data on federal outlays by geographical location provided by the Community Services Administration.
Note: Concentration ratio is the percentage share of each type of outlay divided by the percentage of population in each type of area. Dashes mean not available.

Targeting on declining cities. Recently, the national urban policy debate focused on lagging growth areas, particularly declining cities. Although decline results predominantly from shifts in private sector investments, it is pertinent to ask which types of federal outlays may reenforce or counteract this process.

Defense outlays are least concentrated in declining cities. Per capita defense outlays in declining cities decreased between 1970 and 1976. In all other major functional categories of federal outlays, declining cities received proportionately more funds per capita than growing cities. Concentration of capital development outlays increased between 1970 and 1976, but remained constant or decreased slightly in the other functional categories.

Most of the largest federal grants-in-aid programs and other individual programs listed in Table 4 provided more funds per capita to declining cities than growing cities. There are a number of exceptions, however. Programs with *lower* concentration of outlays in declining than growing cities include DOL's CETA programs, LEAA's law enforcement assistance, HEW's vocational education and work incentive program, and SBA's business loan programs. While construction grants for wastewater treatment works concentrate more funds in declining cities than in slow-growing cities, this concentration remains lower than in rapid-growing cities.

Targeting on low income cities. As could be expected, relief and development outlays are more concentrated in low income than high income cities. Between 1970 and 1976, the concentration of development outlays in low income cities increased, but that of relief outlays decreased. For transportation infrastructure, defense and human capital development low income cities received proportionately less outlays than high income cities. In Fiscal 1976, human capital outlays were the least concentrated in low income cities, experiencing a sharp relative decline since 1970. Most of this decline can be accounted for by a shift in the spatial distribution of health outlays.

All individual federal grants-in-aid programs examined for this study "outlayed" more funds per capita in low income than high income cities. The only exceptions are the UMTA and wastewater treatment works construction grants.

Targeting on high unemployment cities. Most concentrated in high unemployment cities are transportation infrastructure, human capital development, and relief outlays. Concentration of human capital development outlays in high unemployment cities increased markedly between 1970 and 1976. Least concentrated in high unemployment cities are defense and development outlays. Between 1970 and 1976, per capita outlays in high unemployment cities decreased for development, but increased for defense.

Only two of the six largest federal grants-in-aid programs concentrated more outlays in high unemployment than low unemployment cities: revenue sharing and urban mass transportation. A similar pattern can be observed for community action and business development outlays. All other individual grants-in-aid programs considered disbursed more funds per capita in low unemployment than high unemployment cities. These programs include DOL's CETA program and HEW's vocational education and work incentive programs.[15] CDBGs are distributed about evenly between high and low unemployment cities.

Targeting on hardship cities. Except for defense outlays, all major functions of the federal budget outlayed more funds per capita in high hardship cities than low hardship cities. This concentration increased between 1970 and 1976 for human capital development, relief, and transportation infrastructure. Conversely, the concentration of defense outlays in low hardship cities increased during the same period.

With a few exceptions, all individual federal grants-in-aid programs listed in Table 4 outlayed more funds per capita in high than low hardship cities. Exceptions include outlays for law enforcement assistance, and indirect federal outlays for small business loans.

Targeting on large-sized cities. Attention about urban conditions often focuses on the larger cities of the country. Problems facing New York, Detroit, Cleveland, Los Angeles, or Philadelphia not only make attractive front-page stories for the leading newspapers of the country, but also are perceived to be catalysts for federal action and legislation. But, at present, although large cities may be in the popular consciousness, they are not leaders in the funds they receive per capita from the federal budget.

If anything, federal outlays in aggregate and for each major function—including development, human capital development, relief, and defense—of the federal budget are pro-medium-sized cities, that is, cities of 100,000 to 300,000 inhabitants. However, this concentration has decreased between 1970 and 1976 in favor of the larger cities rather than the smaller cities. Only outlays for transportation infrastructure are more concentrated in cities of 300,000 population or more than in medium or small cities.

Smaller cities (less than 100,000 in population) are least "favored" by the federal budget, and the per capita outlays they received from most major budget functions decreased between 1970 and 1976. One exception, however, is per capita outlays for defense, which increased in small cities by 23 percent between 1970 and 1976 and decreased by 8 percent in large cities during the same period.

Like most major functions of the federal budget, the major individual grants-in-aid programs outlay more funds per capita in medium-sized cities than in large or small cities. Exceptions are revenue sharing and, as can be expected, urban mass transportation outlays that are relatively concentrated

---

[15] This finding may be misleading, however. It may reflect the fact that CETA outlays allocated to rest-of-states are attributed to the state capital and not necessarily traced to the location of recipient cities. State capitals typically experience lower unemployment rates than other cities.

in large cities, as are community action outlays. Only one program, EDA's business development assistance, outlayed more funds per capita in small cities than medium- or large-sized cities.

Targeting on central cities. Total federal outlays, federal outlays by major functions of the federal budget, and the major individual grants-in-aid programs concentrated more funds per capita in central cities than in suburban cities. The only exception is for defense outlays, primarily because of a larger concentration of defense prime suppliers in suburban than in central cities. There has been little change between 1970 and 1976.

In summary, the observed distribution of federal outlays going to cities among types of cities suggests that:

- In aggregate, the distribution of total federal outlays appears to have a "neutral" effect on different types of cities, whether characterized by rate of growth, unemployment rate, per capita income, or an index of urban conditions. However, medium-sized cities and central cities typically receive more funds per capita than large and small cities, and suburban cities, respectively.
- The distribution of defense outlays among types of cities generally works at cross-purposes to the other functions of the federal budget.
- Per capita defense outlays are *lowest* in all six types of cities considered: declining, low income, high unemployment, high hardship, large size, and central cities.
- Conversely, all other major functional outlays are *highest* in all six types of cities, except in large cities. Other exceptions include: per capita development outlays are *lowest* in high unemployment cities; per capita transportation infrastructure and human capital development outlays are *lowest* in low income cities.
- Between 1970 and 1976 the pattern noted above has not changed markedly.

PROGRAM CHARACTERISTICS AFFECTING
THE DISTRIBUTION OF OUTLAYS

The observed distribution of federal outlays described above depends on policy decisions about: (1) the classes of jurisdictions (e.g., State and local governments or both), firms, or individuals that are eligible for funds; and (2) the formulae (for formula grants) or the allocation procedures and criteria (for project grants and procurements) for distributing funds among eligible recipients. Although eligibility rules and allocation mechanisms reflect federal goals, there are many possible sets of rules that could be consistent with these goals. Allocations of funds, especially among urban areas, are sensitive to the selected definition of urban areas, to the size that defines eligibility, to the variables selected to measure needs, and to the choice of eligible recipients—states, local governments, firms, or individuals.

Federal programs differ in their methods and criteria used for distributing funds to and among cities. A detailed review of these practices for each of the more than 400 federal programs is beyond the scope of this study. Instead, this section examines how differences in broad program characteristics affect the distribution of federal outlays to and among cities. We compare possible variations in distribution of funds between formula grants and project grant programs; and programs channeling funds to cities *indirectly* through states and *directly* to local governments.

Formula versus project grants

Choices between these two major grant forms may affect the share of federal aid that goes to cities. Under formula grants, funds entitlement going to each eligible grantee is specified by law or regulation, whereas project grants allocate funds on a competitive or discretionary basis.[16] The aid flowing through project grants is small compared with the funds that flow through formula grants.

Project grants are typically intended for narrow categorical purposes and require grantees—states and local governments often compete against each other—to submit specific proposals to the administering federal agency which, in turn, reviews and selects proposals on a merit basis. Federal agencies have considerable discretion in selecting projects, especially if appropriated funds fall short of total grant applications, as is frequently the case. Program legislation typically provides broad guidelines for project selection, and the selection criteria which the agencies are required to make public are also stated in the criteria. These broad guidelines provide flexibility for both federal agencies and applicants to bargain towards approval of a project. They also leave room for political considerations in the bargaining that will bring the agency broad support. The practice of federal administrative agencies toward achieving greatest support suggests that project grants funds will tend to be spread to many areas.[17]

In contrast, formula grants limit the discretion of federal agencies in distributing aid. They are of three types: categorical grants, block grants, and unrestricted grants (revenue sharing). In the past, most formula grants had fairly narrow *categorical* purposes: e.g., law enforcement assistance; highway construction; mass transit facilities and operating assistance, public assistance and medical assistance; and adult and vocational education. Under most of these grants, funds flow initially to states on the basis of population or a specified subset of the population. There are few exceptions. For instance, highway construction formula grants are distributed according to population, area size, and intercity route mileage.

Block and unrestricted formula grants are relatively recent, few in number, but comparatively large in size. They include three of the largest grants-in-aid

---

[16] Federal procurements are also typically allocated on a competitive basis. Their examination is beyond the scope of this study.

[17] Ingram, 1977.

programs considered in the preceding section: revenue sharing, CETA, and CDBG. These programs were instituted in 1972 or after, as outcomes of the Nixon administration's strategy to give State and local governments greater autonomy in the use of federal funds. This shift to block and unrestricted formula grants which allocate funds among areas according to prespecified economic and social characteristics has several implications for the distribution of federal aid.

First, a substantial portion of these grants goes directly to local governments, bypassing State governments—all CDBG funds, 70 percent of CETA (Title I) block grants, and two-thirds of revenue sharing funds. Cities no longer dependent on federal aid passing through and allocated by State governments may benefit from this change.

Second, however, by extending eligibility, these formula grants have tended to spread funds away from central and larger cities to benefit suburban and small cities. One reason is that the shift to block grants folded-in under one program a number of previously existing *project* grants programs.[18] For instance, under CDBG, the number of U.S. Department of Housing and Urban Development (HUD) assisted cities of less than 25,000 inhabitants increased from 794 to 1,313; the number of aided cities of 25,000 to 100,000 increased from 457 to 492. Overall, the number of recipient jurisdictions increased by 40 percent but funds increased only by 15 percent.[19] And in Fiscal 1975, the share received by central cities declined from 82.1 percent under the folded-in programs to 77.1 percent, while the share of urban counties (predominantly suburban areas) increased from 3.7 to 6.0 percent.[20] The CETA Title I formula resulted in a similar shift of funds from central cities to counties. The share going to cities decreased from 41.9 percent under the pre-CETA categorical manpower programs (Fiscal 1974) to 36.1 percent (Fiscal 1975); the share of counties and remainder of states increased by 4.4 and 15 percent, respectively.[21]

And third, the social and economic indicators of needs used in the allocation formula (Table 5), while more restrictive than the single use of population, may still be broader than those employed under the folded-in categorical project grants programs. Any changes in allocation criteria are likely to affect the distribution of funds among types of cities. The use of broad indicators of needs—such as population, unemployment, and per capita income—rather than specific need indicators often seems to have an anti-urban effect.[22] In particular, inclusion of a population factor in aid formulas always has a

---

[18] In 1974, CDBG consolidated seven previously established federal project grants programs including urban renewal, model cities, water and sewer facilities, open spaces, neighborhood facilities and rehabilitation loans, and public facilities loans.

[19] Advisory Commission on Intergovernmental Relations, 1977.

[20] For a detailed discussion of the spreading effect of CDBG, *see* Nathan, January 1977, p. 129.

[21] Mirengoff and Mindler, 1976, p. 40.

[22] Barro, April 1978.

TABLE 5: Factors and Weights in CETA, CDBG, and Revenue Sharing Allocation Formulas

	CETA			CDBG		
	Title I	Title II	Title VI	Pre-1977	Post-1977[a]	Revenue-Sharing[b]
Discretionary amount	20	20	10	18[c]	NA	—
Formula amount	80	80	90	82	NA	100
Total	100	100	100	100		100
Factors						
Prior year's funds	50					
Adults in low-income[d]	12½					
Number unemployed	37½		50			
Above 4.5% rate			25			
Areas of substantial unemployment[e]		100	25			
Population				25		33⅓
Overcrowded housing[f]				25		
Poverty (double weighted)[g]				50	30	
Age of housing[h]					50	
Growth lag[i]					20	
Tax effort[j]						33⅓
Per capita income						33⅓

Note: NA means not available. Dashes mean not applicable.

[a] An area receives the amount computed under the pre-1977 formula or the post-1977 formula, whichever is greater.

[b] For county and local government allocation only. States are allocated the higher between this 3-factor formula and a 5-factor formula (population, urbanized population, per capita income, state income tax collections, and tax effort).

[c] The discretionary amount varies each year. It is equal to the residual of CDBG funds after allocation of formula and hold-harmless amounts and a specific set aside by Congress, which has varied each year.

[d] In FY 1976, families with income below $8000.

[e] Areas with an unemployment rate of 6.5 percent or more for three consecutive months.

[f] Number of housing units with average of 1.01 or more persons per room.

[g] Number of persons below poverty level.

[h] Number of units constructed before 1940.

[i] Difference between current population of the city or county and the population it would have had if its population growth rate between 1960 and 1975 had been equal to the growth rate of all metropolitan cities.

[j] Taxes divided by income.

leveling or spreading effect on the distribution of funds; and the inclusion of per capita income or poverty (unadjusted for interarea cost differentials) usually tends to favor cities in southern states and less urbanized areas. Use of general indicators of needs has been criticized on other grounds as well: unreliability of the statistical indicators, particularly for small areas; lags in reporting; and failure to reflect the problem the program is intended to address.[23]

The discussion above suggests that where block grant programs have been enacted, the result has been less money for cities in general, and large cities in particular, than would have been provided under the superseded categorical project programs. It has been further argued, that because project grants are distributed on a competitive basis, cities, particularly large cities, enjoy an advantage due to their larger and more expert full-time Washington representative and "grantsmen." However, this argument appears ill-founded. Table 6 displays the city concentration ratios for outlays of a selected group of formula and project grant programs in cities of 50,000 inhabitants or more and in large cities of 300,000 inhabitants or more. They indicate that the major formula grants programs typically concentrate a higher proportion of funds to cities than most of the project grants programs considered. The main reason for this outcome is that the first are larger and have more funds to distribute than the latter. They also suggest no systematic pattern of greater concentration of project grant funds in large cities than of formula grants funds. Nor is there a distinct differential pattern between these two grant types in the distribution of funds among cities located in different regions and of different types (Tables 2 and 4).

Pending more systematic research, these findings suggest that achieving higher concentration of funds in cities would involve changes in the criteria and practices used in allocating funds among areas, rather than a choice among alternative forms of grants.

Channelization through states

The amount of aid that flows directly from the Federal government to cities is small compared with the funds that flow from and through the states. Most federal outlays are either channeled through states, are available competitively to both states and local governments, or are channeled directly to profit or nonprofit firms. There are four ways by which states may affect the distribution of federal outlays to within-state areas—all of which should be considered in assessing the distribution of federal outlays to cities and other areas.

First, where federal aid to local jurisdictions is channeled through State governments, the state may have considerable discretion over the intrastate distribution of funds. The broader the state role, the less direct is the connection between federal decisions about the program and the activities and dis-

---

[23] For a discussion of these issues, *see* Vernez, Vaughan, and Yin, January 1979.

TABLE 6: City and Large Cities Concentration Ratios for Selected Program Outlays, Fiscal 1976

Program	Agency	FY 1976 Outlays ($ Millions)	City Concentration Ratio	Concentration Ratio, Cities of 300,000 Inhabitants or More
Formula Grants				
Highway research, planning, & const.	DOT	$4,833.4	a	a
Community dev. block grants	HUD	1,872.5	1.91	0.84
Urban mass trans. assist.	DOT	1,720.3	2.24	1.51
Improving & strengthening law enforcement	LEAA	448.8	2.54	0.86
State & local govt. fiscal assist. (RS)	Treasury	4,111.3	1.00	1.10
Community employment & training assist. (CETA)	DOL	4,438.0	2.41	0.87
Vocational education	HEW		2.39	0.54
Project Grants				
Community action	CSA	307.5	1.82	1.14
Grants & loans for pub. works & dev. facilities	EDA	147.2	0.45	0.89
Special ED & adjustment assist. programs	EDA	76.7	1.22	0.02
Business dev. assist.	EDA			
Grants		49.4	0.54	0.31
Indir. fed. support		NA	1.58	0.05
Small business loans	SBA			
Direct outlays		111.4	1.50	1.06
Indir. fed. support		1,545.6	1.12	0.95
Construction grants for wastewater treatment works	EDA	4,335.5	1.34	0.83
Work incentive program	HEW/DOL	345.0	1.82	0.66

Sources: Compiled from data on federal outlays by geographical location provided by the Community Services Administration.

Note: Concentration ratio is the percentage share of each type of outlay divided by the percentage share of population in each type of area. NA means not available.

a Less than 0.1.

tributional impacts at the local level. Although some argue that states favor rural and suburban areas over cities, no studies comparing the within-state distribution of federal funds passing through and bypassing states are available to support or contradict this assertion.

Second, cities receiving federal aid channeled through states may also receive grants from state revenues. In some cases—including LEAA and highway grants—the local jurisdictions do not receive separate federal and state aid but commingled federal-state assistance. In other cases, the state grants and the federal passed-through grants are nominally for separate projects. In all such cases, states take into account the federal aid available for particular activities and jurisdictions. For instance, it is reasonable to expect that any increment in federal aid will be *partly offset* by a decrease in state aid.

Third, the portion of federal aid earmarked for state-operated programs and projects may indirectly affect the flow of state aid money to local governments. On theoretical grounds, federal aid to states is expected to increase state spending for state-operated programs and increase state assistance to local governments.

And fourth, the federal aid going directly to local jurisdictions is likely to affect states' decisions to aid local governments. If State governments perceive that increased direct federal aid to localities makes the local sector better off, state aid may be reduced or increased by a smaller amount.

The last three considerations above underline the difficulty in separating out the distribution of federal aid from that of state aid. Thus, until we understand better the impact of federal aid to State and local governments on the behavior of states, it may be necessary to account for the composite distribution of federal *and* state outlays in future urban impact analysis.

INTERPRETING THE DISTRIBUTION
OF FEDERAL OUTLAYS TO CITIES

Our findings of "pro-city," pro-southern and Pacific regions, but "neutral" distribution of aggregate federal outlays among types of cities is probably consistent with the perceptions of most urban analysts. The essential question is whether this distribution is desirable. And, if not, how much should be done to change it and how should it be done? However, even before this normative question can be addressed, four major issues that bear on the interpretation of these findings must be considered.

First, the data upon which these findings are based may not be accurate. If this is the case, the true concentration of outlays (for example, among types of cities) could diverge from the observed distribution to an unknown direction. Second, all or a proportion of the outlays attributed to one city (or group of cities) may not actually be spent in that city. If so, again the distribution described may not indicate how federal outlays are truly distributed among cities and other areas. Third, the federal outlays spent in any given area may encourage local governments to reduce their own expenditures, and private firms to reduce their own investments. When this is the case, the net federal outlays spent in an area may be less than observed. And fourth, federal outlays may make a different contribution depending on the program and its location. Below, the extent to which these problems may affect the interpretation of the observed distribution of federal outlays is examined.

Accuracy of the federal outlays data

The analysis reported here is based on the Community Services Administration's (CSA) data-set on federal outlays by agency, program, and indirect federal support for every county and for each city of 25,000 inhabitants or more.[24] It is the only centralized source of data available for analysis of the distribution of federal outlays among regions, states, and types of area. A number of problems make its reliability questionable.

First, there are inaccuracies in reporting total outlays. Some agencies report obligations rather than outlays; obligations may take several years to be actually outlayed, especially in the case of construction grants. The U.S. Congressional Budget Office (CBO) estimated that in 1975 about 30 percent of total outlays were unreliably reported.[25] The bulk of the unreliable data is concentrated in two major functional areas: relief (particularly cash and in-kind transfers) and federal purchases.

Second, there are inaccuracies in the reported geographical distribution of outlays. According to CBO, less than one-fourth of the 1975 total outlays reported by the CSA could be traced to the appropriate county- (or city-) level agency's accounting records. The other three-fourths were allocated using prorating techniques based on population or another criterion (e.g., fraction of the state's special group population in a county).[26] For an estimated 31 percent of all federal outlays, the prorating allocation technique used may be too crude to reflect spending variations among areas accurately. For instance, 1975 Medicare expenditures were apportioned among counties based on 1970 enrollments in the program. Population changes since 1970 and differences in utilization rates and in the price of medical services were ignored. Again, the bulk of the problem is concentrated in relief (for which most outlays are channeled through states) and defense outlays. Because outlays in these two functional areas are the primary determinants of the observed distribution of total federal outlays among areas, as discussed above, the reliability of the latter is seriously in doubt. Any future effort in improving the accuracy of available outlay data should clearly be focused on these two areas.

The geographical pattern for specific federal grants-in-aid (particularly those not channeled through states) is generally reliable. But there are some notable exceptions. For instance, outlays of the CETA programs are reported

---

[24] This data-set was started in 1968 and is available on tape on a yearly basis from the Community Services Administration. Also, the CSA publishes a yearly summary of outlays by program and by states titled *Federal Outlays in Summary*.

[25] U.S. Congressional Budget Office, 1977, Appendix A.

[26] The sensitivity of the distribution of federal outlays to alternative prorating techniques is explored by Anton, in this volume.

to the county or city of residence of the local prime sponsor's main office. Since prime sponsors may be a consortium of counties in an SMSA, including a central city, and since the office is likely to be located in the latter, CETA outlays shown to be spent in cities may be overestimated.

Spillovers

All of the outlays allocated to a city do not necessarily remain in that city. Even excluding the indirect demand for goods and services and induced investments that may be generated by federal outlays, direct outlays for materials and other supporting services will be spent where the supplying industries are located regardless of where it is allocated first. Some suppliers may be located in the suburbs or even other cities or metropolitan areas. This problem is least important for direct cash assistance to persons, but most important for federal outlays in public infrastructure construction and federal purchases.

In construction only about 20 to 50 percent of federal outlays (depending on the type of construction)[27] are spent on on-site labor which is most likely to be recruited within a given jurisdiction. The balance is spent on materials, equipment, and other supplies which may or may not be manufactured in the jurisdiction in question.[28] The problem is amplified for federal purchases— the bulk of which are defense purchases—where nearly 100 percent of outlays are spent for manufactured products. Here there are two issues. First, the U.S. Department of Defense attributes procurement programs outlays to the location of the major work place—possibly headquarters—of the prime contractor. Whenever the contractor has several plants located throughout the United States, all or portions of the actual outlays may take place anywhere but at the "major" location of the prime contractor. Second, an estimated one-half of defense procurements are subcontracted to firms other than those of the prime contractor. According to the author's knowledge, there has been no study of the locational pattern of these subcontractors.

This "spillover" problem may affect up to a third or more of federal outlays: public works and defense procurement outlays alone amounted to some $64 billion in Fiscal 1976. On that basis alone, it is hard to be confident that the observed geographical distribution of outlays determined on a "where it hits first" basis reflects accurately how federal outlays are distributed if spillovers are taken into account. And it will be difficult to assess the effectiveness of any retargeting of federal procurement policies until information on the spatial patterns of subcontracting practices is assembled.

---

[27] For instance, about 50 percent of contract cost is spent on on-site labor in local flood protection and large multipurpose water projects, and only 20 percent is allocated for this purpose in the construction of one-family units and highways.

[28] It should be noted that the focus is on outlays. The long-term return from the completed infrastructure should accrue mostly to the area where the improvement takes place.

Net versus gross outlays

Not all federal outlays flowing to an area are necessarily net additional outlays spent in that area. This may be the case for any one of three reasons.

First, federal outlays in an area may be offset, fully or in part, by the federal taxes levied in the area necessary to finance the federal outlays. In this case net federal outlays equals roughly the difference between observed federal outlays and federal taxes levied in the area. Only one study examined the distribution of federal outlays by per capita federal income taxes paid.[29] Its focus was limited to the distribution of federal grants-in-aid among regions. The results suggest a pronounced general trend toward convergence of the values among regions between 1969–1975, that throughout 1969 to 1975 the East North Central division was the major "net contributor to federal aid," and the East South Central division was the primary net beneficiary. The variance of these findings from our own underlies the importance of netting out from the federal outlays in one area the federal taxes paid by that area. Where the East South Central division ranks first as the primary net beneficiary of federal aid when federal taxes paid are accounted for, it ranks fourth when they are not.

While it will be desirable to account for tax payments in future studies of the distribution of federal outlays among areas, it must also be recognized that it can be carried out comfortably only for federal outlays in aggregate. For functional areas of the federal budget or individual programs, identification of the portion of federal tax payments of the area going to finance portions of the budget or individual programs is difficult. One could attribute the total cost of a program to areas proportionately to taxes paid, but this assumption may be misleading.

Second, federal outlays channeled through State or local governments may induce local governments to reduce their own expenditures (displacement). In this case, the increase in outlays—federal, plus local—in the area may be less than the full amount of the federal outlays. This issue has recently received a great deal of attention, particularly with respect to the federal countercyclical fiscal programs and the revenue sharing program. The few empirical estimates available indicate that for these programs displacement increases over time from 40 to 60 percent after a year to between 80 to 100 percent in the long run. There is some evidence that displacement varies among local governments according to type, size, location, and fiscal condition.[30] Displaced funds can be used for any of the following purposes: (1) tax reduction; (2) tax stabilization, i.e., avoidance of a local tax increase; (3) avoidance of borrowing; (4) increased reserve balances; and (5) increase in pay and benefits. The portion of displaced funds used to increase funds balances or to avoid borrow-

---

[29] U.S. General Accounting Office, 1977.

[30] For a critical review of recent empirical estimates of the displacement effect of federal programs, *see* Vernez and Vaughan, 1978.

ing add no additional outlays within the area. Using displaced funds for any of the other purposes does not affect the volume of outlays actually spent in the area, but the use of those funds, and thus their impacts, would likely differ from those that would have taken place had the federal outlays been used for the original intended purpose. At this time, we know little about how displacement may vary among federal programs and among areas of different type. This is an area where basic research deserves high priority.

A third reason that net outlays in any area may be less than observed federal outlays, is that the latter may be made in lieu of investments that private investors would have made otherwise. For instance, a number of housing economists have argued that regardless of the gross numbers during HUD's peak housing production years in the early 1970s, the *net* contribution of assisted housing programs to total initial starts was very small. Others have argued that some portion of private investments linked to federal public works investments or business development loans would have taken place without the subsidies.[31] The effect of this substitution on net outlays depends on the extent of the substitution and on the use of the substituted funds. If substituted private outlays are invested in the area the total net federal-private outlays will equal gross federal outlays. But the use of funds may differ from those originally intended, and thus, so may the urban impacts. And if substituted private outlays are invested in another area than the area considered, then the gross federal outlays overestimate the net additional federal-private outlays made in the area. Again, at present, we know little about how substitution affects different types of federal outlays and how it may affect different types of areas differentially.

To the extent either or all of these three phenomena take place, the implications for urban impact analyses are two. First, the observed flow of federal outlays to a city or group of cities overstates the actual increase of expenditures taking place in this area. Also to the extent that federal taxes levied, displacement, or substitution vary among areas, the distribution of net additional outlays may differ from that observed for gross federal outlays. Second, the actual use made of federal outlays may differ from the one intended, affecting their effectiveness and thus their impacts.

Problems of aggregation
Some have argued that the primary emphasis of urban impact analysis should be on the urban effects of major policy strategies rather than on the impacts of individual projects or small programs. There is indeed merit to this argument. As we have shown, the distribution of federal outlays varies broadly among programs and even major functional areas of the federal budget. The distributional effects of outlays by a single program or functional area may be swept away by outlays made by other programs or functional

[31] Vernez, Vaughan, and Yin, January 1979.

areas. Also, an aggregate perspective is desirable in order to account for the distribution of federal outlays net of taxes paid.

However, a critical problem with a framework which relies on aggregates like those above is that it implicitly assumes that all dollars outlayed make a uniform contribution. Clearly they do not. The displacement and substitution of these dollars can differ among programs and among areas. Similarly, their impacts can differ tremendously depending on the program and its location. Consider the contrasts in the extreme cases of two Section 8 projects:[32]

A. A Section 8 New Construction project is built in a devastated section of an older central city. Many of the buildings in the neighborhood are abandoned and the rest are deteriorating rapidly. The neighborhood has all of the textbook pathologies of areas of this kind. The Section 8 project provides substantially improved conditions for its tenants, but the area is too far gone for it to create any positive spillover effect. The tenants have moved out of other buildings nearby, which are then abandoned due to the lack of effective demand in the area—thus there is no net addition to the housing stock. Due to the multiple problems of the area, conditions in the Section 8 project itself begin to deteriorate.

B. A series of Section 8 Rehabilitation projects are started in neighborhoods just beginning to show signs of deterioration. The Section 8 investment is sensitively located and significant enough to restore confidence among the residents. Landlords and homeowners begin to make the repairs and improvements to their properties they were not making until they could get a better reading of of the future.

The point is that the impact of a federal dollar can differ not only among cities and other areas, but also among neighborhoods within the same jurisdictional boundaries. Thus, in order to assess the impacts of federal outlays, it is not sufficient to know their distribution among type of cities and among cities, suburbs, and nonmetropolitan areas, it is also necessary to know their distribution among neighborhoods within those areas. At the present time, data on the distribution of federal outlays by neighborhoods within cities are not typically collected. The development of the necessary data base and a reasonable taxonomy of city/neighborhood types may sound like a heroic task. But, with the value of such a system for urban impact analyses, the desirability of such an investment deserves serious consideration.

REFERENCES

Advisory Commission on Intergovernmental Relations. *Community Development; The Working of a Federal-Loan Block Grant.* A-57. Washington, D.C.: U.S. Government Printing Office, March 1957.

Barro, Stephen. *The Urban Impacts of Federal Policies: Fiscal Conditions.* Vol. 3. R-2214-KF/HEW. Santa Monica: Rand Corporation, April 1978.

---

[32] This illustration was supplied by G. Thomas Kingsley of the Rand Corporation.

Dommel, Paul R. "The Cities." In *The 1978 Budget: Setting National Priorities*, edited by Joseph A. Pechman. Washington, D.C.: Brookings Institution, 1977.

Environmental Impact Center. *Secondary Impacts of Transportation and Wastewater Investments*. Washington, D.C., July 1975.

Ingram, Helen. "Policy Implementation through Bargaining: The Case of Federal Grants-in-Aid." *Public Policy* 25 (Fall 1977).

Mirengoff, William, and Mindler, Lester. *The Comprehensive Employment and Training Act*. Washington, D.C.: National Academy of Sciences, 1976.

Nathan, Richard P. *Block Grants for Community Development*. Washington, D.C.: Brookings Institution, January 1977.

———, et al. *Block Grants for Community Development*. Washington, D.C.: U.S. Department of Housing and Urban Development, 1977. Processed.

Rafuse, Robert W., Jr. *The New Regional Debate*. Agenda Setting Series. Center for Policy Research Analysis, National Governors' Conference, 1977.

———. "The State-Local Sector and the Economy: Overall Performance and Regional Disparities." In *State and Local Government Finance and Financial Management: A Compendium of Current Research*, edited by John E. Petersen, Catherine Spain Lavigue, and Martharose F. Laffey. Washington, D.C.: Government Finance Research Center, August 1978.

U.S. Congressional Budget Office. *Troubled Local Economies and the Distribution of Federal Dollars*. Washington, D.C.: U.S. Government Printing Office, August, 1977.

U.S. General Accounting Office. Changing Patterns of Federal Aid to State and Local Governments, 1967–1975. PAD-78-15. Washington, D.C.: U.S. Government Printing Office, 1977.

Vehorn, Charles L. *The Regional Distribution of Federal Grants-in-Aid*. Urban and Regional Development, vol. 3. Columbus: Academy for Contemporary Problems, 1977.

Vernez, Georges, and Vaughan, Roger J. *Assessment of Countercyclical Public Works and Public Service Employment Programs*. R-2214-EDA. Santa Monica: Rand Corporation, October 1978.

———, Vaughan, Roger J., and Yin, Robert K. *Federal Activities in Urban Economic Development*. R-2372-EDA. Santa Monica: Rand Corporation, January 1979.

———. *Federal Activities in Urban Economic Development*. R-2373-EDA. Santa Monica: Rand Corporation, February 1979.

CHAPTER FOUR

Urban Impact Analysis: A Critical Forecast

ANN R. MARKUSEN

INTRODUCTION

The announcement of the birth of the urban impact analysis (UIA) by the Carter administration in early 1978 heartened many urban partisans. Its label led them to believe that their cause would now be empowered with a tool similar to that given the environmentalists in the environmental impact statement (EIS). However, the UIA diverges dramatically from its environmental sibling. First, it heralds an historic shift of presumed culpability for urban problems from the private sector toward the public sector. Secondly, the production process responds to demand and supply incentives in such a way that the forcefulness, representativeness, effectiveness, and the productivity of the UIA can be questioned. Finally, the UIA may turn out to be a disappointing federal initiative unless a number of features akin to the EIS are incorporated into its political and institutional structure. This paper explores each of these points.

THE UIA: A NEW DIRECTION FOR URBAN RESEARCH

The urban impact analysis turns the focus of government research inward, onto its own behavior. Government research traditionally has pursued an understanding of the complexity of the society which was its ward. The behavior of corporations, households, individuals, and even State and local gov-

The author wishes to thank the National Urban Policy Collective in Berkeley, California, for many sessions of discussion on national urban policy which made possible the reflections contained in this paper; Patricia Morgan, Marc Weiss, Madeline Landau, David Wilmoth, and Michael Luger for their critical help; and the Department of Housing and Urban Development, Office of Policy Development and Research, and The Johns Hopkins University for the opportunity to reflect on this aspect of national urban policy.

ernments, has been the object of the analysis. Government-financed economic research in agencies such as the Council of Economic Advisers and the Federal Reserve Board, for instance, probes the aggregate determination of wages and prices via a multitude of economic decisions in the chaotic marketplace in order to aid the engineering of economic policy. It probes the behavior of corporations and banks in determining the supply and demand for investment funds, in order to set monetary policy. Government economic research across-the-board aims at understanding private sector behavior and outcomes, so that it may intervene to stabilize, to compensate, and to perfect market mechanisms.

Public finance theory has justified such studies and intervention by characterizing the outcomes of capitalist production decisions as imperfect, because the pursuit of individual benefits does not always coincide with net social benefits. The government, in the same public finance conception, has been presented as a single, coordinated, self-conscious intervener, that can purposefully plan for the society as a whole and reshape adverse outcomes. The commitment to produce urban impact assessments of its own policy initiatives constitutes an admission on the part of the government that it no longer sees itself as a purposeful and self-aware intervener. It acknowledges that the urban consequences of its own behavior may be severe, counterproductive, unintended and/or inscrutable, even to its architects. It attests to the complexity of bureaucratic structure, within which different bureaus pursue their own and their constituents' ends, indifferent or even hostile to the demands of other constituencies. The UIA is essentially a control device, designed to monitor the actions of one sector of the bureaucracy to guard against adverse impacts for other bureaus and their constituents.

The UIA is by no means the only recent instance of government studying its own behavior. Some econometric models now attempt to make government spending components endogenous rather than exogenous, and several agencies, such as the Advisory Commission on Intergovernmental Relations (ACIR) and the Treasury Department, are interested in the tax and spending behavior of state and local governments, to name just two examples. But the UIA's focus on public sector behavior appears to be symptomatic of a new conception of the object of government research.

The UIA differs dramatically from the EIS, its older more established counterpart. The EIS, because of its project level focus, was designed primarily to monitor private sector actions, to guard against negative environmental consequences from self-interested behavior pursued by one or more independent agents in the capitalist economy. The EIS was justified by a theory in public finance that claimed that externalities—adverse impacts on third parties—occasionally resulted from the production and exchange of commodities contracted between supplier and demander in the market. Only intervention by government, as a representative of the social whole, could restore the appropriate mechanisms to prevent such externalities, whether this was to be done by direct limitations on activity, such as polluting behavior, or by indirect means, such as tax incentives, that would correct price signals. The UIA process is one of an emerging genre that acknowledges that the outcome of government behavior is also frequently imperfect and that it has conflicting and sometimes anarchic decision processes within it.

I find it useful to think of the UIA as a new government product line, with its own characteristic demand structure, production process, and supply behavior. In the following sections, this paper pursues an analysis of the UIA much as a conventional microeconomics text might, beginning with the demand for the UIA and hypothesizing the motivation of its government suppliers in initiating and implementing the analysis. Later sections examine the nature of the production process for UIAs as it is currently shaping up and speculate upon the production process's adequacy in analyzing the urban impacts of the Carter energy policy. The final sections offer a prognosis of the urban impact of the urban impact analysis, and a set of recommendations for its improvement.

DEMAND FOR AN URBAN IMPACT ANALYSIS

The demand for an urban impact analysis might be ascribed to a number of historically evolved features of the federal role in urban settings. First of all, it might be argued that the role of the Federal government has simply grown to such massive proportions that all its actions may have extensive effects on any number of social variables, urban health being one. Proponents of this position might note the growing federal budget, particularly as a source of state and local revenues, as evidence. However, the significance of federal actions reaches far beyond budgeted expenditure, since many forms of regulation and nonbudgetary policy have also affected urban prospects (Markusen and Fastrup, 1978, p. 96). A prime example is the federal land giveaway which accompanied the introduction of continental railroads; this policy alone profoundly influenced the location and growth of many United States cities (Glaab and Brown, 1967). Similarly, the relative prosperity of northern and southern economies has always been strongly shaped by federal actions. It would be difficult to conclude that the Federal government is more of an urban and regional actor today than it has been throughout United States history.

The demand for the UIA might alternatively be ascribed to the severity of Federal government impacts on cities in a number of recently well-publicized cases. This possibility falls closer to the mark. For instance, the post–World War II policy of subsidizing new middle income housing (FHA) has proved a tremendous stimulus for suburban residential construction, and is suspected of accounting for a significant degree of metropolitan urban sprawl. What the Federal government has *not* done may be similarly critical: the failure to standardize welfare payments in all states may have fueled migration of jobs to states with low-welfare rates and therefore, low taxes.

But the severity of federally induced problems is not a sufficient explanation for the particular call for a UIA. The need to *study* past and potential outcomes arises from the concern that they are sometimes unintended, or that their intentions are hidden from the general public. The interstate-freeway network and the location of military facilities are two cases in point. The former was ostensibly designed to facilitate truck and passenger-car travel between cities, yet its belt-loops have completely restructured the location of residential, commercial, and industrial activity in metropolitan areas and may in the longer run contribute to regional restructuring of production. Military bases are ostensibly located with national security foremost in mind, yet their locations are strongly biased toward certain regions of the country where they have provided a strong stimulus to regional economies. Although both these outcomes were probably on someone's agenda (the real estate, oil and gas, automobile, and construction industries; southern congressmen in control of relevant committees), the Federal government as a whole professes to have been unaware of these unfair or adverse outcomes. This aura of surprise and regret tends to evoke a policy of investigation and study, rather than demands for straightforward action that would reverse or compensate for undesirable outcomes.

Even worse, we might suspect that the demand for urban impact analyses may result from the inscrutability of the real results of certain policies whose extensive consequences may be so intertwined, sequential, and convoluted that their net impact may be opaque. To judge from the uncertainty of many partisans over their political stand on certain issues, various parties likely to be affected by a certain action may not in fact be able to tell whether an outcome is in their favor, *even after the fact*. An example from another realm is wage and price controls; within the ranks of both business and labor, there exists every degree of belief that such controls favor business, favor labor, or are bad/good for both. Furthermore, the opaqueness may in some cases be contrived. When a particular policy has been chosen precisely because its bias or its favors to certain groups are less easy to discover, the call for an impact statement may be a first step toward revealing these policies and biases.

Of course, at any particular period the above characteristics shaping the demand for a device, such as the urban impact analysis, will not be effective unless some constituency or set of actors asks for or champions its introduction. In the present case, some combination of urban partisans who expected political results from the Carter administration, and a group of agency actors who (for reasons hypothesized in a later section of this paper) saw a positive program in the UIA, formed the basis of support for the innovation. The urban constituency in turn was a product of both long-run and short-run events in the United States political economy, as discussed elsewhere in recent literature (Alcaly and Mermelstein, 1977; Steinlieb and Hughes, 1978). These larger conditions in the political economy explain the demand for Federal government action on urban problems in general; the issues of severity, intention, and accountability for urban consequences of federal actions explain the transformation of general pressure for urban policy into the specific call, among other things, for urban impact analysis. But such demands have not specified the precise nature of the product to be supplied, a critical weakness.

The explicit proposal for an urban impact analysis of federal policies arose from the business community. Popular demands for a focus on urban problems and urban accountability may have worried business leaders, lest they result in a process similar to the EIS. Any new regulation or monitoring system which might increase private sector paperwork and presume accountability, or threaten to slow down development and location decisions, as occurred in the EIS case, might be expected to arouse business opposition. At the same time, an accountability restricted to *public* actions might aid specific sectors of the business community whose assets were tied to urban locations affected by federal policy.

The business community funded and/or produced, with the help of the Rand Institute and the Urban Institute, two documents that were strategic in shaping the UIA process. Both appeared in the year following the Carter election and preceding the finalization of the Carter urban policy. One, the Committee for Economic Development's *An Approach to Federal Urban Policy* (1977), listed as its first recommendations, "systematic monitoring of the effects of federal policies on the distribution of the labor force and economic activity is essential" (page 9). The other, the four-volume Rand Corporation study, *The Urban Impacts of Federal Policies* (Barro and Vaughan, vol. 1, 1977), was produced under a Kettering Foundation grant. It explores the existing literature and proposed methodologies for looking at the impact of federal policies on the fiscal conditions, economic development, and population and residential location patterns in cities. Through these studies and their authors, it is not hard to detect a strong business input into the urban policy formation process, similar to that which Domhaff documents (1978). The careful channeling of accountability-demands toward the public, rather than the private, realm protected the latter sector from the costs of regulation and uncertainty associated with an EIS-type process.

Given that pro-accountability demands have been vaguely formulated, and that the opposition to urban accountability poses explicit boundaries that it wishes government to observe, the Federal government has enjoyed considerable leeway in shaping the quality and extensiveness of the UIA in ways that would not tread on a regulation-sensitive private sector. Thus, the motivation and behavior of government suppliers and their decisions regarding the nature of the production process for UIAs deserve greater emphasis than they might in a comparable analysis of private sector production.

THE SUPPLIERS OF URBAN IMPACT ANALYSIS

Scholars of public administration and planning, recognizing that government is not a single actor responding to a consensual public mandate, have in recent years produced a growing body of analyses of the relationship between bureaus and constituents, and of decision-making within the bureaucratic structure itself (*see* Wamsley and Zald, 1973; Capitol Kapitalistate, 1977; Niskanen, 1971). These draw on social science models. The modeling of bureaucratic behavior, while yet in its formative stages, permits one to improve upon older naive notions of government behavior. The possibility can be dismissed that government, as some abstract, single entity, has created the UIA because of the superiority, the leadership, and farsightedness of its elite members (the theory of meritocracy) or that it has automatically responded to pressures for urban accountability by well-organized, vocal groups (the theory of pluralism). We can identify several supply groups, whose own agendas may differ significantly from the aims of those making demands and from other supplier groups. Following economic reasoning, we might expect each of them to pursue different goals in shaping the UIA product.

In response to the general demand for Federal government urban accountability, a set of three interdependent but distinct groups of suppliers fashioned the UIA proposal. Two of these are government-lodged: the President's Executive Office and the agencies responsible for urban concerns (such as the U.S. Department of Housing and Urban Development [HUD] and the U.S. Department of Commerce [DOC]). The other is the government-supported research community, including academicians and Washington-based think tanks. Actors from all three groups participated in and around the Carter administration effort to formulate the national urban policy, in the six or so intense months preceding its unveiling by the President in March 1978. Both the Rand Institute and the Urban Institute, following their business-community sponsored research on federal impacts, argued strongly for the UIA. The rapidity with which the UIA plan gained currency among the various task forces and policy advisors attests to its versatility in satisfying the needs of all three supplier groups.

The President needed a means of following through on his promises to urban constituents. Urban coalitions, and black groups in particular, had been strong supporters of Carter's election campaign and had delivered substantial votes. The National Urban League's Vernon Jordan termed the administration's year-long effort to come up with a forceful urban policy "disheartening" and "a missed opportunity." The "frostbelt," industrial states, who had all voted for Carter, were disgruntled with what they felt to be the anti-urban, anti-Northeastern bias of the energy policy, the first Carter initiative. For the President, the UIA promised to be a relatively painless way of demonstrating a commitment to urban consciousness-raising, if nothing else.

The agencies entrusted with addressing and reviving cities also waxed enthusiastic about the UIA process, although differentially and with a competitive watchfulness. For them, the UIA would constitute an empowerment to intervene and participate in the formulation of policy in other agencies of the executive. To quote William Gorham (president of the Urban Institute), the UIA process "legitimizes the role of the cabinet officer in charge of the nation's urban condition, guaranteeing her (him) entrée into the decision-making process" (Gorham, 1979). The UIA would also undoubtedly enhance the prestige of such agencies and garner additional budgetary allocations, if done well.

Urban social scientists and planners, and administrators in think tanks, consulting firms, and academia, are obviously delighted with a new realm in which to apply social science techniques (or to criticize the circumstances of their application). The richness of detail and expansive suggestions for further research represented by the papers in this volume manifest the talent and entrepreneurship of this group in responding to a new opportunity.

This description of supply behavior is oversimplified and speculative. There are undoubtedly subtleties in the particular agendas of particular agencies, and groups within them, that the author is not privy to. A great deal of fruitful theoretical and empirical research could be done on the behavior of public sector suppliers, particularly on their links to those making demands, and on the degree and nature of competition (or more precisely, oligopoly) among them. As is argued in the next section, supply conditions have a profound impact on the shaping of the production process and therefore on the quality of the product that emerges.

THE PRODUCTION PROCESS

The process for producing an UIA is a complicated matter and currently in the formative stages. We can tentatively infer some of its features from Circular A-116. The following characterization may prove inadequate when we eventually evaluate the real thing. It is designed to highlight other possible routes in addition to criticizing the way that the process is currently shaping up.

Determination of product form

Since the demand for urban accountability has not articulated a precise form for its satisfaction, the suppliers of UIAs have considerable power to shape the quality and scope of the product. Several decisions on product-form have been made, all of them limiting the scope of the UIAs application. First, the UIA will be produced for new policy initiatives only, although the Circular A-116 guidelines are vague and do permit expansions in budget outlays as potential candidates. The exclusion of current policies is remarkable, since many in place policies have been named as villains in the urban drama and will undoubtedly continue to play a role, e.g., the energy policy and the interstate-freeway-system completion. The exclusion of individual projects, whose specificity ironically might offer greater technical promise and constituent participation, is also unfortunate.

Secondly, the UIA process will not apparently be applied to the urban policy initiative as a whole, a surprising omission. One suspects that proper account has not been taken, nor has a procedure for evoking accountability been constructed for the direct urban consequences of Carter administration proposals, such as the targeted tax credit, aimed at encouraging new investment to locate in areas of high unemployment which did *not* pass along with the recent extension of the general Investment Tax Credit (ITC). The proposal as it appeared in the Carter package had no analysis similar to a detailed impact statement attached to it. Even worse, unlike the potential accountability for dislocation and other neighborhood effects attached to older urban-renewal programs, the targeted ITC was structured in a way that precluded any public recourse or accountability for adverse impacts. For instance, a targeted ITC-earning project, such as a large capital intensive warehousing operation, could conceivably locate in an urban neighborhood with high unemployment, but eliminate more small-business jobs than it replaces and dislocate neighborhood residents from their homes. Yet nothing in the Carter proposal would require such projects, either before or after the fact, to show that they actually produced net urban benefits in return for the substantial tax break.

Finally, as Norman Glickman also points out in his paper in this volume, the piecemeal consideration of various policy initiatives prevents cognizance of the potential exacerbation of urban problems, or the curtailment of effectiveness of a certain policy, through cumulative effects of interaction. For instance, the energy policy may undermine the efforts of the urban policy. And, the interaction between boom-town impact aid, interstate-freeway extensions, and infrastructure and planning aid from various departments, may fuel the growth of coastal and western small towns as new centers for manufacturing and other new job locations at the expense of cities, far in excess of what would be predicted by analyzing any one policy component.

The production function

The ability to produce an UIA is powerfully constrained by technical possibilities, many of which are addressed by other authors in this volume. Hopefully, these limits can be transcended. However, within these constraints, the production function for UIAs seems to specify a particular combination of labor techniques, whose character, skills, and outlook are quite narrowly defined. First of all, the nomination of initiatives for urban impact scrutiny and the actual production of the UIA rests with the generating department. For example, the Department of Energy will write the impact statement for its own new initiatives as will the Department of Transportation. The Office of Management and Budget (OMB) will review nominations and may request additions or deletions. OMB will also review the statements, although they are not required until *the day* preceding the applying agency's budget hearing. OMB "may request revisions by either the submitting agency or any other agency wth expertise in the area." The process is strangely deferential to the initiating agency, which will face a strong incentive to belittle the adverse urban impacts of a policy initiative that it strongly favors.

Secondly, the preparation of UIAs will most likely involve only professional staff members or contractors, whose primary incentive will be to please the initiating agency. There is no established means for groups affected by the particular policy, either urban constituents or the direct constituents of the policy itself, to participate in the identification and evaluation of impacts. The product will not register the subjective evaluations by such groups of the consequences of various actions; instead technicians will choose some set of proxies for impacts such as those listed in the circular. To take one example, the change in fiscal status of a local government as a result of a new policy does not necessarily indicate the direction or intensity of the change in public services enjoyed by local residents. A highly noxious plant whose location was encouraged by a targeted ITC, for instance, could produce a big increase in local tax receipts but require so much additional public services and clean up, and diminish air quality so severely, that residents could be worse off. The inclusion of such subjective evaluations and distributional consequences may best be achievable by directly involving parties to an action in the production of the UIA itself.

The discipline of competition

Textbook economics insists that competition is the chief way to guarantee that the optimal amount of product is produced at the minimum cost for that level of output. The administration has invested monopoly rights of UIA production in the policy-initiating agency. Even if the possibility of an OMB request to another agency for revisions constitutes an alternative producer (and it is hard to see how this will work if the analysis is not due until the day before the budget hearing), at best one is talking about duopoly or oligopoly. And given the bureaucratic incentives outlined above, the result will undoubtedly be a form of gaming behavior with severe consequences. Since technical limitations make it unlikely that precise determination of future impacts can be achieved, the process is probably headed for much embattlement and bargaining.

Such outcomes can be moderated to the extent that competition over the production of a *general* methodology for producing UIAs can provide an explicit, standardized procedure. It is also possible that the existence of oligopoly could offer outside groups a wedge to gain entrée into the production process. But the lack of competition combines with other absences of marketlike tests to diminish the chances that cost-efficiency and optimal output will be achieved. Following Niskanen (1971), for instance, we might hypothesize that if bureau managers are trying to maximize budgets, they will overspend on UIAs.

Absence of market tests

Because monopolists in the private sector must sell their output, the market constrains their supply behavior. Monopolist suppliers in the public sector confront a political process that intermediates for taxpayers/consumers. In the present case, people affected don't have a direct opportunity to buy or refuse the UIA that is served to them. In other cases, such as the EIS, the missing market test is replaced by political mechanisms which directly require and/or permit the scrutiny of the product by outside parties affected. For instance, the EIS has the force of law behind it and is reviewable and challengeable in the courts. The UIA, established by executive order and implemented by administrative circular, has no such legal status or means of entrée. In fact, its design insulates it from just such review and accountability. Thus its suppliers can all use it to pursue their own ends—to legitimize the administration, to add on to bureaucratic empires, and to increase the demand for social science technicians—without having to directly confront the constituents to whom accountability is owed.

THE ENERGY POLICY AS AN ILLUSTRATION

One of the biggest policy initiatives under the Carter administration has been the creation of the Department of Energy (DOE) and the implementation of a new energy policy. How satisfactory an urban impact analysis of the new energy policy would have been produced under the current guidelines? What are the specific problems that would make such an analysis difficult?

First of all, the main agencies which predated DOE—the Federal Energy Administration (FEA) and the Energy Research and Development Administration (ERDA)—would probably not have been able to pursue an urban impact analysis in an unbiased way. In the bureaucratic turmoil and jockeying for position that accompanied the new agency's birth, careful and critical analysis of the urban impact would not have been a high priority, especially if its pursuit would have uncovered significant negative impacts. And the adverse effects on urban areas are considerable. Consider just the economic stimulus implicit in the energy policy. The quest for energy independence focuses policy initiatives on off-shore oil development, on Western coal development, uranium and oil shale, on nuclear and coal-fired electricity-generating facilities, on pipeline and other energy transmission systems. All of these occur in relatively rural areas, and disproportionately in the Western and Southern sections of the country. Public policies which subsidize these types of energy developments are thus apt to be unwittingly anti-urban and anti-Eastern, at least with respect to their employment and income-generating consequences.

Second, the urban and regional impacts of the new energy policy are so diffuse and extensive that they would hamper an effort to define the relevant initiatives and make an analysis manageable. Almost every aspect of energy policy has spatial impacts: natural gas regulation, capital-intensive technology subsidies, aid to energy-impacted communities, land-leasing policy, strip-mining regulations, air quality regulation, taxation of energy, among others. Many of the policies and programs are not administered by DOE, but by Interior (leasing) or Commerce (offshore-oil impact aid), so that they would not be considered side-by-side with other energy initiatives that might combine to provide unusual stimulus to a particular area. And many are older programs which are proliferating or gaining significance, such as leasing policy, but may not be subject to UIA as new initiatives.

Third, we might expect that the information requirements needed to fully trace the differential spatial economic stimulus associated with the energy package might be impossible to fulfill. Subjective evaluations by community members of the displacement and psychic costs associated with disruptive boom-town growth around energy are currently nonexistent (Markusen, 1978). Precise prediction of future growth impacts stimulated by energy production requires information which is hard to come by. Frequently, such information is monopolized by private-sector companies who may have an incentive to understate or overstate their future production patterns in order to engender local support or to assuage fears of too-rapid development, displacement, and environmental damage. The full impact of even one project would require a sophisticated understanding of the industrial-location decisions of companies and the population-migration decisions of individuals in response to the spatial reordering of energy production, which is now lacking. On balance, one expects gross understatements about the long-run spatial effects of the energy policy because of lack of information and the probability that information might be withheld or biased by particular parties with particular ends.

Much controversy surrounds the capital-intensive high-techonology direction that the United States energy policy is taking under the Carter administration. Many alternative proposals for small-scale, labor-intensive conservation and decentralized strategies have been suggested. These may be less regionally contracted, more amenable to urban adaptation, and more likely to spread the economic stimulus evenly over urban and rural areas. Yet the way that the UIA is presently set up, its application to the energy policy would not have required a comparative study of the urban impacts from these alternatives.

In the long run, the federal policies which will affect urban areas most will probably be those that are hardest to study thoroughly. Currently, most impact studies take into account only the first round macroeconomic impacts associated with direct job creation. Yet growth theory and empirical evidence warn us that supply-induced growth may be even more important in the long run. Growth of a skilled labor force, an enhanced infrastructure, an elaborated service sector and, particularly, a major increase in energy availability may induce producers to relocate and generate long-run growth far in excess of what a multiplier would tell us. Thus we would be apt to underestimate the shifts toward rural and western growth forthcoming from the energy policy and to underestimate the incentive to depopulation of more eastern and more urban areas as workers follow new jobs associated with supply-induced growth. A similar process of southern industrialization was undoubtedly created by the Tennessee Valley Authority (TVA). Yet no decent study has been done of TVA's supply-induced stimulus, and probably it would be difficult to do such a study, even *after* the fact.

Since the UIA is buried in the executive branch, requiring no contributions or comments from outside groups by law (and therefore is not reviewable by the courts), there is little likelihood that in the energy case the results would have had significant consequences for the actual policy-formation process. The energy agencies seem at best to be indifferent to the urban impacts of their policies. The one major facility-location battled over by regional lobbies was the Solar Energy Research Institute, ultimately located in exurban and booming Golden, Colorado, despite several northeastern bids. Without careful and mandatory scrutiny by urban partisans, an UIA of energy policy would not significantly temper its suspected anti-urban bias.

In summary, given the partisan inclinations of energy bureaucrats, the highly anti-urban and regionally skewed bias in the current energy technology and sources being developed, and the leeway afforded initiating agencies in the UIA process, it is unlikely that the UIA process as now constituted would have produced an energy urban impact statement that would have been forceful, comprehensive, comparative, and fully cognizant of the long-run equity and development dynamics in different regions and for city economies.

THE PROSPECTS FOR THE URBAN IMPACT ANALYSIS

Depending on which view of the real purpose of the UIA you hold, you will be more or less sanguine about its ability to deliver. If, as has been suggested in the supply section of this paper, its purpose is to legitimize the Carter administration with its urban constituents without disturbing the business community, and to provide bigger budgets and more jobs for bureaucrats and researchers, then it has fair prospects. If, on the other hand, we expect it to meet its stated purpose to identify major urban impacts, to encourage reconsideration of the more adverse of these impacts, and to help cities in distress—then its prospects are problematic.

Will it identify the full range of adverse urban impacts? Probably it will fall short for both technical and political reasons. Technically, it will be nearly impossible to predict the full set of long-run economic responses to various policy initiatives, particularly the location decisions of both industry and households. Politically, the assignment of the UIA to the lead agency, the lack of legal status, and the absence of a requirement for review by affected parties will work against full disclosure.

Will the UIA process help stem the worst consequences of new federal initiatives on urban areas? It is unlikely to affect the decision-making process that underlies policy formulation. In rare circumstances it may lead to denial in the budget review process or even a presidential veto. As the procedure is set up, the UIA is tacked on to new initiatives after they have been formed; it is not a mandate to the generating agency to consider urban impacts seriously in the design of new initiatives. The EIS process has undoubtedly affected the design of many projects and programs, but only because it has the force of law and requires critical information and response (Teitz, 1978). Affected parties may use the EIS to slow down a project; thus it offers potential sanctions on heedless behavior by proponents. The UIA offers no similar channels to urban partisans, so that it exerts no discipline on the generating agency, which bears little risk that its plans will be interrupted by a UIA challenge.

Will the UIA significantly help cities? This is a different question from the one just posed, for it asks whether or not federal urban impact, even if identifiable and malleable, is really all that important. Past history suggests that it may be. Clearly, the current problems of urban areas stem in part from the post–World War II suburban development and industrial decentralization nourished extensively by federal housing and transportation policies. For these reasons, the advent of a federal self-consciousness about its urban presence is welcome and promising. However, the primacy of the UIA as the newest form of urban research may dangerously deflect from other equally serious research that needs to be done. In particular, it may lead to an overemphasis on the culpability of the public sector and an ignoring of the fundamental role of the private sector in creating urban problems.

The UIA, as it is currently proposed, would be confined to broad federal initiatives. Its exclusion of specific projects prevents the kind of private sector scrutiny often pursued in the EIS. As such, the object is not an understanding of the urban consequences of complex behavior and interaction among private sector agents, in order to intervene, but an understanding of the consequences of the government's own behavior. Implicitly, this focus accepts the gist of the recent social-science trends in the United States, which blame social malfunctions on government intervention rather than on the chaos of the market, the concentration of economic power, or the indifference of capitalist economic structure toward externalities created in the production process.

Private sector actions such as capital relocation and population migration in search of jobs and better living conditions lie at the root of city crises. Our understanding of these processes is still quite primitive. No regional or urban growth model to date can tell us with any certainty what the development implications of any action of import for a regional economy will be beyond five years. The difficulties in modeling economic development will undoubtedly get worse, instead of better, with the increasing pace and ease of internationalization of production, with the increasing large-scale and capital-intensive character of development which introduces more volatile and uncertain production patterns into communities, and with the increasing mobility of households. We badly need study of these processes; otherwise the UIA might unduly focus attention on public sector actions, which may result in distraction from pursuit of a comprehensive understanding of the more fundamental economic forces which they moderate or engender.

Furthermore, understanding the adverse urban impacts of federal policies will not in all cases produce political reversals, even when they might be in the interests of most United States citizens. The gains from private sector movement and policies encouraging it may prompt constituents of particular federal policies to fight hard to preserve their publicly provided incentives. An example is the investment tax credit, which undoubtedly encourages significantly new, non-central city location of jobs. The absence of the extra urban-targeted sweetener, suggested by the President, in the extension of the ITC passed by Congress last fall suggests that even when the results are known, certain client groups, in this case the business establishment, may be too strong to permit urban-based concerns to affect outcomes.

Is the UIA worth the resources we will be spending on it? This is a question which is difficult to answer because the benefits are difficult to discern and the cost of producing UIAs is not known. The latter could be calculated by the administration and might be a worthy exercise. If the concerned agencies are going to spend a large amount on UIA generation and review, the magnitude might provoke a more serious concern with the productivity of the UIA process and with ways to increase efficiency and lower the cost of their generation.

The pessimistic prognosis set forth in this paper could be tempered if the administration would tackle the restrictive character of the institutional setting in which UIAs are produced. The UIA remains, despite the caveats expressed, a promising, if only symbolic, step toward federal self-consciousness about urban consequences of its policy initiatives. The success of the UIA will depend primarily upon the political structuring of its production, rather than upon conquering problems in technique. The current focus on technical innovation, the major direction of this collection of papers, is thus disturbing.

RECOMMENDATIONS FOR AN IMPROVED UIA

Several structural innovations might considerably strengthen the content and political potency of the UIA. They are implicit in the criticisms of the current administrative structure registered above. First, the administration could go to Congress with a proposal giving the UIA legal status akin to that of the EIS. And, in conjunction, the administration could ask for a legal requirement that affected parties and interest groups must review the UIA and agencies must respond to the reviews as part of the written UIA. Second, the UIA should be extended to particular projects and to the aggregate impacts of several interrelated policies. Third, the administration could place lead responsibility for the UIA in an agency other than the policy-initiating agency, particularly in an agency which has urban expertise and stewardship over urban affairs. Furthermore, the agency initiating the policy should be required to involve the urban agency in evaluating urban impacts early on in the decision-making process, and in ways that permit the urban consequences to be a part of the calculus guiding very formulation of the policy. Fourth, any policy initiative which has such urban impacts should be required to present alternatives or to include mitigation measures that will moderate or compensate for adverse impacts.

But even more importantly, the administration should resist the movement of research targets to exclusively public sector actions and consequences at the expense of understanding private sector behavior and urban impacts. Even though the charting of public sector consequences will undoubtedly yield some insight into private sector response, this information will not be produced in a systematic comprehensive way. More research is needed on microlevel decisions, such as the work Harrison et al. (1978) are doing on the impact of relocation decisions by firms and unemployment experience of workers on the New England economy.

Finally, the administration must also confront the necessity to link documentation of private sector impacts with measures to mitigate them. The urban consequences of capital relocation can be thought of as externalities imposed on the people remaining or on people in entered communities, both through unemployment and displacement effects and through abandonment or extraordinary demands on the local public sector (Markusen, 1977). Urban measures that would provide incentives to internalize these costs could be constructed in the manner of exit and entrance fees. The design of such instruments would take much effort, including empirical identification of impacts, but might in the long run constitute a better use of urban-oriented federal resources than a full-scale, exclusively public-sector-focused, pursuit of the urban impact analysis.

REFERENCES

Alcaly, Roger, and Mermelstein, David, eds. *The Fiscal Crisis of American Cities.* New York: Vintage Books, 1977.

Barro, Stephen, and Vaughan, Roger. *The Urban Impacts of Federal Policies*, 4 vols. Santa Monica: Rand Corporation, 1977.

Capitol Kapitalistate. "The Study of Studies: A Marxist View of Research Conducted by the State." *Kapitalistate* 6 (1977): 163–90.

Committee for Economic Development, Research and Policy Committee. *An Approach to Federal Urban Policy.* New York: Committee for Economic Development, 1977.

Domhoff, G. William. *The Powers That Be.* New York: Vintage Books, 1978.

Glaab, Charles, and Brown, A. Theodore. *A History of Urban America.* New York: Macmillan, 1967.

Glickman, Norman. "Methodological Issues and Prospects of Urban Impact Analysis," Chapter 1 in this volume.

Gorham, William. Telephone conversation, January 9, 1979.

Harrison, Bennet; Bluestone, Barry; and Kantor, Sandra. *Private Investment, Public Policy, and the Decline of Older Regions: An Analysis of the New England Economy.* First progress report. Cambridge: Joint Center for Urban Studies of Massachusetts Institute of Technology and Harvard University, July 15, 1978.

Markusen, Ann, and Fastrup, Jerry. "The Regional War for Federal Aid." *The Public Interest* 53 (Fall 1978): 87–99.

Markusen, Ann Roell. "Federal Budget Simplification: Preventive Programs vs. Palliatives for Local Governments with Booming, Stable, and Declining Economies." *National Tax Journal*, 30, no. 3 (1977): 249–58.

———. *Socioeconomic Models for Boomtown Planning and Policy Evaluation: A Critical Review.* Working Paper no. 285. Berkeley: Institute of Urban and Regional Development, University of California, 1978.

National Urban Policy Collective. *Carter's National Urban Policy.* Mimeographed. Berkeley: Department of City and Regional Planning, University of California, April 1978.

Niskanen, William A. *Bureaucracy and Representative Government.* New York: Aldine-Atherton, 1971.

Sternlieb, George, and Hughes, James, eds. *Revitalizing the Northeast.* New Brunswick: Center for Urban Policy Research, Rutgers University, 1978.

Teitz, Michael. *Policy Evaluation: The Uncertain Guide.* Working Paper no. 298. Berkeley: Institute of Urban and Regional Development, University of California, September 1978.

Wamsley, Gary, and Zald, Mayer. *The Political Economy of Public Organizations: A Critique and Approach to the Study of Public Administration.* Lexington, Mass.: Lexington Books, 1973.

PART II

Data and Methodological Issues

CHAPTER FIVE

Outlays Data and the Analysis of Federal Policy Impact

THOMAS J. ANTON

INTRODUCTION

Federal outlays data have been "discovered." Little known and seldom used three or four years ago, the annual compilations of Federal government obligations variously titled *Federal Outlays* or, after Fiscal 1977, *Geographic Distribution of Federal Funds,* recently have provided raw material to structure the so-called "Frostbelt-Sunbelt" controversy (Havemann et al., 1976; and Havemann and Stanfield, 1977), to assess the extent to which federal spending does in fact target on needy areas (Congressional Budget Office, 1977), and even to examine the influence of congressional committee positions (Ritt, 1966). Reasons for increasing interest in outlays data are not difficult to find. Unlike the numerous but fragmentary reports on federal program activity that emerge from the separate federal agencies, outlays data provide a single, comprehensive source of information about *all* federal expenditures, direct and indirect. And, unlike the useful but highly aggregated data that track national income and budget accounts, outlays data are available for all counties and all cities of 25,000 population or more, as well as all states. Finally, outlays data are in principle available for every year since 1968, providing an opportunity to track federal spending for more than a decade. No other annual data source combines these qualities of comprehensiveness,

The author wishes to acknowledge the major contributions to this study made by several of his colleagues in the Intergovernmental Fiscal Analysis Project, Ph.D. Program in Urban and Regional Planning, the University of Michigan; and also would like to thank Jerry Cawley, Kevin Kramer, Kathryn Jones, and Peter Ward for their very different contributions, all of which were essential. In addition, he would especially like to thank Luther Burgess of the Community Services Administration for his very generous assistance in helping the author and his colleagues to understand the outlays data.

program specificity, and area specificity for as long a period of time.[1] These data, therefore, must be regarded as a major national information resource. Our recent "discovery" of this resource, however, can hardly be regarded as an unmixed blessing. Academics and journalists who have begun to use outlays data often produce seriously misleading analyses because they fail to understand the obvious limitations in the data. Increased use by individuals who are undisciplined by awareness of data limitations can more accurately be regarded as "misuse" of a potentially valuable resource (*see*, e.g., Dye, 1978 and Browning, 1973). Curiously enough, there is also a danger that outlays data will not be used enough, precisely because those who recognize the data limitations tend to exaggerate them. Three separate evaluations of the quality of outlays data have been conducted by or for federal agencies within the past two years (see below), each of them pointing to serious problems. Although these evaluations were on the whole favorable, there is some evidence that the negative comments have had a much stronger impact on the Washington policy community (*see*, in particular, *A Report to Congress*, 1978). If so, a potentially powerful tool of policy analysis may well be neglected by those who can profit most from its use. To avoid either neglect or misuse, it is essential that we develop a better appreciation of the character, quality, and potential utility of the outlays series.

OUTLAYS AS DATA

The seed for the federal outlays data series appears to have been planted during a meeting between President Lyndon B. Johnson and a group of state governors, held at President Johnson's Texas ranch in 1968. In preparation for that meeting Johnson had a series of reports made up, showing each governor how much money his state was obtaining from the Federal government. The governors were so pleased with this information that they asked the President to make it available on a regular basis.[2] Johnson obliged, and on June 29, 1967, the Bureau of the Budget (now the Office of Management and Budget [OMB]) issued Circular A-84, titled "Reporting of Federal Outlays by Geographic Location." Circular A-84, effective July 1, 1967, and essentially unchanged through 1978, requires all executive departments and establishments to submit quarterly reports (cumulated annually) of all "obligations" incurred from government-administered funds. Instructions included in the circular require that reports be made according to standardized definitions, with allocations made to the geographic location in which recipients of federal spending are located. Reports must show the lowest possible level of geographic location (cities of 25,000) and provision is made for obtaining

---

[1] For a more complete discussion of various data sets which track federal expenditures, *see* Anton, August 1978.

[2] For background on federal efforts to organize information systems to service State and local governments, *see* Intergovernmental Task Force on Information Systems, 1978.

county and state totals. Each year since 1968, these agency reports have been compiled and published in 53 volumes—one for each state, one for the District of Columbia, one for Trusts and Territories, and a summary volume for the nation as a whole (Community Services Administration, 1968–).

The task of compiling and publishing these volumes was originally assigned to the Office of Economic Opportunity (OEO). A presidential decision to abolish OEO, however, provided an occasion for a thorough evaluation of the outlays data system. Submitted in July 1974, the report of the Interagency Task Team, created by OMB to examine A-84 and related processes, made clear what many had suspected, namely, that much of the information in outlays reports was soft, despite continuous staff efforts to improve it (a recommendation to change the title of the outlays report to "Estimated Geographic Distribution of Federal Funds" was made, but rejected) (Interagency Task Team Report, 1974). A major difficulty was that staff and other resources were modest in the extreme: only five part-time people, with a total budget of under $205,000, were involved in carrying out the enormous and complex job of preparing outlays data for publication. Large increases in both budget and personnel were essential, according to the Task Team, if significant improvements in data quality were to be achieved.

As events turned out, resource increments were considerably less dramatic than the Task Team recommended, and responsibility for outlays reports was shifted to the Community Services Administration (CSA) rather than to OMB, as the Team had suggested. A variety of other proposed reforms were implemented, however, with important results. The outlays format was altered to separate grants from other federal expenditures in the hard-copy volumes; clearer specification of the techniques used to distribute expenditure data among substate units was initiated; an urban-rural index was developed; and efforts were begun to integrate outlays data with other federal data sources, particularly in the *Catalog of Federal Domestic Assistance* (CFDA) and the federal budget. Beginning in 1974, then, outlays data became much harder, more comprehensible, and more accurate.[3]

Intelligent recent efforts to use the improved outlays data, however, repeatedly conclude that the data are not yet as good as they might be. In August 1977, the Congressional Budget Office issued a study entitled *Troubled Local Economies and the Distribution of Federal Dollars* (Congressional Budget Office, 1977). By showing the relationship between federal spending, county income, and county rates of economic growth or decline, this study provided a useful example of the kind of "targeting" analysis for which the outlays data are particularly well-suited. The report also included an Appendix on "Reliability of Data," in which the authors conclude that 69 percent of the outlays data seemed reasonably accurate but that 31 percent

---

[3] Interagency Task Team Report, 1974. The report contains a complete review of the technical changes proposed and adopted.

"seemed open to serious question" (ibid., pp. 53–60). Another study, completed during this same period by two officials of the Economic Research Service, U.S. Department of Agriculture, attempted to show the utility of outlays data in measuring program equity. Their very close examination of the data led authors to conclude that more than three-quarters (76.3 percent) of the information was acceptable, but that just under 23 percent was generated by methods they refer to as "questionable" (Hines and Reid, 1977). A third evaluation was conducted by a Brookings Institution team, led by Richard P. Nathan, at the request of OMB. OMB was interested in judging whether the outlays data might provide a feasible method for "measuring and analyzing the impact of Federal economic and community development outlays on state and local areas." The Brookings response, dated August 19, 1977, made no effort to estimate the overall proportions of "good" and "bad" data, but was generally rather negative. "Although a considerable body of useful geographic information is available in the FIXS [Federal Information Exchange System] reporting system," the study concluded, "a number of problems would have to be resolved before a clean data tape could be prepared for processing." Interestingly enough, Nathan and his associates, who appear not to have come across the 1974 Task Team report, recommended that an "interagency task force" be created to direct production of a clean data tape (Nathan et al., 1977).

It is important to underline the extent to which these studies confirm the general quality of the outlays data. Implementation of several 1974 Task Team recommendations coupled with continuous efforts by CSA staff to upgrade data quality have created an annual information system that intelligent critics find to be 70 to 75 percent accurate. Given the comprehensiveness, program specificity, and substate focus of these data, the current level of accuracy represents both a considerable achievement and a measure of the significance of this information system. But problems remain, and it is equally important to ask whether, and to what extent, these problems can be resolved.

Problems and solutions

In compiling and publishing outlays data, CSA acts as an agent for OMB, the source of authority for all A-84 processes. Two consequences follow from this arrangement. The first is that the outlays data consist entirely of material submitted by the various federal agencies, or to put it differently, CSA is entirely dependent on other federal agencies for the information it publishes as outlays. CSA collects no information by itself and, apart from checking for consistency or obvious inaccuracies, can do little to affect the characteristics of information submitted by other units. The second related consequence is that CSA has little "clout" to exercise in solving problems that arise in the data-gathering process. CSA can cajole, harass, or plead, but it cannot compel other agencies to submit data or change data already submitted if they are unwilling to cooperate. Many other sanctions are open to OMB, of course, but to date OMB has shown considerable reluctance to intervene in the A-84 process. That so much data of such high quality is being submitted each year can thus be seen as evidence of a considerable spirit of cooperation among federal agency officials. On the other hand, the continued existence of data problems may also be attributed in some measure to the decentralized voluntarism of the outlays data system.

A number of these problems seem amenable to relatively straightforward solutions. Some federal expenditure programs, including those in the Department of Housing and Urban Development (HUD), are not reported at all, creating an underreporting problem. Including reports for HUD mortgage- and loan-guarantee programs that become obligations only if defaults occur, on the other hand, creates an overreporting problem. Obviously, improving accuracy in these areas requires special attention to HUD reports, just as improving reporting methods for so-called "indirect federal support" (such as surplus food distributions) will require special attention by Department of Agriculture programs. Improving the accuracy of capital expenditure data presents another difficulty, because spending "obligated" in one year may not in fact be expended until a year or two later. The severity of this problem is unclear, but it may be largely correctable through use of "cumulative approvals" or "cost of active projects" concepts (the latter has been recommended by the Brookings team). For a number of problems such as these, solutions appear readily available through slight increments of intelligence, updated information, or use of more sensible conceptual measures.

The more serious and more difficult problems have to do with the statistical techniques used to allocate some program expenditures to substate areas. OMB Circular A-84 requires that "the primary basis of reporting data by geographic location will be the location of the recipient who received or will receive the payment in liquidation of an obligation." But, "in those cases where data on an actual basis are not available, statistical methods or best estimates may be used" (Community Services Administration, 1976, p. 21). Since only 25 to 30 percent of total annual outlays represent "actual" expenditures, statistical allocation techniques—the so-called "proration" codes —are widely used. In Fiscal 1977 outlays data, some 23 different allocation methods were utilized. Although some of these methods seem quite adequate, others are obviously inaccurate. Fiscal 1977 spending for Child Welfare Services or Vocational Rehabilitation Services, for example, are apportioned through a formula that uses 1970 census and state-reported data. More serious still is use of allocation techniques that really are not codes at all, but simply designations used when no acceptable technique is available. The Department of Health, Education and Welfare (HEW), for example, lists some 40 programs for which expenditures are allocated entirely to the county in which the state capital is located, simply because no convenient method is available to apportion funds among the counties in which expenditures actually are made. Other agencies, too, use this reporting technique—the Law Enforcement Assistance Administration (LEAA) in the Justice Department is a very visible example. Where reporting inaccuracies arise from the use of old data in apportionment formula, remedies can easily be developed. But where allocations stop at the location of the state capital, far more extensive and time-consuming remedies are necessary.

There is yet another major difficulty for which no conceivable remedy exists: the so-called "subcontracting" problem. A number of agencies, most especially the Department of Defense, report expenditures for the procurement of goods and services to the "place of performance" of the prime contractor. Such allocations may be reasonably accurate at the state level, but accuracy degenerates rapidly for reports of county and city spending. The reason, of course, is that prime contractors typically subcontract major portions of their activities to other firms, many of whom are located in a different city, county, or even state. Defense Department reports include allocations to cities and counties but, with many subcontracts let for each prime contract, the substate reports are bound to be misleading. Moreover, there seems to be no feasible method, short of attempting to examine each prime contractor's books, of gaining better information. For the moment, then, there is not, and cannot be, an accurate record of the substate distribution of more than $50 billion in federal expenditures—roughly 12 percent of total 1977 outlays.

Table 1 provides an opportunity to evaluate the significance of these several problems by showing the proportion of total outlays reported by the most important prorations codes used in 1974 and 1977. It is apparent that only a few among the more than 20 codes account for the bulk of agency reports in both years, and that the proportionate amounts remain fairly stable. Allocations based on city and county proportions of total state population declined noticeably between 1974 and 1977, matched by an almost identical increase

TABLE 1: Distribution of Program Expenditures, by Proration Code, 1974 and 1977

	% of Total Outlays	
Proration Code and Explanation	*1974*	*1977*
(5) Allocated to contractor's main office (place of performance)[a]	12.1	12.5
(10) City and county estimates based on state population	10.9	7.1
(12) City and county estimates proportional to special group	32.0	31.6
(15) Prorated by number of employees	9.3	9.5
(99) Actual spending record (no code reported)	25.3	29.5
Total	89.6	90.2

[a] Defense, the main user of this code, reports outlays to a prime contractor's place of performance, rather than the main office.

in reports based on actual spending records. This level of concentration, relatively stable through time, suggests an obvious strategy for achieving further improvement in the outlays data. We know that code 15 is essentially accurate, and we know that little can be done to improve code 5, used primarily by the Defense Department, until the new Federal Procurement Data System and the new Defense Department subcontracting reports begin to be available (*see* Cannata, 1975). Efforts at data improvement can therefore be focused on code 10, used largely by the Department of Agriculture, and code 12, used primarily by HEW and the Veterans Administration. Because the population figures employed in these allocation codes are easily updated, a higher level of accuracy can be achieved through straightforward procedures. Improvements of reports using code 99 may be somewhat more complicated. Sums allocated by this code are said to be accurate "to the level at which they are reported," but a significant fraction of these reports are made at the state level only. The task here, accordingly, would be to sort out those programs for which only state-level data are available and, using state agency reports or other sources, develop more accurate numbers.

But, it may be asked, why should anyone want or need more accurate numbers, particularly if outlays data already are regarded—even by critics—as 70 to 75 percent accurate? To this reasonable question there are several good answers, beginning with the obvious point that outlays are among the most baisc measures of "impact" available to use and as such should be as good as we can make them. Less obvious, except to people who work in the field, is a growing need for a clearer perception of the changes now taking place in intergovernmental fiscal relations. Images currently in circulation capture some aspects of these changing relationships (that is, the flow of funds from "Sunbelt" to "Snowbelt") but exhibit little appreciation either for how the components of intergovernmental relations fit together as a whole or for the ways in which the whole pattern is being changed. A clear and comprehensive image of the "system in transition" is necessary if we are to properly interpret evidence derived from studies of the "impact" of some component part or program. Outlays data, which combine comprehensiveness with program specificity, provide an opportunity to develop both a more useful image of the "system" and a better sense of program impact. If we seize that opportunity, we can expand our perspectives on "impact" as well, as described below.

Toward more comprehensive imagery of "system"

Perhaps the most persistently popular image of the intergovernmental fiscal system during the past several years has been that of a "bias" in federal spending in favor of the so-called "Sunbelt," at the expense of the "Snowbelt." This image, built upon state-by-state calculations of the ratio of federal taxes paid to federal expenditures received, has been persuasively argued and may well have contributed to the recent shift in federal grant expenditures toward the North and Northeast (General Accounting Office, 1977). But consider what happens when we calculate per capita federal outlays, using total outlays (including indirect activities) rather than the more restrictive set of obligations as totaled in the printed outlay volumes. Table 2 reports these per capita calculations for 1971 and 1977, and along with rank orders for both years, for the nation as a whole and for the nine regions. Total federal outlays more than doubled during this period, from $226 billion to $464 billion but, because population increased as well (206 to 216 million), average per capita outlays increased somewhat less (96 percent). Considerable variation between regions is apparent in both years, particularly in 1977, when a gap of more than $1,000 appears between the lowest and highest region.

The relative position of these regions does not change a great deal, however. New England moves from eighth place in 1971 to sixth in 1977, West North Central moves from sixth to fifth, and West South Central (Arkansas, Louisiana, Oklahoma, and Texas) drops from fifth to eighth place. The top four regions remain on top, although the Middle Atlantic area (New York, New Jersey, Pennsylvania) required a 108 percent increase, second only to New England's 111 percent increase, to retain its position. Neither these numbers nor rank orders would easily support a conclusion of "Southern" bias, particularly since one "Southern" region, South Atlantic, shows numbers that are inflated by the inclusion of the District of Columbia, with its very high per capita amounts for government salaries. To the extent that Mountain states, such as Arizona, or Pacific states, such as California, represent a "Sunbelt" conception, their high per capita amounts may reflect an earlier bias, but New England and the Middle Atlantic region are far behind these areas in rate of increase. If there is a bias in these figures for 1971 and 1977, it is toward the Northeast rather than the South or West. Even the East North Central region, long the least-favored area for federal disbursements, achieves the third-highest rate of increase among the several regions, although its per capita sums remain low.

Whether measured in per capita dollar amounts or rank orders, then, the intergovernmental system of the 1970s shows an image of low disbursements to the North and Northeast getting better; high disbursements to the South Atlantic, Mountain, and Western regions going higher; and low disbursements to the South increasing less rapidly than other regional outlays. The "Sunbelt-Snowbelt" image is clearly too simple to capture these differences, since part of the "Sunbelt" and part of the "Snowbelt" are in very similar relative positions. If we use these same numbers to calculate regional differences from the national mean in both years (Table 2), for example, we see that regions in the Midwest and the South are the only regions that are not only below the national mean in both years, but moving further away from it. Perhaps we should begin referring to a bias in favor of a "ski-and-sunbelt," and against the "middle belt."

These kinds of images, of course, can be little more than directional indicators for further analysis. It would be interesting to know, for example,

TABLE 2: Regional Deviation from National Mean Per Capita Federal Outlays, and Rank Order of Regions, 1971 and 1977

	1971	1977	% Change	Variation from Natl. Mean, 1971	Variation from Natl. Mean, 1977	Rank as Recipient of Federal Outlays 1971	1977
U.S.	1,096.43	2,144.33	96			1. Mountain	1. Mountain
New England	992.41	2,096.40	111	−104.02	− 47.93	2. Pacific	2. Pacific
Middle Atlantic	1,136.04	2,361.58	108	+ 39.61	+217.25	3. South Atlantic	3. South Atlantic
East North Cent.	765.17	1,584.66	107	−331.26	−559.67	4. Middle Atlantic	4. Middle Atlantic
West North Cent.	1,071.27	2,110.53	97	− 25.16	− 33.80	5. West South Cent.	5. West North Cent.
South Atlantic	1,300.29	2,417.73	86	+203.86	+273.40	6. West North Cent.	6. New England
East South Cent.	1,025.26	2,061.29	101	− 71.17	− 83.04	7. East South Cent.	7. East South Cent.
West South Cent.	1,117.05	1,859.12	66	+ 20.62	−285.21	8. New England	8. West South Cent.
Mountain	1,331.44	2,596.38	95	+235.01	+452.05	9. East North Cent.	9. East North Cent.
Pacific	1,308.09	2,469.85	89	+211.66	+325.52		

whether certain kinds of outlays are associated with these regional trends. Outlays data include some eleven "types" of expenditure activity, of which nine account for the bulk of annual obligations. By calculating the proportion of annual outlays included in each type of activity it is possible to get a closer look at system change. Between 1971 and 1977, as Figure 1 reveals, procure-

FIGURE 1: Change in Type of Federal Outlays, 1971–1977

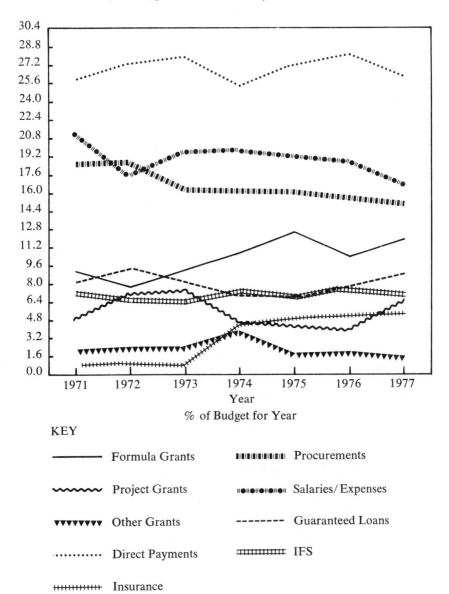

% of Budget for Year

KEY

————— Formula Grants   ⅢⅢⅢⅢⅢⅢ Procurements

〜〜〜 Project Grants   ⅠⅠⅠⅠⅠⅠ Salaries/Expenses

▼▼▼▼▼▼ Other Grants   - - - - - - Guaranteed Loans

············ Direct Payments   ⊞⊞⊞⊞⊞ IFS

++++++++ Insurance

ments and salaries/expenses, two major components of federal outlays declined noticeably as a percent of total outlays. Direct payments, a category dominated by payments to individuals, increased slightly, as did guaranteed loans and project grants. Major increases were experienced in two categories: formula grants, which moved from 9 to 12 percent of annual outlays, and particularly the insurance category, which represented less than 1 percent of total outlays in 1971, but 5.40 percent in 1977.

Large new programs, aimed at cities and based on population or employment formula, account for the rise in formula grant spending. The dramatic increase in insurance outlays reflects large obligations incurred for Medicare hospital insurance beginning in Fiscal 1974. Although insurance outlays remain a small fraction of total outlays, it is worth noting that, with annual outlays as large as they have become, even small fractions involve large dollar amounts. Per capita outlays for insurance, for example, jumped from $4.54 in 1971 to $124.69 in 1977 in the New England region and, even more dramatically, from $3.98 to $147.98 in the East North Central region during the same period. Together, Medicare hospital insurance and Medicare supplementary medical insurance amounted to $21 billion in Fiscal 1977.

Knowing something about the national pattern is helpful in understanding regional and state variations from that pattern. Michigan (Figure 2) is similar to the national pattern, with a consistently high proportion of federal outlays devoted to direct payments, rapidly increasing fractions devoted to insurance and formula grants, and a noticeable decline in payments for salaries/expenses. Whereas procurements as a fraction of total outlays declines for the nation as a whole, however, this category records an increase in Michigan, although the increase is slight and, in keeping with Michigan's location in the East North Central region, begins from a low per capita base. Within this region, incidentally, only Wisconsin closely resembles this distribution of outlay types, a point that suggests a certain artificiality to the regional divisions used here.

California (Figure 3) shows still a different pattern of federal funding. salaries/expenses declines drastically as a portion of outlays in California between 1971 and 1977, in keeping with the national trend. Procurements declines as well, but only slightly, retaining its position as the most prominent type of federal activity in this "sun-and-ski" state. Formula grants increase as a share of outlays, but not as rapidly as the national average, no doubt because such grants were already fairly important in 1971. Note also that insurance obligations increase in California, but do not achieve as significant a position as they reach in Michigan. While reflecting national patterns in some ways, then, these two states show interesting differences in the significance of various outlay types, the rates of change in outlays, and even the direction of change. Despite admitted inaccuracies in the procurement data, these calculations nevertheless produce state images that do no great violence to what is known about Michigan and California from other sources.

The outlays pattern for New York State (Figure 4) provides a final example.

Grossly fitted curves for formula grants and insurance move in the expected direction, and at magnitudes roughly resembling national averages. Plotted curves for procurement and salaries also move in the expected direction, although the magnitude of these two categories seems less significant in New

FIGURE 2: Change in Type of Federal Outlays in Michigan, 1971–1977

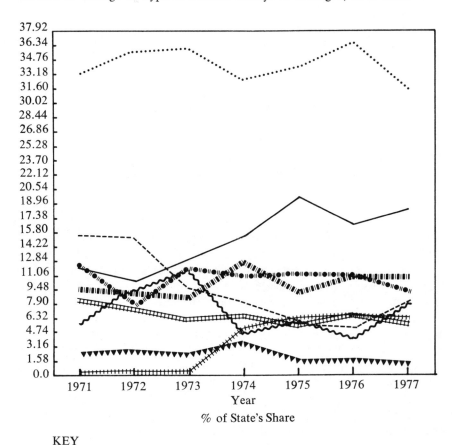

KEY

———— Formula Grants   ıılıılıılıılıılı Procurements

∿∿∿∿ Project Grants   ▸ıı●ıı●ıı●ıı●ıı Salaries/Expenses

▼▼▼▼▼▼▼▼ Other Grants   - - - - - - - Guaranteed Loans

············ Direct Payments   +++++++++++ IFS

+++++++++++ Insurance

FIGURE 3: Change in Type of Federal Outlays in California, 1971–1977

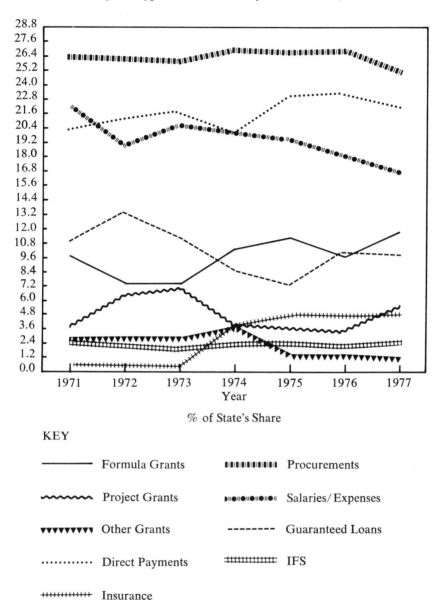

% of State's Share

KEY

——————— Formula Grants   ▮▮▮▮▮▮▮▮▮▮ Procurements

∿∿∿∿∿∿∿ Project Grants   ▮●▮●▮●▮●▮●▮● Salaries/Expenses

▼▼▼▼▼▼▼▼▼ Other Grants   – – – – – – Guaranteed Loans

············ Direct Payments   ⫲⫲⫲⫲⫲⫲⫲⫲⫲ IFS

+++++++++ Insurance

York than elsewhere. The real interest in this plot is the direction of change for direct payments, which appears to be decreasing in significance, in contrast to the national pattern. More interesting still is the appearance at the top of the list in proportional significance of a type of fiscal activity labelled "Indirect Federal Support" (IFS). In neither the national nor the state plots discussed earlier was indirect support sufficiently significant to warrant much comment, yet this category is by far the most significant component of federal fiscal activity in New York. What significance should be accorded this apparent peculiarity?

First it is necessary to establish that this pattern is peculiar to New York

FIGURE 4: Change in Type of Federal Outlays in New York, 1971–1977

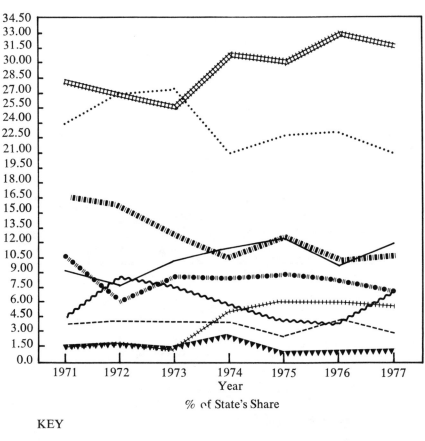

% of State's Share

KEY

——————— Formula Grants   ▮▮▮▮▮▮▮▮▮▮ Procurements

∿∿∿∿∿∿ Project Grants   ▮●▮●▮●▮●▮● Salaries/Expenses

▼▼▼▼▼▼▼▼ Other Grants   - - - - - - - Guaranteed Loans

············ Direct Payments   ▭▭▭▭▭▭▭ IFS

++++++++++ Insurance

TABLE 3: State Proportions of Total IFS, Top
Five States, 1977 and 1973

	Percent of Total National IFS	
State	*1977*	*1973*
New York	51.68	46.36
New Jersey	7.25	13.78
California	4.35	3.44
Illinois	3.30	3.50
Pennsylvania	2.72	2.68
Total	69.30	69.76

and explain why and how this fact can be established. In Table 3 the proportion of total indirect support reported by the 5 top states in 1977 and
1973 is shown. In both years only 5 states accounted for nearly 70 percent
of all such reports across the nation, with New York clearly dominating in
IFS reports for both years. As of Fiscal 1977 more than half of all sums reported in this category were allocated to New York alone. In recent discussions about New York finances Senator Moynihan, among others, has focused
attention on the outlays included in this category, which are predominantly
interest payments on the national debt and outlays destined for use in other
countries (Moynihan, 1978). His argument, which seems quite reasonable,
has been that including such outlays in the sums allocated to New York has
artificially inflated the amount of federal assistance available *in* New York,
and thus exaggerated the amount of help the Federal government has given
to that state. Funds destined to support maintenance or construction of
buildings abroad may be deposited in New York banks before transfer out
of the country, but that hardly seems a sufficient reason to regard them as
outlays *for* New York. Senator Moynihan has made his case persuasively and,
beginning with the outlays reports for Fiscal 1977, these kinds of obligations
are reported separately from other outlays data.[4]

Politically and economically, the treatment of these sums makes an enormous difference, in part because IFS outlays nearly doubled between 1971
and 1977, rising to $32 billion in the latter year. If we compare per capita
outlays in New York in 1971 and 1977 with per capita outlays for the nation
as a whole for those years (Table 2), New York appears to be doing very
well indeed. Per capita outlays in 1971 (Table 4) were $252 higher in New
York than in the nation, and this difference in favor of New York grew to
more than $763 in 1977. When we remove the IFS obligations, however,

---

[4] As noted in the user's guide to Hines and Reid, 1977, "Indirect Federal Support
activity dollars are listed separately from the dollar outlays of programs at each governmental level," p. 1.

TABLE 4: Per Capita Outlays for U.S. and New York 1971 and 1977, Total and Adjusted for Indirect Support

	National Per Capita	New York Per Capita	Difference
1971			
Total	$1,096.43	$1,348.78	$252.35
Excluding indirect support	1,017.66	968.89	−48.77
1977			
Total	2,144.33	2,907.91	763.58
Excluding indirect support	1,996.11	1,983.38	−12.73

federal outlays in New York fall below the national mean in both years. Whether or not we view New York as disadvantaged or increasingly advantaged in the flow of federal outlays thus depends on whether we include the $16.6 billion in foreign assistance and interest payments (in 1977) as part of New York's receipts. For 1977, this choice makes a difference of $925 *per capita*!

If the political point seems obvious, there is also an analytical point that may be less obvious. Presumably, IFS allocations that are of questionable validity when applied to New York are equally questionable elsewhere, and for past years as well as for 1977, when these sums were reported separately for the first time. By identifying the programs included in the IFS allocations for 1977 and tracking those programs back in time, we have been able to isolate IFS expenditures for 1971–76, as well as 1977. All of the plots and all of the tables reported here, therefore, are based on this improved data set, which makes it possible to include or exclude IFS outlays for any or all years, any level of analysis desired, or any jurisdiction. These sums have been treated separately here in order to clarify the unique position of New York. By comparing the New York "profile" derived from the old as well as the "improved" data, we can observe another difference in interpretation (Figure 5). It seems apparent that funds classified as "indirect support" in 1977 had been classified as "direct payments" in prior years, which seems reasonable enough. Separate treatment of IFS obligations permits us to see a declining trend in the state's proportion of payments, primarily to individuals, that previously had been masked. Exposing previously unrecognized trends, and thus raising new problems for detailed exploration, is of course an important benefit that flows from improvement in the outlays data.

The utility of focusing attention on the different kinds of assistance offered to states and localities by the Federal government is twofold. First, it enables us to go beyond mere description of regional or state variation in spending patterns to analysis of the mechanisms through which such patterns are produced. Second, by observing changes in the "mix" of such mechanisms over time, at both the federal and state levels, we can begin to track changes in the pattern that may in fact be important components in policy. Whether or not "loans" are a substitute for more direct forms of spending or whether grants replace or supplement salaries, and in what units and for what functions, are the kinds of questions that we can begin to ask and answer. Good answers require improved informational quality, but, as indicated, significant improve-

FIGURE 5: Change in Type of Federal Outlays in New York, with Indirect Federal Support Incorporated, 1971–1976

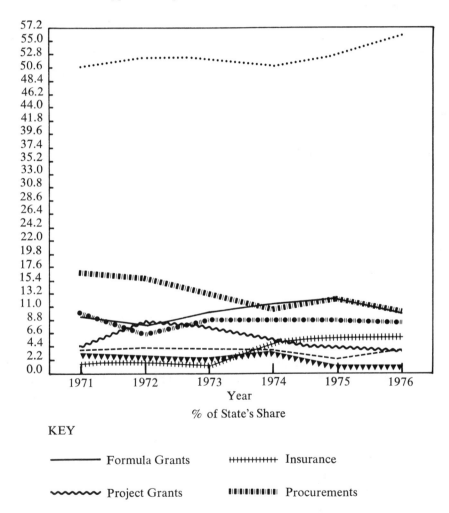

% of State's Share

KEY

——————— Formula Grants   ++++++++++ Insurance

∿∿∿∿∿ Project Grants   ▮▮▮▮▮▮▮▮▮▮ Procurements

▼▼▼▼▼▼▼ Other Grants   ●●●●●●●● Salaries/Expenses

············ Direct Payments   -------- Guaranteed Loans

ments are clearly within reach. With continued improvement, far more useful images of system change are possible.

USING OUTLAYS DATA FOR PROGRAM OR POLICY EVALUATION

Just as the comprehensiveness of outlays data permits investigation of the larger dimensions of system change, at the national, regional, or state levels, the specificity of these data permit analyses couched in the more conventional mode of program/policy evaluation. Recall that outlays data are reported, in principle, to all cities of at least 25,000 population, to all counties, and to all states. Outlays data, in fact, provide a more comprehensive listing for cities than is available in the *County and City Data Book*, issued by the Census Bureau (1977). The Census Bureau reports data only for "incorporated" places of 25,000 and above, thus missing more than 160 municipal units that have the requisite population but not legal status, including very large "towns" in New York and metropolitan suburbs in Maryland.[5] Recall, too, that outlays data are records of expenditure *by program*, within agency, that are keyed to other sources of fiscal information put out by OMB. A three-digit budget-function code, as used in the federal budget, is attached to each record and, since 1975, the code used to identify programs in the *Catalog of Federal Domestic Assistance* (CFDA) also has been included in the outlays record.

These qualities imply the capacity to construct records of expenditure over time in a city, or cities, by program, by function (as used in the budget or as constructed by the analyst), by agency or subagency, or by some aggregation of any of these categories. (The word "imply" is used because certain problems remain to be resolved before all of these implications can be realized.) One problem is that CFDA codes are not available for outlays data prior to 1975, limiting opportunities for time-series analysis. This is an important consideration for analyses of "impact," which often are confounded by insufficient passage of time in which to generate measures of effect. Another problem is the instability in definitions of "functions," which are changed frequently by OMB. A third, very serious problem is that some large expenditure programs are not reported to the municipal level (Medicaid and welfare obligations, for example, are allocated to counties) while other programs, as noted earlier, allocate all obligations to the county in which a state capital is located, for want of good techniques to identify the locations in which funds are actually spent. The result is that expenditure records for cities, even for large cities, do not contain records for all important programs, while county-level records exhibit a "lumpiness" caused by artificially high allocations to the state capital county.

There are solutions to these problems, but they have not yet been achieved. Until they are, most city-focused analyses are bound to produce more "noise"

---

[5] Examples of such towns include Silver Spring, Maryland, and Babylon, New York.

than insight. Nevertheless, there are some intelligent uses that can be made of outlays data, even now, as the following two examples—one an analysis of a federal program for which city data are available and the other a county-level exercise in "pre-evaluation" or prediction—illustrate.

Tracking the Community Development Block Grant (CDBG) program

The CDBG program, enacted in 1974, consolidated seven previously existing grant programs into a single new program activity, with authorized expenditures of $8.3 billion over a three-year period. In contrast to funding procedures followed in the old, "folded in" programs, which were based on federal evaluation of detailed proposals submitted by interested local governments, the new CDBG program created a designation of "entitlement" jurisdictions, for which money was set aside on the basis of formula calculations (population, overcrowded housing, poverty). Although the new program continued to require submission of applications, such proposals were automatically approved after 75 days unless vetoed by the HUD Secretary. Vetoes were authorized, however, only for applications which proposed uses of funds that were "plainly inappropriate" to the purposes of the program or "plainly inconsistent" with known facts. (Only three applications from entitlement jurisdictions were vetoed in the first nine months of the program.) In addition to funds set aside for entitlement communities, which were primarily urban jurisdictions, funds were made available to nonmetropolitan areas on a discretionary basis, and a "hold harmless" provision guaranteed communities already participating in the old programs against any significant reduction in federal funds for a three-year period. In this, as in other "block grant" efforts of the early 1970s, the intent was to reduce the scope of federal intervention in local affairs and enlarge the scope of local initiative (Nathan et al. 1977).

By distributing funds according to formula-based entitlements rather than project applications, the CDBG program initiated changes of considerable fiscal and institutional significance. And because these funds are distributed directly to local governments, rather than to states for later distribution to local units, outlays data can be used to track some of these changes. For example, CDBG allocations to cities of various size classes can be measured against indices of economic or fiscal "need" in those cities in order to estimate the extent to which allocations are affected by need. Or the effect of using different formula terms in calculating CDBG impact can be estimated. If one were interested in estimating the per capita CDBG distributions, for example, Table 5 suggests that such estimates would be very different using 1975 estimates than they are with 1970 population counts.

Outlays data can also be used to track the so-called "spreading effect" associated with the CDBG program. Creating entitlement cities by formula had the effect of distributing funds for urban-type programs to a number of cities that previously had not participated in any of the "rolled up" programs. A

TABLE 5: 1975 Per Capita CDBG Allocations, by City Size
(1970 and estimated 1975 populations as base)

	Per Capita CDBG 1975	
City Size (population)	*Base = 1970 Pop.*	*Base = 1975 Est. Pop.*
25,000– 49,999	$13.05	$13.30
50,000– 99,999	15.25	14.59
100,000–299,999	24.34	24.13
300,000–999,999	23.61	23.32

similar effect followed designation of discretionary funds for use in non-metropolitan areas. Thus, units such as Mesquite, Texas, with no allocations for any of the seven pre-CDBG programs during 1970–72, achieves a 1975 CDBG grant of $166,000, which later (1977) rises to $1,026,000. The post-CDBG spreading effect can be observed in Table 6, which reveals a total of 620 units participating in the program in 1977, compared to only 321 that participated in the seven programs in 1970. Most of this increase, moreover, is accounted for by units in the smaller size categories: participation by cities of 100,000 or less doubled between 1970 and 1975, and the trend continues upward. These increases in participation are most noticeable in the Midwest and Pacific regions, thus confirming a Brookings Institution conclusion that

TABLE 6: Participation in CDBG by City Size and Region

	Number of Units Participating			
	1970	*1972*	*1975*	*1977*
City Size (pop.)				
25,000–49,999	103	176	222	262
50,000–99,999	88	131	214	212
100,000–299,999	83	89	106	100
300,000–999,999	41	42	41	41
over 1,000,000	6	6	6	5
Region				
New England	36	65	73	80
Middle Atlantic	56	69	89	90
East North Central	58	71	116	121
West North Central	29	38	53	51
South Atlantic	49	63	80	81
East South Central	24	29	36	39
West South Central	22	41	55	62
Mountain	15	29	32	39
Pacific	42	63	92	96

CDBG "spreading" in effect redistributes money from the Northeast to other portions of the country (Nathan et al., 1977, pp. 75–183).

In spreading money, of course, CDBG is also spreading access to the system—an urban "impact" that may be quite difficult to evaluate at the moment, but one that may be the most significant impact of all. Like its predecessor program, General Revenue Sharing, CDBG increases the number of actors with a financial stake in the federal aid system as it increases the amount of aid distributed. One consequence of higher rates of participation by small communities, for example, is to increase the number of city managers brought into this portion of the grants economy. From 1970 to 1977 the proportion of cities involved in CDBG-type activities that had managers increased from 48 to 54 percent, while the fraction of mayor-council cities declined from 43 to 37 percent.[6] Does this shift have any significance for further development of the CDBG program, or for grant programs other than CDBG, or for the demand for federal aid in general? Would analysis of the mix of federal programs by political or governmental characteristics, as well as geographic location, reveal something about the changing dynamics of urban-oriented programs?

For the time being, these questions can be no more than suggestive, so long as city-reported data are as fragmentary as they are. Even CDBG outlays, presumably based on "hard" reports, are partially ambiguous. New York City and some other cities, for example, are treated as counties in the outlays data, which means that different modes of access to the data must be developed for these places. The account structure for CDBG expenditures has changed from one year to the next, causing confusion in both the data and their interpretation. Outlays reports are not always consonant with reports produced by HUD or OMB, and so on. In short, these data, for a direct federal-local program are considerably better than data for many other urban-focused programs, but problems remain to be worked out. When these difficulties are resolved, not only the measurement of "impact" in conventional ways but the exploration of a variety of interesting questions arising from structural changes in intergovernmental finance can be done.

ANALYSIS OF A MICHIGAN TAX-REDUCTION PROPOSAL

In November 1978, Michigan voters were confronted with three tax limitation proposals. One of these, similar in some ways to California's Proposition 13, proposed to cut property tax assessments by half. Since federal grants to Michigan were increasing rapidly—grants rose by some 128 percent between 1974 and 1977 alone—and since many federal grants are tied to local revenues through matching requirements, it would be useful to attempt an estimate of the impact of property tax reduction on the flow of federal

---

[6] Data on form of government was taken from *County and City Data Book*, 1977.

grant dollars into Michigan (Anton et al., 1978). More than 400 programs active in Michigan in 1977 already had been identified, as well as a matching rate for each program, by using the CFDA code as a guide to the appropriate program description. Assuming that the 1978 range and mix of federal programs would be similar in 1979, what impact might a 50 percent property assessment reduction have?

Deriving an answer to that question was somewhat complicated. First, it was known that the property tax was more important in some areas than others. Obviously, the more revenue generated from sources other than property, the less affected local governments would be by a loss in property tax revenue. To deal with this complication a *property tax dependency ratio* was developed for each of Michigan's 83 counties, defined as total property tax divided by total local revenues for all units of government within a county.[7] Since the 40 counties that derived 90 percent or more of their revenue from property taxation were found to be concentrated in the more urban, southern portion of the state—including the heavy populated Wayne (Detroit), Washtenaw (Ann Arbor), and Kent (Grand Rapids) areas—and since we knew that these more urbanized areas had more programs and more federal dollars than the less urbanized areas, we could anticipate the locations of maximum potential impact.

A second complication, however, was how local decision-makers might react to a 50 percent property tax loss was unknown and difficult to predict. Indeed, it was strongly doubted that a 50 percent assessment reduction would translate *directly* into a 50 percent revenue reduction: tax base growth might recapture a portion of lost values in some communities, or local officials might choose to reduce expenditures or find other revenue sources rather than cut matching funds, and so on. Rather than guess what these outcomes might be, three plausible alternatives were calculated. At one extreme it was imagined as a theoretical possibility that a 50 percent assessment reduction would translate into a 50 percent revenue reduction, which in turn would cause a loss of 50 percent in federal dollars. At the other extreme, the possibility was conceived that, with strict economies and good luck, some communities might be able to replace as much as 40 percent of property revenues, producing a net impact of not more than a 10 percent loss in revenue to match federal grants. The most plausible outcomes, it was thought, would fall between these extremes, suggesting a 30 percent loss approximately in local, hence also federal, dollars.

Tables 7 and 8 show the results of calculations predicated on these considerations. All Michigan counties are grouped by property tax dependence; up to 80 percent reliance on property taxes, 80 to 90 percent reliance, and

---

[7] Data on local government revenues were taken from the *1972 Census of Governments*, 1972.

90 percent or higher dependence. For each county within each group the number of federal grant programs active in Fiscal 1977 is listed and, based on 1976 population estimates as shown in the last column, per capita losses are reported based on assumptions of maximum (50 percent), moderate (30 percent), and minimum (10 percent) impact. For each impact level, per capita losses are calculated first on the basis of *total* losses in program dollars, that is, federal plus local dollar reductions. Per capita losses are calculated in federal dollars only. Finally, Table 8 presents a summary of the per capita dollar effects by level of property tax dependency, under the different assumptions of impact. It should be noted that these calculations of dollar loss per person were based on matching rates *by individual program* and that the estimates are conservative: more than $73 million in program dollars for which no specific matching rates could be identified are excluded from the analysis. Excluding these "variable match" programs, of course, significantly *understates* the potential loss in federal grant funds. These procedures led to the conclusion that as little as $76 million or as much as $378 million in federal dollars might be lost if property taxes were reduced by half in Michigan.

Whether or not these estimates were more or less correct is, for present purposes, less important than the ability to contemplate this kind of analysis at all (the proposal was not implemented, thus preventing a natural test). Outlays data permit analysis of several characteristics (amount, matching provision, location) of a large number of separate federal programs, and this permits derivation of plausible estimates, in advance, of policy impacts in a large number of jurisdictions. More sophisticated extensions of this kind of analysis might have aggregated programs to examine impacts by function or agency, extended the analysis ahead or back in time, or even made use of "multiplier" estimates by jurisdiction to project a more comprehensive image of impact. Only preliminary exploration of these possibilities has been attempted to date, but it seems clear that outlays data, with their program specificity and depth, offer unique opportunities to track the multiple impacts of "shocks" to the intergovernmental fiscal system.

CONCLUSION

In their present form, outlays data represent an extraordinarily useful source of insight into American fiscal patterns. State-level analyses of federal expenditures over the past decade, by program, agency, function, and type of spending, can be done now, with a generally high level of accuracy. For certain purposes and functions, county-level analyses of generally high accuracy can also be done now, and it is now possible to integrate state- and county-level outlays data with other demographic, economic, or social data sets (i.e., census data) to analyze a variety of major policy issues. Alternative analytic strategies for use of outlays information have only begun to be ex-

TABLE 7: Per Capita Effect of a 50 Percent Assessment Reduction in the Flow of Federal Funds into Michigan, by County and Level of Property Tax Dependency

| County | No. Fed. Programs | Net Per Capita Reduction | | | | | | Population Estimate (Base = 1976) |
| | | Maximum Impact (50%) | | Moderate Impact (30%) | | Minimum Impact (10%) | | |
		Loss in Total $	Loss in Fed. $	Loss in Total $	Loss in Fed. $	Loss in Total $	Loss in Fed. $	
80% property tax dependent or less								
Baraga	12	48.13	32.04	28.88	19.22	9.63	6.41	8,000
Branch	10	17.61	11.15	10.57	6.69	3.52	2.23	38,400
Chippewa	32	41.12	27.43	24.67	16.46	8.22	5.49	37,100
Dickinson	12	109.48	75.75	65.69	45.45	21.90	15.15	25,100
Gogebic	21	34.96	20.70	20.98	12.42	6.99	4.14	20,200
Lapeer	12	35.73	27.26	21.44	16.36	7.15	5.45	62,800
Luce	8	31.18	17.45	18.71	10.47	6.24	3.49	7,300
Manistee	12	32.31	19.92	19.39	11.95	6.46	3.98	21,800
Missaukee	7	21.61	10.03	12.97	6.02	4.32	2.01	9,200
Schoolcraft	15	105.19	75.00	63.11	45.00	21.04	15.00	8,900
Tuscola	14	23.98	12.57	14.39	7.54	4.80	2.51	54,500
80–90% property tax dependent								
Antrim	12	32.04	18.33	19.22	11.00	6.41	3.67	15,400
Barry	9	19.31	9.98	11.58	5.99	3.86	2.00	41,900
Bay	26	141.90	103.08	85.14	61.85	28.38	20.62	119,300
Benzie	9	47.04	21.60	28.23	12.96	9.41	4.32	10,400
Cass	13	17.15	9.31	10.29	5.59	3.43	1.86	45,800
Charlevoix	14	22.36	11.49	13.41	6.89	4.47	2.30	19,200

Clinton	25	530.87	292.99	318.52	175.80	106.17	58.60	51,900
Crawford	13	45.86	31.14	27.52	18.68	9.17	6.23	9,000
Eaton	13	68.50	50.56	41.10	30.34	13.70	10.11	78,100
Emmet	10	31.65	17.26	18.99	10.36	6.33	3.45	21,100
Genesee	33	36.94	24.37	22.16	14.62	7.39	4.87	445,800
G. Traverse	14	26.59	15.06	15.96	9.03	5.32	3.01	45,900
Gratiot	17	37.16	22.34	22.29	13.41	7.43	4.47	39,200
Hillsdale	9	21.75	11.08	13.05	6.65	4.35	2.22	40,300
Houghton	28	185.67	125.19	111.40	75.11	37.13	25.04	36,700
Huron	9	36.91	18.92	22.15	11.35	7.38	3.78	35,400
Iosco	13	25.66	10.49	15.40	6.30	5.13	2.10	28,700
Iron	17	50.08	33.01	30.05	19.81	10.02	6.60	14,900
Isabella	15	21.97	14.54	13.18	8.72	4.39	2.91	51,400
Jackson	24	28.11	18.21	16.87	10.93	5.62	3.64	147,000
Kalkaska	8	49.99	37.37	30.00	22.42	10.00	7.47	10,000
Keweenaw	4	30.60	27.49	18.36	16.49	6.12	5.50	2,300
Lenawee	16	169.54	121.94	101.72	73.16	33.91	24.39	86,600
Mackinac	15	105.75	72.01	63.45	43.20	21.15	14.40	10,300
Marquette	25	38.01	26.25	22.80	15.75	7.60	5.25	70,900
Mason	11	57.22	38.35	34.33	23.01	11.44	7.67	24,900
Monroe	21	30.78	20.90	18.47	12.54	6.16	4.18	127,400
Newaygo	9	43.45	29.19	26.07	17.51	8.69	5.84	31,200
Oakland	57	45.51	32.26	27.30	19.35	9.10	6.45	967,100
St. Joseph	9	22.78	14.05	13.67	8.43	4.56	2.81	51,200
Sanilac	10	22.06	10.72	13.23	6.43	4.41	2.14	39,600
Van Buren	17	65.29	37.51	39.17	22.51	13.06	7.50	62,000

90% property tax
dependent or greater

Alcona	12	35.38	19.77	21.23	11.86	7.08	3.95	8,800
Alger	15	26.55	14.75	15.93	8.85	5.31	2.95	9,400

TABLE 7 (continued)

| County | No. Fed. Programs | Net Per Capita Reduction | | | | | | Populaiton Estimate (Base = 1976) |
| | | Maximum Impact (50%) | | Moderate Impact (30%) | | Minimum Impact (10%) | | |
		Loss in Total $	Loss in Fed. $	Loss in Total $	Loss in Fed. $	Loss in Total $	Loss in Fed. $	
Allegan	16	53.34	36.08	32.00	21.65	10.67	7.22	71,700
Alpena	20	51.75	31.09	31.05	18.65	10.35	6.22	33,000
Arenac	11	34.09	17.79	20.45	10.67	6.82	3.56	13,200
Berrie	26	40.91	23.60	24.55	14.16	8.18	4.72	172,000
Calhoun	27	44.41	28.75	26.64	17.25	8.88	5.75	140,400
Cheboygan	11	103.17	79.19	61.90	47.51	20.63	15.84	19,800
Clare	9	25.17	11.58	15.10	6.95	5.03	2.32	22,400
Delta	17	39.68	23.58	23.81	14.15	7.94	4.72	39,300
Gladwin	13	38.16	23.17	22.89	13.90	7.63	4.63	17,000
Ingham	132	213.51	142.94	128.10	85.76	42.70	28.59	268,800
Ionia	9	26.85	15.09	16.11	9.05	5.37	3.02	48,600
Kalamazoo	41	43.80	27.34	26.28	16.40	8.76	5.47	202,200
Kent	49	43.56	27.25	26.14	16.35	8.71	5.45	425,900
Lake	16	69.39	35.64	41.63	21.38	13.88	7.13	6,800
Leelanau	11	26.14	13.40	15.69	8.04	5.23	2.68	12,500
Livingston	11	29.95	20.86	17.97	12.52	5.99	4.17	81,400
Macomb	24	42.48	31.72	25.49	19.03	8.50	6.34	670,600
Mecosta	14	40.85	26.00	24.51	15.60	8.17	5.20	34,400
Menominee	15	43.79	21.00	26.27	12.60	8.76	4.20	25,200
Midland	14	24.75	14.54	14.85	8.73	4.95	2.91	67,500
Montcalm	10	22.48	9.51	13.49	5.70	4.50	1.90	44,400
Montmorency	8	25.11	10.73	15.07	6.44	5.02	2.15	7,100

Muskegon	26	40.23	20.80	24.14	12.48	8.05	4.16	157,600
Oceana	9	201.82	166.40	121.09	99.84	40.36	33.28	20,700
Ogemaw	10	27.36	13.42	16.42	8.05	5.47	2.68	14,900
Ontonagon	16	57.87	33.30	34.72	19.98	11.57	6.66	11,500
Osceola	14	47.92	22.74	28.75	13.65	9.58	4.55	17,800
Oscoda	7	19.60	8.32	11.76	4.99	3.92	1.66	6,600
Otsego	11	69.52	45.16	41.71	27.09	13.90	9.03	14,100
Ottawa	22	25.13	12.86	15.08	7.72	5.03	2.57	142,200
Presque Isle	9	47.82	24.38	28.69	14.63	9.56	4.88	13,900
Roscommon	13	69.35	46.78	41.61	28.07	13.87	9.36	15,100
Saginaw	28	40.55	22.50	24.33	13.50	8.11	4.50	226,100
St. Clair	19	71.02	51.72	42.61	31.03	14.20	10.34	130,100
Shiawassee	12	31.26	19.90	18.76	11.94	6.25	3.98	68,900
Washtenaw	124	254.93	189.88	152.96	113.93	50.99	37.98	248,100
Wayne	135	53.52	35.94	32.11	21.56	10.70	7.19	2,477,900
Wexford	12	170.97	119.42	102.58	71.65	34.19	23.88	22,000
State-wide per capita loss	—	61.86	41.50	37.11	24.90	12.37	8.30	—

Sources: Community Services Administration; U.S. Bureau of the Census (1977); Office of Management and Budget (1977).

TABLE 8: Impact of a 50 Percent Assessment Reduction in the Flow
of Federal Funds to Michigan, under Net Reduction Assumptions of 10, 30, and 50 Percent

	Per Capita Reduction		
	Maximum Impact (50%)	*Moderate Impact (30%)*	*Minimum Impact (10%)*
80% property tax dependent or less			
Total dollars lost	39.75	23.85	7.95
Federal dollars lost	26.39	15.84	5.29
80–90% property tax dependent			
Total dollars lost	59.20	35.52	11.84
Federal dollars lost	39.13	23.48	7.83
90% or more property tax dependent			
Total dollars lost	64.15	38.49	12.83
Federal dollars lost	43.32	25.99	8.66

plored but it seems obvious, even now, that careful use of this resource can help achieve a far more precise, yet comprehensive, understanding of fiscal flows and their impact on our lives than is now available.

Useful as these data may be now, their potential utility is even greater. Full development of the recently created Federal Procurement Data System is expected to produce procurement data, reported to communities, that is as much as 85 percent accurate—and these data can be integrated into outlays data files. Significant improvements have already been achieved by identifying and reporting "indirect" transactions from 1971 through 1977, and by developing useable crosswalks between outlays data and other federal information sources. Other improvements in the accuracy of outlays reports for past years are within reach—in some cases through simple adjustments based on updated population or economic estimates. In short, we stand on the threshold of access to a remarkably comprehensive, accurate, and thus, useful record of federal expenditure trends.

But that threshold has not yet been crossed, however, and caution should therefore be exercised. Outlays data remain fragmentary at the city level either because outlays are reported only to counties or because lack of good statistical estimates confounds reports made at the city level. Efforts to use outlays reports to analyze federal expenditure impacts in cities, therefore, are bound to be misleading unless great care is used in the selection of cities and programs for analysis. In time, solutions will be found to the "pass through" difficulties that currently undermine the quality of city-level outlays data.

When those solutions are found, outlays data promise to become as important a resource in understanding the federal impact on cities as they now are for developing more useful images of the intergovernmental fiscal system as a whole.

REFERENCES

Anton, Thomas J. *Creating a Data Base for Intergovernmental Fiscal Analysis.* Analysis Series Paper no. 1. Ann Arbor: Intergovernmental Fiscal Analysis Project, August 1978.

————, et al. *The Impact of the Tisch Amendment on Federal Aid to Michigan.* Analysis Series Paper no. 2. Ann Arbor: Intergovernmental Fiscal Analysis Project, October 1978.

Browning, Clyde. *The Geography of Federal Outlays: An Introduction and Comparative Inquiry.* Studies in Geography no. 4. Chapel Hill: University of North Carolina, 1973.

Cannata, Joseph. "Federal Procurement Data System." Paper prepared for the Federal Procurement Data System Committee by the Subcommittee on Data System Design. Washington, D.C., July 1975.

Community Services Administration. *Geographic Distribution of Federal Funds: A Report of the Federal Government Impact by State, County and Large City.* Washington, D.C.: Community Services Administration, 1968 to the present.

————. "Instructions for Reporting of Federal Outlays by Geographic Location." Interagency memo to heads of executive departments and agencies. Mimeographed. Washington, D.C.: Community Services Administration, March 1976.

Congressional Budget Office. *Troubled Local Economies and the Distribution of Federal Dollars.* Washington, D.C.: U.S. Government Printing Office, 1977.

Dye, Thomas. "The Responsiveness of Federal and State Governments to Urban Problems," *Journal of Politics* 40 (1978): 196–207.

General Accounting Office. *Changing Patterns of Federal Aid to State and Local Governments, 1969–75.* DAD-78-15. Washington, D.C.: U.S. Government Printing Office, December 1977.

Havemann, Joel, et al. "Federal Spending: The North's Loss is the Sunbelt's Gain," *National Journal* 8 (1976): 878–91.

————, and Stanfield, Rochelle. "A Year Later, the Frostbelt Strikes Back," *National Journal* 9 (1977): 1028–37.

Hines, Fred, and Reid, J. Norman. *Using Federal Outlays Data to Measure Program Equity—Opportunities and Limitations.* Working Paper No. 7711. Washington, D.C.: U.S. Department of Agriculture, 1977.

Interagency Task Team Report. *Interagency Task Team Report on Improvements to the Federal Outlays Report by Geographic Region.* OMB Circular A-84, Policy and Associated Processes. Washington, D.C.: Community Services Administration, July 1974.

Intergovernmental Task Force on Information Systems. *The Dynamics of Information on Federal Assistance Programs.* Washington, D.C.: U.S. Government Printing Office, December 1978.

Moynihan, Daniel P. "The Politics and Economics of Regional Growth." *Public Interest* 51 (1978): 3–21.

Nathan, Richard, et al. *Block Grants for Community Development.* First Report of the Brookings Institution Monitoring Study of the Community Development Block Grant Program, prepared under Contract H-2323R. Washington, D.C.: U.S. Department of Housing and Urban Development, January 1977.

———. "Feasibility of Measuring the Geographic Impact of Federal Economic and Community Development Programs." Mimeographed. Washington, D.C.: Brookings Institution, August 1977.

A Report to Congress: Improving the Distribution of Information on Federal Assistance Programs. Washington, D.C.: U.S. Government Printing Office, December 1978.

Ritt, Leonard. "Committee Position, Seniority, and the Distribution of Governmental Expenditures." *Public Policy* 24 (1976): 463–89.

U.S. Department of Commerce, Bureau of Census. *1972 Census of Governments.* Washington, D.C.: U.S. Department of Commerce, 1972.

U.S. Department of Commerce. Bureau of Census, *County and City Data Book, 1977, A Statistical Abstract Supplement, Regions, Diversions, States, Counties, Metropolitan Areas, Cities.* Washington, D.C.: U.S. Department of Commerce, 1977.

———. *Population Estimates.* Series P-26, no. 77-22. Washington, D.C.: U.S. Government Printing Office, 1977.

U.S. Office of Management and Budget. *1977 Catalog of Federal Domestic Assistance.* Washington, D.C.: U.S. Government Printing Office, 1977.

CHAPTER SIX

Impacts of Defense Spending on Urban Areas

ROGER BOLTON

INTRODUCTION

National defense is not generally considered a policy or program designed to affect individual cities, or to remedy "urban problems." Nor does one think of it as targeting demand or income support toward particular areas, or as shifting supply functions in urban areas in the way manpower training or public works do. Rather it is thought of as an expenditure program designed primarily to withdraw resources from the private sector and to be used to produce a public good on the national scale. Thus, the effects on urban areas are *incidental* to the more basic function of defense spending.

But those incidental effects can be very significant, which is why defense is a topic for this volume. They are significant because the scale of defense spending is large and because its effects are often concentrated on particular cities, even if not by conscious design. The "base program" is a large one. In addition, *changes* in defense spending often have great effects in some areas. Although those changes are not often thought of as "new initiatives," as that phrase is used in rules requiring urban impact statements, the fact is that in their quantitative and qualitative dimensions the changes are comparable to "new initiatives" in other programs. Indeed, the incidental and implicit effects of defense spending and its changes are undoubtedly much larger than the

The author would like to acknowledge recent helpful conversations with many persons on matters covered in this paper: John Lynch, Marvin Stern, Stanley Tesko, Lou Schenck, James Beller, and Neil Singer of the Department of Defense; James Delaney and Paul Bryant of the General Services Administration; George Moll, George Neidich, and Tom Trimboli of the House Small Business Committee; Larry Zabar of the Northeast-Midwest Congressional Coalition; and Ben Chinitz. The author has also benefited from association with Ben Stevens, Bob Coughlin, and the staff of the Coalition of Northeast Governors Policy Research Center on a study of the impact of defense expenditures on the Northeast and Midwest.

conscious and explicit effects of many of the other "urban programs" discussed elsewhere in this book.

"Incidental" is not the right word, because it suggests unimportance. "Unintended" is not right either, because it suggests that defense planners are unaware of the effects. That is certainly not true—our political system makes sure they are aware. Nor should we use "indirect," for it has a special use in regional analysis. Perhaps the best word, and the one that will be used in this chapter, is "unprogrammed."

THE IMPORTANCE OF DEFENSE ACTIVITY

There are three reasons why the unprogrammed effects can be very significant. Specifically, they are important enough to be forecast and analyzed carefully in urban impact statements.

Total size and uneven distribution

First there is the sheer size of defense activity, and its uneven distribution. At about 5 percent of gross national product (GNP), it is somewhat lower than in the nonwar periods of the 1950s and 1960s, which helps explain why there is less concern with the *national* macroeconomic effects of a large reduction (as with "disarmament"). But it is still large enough that changes in the defense budget can have macroeconomic effects, which are pervasive and affect many urban areas. But these effects, while pervasive, are nonetheless more important for some areas than others, because some cities and their metropolitan areas are much more specialized or dependent on defense demand. If the total (real) defense budget rises or falls by 5 percent, defense-related demand may vary by 20 percent in a particular area. Even if the total is unchanging, the composition of it may change, due to new emphases in weapons systems, forces structure, or base locations; these can have profound effects on some areas.

Dynamic adaptation

Over decades of time there may be a dynamic adaptation process by which the industrial structure and political culture of an urban area, in which defense once becomes important, make it more suited for further increases in defense. Some initial defense activity may increase the specialization of firms and workers which are efficient in defense, and that may make the area more competitive. Research and development may lead to production work. Once the nucleus of a military base is established, chances are it will be a good place to expand training and support operations.

This positive feedback process may lead to an unhealthy degree of dependence, and a vulnerability to changes in defense technology and policy. The political culture also adapts: if a highly specialized area is threatened by loss of defense business, its political and business leaders may refuse to begin adjustment planning. To plan to do so is to admit the possibility that the business will be lost, and the leaders may believe it unwise to admit that while they are still struggling politically to hold on to the business. That is the explanation given by two communities for their recent failure to ask for help from the Office of Economic Adjustment in the Department of Defense (DOD) even though their military bases have been declared "candidates" for cutbacks.

This raises the question of whether the urban impact analysis should attempt to forecast such a dynamic process. Perhaps it should, for the long-term structural changes are undoubtedly more significant than any structural changes wrought by other specifically "urban programs." The issue is raised especially sharply by proposals—which certainly would be "major initiatives" —to maintain defense spending in some "problem regions" where it would otherwise decline. This is the situation for some areas in the Northeast and Midwest, whose political leaders have vigorously urged reallocation of defense expenditure and incorporation of nonbudgetary cost criteria in procurement and base location (CONEG, 1977; U.S. Congress, 1977, 1978a, 1978b; Zabar, 1977; Zabar and Travis, 1978). Such proposals raise a dilemma—maintaining defense activity in an area may perpetuate or reinforce the vulnerability to a day of reckoning when defense reductions become inevitable, even as it postpones that day of reckoning. They especially raise a dilemma when they are justified strictly on grounds of equity, as a "prop" for a declining region, or on the grounds of a "fair share" based on share of population or federal tax payments (*see* discussion in Bolton, 1966a, and an example of justification in CONEG, 1977).

The vulnerability referred to, and which an urban impact analysis should properly measure, is measured not simply in the proportion of economic activity—income or employment—directly or indirectly dependent on defense. One must also take into account the ability of the local economy to shift its resources into alternative production if defense demand declines. Two areas may be identical in their "dependence" as measured by the proportion of resources currently dependent on defense, but may be very different in their ability to compete successfully in other industries or to work off unemployment and excess capacity with little distress for residents.

Federal policy issues

Finally, some significant federal policy questions stem from, and are implicit in, the preceding two characteristics. They involve both efficiency and equity (*see* Bolton, 1971 and 1977).

Efficiency is involved because the real resource cost of the nation's defense burden is affected by its regional distribution. Some years ago I wrote a piece called, "Defense Spending: Burden or Prop?" (Bolton, 1966b). I pointed out that while many regions and industries see such spending as a prop, for citizens in general, defense imposes a burden, and we ought to make sure it is produced at as low a real resource cost as possible. However, the budgetary cost to the Federal government is not necessarily the opportunity cost to the economy. Along the same line, the budgetary cost to the DOD is not even the budgetary cost to the entire Federal government. Consider a case where defense decision-makers are considering whether or not to use resources in a given area, where the resources otherwise would be idle for a significant period of time. Then, if the resources are used in production of defense, there will be some increased real product, and increased federal tax revenue (which is a sharing of the increased real product with federal taxpayers). There will also be reduced unemployment insurance and welfare payments (which reflect redistribution of already existing national product). In either case, the effects on the whole federal budget are more complicated than the effects on DOD's own budget.

Thus, neither the budgetary cost to the entire Federal government nor the opportunity cost to the entire economy is accurately measured by the budgetary cost to the Defense Department. Yet our budgetary practices, and the incentives to defense decision-makers, allow only the latter to be considered. Theoretically, urban impact statements would be helpful if they estimated relevant costs more correctly. However, while law and regulations require urban impact statements, they also explicitly insist on DOD's budgetary cost as the cost criterion in decisions on where to spend the defense dollar.

On the equity side, the central question is the impact of *changes* in defense activity on the distribution of income. An important aspect here is the prolonged spell of unemployment and idle capacity after a defense cutback in a city heavily specialized in defense and unable to reach a new full employment equilibrium quickly. Another is the permanent losses in personal income and property value which must be suffered as a result of having to move to a new equilibrium. Again, urban impact analysis is necessary to describe these effects in detail.

Still another question on distribution policy is whether defense can legitimately be used as a tool for *remedying* distributional problems created by *other* market forces (U.S. Congress, 1977, 1978a, 1978b; Zabar, 1977). Should decisions on awarding of procurement contracts, or on using military bases, for example, be affected by whether the added employment would reduce distress in a declining or stagnating urban area? Many politicians think so, although Congress has been persuaded by defense planners to reject this alternative explicitly in defense appropriations acts. The issue is a complicated one. It would appear that such preferences can be helpful to a small number of areas if granted in a very limited way. The reasons are several: first, there is a lot of "leverage" in preferences as is discussed below. Second, defense spending may alleviate distress while at the same time increasing real output, by virtue of employing resources which would otherwise remain idle. Third, there are psychological advantages in alleviating distress by creating jobs rather than giving transfers. Unfortunately, against these considerations we have the powerful counter-argument that preferences are a bottomless pit, and once begun cannot be cut off, not even long after the opportunity costs cease to be low because the resources would have been employed in some alternative use. Preferences which are theoretically justified as a short-term adjustment policy might inevitably become entrenched as a continuing program which interferes with necessary long-run adjustments to changing demand patterns and technological changes in the economy. The strong tradition of "politics" in the regional allocation of defense strengthens this unfortunate possibility, and so does the "political culture" effect I mentioned above. Thus, any preference program can accomplish both equity and efficiency objectives simultaneously only if it is cleverly designed, implemented with an iron will, and used in combination with manpower and mobility policies. And the program could never affect enough areas to be a major weapon in the Federal arsenal of policies on urban problems.

THE CRITICAL ELEMENTS IN URBAN IMPACT ANALYSES

Below is a review of the elements in an urban impact analysis which are critical for the choice of a methodology and for understanding the range of federal policy choices which the analysis is presumably designed to illuminate. This review has been influenced by Norman Glickman's discussion in Chapter 1 of this volume, but his outline is not followed systematically.

Time and timing

Glickman's distinction is between the short-run impacts of construction of public works projects and the long-run supply effects of the projects. In defense, however, new construction is now relatively unimportant except in a few areas, and it is the production activity in existing public and private facilities which is most important. However, it is important to forecast the temporal pattern of that activity.

Thus, there are some distinctions between short-run and long-run impacts. For one thing, the dynamics of private and public investment complicate the temporal pattern of demand after an exogenous change in defense activity. For another, a change in defense demand has temporary results which lead to mitigating or offsetting supply changes after some delay. This is a common-sense application of the standard microeconomic theory of short- and long-run supply. An increase or decrease in demand leads eventually to supply effects which partially reverse the temporary effects on the unemployment rate, business profits, housing markets, and government budgets. Some of the offsetting forces are stronger and come faster in the case of defense, for reasons discussed below.

Our customary regional models may find it hard to pick up some of the supply reactions to a *decrease* in defense demand. Models which incorporate supply reactions do so by specifying a link between business costs in the region relative to the nation, rather than through unemployment and excess capacity. To the extent that wages and prices are sticky and do not fall, the models may underestimate the competitive effects of unemployment and excess capacity (*see* Bolton, 1978a and forthcoming).

Direct, indirect, and induced effects
    The classification of demand effects between direct, indirect, and induced is a traditional one in regional economics and impact analysis. There are good reasons for this, which need emphasizing here.
    In an analysis of defense, it is useful to use the classification in conjunction with another one, which is by type of expenditure: military payrolls, civilian employee payrolls, and defense procurement. Table 1 shows totals for each type in Fiscal 1977 and 1978. (In addition, military retirement pay is about $9 billion per year.)
    Military payrolls are cash wages of military personnel. The military pay system raises some problems in measuring these wages in impact analysis which are mentioned later in discussing data problems. Civilian payrolls are wages of civilian employees on military bases, in research and industrial facilities, and in administrative offices. "Procurement" here is a broader term than it is in budgetary language; it is all purchases of goods and services from outside the Defense Department, including the budgetary categories of procurement, research and development, operations and maintenance, and construction.
    This classification by type is necessary for sophisticated, fine-grained analysis of an urban area. It would be misleading to lump all three types together into a single total for input-output or economic base analysis, for example. The indirect and induced effects are different for each type. In addition, the

TABLE 1: Total Defense Spending in the United States, Fiscal Years 1977 and 1978

	Expenditures ($ thousands)	
	1977	*1978*
Military payrolls		
Active duty personnel	(14,480,808)	(15,316,884)
Reserve and national guard personnel	(1,385,870)	(1,716,589)
Total mil. payroll	15,866,678	17,033,473
Civilian employee payrolls	14,189,295	15,572,706
Procurement (prime contracts)	52,751,721	61,174,090
Total expenditures	82,807,694	93,780,269

Source: Office of the Secretary of Defense.
Note: Covers 50 states and the District of Columbia.

suitability of the data for measuring direct impact also varies by type (*see* Bolton, 1968 and 1971).

Regarding the direct-indirect-induced classification, the direct demand for military and civilian payrolls is measured by the payrolls themselves. There is no indirect demand. Induced demand is the additional demand in a region caused by the presence and consumption of the employees who received the payrolls; it includes the multiplier and accelerator effects of their consumption, new housing investment, private investment, and public sector consumption and investment. In all cases, the effects in the region must be estimated by allowing for import leakage out of the region.

For procurement, the direct demand is measured by the value added, and thus the demand for factors of production in the firm which is the last stage of production, that is, the firm which does the final assembly of a manufactured product or which performs the service directly for the military buyers. (Not every empirical researcher would agree; some would count the entire value of the final product as the direct effect, rather than only the value added in the last stage.) The indirect effect, then, is the value added in all firms which produce and sell inputs and supplies to the firm producing (or "assembling") the final product. These indirect effects must be estimated by tracing the production process back through all the stages of production and measuring the value added at each stage. Some of the indirect value added is produced in the same region where the direct value added is, but much of it is not. The proportion depends on the size of the region in which the direct effect occurs, its industrial structure, and the degree of vertical integration in the plant where final assembly occurs. These definitions of direct and indirect insure that the sum of the two exactly equals the value of the product.

The induced effect of procurement is the same as with payrolls, except that the employees and capital owners of the firms produce the value added counted in the direct and indirect effects, rather than DOD's employees.

In conventional practice, direct, indirect, and induced effects are measured on a partial equilibrium basis, that is, on the assumption that relative prices of intermediate goods and factors of production are constant, or that supplies are perfectly elastic at existing relative prices. This is, of course, not always valid, but the complications of rising supply prices and supply-demand equilibration are best called "supply effects," and are best handled as separate modeling problems, rather than trying to allow for changes in prices in measuring direct, indirect, and induced effects.

Importance of the classification of direct, indirect, and induced

Although some of the basic material of regional input-output and economic base analysis is familiar, the question of *why* the classification of direct, indirect, and induced is important must be asked. There are several reasons. Although not surprising, they are so important for urban impact analysis that they need repeating because politicians, local boosters, and regional analysts often forget the importance of the distinctions in their rush to count up every dollar of effect in one grand total which can be used for political purposes.

One reason is the *regional multiplier*. As a qualitative phenomenon, the multiplier is extremely important, although the widespread misuse of it is one of the worst things that ever happened to applied regional economics. The important idea here is that the total demand effect is greater than the direct effect alone. Maybe not much greater, for surely the multiplier is very low for some types of defense spending in some areas. But as a general rule, it is more than one. That is important to know. In his paper, Glickman refers to size of impact relative to size of program as critical, for example; the "size" of the program is presumably the budgetary expenditure, which is the total of direct and indirect demand in my terminology. Eliminating 1,000 civilian jobs at an Army base will affect somewhat more than 1,000 families, in the short run at least. We need to know that.

A second reason is that the classification helps us understand the *temporal pattern of induced effects*. Even if direct and indirect defense demands rise, and the increases are sustained permanently, the regional multiplier effect will not simply raise induced nondefense demand smoothly to a permanently higher level. The regional multiplier combines what in national macroeconomic models are two separate effects, the consumption multiplier and the investment accelerator (both net of imports from outside the region). Although it grossly oversimplifies any regional economy, a multiplier-accelerator model nonetheless signals that the temporal pattern of total activity in the region is difficult to predict and depends on many parameters.

A third reason is that the *indirect and induced effects are less concentrated geographically than direct effects*. There may be only one region directly affected by a military procurement or operating base, but many are indirectly affected by the purchases of intermediate inputs and the multiplier effects. This has some implications. An area may be significantly affected by—even vulnerable to shifts in—defense spending even if no defense activity takes place in it. That, of course, is especially likely if the region getting the direct effect is defined as a small one. The diffusion of indirect and induced effects helps to reduce the multiplier in the region of direct impact. The diffusion is the main reason why the regional multiplier in the area of direct impact is often rather low (even if one ignores supply effects which might offset defense increases [decreases] by reducing [increasing] competitiveness in nondefense markets). In addition, the range of industries and workers affected by indirect and induced effects in a region is more varied than the range of those affected directly. Defense spending in a region may be heavily concentrated on the final products of a few industries—aircraft, shipbuilding, or electronics. But indirect and induced effects will range over a whole variety of industries supplying intermediate inputs, consumer goods, construction, and goods purchased by local governments.

The fourth reason, and perhaps the most important one, is that *resources directly affected are the most vulnerable* to sharp reductions in defense spending. Resources indirectly affected are much less vulnerable. It is harder to generalize for resources affected by induced demands; their vulnerability depends both on where they are located and on the geographic extent of the markets of the industries employing them. They are more vulnerable if employed in local market industries located in the same region where there is a direct effect, for example, but much less so if employed in national or regional market industries located in other regions. These generalizations are not hard-and-fast; they depend on various assumptions about specialization of resources, resource mobility, sizes of labor market areas, and other things. However, the classification of effects between direct, indirect, and induced in any region gives us important clues as to vulnerability to unemployment, wage and profits losses, and public sector fiscal pressures. Again, this is a point sometimes glossed over by people who are interested only in totaling up *all* the effects they can find, no matter what kind.

To elaborate on the point, and for reasons of simplicity, workers, rather than "resources" in general, will be examined. The following comments can be applied to other income earners with a slight change in wording.

The word "vulnerability" means ideally a quantitative measure for any given worker of the expected value of the loss in lifetime wage income, suffered as a result of a change in defense spending of some given size. The expected value is the mean of a probability distribution of income losses of various amounts and durations; in order to measure it one needs to predict the dynamic path of incomes during the period of adjustment to a new equilibrium, and also to use comparative statics to compare the long-run equilibrium after the change to the one before. This is a very hypothetical measure, because the long-run equilibrium toward which a region is moving is undoubtedly changing constantly. It is also an extremely difficult number to estimate. But in theory it is a good measure of "vulnerability," and it is one of the important things people have in mind when they speak of the urban impacts of defense. It should be an important ideal measure toward which the imperfect urban impact analysis gropes in practice.

Workers directly affected are generally more vulnerable because the plants they work in are more specialized in defense, because of their location or the characteristics of the capital goods in them, or both. We may assume that in the case of a cutback in defense spending, federal policy-makers will attempt to maintain macroeconomic stability in the nation as a whole by fiscal and monetary stimuli. However, the plants which specialize in defense production are unlikely to get an equivalent share of the replacement demand generated by those stimuli. As a rule, however, the plants producing intermediate inputs—the indirect effects—are more likely to get a greater share of the replacement demands because they are less specialized and are less concentrated geographically. This relative advantage of the intermediate goods suppliers is all the greater, the more selective is the original cutback—that is, the more concentrated it is on particular weapons systems or installations. In some cases, where the cutback in defense is very comprehensive, the relative advantage of the intermediate goods suppliers will be sharply diminished, especially in the stages of production just beyond the final assembly stage. Plants in these late stages may also be extremely adversely affected if their products are very specialized inputs into military weapons systems. It is in fact conceivable that some first-tier subcontractors are more specialized than the prime contractors they serve. They may be even less likely to share in the replacement demands than the prime contractors. There is the additional problem for them that, in the event of a sharp reduction in defense orders, prime contractors often pull subcontract work back into their own plants, increasing the vertical integration. Lynch reports this happened in the 1968–71 phase-down from the Vietnam War; small business subcontractors were especially affected, notably small machine shops, blueprint firms, small component manufacturers, and small metal fabricators, etc., and notably in Bridgeport, Seattle, Wichita, and Southern California (*see* Lynch, 1976).

What about the workers who are employed due to induced demands? How they fare in a cutback will depend largely on whether the markets for the goods they produce are "local" as opposed to regional or national. Let A be the labor market area in which the direct effect was suffered; let X be the plants directly affected. The workers producing for a local market in A will be adversely affected, in the sense that a large proportion of their employees will lose jobs and income; expected value of losses will be high for them. That is because their plants' markets are heavily dependent on consumer purchases by employees of X, whose incomes have fallen, and their plants will not pick up sales from increases in the replacement demands in other areas. The effects on these workers will be pervasive; those in grocery stores, repair shops, personal services, utilities, and construction will all be affected. How vulnerable these industries are depends not so much on the type of product they produce, as it did for the intermediate input industries above, but rather on the geographical domain of their markets. However, the depressing effects will be less than on workers in X, for the depressing effects are averages of large effects of laid-off X employees and the smaller effects of laid-off employees of firms which sold intermediate inputs to X; the average is less than for X alone. There is also an offset because these workers will benefit from some increases in production of goods for replacement demands in A.

The picture is better for workers in A, who were employed to serve induced demand, but whose plants serve national or large regional markets. They were not so heavily dependent on city sales in A, so will lose *relatively* less. They are also more likely to pick up sales to meet replacement demands. Some of these employees will in fact benefit due to the change in composition of demand, rather than be hurt.

The picture is best for workers in *other* areas from the one in which the direct effect was felt. They will suffer little, on average, and will probably even benefit because of the replacement demand. While one might say they had felt some favorable effects of the defense activity in *A*, in fact they would benefit from the loss of that defense activity, if there were compensating fiscal and monetary policies. The only exception would be if there was a heavy concentration of them in a small, labor market area.

The measure of vulnerability depends on the *probability* that a worker who lives in a given labor market area will be adversely affected. This does not negate the fact that *some* workers will lose income, perhaps a lot, in some areas, *no matter* whether they were originally affected directly, indirectly, or by induced demands. This distributional problem must, of course, be mentioned in any analysis. But surely in practice the probabilities and expected losses will deserve much more attention.

The relationships sketched herein are not hard-and-fast ones; there are exceptions. The main cause of exceptions is that vulnerability depends not only on demand characteristics but also on supply characteristics. The *alternatives* open to a worker or owner of capital will shape the degree and the duration of his loss. Even if a worker is almost certain to lose his job, it is possible he can move easily to another one, within the region or outside it, without suffering much reduction in lifetime income. It is possible that in the foregoing example, the workers in *X* are actually less vulnerable than workers in other plants, if they can move more easily.

Supply effects

The preceding discussion has already slipped into a consideration of supply effects. Supply effect means any effect which changes the relative supply prices of resources in a region. Changes in the distribution of demand inevitably set up some responses on the supply side. The ultimate impact of a change in defense demand in a region is the result of the equilibrium between the demand forces and the supply forces the program also creates, or which respond to the initial defense demand. This is, of course, a very general problem in modeling the impacts of *anything* on urban areas, and an analysis of defense must model some of these supply forces in the same way as the analysis of any other change. However, there are some unusual supply forces which merit attention here.

A very important example arises in the case of military personnel. An increase or decrease in military personnel strength in a region is automatically and simultaneously an increase in both demand and supply. If military personnel are increased, the persons involved are not present residents in the area, but are brought into it for the first time. Thus demand for direct employment creates its own supply, on an immediate one-for-one basis. An econometric model may have trouble catching that. To a lesser extent, the supply of labor for indirect and induced demand is also automatically increased, because military personnel moonlight in civilian jobs and in some cases are accompanied by dependents who join the civilian labor force (whether this is true depends on the nature of the base). There are also automatic offsetting supply effects if there is a reduction in military personnel; the personnel leave the area, and so do their dependents. This will soften the impact on the unemployment rate and make the total impact less than it would be if a private firm laid off the same number of civilian residents, many of whom would remain in the region looking for jobs.

Size of impact relative to size of program

Another critical element mentioned by Glickman is the size of impact relative to size of program: this is the "leverage." In defense, we have a large program to start with, and its effects are large. There seems no *a priori* reason why the leverage per dollar is higher than for civilian activity. Many analyses have found that the employment/dollar ratio is, in fact, less for defense. And the leverage effect of military payrolls on a particular urban area is often low because lower-rank military personnel are frequently unaccompanied by families and send some of their pay to relatives in other areas.

However, there is a special case where leverage might be quite high indeed. For example, where a military base is in city *A*, and DOD is thinking of moving it to city *B*. Or, alternatively, it is deciding whether to give a prime contract to a firm in *A* or one in *B*. Assume that monetary costs to the DOD are higher in *A* in either case—$110 million compared to $100 million. However, for some reason, the employment and income impact would be much higher in *A* than in *B*; the $100 million is much larger relative to the economy of *A* than of *B*, or *A* is more vulnerable than *B*, because of extreme specialization or long-term secular decline. One way of seeing DOD's decision is that it will buy $100 million of goods and services in any event, but that the crucial decision is whether or not to spend $10 million in order to reduce socioeconomic distress in *A*. If that is a legitimate federal goal, then for a small "program expenditure" of $10 million, a very large effect might be achieved. The case for the $10 million "program" would be strengthened if the opportunity cost of resources is much lower in *A* than in *B*, which might be the case. But even if we ignore an efficiency argument, the point remains that if we define "program" in an unorthodox but meaningful way, some "programs" associated with defense activity have tremendous leverage, precisely because some cities are so heavily dependent on defense activity and because a single defense decision can involve hundreds of millions of dollars in demand over a good many years.

DOD decision-makers have vigorously rejected any thoughts of defining "programs" in this way, and their refusal to entertain such a definition has been supported by congressional legislation. However, the opportunity cost and leverage arguments have been used to support preferences for high unemployment, labor market areas for *nondefense* procurement and Congress has recently explicitly permitted such preferences, even at the expense of extra budgetary costs. This policy allowing preferences is the "Defense Manpower Policy No. 4." It calls for encouraging defense and nondefense procurement and facility location in "labor surplus" areas, but Congress has persistently refused to allow any price differentials on the defense parts of procurement and facility location. How a "Defense Manpower Policy" permits more meaningful regional preferences for nondefense activity than for defense activity is a fascinating story, too long to be told here. (*See* Bolton, 1977; U.S. Congress, 1978a; and Zabar, 1977.)

Spatial units of analysis

Differential interregional, intraregional, intrametropolitan, and intraurban effects are all important. Because defense impacts are primarily ones through demands for resources, labor market areas, or combinations of them, make the most sense, but naturally states are important enough political units to demand attention. The emerging regional "coalitions" will lead to analyses of large multistate regions.

There is extensive case-study literature on individual metropolitan areas. The context is often a hypothetical sharp reduction in defense in the area, perhaps with an assumed pattern of replacement demand in the nation as a whole. Data problems and the nature of large-scale multiregional models have made it difficult to do *inter*regional analysis of differential effects on them.

*Intra*urban effects are important because of the effects of immobile physical capital on military bases or other installations (such as arsenals or shipyards). The capital is located in a particular place and affects the "neighborhood" environmentally, economically, and socially. As discussed below, the *reuse* of the capital in the event of a closing can have profound intraurban effects. Witness the reuses planned or already under development in the Boston area, where significant industrial facilities, luxury housing, and recreational spaces may result. Reuse is getting more attention these days, but the intraurban effects of the defense facilities themselves, while still in operation, is very much underexplored in the literature. There are also some ongoing studies of the few communities where defense bases are being significantly *expanded*.

There has not been much research on the distribution between metropolitan areas and nonmetropolitan areas. There are some data, especially on payrolls, which could be used for this. It has been noted that nonmetropolitan counties with large concentrations of military personnel in 1970 did not generally share in the resurgence of population growth in nonmetropolitan America in the seventies; they have been conspicuous exceptions to the trend. The reason is, of course, the sharp reduction in military personnel strengths after the end of the Vietnam War, which reversed the earlier trend which had made "[m]ilitary work . . . a major rural growth industry in the post World War II decades." (Beale, 1976, pp. 11–12.)

REUSING THE PHYSICAL CAPITAL ON MILITARY BASES

An essential factor in the regional supply picture, after a loss of demand, is the ease with which the capital goods can be switched over to new uses. These are familiar problems in impact analysis, and many tools of regional analysis can be used. However, in the case of a military base closing, there is an unusual collection of capital goods in the form of the base property itself, and it requires special attention. Despite the importance of this capital, there has not been extensive empirical research on the patterns of its reuse and the implications for readjustment, in the context of analytical regional models. This was noted above in the comments on intraurban impacts, and it is also true for analyses of whole labor market areas. There is a lot of descriptive case-study information, however (U.S. President's Economic Adjustment Committee, 1977 and 1978).

Operating bases have a wide variety of buildings, equipment, and public works-like facilities which have the potential to be reused in private production or as infrastructure contributing to low business costs or a high quality of life in the region. A base may have an airport, streets and roads, unloading docks, housing, school buildings, cafeteria and recreational buildings, hospitals and infirmaries, warehouses, retail stores, industrial buildings, machine shops, laboratories, golf courses, large open and/or wild areas (with extensive wild animal life), and sewage and water supply systems (with sewage treatment plants and water treatment plants).

Various reports of the President's Economic Adjustment Committee make clear that the physical capital on bases has considerable potential in civilian reuse, but in many cases successful reuse requires careful planning, the building of complementary capital in the community, and a willingness to use the property in a variety of uses rather than attempting to "recycle" it in one piece.[1]

A survey of 75 military base closures with completed base reuse programs, from 1961 to 1977, was conducted in early 1977. In those 75 cases, 85,402 military personnel were relocated, and 68,800 DOD civilian or contractor employees lost their positions. A total of 78,765 new civilian jobs are now located *on the former defense facilities*, of which 69,542 are new jobs in the community and 9,223 relocated to the base from elsewhere in the community. Thus the new nondefense jobs on the bases more than offset the

---

[1] All of the factual material in this and following paragraphs is based on two recent reports by the President's Economic Adjustment Committee (1977 and 1978). *See also* Lynch (1975).

loss of defense civilian jobs, but do not offset the military personnel reloca-tions. These data suggest that the physical capital on the base can have an important "supply effect" in offsetting the direct impact from a base closing. In the 75 cases, the physical capital was reused in a great variety of ways, with education, air transportation, and light industry most prevalent. Seven four-year colleges, 26 postsecondary vocational-technical institutes and six high school vocational-technical programs have been established; in early 1977, there were 52,512 postsecondary and 4,215 high school students, and 5,309 job trainees on former bases. Industrial parks had been established at 47 bases; three former defense manufacturing plants were operated as private plants; all or part of 31 bases had municipal and general aviation airports. Other miscellaneous examples of reuses for facilities are: state and city gov-ernment and school offices; parks; U.S. Postal Service bulk mail center; Vet-erans Administration hospital; municipal recreation center; prison; and retire-ment communities. Many units of military housing had been converted to civilian use.

The flexibility of existing defense capital must not be overemphasized, how-ever. Successful reuses often depend on extensive development of new com-plementary facilities, such as transportation access, replacement of road and utility systems, and demolition of outmoded buildings. Reconversion of mili-tary housing may require especially extensive modernizations. The general economic picture of the community and the location of its base are obviously important. Another important problem is that a military base is originally designed and built for a single user who controls allocation of all space and facilities. Usually, the base is *re*developed for a variety of new owners and users, so there must be extensive legal and engineering changes to create street and utility easements, new property lines, decentralization of heating and communications facilities, among other things.

Naturally, reuse experience is not uniform. In the 75 projects referred to earlier, there were large net losses of civilian jobs in some and large net gains in others. For example, there were large net losses in the following cases (minus indicates number of civilian jobs lost, plus represents jobs gained, not counting jobs relocated to the base from elsewhere in the area): Brookley Air Force Base and Mobile air material area, Mobile, Alabama, −12,300, +4,300; Hunters Point Naval Shipyard, San Francisco, −4,650, +690; Watertown Arsenal, Massachusetts, −2,306, +0; Erie Army Depot, Port Clinton, Ohio, −1,885, +800; and Olmstead Air Force Base, Harrisburg, Pennsylvania, −10,050, +3,010. Large net gainers included: Theodore Army Terminal, Mobile, Alabama, −14, +2,075; Decatur, Illinois, Army Signal Depot, −1,310, +2,400; Schilling Air Force Base, Salina, Kansas, −326, +3,135; Dow Air Force Base, Bangor, Maine, −328, +1,603; Grenier Air Force Base, Manchester, New Hampshire, −138, +2,000; Raritan Arsenal, Metuchen, New Jersey, −2,610, +4,450; Camp Kilmer, New Brunswick, New Jersey, −578, +1,626; Rossford Arsenal, Toledo, Ohio, −1,654,

+3,640; Marietta Air Force Station, Lancaster, Pennsylvania, −750, +2,000; Donaldson Air Force Base, Greenville, South Carolina, −672, +3,500; Steward Air Force Base, Smyrna, Tennessee, −470, +1,910. These examples are all the cases on the list of 75 for which the net change was 1,000 civilian jobs or more.

There are some caveats in interpreting these data. First, the comparisons are of civilian jobs on the former base, not the total employment effect in the urban area. The comparisons relate only to the supply effect of the base capital. In fact, in four of the eleven examples of net positive job change listed, the loss of military personnel was greater than the net change. Second, many of the base-reuse programs were completed only over many years, and with unknown expenditures for complementary physical works and planning. Many more base-reuse programs remain to be completed. Third, the degree of success undoubtedly depended somewhat on the general health of the national economy at the time reuse efforts were going on. Finally, we have no systematic information on wage levels in new versus old jobs.

Under the laws governing surplus property disposal, property may be transferred free of charge to local public and nonprofit agencies for certain uses, such as public health and education (including water and sewer facilities), civilian airports, park and recreation facilities, wildlife conservation, and historic preservation property (U.S. President's Economic Adjustment Committee, 1978). In some cases, there are deed restrictions which require use for the designated purpose in perpetuity; for public health or education property, full ownership is transferred only gradually over a 30-year period.

Public agencies have the option to acquire property for industrial and commercial use, and housing, in a negotiated purchase from the General Services Administration (GSA) at fair-market value, without deed restrictions on resale or use. If the community rejects this option, GSA will put up the property for open bidding. The community then has a chance to buy it at a price less than GSA would demand in a negotiated sale, but runs the risk of losing control if someone else puts in a higher bid (although local zoning controls would still apply).

There are significant policy issues involved in the community adjustment process, which cannot be analyzed in detail here. Neither the legislation on surplus property disposal nor the administration of the disposal process by GSA is without criticism. In some communities, GSA is very much criticized for delays and unrealistic demands in the negotiated sale of property for commercial and industrial use. The role of the Office of Economic Adjustment (OEA), which provides staff work for the President's Economic Adjustment Committee, is not without controversy. Critics have accused it of being biased, because it is located in the Defense Department, or ineffectual, for the same reason. Although the President's Economic Adjustment Committee includes representation from outside the Defense Department, there is still suspicion that the reports of OEA and its work with the communities are influenced by the need to put a good light on the actions of the military department that is closing the base. On the other hand, defenders argue that a location within DOD is actually helpful in keeping a link between the affected communities and the military department which still controls the base property during the early stages of reuse planning. When a base is cut back but not closed completely, decisions on just which property to retain under military control affect reuse planning greatly. Early in the Carter administration, an extended review of the OEA was conducted, in the context of proposals by some observers that it be moved to the White House itself. The proposals were rejected.

Some have also criticized the methodology used in OEA's reports on the impacts and adjustment possibilities (Zabar and Travis, 1978). Space does not permit evaluation of the OEA reports and the critics' arguments here; a scholarly review would be useful in illuminating the possibilities and problems of urban impact analysis as applied to defense programs. In many cases both the OEA reports and the studies cited by the critics as the better ones are very simple applications of economic base concepts, in the absence of more sophisticated models of the affected areas. The essential points of disagreement seem to be the methodology for measuring the multiplier; the choice between employment multiplier or income multiplier; the size of the region in which to measure impacts; and whether or not to calculate employment impacts after subtracting some of the mitigating supply effects, such as civilian employee retirements and relocations. Critics who argue that OEA deliberately minimizes estimates of impact also admit that some others maximize them (Zabar and Travis, 1978).

MODELS FOR REGIONAL MACROECONOMIC IMPACT ANALYSIS

There are two different contexts for analysis, requiring two kinds of models. One is the multiregional allocation or redistribution, in which the analyst forecasts the impact on many areas of national-scale changes in the total and/or composition of the defense budget. There are a variety of multiregional models, including two input-output models (the Leontief "balanced" model and Polenske's Multi-Region Input-Output [MRIO] model) and several econometric models.

The second context is in the sharp change in defense demand in a single region, as with more or less prime contracts or the expansion or closing of a base. The economic base model is still widely used, because nothing else is available. But for some states and urban areas, more sophisticated input-output or econometric models, or combinations of the two types, are available.[2]

---

[2] The literature on multiregional and single-region models is of course extensive. As my present purpose is not to review these models in detail, I shall forgo numerous citations. For multiregional models, see two survey papers of my own (Bolton, 1978a

Criteria for models

The earlier review of "essential elements" suggests useful characteristics for models to analyze defense impact, in addition to more general criteria for models in any policy analysis. First, if one wants to analyze national-scale changes, there must be a good *national* model to produce control totals for the region(s), to determine national variables simultaneously with regional variables (the latter is the so-called "bottoms up" approach, which is a welcome trend in multiregional modeling).

Second, a model should have an explicit variable for defense demand in the region(s), and it should be disaggregated by the three types of spending: military payrolls, civilian payrolls, and procurement. Ideally, procurement should be further broken down by major product or weapons system. An input-output model will usually have defense as an explicit variable; most econometric models do not. In practice, most econometric models include defense spending as an explicit variable in only a few equations, the ones for the most dependent industries (aircraft, for example). Thus, "constant term adjustments" are required to reflect changes in defense demand in the whole array of industries which are affected. Glickman (1977, pp. 180–81) used input-output information for Philadelphia in making such adjustments; Harris (1973, p. 191), in a *multi*regional simulation of a general defense reduction, assumed arbitrarily that decreases would be concentrated more heavily in the urban areas that had a high proportion of personnel or prime contracts in the base situation.

Third, the model should permit a clear separation of direct, indirect, and

---

and forthcoming) and a forthcoming symposium in the *Journal of Regional Science*, to which several multiregional model builders and I will contribute. For a full treatment of single-region models, see Glickman's recent survey (1977) and my own less complete one (1978b). Neither of those surveys is really complete, and neither covers some interesting proprietory models by some consulting firms, including Chase Econometrics and Data Resources Incorporated. Details on the proprietory models are generally not freely available, but they are obvious candidates for use in single-region impact analysis. Prominent published examples of defense analysis with multiregional models include three with the Leontief balanced model: Leontief et al. (August 1965); Dresch (December 1972), using a prototype of IDIOM, the currently operational version of the balanced model; Dresch and Updegrove (1978), with the fully developed IDIOM. The first two analyzed general reductions in defense, the third a cutback in military export sales. All three produced results for states. Examples of use of Curtis Harris's large econometric model, with states and metropolitan areas as the regions, are in Cumberland (1973) and Harris (1973).

Applications of single-region models include many with input-output models; perhaps the best known is on the impact of the Vietnam War on Philadelphia by Isard and Langford (1969). Econometric models were used in Glickman, for Philadelphia (1977); by Treyz (1977), for Massachusetts (1977); L'Esperance (1968, 1977a, and 1977b) for Ohio, including a simulation with defense contracts as a policy instrument. Bourque, Conway, and Howard (1977) analyzed the impact of aerospace industry on Washington with a combined input-output econometric model, but did not limit it to defense business of the industry.

induced effects in each region. This is a relatively easy thing to do with an input-output model, although most operational models do not have endogenous investment and state and local purchases, which is a shortcoming. Econometric models do not usually permit this clear separation. A good example of how important is the separation of the effects is in Dresch and Updegrove's (1978) analysis with IDIOM, a balanced input-output model. They simulated a decline in military export sales compensated, first, by personal tax cuts, and, alternatively, by public works construction *targeted* to states suffering the greatest negative direct-plus-indirect effect from defense. In the second case, defense-dependent states lost much less employment than in the first case, but they did lose some employment, because they had smaller shares of the indirect and induced demands from public works than their shares of direct and indirect defense demand.

Finally, a model should include supply responses, in order to predict the probability and duration of unemployment which I argued earlier were important for "vulnerability." Input-output models do not include these; they are purely demand allocation models. As such, however, they are useful in indicating in a general way the extent and direction of movements of labor which would be needed to restore full employment, in the extreme case where relative prices did not change (*see* Leontief et al., 1965).

DATA FOR DEFENSE IMPACT ANALYSIS

The Defense Department publishes data for each type of spending—military payrolls, civilian payrolls, and procurement—in each state, and submits county and city data for the Community Services Administration reports on federal outlays (*see* Chapter 5 in this volume). A convenient compilation of data for all three types for selected years can be found in McBreen (1977).

Military payrolls. Amounts are reported for the region where the military installation is located; they include allowances for uniforms and quarters, but not the value of food, clothing, and lodging provided in-kind. DOD purchases of this food and clothing, and its construction of military housing, are of course included in data for procurement. Pay is measured before deductions of amounts withheld to be sent to dependents elsewhere.

Because some income is sent to dependents living elsewhere, we can assume the marginal propensity to consume is less than for a permanent civilian resident earning the same cash income. Because some income is received in-kind, the serviceman's consumption patterns in the local economy are different. Multiplier effects will be overstated if based on consumption coefficients for civilian families, and the effects on some industries will be especially overstated. One way to see this is to note that a civilian family spends some of its income on retail trade services embodied in consumption goods, while many servicemen are provided those services by other military personnel or civilian employees on base (such as food handlers, supply clerks), whose pay is included in DOD payrolls. If civilian consumption coefficients are used, there is, in a sense, double counting of those other personnel. Fortunately, the double counting is reduced by DOD's practice of excluding PX and other retail-store-employees' wages from the payroll figures.

Civilian payrolls. These are reasonably straightforward, with amounts recorded in the region of location of the employing installation. However, as with military payrolls, there are no residence adjustments, which complicates intraurban impact analysis. Most civilian employees, and even many military personnel, live off the base.

Procurement. This is the greatest kind of spending, has the indirect effects to complicate analysis, and has the least satisfactory data! The only data by region are on prime contracts, which have a timing much different from actual demand, and which do not show the regions where value added actually is produced. DOD reports contracts by major program (such as aircraft, aircraft engines, ships, missiles, electronic systems, tank-automotive, food, clothing, construction) in each state; the Community Services Administration reports total contract value for states, counties, and cities over 25,000, but for only four "programs" (supply, services, R and D, and construction). There are no contract data by Standard Industrial Classification (SIC) code; there are some by-products, based on the Federal Supply Classification System, but they are not by region.

The region under which the prime contract is recorded is almost always the location of final assembly of the item or where a service is performed. An earlier tendency to assign some contracts to the state of the prime contractor's headquarters has been almost eliminated. But, of course, the region of final assembly or performance of service is not where all the value added is produced; the prime contractor buys intermediate goods and services from other regions and so do his subcontractors, even if they are in the same region. This problem exists in the impact analysis of any kind of exogenous demand in a region, of course, not just for defense. In tracing the value added to regions, analysts traditionally have had to know general interindustrial and interregional trade patterns and then assume the patterns for defense production are the same. We do not know if that assumption is valid or not, in the absence of data on subcontracting. Some suspect the defense patterns are *not* the same, that some pairs of firms in different regions are more likely to have a prime contractor/subcontractor relationship for a defense item than for a nondefense item. The suspicion is based on the specialization of many firms in defense and the emphasis on quality control and specifications, which may prompt primes to maintain long-standing connections with particular subcontractors.

We very much need some data on the interregional flows of intermediate goods in defense production. There have been no regular data; some sample studies in the 1960s did show that subcontracts were if anything more concentrated regionally than prime contracts (Lynch, 1976). In 1977 Congress, under pressure from regional groups, required DOD to initiate a data collection effort, which is now in progress, and which is expected to produce regular reports beginning later this year. For every prime contract of $500,000 and up, the prime contractor and his subcontractor will both report on any subcontract or other purchase of $100,000 or more; in addition, the subcontractor will report on his own (second-tier) subcontracts to others of $10,000 and up. Values will be reported by principal place of performance or assembly of the prime and of the subcontract; however, no program or SIC code will be included, which will sharply limit the usefulness of the data.

One problem in the prime contract data is very revealing. DOD does not publish regional data for contracts under $10,000 or for miscellaneous ones which cannot be assigned to a region; these amount to about 14 percent of the total. In Fiscal 1978 they amounted to about $7.5 billion, which is a lot bigger than many "urban programs"! In the CSA data, these are assigned to the county in which the procurement office granting the contract is located, even though that is known to be different from where production will take place. This complicates interregional analysis with CSA data; for example, in the CSA data the District of Columbia is credited with about 10 percent, which is far more than it conceivably could produce, because so many procurement offices are located there. The practice by CSA also complicates intrametropolitan area analysis, for even though a lot of the items procured under small contracts are produced in the same metropolitan area, they are not produced in the same county as the procurement office.

Another problem relates to "government furnished equipment." Consider an aircraft engine or electronics subsystem which is to be incorporated into a military airplane. The airframe, engine, and electronics may be bought under three different contracts, in three different regions. There are similar examples for other weapons systems. Now, the prime contractor will not have to make an intermediate purchase of the engine or electronics. But a nondefense manufacturer does make such purchases, and the usual input-output table will have coefficients which are averages of the defense and civilian plane manufacturer's requirements; the coefficients thus are *over*estimates for defense production. This may lead to an overstatement of the value added in regions specializing in items purchased separately as "government purchased equipment"; they will be credited with both the prime contract for the equipment and the intermediate purchases which only a civilian manufacturer would make.

U.S. Census Bureau data. There is a wholly different set of data on defense production, but one which is incomplete in coverage. The U.S. Census Bureau annually publishes data on shipments from defense-oriented manufacturing plants. These are from a sample of 7,000 plants (including all with 500 employees or more) in 94 SIC 4-digit industries known to do a lot of work for the Federal government. The plants report value of shipments and employment, but not value added, for work they know is under a defense prime or subcontract. Data are published for states, for industries, and for about 160 metropolitan areas, but there is no cross-classification by region and industry.

These data are somewhat helpful in indicating dependence on defense production. However, not all manufacturing industries, and no nonmanufacturing industry, are covered. And even some firms in the sample do not know whether or not one of their products will or will not be incorporated into a final product to be delivered to defense buyers. The total amounts reported by Census for value of shipments always fall far short of total procurement expenditures, in spite of the fact that they inevitably involve some double counting.

REFERENCES

Beale, Calvin. *The Revival of Population Growth in Nonmetropolitan America.* ERS-605. Economic Research Service. Washington, D.C.: U.S. Department of Agriculture, 1976.

Bolton, Roger. *Defense Purchases and Regional Growth.* Washington, D.C.: Brookings Institution, 1966*a*.

―――. "Statistics on Industrial and Regional Defense Impact." In *1967 Proceedings of Business and Economic Statistics Section.* American Statistical Association, 1968.

―――. "Defense Spending and Policies for Labor-Surplus Areas." In *Essays in Regional Economics,* edited by J. Kain and J. Meyer. Cambridge: Harvard University Press, 1971.

―――. "Defense Manpower Policy No. 4." Unpublished paper. 1977.

―――. "Regional Models for Policy Analysis." Paper read at Regional Science Association Meetings, November 1978*a*, Chicago. Mimeographed.

―――. "Review of the Literature on Regional Econometric Models and Regional Business Cycles." Unpublished paper. 1978*b*.

―――. "Multiregional Models." Paper submitted to *Journal of Regional Science,* forthcoming.

―――, ed. *Defense and Disarmament.* Englewood Cliffs: Prentice-Hall, 1966*b*.

Bourque, Philip J.; Conway, Richard S.; and Howard, Charles. *The Washington Projection and Simulation Model.* Seattle: University of Washington, 1977.

CONEG (Coalition of Northeast Governors) Policy Research Center and Northeast-Midwest Research Institute. *A Case of Inequity: Regional Patterns in Defense Expenditures, 1950–77.* New York: CONEG, 1977.

Cumberland, John. "Dimensions of the Impact of Reduced Military Expenditures on Industries, Regions, and Communities." In *The Economic Consequences of Reduced Military Spending,* edited by Bernard Udis. Lexington: D.C. Heath, 1973.

Dresch, Stephen. "Disarmament: Economic Consequences and Development Potential." Report to the U.N. Department of Economic and Social Affairs, December 1972.

————, and Updegrove, Daniel. "IDIOM: A Disaggregated Policy-Impact Model of the U.S. Economy." New Haven: Institute for Demographic and Economic Studies, 1978. (Prepared for NSF Conference on Microeconomic Simulation Models for the Analysis of Public Policy, 1978.)

Glickman, Norman. *Econometric Analysis of Regional Systems.* New York: Academic Press, 1977.

Harris, Curtis. *The Urban Economies 1985.* Lexington: D.C. Heath, 1973.

Hoover, Edgar. *An Introduction to Regional Economics.* 2d ed. New York: Alfred Knopf, 1975.

Isard, Walter, and Langford, Thomas. *Impact of Viet Nam War Expenditures on the Philadelphia Economy.* Discussion paper No. 29. Philadelphia: Regional Science Research Institute, 1969.

Leontief, Wassily, et al. "The Economic Impact—Industrial and Regional—of an Arms Cut." *Review of Economics and Statistics* 47 (August 1965): 217–41.

L'Esprance, Wilford. "Optimal Stabilization Policy at the Regional Level." *Regional Science and Urban Economics,* 1977a, pp. 25–48.

————. "The Optimal Control of a Regional Econometric Model." Columbus: Ohio State University, 1977b. Mimeographed.

————; Nestel, G.; and Fromm, D. "Gross State Product and an Econometric Model of a State." *Journal of the American Statistical Association,* September 1968, pp. 787–807.

Lynch, John. *Local Economic Development after Military Base Closures.* New York: Praeger, 1970.

————. "Regional Impact of the Vietnam War." *Quarterly Review of Economics and Business* 16, no. 2 (1976): 37–50.

McBreen, Maureen. "Regional Trends in Federal Defense Expenditures: 1950–1976." In U.S. Senate, Committee on Appropriations, *Selected Essays on Patterns of Regional Change.* Washington, D.C.: U.S. Government Printing Office, 1977.

Treyz, George. *The Massachusetts Economic Policy Analysis: Econometric Model Project.* Amherst: University of Massachusetts Press, 1977.

————. Personal communication, 1978.

U.S. Congress. House of Representatives. Committee on Small Business. *Hearings, Defense Manpower Policy Four and DOD Minority Enterprise Subcontracting Program.* Washington, D.C.: U.S. Government Printing Office, 1977.

————. *Hearings, Labor Surplus Program, Part 1* and *Labor Surplus Program, Part 2.* Washington, D.C.: U.S. Government Printing Office, 1978.

————. *Hearings, DOD Procurement Policies and Practices.* Washington, D.C.: U.S. Government Printing Office, 1978.

U.S. Department of Commerce, Bureau of the Census. *Shipments of Defense-Oriented Industries, (MA-175).* Washington, D.C.: U.S. Government Printing Office, annual.

U.S. President's Economic Adjustment Committee. *Planning Civilian Reuse of Former Military Bases.* Office of Economic Adjustment. Washington, D.C.: Department of Defense, 1978.

————. *Communities in Transition.* Office of Economic Adjustment, Washington, D.C.: Department of Defense, 1977.

Zabar, Laurence. *Federal Procurement and Regional Needs: The Case of Defense Manpower Policy No. 4.* Washington, D.C.: Northeast-Midwest Research Institute, 1978.

————, and Travis, Paul. *The Aftermath: The Problems Communities Face after a Military Installation Closes.* Washington, D.C.: CONEG (Coalition of Northeast Governors) Policy Research Center and Northeast-Midwest Research Institute, 1978.

CHAPTER SEVEN

"People" versus "Places" in Urban Impact Analysis

MATTHEW EDEL

INTRODUCTION

The issue of spatial formulation

Government actions may have differential benefits and costs for different areas. Some policies are designed deliberately to develop specific areas, to equalize opportunities between the different places in which people may live or invest or otherwise to shape how a country uses its geographic resources. Other policies may have unintended spatial effects. Knowledge of these differential effects is useful for the formulation and evaluation of policy.

Adoption of the urban impact analysis requirement brings consideration of these effects into the federal executive budget-making process. Up to now, the principal method for taking into account local effects of policy has been legislative. The localized nature of congressional representation was designed to protect states and regions from adverse national policies. But congressional "logrolling," while sometimes successful at ensuring local interests, has not always worked. The new initiative may be a useful supplement to it.

The author has argued in the past for more concern with the spatial effects of policies (Edel and Rothenberg, 1972, pp. 1–11; R.R.P.E. Editorial Collective, 1972), and logically should welcome this new requirement. But enthusiasm is tempered by a potential danger: the spatial dimension is never the only effect of policies. Many programs may be designed to affect incomes or opportunities for different groups of people—wage earners, investors, or recipients of transfer income. It is feared that spatial concern will *replace*, rather than *supplement*, attention to the needs of population groups such as minorities, the poor, and the unemployed. These groups have received at least sporadic recognition in past "urban" and "regional" policies. But concern with places may be replacing whatever concern with people existed in the making of "urban" policy. Some reasons why the urban impact analysis requirement may worsen this danger will be suggested in this paper.

Policy-making and analysis have often confused individual or group "people" impacts with "place" impacts. For example, as Robert A. Levine has suggested, "some tendency exists to confuse poor people with poor areas," with the result that regional development and antipoverty objectives have often been substituted for each other (Levine, 1970, p. 41). At times this confusion has been benign. But these objectives cannot be considered as perfect substitutes.

It shall be argued that a spatial formulation for a program designed to assist people may have several adverse effects. First, eligibility criteria, or ex post evaluations of who was helped, may be incorrectly specified by the *ecological fallacy*. Second, benefits themselves may be diverted, not strictly from "people" to "place," but from initial recipients to the owners of places (that is, land owners or others who can control the use of places), by a process of *capitalization*. Third, attempting to understand social and economic relationships by thinking of places, rather than individuals or groups of people, as active participants may cause ideological confusion.

Distinguishing the effects of programs on groups or categories of *people* from these effects on *places* can help dispel this confusion, and perhaps help combat some biases in program design.

In the next section some reasons for concern with the issue of "people" versus "places" impacts will be discussed. Subsequent sections of this paper discuss the possibilities of conflict between people-oriented and place-oriented formulations of urban programs and the process by which thinking about spatial goals has displaced thinking about goals of benefiting groups of people. Finally, it is suggested that urban impact statements could be designed to prevent the exclusion of effects on people.

The author proposes that the urban impact analyses be required to specify *both* effects on spatially defined "urban" places, and on relevant population groups, in order to make the results of policy as explicit as possible.

Reasons for concern

Devoting attention to the precise formulation of urban impact analyses is worthwhile only if first, the analyses themselves are not a mere formality, and second, the formulation can either affect or expose policy choices. Neither of these aspects of the urban impact analysis is self-evident.

There is, first of all, a question of whether the new requirement is simply window-dressing. Many government studies "are public relations efforts directed to the general public to bolster the government's claim that it acts in the public interest" (Capitol Kapitalistate Collective, 1977, p. 167). The present requirement may simply be a move to appease big-city mayors with the appearance of federal involvement, and to disguise the fact that urban aid is being cut by claiming that other programs have positive urban impact. That the urban impact analysis is not officially subjected to any approval or hearings mechanism or legal review process suggests it is not considered very important. If the study is purely window-dressing, no further critique of its specific form would seem necessary.

It is, however, too pessimistic to say the new requirement is too meaningless to study. A formal requirement may be made the occasion for community mobilization, a forum for struggle,[1] even if that were not its initial intent. This seems to have happened with the environmental impact statement. What is more, if the wording of the statement *does indicate* a real transformation of program goals, this can be subjected to critique if it is made more visible. The urban impact requirement comes just at a time in which poverty programs —some of which were thought of initially as "urban"—are losing importance within federal priorities. An urban impact requirement may accelerate, combat, or simply mask this tendency to devalue assistance to the poor. It thus requires close scrutiny.

The second question, the potential relevance of the choice of "people" or "place" criteria, can be answered by an appeal to recent history. The substitution of spatial for individual criteria has often occurred in the formulation of poverty programs. In the 1960s, many programs defined poverty in terms of urban poverty areas, or occasionally in terms of depressed rural districts as well (*see* Levine, 1970, and Levitan, 1969). The Area Redevelopment Act, the first of the Kennedy domestic proposals to respond to a concern with poverty, was concerned with nonurban depressed areas. Its successor, the 1965 Economic Development Act, added some urban districts to the list of eligible places. The 1964 Economic Opportunity Act, while ostensibly concerned with family poverty and individual opportunity, had a strong community development component. Poverty areas were defined, and Community Action programs, Neighborhood Youth Corps programs, and other local area programs established.

A similar spatial focus was given to opportunity programs in the 1965 Elementary and Secondary Education Act. Title I set aside funds for school districts with specific proportions of children from poor households. A number of later programs, including Model Cities, the Special Impact Program, and the Concentrated Employment Program, picked selected spatial targets. Community Development Block Grants (CDBG) and some other recent revenue sharing programs use area criteria to determine funding levels.

All of these programs were concerned, in their conception, with lifting individuals above a poverty line. In their rationale, it was often explicitly stated

---

[1] Capitol Kapitalistate Collective, 1977, p. 165, criticizes other government analyses for not providing such a forum. For a further elaboration of the critique, *see* ibid., p. 191, and Chapter 4, above.

that regional or neighborhood development could increase individual opportunities. Certainly no necessary conflict between community betterment and the improvement of individual incomes or opportunities was foreseen (Levine, 1970, p. 157). As will be suggested later, the spatial focus of these programs had much to recommend it in terms of ability to take advantage of social processes and administrative convenience.

The substitution of locational for income criteria did, however, involve a degree of self-deception. "Urban program" became something of a "codeword" for "poverty program." In the 1960s, this could rally support among the urban nonpoor for poverty programs, and diffuse some conflict over racial criteria. In the 1970s, however, it has become a rationale for diverting poverty efforts toward other urban goals—as for example, in the utilization of Comprehensive Employment and Training Act (CETA) funds for the maintaining of city services instead of for the training of the hard-core unemployed.

To a degree, urban policy is still a term for antipoverty policy. President Carter was responding, in part, to a perceived poverty issue and to pressure by the Black Caucus in Congress on his urban program. But, increasingly, issues other than poverty are being conceived of as "the urban problem." Fiscal crisis has become important, and many new policies seek to help urban government units rather than any population subgroup, at least at the first level of impact.

The promulgation of the August 18, 1978 Executive Order came in the same year as the passage of another Black Caucus priority, the Humphrey-Hawkins bill. But this legislation, as passed, *removed* many of the employment impact analysis requirements suggested in earlier versions of the bill. That urban but not employment impacts are to be evaluated may be a significant policy choice by the government, at least if "urban" is interpreted only spatially. To oppose a narrow geographic drawing of the urban impact requirement is thus to attempt to retain some of the initial antipoverty focus of urban policy within the definition of urban impacts.

POTENTIAL CONFLICTS BETWEEN "PEOPLE"
AND "PLACES" IMPACTS

There are two principal ways in which programs that are designed for the benefit of a group of people, but that are formulated in spatial terms, may have their effects diverted from the intended beneficiaries. The first is a skewing of eligibility so that initially ineligible people become beneficiaries by their place of residence, while some intended beneficiaries are excluded for the same reason. The second is a shifting of benefits from the original beneficiaries to the owners of land or of other immobile factors of production, a shifting which may sometimes involve the actual removal of the intended beneficiaries from the target area. The process by which each distortion occurs will be discussed in turn.

Eligibility by location and the ecological fallacy

A number of federal programs designed to assist the poor have eligibility standards based not on income but on residence in areas whose average income is below a poverty threshold. These programs frequently reach the poor because of the relatively segregated nature of the modern American city. For more than half of this country's two centuries of independence, economic and social forces have been quite effective in sorting out different income strata into different neighborhoods. In part, this is an automatic result of a land allocation system based on individual bidding for homesites or apartments, in which those with higher incomes or particular tastes (when backed up by sufficient incomes) can outbid others for the sites they consider prime. In part it is a result of zoning and other government policies which militate against mixed land uses. And, in part, it is a result of self-segregation or involuntary exclusion by different social groups, defined by class, racial, ethnic, or lifestyle criteria. The pattern as a whole may be socially damaging, but from a program design standpoint, it makes it easier to serve selected population subgroups by locating programs where they live.

However, segregation is not "perfect" from a program design viewpoint. Very few districts large enough to be service catchment areas are completely segregated, even in racial terms (Taeuber and Taeuber, 1965). Income segregation is also imperfect. The dynamics of residential location ensure this. Neighborhoods change, but not all individuals move or recontract for their locations at once. Thus, even if market or social forces are ensuring uniformity of *new* entrants into an area, not all old residents will share the same characteristics.

This means that, under most reasonable systems of boundary-drawing, service or eligibility districts will encompass residents with a variety of income and other characteristics. To attribute individual characteristics (like presumed income eligibility) on the basis of the area of residence, is to commit the "ecological fallacy" well known in the statistical literature (Simon, 1958, p. 327). As Levine shows, in 1966 fewer than half of the poor in central cities were in designated poverty areas (Levine, 1970, p. 21). Nor were all poverty-area residents themselves poor.

A program that defines eligibility in terms of residence in a poor district will make eligible many nonpoor residents, while excluding poor persons who form a minority of the population of nonpoor areas. For example, Title I educational funds are distributed to school boards for use in schools with a designated percentage of children from poor families. But they need not be spent directly for the poor children and thus may disappear into the general budget. As Levitan states, they are often used for "traditional educational activities" (Levitan, 1969, p. 80). The poor who live outside the poverty areas do not benefit. There may be some further incentive for school district lines to be gerrymandered to maximize Title I fund inflow for general budgetary purposes.

Benefit capitalization

A second problem with targeting the site as the beneficiary of a program may shift benefits from the intended individual beneficiaries to landowners or to people who move into the area later. By making residence in an area more desirable, in terms of eligibility for program benefits or in terms of general neighborhood environment, programs may increase the amount some individuals would be willing to pay to live there. To the extent that market conditions allow these people to make their desires effective, they will bid away the use of sites from prior users, in the process raising the effective rents or property values in the area. If the previous residents do not have ownership rights in the area, they will not benefit from the increased value. Indeed, unless housing supply is extremely elastic, they may have to move away or pay significantly higher rents in order to stay.

If one takes literally the market model used in contemporary urban economics, one can posit conditions in which *all* of the positive benefits of geographically targeted programs are capitalized into land values, and thus accrue to landowners (*see* Edel, 1972). If the neoclassical assumptions of labor and capital mobility prevail, wage-and-profit rates will tend to be equalized between places. Thus local benefits cannot take the form of localized higher wages or profits. If the program area is itself a *small enough* part of the overall national economy in which high mobility prevails, so that the impact on the national average wage-and-profit rates can be ignored, then immobile local factors of production can capture all the benefits. In the simplest model, the landowner gets it all. In more complex cases, taxes and local monopoly returns can also be increased.

Even if a large category of areas, such as metropolitan areas in general, are affected by a program, landowners may capture much, or conceivably all, of the benefit. What one expects at this level of analysis depends, of course, on the paradigm one has for understanding the economy. Under *neoclassical assumptions*, benefits should be divided among all factors of production, depending on their elasticities of supply and substitution. Landlords generally receive only part of the gain, although this is not inevitable. However, if "natural" equilibrium wage-and-interest rates are presumed, on Malthusian, Austrian, or other grounds, the landlord's share of the product should rise. *Radical economic models* yield somewhat different macrolevel results. Henry George's model included a special case of assumed "natural" wages-and-interest rates governed by a geographical frontier. He derived a rising landlord share. (Indeed, *Progress and Poverty*, written a century ago, contains discussion of the urban impact of several policies and innovations including agglomeration and clean government, suggesting benefits can accrue entirely to landowners.) Finally, in a Marxist model, returns to *general* improvement will normally be captured entirely by capital. This will prevail unless the power positions of working or landlord classes are strong enough to allow them to gain a share (Edel, 1977; George, 1938; Engels, n.d.).

The differences between these paradigms do not, however, prevent agreement that if improvements are *localized*, and capital and labor are mobile, the gains appear as local land rents (which landowners or government may acquire).

The capitalization of local advantages or disadvantages into land values has been used as the basis for cost or benefit measurement in a number of recent studies. Costs of pollution, and the benefits of public services, transport access, and urban agglomeration (city size) have all been approached in this way (*see* Ridiker and Henning, 1967, pp. 246–57; Oates, 1969, pp. 957–71; and Edel, 1972).

These studies have some difficulties which are admitted in the extant literature (Mohring, 1961; Edel and Sclar, 1974). It is recognized that capitalization may not be complete. If consumers of space in the benefited (or damaged) areas vary in incomes or tastes, marginal rather than total benefits will be capitalized, leaving a consumers' or producers' surplus to the nonmarginal users. Measurement only of marginal benefits makes extrapolation to total benefits impossible. The proportion capitalized is unknowable if total benefits cannot be estimated independently. Benefit measures that *are* independently obtained, however, may include part, but not all, of the capitalized portions of the benefits. Merging the two types of measures, therefore, is risky. It has also been recognized that if the impact area is large enough, effects on land values in other areas must also be considered. But with all of these caveats, capitalization studies have remained an accepted rough tool of impact analysis.

What is not always apparent in these studies, however, is the *distributional* side of capitalization. If the ultimate user of space in an impact area is not also the initial landowner, benefits that one is measuring by capitalization are precisely those benefits that the user is not receiving. They are being transferred to landlords. Or, if they were foreseen, former owners may have already acquired them through higher land-sale prices. These effects have been ignored in some studies which deal with communities of homeowners, perhaps with little damage done. But they cannot be ignored safely if some residents are not owners.

This has been argued by Charles M. Eastman, in a critique of neighborhood development programs:

> Any effective neighborhood development programs should increase the value of property within the designated area due to the improved services it provides. Inhabitants of the neighborhood who own their place of residence would receive those benefits resulting from the program itself, as long as they remained. If they chose to sell their property, then they would gain in capital the marginal net worth of the neighborhood development program in existence. . . . However, the most needy residents of a neighborhood are not likely to be homeowners. They will rent their dwellings. For these people, the market operates in a negative way. The increased value of locations within the program area can be charged to them in higher rents. (Eastman, 1972, p. 290)

That locally focused programs may show positive benefits by a land value criterion, yet leave initial residents worse off, indicates clearly the potential conflict between "people" and "place" impacts of a program. It also suggests that when we talk of "places" we may be really referring to a particular set of people—the owners of the land.

The designers of urban programs which are spatially defined may be sometimes concerned primarily with bolstering land values or quality as it will be perceived by potential buyers. Downtown urban renewal, suburban infrastructure improvement, and programs to sustain tax bases by attracting the middle class to inner cities may have this deliberate aim. Land value increases wrought by these programs may even have positive benefits for the poor, if they are not made at the cost of excessive tax abatement, since the tax base for local government service provisions may increase. But often programs, which appear to have benefits for poor people as their goal, ignore the fact that the primary benefits can spill over to landowners.

One possible reason for this is an assumption that neighborhoods that have remained poor contain immobile people, a situation which would prevent capitalization. However, the poor are not immobile. They frequently move either in search of jobs or because they are evicted (*see*, for instance, Knights, 1969, pp. 258–74).

It can be seen that there is a potential for programs which are intended to benefit categories of people, but which are targeted in geographical terms that miss their intended beneficiaries. The latter may not all be located in the eligible area, while some unintended recipients become eligible due to residence. Or, if intended beneficiaries are (voluntarily or involuntarily) mobile, benefits may be diverted by capitalization. Programs, like urban renewal or neighborhood "upgrading," may sometimes benefit the owners of land, while missing or even damaging the welfare of initial residents. There is, therefore, good reason to be wary of substitution of geographical for individual criteria in program design. Similarly, evaluation of programs may ignore important effects if ecological fallacy and capitalization effects are not accounted for.

FACTORS FAVORING SPATIAL CRITERIA

If there are dangers in the place-oriented design or evaluation of federal efforts to assist categories of individuals, it is worth inquiring what factors favor the spatial focus. A number of factors have made spatial program design increasingly popular, particularly in the poverty program area, and have led to increased attention to spatial factors in program evaluation. These factors, up to a point, justify an increasing spatial concern as beneficial. But they also suggest such a concern can be exaggerated to the exclusion of concern for individuals.

Administrative convenience

A first reason for spatial delimitation of programs has been administrative convenience or feasibility. The United States operates on a federal system with geographically defined units of government. Although the Federal government can in some cases administer programs centrally and uniformly, most programs are decentralized. State, county, and municipal governments take part in their implementation. Even where this is not the case, federal programs may be administered more effectively through regional offices which cannot be located everywhere at once. Thus, an "aspatial" set of rules and a centralized system of administration for federal antipoverty and educational programs could be envisioned. That is, negative income tax administered by the Internal Revenue Service and federally issued vouchers for education could be added to present centrally administered food stamp and social security programs. But greater sensitivity to local differences in needs, political accommodation to local forces, and more effective administration of complex services can be achieved through administrative decentralization. Even food stamp programs allow some unofficial flexibility at the local level, in terms of treatment of issues like whether part-time students are "emancipated" from parental support.

If programs are administered in a decentralized manner, certain areas will, deliberately or not, be recipients of greater attention to the program. It is a short step from the locating of administrative centers for a program near the greatest concentrations of potential users to adoption of residential- or workplace-location criteria for eligibility to use programs. Even when eligibility is originally thought of in terms of income level, minority status, or some other personal characteristics of categories of individuals, this shift may occur.

Residential-location criteria for eligibility have a number of obvious administrative advantages over income criteria. It is easier to ask a person his address than his taxable income—and far easier to verify the accuracy of the answer. In many cases, no formal eligibility test need be made visible to recipients at all. The physical location of a service in a geographical area will ensure that most clients will come from places with easy transportation access. Since the determination of individual eligibility for programs is costly, in terms of staffing and sometimes in terms of frictions between staff and clients, a geographical shortcut may cut costs substantially. As indicated above, this substitution of eligibility criteria may leave some otherwise eligible people unserved. A system at first beneficial may have diminishing benefits if extended too far.

Displacement of conflict

A spatial definition of programs may also be attractive because it partially obscures the fact that one group of people may be in conflict with another over program funds or other benefits. Thus, funding programs may be directed to minority groups without explicitly recognizing any racial benefits. The selection of certain neighborhoods for community development or other funding can be done on the basis of "objective" (measurable, quantitative) criteria of places, rather than on racial grounds, and yet minority neighborhoods will predominate among those chosen, if the criteria are carefully chosen. Thus when objections exist, either in law or in public opinion, to racial criteria, programs may still be implemented which are more or less targeted on racially defined groups. For example, the SEEK program, a special opportunities program in the City University of New York, initially had both personal income ceilings and the requirement of residence in a designated poverty area as admission criteria. This ensured an *overwhelmingly minority* eligibility pool, without compromising the official stance of the university as provider of opportunities for all, although some students from poor families, black as well as white, were excluded.

An occasional spatial subterfuge to ensure the acceptance of compensatory opportunity programs may be condoned, although it is doubtful that many people will be fooled for long by attempts to disguise minority opportunity programs. But once spatial defining of problems and programs begins, it may be used in other groups' interest as well. For example, the definition of present problems of local unemployment as part of a "Northeast" versus "Sunbelt" conflict over jobs obscures several lines of conflict and militates against some possible solutions. It has been argued that the use of regional differences in wages, working conditions, and local service costs may be used by business as a source of advantage in labor-management conflict.[2] To ask for assistance to "Snowbelt" industries, however, substitutes a perception of labor-management conflict with perceptions of competition among workers in different regions for jobs, among businesses in different regions for federal contracts, or among industrial park owners in different regions for tenants. A focus on such competition makes any remedial legislation unlikely. It also diffuses possible labor demands for a more effective *national* full employment program, or for action to force southern wages upward to northern levels. The geographic focus, in short, is not neutral in terms of labor-employer conflict.

That government may wish to obscure or deflect racial or class conflicts is understandable. It provides a basis for the popularity of spatial program definitions (and hence for the thinking of impacts in spatial terms). Individuals will vary as to when they think this process goes too far, depending on their political orientation. But that it may be counterproductive should be obvious.

The rise of "urban" disciplines

Another factor favoring spatial program design and evaluation criteria has been the rise of spatially defined urban subfields in a number of academic

---

[2] *See* R.R.P.E. Editorial Collective, 1972, and other articles in the same journal issue.

disciplines. Urban sociology, urban economics, and environmental psychology have followed the more overtly spatial urban planning, urban geography, and regional science in their central concerns. The determination of patterns of land use and spatial grouping of activities, and the effects of location on behavior and perception, have become the principal objects of their study.

The rise of these fields, focusing their attention on spatial phenomena, responded in part to a neglect of important spatial dimensions in the existing social sciences. In economics, the rise of Keynesian macroeconomics had diverted concern from a wide variety of microeconomic issues. General equilibrium analysis generally took on an "aspatial" form as it was evolving. Locational investigations and studies of the interaction of location and other economic phenomena were clearly needed. Locational studies became the core of an evolving "urban economics" field, however, only in part, because they were useful in themselves. In part, interest and funding, were attracted to urban economics because of political events of the 1960s, particularly racial conflict located in urban areas. Urban economics programs were expanded and their studies spread into areas traditionally considered by other subfields (labor economics, for example).

This left urban economics professionally unsatisfying to many economists. It was diffuse, but professionals expect a discipline to have an analytical core of interrelated models which can be honed and developed. Its borders to other fields were open, when institutionally a thriving field should be able to delimit itself. It was for professional development reasons, therefore, that spatial modeling became the core, rather than just one part of, urban economics.[3] A similar phenomenon has occurred in urban sociology, with the ecological tradition of the "Chicago School" playing the role there that locational models play in urban economics.

These conceptions of urban disciplines have been criticized, of late, from a number of quarters. Harry Richardson criticizes the narrowness of recent spatial modeling—the "New Urban Economics"—for divorcing itself from any policy-relevant issues (Richardson, 1978). Manuel Castells and Michael Ball have gone further, in critiques based on the epistemology of Marx and Althusser. They claim the object of studying urban sociology and economics is nonscientific, rather than merely of low priority. Most urban studies artificially divide phenomena into "spatial" and "aspatial" components, in order to then determine how the two interact. Or they group under the label of "urbanization" a variety of effects (changes in residence, in occupation, and in attitudes) which may be roughly correlated with each other, but which are conceptually distinct. Since these initial divisions and groupings are arbitrary, Castells and Ball argue, the basic thrust of the urban studies field is founded on logical inconsistencies (Castells, 1977; Ball, unpublished paper).

---

[3] Edel and Rothenberg, 1972, reflects this narrowing process in what now appears to be a regrettably uncritical way.

The criticism made by Castells and Ball goes beyond the discussion of the object of urban analysis. They criticize the empiricist inference from correlation to causality used in orthodox econometrics and sociology. They set their critique within a general analysis of the ideological elements that shape social theory. But whether the wider philosophic position be adopted or not, their criticism of spatial orientations of urban studies is relevant to the issue of program evaluation.

Castells and Ball are clearly concerned that a spatial definition of urban studies diverts attention from issues of the place of "urban problems" in the operations of capitalism, in the accumulation of capital and power by capitalists, and in the subsistence and organization of the working class. Castells even proposes, as a more proper focus for urban studies, the issue of "the social reproduction of the proletariat" (Castells, 1977). Even if one is concerned with groups of people defined in ways other than the Marxian categories of class, the point would seem to hold that the definition of urban fields, a result of professional rather than social needs, has directed attention away from people and toward places. The focus of disciplines, in turn, may affect policy as urban studies practitioners are called on for policy analysis.

Theories of community and poverty

A spatial focus in thinking about programs also was fostered by many of the analyses of poverty which were advanced in the 1960s. The apparent concentration of poverty in central city ghetto neighborhoods led to suggestions that neighborhood effects might be either causes of problems or avenues to solutions.[4]

One line of analysis suggested that residential segregation was limiting access of the poor to better schools, better jobs, and less costly consumer goods. Ghetto dispersal, or residential integration, therefore, was presented as desirable. Residential relocation came to be seen as a program to help poor people. The excesses of urban renewal, and resistance to forced relocation, eventually weakened the simple view that clearing slums (fixing places) was an antipoverty program.

The next approach tried, however, was equally spatial: the poor community itself could be a source of strength to poor people. Both the Ford Foundation's Gray Areas Program and its other pilot programs, which became the War on Poverty in the Johnson administration, concentrated on community upgrading as a way of reaching poor people. An influx of foreign aid and Peace Corps strategists into the poverty program reinforced the analogy between ghettos and underdeveloped countries, for which spatially delimited programs were customary. Community organizing was seen as a focus for anti-establishment efforts, too, in the early efforts of the Students for

---

[4] For a review *see* Matthew Edel, "Development vs. Dispersal: Approaches to Ghetto Poverty," in Edel and Rothenberg, 1972, pp. 307–24.

a Democratic Society (SDS) and other radical organizations. The eventual rise of a Black Power movement reinforced this spatial orientation, by demanding greater self-government or community control.

This position has been criticized, both by conservatives and radicals, for romanticizing community and neglecting class issues. In short, it is seen as ignoring intra-locality differences, and assuming common areas of residence always meant group unity. But it should be noted that even the leading critic of this view, Daniel P. Moynihan, had offered a spatial view of the ghetto as "a tangle of pathology" which drew back individuals who tried to advance themselves (Moynihan, 1965 and 1969).

The neoconservative reformulation of the poverty issue, when not simply neglecting the issue, has tended to return to the urban renewal approach. This is done not so much with the original faith that new housing could make people middle class, but simply with the view that minimal maintenance of the poor away from inner cities would be cheaper, and that tax bases could be improved were the poor not there.[5] Even the discussion of welfare reform has tended to focus on its possible effects on city-country migration and on urban fiscal balance. Similarly, the Nixon administration's substitution of revenue sharing and state control for federal program administration gave many programs a spatial definition, by increasing jurisdictional variation.

For the Left, the community ideology was thrown into disrepute by its appropriation by white communities that opposed busing. If some writing on the Left now involves a serious attempt to explore the interrelationships of class, race, and location, it has not led yet to any programmatic experiment such as the community-organizing campaigns of the 1960s. Rather, sides are taken, often uncritically, for or against existing spatial trends or organizational forms (busing, black mayoral campaigns, defense of city services, and campaigns versus runaway shops from the Northeast, for example).[6]

In short, the ideologies on the Right and on the Left that favored spatial thinking and program design in the 1960s have come under attack. But how to subsume spatial considerations within a wider approach has not been formulated by either side.

The fiscal crisis

The final reason for increasing concern with the spatial effects of public policies, sometimes to the exclusion of effects on people, is that in recent years budgetary imbalances or restrictions have faced many local governments in the United States. This "fiscal crisis," rather than continuing levels of poverty, unemployment, or immediate racial conflicts, is what prompted mayors and other local officials to pressure President Carter, which in turn resulted

[5] The extreme case is Forrester, 1969. But frequent statements by New York City public officials present a similar view.

[6] For discussion *see* Green and Hunter, 1978, pp. 271–96.

in his urban policy. The urban impact analysis requirement is thus a direct effect of the fiscal crisis, even if its specific form, requiring spatial analysis, is influenced by wider currents.

But even before the immediate policy demands that led to the U.S. Office of Management and Budget Circular A-116, a trend began to consider fiscal impacts, instead of global cost-benefit comparisons or analysis of the effects of programs on the "urban" poor. This tendency was not reflected directly in much academic writing on evaluation until quite recently; it has become more important in the impact studies commissioned by units of local government, which have been concerned with the service cost of allowing new housing or other facilities to be built, and with the comparison of these with tax revenues generated.[7] Consulting firms have developed fiscal impact analysis capacity which will no doubt be an influence in the formulation of many urban impact analyses.

The fiscal squeeze on local governments is without a doubt a serious problem in this country. That the local tax base and fiscal effects of proposed federal policies be considered carefully is all to the good. However, distributionally distinct methods for balancing budgets may meet the same fiscal criteria. For this reason an exclusive emphasis on the fiscal side can mask a variety of programs with different implications for intergroup or interindividual equity. It has been suggested that the fiscal crisis be analyzed as a method used to reduce the real incomes of workers and/or the poor, in a period of difficulty for capitalism, rather than simply as a budgetary problem caused by local decisions (O'Connor, 1973; Arcaly and Mermelstein, 1977). Since some proponents of fiscal improvement have recommended improving tax bases by moving the poor out, it is clear that fiscal crisis solutions may have negative consequences for specific groups of people. A purely fiscal approach to urban equity impacts would ignore these consequences.

CONCLUSIONS AND RECOMMENDATIONS

The institution of a new requirement for urban impact analyses provides an opportunity to clarify the relationship between individual and spatial goals of federal programs. It allows recognition that some programs have adversely affected people because of where they live. It can clarify the local fiscal impact of federal expenditure. But the requirement also bears with it a danger that, because of the spatial orientation of impact analyses, program goals will be reconstructed toward an emphasis on "place" impacts over "people" impacts. This could provide the occasion for a redirection of funding which would alter the nature of benefiting groups significantly and probably regressively (for example, shifting priorities away from programs aimed at the poor toward the owners of real estate in poor areas). Even if this does not happen, a probable effect will be to increase the degree to which programs

---

[7] This is discussed by Mason Gaffney in an unpublished paper.

designed for poor people will have to be formulated spatially. This will accentuate an extant trend which is both confusing to the public and potentially a distortion of programs. As has been shown above, spatially limiting a program that is designed to benefit individuals may result in diverting all or part of its benefits to land value change.

There is, actually, some recognition on the part of the framers of the urban impact analysis requirement that antipoverty and equal opportunity goals of a nonspatial nature somehow are to be proper targets of urban impacts.

Circular A-116 includes a number of equity factors as subjects for investigation. These include employment, especially of minorities; population size and composition, including the degree of racial concentration or deconcentration; and income, especially that of low income households. But the wording, particularly the reference to racial concentration or deconcentration, suggests the concern is with spatial phenomena—where the minorities live—rather than with individuals' welfare.[8]

Impacts on people, rather than on places, receive further emphasis in the convening document for this conference. Norman J. Glickman initially states: "Urban impact analyses consist of attempts to gauge the *spatial dimensions* of public policies. That is, how do policies affect central cities, suburbs, nonmetropolitan, and other spatial units, absolutely or relatively?" (Glickman, Chapter 1, above). Impact analysis is referred to throughout as "spatial policy analysis." However, in defining variables to consider the impact evaluation, Glickman indicates a particular concern with population mix, migration, employment, and per capita or total income levels, particularly with respect to minorities or low income individuals. In discussing equity, he further indicates, "consideration should be given to *intraarea, interarea,* and *interpersonal* income differentials," and admits "there may be conflicts between 'place' and 'people' equity" (ibid.).

This unease over the people versus place problem is well founded. Ecological fallacy and capitalization considerations indicate spatial program eligibility may have very different effects from population category eligibility. A shifting of benefits of poverty programs to nonpoor residents of low income areas and to owners of land in benefited areas (of poverty or other programs) may occur.[9] The essential point is that since people are not completely immobile between locations, people and place cannot be interchanged definitionally without problems occurring.

The argument is not for a lack of attention to geographic location of benefits. Where things happen is important. Agglomeration affects both economic

---

[8] U.S. Office of Management and Budget Circular A-116, August 16, 1978.

[9] Similarly, when programs are designed to improve the profitability of capital invested by a set of enterprises (e.g., small farms), general mobility of capital may lead to shifting of benefits as more capital is invested in the favored sector, driving down prices of goods. Land values may capture some of the benefits. *See* the various annual conference volumes of the Committee on Taxation, Resources, and Economic Development, published by the University of Wisconsin Press.

and political activity. Some people and investments are immobile geographically. Spatially focused programs, for the ghetto, the Appalachians, or the Northeast may be beneficial in certain program categories. Other programs may inadvertently affect immobile populations or past investments. We should know this, just as we should know in which categories a spatial definition is insufficient to prevent ecological fallacy spillovers.

Even when factors are mobile, and in the long-run view "urban impact" really means "landowner impact," government may be concerned with land value effects. Since land values are an important part of the tax base for cities, and since large-scale mortgage defaults can contribute to financial crisis, government can hardly stand aloof from the impacts of policy on landowners. But we should know whether effects we are measuring, or trying to induce, will be effective on population categories defined by income or income source other than landownership, or whether we are talking about aid to landlords.

What this means is that an urban impact statement must be concerned both with "people" and "places"—or more precisely with mobile and nonmobile factors of production and their owners. In knowing how a city, a metropolitan area, a rural district, or a broad geographic region is affected by a program, we should ask *specifically* both for the effects of the program on incomes or welfare of groups within the area and on those aspects of income or welfare of groups outside the area that may be affected. We should be particularly concerned, when targeting programs for specific areas, to inquire whether people are left ineligible by residence in the wrong place (ecological fallacy effect), and which are led to migrate in or out (to gain benefits, or because rent increases make it too costly to afford eligibility). And we should particularly be alert to the issue of capitalization of benefits. There is no easy shortcut to this knowledge. No single statistic sums it up. Learning the effects on total or group incomes in the impact area studied, and on groups excluded from, expelled from, or attracted to the area, and on land rents or values, which may accrue to residents or nonresidents, may add steps to the preparation of an impact analysis. But taking these steps may be necessary to avoid severely biased descriptions of benefit and cost patterns.

The guidelines for urban impact analysis should be expanded to require explicit treatment of both "people" and "place" effects, and to determine whether migration and capitalization are among the impacts.

REFERENCES

Alrcaly, Roger, and Mermelstein, David. *The Fiscal Crisis of American Cities.* New York: Vintage, 1977.

Ball, Michael. "A Critique of Urban Economics." Unpublished. Birkbeck College Department of Economics, London, 1978. (To be published in *Int. J. Urb. and Reg. Res.*)

Capitol Kapitalistate Collective. "A Study of Studies: A Marxist View of Research Conducted by the State." *Kapitalistate: Working on the Capitalist State* 6 (Fall 1977).

Castells, Manuel. *The Urban Question*. Cambridge: MIT Press, 1977.

Eastman, Charles M. "Hypotheses concerning Market Effects on Neighborhood Development Program." *Urban Affairs Quarterly* 7 (March 1972): 287–300.

Edel, Matthew. "Land Values and the Costs of Urban Congestion: Measurement and Distribution." In *Political Economy of Environment: Problems of Methods*, edited by I. Sachs. Paris: Mouton, 1972.

———. "Rent Theory and Labor Strategy: Marx, George, and the Urban Crisis." *Review of Radical Political Economics* 9 (Winter 1977): 1–15.

———, and Rothenberg, Jerome. "Introduction: Urban Economics as a Discipline." In *Readings in Urban Economics*. New York: Macmillan, 1972.

———, and Sclar, Elliott. "Taxing, Spending, and Property Values: Supply Adjustment in a Tiebout-Oates Model." *Journal of Political Economy* 82 (1974): 941–54.

Engels, Frederick. *The Housing Question*. New York: International Publishers, n.d.

George, Henry. *Progress and Poverty*. New York: Modern Library, 1938. Originally published, 1879.

Glickman, Norman J. "Methodological Issues and Prospects for Urban Impact Analyses." Chapter 1 in this volume.

Green, Jim, and Hunter, Alan. "Racism and Busing in Boston." In *Marxism and the Metropolis*, edited by W. K. Tabb and L. Sawers. New York: Oxford University Press, 1978.

Knights, Peter. "Population Turnover, Persistence, and Residential Mobility in Boston, 1830–60." In *Nineteenth-Century Cities*, edited by S. Thernstrom and R. Sennett. New Haven: Yale University Press, 1969.

Levine, Robert A. *The Poor Ye Need Not Have with You: Lessons from the War on Poverty*. Cambridge: MIT Press, 1970.

Levitan, Sar A. *Programs in Aid of the Poor for the 1970s*. Baltimore: Johns Hopkins Press, 1969.

Mohring, Herbert. "Land Values and the Measurement of Highway Benefits." *Journal of Political Economy* 69 (June 1961): 236–49.

Moynihan, Daniel P. *Maximum Feasible Misunderstanding: Community Action in the War on Poverty*. New York: Free Press, 1969.

———. *The Negro Family*. Washington, D.C.: U.S. Department of Labor, 1965.

Oates, Wallace E. "The Effect of Property Taxes and Local Spending on Property Valuation." *Journal of Political Economy* 77 (December 1969): 957–91.

O'Connor, James. *The Fiscal Crisis of the State*. New York: St. Martin's Press, 1973.

R.R.P.E. Editorial Collective. "Uneven Regional Development in Advanced Capitalism." *Review of Radical Political Economics* 10 (1972): 1–15. Special issue.

Richardson, Harry. *The New Urban Economics—and Alternatives*. New York: Academic Press, 1978.

Ridker, Ronald G., and Henning, John A. "The Determinants of Residential Property Values with Special Reference to Air Pollution." *Review of Economics and Statistics* 49 (May 1967): 246–57.

Simon, Julian L. *Basic Research Methods in Social Science*. New York: Random House, 1958.

Taeuber, Karl E., and Taeuber, Anne F. *Negroes in Cities*. Chicago: Aldine, 1965.

CHAPTER EIGHT

Using a Multiregional Econometric Model to Measure the Spatial Impacts of Federal Policies

KENNETH P. BALLARD, NORMAN J. GLICKMAN,
AND ROBERT M. WENDLING

INTRODUCTION

In recent years there has been considerable debate concerning two important issues: the impacts of federal programs and the distribution of these activities on different regions. The first issue has been raised through President Carter's National Urban Policy that requires urban impact analysis (UIA) of federal policies. Accordingly, agencies must estimate the absolute and differential effects of their policies on cities and regions. The second issue has been brought to the public's attention through arguments over the *allocation* of funding. For instance, many have argued that the "Frostbelt" states have not been receiving a fair share of grants and procurements. Alternately, others have said that this shortfall does not exist or has been significantly overstated. To date, however, little rigorous analysis of this debate has been undertaken. This paper attempts to provide an analytical mechanism which can view these types of situations in an unbiased manner.

For analytical purposes, differences in the interregional impacts of federal policies can be divided into two major sources. First, the *direct* effects of each program—that is, the amount of money spent by the Federal government in a particular area. Second, the *indirect* effects or multiplier impacts that are generated by the increased income flows resulting from direct spending. These impacts can be measured by many, currently available impact models. However, both the direct and indirect effects have important *spatial*

The authors thank Robert Dubinsky, A. Ray Grimes, Richard D. Gustely, G. Thomas Kingsley, W. Warren McHone, Georges Vernez, and Kelly Dawson for helpful comments and assistance on this paper.

dimensions which are often overlooked in policy analyses. While it is possible to use other analytical methods, models which can comprehensively capture impacts in both time and space can help provide a fuller understanding of policies' spatial implications. The use of models in UIA is demonstrated in other papers in this volume[1] as a method of aggregating disparate types of programs, and, in general, of providing a coherent analytic framework.

This paper addresses both issues by applying a modeling framework that looks at the federal funding distribution and impact analysis through integrating spatial and economic elements. This is done by employing the National-Regional Impact Evaluation System (NRIES) developed by the Bureau of Economic Analysis (BEA). The model combines 51 individual regional models into an integrated, multiregional econometric model of the United States economy. With relationships between variables based upon time series regression estimations, NRIES is used to forecast for short- and medium-term periods and to measure the impacts of individual as well as clusters of federal program policies. In the framework of UIA, the model can be used, when suitably extended, to gauge the direct and indirect spatial impacts of federal policies while providing a detailed measurement of changes to output, employment, income, and other variables.

Multiregional econometric models[2] have been used in other countries for planning and forecasting purposes. In France, for example, there is the detailed REGINA model (Courbis, 1972) which has been used in the formulation of the last two French national plans; REGINA has been successful in setting out the spatial implications of the plans. Similarly, the RENA model (Thys-Clement et al., 1973) has been used within the Belgian planning system, and CANDIDE-R has been employed in Canada (Canadian Government, 1975). These models, which build upon previous work with single-region models,[3] have demonstrated their viability for handling a wide range of policy problems. The NRIES model, though structured differently from those of other countries, is in the same tradition.

In the next section of this paper the nature and workings of NRIES are briefly described. Then, in the third section, two sets of policy simulations involving federal policies are discussed. First, there is an analysis of the spatial effects of a change in the Department of Housing and Urban Development (HUD) budget.[4] Second, the regional impacts of the federal grants-in-aid (GIA) program are examined. Here, federal GIA are artificially redistributed on an equal per capita regional basis and compared to the pres-

---

[1] *See* the chapters in this volume by Danziger et al., Holmer, and Putman for other uses of models in urban impact analysis.

[2] For other examples of multiregional econometric models, *see* Ballard and Glickman, 1977; Quantitative Analysis Unit, 1975; Courbis, 1972; Crow, 1973; Milne, Glickman, and Adams, 1978; and Thys-Clement, van Rompuy, and deCorel, 1973.

[3] *See* Glickman, 1977, for an example of a large single-region model and a review of other models.

[4] For further details, *see* Glickman and Jacobs, 1979.

ent regional distribution. In both cases the indirect (multiplier) effects generated by federal policies are estimated by NRIES. Also, in the GIA simulation, questions of interregional equity are examined. In the final section, this paper concludes with a discussion of the use of NRIES in undertaking UIAs by extending it to a Standard Metropolitan Statistical Area (SMSA) level and by integrating it with BEA's Regional Industry Multiplier System (RIMS), a process that is now being implemented in a joint HUD-BEA project.

THE NRIES MODEL[5]

NRIES is comprised of 51 state-area[6] econometric models that are integrated into a model of the United States economy (*see* Figure 1). In contrast to most other multiregion models, NRIES takes a "bottom-up" approach to regional analysis: the national model is the summation of the 51 independently constructed state models. First, each state model generates individual growth patterns as if there were 51 separate, single-region econometric models. National growth trends, in this bottom-up approach, are therefore determined by regional growth patterns, and not vice versa.

However, regions do not grow independently and this is reflected in an important feature of the NRIES model: the explicit set of interregional linkages in economic activity among all states. *Interaction variables*, derived for each state and representing distance-deflated economic activity in all other states, are included in the state variable estimations. The interaction variables are calculated individually for each state (r), variable x^j and time period (t) based upon the following formula:

$$
{}^r g_t^{x^j} = \sum_{\substack{k=1 \\ k \neq r}}^{r} \frac{{}^k x_t^j}{{}^{rk} d}
\tag{1}
$$

The activity levels of the variables x^j in all other states are scaled by the distance ${}^{rk}d$ from the own-state (r) and summed. The distance scalar ${}^{rk}d$ currently used is the geographic distance between the population centroids of each region.[7] Since interaction variables are distance-deflated, the linkages are also spatially proportioned. Thus, for example, while economic activity in California affects the economies of both Nevada and New Hampshire, the influence on Nevada is greater due to its proximity. The interaction variables

---

[5] For a more detailed description of NRIES and its structure, *see* Ballard and Wendling, 1978.

[6] For simplicity, Washington, D.C. is referred to as a "state."

[7] There are several theories explaining spatial relationships in a gravity-potential context. The simple linear distance technology has certain advantages: it is computationally simple and does not constrain the forecasting to point-in-time trading or spatial interaction patterns. *See* Carrothers, 1956, for a more detailed discussion on this topic.

FIGURE 1: NRIES Model System Flow Diagram.

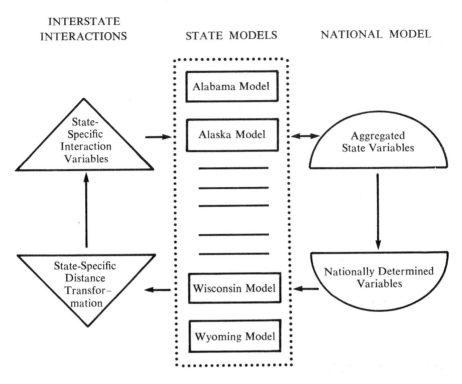

INTERSTATE
INTERACTIONS   STATE MODELS   NATIONAL MODEL

are also weighted by the mass (levels of economic activity) of the states. Here, for example, New York and Connecticut are nearly the same distance from Louisiana but the influence of New York on the Louisiana economy is much greater than Connecticut's due to New York's larger size.

The NRIES behavioral equations are econometrically estimated by Ordinary Least Squares regression for each variable in each region using annual time series data from 1955 to 1976. This results in a total of 11,730 equations (230 variables times 51 regions). All equations in a given region are aggregated to form the state "model"; the state models are then aggregated to form the complete NRIES model.

Looking again to Figure 1, the structure of NRIES can be represented simply by the three columns. In the middle column are the state models, the core of the multiregional system. The left column represents the interaction variables that provide the interregional linkages. The right column shows that the national model is two integrated components: variables that are regionally derived (from the middle column) and variables that are always the same for each state. In equation 2 the structural relationship is presented in the more common modeling matrix format.

$$^r\mathbf{X}_t = A \, ^r\mathbf{X}_t + B \, ^r\mathbf{Z}_t + C \, ^r\mathbf{N}_t + \, ^r\mathbf{U}_t \qquad (2)$$

The value of activities of economic and demographic variables (X) within region (r) in time period (t) is determined by three types of explanatory variables: (1) *regional endogenous* (X), (2) *regional and national exogenous* (Z), and (3) *national* and *interregional endogenous* (N). U represents the stochastic error term. A, B, and C are matrices of estimated coefficients. Regional endogenous variables include the region-specific variables that determine regional economic or demographic activity. For example, regional endogenous variables include local manufacturing employment which is determined in the model by local manufacturing output. Exogenous variables include federal GIA payments to Hawaii (regional exogenous) and Federal Reserve Bank policies (national exogenous). The national and interregional endogenous variables include the national aggregates, national variables estimated stochastically, and the interaction variables.

There are several advantages to the approach employed here. First, because it is an interregional model, NRIES can be used to analyze the regional or spatial distribution of policy impacts. For example, the model can measure the effects of changes in one region upon all other regions in the economy. Second, the system can simultaneously determine the level of both national and regional activity. In contrast, most existing multiregional models distribute given national totals among regions (a "top-down" approach), and thereby ignore the effects that changes in regional activity could have on the Nation as a whole. Third, by integrating regional and national models (the totals in the national model equal the sum of the 51 regional models), the NRIES structure insures that the regional activity will always be consistent with forecasts of national activity. In contrast, individual state models often produce inaccurate forecasts of growth when no national framework is present. Finally, NRIES is able to examine the effects of concurrent national and regional policy changes. This type of application might include the analysis of the effects of a construction project built in one state but funded by a federal tax imposed on all states.

THE SPATIAL IMPACTS OF FEDERAL PROGRAMS

The following analysis examines the empirical results from using the NRIES approach to spatial policy study. While not explicitly "urban," this study focuses on interstate activity in an attempt to capture the differential effects that flows generated by federal programs will have on state economies. When presenting the results, emphasis is given to the *macroeconomic* effects of Federal government programs: the implications for the income, employment, and output sectors of the economy due to changes in government spending.

In order to estimate the levels of impacts, the NRIES model first simulates the growth of the U.S. economy over a 1978 to 1982 forecast period under a "most likely" scenario about economic development. This is called a *control solution* and forms a baseline for comparison with our policy simulation experiments. In a second, or *alternate*, simulation, the model forecasts the same time period but with a changed set of federal policy variables. The results, obtained by contrasting the two forecasts, are presented and discussed for the United States as a whole, the eight BEA multistate regions, and the 50 states and the District of Columbia.

The two sets of scenarios discussed involve the effects of changes in federal spending policies and GIA programs in a multiregional framework. First is an analysis of the economic impact of an increase in the HUD budget. Second, in a hypothetical scenario, the Federal government grants-in-aid payments to state and local governments are redistributed based solely on regional population levels. This second simulation is intended to look at the income-generating and redistributive properties of federal aid payments.

The spatial impacts of the HUD budget

As Glickman notes in Chapter 1 of this volume, HUD, as most other Federal government agencies, is now required to submit UIAs for each of its *major new initiatives*. While the idea of impact analysis, as contained in Environmental Impact Statements, is not new, the relevance of UIAs for Federal government policy and planning efforts may be quite significant. Federal government programs are unlike the activity of many business and local government agencies because most federal programs are spread over the entire country. Thus, it is not only necessary to measure the impacts *within* each area but also those representing the *interaction* among the different areas.

The first simulation examines the macroeconomic impact that a doubling of the HUD budget expenditures in 1978 might have on the growth of the United States and the individual state economies. This analysis goes beyond the directives of the Office of Management and Budget (OMB) and looks at the *entire budget*, not just HUD's new initiatives.[8]

HUD has responsibility for a wide variety of programs, with budgetary authority of nearly $34 billion and outlays of $6 billion in FY 1977. The two dominant program types are subsidized housing (which includes Section 8 and public housing) and Community Development Block Grants (CDBG). Between them they involve about three-quarters of HUD's annual outlays. For instance, subsidized housing accounted for 42 percent of all outlays and CDBG for 36 percent in Fiscal 1977. The remainder of the direct spending was allocated among a number of smaller programs. In addition to the direct spending, the existence of long-term HUD housing subsidies (primarily in assisted housing programs) through its budget authority, induces large amounts of private construction activity. This "induced" construction was estimated at $3.6 billion in Fiscal 1977 and is discussed in detail in Glickman and Jacobs (1979). The major categories of the HUD budget and induced

---

[8] This extension has been proposed by Glickman earlier in this volume and is carried out here as a prototype analysis.

construction that are considered in the modeling effort are listed below and in Table 1:

Community development block grants: These payments account for one-half of the current budget. Funds are distributed by formula to localities for spending on urban development projects.[9]

Section 8: Subsidies for building and operating low income housing units. The program consists of three components: new, existing, and substantial rehabilitation. (*See* Rasmussen in this volume for a detailed discussion of these programs.)

Public housing assistance: The current year's expenditures for the operating, modernization, and debt service in public housing units.

Leased housing subsidies: Subsidies to low income rentals. This is the predecessor to Section 8—Existing. Here, a local public housing authority rents private units and sublets them to eligible individuals at a reduced rent. The difference between the cost to HUD and the receipts from renters is the subsidy.

Induced construction: New building and rehabilitation of older buildings that result from a HUD commitment to subsidize future operations from Section 8 and new public housing. Unlike the other categories, this is not a budgetary item. Increases in private construction activity in a given year are *induced* by a HUD guarantee to builders to subsidize rents over the useful life of the units. Since this HUD-induced activity creates important additional impacts on local economies, it is included in the analysis.

Section 701 planning grants: Aid for local land use planning and zoning efforts.

These categories do *not* comprise the entire HUD budget or activities. Specifically excluded are the secondary mortgage market (GNMA) and mortgage insurance (FHA), which, although important, have ambiguous macroeconomic effects. The $5,092-million total HUD spending, noted in Table 1, *does* represent 83 percent of all HUD outlays in fiscal 1977. It is assumed in the modeling exercise that all programs are doubled in 1978 and that the spatial allocation of each remains the same as in the previous year. Table 1 shows HUD's direct outlays and induced construction, by state and BEA multistate region, for the nine categories examined in the analysis.

While the Department operates in all states, the levels of direct expenditures and commitments vary considerably among the different programs and states. In Fiscal 1977 for example, CDBG funds were distributed roughly in proportion to the relative population of each state: from New York and California, with about 10 percent apiece, down to the less urban states of Wyoming and Nevada. In contrast, the levels of Section 701 planning grants show much less of a relationship with spatial demographics. Section 8 expenditures were much greater in California, almost twice its population weight. New York received over 17 percent of the Section 8—new and

---

[9] *See* Glickman and Bunce (Chapter 22) for a discussion of the CDBG formula for allocating funds. Under a 1978 formula change, less emphasis in CDBG funding is given to population and a higher emphasis to poverty, age of housing stock, and the lag in the population growth rate.

TABLE 1: MAJOR EXPENDITURE & COMMITMENT CATEGORIES IN THE DEPARTMENT OF HOUSING AND URBAN DEVELOPMENT (FISCAL 1977)

	COMMUNITY DEVELOPMENT BLOCK GRANTS	SECTION 701 PLANNING GRANTS	SECTION 8 NEW AND REHABIL.	SECTION 8 EXISTING	PUBLIC HOUSING OPERATING SUBSIDIES	PUBLIC HOUSING MODERNIZATION EXPENDITURES	DEBT SERVICE	LEASED HOUSING SUBSIDIES	H.U.D. TOTAL	DIRECT SPEND. PER CAPITA DOLLARS	CONSTRUCTION "INDUCED" BY COMMITMENTS Mil. $
				MILLIONS OF DOLLARS							
UNITED STATES	3040.1	61.5	40.6	326.6	522.0	52.9	858.9	188.4	5091.7	23.4	3564.8
NEW ENGLAND	220.3	3.2	3.7	23.4	53.2	3.8	54.3	10.6	372.6	30.4	318.2
MIDEAST	742.1	9.4	13.2	60.1	144.3	6.6	229.3	32.7	1238.1	29.3	1118.8
GREAT LAKES	470.2	9.7	6.2	35.6	76.4	10.6	135.7	23.0	767.2	18.6	546.2
PLAINS	222.5	5.6	3.1	23.5	25.2	1.9	60.7	9.1	351.8	20.7	265.9
SOUTHEAST	648.5	17.7	8.2	68.6	95.5	21.7	213.3	39.2	1113.4	22.6	738.3
SOUTHWEST	271.7	6.3	1.5	24.6	38.1	1.2	79.3	10.7	433.2	22.2	157.9
ROCKY MOUNTAIN	65.6	2.3	1.5	4.9	5.0	1.5	11.8	2.5	94.7	15.7	64.0
FAR WEST	399.1	7.4	3.9	85.8	84.1	5.6	74.5	60.2	721.0	25.8	355.0
1. ALABAMA	51.3	1.6	.7	.3	9.0	4.5	25.0	3.9	96.3	25.7	66.7
2. ALASKA	7.3	.4	.4	2.0	1.1	.2	6.3	.3	18.0	44.3	9.8
3. ARIZONA	22.9	.7	.2	3.9	5.2	.4	9.9	3.7	46.6	19.5	20.5
4. ARKANSAS	40.7	1.0	.2	3.5	.4	.4	11.3	.7	62.7	28.9	13.6
5. CALIFORNIA	310.4	4.5	3.2	67.4	68.3	1.2	27.9	48.9	532.0	23.9	274.2
6. COLORADO	30.5	.8	.5	4.6	2.9	.3	7.2	1.6	45.9	17.2	37.6
7. CONNECTICUT	68.2	.3	.1	1.0	11.2	1.1	12.6	2.2	101.3	32.6	49.5
8. DELAWARE	7.4	.1	.0	1.5	1.5	.0	2.5	.2	13.1	22.5	8.2
9. DISTRICT OF COLUMBIA	41.0	.0	.4	.0	8.4	.7	8.4	1.4	60.7	85.6	34.0
10. FLORIDA	105.4	2.4	.8	14.9	19.8	.7	24.9	9.0	172.9	20.1	76.2
11. GEORGIA	70.9	1.9	.5	6.1	14.4	.5	31.4	7.2	133.9	26.3	57.8
12. HAWAII	12.9	.2	.2	3.3	1.8	.1	3.6	1.7	24.0	25.7	16.9
13. IDAHO	10.3	.1	.1	.9	.6	.5	.9	.7	13.7	15.4	9.0
14. ILLINOIS	130.7	2.4	1.9	7.3	30.7	7.1	56.4	9.4	245.8	21.8	177.0
15. INDIANA	51.3	1.3	.4	4.1	9.0	.7	14.1	2.6	83.7	15.7	29.4
16. IOWA	31.6	.9	.4	2.7	2.3	.2	2.0	.8	40.9	14.1	29.4
17. KANSAS	37.2	.6	.4	.7	1.4	.1	8.3	.9	49.0	20.2	35.9
18. KENTUCKY	37.3	1.6	1.1	2.5	6.2	2.1	16.7	1.9	87.3	23.0	89.5
19. LOUISIANA	44.2	1.3	.3	8.1	8.9	1.3	25.1	2.9	89.2	23.0	34.6
20. MAINE	15.3	.5	.4	2.4	2.5	.3	16.5	.2	25.2	23.0	28.6
21. MARYLAND	54.7	1.1	2.0	12.8	32.6	1.4	25.7	6.7	89.6	21.7	63.4
22. MASSACHUSETTS	104.2	1.2	2.8	8.6	5.6	.4	19.7	1.6	187.0	32.5	171.9
23. MICHIGAN	117.3	1.9	1.0	8.7	5.8	.4	18.3	2.6	152.4	16.5	109.0
24. MINNESOTA	60.4	1.2	.8	2.1	3.1	4.0	7.2	1.4	56.9	25.3	84.1
25. MISSISSIPPI	62.5	.8	.1	6.5	7.9	.1	19.2	2.8	102.0	23.7	39.5
26. MISSOURI	62.5	.5	.2	6.5	7.9	.6	19.2	2.8	102.0	21.1	72.5
27. MONTANA	9.0	.2	.1	1.2	.1	.3	2.1	.1	13.6	17.7	8.8
28. NEBRASKA	12.8	.3	.1	1.4	1.6	.1	5.5	.8	23.6	15.1	18.6
29. NEVADA	3.6	.2	.1	.7	2.1	.1	2.9	1.1	30.1	44.9	16.2
30. NEW HAMPSHIRE	8.2	.1	.1	1.6	1.6	.1	2.5	.8	16.4	18.9	11.5
31. NEW JERSEY	103.5	1.0	2.5	9.7	26.8	3.3	40.3	6.8	193.9	26.4	210.0
32. NEW MEXICO	21.2	.7	2.0	2.4	1.4	.1	8.7	1.8	34.1	28.0	55.4
33. NEW YORK	320.9	3.7	7.0	29.2	68.2	2.3	106.7	17.4	555.5	31.2	580.7
34. NORTH CAROLINA	72.6	7.6	.6	12.6	10.5	1.4	26.8	5.0	131.1	27.2	57.1
35. NORTH DAKOTA	8.9	.1	.1	2.4	1.7	.2	3.8	1.0	17.8	27.2	9.9
36. OHIO	133.9	1.3	1.3	11.0	25.1	2.2	30.8	1.6	219.8	20.5	123.4
37. OKLAHOMA	41.6	1.1	.2	2.6	5.5	.6	4.3	1.6	72.4	25.4	25.3
38. OREGON	19.2	.2	.2	5.6	5.8	.4	55.1	5.3	40.8	17.0	216.3
39. PENNSYLVANIA	20.4	2.7	2.5	11.6	30.2	.7	6.1	.6	325.3	27.7	43.2
40. RHODE ISLAND	28.2	.5	.1	2.1	3.2	.2	4.5	.6	34.5	36.8	52.6
41. SOUTH CAROLINA	9.1	.2	.2	2.8	2.8	.2	22.9	4.3	45.8	15.8	15.5
42. SOUTH DAKOTA	62.8	1.4	.4	1.4	9.0	.2	40.5	5.4	17.5	25.5	98.6
43. TENNESSEE	186.0	3.8	.9	6.7	26.1	.6	40.3	.4	280.1	21.4	96.7
44. TEXAS	186.0	1.2	.9	16.8	26.1	.6	40.3	.2	16.5	12.6	6.6
45. UTAH	12.2	.4	.4	.9	1.1	.7	1.3	.2	16.5	12.6	6.6
46. VERMONT	3.8	.3	.3	.9	1.3	.7	4.0	.2	8.2	16.7	13.5
47. VIRGINIA	77.7	1.5	1.3	5.6	6.5	.7	14.0	1.1	108.4	20.9	102.3
48. WASHINGTON	45.9	1.0	.2	6.8	5.4	3.4	9.5	3.8	76.1	20.6	25.4
49. WEST VIRGINIA	25.0	1.6	.6	1.9	2.0	.2	5.7	.6	36.5	19.6	49.7
50. WISCONSIN	36.9	1.3	1.0	8.6	6.1	1.0	9.7	6.5	65.5	14.0	77.6
51. WYOMING	3.6	.2	.0	.1	.2	.0	.5	.2	5.0	11.7	2.6

rehabilitation subsidies (and the Mideast received more than any of the other seven regions), while California received over 20 percent of the Section 8—existing subsidies (and the Far West received more than any other region). Public housing assistance is divided into three groups: operating subsidies, modernization expenditures, and debt service. As can be seen in Table 1, the net gainers in these expenditures were Illinois and the Southeast states (for example, Alabama and Georgia). Leased housing subsidies were heavily weighted to the Far West and, in particular, to California, which received 26 percent of the total. Induced construction was concentrated in New England and the Mideast (primarily Massachusetts and New York), while California and the Southwest showed percentages far below their population weights.

Since NRIES uses budgetary accounting data that employs a National Income and Products Accounts (NIPA) and a U.S. Bureau of the Census framework, it is necessary first to translate the fiscal data (shown in Table 1) into an accounting system that is consistent with the model.[10] This translation (*see* Appendix 1 for detailed methodologies) has been provided for the HUD categories and is given in Table 2. The eight major NIPA-Census categories are (1) GIA payments to local governments, primarily composed of the CDBG and Section 701 Grants; (2) income transfers to persons, payments for subsidized housing under Section 8, public housing, and leased housing; and (3) to (8) six gross-output categories that result from the direct provision of goods and services to the community from the industrial or business sectors. Estimates of each output sector's level is made by allocating the HUD activities to the supplying sectors, primarily through input-output relationships. As can be seen in Table 2, gross-output originating is the largest of the three major categories, making up over 80 percent of HUD total direct impact. The construction sector (owing primarily to public housing modernization expenditures and induced construction) contains the largest level of gross-output originating (almost one-quarter). GIA and income transfers ot persons account for 14 and 5 percent, respectively, of the total HUD expenditures and commitments.

Having transformed the data to fit the model's specifications, the alternate simulation was calculated and compared to the control solution. Table 3 lists the resulting regional impacts of the HUD budget on personal income and gross output originating by state and by BEA region. Each of the table's two sections contains a column listing the initial impacts (year 1), the "dynamic" impacts (years 2 to 5), the total impact, and the resultant "augmented" multiplier. The multiplier is calculated here as the total impact divided by the total HUD outlays in 1978, but includes the effects of induced construc-

---

[10] The approximations of the nature of HUD impacts are in some instances dictated by the structure of NRIES.

TABLE 2: TRANSLATION OF MAJOR H.U.D EXPENDITURE-COMMITMENT CATEGORIES INTO ECONOMETRIC MODEL ACCOUNTING FRAMEWORK

	GRANTS-IN-AID TO LOCAL GOVERNMENTS	INCOME TRANSFERS TO PERSONS	CONSTRUCTION	MANUFACTURING	UTILITIES	TRADE	FINANCE	SERVICE
				GROSS OUTPUT ORIGINATING — MILLIONS OF DOLLARS				
UNITED STATES	1178.1	472.3	2133.7	1398.3	495.7	880.2	1109.4	988.1
NEW ENGLAND	84.5	32.0	177.7	116.5	44.4	73.3	73.9	88.4
MIDEAST	282.4	90.1	613.8	402.3	140.7	253.3	253.3	280.6
GREAT LAKES	182.2	55.1	328.9	215.5	75.1	135.7	171.2	149.8
PLAINS	87.0	30.4	157.2	103.0	32.3	64.8	78.4	64.5
SOUTHEAST	255.4	98.7	450.5	295.2	100.0	185.8	266.0	199.5
SOUTHWEST	105.9	31.3	127.7	83.7	31.0	52.7	66.8	63.4
ROCKY MOUNTAIN	26.2	7.7	41.4	27.1	2.7	17.1	16.3	15.7
FAR WEST	154.4	127.5	236.8	155.0	63.4	97.6	115.5	125.9
1. ALABAMA	20.4	4.1	39.9	26.1	9.0	16.5	28.9	18.0
2. ALASKA	9.4	2.4	5.6	3.7	1.2	2.3	7.2	2.4
3. ARIZONA	9.1	6.8	13.5	8.8	3.7	5.6	12.2	7.4
4. ARKANSAS	15.9	5.0	15.3	10.1	3.5	6.3	13.4	6.9
5. CALIFORNIA	118.9	101.6	182.1	119.3	49.9	75.1	60.1	99.1
6. COLORADO	12.0	3.5	22.0	14.4	4.3	9.1	9.6	8.6
7. CONNECTICUT	25.8	6.2	36.2	23.7	9.2	14.9	3.1	18.2
8. DELAWARE	3.0	1.1	5.0	3.3	1.3	2.1	3.1	2.5
9. DIST OF COLUMBIA	15.9	1.5	23.2	15.2	6.3	9.6	10.5	12.5
10. FLORIDA	39.4	21.0	54.2	35.5	14.7	22.4	32.8	29.1
11. GEORGIA	28.0	11.7	40.2	26.3	10.8	16.6	21.4	21.4
12. HAWAII	5.0	4.5	9.7	6.3	2.1	5.1	5.4	4.1
13. IDAHO	4.1	1.2	6.1	4.0	1.1	2.5	1.4	2.3
14. ILLINOIS	50.6	6.3	108.8	67.4	23.4	42.4	67.2	51.0
15. INDIANA	14.1	6.3	35.6	23.3	8.3	14.7	18.0	16.6
16. IOWA	14.1	3.2	19.1	12.5	3.7	7.9	4.1	7.2
17. KANSAS	15.3	5.5	22.9	15.0	4.0	9.4	10.3	8.0
18. KENTUCKY	17.5	8.7	44.3	29.0	8.8	18.3	21.1	17.6
19. LOUISIANA	6.1	2.8	24.6	16.1	6.6	10.2	24.9	13.2
20. MAINE	6.1	1.2	14.8	9.7	3.1	6.1	5.1	6.1
21. MARYLAND	21.1	6.8	37.9	24.8	8.8	15.6	20.5	17.5
22. MASSACHUSETTS	39.9	18.3	92.2	60.4	24.7	38.0	36.2	49.2
23. MICHIGAN	44.6	10.5	70.6	46.3	12.7	29.1	26.4	25.4
24. MINNESOTA	23.3	3.4	47.2	30.9	10.1	19.5	23.9	20.1
25. MISSISSIPPI	14.8	8.6	25.8	16.9	5.2	10.7	9.8	10.0
26. MISSOURI	24.5	7.4	43.4	28.4	9.2	17.2	24.1	18.8
27. MONTANA	3.7	1.2	10.4	6.8	2.3	4.3	2.7	3.3
28. NEBRASKA	5.2	2.0	7.1	4.7	1.7	4.7	6.6	4.7
29. NEVADA	1.6	1.6	6.5	4.3	1.6	2.7	2.3	3.3
30. NEW HAMPSHIRE	3.3	1.8	10.4	6.8	2.2	4.3	3.2	3.3
31. NEW JERSEY	39.2	16.1	107.3	70.3	24.1	26.7	51.5	50.4
32. NEW MEXICO	8.4	15.6	40.2	4.3	2.2	4.6	4.3	4.4
33. NEW YORK	121.9	45.6	304.7	199.7	68.4	125.7	138.6	137.2
34. NORTH CAROLINA	3.6	15.5	40.7	26.4	9.5	16.6	32.7	29.0
35. NORTH DAKOTA	4.0	3.0	6.0	4.0	1.5	2.5	7.8	1.0
36. OHIO	52.1	16.0	81.1	53.2	20.5	33.5	45.1	40.9
37. OKLAHOMA	16.3	3.3	20.1	13.2	4.8	8.3	22.2	9.6
38. OREGON	8.2	19.0	9.8	6.4	3.4	8.0	6.5	9.4
39. PENNSYLVANIA	81.3	8.0	135.8	89.0	30.5	56.0	69.1	60.9
40. RHODE ISLAND	7.7	4.2	21.8	14.3	5.2	11.6	9.0	8.8
41. SOUTH CAROLINA	11.5	1.9	28.0	18.4	5.2	11.6	5.5	10.5
42. SOUTH DAKOTA	3.8	10.3	5.4	3.6	1.1	3.4	9.0	3.4
43. TENNESSEE	24.7	19.6	54.1	35.4	11.2	22.3	28.9	22.4
44. TEXAS	72.0	1.2	83.0	54.1	21.1	34.2	50.5	42.0
45. UTAH	4.8	1.7	5.6	5.4	1.2	2.5	1.9	2.7
46. VERMONT	1.7	6.8	2.3	3.6	1.4	2.3	2.0	2.9
47. VIRGINIA	29.9	9.2	58.5	38.3	11.1	24.1	19.7	22.7
48. WASHINGTON	17.8	2.5	22.3	14.6	5.2	9.2	12.9	10.3
49. WEST VIRGINIA	9.7	9.7	25.3	16.6	4.5	10.4	8.1	9.1
50. WISCONSIN	14.9	9.7	38.8	25.5	7.9	16.0	14.5	15.9
51. WYOMING	1.5	.3	1.9	1.3	.4	.8	.7	.7

TABLE 3 : REGIONAL IMPACTS OF THE H.L.D. BUDGET ON PERSONAL INCOME AND GROSS (STATE) PRODUCT ORIGINATING

| | ADDITIONS TO PERSONAL INCOME | | | | ADDITIONS TO GROSS OUTPUT ORIGINATING | | | |
| | – – – – MILLIONS OF DOLLARS – – – – | | | AUGMENTED MULTIPLIER | – – – – MILLIONS OF DOLLARS – – – – | | | AUGMENTED MULTIPLIER |
	YEAR 1	YEARS 2-5	TOTAL		YEAR 1	YEARS 2-5	TOTAL	
UNITED STATES	6476.9	11568.1	18445.0	3.6	14319.1	13182.4	27501.4	5.4
NEW ENGLAND	358.4	740.6	1099.0	2.9	1006.8	852.5	1859.2	5.0
MIDEAST	1766.2	3426.1	5192.3	2.9	3917.7	4055.3	7972.0	6.4
GREAT LAKES	1160.6	2567.6	3728.2	4.0	2629.3	2727.2	5356.9	7.0
PLAINS	402.5	659.0	1061.5	3.0	896.9	469.0	1365.9	5.0
SOUTHEAST	1535.0	2755.9	4290.9	3.1	3128.7	2735.6	5864.3	5.3
SOUTHWEST	379.1	769.6	1148.7	2.7	907.3	799.8	1707.2	3.0
ROCKY MOUNTAIN	109.0	100.8	205.8	2.2	213.5	87.9	301.4	3.2
FAR WEST	788.1	1036.4	1824.5	2.5	1618.8	1455.1	3073.5	4.3
1. ALABAMA	101.4	142.2	243.6	2.5	221.1	125.4	346.5	3.6
2. ALASKA	9.1	9.1	18.1	1.0	26.2	27.3	53.5	3.0
3. ARIZONA	64.8	126.0	190.9	4.1	118.6	170.0	288.6	6.2
4. ARKANSAS	43.7	104.3	148.0	2.4	122.9	129.2	252.1	4.2
5. CALIFORNIA	610.7	745.5	1356.1	2.5	1230.9	1086.5	2317.3	4.0
6. COLORADO	74.2	81.9	156.1	3.0	126.2	32.9	159.1	3.5
7. CONNECTICUT	75.1	180.0	255.1	5.1	234.1	200.2	434.2	9.1
8. DELAWARE	18.8	118.6	137.4	5.2	175.7	172.4	348.1	4.1
9. DIST OF COLUMBIA	297.4	598.9	896.3	5.3	484.7	377.4	862.1	4.5
10. FLORIDA	212.1	357.9	570.0	4.3	425.6	377.8	805.3	5.5
11. GEORGIA	23.6	37.5	61.2	2.5	46.3	44.5	90.8	6.0
12. HAWAII	8.7	12.6	21.2	1.6	31.9	23.0	54.5	3.8
13. IDAHO	304.7	829.6	1134.2	4.6	658.1	810.1	1468.2	4.0
14. ILLINOIS	180.4	346.4	526.8	6.3	344.1	374.3	718.4	6.0
15. INDIANA	51.1	90.4	141.5	3.5	99.9	68.9	168.8	8.6
16. IOWA	56.5	87.8	144.2	2.9	140.3	68.8	209.2	4.1
17. KANSAS	115.9	188.9	304.9	4.3	252.3	203.5	455.5	4.3
18. KENTUCKY	86.1	173.3	254.4	3.0	169.2	202.3	371.5	6.5
19. LOUISIANA	31.7	91.5	123.2	4.9	69.7	87.8	157.4	4.3
20. MAINE	122.4	199.5	321.9	3.6	228.8	224.6	453.4	6.2
21. MARYLAND	154.0	328.3	482.3	2.6	488.5	399.8	888.3	4.8
22. MASSACHUSETTS	249.7	483.8	733.5	4.8	638.5	646.2	1284.7	5.1
23. MICHIGAN	124.4	196.2	320.6	3.2	268.0	112.4	380.4	8.4
24. MINNESOTA	108.4	55.9	112.5	2.2	121.7	81.8	213.4	3.8
25. MISSISSIPPI	10.4	213.3	402.2	1.3	265.1	187.7	457.7	4.5
26. MISSOURI	26.8	5.6	17.1	3.7	58.0	7.7	65.7	3.8
27. MONTANA	31.9	29.1	86.4	2.0	78.4	26.6	85.7	2.4
28. NEBRASKA	307.4	58.0	61.0	5.0	61.1	35.0	113.4	3.6
29. NEVADA	35.2	657.0	82.7	5.0	65.5	71.4	132.4	8.1
30. NEW HAMPSHIRE	827.7	49.0	964.4	2.8	655.5	513.2	1169.8	6.0
31. NEW JERSEY	153.3	1283.3	84.2	3.3	73.7	66.6	140.3	4.1
32. NEW MEXICO	16.0	278.6	2111.1	1.4	1911.0	1997.0	3908.0	7.0
33. NEW YORK	308.4	8.1	431.9	4.3	336.4	348.1	684.6	5.2
34. NORTH CAROLINA	54.8	645.6	24.1	3.2	27.9	-.3	27.6	1.6
35. NORTH DAKOTA	53.2	91.8	954.0	4.8	722.6	680.7	1403.3	6.4
36. OHIO	413.2	86.2	146.6	6.4	149.0	82.6	231.6	3.2
37. OKLAHOMA	55.3	1150.2	129.5	6.7	872.2	109.8	197.1	4.8
38. OREGON	74.2	153.1	1563.4	2.1	951.9	1123.3	2075.2	6.4
39. PENNSYLVANIA	19.3	33.5	222.5	7.0	151.0	65.2	185.2	6.7
40. RHODE ISLAND	190.2	336.8	222.8	3.7	151.2	154.2	357.6	2.1
41. SOUTH CAROLINA	224.3	502.7	22.2	2.4	33.1	403.0	771.1	7.0
42. SOUTH DAKOTA	12.2	14.3	527.0	4.2	358.1	480.7	1046.7	3.7
43. TENNESSEE	13.5	20.6	727.0	1.6	566.0	1.5	3.9	2.4
44. TEXAS	156.3	202.0	64.4	4.2	23.8	28.2	61.6	7.5
45. UTAH	69.5	129.0	34.1	3.2	33.5	162.6	503.9	4.6
46. VERMONT	58.0	70.0	352.3	2.6	341.3	152.0	301.8	4.0
47. VIRGINIA	117.4	262.4	198.5	3.5	149.8	78.4	202.6	5.6
48. WASHINGTON	3.5	5.4	128.0	5.8	124.2	215.9	481.9	7.4
49. WEST VIRGINIA			379.8		266.0		15.5	3.1
50. WISCONSIN			8.9	1.8	6.6	8.9		

tion in the numerator and excludes government expenditures in the denominator. The multiplier is therefore larger than a standard multiplier.

Generally, the initial effects to key economic indicators primarily reflect the size of the initial HUD stimulus for that particular region. As can be seen from column 2, the dynamic effects to regions (and the United States as a whole) are usually of greater magnitude than the initial impact. This occurs because the region is no longer affected solely by the initial impact, but rather benefits from a continuing demand, or stimulus, of economic activity flowing over time and space throughout the economy.

For the United States as a whole, the 1978 HUD outlays and induced construction of $8,655.8 million (the sum of row 1 of Table 2) generated a total impact of $18,445 million on personal income and $27,501.4 million on the gross national product (GNP). The ratio of the impacts on personal income and GNP to 1978 HUD spending and commitments is 2.1 and 3.2, respectively. The multipliers in columns 4 and 8 are, however, larger since the construction induced by HUD commitments has no current cost to the Federal government and, as mentioned earlier, has been excluded from the denominator of the augmented multiplier calculations.

Table 3 shows that there are appreciable differences in both the size of impacts and multipliers among regions. The Mideast, Southeast, and Great Lakes (and the states of New York and California) showed the greatest first-year impact to personal income. The indirect impacts generated in the next four years were relatively larger in industrial states such as Illinois, Michigan, and Indiana. Overall, however, New York had the largest absolute impact ($2.1 billion) over the five years, followed by Pennsylvania ($1.6 billion). The augmented personal-income multipliers, listed in the fourth column, can be ranked by comparing regions that benefited the most per dollar of HUD expenditure. The average for the United States was 3.6, with the Great Lakes having the highest (4.9) and the Rocky Mountains the lowest (2.2). Indiana had an extremely high personal-income multiplier, as did other states with a high concentration of manufacturing activity. This is expected since manufacturing demand is the most "elastic" economic sector, given changes in the United States economy growth, generated here by the HUD budget. States that did not benefit relative to HUD expenditures (for example, those with low multipliers) were basically those that do not have diversified industrial bases or have very "open" economies, such as Alaska, North and South Dakota, and Montana.

Additions to gross-output originating were generated in a similar regional pattern to the personal-income impacts. This is expected due to the close relationship between income and output. New York, California, Pennsylvania, and Illinois registered the greatest total gross-output impacts over the five-year period. While New York had one of the highest augmented gross-output multipliers, California's was well below the nation's average of 5.4. California's high proportion of service industries and government makes it more stable and thus not as conducive as are some other states to incremental feed-back effects from United States economic growth. Such effects are highlighted again by extremely high gross-output multipliers for the states which have the highest proportions of manufacturing relative to the state's total economy —Delaware, Indiana, and Michigan. The manufacturing belt (the Great Lakes and Mideast) had the highest augmented gross-output multiplier among BEA regions at 7.0 and 6.4 respectively, with the lowest at 3.2 for the Rocky Mountains.

Tables 4 and 5 list the regional impacts of the HUD budget on employment, construction output, the net change on per capita income, and the major impacts expressed as a percent of the United States total by state and BEA region. The first three columns in Table 4 show that changes in employment were generated in a similar pattern to the personal income impacts. Nearly one million jobs were created nationally, mostly in the Mideast, Southeast, and Great Lakes. The impacts on the construction sector were the most varied and, unlike the other major economic indicators, nearly three-quarters of the impact occurred in the first year. Additions to construction industry output amount to $2.2 billion over five years, over half in the Mideast and Southeast.

The last two columns of Table 4 are of major significance for they help to answer a crucial question: Defining per capita income as the measure of benefit, who gained the most by the regional distribution pattern of HUD expenditures? The District of Columbia registered the highest per capita increase to personal income at $194. This was followed by net gains in Pennsylvania, New Jersey, and Rhode Island. Utah registered the smallest increase, $20, followed by Wyoming at $21, then Montana and Idaho. The Rocky Mountains showed the lowest per capita regional increase, $35, compared to the Mideast which showed the highest, $122. This regional difference occurs in part because of the lower proportion of urban dwellers in the Rocky Mountain region. The United States averaged a per capita income gain of $85 that, based upon the personal-income multiplier mentioned earlier, was about three and one-half times greater than the initial HUD expenditure increase.

Table 5 also shows the regional output impacts expressed as a percent of the United States. About 70 percent of the impacts went to three regions: the Mideast, Great Lakes, and Southeast. Since these regions have only 61 percent of the Nation's population, they were the main gainers on a per capita basis as shown in Table 6. The shares of gross-output impacts for those regions compared to their population proportions were 1.50, 1.06, and 1.01, respectively. A value of 1.00 would denote that a region benefited in exact proportion to its population. The regions gaining least on a per capita basis were the Rocky Mountains (0.39) and the Far West (0.63). Comparisons to income are also made in Table 6. The Mideast has the highest ratio of output impacts to personal income (1.38); the other principal gainers were New England (1.17) and the Southeast (1.14).

	ADDITIONS TO EMPLOYMENT (THOUSANDS OF MAN YEARS)			ADDITIONS TO CONSTRUCTION OUTPUT (MILLIONS OF DOLLARS)			NET CHANGE IN PER CAPITA INCOME	
	YEAR 1	YEARS 2-5	TOTAL	YEAR 1	YEARS 2-5	TOTAL	DOLLARS	RANK
UNITED STATES	342.5	577.5	919.9	1657.7	535.9	2193.7	84.6	
NEW ENGLAND	21.1	37.2	58.2	132.9	63.2	196.1	89.7	3
MIDEAST	78.3	145.3	223.7	478.6	192.5	671.1	122.5	1
GREAT LAKES	60.8	115.1	175.9	238.6	50.5	288.5	99.5	2
PLAINS	22.7	35.1	57.9	101.5	-20.3	81.2	62.6	5
SOUTHEAST	94.4	146.7	241.1	398.0	122.7	520.7	85.2	4
SOUTHWEST	23.5	41.4	64.9	114.2	55.8	170.0	58.8	7
ROCKY MOUNTAIN	5.9	4.3	10.1	29.0	-1.0	28.0	34.7	8
FAR WEST	35.9	52.4	88.4	169.6	72.5	242.1	60.2	6
1. ALABAMA	6.1	7.9	14.0	29.4	9.6	39.0	65.1	34
2. ALASKA	.5	.3	.8	3.4	2.1	5.5	44.7	46
3. ARIZONA	3.9	8.3	12.2	13.0	20.5	33.6	80.0	20
4. ARKANSAS	3.1	6.6	9.7	10.2	12.1	22.3	68.1	29
5. CALIFORNIA	27.0	38.0	64.9	125.7	62.4	188.1	61.0	36
6. COLORADO	4.0	2.5	6.5	16.7	-2.1	14.7	82.0	18
7. CONNECTICUT	4.5	8.0	12.6	21.7	8.5	30.2	82.1	15
8. DELAWARE	.8	1.7	2.5	3.2	4.8	8.0	128.0	5
9. DIST OF COLUMBIA	1.8	2.0	3.7	19.1	-2.4	16.6	193.2	1
10. FLORIDA	16.2	29.4	45.6	78.1	-12.4	66.6	104.1	10
11. GEORGIA	13.7	19.5	33.3	44.0	24.0	69.0	112.0	9
12. HAWAII	1.1	1.8	2.9	5.8	.9	5.8	67.3	31
13. IDAHO	1.6	.7	2.3	4.2	.0	4.2	24.3	48
14. ILLINOIS	15.4	35.6	51.0	66.4	28.6	95.0	100.7	11
15. INDIANA	6.8	15.0	23.9	28.6	14.6	43.1	98.6	12
16. IOWA	2.9	5.4	8.5	12.1	-.0	12.1	48.8	43
17. KANSAS	3.5	5.0	8.5	16.0	3.2	19.2	61.7	35
18. KENTUCKY	6.9	11.6	18.4	35.8	15.8	51.6	87.4	16
19. LOUISIANA	4.6	8.6	13.2	19.0	27.3	46.3	65.3	33
20. MAINE	2.1	5.6	7.7	9.9	2.7	12.6	112.6	8
21. MARYLAND	7.3	11.9	19.2	27.6	8.1	35.7	77.8	25
22. MASSACHUSETTS	12.9	15.9	24.1	74.0	41.2	115.2	83.7	17
23. MICHIGAN	12.9	19.5	32.4	42.4	42.0	75.6	75.6	22
24. MINNESOTA	6.5	10.0	16.5	30.4	-11.3	42.4	80.0	44
25. MISSISSIPPI	3.7	3.4	17.2	18.2	-9.0	20.6	66.8	32
26. MISSOURI	6.0	11.2	17.2	3.5	2.7	3.7	22.2	49
27. MONTANA	1.5	3.2	4.7	3.5	-2.0	7.3	52.2	38
28. NEBRASKA	1.6	1.2	2.8	11.6	-4.7	5.3	91.0	14
29. NEVADA	1.9	3.3	5.2	6.6	-4.7	6.8	95.5	13
30. NEW HAMPSHIRE	1.9	27.7	42.8	74.9	12.6	13.1	131.5	3
31. NEW JERSEY	15.1	2.9	5.5	9.9	12.6	87.6	69.1	27
32. NEW MEXICO	2.6	53.3	85.2	259.7	6.0	16.0	118.6	7
33. NEW YORK	31.4	15.3	24.9	37.3	115.5	375.3	37.6	24
34. NORTH CAROLINA	9.6	.1	.9	4.2	17.9	55.2	89.1	46
35. NORTH DAKOTA	.9	20.9	46.9	63.6	-1.2	3.0	51.4	15
36. OHIO	17.0	4.9	8.9	12.6	-2.9	60.7	53.8	41
37. OKLAHOMA	4.0	4.5	8.9	12.6	1.7	14.3	133.3	39
38. OREGON	2.0	48.7	70.2	92.6	3.4	108.8	129.6	2
39. PENNSYLVANIA	21.4	3.3	8.9	15.4	53.9	146.6	38.2	4
40. RHODE ISLAND	3.6	9.4	14.7	22.2	5.0	17.2	121.3	23
41. SOUTH CAROLINA	5.3	4.5	31.5	37.6	5.2	27.4	55.5	47
42. SOUTH DAKOTA	1.2	19.0	39.3	78.6	-2.9	2.4	20.3	6
43. TENNESSEE	12.5	25.4	3.2	5.4	25.5	63.3	38.2	37
44. TEXAS	12.1	1.0	31.5	78.6	27.5	106.2	121.3	51
45. UTAH	.8	1.6	1.8	5.4	2.3	5.4	55.5	26
46. VERMONT	9.7	12.4	22.2	46.6	-8.9	7.7	69.7	30
47. VIRGINIA	3.8	6.7	10.4	15.6	9.4	37.7	68.1	40
48. WASHINGTON	3.8	3.6	6.6	18.5	5.5	25.0	53.8	28
49. WEST VIRGINIA	6.6	15.1	21.7	33.0	10.3	21.9	81.0	19
50. WISCONSIN	.2	.2	.4	1.1	.0	43.3	20.9	50
51. WYOMING						1.1		

TABLE 5 : H.U.D. SPENDING TOTALS, PER CAPITA INCOME AND SELECTED IMPACT STATISTICS

	1978 (EST.) PERSONAL INCOME - - - - PER CAPITA - - - - DOLLARS	RANK	IMPACTS EXPRESSED AS A PERCENT OF U.S. TOTAL INCOME	OUTPUT	CONSTRUCTION	EMPLOYMENT
UNITED STATES	7874.0		100.0	100.0	100.0	100.0
NEW ENGLAND	7952.5	4	6.0	6.8	P.9	6.3
MIDEAST	8533.0	1	28.0	29.0	30.6	24.3
GREAT LAKES	8427.4	3	20.2	19.5	13.0	19.1
PLAINS	7652.7	5	5.8	5.0	3.7	6.3
SOUTHEAST	6819.0	8	22.8	21.3	23.7	26.2
SOUTHWEST	7304.0	7	6.2	6.2	7.7	7.1
ROCKY MOUNTAIN	7395.0	6	1.1	1.1	1.3	1.1
FAR WEST	8474.4	2	9.9	11.2	11.0	9.6
1. ALABAMA	6367.4	47	1.3	1.3	1.8	1.5
2. ALASKA	10099.3	2	.1	.2	.3	.1
3. ARIZONA	7237.3	31	1.0	1.0	1.5	1.3
4. ARKANSAS	6255.6	50	.8	.9	1.0	1.1
5. CALIFORNIA	8585.2	9	7.4	8.4	8.6	7.1
6. COLORADO	8015.3	16	.7	.6	.7	.7
7. CONNECTICUT	8983.4	6	1.4	1.6	1.4	1.4
8. DELAWARE	8729.0	7	.4	.4	.4	.3
9. DIST OF COLUMBIA	10769.7	1	.7	.9	.8	.4
10. FLORIDA	7461.7	28	4.9	3.5	3.0	5.0
11. GEORGIA	6784.2	36	3.1	2.9	3.1	3.6
12. HAWAII	8251.7	12	.3	.3	.3	.3
13. IDAHO	6629.8	39	.1	.2	.2	.1
14. ILLINOIS	9089.6	3	6.1	5.3	4.3	5.5
15. INDIANA	7998.0	17	2.9	2.6	2.0	2.6
16. IOWA	8238.5	13	.8	.6	.5	.9
17. KANSAS	7737.9	25	.8	.8	.9	.9
18. KENTUCKY	6799.5	35	1.7	1.7	2.4	2.0
19. LOUISIANA	6472.2	43	1.4	1.4	2.1	1.4
20. MAINE	6427.5	44	.7	.6	.6	.8
21. MARYLAND	8501.1	11	1.7	1.6	1.6	2.1
22. MASSACHUSETTS	7928.6	20	2.6	3.2	5.3	2.6
23. MICHIGAN	9023.8	5	4.0	4.7	1.9	3.5
24. MINNESOTA	7775.4	22	1.7	1.4	.9	1.8
25. MISSISSIPPI	5719.7	51	.6	.8	.9	.8
26. MISSOURI	7443.0	29	1.7	1.7	.8	1.9
27. MONTANA	7111.9	32	.1	.1	.2	.1
28. NEBRASKA	7770.5	23	.5	.3	.2	.5
29. NEVADA	8611.1	8	.3	.4	.3	.3
30. NEW HAMPSHIRE	7098.5	33	.4	.5	.6	.6
31. NEW JERSEY	9050.6	4	5.2	4.3	4.0	4.7
32. NEW MEXICO	6261.9	49	.5	.5	.7	.6
33. NEW YORK	8584.8	10	11.4	14.2	17.1	9.3
34. NORTH CAROLINA	6732.1	38	2.3	2.5	2.5	2.7
35. NORTH DAKOTA	6378.0	46	.1	.1	.1	.1
36. OHIO	7873.0	21	5.2	5.1	2.8	5.1
37. OKLAHOMA	6976.0	34	.8	.8	.7	1.0
38. OREGON	7761.3	24	.7	.7	.5	.7
39. PENNSYLVANIA	7997.0	18	8.5	7.5	6.7	7.6
40. RHODE ISLAND	7986.4	19	.7	.7	.8	.7
41. SOUTH CAROLINA	6351.6	48	1.2	1.1	1.2	1.6
42. SOUTH DAKOTA	6565.2	41	.1	.1	.2	.2
43. TENNESSEE	6774.2	37	2.9	2.8	2.9	3.4
44. TEXAS	7484.5	27	3.9	3.8	4.8	4.2
45. UTAH	6600.8	40	.1	.1	.2	.1
46. VERMONT	6551.0	42	.2	.2	.4	.2
47. VIRGINIA	7678.1	26	1.9	1.8	1.7	2.4
48. WASHINGTON	8122.8	14	1.1	1.1	1.1	1.1
49. WEST VIRGINIA	6403.6	45	.7	.7	1.0	.7
50. WISCONSIN	7419.6	30	2.1	1.8	2.0	2.4
51. WYOMING	8019.4	15	.0	.1	.1	.0

TABLE 6: Ratios of Gross-Output Impact Shares to Population and Personal Income Shares, by Region

| | Share of Output Impacts Relative to: | |
	Population Share	Income Share
New England	1.15	1.17
Mideast	1.50	1.38
Great Lakes	1.06	0.94
Plains	0.67	0.69
Southeast	1.01	1.14
Southwest	0.72	0.78
Rocky Mountain	0.39	0.44
Far West	0.63	0.57

The spatial impacts of the Federal government GIA program

In the second NRIES simulation, a hypothetical situation is examined in which the Federal government distributes its GIA payments solely on a per capita regional basis. This, in effect, measures the equality in the dispersion of GIA programs, the most general type of federal expenditures. Measuring equity, however, is far from a clear-cut process. Before detailing the results of the simulation, it is first necessary to discuss briefly a few of the underlying issues concerning the definition of equity.[11]

The most important issue in an analytical context involves the "place" versus "people" prosperity distinction, as Edel shows in Chapter 7 above. If a program aids an economically poorer area, *ceteris paribus*, then it is progressive regarding the place of incidence. A program can, however, aid nonpoor individuals in a relatively poor area. This latter type would not be progressive regarding equity incidence on people. As a result, aid to poor places does not guarantee a benefit to poor people.

Second, the redistribution of wealth or income is not the purpose of many federal programs. The Department of Defense and the National Park Service, for example, have firm policies and objectives that often do not take into account regional equity considerations. Other agencies have objectives and goals that are necessary but, in many cases, have nothing to do with equity.

The final issue is the measurement of equity itself. For example, although per capita income is one index for judging relative economic prosperity, the relative cost of living in different areas will alter nominal income. Also, other variables may be used to measure the interregional differences in equity: environmental quality, levels of social infrastructure, or other socioeconomic

---

[11] For a general discussion of regional equity *see* Richardson, 1978.

factors, such as unemployment rates. As Bloomenstein et al. (1978) and Richardson (1978) have shown, multidimensional criteria might produce a more comprehensive measure of equality than per capita income.

The obvious conclusion is that neither NRIES nor any other existing model can adequately take all of these factors into consideration simultaneously. Given the nature of NRIES, the analysis has, therefore, been strictly limited to statements about per capita income and is directed at a *place* equity.

The second simulation examines the spatial equity and interregional impacts of GIAs, and emphasizes the relative nominal macroeconomic income effects on place equity. Columns 1 and 3 in Table 7 list 1978 state and local GIA received by state and by BEA region. Columns 2 and 4 give these in terms of their shares of the federal GIA. A comparison of the columns shows that state and local GIA distributions are spatially proportioned similarly across the country. One exception is the Mideast, which receives a much higher weight of local GIA compared to state expenditures (of course, the District of Columbia receives no "state" revenues). Column 6 lists the percent of the combined programs that each state or region received. The last column ranks the levels of these combined programs and they can be compared to the population rank in column 7.

Table 8 shows the simulated redistribution of 1978 GIA as if the allocations were based solely upon population levels. Columns 2, 4, and 6 list the change in aid for a particular state or region from the current distribution pattern given in Table 7. There is no *initial* macroeconomic impact from the redistribuiton since, for both state and local GIA programs, the United States total remains at the previous level. Looking at the last three columns, the Southeast receives the most GIA when based upon population, whereas under the current pattern the Mideast receives the most. The Mideast loses the most (almost $2.2 billion), followed closely by the loss in the Far West (almost $1.9 billion), when allocations are based upon population. Column 6 shows that the major beneficiaries of the redistribution are the Great Lakes, Southeast, and Southwest. As can be seen from the last column, the greatest per capita loss in aid is in the Far West ($63) while the greatest gain is in the Southwest ($56).

The first-year economic changes under the new spatial distribution pattern reflect primarily the initial impact upon an area. This, in turn, generates the dynamic changes in the following years. Looking at columns 1, 3, and 5 in Table 9 (which give first-year impacts of the GIA redistribution pattern on personal income, employment, and gross product), a similarity of direction and magnitude can be seen with the initial change in expenditures. However, as mentioned earlier, the more important measurement of effects must include the indirect and induced impacts on the area that extend many years after the original expenditure. These are listed in columns 2, 4, and 6 in Table 9. When the total five-year impacts are considered, Texas and Ohio netted the largest advances to personal income, employment, and gross-product origi-

	STATE GRANTS-IN-AID		LOCAL GRANTS-IN-AID		TOTAL GRANTS-IN-AID		1978 RANK	
	MIL. $	% OF TOTAL	MIL. $	% OF TOTAL	MIL. $	% OF TOTAL	POP.	AID
UNITED STATES	53015.6	100.0	17592.7	100.0	70608.3	100.0		
NEW ENGLAND	3213.8	6.1	1036.7	5.9	4250.5	6.0	7	7
MIDEAST	11217.4	21.2	4656.3	26.5	15873.8	22.5	2	1
GREAT LAKES	8690.6	16.4	2818.1	16.0	11508.7	16.3	1	4
PLAINS	3808.3	7.2	1220.6	6.9	5028.9	7.1	6	6
SOUTHEAST	11311.4	21.3	3423.8	19.5	14735.2	20.9	3	2
SOUTHWEST	3887.2	7.3	1359.8	7.7	5247.0	7.4	5	5
ROCKY MOUNTAIN	1865.4	3.5	386.0	2.2	2251.4	3.2	8	8
FAR WEST	9021.4	17.0	2691.4	15.3	11712.8	16.6	4	3
1. ALABAMA	957.3	1.8	221.7	1.3	1179.0	1.7	21	21
2. ALASKA	330.3	.6	42.0	.2	372.3	.5	51	42
3. ARIZONA	400.6	.8	185.3	1.1	585.8	.8	33	35
4. ARKANSAS	557.3	1.1	135.4	.8	692.7	1.0	31	32
5. CALIFORNIA	6405.5	12.1	1918.8	10.9	8324.3	11.8	1	1
6. COLORADO	702.6	1.3	189.7	1.1	892.3	1.3	28	26
7. CONNECTICUT	627.4	1.2	192.6	1.1	820.0	1.2	24	29
8. DELAWARE	152.8	.3	64.0	.4	216.8	.3	48	50
9. DIST OF COLUMBIA	.0	.0	750.7	4.3	750.7	1.1	44	31
10. FLORIDA	1335.8	2.5	675.5	3.8	2011.3	2.8	8	10
11. GEORGIA	1265.7	2.4	391.5	2.2	1657.2	2.3	14	11
12. HAWAII	390.7	.7	108.9	.6	499.6	.7	40	36
13. IDAHO	256.6	.5	52.6	.3	309.2	.4	41	44
14. ILLINOIS	2478.1	4.7	770.1	4.4	3248.2	4.6	5	5
15. INDIANA	846.1	1.6	249.0	1.4	1095.0	1.5	12	23
16. IOWA	630.1	1.2	190.5	1.1	820.6	1.2	26	28
17. KANSAS	474.4	.9	135.5	.8	610.0	.9	32	34
18. KENTUCKY	889.2	1.7	228.1	1.3	1117.3	1.6	22	17
19. LOUISIANA	1053.5	2.0	293.2	1.7	1346.7	1.9	20	22
20. MAINE	325.8	.6	107.3	.6	433.1	.6	38	39
21. MARYLAND	939.7	1.8	439.6	2.5	1379.3	2.0	18	16
22. MASSACHUSETTS	1584.3	3.0	571.9	3.3	2156.2	3.1	10	7
23. MICHIGAN	2264.6	4.3	875.8	5.0	3140.4	4.4	7	6
24. MINNESOTA	1087.0	2.0	332.5	1.9	1419.5	2.0	19	15
25. MISSISSIPPI	886.9	1.7	175.2	1.0	1062.1	1.5	30	30
26. MISSOURI	1354.7	2.6	457.6	2.6	1812.3	2.6	15	19
27. MONTANA	277.3	.5	53.4	.3	330.7	.5	43	43
28. NEBRASKA	322.6	.6	99.1	.6	421.8	.6	35	40
29. NEVADA	170.5	.3	42.3	.2	212.7	.3	46	51
30. NEW HAMPSHIRE	179.0	.3	54.6	.3	233.6	.3	42	49
31. NEW JERSEY	1622.0	3.1	576.9	3.3	2198.9	3.1	9	8
32. NEW MEXICO	361.7	.7	115.0	.7	476.7	.7	37	37
33. NEW YORK	5964.2	11.2	1893.7	10.8	7857.9	11.1	2	2
34. NORTH CAROLINA	1289.2	2.4	362.1	2.1	1651.3	2.3	11	12
35. NORTH DAKOTA	208.1	.4	35.4	.2	243.5	.3	47	47
36. OHIO	1892.9	3.6	657.0	3.7	2549.9	3.6	6	9
37. OKLAHOMA	661.5	1.2	233.6	1.3	895.1	1.3	27	25
38. OREGON	715.9	1.4	292.4	1.7	1008.3	1.4	29	24
39. PENNSYLVANIA	2538.8	4.8	931.3	5.3	3470.1	4.9	4	3
40. RHODE ISLAND	299.6	.6	73.6	.4	373.2	.5	39	41
41. SOUTH CAROLINA	715.2	1.3	165.1	.9	880.1	1.2	25	27
42. SOUTH DAKOTA	206.2	.4	50.4	.3	256.5	.4	45	45
43. TENNESSEE	928.8	1.8	325.1	1.8	1253.8	1.8	17	20
44. TEXAS	2463.4	4.6	826.0	4.7	3289.4	4.7	3	4
45. UTAH	391.3	.7	73.5	.4	464.8	.7	36	38
46. VERMONT	208.2	.4	86.2	.5	294.4	.4	48	45
47. VIRGINIA	1057.4	2.0	233.5	1.3	1290.9	1.8	13	14
48. WASHINGTON	1008.6	1.9	288.0	1.6	1296.6	1.8	22	18
49. WEST VIRGINIA	585.2	1.1	86.4	.5	671.6	1.0	34	33
50. WISCONSIN	1289.0	2.4	382.6	2.2	1671.6	2.4	16	13
51. WYOMING	237.7	.4	16.7	.1	254.4	.4	50	46

TABLE 8: 1978 FEDERAL GRANTS-IN-AID PAYMENTS REDISTRIBUTED BASED ON THE DISTRIBUTION OF POPULATION

| | - - STATE - - GRANTS-IN-AID | | - - LOCAL - - GRANTS-IN-AID | | - - TOTAL - - GRANTS-IN-AID | | PER CAPITA CHANGE |
	MIL. $	CHANGE	MIL. $	CHANGE	MIL. $	CHANGE	DOLLARS
UNITED STATES	53015.6	.0	17592.7	.0	70608.3	.0	.0
NEW ENGLAND	2981.8	-252.0	989.5	-47.2	3971.3	-279.2	-22.8
MIDEAST	10288.6	-928.9	3414.2	-1242.2	13702.7	-2171.0	-51.3
GREAT LAKES	10025.0	1334.4	3326.7	508.6	13351.7	1843.0	44.7
PLAINS	4127.5	319.2	1369.7	149.1	5497.2	468.3	27.6
SOUTHEAST	11997.6	686.2	3981.3	557.5	15978.9	1243.6	25.2
SOUTHWEST	4975.0	867.8	1577.9	216.1	6552.9	1095.9	65.4
ROCKY MOUNTAIN	1470.0	-395.4	485.6	101.8	1955.8	-295.6	-49.6
FAR WEST	7370.2	-165.2	2445.7	-245.7	9815.9	-1297.0	-62.6
1. ALABAMA	910.6	-46.7	302.2	80.4	1212.1	33.7	9.0
2. ALASKA	98.8	-231.5	32.8	-9.2	131.6	-240.7	-592.7
3. ARIZONA	580.2	179.7	192.5	7.3	772.8	186.9	78.4
4. ARKANSAS	528.4	-28.9	175.3	39.9	703.7	11.0	5.1
5. CALIFORNIA	5405.0	-1003.5	1793.6	-125.3	7198.5	-1125.8	-50.7
6. COLORADO	649.2	-53.3	215.4	25.7	864.7	-27.6	-10.4
7. CONNECTICUT	755.6	128.2	250.7	58.1	1006.4	186.3	60.0
8. DELAWARE	141.5	-11.4	46.9	-17.0	188.4	-28.4	-48.8
9. DIST OF COLUMBIA	.0		229.9	-520.8	229.9	-520.8	-734.2
10. FLORIDA	2095.3	759.5	695.3	19.9	2790.6	779.4	50.5
11. GEORGIA	1238.1	-27.6	410.8	19.3	1648.9	-8.3	-1.6
12. HAWAII	221.2	-169.5	73.4	-35.5	294.6	-205.0	-225.5
13. IDAHO	212.4	-44.1	70.5	17.9	282.9	-26.3	-30.1
14. ILLINOIS	2739.9	261.8	909.2	139.1	3649.1	400.9	35.6
15. INDIANA	1300.2	454.1	431.4	182.4	1731.6	636.5	115.1
16. IOWA	705.7	75.6	234.2	43.7	939.8	119.2	41.1
17. KANSAS	568.3	93.9	188.6	53.0	756.9	146.9	62.6
18. KENTUCKY	848.3	-40.9	281.5	-5.4	1129.8	-46.3	-13.6
19. LOUISIANA	966.4	-77.5	323.6	-27.4	1290.0	-104.9	-15.1
20. MAINE	266.4	67.2	88.4	-23.6	356.8	-34.8	-17.3
21. MARYLAND	1008.8	-182.5	465.2	-106.7	1134.0	-289.2	-50.2
22. MASSACHUSETTS	1401.8	-23.6	465.2	-132.2	1867.0	-155.8	-18.4
23. MICHIGAN	2241.0	-104.9	743.6	-15.0	2988.6	-119.9	-29.4
24. MINNESOTA	975.1	-93.7	323.6	5.4	1298.7	-35.4	-14.8
25. MISSISSIPPI	583.4	287.5	193.6	18.7	776.9	306.2	106.2
26. MISSOURI	1174.4	-90.2	389.7	8.6	1564.2	-81.6	6.4
27. MONTANA	187.0	58.5	62.1	27.3	249.1	85.8	54.8
28. NEBRASKA	381.1	-7.5	126.5	11.8	507.6	4.3	6.4
29. NEVADA	163.0	31.6	54.1	15.3	217.1	47.0	54.3
30. NEW HAMPSHIRE	210.7	162.4	69.9	15.2	280.6	177.6	24.2
31. NEW JERSEY	1784.3	-65.3	592.1	-16.6	2376.4	-81.9	-117.5
32. NEW MEXICO	296.4	-65.3	98.4	-457.0	394.8	-2091.5	-26.6
33. NEW YORK	4329.6	-1634.5	1436.7	86.0	5766.4	-36.0	-56.3
34. NORTH CAROLINA	1350.6	61.3	448.2	1.6	1798.7	147.4	26.6
35. NORTH DAKOTA	155.7	-52.3	51.7	3.5	207.4	-36.0	-56.3
36. OHIO	2603.9	711.0	864.1	207.1	3468.0	918.1	85.8
37. OKLAHOMA	693.4	31.9	230.1	-3.5	923.5	28.4	10.0
38. OREGON	585.1	-130.8	194.2	-98.3	779.2	-229.1	-95.2
39. PENNSYLVANIA	2853.7	314.9	947.0	15.6	3800.7	330.5	28.2
40. RHODE ISLAND	228.2	-60.8	75.2	-8.5	303.5	-69.4	-29.1
41. SOUTH CAROLINA	733.6	-33.0	243.6	8.5	977.2	-34.4	33.5
42. SOUTH DAKOTA	167.2	128.4	55.5	5.1	222.6	-34.0	-63.8
43. TENNESSEE	1557.1	-33.1	350.8	25.7	1408.0	154.1	35.5
44. TEXAS	3184.9	721.5	1056.9	230.9	4244.8	952.4	72.8
45. UTAH	317.4	-73.9	105.3	31.8	422.7	-42.1	-32.3
46. VERMONT	119.1	-89.0	39.5	13.3	158.7	-75.7	-154.6
47. VIRGINIA	1259.1	201.7	417.8	13.3	1676.9	215.0	41.5
48. WASHINGTON	897.2	-111.4	297.7	10.7	1194.9	-100.7	-27.3
49. WEST VIRGINIA	453.5	-131.3	150.6	64.2	604.5	-67.1	-36.0
50. WISCONSIN	1140.1	-68.9	378.3	112.2	1518.4	43.3	9.2
51. WYOMING	103.9	-133.7	34.5	17.7	138.4	-116.0	-271.6

	CHANGE IN PERSONAL INCOME (MILLIONS OF DOLLARS)		CHANGE IN EMPLOYMENT (THOUSANDS OF MAN YEARS)		CHANGE IN GROSS PRODUCT (MILLIONS OF DOLLARS)		NET CHANGE IN PER CAPITA INCOME	
	YEAR 1	TOTAL	YEAR 1	TOTAL	YEAR 1	TOTAL	DOLLARS	RANK
UNITED STATES	-118.9	650.0	32.1	111.5	531.9	161.6	3.0	
NEW ENGLAND	-127.9	-299.6	-9.9	-16.6	-231.8	-530.7	-24.0	7
MIDEAST	-1191.3	-2269.0	-60.1	-101.6	-1984.6	-3987.0	-53.7	8
GREAT LAKES	652.0	1567.1	50.5	98.4	1785.0	2919.5	38.0	2
PLAINS	87.0	299.9	8.1	22.6	219.0	389.5	17.7	4
SOUTHEAST	310.8	915.5	28.7	65.3	840.4	1389.9	18.5	3
SOUTHWEST	410.2	1119.0	31.6	79.3	817.5	1518.9	57.3	1
ROCKY MOUNTAIN	-19.1	-36.1	-1.7	-2.9	-71.2	-101.4	-6.0	5
FAR WEST	-240.5	-649.8	-15.1	-32.8	-842.2	-1437.1	-21.5	6
1. ALABAMA	3.0	28.5	.4	2.3	12.1	39.9	7.6	17
2. ALASKA	-1.2	-3.0	-.1	-.1	-4.2	-7.3	-7.3	32
3. ARIZONA	208.3	301.7	14.6	21.1	300.4	452.1	126.9	1
4. ARKANSAS	1.8	87.1	.3	1.5	7.0	122.1	-19.2	16
5. CALIFORNIA	-151.4	-425.4	-9.2	-20.5	-626.8	-1059.2	-19.3	28
6. COLORADO	-2.8	-30.6	-.2	-.6	31.7	-20.7	-9.8	34
7. CONNECTICUT	-3.3	-8.2	-.2	-.6	-10.9	-24.6	-14.1	35
8. DELAWARE	-106.9	-120.2	-4.6	-4.7	-161.1	-195.4	-169.5	51
9. DIST OF COLUMBIA	228.6	494.5	19.0	31.1	495.6	664.5	57.4	5
10. FLORIDA	3.5	35.7	.6	3.0	17.5	53.4	7.0	19
11. GEORGIA	-28.5	-56.9	-2.0	-3.2	-53.9	-91.1	-62.6	47
12. HAWAII	-1.0	-1.7	-.0	-.0	-22.2	-26.6	-1.9	26
13. IDAHO	200.2	446.1	13.8	24.4	284.7	581.9	39.6	7
14. ILLINOIS	164.4	44P.0	14.0	31.9	432.7	683.7	83.8	2
15. INDIANA	6.3	25.7	.7	2.2	17.6	30.9	8.9	14
16. IOWA	14.2	72.6	1.4	5.8	55.7	105.3	31.1	10
17. KANSAS	-2.3	14.0	.3	2.0	10.6	44.7	8.6	15
18. KENTUCKY	-3.0	-28.6	-1.3	-1.2	-29.3	-56.9	-31.5	21
19. LOUISIANA	-13.0	-135.5	-3.1	-7.7	-131.5	-310.4	-6.9	4
20. MAINE	-42.9	-151.8	-3.7	-6.8	-192.8	-221.8	-24.2	31
21. MARYLAND	-61.1	-3.6	-.5	-.2	-10.2	-9.0	-16.5	41
22. MASSACHUSETTS	-7.4	-5.1	-.7	-.2	-6.6	-1.5	-1.9	37
23. MICHIGAN	-7.4	184.5	5.4	13.3	126.0	230.2	-24.2	25
24. MINNESOTA	60.7	-18.9	-.7	-1.9	-25.0	-39.2	-16.5	27
25. MISSISSIPPI	-8.7	34.2	2.2	2.9	47.3	58.6	-1.9	8
26. MISSOURI	23.6	.3	.0	.1	1.2	69.7	-2.1	42
27. MONTANA	-.2	32.8	1.1	2.5	49.0	-242.6	38.2	11
28. NEBRASKA	12.3	-183.3	-5.1	-5.1	-50.9	-75.7	-24.8	23
29. NEVADA	-23.3	-44.1	-1.3	-2.9	-42.7	-377.8	21.4	9
30. NEW HAMPSHIRE	-15.2	-181.6	-54.1	-86.4	-1693.4	14.4	37.8	43
31. NEW JERSEY	-1028.1	7.7	-.2	1.1	6.9	-5.2	-25.0	45
32. NEW MEXICO	-1.5	-2.3	.2	.2	-5.2	185.1	-36.2	49
33. NEW YORK	34.8	789.4	25.9	46.0	1245.2	-179.6	-102.2	22
34. NORTH DAKOTA	26.0	5.5	2.7	-.5	-115.1	-191.7	-1.4	29
35. OHIO	-31.9	-89.5	-2.5	-5.5	-41.4	-108.4	-3.6	12
36. OKLAHOMA	-16.0	-110.1	-.5	-3.7	-81.8	60.8	20.8	46
37. OREGON	-42.2	-63.3	-2.8	-3.4	36.8	-16.4	-37.2	33
38. PENNSYLVANIA	16.8	4.1	1.7	3.7	-12.1	404.9	-9.4	48
39. RHODE ISLAND	-8.9	-11.2	-1.5	-1.1	217.6	1045.3	-67.5	13
40. SOUTH CAROLINA	52.3	226.1	5.6	17.1	507.4	-16.7	14.2	36
41. SOUTH DAKOTA	191.1	801.8	15.5	55.9	-10.7	-103.9	-16.3	6
42. TENNESSEE	-3.4	-7.7	-.3	-.5	-69.4	57.1	52.0	4
43. TEXAS	-40.3	-59.4	-4.1	-4.8	43.9	-98.6	61.3	30
44. UTAH	14.4	25.2	1.5	3.3	-43.3	-5.5	-5.9	50
45. VERMONT	-19.7	-75.2	-1.4	-3.5	-4.7	50.3	-121.4	20
46. VIRGINIA	-3.3	-5.1	-.2	-.5	15.2	-11.0	5.6	40
47. WASHINGTON	-3.6	35.3	.5	2.8	-6.2		-20.4	28
48. WEST VIRGINIA	-4.3	-8.7	-.4	-.8			-2.8	18
49. WISCONSIN							7.5	18
50. WYOMING							-20.3	39

nating; much further behind were Indiana and Florida. The largest negative effects to the economic indicators were reflected by New York and California, the two most populous states, followed by New Jersey, Michigan, and Massachusetts. Regionally, the Great Lakes and Southwest registered the largest gains to the economic indicators and the Mideast and Far West registered the largest declines.

These changes in the states' economies must be converted to a per capita basis in order to examine the effects on the residents of those states. The last two columns of Table 9 list the personal income per capita impact caused by a redistribution of federal GIA on a population basis. The Southwest and Great Lakes registered advances of $57 and $38, respectively. These regions included state gains of $126 in Arizona (the largest), $84 in Indiana, $74 in Ohio, and $67 in Texas. The largest net losses to personal income per capita were in the Mideast and New England, at −$54 and −$24, respectively. The District of Columbia registered the largest decline (−$170), followed by state losses—Vermont (−$121), New York (−$102), and Rhode Island (−$68)—in the two regions mentioned. California showed a relatively mild $19 loss, a rate which was exceeded by losses in 13 other states.

An interesting phenomenon results from this situation, and is shown in the first line in Table 9. Although there were no net direct expenditure changes by the Federal government, there was a net positive increment to United States gross product ($162 million), personal income ($650 million), and employment (112,000 man-years) resulting from the redistribution of GIA. The reason for this is clear: there has not only been a redistribution on a population basis, but one from low- to high-multiplier states, as well. The result of a positive impact due only to a spatial redistribution may be called the "spatial balanced budget multiplier effect."

Turning now to equity issues, one simple measure of the spatial equity that can be derived from this analysis is the comparison of the *coefficient of variation* for per capita income before and after the GIA redistribution. The coefficient of variation is defined as the standard deviation divided by the mean and, in this case, measures the dispersion of income among the states. Before the redistribution, the coefficient of variation of personal income was 0.1374. After the *direct* effects of the initial redistribution are taken into account, the coefficient *falls* to 0.1302. This signifies that the new distribution of state per capita income is more equally distributed than before the change in GIA allocation. However, when the *indirect* effects of interregional income flows are generated by NRIES, the coefficient of variation *rises* to 0.1359. This shows that indirect purchases of goods and services accrue primarily to higher income states. Overall, the coefficients of variation show that a redistribution of GIA based on population would produce a more equal, spatial income distribution at the state level than the present system. Therefore, given that aggregate economic activity has also increased, the redistribution of GIA can be described as having both small positive efficiency and equity effects.

FURTHER DEVELOPMENTS

In the previous sections, the manner in which a multiregional modeling framework can provide relevant and timely information about the macroeconomic impacts of Federal government policies through its expenditure patterns was discussed. The two simulation experiments using the current NRIES model have provided specific measurements of state and multistate impacts. The next logical step is to provide impact measurement and analysis at the substate level, particularly the impacts associated with urban areas. This will allow for urban impact analysis that can be applied to a broad variety of federal policies.

As noted earlier, the most important feature of NRIES is its ability to model interactive flows among different areas within the United States economy. At BEA there exists a working model called the Regional Industry Multiplier System (RIMS) (U.S. Water Resources Council, 1977). RIMS was designed to estimate industry-specific input-output (I-O) multipliers for any single region, with a region defined as a county or group of counties in the United States, and industries defined as any of the 478 industries included in the national input-output table. Although RIMS has no interregional feedbacks, it presents a clear improvement over NRIES in its ability to provide a high level of spatial flexibility and interindustry detail. Thus, one way to measure and analyze inter- *and* intraregional impacts at a much finer level of regional detail would involve the linking of these two model systems.

There are several advantages of combining the two models: (1) the new model would have both I-O and econometric features which include both a finer level of industrial detail and time series estimation techniques; (2) any combinations of states or counties can be aggregated into regions; (3) all areas are, in effect, modeled independently and interact fully with other areas; and (4) there would be no need to restructure an expanded NRIES model for small areas.

The following steps would, in effect, link the two models and provide an avenue for the measurement of interactive, intrastate impacts on urban areas. First, using expenditure data from the Community Service Administration (Anton, Chapter 5, above), the RIMS model would estimate the impacts of federal expenditures for urban areas. This analysis would include the direct and indirect impacts caused by increased income flows *within* each of the areas, but excluding all interregional flows. Second, also using RIMS, the impacts for each state would be estimated by summing the substate components. At this stage the *intrastate* impacts have been measured but as yet there is no *interstate* analysis. Third, NRIES can now be used to derive the interregional flows for the United States that are generated by changes in state activity. This includes all direct and indirect impacts at the state and multistate level as well as flows among states. The final step involves consolidating the sums of intra- and interstate impacts and allocating them to the county and SMSA level. The resultant allocation of impacts would be to the urban areas under study, the remaining portions of the states, and the remaining state and multistate areas. For each area the impacts would be divided into three categories: the direct effects, the indirect effects that are generated within each area, and the effects generated by interregional flows among areas.

In summary, this modeling process is designed to detail the important differences in multipliers between central cities and suburbs, and between selected SMSAs. Starting with a given set of federal policies, the RIMS and NRIES modeling analysis would be combined to yield the total impacts accruing to small areas. In this manner, UIA can be simultaneously conducted for a large number of SMSAs and for a wide variety of federal programs.

APPENDIX 1

This appendix details the methodology used to transform the 1977 fiscal year data for the major HUD programs (shown in Table 1) into an econometric model accounting framework (shown in Table 2). The methodology employs several surveys and studies which, for purposes of brevity, are not documented at this time. The transformations are intended to convert the fiscal disbursements and commitments into the individual output and income categories for which the money is spent. Since it is intended that most of the intermediate transfers be netted out of the analysis, the transformation does not directly conform to the exact National Income and Product Accounts (NIPA) accounting in certain instances. For the lack of more specific data, the regional expenditures and commitments are allocated to output and income using national factors.

Community Development Block Grants (CDBG)
The allocation factors for this category are taken from HUD program reports. The distribution is shown below:

Type of Distribution	Percent	Model Category
Administrative	14.4	Grants-in-aid to local governments
Construction and repairs	63.7	Construction (see Section 8, part B below)
Services	21.9	Grants-in-aid to local governments

Section 701 Planning Grants
The entire expenditure of this category is considered as grants-in-aid to local governments.

Section 8
The distribution of this category is based upon a consensus of several surveys and research reports compiled by researchers at HUD, the Rand Cor-

poration, and the U.S. Department of Commerce. The distribution is divided into categories shown below:

A. Current expenditures

Income transfers to persons	85 percent
Output in finance, insurance and real estate	15 percent

B. Construction "induced" by HUD commitments

Type	Percent
Output in construction	38.3
Output in manufacturing durables	23.3
Output in manufacturing nondurables	1.8
Output in transportation, communications, and utilities	5.9
Output in wholesale and retail trade	15.8
Output in finance, insurance, and real estate	3.0
Output in services	11.9

Public Housing

A. Operations

This is divided into four components based upon a HUD survey.

Type	Percent	Model Category
Utility payments	32.0	Output in transportation, communications, and public utilities
Taxes	2.5	Grants-in-aid to local governments
Extraordinary maintenance	3.2	Construction (see Section 8, part B)
Other	62.3	Output in services

B. Modernization

All expenditures of this type are put into the model category of construction (see *Section 8,* part B).

C. Debt Services

All expenditures of this type are put into the model category of Output in finance, insurance, and real estate.

Leased Housing

All expenditures of this type are put into the same model category as *Section 8,* part A.

REFERENCES

Ballard, K. P., and Glickman, N. J. "A Multiregional Econometric Forecasting System: A Model for the Delaware Valley." *Journal of Regional Science* 17 (August 1977): 161–77.

————, and Wendling, R. M. "The National-Regional Impact Evaluation System: A Spatial Model of U.S. Economic and Demographic Activity." U.S. Department of Commerce, Bureau of Economic Analysis, November 1978; forthcoming, *Journal of Regional Science.*

Bloomenstein, H. J.; Nijkamp, P.; and Rietveld, P. "A Multivariate Analysis of Spatial Inequalities." Amsterdam: The Free University, 1978.

Carrothers, G. "An Historical Review of Gravity and Potential Concepts in Human Interaction." *Journal of the American Institute of Planners* 22 (1956): 94–101.

Courbis, R. "The REGINA Model: A Regional-National Model of the French Economy." *Economics of Planning* 12 (1972): 133–52.

Crow, R. T. "A Nationally Linked Regional Econometric Model." *Journal of Regional Science* 13 (August 1973): 187–204.

Glickman, N. J. *Econometric Analysis of Regional Systems.* New York: Academic Press, 1977.

————, and Jacobs, S. S., eds. *The Urban Impacts of the Budget of the Department of Housing and Urban Development.* Washington, D.C.: U.S. Department of Housing and Urban Development, 1979.

Milne, W. J.; Glickman, N. J.; and Adams, F. G. "A Framework for Analyzing Regional Decline: A Multiregional Econometric Model of the United States." Department of Economics Discussion Paper no. 398. Philadelphia: University of Pennsylvania, 1978; forthcoming, *Journal of Regional Science.*

Quantitative Analysis Unit, Economic Analysis Division. *Working Paper No. 1: An Overview of CANDIDE-R.* Ottawa: Department of Regional Economic Expansion, Canadian Government, 1975.

Richardson, H. W. "The State of Regional Economics: A Survey Article." *International Regional Science Review* 3 (1978): 1–48.

Thys-Clement, F.; van Rompuy, P.; and deCorel, L. *RENA: Un Modèle économetrique pour l'élaboration du Plan 1976–1980.* Brussels: Bureau du Plan, 1973.

U.S. Water Resources Council, *Guideline 5: Regional Multipliers.* Industry-Specific Gross Output Multipliers for BEA Economic Areas, prepared by Bureau of Economic Analysis, U.S. Department of Commerce. Washington, D.C.: U.S. Government Printing Office, 1977.

PART III

Urban Impact Analysis 1: Income Transfer Programs

CHAPTER NINE

The Urban Impacts of the Program for Better Jobs and Income

SHELDON DANZIGER, ROBERT HAVEMAN,
EUGENE SMOLENSKY, AND KARL TAEUBER

INTRODUCTION

In August 1977, President Carter announced his plan for welfare reform—the Program for Better Jobs and Income (PBJI). The plan would have consolidated three major components of the current welfare system and provided, for the first time, a nationwide minimum federal cash payment for all the poor. In addition, a public service job would have been provided for those able and expected to work. Earnings, welfare, manpower policy, and taxes would have been interrelated through an expanded earned income tax credit and a new, nationally uniform system of basic income support payments. PBJI represented a small increase in government spending, and thus, if it had been legislated, it would have had only a limited impact on various measures of economic well-being. However, these impacts would have varied widely by region and among urban areas within regions.

In this paper we describe the major components of PBJI in the first section, and, in the second section, analyze their impacts on various measures of economic well-being for individuals and urban areas. The program's effects on income flows, job creation, poverty reduction, and fiscal relief are emphasized. In the third section we discuss the long-term effects of PBJI on regional income convergence, migration, and residential segregation.

The authors wish to acknowledge the assistance of Martin Holmer and Jeffrey Sibner of the Office of the Assistant Secretary for Planning and Evaluation of the Department of Health, Education, and Welfare in providing much of the data that appear in this paper, and of Elizabeth Haveman in the preparation of the tables. George Jakubson provided valuable comments on a previous draft.

THE PROGRAM FOR BETTER JOBS AND INCOME[1]

Compared with the current system, PBJI would have accomplished several goals:

1. Welfare would have been integrated with earnings and both coupled with the tax system;
2. consolidation would have streamlined administration;
3. work would always have paid more than welfare;
4. family stability would have been enhanced by allowing married couples with children to benefit in the same manner and to the same extent as single-parent families;
5. the relatively high national minimum payment would have reduced incentives for migration from low to high benefit states; and
6. states and localities would have received fiscal relief.

Major components of PBJI

The details of the Carter administration's program can best be understood by focusing on its four major components: special public service jobs, the work benefit and income support provisions for those expected to work, income support payments for those not expected to work, and tax reductions.

Special public service jobs. PBJI would have allocated $8.8 billion to create up to 1.4 million minimum-wage, public service jobs for adult workers with children who could not find regular public or private jobs. Basically, one adult per family would have been eligible for these jobs and expected to work, unless all the adults in the family fell into a special category: aged, blind, disabled, or parents without spouse whose youngest child is less than seven years old. Mothers without husbands (or fathers without wives) whose youngest child is between seven and 14 years would have been expected to work part time, whereas such parents whose youngest child was over 14 would have been expected to work full time. Because earnings from employment in a regular job would have been accompanied by a subsidy (the earned income tax credit [EITC]), a regular job would have paid more than a special public job, and workers would have had an incentive to use the public service jobs only as a last resort.

Work benefit and income support for those expected to work. Earnings of all low-wage workers would also have been supplemented by a cash payment which would have depended upon the amount of earnings, other income, family size, and whether the family was expected to have had a working member. Cash supplements for a four-person family would have started at $2,300 when a family member was expected to work, and remained at that level as long as earnings were less than $3,800. The cash supplement would have declined by 50 cents for every dollar of earnings in excess of $3,800,

---

[1] A more complete analysis of PBJI can be found in Danziger, Haveman, and Smolensky, 1977.

becoming zero at $8,400, and would have declined by 80 cents for every dollar of unearned income.

Income support for those not expected to work. For a family of four in which no one was expected to work, the basic income support payment would have been $4,200, exceeding the payment for a family expected to work. For this group, benefits would also have decreased by 50 cents for every $1 of earnings, but without a $3,800 "disregard" range. The not-expected-to-work group would have included most current welfare recipients (all aged, blind, or disabled recipients), and for many of them benefits would have increased under the proposed program.

Tax reduction. Since 1975, the earned income tax credit has provided benefits ranging up to $400 for families with children. Under PBJI, benefits would have been increased for all families with regular earnings (that is, earnings that do not come from special public jobs) of more than $4,000 but less than $15,620. Families earning between $8,000 and $15,620 would have received a benefit for which they are not now eligible. The new maximum benefit would have been $654. In addition, the level of income at which families would have been liable for income taxes would have been raised.

The cost of PBJI

The provision of jobs for those expected to work, plus the increased income support for those not expected to work, the expanded EITC, and the raised tax threshold for those who do work, would have increased the income flowing to the low and lower-middle income population by at least $4 billion in the first year. The two main components of outlays would have been the cash benefits of $19.2 billion and the public service jobs of $8.8 billion (cost estimates by the administration are shown in Table 1). Offsetting expenses would have come from the phaseout of three existing transfer programs ($17.6 billion),[2] the reduction in manpower training and other public employment programs because of the PBJI jobs ($6.9 billion), and several smaller items. Considering both pluses and minuses, the federal budget in 1978 would have increased by about $2.8 billion according to official estimates.[3]

PBJI and poverty

PBJI was conceived to reform the welfare system, and not to eliminate poverty. Its primary goals were to raise cash payments to those in low benefit states, to increase the proportion of welfare recipients holding jobs, and to increase the income gap between the working and non-working poor.

---

[2] The three transfer programs to be phased out were Aid to Families with Dependent Children (AFDC), Supplemental Security Income (SSI), and Food Stamps.

[3] An analysis of these cost estimates and some alternatives is discussed in Congressional Budget Office, 1978. This analysis suggests that the total budgetary cost would have been closer to $15 billion than to $3 billion.

TABLE 1: Administration Estimate of the Costs of PBJI
          (billions of 1978 dollars)

OUTLAYS

Basic federal income supplement program		
Cash grants to participants, plus adjustments	16.97	
Administration	2.20	
Cost, basic program		19.17
Federal costs for matching state supplements		1.49
Adjustments for hold harmless, state share calculation, and		
Puerto Rico		−.49
Earned income tax credit[a]		1.50
Emergency assistance		.61
Employment program:		
Full-time jobs	7.88	
Part-time jobs	.52	
Administration	.40	
Cost, employment program		8.80
Total outlays		*31.08*

SAVINGS (from reductions in expenditure on other programs
or increases in taxes)

Abolition of AFDC[b]	6.40	
Abolition of SSI	5.70	
Abolition of Food Stamps	5.50	
Reductions in EITC from additional earnings	1.10	
Reduction in CETA, WIN, and UI[b]	6.90	
Reduction in housing programs	.30	
Increased payroll taxes	.70	
Reduction in fraud	.40	
Wellhead tax	1.30	
Total savings		*28.30*
NET COST OF BPJI		*2.78*

[a] Tax benefits of $3 billion for those who will not receive income supplements are not considered by the administration to be a cost of the welfare program.

[b] Aid to Families with Dependent Children (AFDC), Comprehensive Employment and Training Act (CETA), Work Incentive tax credit (WIN), Unemployment Insurance.

Under PBJI, the income guarantee for a family of four in which the head was not expected to work would have been about 65 percent of the poverty line for that family. Only for the aged, blind, or disabled would the guaranteed cash assistance payment have reached the poverty line. Those who did not work (and were not aged, blind, or disabled), even if they were not expected to work, would have remained poor. In fact many current welfare recipients would have suffered income losses if their states had not been required to "grandfather" benefits for three years. Although many current recipients in high benefit level states could not have benefited unless they worked, the extension of cash benefits to all persons would have increased the incomes of many currently ineligible for cash assistance—childless couples, unrelated individuals, and two-parent families in states without an AFDC program for unemployed parents.

PBJI would have represented a significant departure from previous welfare policies for those who worked. Because it emphasized the provision of jobs and the supplementation of earnings, it would have benefited all those who worked at low wages, regardless of family composition or region of residence, and in many cases, removed them from income poverty. Moreover, by providing a nationally uniform, minimum cash payment for all individuals, it would have become the nation's first universal, guaranteed annual cash income.

THE URBAN IMPACTS OF PBJI

Overview

The introduction of PBJI would have had an impact on urban areas of the United States. The increased transfer-income flows and increased job opportunities and earnings that would have resulted for low-income families would have affected urban areas more than the country as a whole, since urban areas generally contain high concentrations of poor families. Although most metropolitan areas would have gained for this reason, some would have been adversely affected. Because some regions have lower incomes and more poor people than other regions, the changes in incomes and jobs induced by PBJI would have had differential effects.

PBJI would have created incentives which would have altered individual behavior—particularly, labor supply and consumption behavior—as people responded. As a result, income flows in the economy would have changed. For example, families with increased income would have spent more on consumption, and this would have altered the level of demand, first in their region of residence and then in other regions, as second and third round demands would have trickled through the economy and altered the pattern of regional output and employment. By altering regional and locational income and employment disparities, PBJI might even have changed migration patterns, since they depend in part upon economic conditions in various regions and urban areas. Higher income regions or urban areas, or places with low unemployment rates or generous income support policies tend to attract people from those regions or areas with fewer income possibilities.

One of the items to which PBJI-induced spending would have been devoted is housing. PBJI would have increased current income and, by providing an income floor, future income. This provision of economic security would have increased purchases of durable goods, such as long-term rental leases or mortgages for owner-occupied housing. In addition, because the economic and residential characteristics of black and white families differ, PBJI might have affected the level and pattern of racial residential segregation in urban areas.

Besides altering income flows and associated demand patterns, PBJI would have provided employment opportunities to those now relying on cash transfers, leading to an increase in the labor force and a decrease in measured unemployment (the size of this response varying from Standard Metropolitan Statistical Area [SMSA] to SMSA). PBJI would have induced changes in the demand and supply of labor through three channels. First, with the direct provision of 1.4 million public service jobs, the demand for low-level skilled labor would have shifted. Second, the increased spending stimulated by the increased income flows would have stimulated changed demands for production and labor. Third, the increased provision of transfers would have altered the work incentives of recipients, and hence their labor supply. These demand and supply shifts would have had differential impacts on labor markets and, hence, wage rates in various urban areas.

Finally, PBJI would have provided fiscal relief to State (and a few local governments. The amount of relief would have depended on the generosity of current state welfare programs and the extent to which states would have supplemented PBJI benefits. As a result, relief would have varied widely among states.

In the following subsections, the urban impacts discussed in this overview are analyzed, using data derived from two sources. The first is a set of simulations done by the Department of Health, Education, and Welfare, employing the microdata model used to estimate cost and incidence effects of welfare reform alternatives (Betson, Greenberg, and Kasten, forthcoming). This computer model is based on the 1976 Survey of Income and Education data and applies the rules and benefit schedules of PBJI to individual families in the data base. The model incorporates labor supply and employment responses, and income and job creation effects are estimated for each of the families. These individual household-based impacts are aggregated for each of the largest SMSAs.

Other estimates of PBJI's impacts come from simulations of the Poverty Institute Regional and Distributional Model (Golladay and Haveman, 1977). This model employs several microdata and sectoral data sets to trace the results of a change in income on alterations in the level and composition of consumption spending. As the composition of demands for goods and services changes—by industry and by region—various firms in various regions alter their production levels and call for a new constellation of indirect demands and employment patterns. After the economy has adjusted to new demands created by the policy, some sectors—occupations, industries, regions, income classes—will gain and others will lose. The Poverty Institute model is designed to estimate these induced sectoral effects.

Some specific urban impacts of PBJI

This section describes the effects of PBJI on income flows, employment, poverty incidence, and fiscal relief for urban areas, and on income inequalities among regions. These estimates represent the direct effects of the program. Possible induced responses (e.g., migration and racial segregation) are described in the third section of this paper. Unless otherwise noted, estimates are based on the unlikely assumption that the states would not have supplemented PBJI benefit levels. If they would have provided supplementation, income flows and poverty reductions would have increased, but fiscal relief to the states would have decreased.

On an aggregate level, the program would have produced an increase in total disposable income of $4.1 billion (Table 2). Although private sector earned income (PSE) and cash transfers would have fallen, PSE earnings would have more than compensated for the reduction. The $2.8 billion reduction in taxes from the expanded EITC would have exceeded the increase in other taxes stemming from the increased earnings.

Table 3 shows the distribution of this $4.1 billion change in disposable income by income class. Families with incomes of less than $2,000 would have experienced an increase in per family disposable income of $310. The aggregate increase for this income class would have been almost as large as that of the $6,000–$12,000 group. However, because the lowest income class contains only 5.4 percent of the nation's families, the per family disposable income increase would have been nearly seven times that of the higher income group. Because of the abolition of several transfer programs, the

TABLE 2: Changes in Disposable Income, by Income Source (billions of 1975 dollars)

	Income Change	
Source of Income	*Losses*	*Gains*
Private earned income	1.5	
Public service earned income		6.3
Income-conditioned cash or in-kind benefits	2.3	
Unemployment benefits	0.6	
Earned income tax credit		2.8
Federal income taxes	0.2	
Social security taxes	0.3	
State income taxes	0.1	
Totals	5.0	9.1
Net Gain		*4.1*

Source: Simulations by the U.S. Department of Health, Education and Welfare.

TABLE 3: Distribution of Change in Disposable Income, by Income Class

Current Family Disposable Income	Total Change in Disposable Income (millions of 1975 dollars)	Per Family Change in Disposable Income (all families)	Per Family Change in Disposable Income (families with a change)
Less than $2,000	$1,286.5	$310.37	$448.07
$2,000– 3,000	312.0	59.06	93.89
$3,000– 4,000	403.4	77.58	160.78
$4,000– 5,000	421.5	77.97	204.73
$5,000– 6,000	392.0	69.47	184.82
$6,000–12,000	1,322.9	44.86	145.96
Over $12,000	−50.4	−2.29	−29.35
All income groups	$4,087.8	$ 52.95	$172.96

Source: Simulations by the U.S. Department of Health, Education and Welfare.

increase in disposable income for the $2,000–$3,000 and $3,000–$4,000 income groups would have been low relative to that of the other income classes. It should be noted that because Table 3 summarizes average results within income classes, it disguises the fact that there would have been a distribution of effects within each class. Thus, even in the lowest income classes there are some families who would have been adversely affected by the program (for example, current AFDC recipients in high benefit states). In addition, the analysis assumes that the additional costs of PBJI would have been borne through deficit spending. If they would have been covered by tax increases, the total income flows would have been smaller, and many high and middle income households would have had negative income flows.

Impacts on aggregate urban income

As suggested above, PBJI would have altered the flow of aggregate income[4] among the nation's metropolitan areas (SMSAs). Here we present estimates of these income impacts for the 40 largest SMSAs.[5] Table 4, column 1, indi-

---

[4] Aggregate income is here defined as Census Bureau money income plus the Food Stamp bonus less Federal and State income taxes and social security payroll taxes.

[5] A few large SMSAs are not included. The location of residents in these SMSAs was suppressed by the Census Bureau to insure confidentiality of respondents. Although Table 4 presents data for the largest 40 SMSAs, the impacts were estimated for 84 SMSAs. The detailed SMSA estimates in the tables are point estimates based on the sample observations included in the SIE for an area. For the large SMSAs, the 95 percent confidence interval fits tightly around the point estimate. However, for the smaller SMSAs, the 95 percent confidence interval is large. Especially for the smaller SMSAs then, the results should only be taken as suggestive, and little significance attached to differential impacts among the smaller areas. On this matter, see Holmer, Chapter 21, below.

cates that only two of the SMSAs would have experienced a reduction in the aggregate flow of income. The changes in income would have ranged from a loss of .02 percent to a gain of 1.1 percent of preprogram income.

An analysis of the SMSA income changes, using the regressions shown in Table 5, reveals the following: SMSAs with higher per capita incomes would have experienced a smaller change in income than those with lower per capita incomes. Whereas the change in income would have averaged .4 percent of preprogram income for an SMSA with mean per capita income, an SMSA with $1,000 more than the mean would have averaged an increase of .64 percent, and one with $1,000 less than the mean would have averaged an increase of only .16 percent. PBJI-induced income changes would have been higher in those areas with a higher incidence of poverty, but there would have been no clear relationship between income changes and unemployment rates across SMSAs.

By and large, the regional pattern of income change would have been consistent with that of per capita income. Column 1, Table 6 shows that, on

TABLE 4: Program Impacts for Selected Metropolitan Areas

SMSA (by population size)	Program-Induced Change in Income (% of preprogram income)	Public Service Jobs (% of unemployed)[a]	Reduction in Total Poverty (%)
New York	0.07	32.9	14.2
Los Angeles-Long Beach	0.17	31.7	21.1
Chicago	0.11	42.3	7.7
Philadelphia	0.30	25.0	18.2
Detroit	0.35	26.6	13.9
San Francisco-Oakland	−0.02	12.6	15.2
Washington	0.10	33.7	2.7
Boston	0.34	15.6	13.4
Pittsburgh	0.13	34.4	7.6
St. Louis	0.33	29.5	6.5
Baltimore	0.25	36.8	3.7
Cleveland	0.32	39.6	2.4
Houston	0.50	40.4	18.6
Newark	0.20	25.8	23.9
Minneapolis-St. Paul	0.10	25.1	3.8
Dallas	0.38	40.3	18.0
Seattle-Everett	0.27	20.8	19.2
Anaheim-Santa Ana-Garden Grove	−0.02	49.1	−0.4
Milwaukee	0.09	29.0	6.2
Atlanta	0.51	28.9	14.2

TABLE 4 (continued)

SMSA (by populatoin size)	Program-Induced Change in Income (% of preprogram income)	Public Service Jobs (% of unemployed)[a]	Reduction in Total Poverty (%)
Cincinnati	0.63	37.1	12.3
Paterson-Clifton-Passaic	0.15	34.7	5.0
San Diego	0.09	37.2	8.1
Buffalo	0.34	28.5	18.4
Miami	0.49	31.7	4.4
Kansas City	0.30	31.3	5.8
Denver	0.20	29.6	8.3
Indianapolis	0.42	45.9	17.1
San Jose	0.12	28.6	16.7
New Orleans	0.56	45.4	48.7
Tampa-St. Petersburg	0.61	34.2	5.8
Portland (Oregon)	0.28	22.6	9.6
Phoenix	0.69	26.8	14.3
Columbus	0.03	22.3	−9.5
Rochester	0.15	38.3	0.6
San Antonio	0.78	36.1	8.6
Dayton	0.62	57.3	14.7
Louisville	0.45	25.4	6.7
Sacramento	1.10	77.2	46.2
Memphis	1.00	62.5	3.7

Source: Simulations by the U.S. Department of Health, Education and Welfare.
[a] Because each PSE job, on average, would have employed two individuals during a year, the size of this ratio does not indicate the extent of the reduction in unemployment.

average, SMSAs in the Southeast and Southwest regions would have experienced increases in income of .6 percent, whereas increases in most other regions would have averaged about .35 percent. SMSAs in the Far West would have experienced increases of less than .2 percent.

A state-by-state analysis of the regional income impact of PBJI is summarized in Table 7, column 1, where the full regional allocation of the $4.1 billion change in disposable income is shown. These estimates include the changes in disposable income to all families in a region. On balance, the South would have experienced an increase in disposable income of $2.1 billion, over 50 percent of the total increase of $4.1 billion. The North Central region would have experienced an increase of nearly $1 billion and the Northeast and West, together, would have accounted for the remaining $1 billion. The two surprises among the detailed regions are the changes recorded for New York (region 2) and California (region 23). The gains in income

TABLE 5: Program Impacts, by SMSA Characteristics

		SMSA Characteristics			
Program Impacts (mean value)	*Constant*	*Per Capita Income in Thousands*	*Unem- ployment Rate*	*Incidence of Poverty*	R^2
Program-induced change in income as a percent of	1.64	−0.24 (5.74)			.287
preprogram income (0.395)	0.44		−0.006 (0.39)		.002
	−0.12			0.04 (6.38)	.332
Public service jobs as a percent of unemployment	58.22	−4.66 (1.95)			.044
(33.41)	49.30		−1.87 (2.73)		.083
	14.94			1.30 (4.04)	.166
Percent reduc- tion in poverty	19.18	−1.43 (0.79)			.008
(11.59)					
	2.99		1.02 (1.95)		.044
	5.22			0.45 (1.75)	.036

Note: Univariate regression; 84 observations; t-statistic appears below regression coefficients.

would have been small for these states because existing programs, which would have been abolished, provide very high benefit levels.

PBJI would also have favored metropolitan areas in fast- rather than slow-growing states. In part, this is due to the fact that the South, which would have experienced large income gains, is both a relatively low income and fast-growing region.[6] The 20 SMSAs in states designated as fast-growing

---

[6] The designation of fast- and slow-growing states is from Bretzfelder, 1977. The two types of regions are defined as follows: *fast-growing*—Alaska, Maine, Wyoming, Texas, Michigan, Utah, Louisiana, Mississippi, New Mexico, New Hampshire, Nevada, West Virginia, Oregon, South Carolina, Alabama, Tennessee, Kentucky; *slow-growing*—North Dakota, South Dakota, Nebraska, Montana, Iowa, Minnesota, Illinois, New York, District of Columbia, Hawaii, Connecticut, Massachusetts, Delaware.

TABLE 6: Program Impacts, by Region of SMSA

	Mean of:			
Region of SMSA	Program-Induced Ch. in Inc. as % of Prepro-gram Inc.[a]	Pub. Serv. Jobs as % of Unem-ployed[a]	% Reduc-tion in Total Poverty[a]	Fiscal Relief as % of Current Welfare Expend.[b]
New England	0.37	21.1	21.8	7.1
Mideast	0.31	29.8	10.2	18.3
Southeast	0.63	39.7	12.1	4.4
Great Lakes	0.37	33.9	9.0	11.0
Plains	0.34	28.5	6.5	4.6
Southwest	0.60	38.2	10.6	7.3
Rocky Mountains	0.35	35.7	9.3	4.6
Far West	0.17	41.5	11.2	8.3

Source: Simulations by the U.S. Department of Health, Education and Welfare.
[a] Means computed for SMSAs in each region (84 SMSAs total).
[b] Means computed for states in each region.

would have experienced an income gain of .56 percent, whereas those in slow-growing states—primarily New England and the Mideast—would have experienced an average income gain of .26 percent.

Impacts on urban employment

In part, PBJI was designed to move low-income people from unemployment and welfare rolls into employment. The primary instrument for accomplishing this would have been the 1.4 million public service jobs (PSE) created for primary earners in low income (primarily welfare) families. Because many accepting these jobs would have held them for less than one year, a single PSE job would have provided work to more than one individual over the course of a year.[7]

Some of the individuals who would have occupied these jobs would have been unemployed. Others would have entered the labor force to accept these jobs. Still others would have left existing jobs for a PSE job. Because of these various patterns, PBJI would have decreased measured unemployment where PSE jobs were located, and simultaneously increased labor force participation and employment. The reduction in measured unemployment would have been smaller than the increase in employment.

An indicator of the differential effect of PBJI on measured unemployment in an urban area is the ratio of the number of individuals who would have

[7] It is estimated that on average each PSE job would have been held for about 24 weeks. Hence, each job would have employed two individuals.

TABLE 7: Change in Disposable Income, Gross Output, and Labor Demand, by Region

Area and Region (numbered)	Change in Disposable Income (millions of dollars) (1)	Change in Gross Output (millions of dollars) (2)	Ratio of Col. (2) to Col. (1) (3)	Change in Labor Demand (thousands of man-years) (4)
Northeast	629.1	1,086.7	1.73	42.3
1. (Connecticut, Maine, Massachusetts, New Hampshire, Rhode Island, Vermont)	200.8	353.6	1.76	13.5
2. (New York)	126.2	327.8	2.60	12.0
3. (Pennsylvania, New Jersey)	302.1	405.3	1.34	16.8
North Central	957.1	1,634.3	1.71	62.0
4. (Ohio, Michigan)	431.6	512.2	1.19	20.0
5. (Indiana, Illinois)	244.2	372.2	1.53	14.0
6. (Wisconsin, Minnesota)	86.9	253.1	2.92	8.8
7. (Iowa, Missouri)	95.7	252.2	2.64	10.0
8. (Kansas, Nebraska, North Dakota, South Dakota)	98.7	244.6	2.49	9.2
South	2,115.3	3,653.4	1.73	159.0
9. (Delaware, District of Columbia, Maryland)	64.0	262.7	4.11	8.6
10. (Virginia, West Virginia)	187.0	330.6	1.77	13.6
11. (North Carolina)	219.6	338.1	1.54	15.8
12. (South Carolina)	126.7	271.9	2.15	12.9
13. (Georgia)	173.8	282.7	1.63	10.1
14. (Florida)	264.8	352.4	1.33	16.6
15. (Kentucky, Tennessee)	235.9	352.5	1.49	15.2
16. (Alabama)	121.3	267.1	2.20	11.0
17. (Missouri)	114.2	247.7	2.17	14.3
18. (Arkansas, Oklahoma)	135.7	268.7	1.98	11.7
19. (Louisiana)	119.5	256.4	2.15	10.9
20. (Texas)	352.8	422.6	1.20	18.3
West	386.5	795.3	2.05	29.2
21. (Arizona, Colorado, Idaho, New Mexico, Utah, Nevada, Wyoming, Montana, Alaska)	225.1	319.7	1.42	13.8
22. (Washington, Oregon, Hawaii)	105.9	237.5	2.24	8.2
23. (California)	55.4	238.1	4.30	7.2
U.S.	4,087.8	7,169.9	1.75	292.6

Source: The Poverty Institute Regional and Distributional Model simulations of PBJI.

received some earnings from public service jobs in a year to the number of unemployed individuals.[8] Column 2, Table 4 presents this indicator for each of the largest SMSAs. The indicator would have ranged from a high of 77.2 percent (Sacramento) to a low of 12.6 percent (San Francisco).

The second group of regressions in Table 5 shows that the distribution of PSE impacts would have been similar to the pattern of income flows across SMSAs. PSE jobs would have decreased with per capita income and increased with the incidence of poverty. Surprisingly, the allocation of PSE jobs does not appear to favor those SMSAs with more serious unemployment problems. The jobs impact would have declined by about 2 percentage points for each 1 percent increase in the unemployment rate.

The regional pattern of PSE jobs, shown in column 2, Table 6, would have been quite different from the pattern of income flows. The region with the highest jobs-unemployed indicator would have been the Far West. Following the Far West would have been the two southern regions. New England, which has a serious unemployment problem, would have had the lowest indicator.

These results reveal that the South and the West, which are already fast-growing areas, would have experienced greater increments to labor demand from PBJI than other, slow-growing regions. Because fast-growing areas generally experience greater upward wage pressure than slow-growing regions, the program would have increased upward wage pressure in these areas even more. Because the South—a relatively low wage area—would have had one of the largest indicators, this wage effect of PBJI would have tended to narrow wage differentials nationally. The extent of this wage pressure, however, would probably not have been very large, given the low wage rate of the PSE jobs.

The evidence presented so far concerns the increase in labor demand from the PSE jobs. Another source of labor demand would also have developed— the demand for labor to produce the direct and indirect outputs stimulated by PBJI-induced consumption. Columns 2, 3, and 4, Table 7 summarize these output and employment effects. Column 2 shows that, for the entire nation, gross output would have increased by about $7.1 billion because of PBJI. About 51 percent of this increase would have accrued to the South, while the North Central region would have received almost a quarter. The Northeast and West would have accounted for 15 and 11 percent, respectively. Column 3 shows the ratio of induced gross output to the change in disposable income for each of the regions and the United States. For the entire nation, this ratio would have been 1.75. Among the various regions,

[8] Because the number of individuals working at a PSE job during a year exceeds one, the absolute size of this ratio does not indicate the extent of reduction in unemployment. If it is assumed that no increase in labor force participation would have resulted from PBJI, and if job duration in PSE jobs equaled the duration in the pool of unemployed, the percentage of reduction in unemployment would have been equal to about one-half the value of this indicator.

this ratio would have varied from 4.30 in California to 1.19 in the Ohio-Michigan region. In general, this distribution of gross output by region would have been less unequal than the distribution of changes in disposable income. Hence as the induced expenditure demands stimulated by PBJI would have been reflected in gross output patterns, the regional disparities in the distribution of net transfers would have been reduced.

That the induced output would have reflected the general geographic location of productive capacity is also shown in column 4 of the table. It reveals the regional distribution of the nearly 300,000 additional man-years of employment that additional consumption from the program would have induced. Over one-half of this increase would have been in the South. However, the West would have experienced only a small increase in labor demand—about 10 percent of that of the nation as a whole. This effect would have offset the pattern of labor demand and wage pressures from PSE jobs in this region relative to other regions.

Impacts on poverty reduction

Although the elimination of poverty was not one of the primary goals of PBJI, a considerable reduction in the poverty population would have resulted. Detailed estimates of poverty reduction[9] in the largest SMSAs are shown in column 3, Table 4. Because changes in aggregate income in an SMSA are related to changes in poverty reduction, the patterns shown in these estimates parallel those shown earlier.

If we assume that states would not have supplemented benefit levels, the largest metropolitan areas would have experienced, on average, an 11.59 percent decrease in the number of poor people. A few SMSAs would have experienced an increase in the number of poor. The persons who most likely would have suffered income losses from PBJI are those working in states with high current-benefit levels. Because blacks have a higher incidence of welfare recipiency in these states, they would have experienced disproportionate increases in poverty. As the third panel of Table 5 suggests, the reduction in poverty would have been higher in SMSAs with lower per capita incomes, higher unemployment rates, and a higher incidence of preprogram poverty.

Table 6 shows that urban areas in the New England region would have had the greatest reduction in poverty, while those in the Plains states would have had the smallest. The large reductions in New England and the South would have occurred because of the low benefit levels provided by current welfare programs in several of these states.

Impacts on fiscal relief

The existing federal welfare system tends to impose financial responsibilities on states rather than on local governments. These responsibilities include

[9] The indicator of poverty reduction is the percentage of reduction in the number of poor people, using the official poverty level as a criterion.

cost sharing in the Aid to Families with Dependent Children (AFDC), Medicaid, Emergency Assistance, and Food Stamp programs. In addition, states can, and are encouraged to, supplement federal benefits under the Supplemental Security Income (SSI) and General Assistance programs. In 1975, State and local governments spent about $27.2 billion on these programs, of which $14.4 billion was financed by federal grants. In that year, welfare expenditures by State and local governments were about 12 percent of their general expenditures, up from 8.5 percent only a decade earlier. That rapid increase came from two sources. One was the accelerated rise in AFDC benefit levels and in the participation rate among the eligible population in the 1968–1973 period. This rapid growth of AFDC payments ended in the early seventies. The second source of major expansion during the past decade was the Medicaid program. Its growth has not slackened. Because of these increased costs, fiscal relief to the states became a major objective of welfare reform.

Various aspects of PBJI would have affected the aggregate liability of the states for welfare payments. The Federal government would have paid 90 percent of the federally mandated national guarantees. In some high benefit states that would have constituted an increase in the federal share, and would have provided direct fiscal relief if those states would not have altered their policies. In many low income, low benefit level states of the South, their 10 percent share of the national guarantees would have exceeded their current spending and, unless other changes were made, the fiscal burden for them would have increased. Other factors would have also affected the states' expenditures. States, for example, could have chosen to supplement both cash assistance and the wage paid on public service jobs. If they had done so within rigorously prescribed rules, the Federal government would have paid part of that supplementation. The states would have been required to "grandfather" most current beneficiaries and to "maintain effort," i.e., spend on a range of social programs what is currently spent on welfare. Also, the states would have had to establish an emergency needs program for which federal funds could have proven insufficient. The net effect of all these complex interconnections would have been uncertain. Hence, a final assurance of fiscal relief was established: All states would have been guaranteed at least a 10 percent reduction from current spending.

Tables 6 (column 4) and 8 reveal how fiscal relief would have been distributed across states and regions. These estimates embody expectations about state supplementation as provided by the states themselves. As expected, the low income, low benefit states of the South would have received the smallest fiscal relief, both absolutely and as a percentage of their current welfare expenditures. Fiscal relief as a percentage of welfare expenditures would have been higher in states with higher levels of per capita income. Relative gains would have been largest in the Mideast and Great Lakes states. Within those regions the big gainers would have been the states with both

TABLE 8: Fiscal Relief, by State

	Fiscal Relief (millions of dollars)	Fiscal Relief as % of Welfare Expenditures		Fiscal Relief (millions of dollars)	Fiscal Relief as % of Welfare Expenditures
Northeast			*North Central*		
Connecticut	9.7	5.7	Ohio	84.4	13.6
Maine	3.8	6.1	Michigan	98.8	10.6
Massachusetts	112.5	13.2	Indiana	5.2	2.6
New Hampshire	1.5	3.2	Illinois	195.7	25.0
Rhode Island	7.9	8.9	Wisconsin	11.7	3.4
Vermont	1.7	5.5	Minnesota	10.0	3.6
New York	424.5	21.9	Iowa	5.0	3.1
Pennsylvania	145.4	15.4	Missouri	17.9	9.3
New Jersey	66.6	12.4	Kansas	3.9	4.1
			Nebraska	1.6	2.4
South			North Dakota	0.5	3.7
Delaware	5.8	16.4	South Dakota	1.4	5.9
District of					
Columbia	34.0	24.1	*West*		
Maryland	44.9	19.8	Arizona	2.7	4.7
Virginia	7.7	3.7	Colorado	4.7	5.1
West Virginia	2.4	5.5	Idaho	1.2	5.7
North Carolina	5.7	4.4	New Mexico	2.6	10.9
South Carolina	3.7	8.0	Utah	1.4	4.9
Georgia	8.4	5.2	Nevada	1.7	6.6
Florida	10.7	5.1	Wyoming	0.3	3.1
Kentucky	4.8	3.3	Montana	0.8	4.4
Tennessee	5.3	4.7	Alaska	1.4	6.3
Alabama	5.3	6.0	Washington	23.5	12.7
Mississippi	1.8	3.1	Oregon	7.6	5.9
Arkansas	1.7	0.3	Hawaii	4.7	5.9
Oklahoma	7.8	8.5	California	316.7	12.2
Louisiana	7.6	6.8	U.S.	1,750.3	12.7
Texas	12.7	5.0			

Source: Simulations by the U.S. Department of Health, Education and Welfare.

high benefit levels and large numbers of welfare recipients. In fact, about 60 percent of the total fiscal relief would have been received by four states: New York, Pennsylvania, Illinois, and California.

The few cities which both administer and have a financial stake in the welfare system, of which New York is the primary example, would have directly benefited from PBJI. In most states, however, any benefits to the cities would have come only indirectly, depending on how these states would have allocated their savings among alternative policies. Since we do not know how states would actually have distributed the relief, we cannot estimate fiscal relief to cities.

Impacts on intraregional income inequality
Table 3 indicates that the distribution of disposable income gains from PBJI would have been distinctly pro-poor. However, these impacts were only the first-round redistributional impacts. Because of the pattern of consumption and production induced by PBJI, additional labor would have been hired. These workers would have had a particular skill composition and would have generated earned income with a distinct distributional pattern. The effect of the program on the distribution of induced earnings is shown for regional groupings of states in Table 9. One pattern dominates these

TABLE 9: Earnings Class Impact Indicators, by Region

| | Impact Indicators by Earnings Class | | | | |
Area and Region (numbered)	Less than $4,000	$4,000– 10,000	$10,000– 20,000	Over $20,000	Regional Impact Indicator
Northeast	1.56[a]	1.89	2.00	2.34[b]	1.79
1. (Connecticut, Massachusetts, Maine, New Hampshire, Rhode Island, Vermont)	2.13[a]	2.46	2.57	3.22[b]	2.36
2. (New York)	1.03[a]	1.49	1.58[b]	1.52	1.32
3. (Pennsylvania, New Jersey)	1.73[a]	1.94	2.12	2.83[b]	1.91
North Central	2.22[a]	2.43	2.58	2.88[b]	2.38
4. (Ohio, Michigan)	2.17[a]	2.19	2.43	2.96[b]	2.24
5. (Indiana, Illinois)	1.69[a]	1.87	2.02	2.54[b]	1.85
6. (Wisconsin, Minnesota)	1.98[a]	2.47	2.75[b]	2.47	2.29
7. (Iowa, Missouri)	2.48[a]	3.19	3.47[b]	3.19	2.90
8. (Kansas, Nebraska, North Dakota, South Dakota)	3.69[a]	4.32	4.53[b]	4.19	4.02
South	5.34[a]	6.33	6.80	7.13[b]	5.94
9. (Delaware, District of Columbia, Maryland)	3.28[a]	3.73	3.89	4.01[b]	3.75
10. (Virginia, West Virginia)	4.68[a]	5.99[b]	5.67	5.30	5.33
11. (North Carolina)	6.06[a]	6.84	9.24	12.87[b]	6.69
12. (South Carolina)	8.39[a]	12.13	15.21	20.25[b]	10.33
13. (Georgia)	4.40[a]	5.16	6.61	7.05[b]	4.97
14. (Florida)	5.24[a]	6.62	6.53	7.15[b]	5.94
15. (Kentucky, Tennessee)	4.49[a]	5.14	6.97	7.67[b]	5.03
16. (Alabama)	6.84[a]	8.56	10.26[b]	9.35	7.86
17. (Mississippi)	13.92	20.10	23.78[b]	12.72[a]	16.62

TABLE 9 (continued)

18. (Arkansas, Oklahoma)	5.30[a]	6.63	7.52	8.07[b]	6.04
19. (Louisiana)	6.97[a]	8.44	9.91	10.10[b]	7.92
20. (Texas)	3.43[a]	3.97	4.17	4.69[b]	3.76
West	1.77[a]	2.10[b]	1.87	1.89	1.91
21. (Arizona, Colorado, Idaho, New Mexico, Utah, Nevada, Wyoming, Montana, Alaska)	3.29[a]	3.92	4.06	4.09[b]	3.65
22. (Washington, Oregon, Hawaii)	2.48[a]	4.88[b]	3.22	3.35	3.31
23. (California)	0.74[a]	0.82	0.87	0.92[b]	0.80
U.S.	3.01[a]	3.35	3.18	3.55[b]	3.18

Source: The Poverty Institute Regional and Distributional Model simulations of PBJI.
[a] Minimum for region.
[b] Maximum for region.

estimates. The lowest skill/lowest earnings class (less than $4,000) would have had the lowest impact indicator[10] in 22 of the 23 regions, Mississippi being the only exception. Conversely, the highest earnings class (more than $20,000) would have had the largest impact indicator in 15 of the 23 regions. For the four Census Bureau regions and for the United States, the lowest skill/lowest earnings class would have had the lowest impact indicator and, with the exception of the western region, all of the highest earnings classes would have had the highest impact indicators. For the United States as a whole, the impact indicator for the highest earnings class (3.55) would have been 18 percent greater than that of the lowest earnings class.

These comparisons indicate that the final income distributional impact of PBJI would probably have been weaker than that indicated by the high concentration of disposable income changes in the lowest income classes. Although the induced consumption and production decisions would have been less pro-poor than the initial redistribution, these induced effects, in fact, would also have tended to offset in part the initial redistribution. The lower income families experiencing the increased income would have spent their income increments on goods and services produced by relatively high earn-

---

[10] The earnings class indicator is the ratio of induced labor demand in a regional earnings class to 1970 employment in that earnings class times .001. Symbolically,

$$S_i = \frac{M_i}{.001\,(E_i)},$$

where S_i is the impact indicator for a regional earnings class, M_i is the program-induced change in employment in that earnings class, and E_i is the total 1970 employment in that earnings class.

ings groups. The program would have achieved a reduction in inequality, but the indirect effects would have shifted the structure of employment away from low skill/low earnings classes and toward high skill/high earnings classes.

SOME LONG-TERM AND DYNAMIC IMPACTS OF PBJI

Impacts on regional income disparities

In 1840, per capita income in the Northeast was 80 percent greater than per capita income in the South; by 1940 the income advantage of the Northeast over the Southeast had declined to about 30 percent. Since the Northeast has traditionally been the highest per capita income region and the Southeast the lowest, comparing them is suggestive of the long-term trend in regional income differentials. That comparison reveals that income differentials across regions have been large and persistent. Although they have narrowed through time, there has been no significant change in the rank order of regions.

An important source of convergence during the recent past has been the relatively rapid growth of transfer payments in the low income states (Labovitz, 1978). Although old-age and survivor payments dominate this flow, SSI benefits and AFDC payments also play a part. PBJI would have reinforced this development. PBJI would not have significantly affected the flow of federal funds to SSI recipients, but its cash supplements would have directed larger federal flows to the low income Southeast than the AFDC and Food Stamp programs combined. The magnitude of those changes, as indicated in the previous section of this paper would not have been large, but the direction toward the low income and rapidly growing regions would have been clear.

Hence, the direct effect of the cash assistance portion of PBJI would have been to accelerate the ongoing convergence pattern. Although less certain, the same would have probably been true of the jobs component. One question remains: Would the long-run indirect effects have countered the short-run direct effects? The argument here would be as follows. Convergence results in large part from the migration of industry south. Would higher welfare benefits and more competition for workers by the public sector have slowed this migration, thus offsetting the direct transfer and employment effects of the program? Because PBJI would have had small income and employment effects, such indirect effects seem unlikely. However, as transfer recipients would have spent their income and the multiplier effects of the income redistribution would have worked themselves out nationwide, benefits would have become more equally distributed among regions and the convergence impact would have been reduced.

Impact on regional and urban-rural migration patterns

The demographic history of the United States has been dominated by massive migratory transformations. Four pervasive patterns may be identified: immigration, westward settlement, urbanization, and suburbanization.

Immigration has been a fundamental source of growth in the United States. In the most recent period, however, restrictive legislation has kept immigration tightly controlled. PBJI would not have had any discernible impact on the pattern of legal immigration. Although there has been a major increase in the volume of illegal immigration, these persons are outside the current statistical system, so there is little basis for speculation about the illegal immigration impact, if any, of PBJI. To the extent that illegal immigrants are able to obtain welfare benefits, the increased benefits under PBJI might have increased illegal immigration by a small amount.

Westward movement was the dominant regional migration pattern throughout the settlement of the continent. Right through the postwar decades, the West continued as the primary destination of long-distance migrants. Florida and Texas also received immigrants, but much of the South was still sending out migrants from rural areas and small towns. However, in the 1970s a sharp change in regional migration occurred. The "Sunbelt" became the highly publicized new growth center.

There is no consensus on the precise influence of differential welfare and income-security programs on migration flows, except that such factors, if influential, are of minor impact in explaining gross regional patterns and the rise of the Sunbelt. From the discussion above, it is apparent that the direct effect of PBJI would have been to augment income in the fast-growing metropolitan areas of the Sunbelt more than in other areas. To the extent that these income effects add to the relative demographic retentive and attractive power of the Sunbelt the current regional migration patterns toward this area would have been slightly reinforced by PBJI.

Another centuries-long migration pattern has reached a turning point in the 1970s. The growth of metropolitan areas had been the dominant feature of demographic change. The great "nonmetropolitan turn around" of the 1970s was the culmination of a concentration process that could not continue forever. The role of urban social service and welfare programs as a stimulus to metropolitan growth cannot have been a dominant one, as compared to the massive economic and social determinants of population concentration. Nor has it been demonstrated that the Food Stamp program and other welfare changes of recent years had a significant effect on the genesis or magnitude of the nonmetropolitan turn around. Our simulation estimates indicate that the income and jobs effects of PBJI would have been greater in the fast-growing states, which tend to be southern states that are less highly metropolitan. Because PBJI would have produced a more standardized national level of aid, the possible slight effects of PBJI on metropolitan migration would have reinforced the existing patterns of the 1970s.

The black population has been thought to be more susceptible to welfare program influences on migration than the white population. Throughout recent decades a far higher proportion of blacks were poor and were concentrated in low income regions with low welfare benefits. Some empirical analyses conclude that welfare benefits fostered black migration; some do not. Others indicate that black migrants to cities generally found jobs and avoided welfare programs. PBJI probably would have reinforced slightly the recent pattern of a more balanced flow of black migrants between regions and increased the similarity between black and white intermetropolitan flows.

The fourth pervasive migration pattern in American history is suburbanization. Peripheral growth has been part of the metropolitan growth process for at least two centuries. However, in recent decades welfare benefit levels in a number of large central cities may have deterred the out-movement of the poor, and hence contributed to a cycle of selective out-movement of the middle classes and the relative reduction of the fiscal capacity and economic and social viability of cities. The research results again are inconclusive.

PBJI might have reduced some of the welfare system incentives for selective city-suburban migration. The fiscal relief offered by PBJI would have been relatively larger in the highly metropolitan states with current high welfare benefit levels, and this, too, might have produced some slight relief of the composite urban crises. These effects, however, would have been small relative to the other economic and social forces influencing the pace and character of suburbanization. Hence PBJI would have become only a minor component of the nation's broader urban policy.

Impact on urban racial segregation patterns

When the twentieth century began, the black population was residentially concentrated by region (in the South), by type of place (rural), and by location within places (the "other side of the tracks"). By 1970 there had been a massive demographic redistribution. Nearly half the black population lived outside the South, and a higher percentage of blacks than whites lived in metropolitan areas. Racial residential segregation within places, by contrast, has persisted and in certain respects intensified.

If racial economic differentials and locality differentials in welfare systems were an important cause of racial residential segregation, then a program such as PBJI might have had some effect on patterns of segregation. Although our conclusions about the impact of PBJI on residential segregation are foreshadowed by our conclusions that PBJI would have had little impact on racial migration patterns, there are some additional considerations.

Despite the stereotypical image of wealthy suburbs and undesirable central-city housing, nondiscriminatory economic factors have not been a major cause of black concentration in the cities and white concentration in the suburbs. Both cities and suburbs are highly diversified in the price levels of their housing stock. With a few exceptions, urban whites at all income levels tend to be similarly distributed between city and suburban locations. At all income levels, blacks tend overwhelmingly to be central-city rather than suburban residents. Central-city concentration is a function of race far more than of income.

To the extent that PBJI would have provided a stable income floor, it might have increased spending by both poor whites and poor blacks on housing. According to the estimates in column 2, Table 10, the effects of PBJI on the aggregate income of black families in most metropolitan areas would have been less than 2 percent. This is so, even though, as column 3 shows, blacks would have received a disproportionate share of the special public jobs. Experience from the housing allowance experiments and other evidence on the housing consumption behavior of black families suggest that, at least in the short run, few locational changes would have occurred from such small income changes.

However, this is a general conclusion, and it is possible that there might have been some discernible impact of PBJI in a few metropolitan areas. The conjunction of a high PBJI impact in a metropolitan area that has an active program to assist minority residential dispersal might have fostered black suburbanization with some degree of lessened segregation.

TABLE 10: Program Impacts, SMSAs with Large (over 250,000) Black Populations

SMSA	Black Pop. (thousands)	Program-Induced Change in Income (as % of preprogram income)	PSE Jobs to Blacks (as % of all PSE jobs)	% Reduction in Total Poverty
New York	1,849	−0.79	37.6	3.4
Los Angeles-				
Long Beach	968	−0.15	32.9	12.6
Chicago	1,372	0.16	51.6	11.3
Philadelphia	754	0.57	50.5	21.7
Detroit	777	0.47	34.5	22.0
San Francisco	318	−0.33	18.4	12.1
Washington, D.C.	807	0.26	59.3	6.6
St. Louis	420	1.57	55.6	11.7
Baltimore	492	0.39	57.2	2.7
Cleveland	326	0.71	35.9	4.9
Houston	393	2.26	50.0	28.2
Newark	298	0.11	47.3	31.2
Dallas	306	2.50	51.6	27.3
Atlanta	460	1.92	72.2	17.4
Miami	344	1.46	34.8	0.0
New Orleans	293	1.48	70.9	6.7
Memphis	322	2.41	74.3	5.1

Source: Simulations by the U.S. Department of Health, Education and Welfare.

CONCLUSION

The urban impact of the Program for Better Jobs and Income would not have been substantial, but it would have slightly ameliorated some current urban problems. In particular, PBJI would have achieved the following:

• Reduced the incidence of poverty, and concentrated this reduction in areas with low per capita income and a high preprogram incidence of poverty.
• Reduced income disparities among persons in urban areas and among urban areas themselves.
• Reinforced current trends in relative regional growth, and hence, favored the fast-growing, but relatively poor Sunbelt region over the higher income, but relatively slow-growing Snowbelt region.
• Distributed PSE jobs toward urban areas with low per capita income and high levels of poverty, although failing to target these jobs in high unemployment areas.
• Concentrated fiscal relief on those states now making relatively high welfare payments to relatively large numbers of recipients.

PBJI, then, is consistent with a broader urban policy that seeks to enable distressed urban areas to regain economic viability and to attack the residential segregation that pervades the housing delivery system. This analysis has uncovered only two areas of potential conflict with such an urban policy —its reinforcement of the growth and migration patterns central to the "Sunbelt-Snowbelt" controversy, and its failure to target new public job slots in those areas with the most serious unemployment problems.

REFERENCES

Betson, David; Greenberg, David; and Kasten, Richard. "A Micro-Simulation Model for Analyzing Alternative Welfare Reform Proposals." In *Microeconomic Simulation Models for the Analysis of Public Policy,* edited by Robert Haveman and Kevin Hollenbeck. New York: Academic Press, forthcoming.
Congressional Budget Office, *The Administration's Welfare Reform Proposal.* Washington, D.C.: U.S. Government Printing Office, April 1978.
Danziger, Sheldon; Haveman, Robert; and Smolensky, Eugene. *The Program for Better Jobs and Incomes—A Guide and a Critique.* U.S. Congress, Joint Economic Committee. Washington, D.C.: U.S. Government Printing Office, October 1977.
Golladay, Frederick, and Haveman, Robert. *The Economic Impacts of Tax-Transfer Policy.* New York: Academic Press, 1977.
Bretzfelder, R. B. "State Personal Income, 1975–76." *Survey of Current Business,* August 1977.
Labovitz, I. M. "Federal Expenditures and Revenue in Regions and States." *Intergovernmental Perspective,* Fall 1978, pp. 16–23.

CHAPTER TEN

The Urban Impacts of the Section 8
Existing Housing Assistance Program

DAVID W. RASMUSSEN

This paper considers the urban impacts of the Section 8 Existing Housing program. This analysis represents an attempt to evaluate urban impacts with a method that can be used by program offices. In the first part the program is described and the general urban impacts of Section 8 are analyzed. The second part shows how program funds are distributed among geographic areas, income groups, and race. An evaluation of the spatial impacts of Section 8 Existing is presented in the third part. Alternatives are evaluated in the final section.

BACKGROUND AND DESCRIPTION

Description of the program

The Section 8 Existing Housing Assistance Payments program was authorized by the Housing and Community Development Act of 1974. It was developed from two previous housing programs: the Section 23 Leased Housing Program (LHP) and the Experimental Housing Allowance Program (EHAP). The LHP was made possible by a 1965 amendment to the U.S. Housing Act of 1937, which allowed a local housing authority to lease units from the private sector for subleasing to low income tenants. Families participating in the Section 23 program paid rent limited to 25 percent of their income adjusted for family size.

EHAP, which will be described in greater detail below, was begun in 1970 to demonstrate the potential use of housing allowances to improve the housing of the poor. EHAP differed from Section 23 by taking the local housing authority out of the rental business: housing assistance payments were paid

The author wishes to thank Norman Glickman, Susan S. Jacobs, Deborah Both, Edgar Olsen, and Thomas Kingsley for their comments on a previous draft of this paper.

directly to the eligible families. The Section 8 program is a hybrid of these two programs. It has three components: New Construction, Substantial Rehabilitation, and Existing. This urban impact analysis will focus on the Existing program, although important differences among these component programs will be noted.

Under the Existing program, Public Housing Authorities (PHAs) issue certificates which promise assistance to families with incomes less than 80 percent of the area's median income. Funds are sufficient to cover only a portion of the income-eligible families. The certificate holder must find a unit that meets Section 8 standards and rents for less than the maximum allowable rent. The maximum allowable rent is called the Fair Market Rent (FMR). FMRs are higher for dwellings with more rooms and for "recently completed" housing constructed or substantially rehabilitated within the last six years. They are calculated each year by the Economic Market Analysis Division of the U.S. Department of Housing and Urban Development (HUD).

The housing assistance payment is equal to the difference between the rent paid and 25 percent of family income adjusted for family size. Under this payments formula the assistance payment is larger when a family is larger or poorer. If a recipient household rents a unit for less than the FMR, the tenant's contribution is reduced by a fraction of the difference. This is the Rent Reduction Credit which is designed to provide an incentive to lower program costs.[1] A contract between the PHA and the landlord provides that the payment goes directly to the landlord as does a tenant contribution of 25 percent of adjusted family income.[2]

History of funding

Section 8 began in mid-1975 and by the end of Fiscal 1976 only 171,773 units had been allocated. Subsequently the program expanded rapidly, with a total of 531,357 units by the close of Fiscal 1977 and over 665,245 units by the end of 1978. Table 1 shows the growth of the Section 8 Existing program which is now the nation's second largest low income housing program, smaller than only Low Rent Public Housing.

The number of units reserved is used as the indicator of program size in Table 1. A reservation is made when a PHA application has been accepted. Before occupancy can be achieved, an Annual Contribution Contract (ACC) must be completed so that funds can be transmitted to the local area. Unit

[1] At present the Rent Reduction Credit is not working well, partly because it is not widely understood. This aspect of the program has been analyzed by Jill Khadduri, 1978.

[2] Under the New Construction and Substantial Rehabilitation programs the housing assistance contract is made between HUD and the sponsors of certain types of new or substantially rehabilitated projects that are designed for use by low income households. These contracts are for five years and renewable at the owners' discretion for twenty to forty years, depending on the type of sponsor and the kind of financing used. Once the project is in operation, it works like the Section 8 Existing program except that the subsidy is tied to the specific unit and the FMR is typically higher.

TABLE 1: Growth of the Section 8 Existing
Program, 1975–1978

Fiscal Year	No. Units Reserved
1975	55,322
1976	171,773
Transition quarter[a]	142,721
1977	161,581
1978	133,848
Total	665,245

Source: Budget Office, U.S. Department of Housing and Urban Development.
[a] Resulted from one-time change in the end of the fiscal year, from June 30 to September 30.

reservations are always greater than units occupied for three reasons. First, a period of time passes before reservations have a completed ACC. Second, units in an ACC allocation are not immediately occupied due to the time required for recipient search and program administration. And third, there is a normal turnover among participants. While this measure of program size is biased upward, the urban impacts measured using these data will represent the maximum impact from existing program commitments. However, there is no reason to believe the distribution of program impacts is affected. Variations in the difference between reservations and occupancy are not likely to vary significantly among regions.

General urban impacts of the Section 8 Existing program
This urban impact assessment of the Section 8 Existing program focuses on six variables: housing quality, neighborhood quality, employment, income, fiscal condition, and population. The urban impacts of the Section 8 Existing program stem from two fundamental forces. First, its impacts on the housing stock affect variables such as housing quality, neighborhood quality, and fiscal condition. Second, and of greater magnitude, are the effects of the income transfers that are associated with the Section 8 program. The program reduces the rent burden of participating households from an average of 40 percent of income to less than 25 percent, thus accomplishing a major redistribution of income independent of direct housing effects. This redistribution of income has a significant impact on the spatial distribution of employment and income.

Once the spatial distribution of program expenditures are known, impacts on the relevant variables must be ascertained. For example, what is the impact of housing allowances on employment or neighborhoods or fiscal condition? One way to determine these impacts is through theoretical reasoning. Approaching urban impact analysis in this way is more effective for some variables than others. For example, program expenditures are likely to have multiplier effects which tell us that the impacts are larger than the initial outlays. If no more specific data are available, theory can point to the expected *direction* of impact without providing an estimate of its magnitude.

Even the direction of impact on some variables cannot be determined by theory. Consider neighborhood quality. Housing allowances could, theoretically, work to improve neighborhoods by raising the rate of return to landlords, causing them to improve their property. In response to the program's direct effect, other owners might be encouraged to improve their property. Thus, theory might suggest a positive program effect on neighborhood quality. An equally strong case can be made that the program would have no impact on neighborhoods. Rather than investing in response to a higher rate of return, owners may not improve their property in some neighborhoods because the profit-maximizing strategy for each is to let other owners improve their property while making no investment. The ambiguity of theory points to a need for other tools to understand the direction and magnitude of urban impacts. Three such tools are simulation studies, program evaluations, and social experiments.

Simulations are an extension of theory that use statistical relationships to estimate program effects. This very useful tool is not likely to be used on a regular basis because of the high start-up costs. Currently operating simulation models have been employed for this purpose with considerable success.[3] Program evaluations and social experiments share the unfortunate attribute of high cost. An urban impact analysis can only use these if they happen to be available for the program under consideration or a similar program. In the case of Section 8 Existing, there is the good fortune of having a recently completed evaluation of Section 8 and the experience of a huge social experiment to draw on—the Experimental Housing Allowance Program (EHAP).

Much of the evidence presented here on the urban impacts of the Section 8 Existing program is drawn from EHAP. This experiment was performed in three parts: (1) the Demand Experiment in two large cities, Phoenix and Pittsburgh, was designed to test the response of recipients to the program; (2) the Supply Experiment tested the effects of an open enrollment program in two small markets, Green Bay and South Bend; and (3) an eight-city Administrative Agency Experiment tested the efficiency of alternative methods of program delivery.

Complete with control groups, this experiment presents a unique opportunity to evaluate Section 8 in the critical areas of housing and neighborhood quality, mobility, and fiscal condition. One caveat is in order: there are two

[3] The University of Wisconsin Poverty Institute's Regional and Distributional Model was used to evaluate the Program for Better Jobs and Income. An evaluation of the Section 8 program was simulated on the Urban Institute's Model. *See* Danziger et al., Chapter 9, above, and Struyk et al., 1978.

fundamental differences between EHAP and Section 8 Existing that may affect the quality of the evidence. First, housing assistance payments under EHAP were made directly to recipients rather than to the landlord as in Section 8. Second, the FMR in Section 8 is a maximum allowable rent, in EHAP it only served to determine the size of the subsidy and did not limit a household's consumption of housing. Nevertheless, the EHAP offers a unique opportunity to investigate the impacts of Section 8 wtih more precision than would otherwise be possible.

The problem of substitution. Estimating the absolute employment and income impacts of a program is relatively easy. Of greater difficulty is the measurement of the impacts compared to what they would have been in the absence of the program. This is the problem of substitution. Program substitution is the extent to which expenditures, and hence program impacts, merely replace expenditures that would have been made in the private sector. Examples are in ready supply. When HUD subsidizes the construction of a new housing unit it is difficult to know whether to count this as an additional housing start or a substitute for a dwelling that would have been built by the private sector. Expenditures, made as a result of transfer payments to the poor, might have been spent by taxpayers if they had paid fewer taxes in the absence of the program. The problem of substitution is an element that must be considered in the evaluation of any program.

Complicating the situation is the fact that the degree of substitution is likely to vary over the business cycle. Under a traditional fiscal stabilization program, budget deficits rise in recessions and fall during expansions. Program expenditures made during a recession are more likely to be financed out of budget deficits, acting thus as an addition to aggregate demand and a stimulus to the economy. During such times the problem of substitution is relatively unimportant. Of course, since all programs are equally funded from the deficit, it is hard to argue that any one program avoids substitution even in a recession. In expansions, when private demand is brisk, program expenditures are more likely to be siphoned off from private demand through tax revenues. Thus, the problem of substitution is particularly difficult to measure since its extent is likely to vary over the business cycle.

This difficulty need not paralyze our efforts to evaluate the spatial impacts of various programs. While the problem of substitution is severe when attempting to determine the total effects of a program, it is less of a problem when the primary concern is the spatial distribution of the impacts. If a program's expenditures are highly concentrated in the central city, the problem of substitution suggests that the level of impacts is uncertain, but the distribution of impacts may be unaffected if the degree of substitution does not vary by geographic areas. To the extent the degree of substitution is not invariant over areas, it is probably highest in suburban areas, where there is more private sector activity. Hence if a bias exists, the distribution of employment and income impacts will be understated in central cities and overstated in the suburban ring. Furthermore, when comparing the spatial impacts of alternative programs, the extent of substitution may not affect the outcome so long as the same method of calculation is used in each case. As long as programs have a similar degree of substitution, the relative merits of the alternatives will not be influenced by this factor. As already noted, the problem of substitution is most severe when evaluating whether the program's benefits justify the expenditures. It is of less importance when evaluating the distribution of urban impacts among programs.

ALLOCATION OF PROGRAM FUNDS

Section 8 assistance is allocated to conform with Section 213 of the Housing and Community Development Act of 1974. This legislation requires that allocations to geographic areas respond to the relative needs of communities as measured by population, poverty, housing overcrowding, housing vacancies, amount of substandard housing, or "other objectively measurable conditions." Between 20 and 25 percent of all assistance payments must be allocated to nonmetropolitan areas. Once program funds are allocated to jurisdictions, certificates are allocated directly to families as described in the previous section.

A significant portion of the Section 8 Existing program has been allocated to Loan Management projects. Loan Management Section 8 is designed to stabilize the finances of HUD-insured housing projects. The purpose of this assistance is to reduce claims on HUD insurance funds and to assure the continued availability of the units for lower income families. Since units under the Loan Management assistance are tied to specific projects, these allocations do not offer the freedom of residential choice that is characteristic of the Section 8 Existing program. Almost 170,000 units, about 25 percent of the total, were reserved for Loan Management assistance by the end of Fiscal 1978. Loan Management allocations have been discontinued but in their place is a Property Disposition program that will earmark Section 8 Existing funds for HUD-held properties to be sold to private management interests. Data presented in this paper include Loan Management assistance, unless otherwise noted.

Allocation by area

Table 2 shows the distribution of Section 8 Existing units by area. Among the four major regions, the Northeast has 187,599 units reserved, slightly over 28 percent of the total; the South has 184,805 units, almost 28 percent of the total; the West has 157,331 units, which account for 24 percent; and, last, the North Central region has 135,510 units or 20 percent of the total.

Within these regions, central cities dominate the program with almost 46 percent of the units. Central cities in the North Central and South are above average, accounting for 52.3 and 47.1 percent, respectively, of the regional

TABLE 2: Distribution of Section 8 Existing Reservations, by Region (Cumulative through Fiscal 1978)

Region[a]	Number	%	% of Substandard Units
Northeast			
Central city	80,561	12.11	
Suburban	72,977	10.97	
Nonmetropolitan	34,061	5.12	
Total	187,599	28.20	27.18
North Central			
Central city	70,915	10.66	
Suburban	43,441	6.53	
Nonmetropolitan	21,154	3.18	
Total	135,510	20.37	22.18
South			
Central city	87,014	13.08	
Suburban	45,370	6.82	
Nonmetropolitan	52,421	7.88	
Total	184,805	27.78	39.02
West			
Central city	65,859	9.90	
Suburban	69,518	10.45	
Nonmetropolitan	21,954	3.30	
Total	157,331	23.65	11.67
Total United States			
Central city	304,350	45.75	43.14
Suburban	231,305	34.77	18.92
Nonmetropolitan	129,590	19.48	37.94
Total	665,245	100.0	100.0

Source: Budget Office, U.S. Department of Housing and Urban Development.

[a] Defined by Federal rather than Census region in this paper. The Federal Northeast (regions 1, 2, and 3) includes Delaware, the District of Columbia, Maryland, and West Virginia (all in the Census South region). Federal North Central (regions 5 and 7) does not include North and South Dakota, as the Census grouping does; these two states are in the Federal West region. The Federal South (regions 4 and 6) includes New Mexico; the Census grouping places this state in the West. The Federal West consists of regions 8, 9, and 10.

total. Almost 43 percent of the units reserved in the Northeast are in central cities, while the corresponding figure for the West is 41.9 percent.

Comparing these data with indices of housing inadequacy sheds light on the allocation by region.[4] The Northeast and North Central regions received 28 and 20 percent, respectively, of the reservations—figures close to their relative shares of substandard units in 1976, that is, 27 and 22 percent, respectively. The South, on the other hand, received 28 percent of the Section 8 reservations but had 39 percent of all deficient units. The West benefited from this imbalance, having only 12 percent of the deficient units but receiving twice that proportion of all Section 8 reservations. This imbalance is related to the distribution of program funds within regions. Regulations limit non-metropolitan allocations of Section 8 assistance to 20 to 25 percent of the total. This means that these areas, with almost 38 percent of all substandard housing, receive a small number of units relative to need. Suburban areas gained most from this regulation, receiving 35 percent of the unit allocations while having the fewest substandard dwellings.

Allocations by income class

Families up to 80 percent of the median income of an area are eligible for Section 8 Existing assistance. Regulations require that 30 percent of all recipients have "very low income," that is, below 50 percent of the area's median income for a family of four. A study of the early experience under Section 8 shows this targeting to very low income families had been surpassed: 82 percent of all recipients were in this category (Drury et al., 1978, p. 15).

The extent to which Section 8 Existing serves low income families is shown in Table 3. Almost 38 percent of all recipient households had incomes under $3,000; over-three fourths had incomes below $5,000.[5] The low income of recipients is partly explained by the fact that 47 percent are elderly and 84 percent receive welfare or benefit income as well as wages. Only 16 percent have only wage income and 27 percent receive only welfare income. Females head 73 percent of all recipient households. These data confirm earlier work that Section 8 Existing is well-targeted on low income families.

Allocations by race and age

Table 3 also shows the distributions of Section 8 Existing recipients by race. Black families accounted for 22 percent of all recipients and Hispanic

---

[4] Standard units must have complete plumbing and kitchen, a dependable sewerage system (e.g., toilets not out of order more than three times for more than six hours in the past three months), reliable heat, not be in need of significant maintenance (e.g., have substantial cracks in the walls), and public halls must be in adequate condition. All data presented here come from the U.S. Bureau of the Census, 1978b.

[5] Data in Table 3 do not include families receiving Loan Management assistance. The median income of 37,447 Loan Management families entering the program during the last half of 1977 was $4,380, about 25 percent higher than the median for other Section 8 Existing families. About 60 percent of Loan Management recipients had incomes below $5,000.

TABLE 3: Distribution of Section 8 Existing Recipients, by Income and Race, 1977

	White	Black	Other Minorities[a]	Total
Income (dollars)				
0–2,999	25,357	9,828	3,940	39,125
3,000–4,999	28,435	6,926	4,113	39,474
5,000–7,999	12,863	4,837	3,001	20,701
8,000–9,999	1,966	825	661	3,452
over 10,000	600	271	305	1,176
Total cases	69,221	22,687	12,020	103,928
Mean income	$3,894	$3,866	$3,785[b]–$5,947[c]	$3,938
Median income	$3,490	$3,380	$3,480[b]–$5,600[c]	$3,510

Source: Section 8 Certifications, Table 1, Report RIS AECA, December 31, 1977.
[a] Includes American Indians, Hispanic Americans, Oriental Americans, and others.
[b] American Indians.
[c] Oriental Americans.

Americans, Oriental Americans, and other minorities, accounted for 11 percent of the total. The early experience showed a slightly higher participation rate for these groups: 27 percent for blacks and 10 percent for other minorities. In 1976, these minorities accounted for 35 percent of the eligible population.

The early evaluation of Section 8 showed about 33 percent of recipients were elderly, accounting for 37 percent of the eligible population. More recent evidence shows a higher rate of elderly participation. During the last six months of 1977, almost 46 percent of all program entrants were elderly. Because Section 8 Existing allows households to rent their current dwelling, if it meets program standards, the program is particularly attractive to this relatively immobile population.

URBAN IMPACTS

In this section the spatial impacts of the Section 8 Existing program are evaluated. The effects of the program on central cities, the suburban ring, and nonmetropolitan areas with respect to six variables are investigated: housing units, neighborhood quality, employment, income, fiscal condition, and population. When it is impossible to quantify the program's impact, qualitative judgments are made.

Housing units

The Section 8 Existing program affects households and housing units in two ways. First, low income households receive subsidies to improve the quality of their housing and to lower the proportion of income devoted to housing. Second, the program can induce extra repair of dwellings, either by the imposition of the housing standards or by increasing the rate of return to landlords. In this section these effects are estimated for central cities, the suburban ring, and nonmetropolitan areas. Table 2 showed the absolute number of units, 665,245, that will be directly affected by the assistance payments.

There is no direct evidence on the effect of Section 8 Existing or maintenance and repair activity. As noted earlier, theoretical reasoning is somewhat ambiguous on this point. On the one hand, a higher expected rate of return could cause landlords to improve their units. On the other hand, it might discourage such expenditures. Data from the supply side of the EHAP provide evidence that Section 8 Existing may cause an increase in maintenance activity for some units. Thus, among those units that are affected by receiving a housing assistance payment, there is a subgroup that is also actually in better condition as a result of the program.

Considerable resources in EHAP were spent to estimate repair expenditures for recipients and nonrecipients. In the supply experiment, expenditures were divided into initial repairs made at the onset of an enrollee's participation and annual repairs that were not required by the program. EHAP data on improvements to renter-occupied units are inadequate because the tenant, who is not likely to have an accurate idea of maintenance expenditures made by the landlord, responded to the questions. Hence, EHAP homeowners provide the only comparisons which can be used to the evaluate effects of Section 8 Existing.

Even though Section 8 is exclusively a rental program, the EHAP experience is useful for the purposes of this study. There is some evidence that owners of rental property and owners who occupy their units have a similar propensity to repair their dwellings. Landlords tend to spend as much or more than owner occupants. In 1976, landlords of single-unit dwellings spent an average of $456 on repairs, while owner occupants of comparable units spent $450 (U.S. Bureau of the Census, 1978b). Given this similarity of maintenance expenditures, it is assumed that homeowners provide a reasonable estimate of how owners of rental property will respond to the program. Hence, we can use the data for homeowners in EHAP to evaluate the maintenance and repair response of landlords in Section 8 Existing.

Table 4 shows that initial repairs under Section 8 are from 3.5 to 5 times higher than those reported for homeowners in the EHAP. To the extent these initial repairs are actually accelerated repairs that would have been made at a later date, they exaggerate the program's impact. Average annual cash outlay per repaired dwelling is available for the EHAP but not, unfortunately, for Section 8. Inasmuch as initial Section 8 repairs are over 60 percent of annual EHAP outlays, we assume that annual expenditures will not be lower than those under EHAP.

The significance of these expenditures depends on the extent to which they

TABLE 4: Maintenance Expenditures for Repaired Dwellings under EHAP and Section 8

	Average Cash Outlay Per Repaired Dwelling	
	Initial Repairs	*Annual Repairs*
EHAP		
Brown County	$ 55	$437
St. Joseph County	81	467
Section 8	284	n.a.

Sources: Rand Corporation (1978); Urban Institute (1978).

TABLE 5: Actual Maintenance Expenditures for EHAP Homeowners Compared to All Low Income Homeowners

	Annual
Brown County	
EHAP	$324
All low income owners	182
St. Joseph County	
EHAP	347
All low income owners	268
Average (2 counties)	
EHAP	335
All low income owners	225

Source: Rand Corporation (1978).

were induced by the program. If the repairs would have been made anyway, the program did not contribute to the maintenance of the housing stock. EHAP homeowners spent $335 annually; all low income homeowners in these counties allocated $225 for repairs. This latter figure can be viewed as an estimate of repair activity in the absence of the program.[6] One could infer from the data in Table 5 that Section 8 landlords may spend almost 50 percent more on repairs than nonprogram owners. Assuming that initial repairs and differences in annual repairs are stimulated by the program, induced maintenance expenditures would account for almost 20 percent of all allowance payments in Brown County and 13 percent in St. Joseph County. These estimates are shown in Table 6.

[6] The $225 for all low income homeowners is virtually identical to an estimate derived from a regression analysis of census data based on a sample of 5,539 homeowners. In a household with an income of $7,000 and a housing value of $20,000, figures comparable to EHAP families, Mendelsohn estimates annual expected repairs to be $226 (Mendelsohn, 1977, pp. 459–68).

TABLE 6: Program-Induced Repairs by Homeowners (Estimated through June 1978)

	Brown County		St. Joseph County	
	Added Outlay (thousands)	*% of Allowance Payments*	*Added Outlay (thousands)*	*% of Allowance Payments*
Initial repairs	$ 44		$136	
Annual repairs	562		542	
Total	606	19	678	13

Source: Rand Corporation, unpublished data on the Housing Allowance Supply Experiment.

Frequency-of-repair data provide the best estimates of the number of units that will be of higher quality because of the Section 8 Existing program. About 57 percent of all owner-occupied units valued under $20,000 were repaired in 1976. In contrast, 74 percent of all owned units evaluated in the EHAP made annual repairs that were not required to meet program standards. The difference in frequency of repair between EHAP participants and similar homeowners suggests that a demand-side housing program, such as Section 8 Existing, may stimulate repair activity in as many as 17 percent of the units. Assuming the 17 percent figure is relevant for the three area designations used here, about 52,000 units would be improved in central cities, 39,000 in suburban rings, and 22,000 in nonmetropolitan areas. Of course, the added demand for housing caused by the program may have caused other landlords to increase their maintenance activity. This effect cannot be measured, but it would work to increase the number of units which are improved as a result of the program. Given the small portion of the eligible population served by the program, this positive effect is probably insignificant.

Neighborhood quality

Housing programs should not disrupt neighborhoods. At the same time they should not completely inhibit changes that are inherent in urban dynamics. The goal of neighborhood stability, therefore, is to seek a middle ground of orderly change that does not cause the displacement of poor households or rapid deterioration of neighborhoods. Rapid changes in property values in a community, relative to the surrounding area, signal neighborhood instability. Very rapid increases in property values raise market rents and are associated with the displacement of poor households. Declining or constant property values in an inflationary setting signify neighborhood deterioration. While normal market processes may cause these outcomes, neither event should be the product of public policy. Section 8 Existing could cause neighborhood instability in one of two ways. First, the increase in demand for housing as a result of the housing allowances could raise property values. This could cause residential displacement among income-eligible households which are unable to get Section 8 assistance because program funds are limited. Second, the program subsidies could induce recipients to move out of the worst housing and neighborhoods, causing accelerated abandonment and decline. As we will see below, neither of these effects is a likely consequence of Section 8 Existing.

Rapidly increasing property values are not likely to accompany this program. The EHAP showed that demand-side subsidies to low income households do not cause significant increases in housing demand. The supply part of the experiment consisted of a big allowance program in two small markets, the counties surrounding Green Bay, Wisconsin, and South Bend, Indiana. As many as 20 percent of the households in some census tracts were participants. Contrary to initial expectations, the experiment showed few signs of induced rent inflation (Rand Corporation, 1978, p. 100). One reason for this is that the change in housing expenditures in response to a change in income among recipients is relatively low (Abt Associates, 1977, p. 20). Another is that many households do not immediately move to a better dwelling when they receive a subsidy. The program's impact is spread over time, thus minimizing market disruption. The long-run effect on the market of a large-scale program is not known. It would clearly depend on variables, such as housing standards and the size of the subsidies. Given the current structure of the program, it is reasonable to conclude that Section 8 will not cause neighborhood instability by increasing the demand for low income housing under any feasible funding level.

More probably neighborhood instability might be generated by Section 8 recipients who move out of the worst housing and neighborhoods, causing accelerated abandonment and decline. The early evaluation of Section 8 sheds some light on this issue. Mobility among Section 8 households is considerable—46 percent of all recipients moved upon entering the program. Of these, about 70 percent changed neighborhoods. One half of the households that changed neighborhoods thought they had moved to better neighborhoods. Thus, about 16 percent of all Section 8 recipients moved to what they thought was a better neighborhood (Yap et al., 1978, pp. 61–62). A few moved to neighborhoods they thought to be less desirable. The EHAP shows the same pattern of participant mobility away from less desirable neighborhoods. In both Pittsburgh and Phoenix, census tracts, with a net loss-of-demand experiment households, were of lower quality, that is, had fewer owner-occupied units, more units built prior to 1950, and more low income households.

The large-scale EHAP supply experiment in small markets reported modest net changes in neighborhoods. In Green Bay net moves of participants over a two-year period never exceeded 1.2 percent of all households in either the origin or destination census tract. The maximum loss in absolute terms was Green Bay's Central Business District East, which lost 7.2 percent of its 639 participants or about 46 households. Neighborhood deterioration should have been more pronounced in South Bend which had a large stock of old housing and a large minority population. The Core West of South Bend, the site of the worst housing and highest crime rate, lost 53 of its 986 participating households or 5.4 percent (Rand Corporation, 1978, p. 128). Thus, evidence from both Section 8 and the EHAP suggests a slight tendency of recipients of a housing subsidy to move from the poorest areas. This could speed the decay of these neighborhoods, although the key question is the degree to which the program induces this mobility.

To the extent a subsidy increases mobility, it could encourage people to move out of beleagured neighborhoods more rapidly than otherwise. If participants move no more than nonparticipants and the program subsidy does not influence the pattern of mobility, neighborhood stability is unaffected by Section 8. Evidence from the EHAP suggests that the propensity to move is not appreciably affected by a demand-side subsidy for housing. Analysis of mobility suggests there are some significant differences between program and control households, but that "the pace at which participants move to better housing or neighborhoods is largely determined by their normal mobility patterns" (MacMillan, 1978, p. S-3). In its work on the supply side of the experiment, the Rand Corporation reported that the housing allowances appeared to have "induced or facilitated some shift from residentially deteriorating neighborhoods to areas that offer better housing and neighborhood services" (Rand Corporation, 1978, p. 129). Nevertheless, the relatively small number of net gains or losses in any district of origin or destination suggest this impact is modest.

The Section 8 program probably does not contribute to neighborhood instability in the short run. Mobility induced by the program is modest, but the cumulative long-run effect of even a small increase in mobility away from distressed neighborhoods can be substantial. Even modest mobility in the long run can create vacancies and lower the expected rate of return to landlords. Repair activities are curtailed, encouraging still more households to leave the neighborhood. As the vacancy rate continues to rise, the distressed neighborhood falls into a spiral of dynamic decay. Although this long-term scenario is a possible consequence of Section 8, it is not a probable one. The program, in its present form, is so small that it will certainly not be a major cause for any neighborhood being caught in a cycle of dynamic decay.

Neighborhoods not now deteriorating, but which are in danger of becoming distressed, could be strengthened by the presence of the Section 8 program. As already shown above, landlords in the program are likely to spend more on repair and maintenance than similarly situated nonprogram owners, largely because the program provides increased rental income and a lease providing some protection against nonpayment of rent. Strengthening of neighborhoods is not likely unless there is a significant concentration of Section 8 funds. At current funding levels, this will not occur unless there is special targeting. The Urban Reinvestment Task Force has demonstrated the potential stabilizing influence of Section 8 Existing by using special allocations in its Neighborhood Housing Service programs that are designed to stabilize threatened communities.

Employment

Section 8 Existing can create employment in two ways. First, to the extent it increases maintenance and repair expenditures beyond what they would be without the program, the program increases the demand for building supplies and workers in the repair trades. The second source of employment stems from the increased demand for goods and services that results from the increased flow of income to Section 8 recipients.[7] Since both maintenance expenditures and the subsidy payments are flows that extend over time, the employment effects that result will continue as long as Section 8 assistance continues. Current program commitments extend five years from the time a unit is allocated.

Measuring the employment effects. Expenditures generated by the Section 8 Existing program are used to estimate employment effects. Most program dollars—over 80 percent according to EHAP estimates shown in Table 6—are essentially transfers to the recipients. These transfers reduce the rent burden of Section 8 households from an average of 40 percent to 22 percent. Because of the low income of recipients, it is assumed this money is spent entirely in the wholesale and retail trade sector. The remainder is spent on maintenance and repair activity. There are two components to this activity: one is retail sales of materials and tools and the other is the construction sector. Since most maintenance work does not involve a contractor, expenditures for the repairs are also assumed to be made in the wholesale and retail trade sector.[8]

The method of calculating employment effects is straightforward. Expenditures generated by the program create jobs in the wholesale and retail trade sector. It is assumed that program expenditures create the same number of jobs that are created per dollar expenditure in that sector. Hence, the number of jobs generated by Section 8 Existing is the product of program expenditures and the employment/output ratio for the wholesale and retail trade sector. Earnings generated by these jobs are the product of the number of jobs times the average wage in the sector.

[7] The employment and income effects of the Section 8 New Construction and Substantial Rehabilitation program come in two stages. First is the phase in which jobs and income are created by expenditures for labor and material used in the construction or rehabilitation process. This construction activity is undertaken because the supplier of housing services has been promised a flow of subsidy payments for eligible families that help realize a satisfactory rate of return. This flow of subsidy payments generates the same employment and income impacts under all versions of the Section 8 program.

[8] The net effect of this assumption is to lower the employment estimates from what they would be if construction data were used for maintenance and repair expenditures. However, since the estimate is lowered about 1 percent, this assumption is without consequence.

TABLE 7: Estimates of Employment Generated by Section 8 Existing, by Area

	No. Jobs Created (max.)		Employment Distribution		
	FY 1977	Cumulative through FY 1978	Section 8	Total	Ratio of Section 8 to Total
By region					
Northeast	3,672	11,220	28.2%	30.9%	.91
North Central	2,657	8,117	20.4	27.7	.74
South	3,620	11,061	27.8	24.5	1.13
West	3,073	9,390	23.6	16.9	1.40
Total	13,022	39,788	100.0	100.0	
By population dist.					
Central cities	5,951	18,183	45.7	27.9	1.64
Suburban	4,532	13,846	34.8	40.9	.85
Nonmetro- politan	2,539	7,759	19.5	31.2	.63
Total	13,022	39,788	100.0	100.0	

Sources: U.S. Bureau of the Census (1977); *County and City Data Book,* 1977.

Total program expenditure is the average housing allowance payment times the number of units in the program. The average housing allowance payment is about $1,500.[9] Multiplying this number times the number of units reserved yields program expenditures of almost one billion dollars. The total number of jobs generated by this expenditure is $997.9 million times the employment/ output ratio—.000039872,[10] or 39,778 jobs. This is an estimate of the number of jobs created by Section 8 Existing, and is shown in Table 7. Employment generated by Fiscal 1977 expenditures of $326.6 million and the spatial distribution of these jobs are also shown in the table.

It is unlikely the entire subsidy will enter the economy as new expenditure. Much of this amount is consumption diverted by taxes from the rest of the population. The incremental demand due to Section 8 Existing is the difference between what recipients spend and what taxpayers would have spent had there been no income transfer. To estimate this, we assume the marginal propensity to consume (MPC) among program recipients is 1.0 and the MPC among taxpayers is equal to the national average propensity to consume of .935. The increased expenditure due to Section 8 Existing is, therefore, the difference, .065 of the total income transfer. This revised expenditure estimate

[9] This figure is an estimate that increases the 1976 figure by the rate of inflation. The 1976 subsidy figure is found in Drury et al., 1978, p. xvii.
[10] This figure was derived from Vernez et al., 1977.

times the employment/sales ratio is a minimum employment estimate: 846 jobs in Fiscal 1977 and 2,586 cumulative through Fiscal 1978. As noted earlier, the extent of substitution will vary over the business cycle and perhaps be greater in suburban areas than in central cities.

The methodology employed here assumes that employment is generated in the area in which program expenditures occur. This assumption is required since it is difficult to allocate among areas the jobs that result from Section 8 spending. Thus the data in Table 7 show that jobs are distributed in proportion to the number of units in each area. The distribution of employment generated by Section 8 Existing is compared to that of the total in the last column of Table 7. Areas that gain employment have a ratio of greater than one; the ratio is less than one for those that lose employment. The South and West regions gain at the expense of the rest of the nation. The data show central cities also gain, but, given the significant mobility between central cities and the suburban ring, the Section 8/total ratio for central cities probably has a significant upward bias.

Income

The Section 8 Existing program gives an average subsidy of over $1,500 per year to each recipient. For the almost 665,000 households in the program, this amounts to an increased aggregate income of $997.7 million. Since the program transfers purchasing power from more affluent to lower income families, the spatial distribution of income can be influenced. As shown in Table 8, there is a substantial redistribution of income among areas. The

TABLE 8: Percentage Distribution of Section 8 Allocations Compared to Aggregate Income, by Area

	Section 8 Allocations	Aggregate Income	Ratio of Allocations to Income
By region			
Northeast	28.2	29.6	.95
North Central	20.4	27.3	.75
South	27.8	23.4	1.18
West	23.6	19.7	1.19
Total	100.0	100.0	
By population dist.			
Central cities	45.7	27.4	1.67
Suburban	34.8	39.5	.88
Nonmetropolitan	19.5	33.1	.59
Total	100.0	100.0	

Source: U.S. Bureau of the Census (1978).

spatial distribution of Section 8 allocations is compared to the distribution of aggregate income. This comparison is summarized in the last column which shows the ratio of these two variables. If the allocations/income ratio is unity, it means that the area is receiving funds in proportion to its aggregate income. If it is less than one it is supporting other regions, and if greater than one it is subsidized by the rest of the country. The highest per capita income regions of the nation, the Northeast and North Central, are subsidizing the lower income per capita areas in the South and West. Higher income suburban areas transfer income to the relatively poor central cities, and nonmetropolitan areas receive the fewest funds relative to their share of aggregate income.

Fiscal condition

Section 8 Existing will not have a substantial impact on the fiscal condition of local governments. Aggregate property values, and hence property tax revenues, are not affected by Section 8 Existing, as has been discussed. Aggregate income and spending in central cities are increased, and to the extent sales and income taxes provide local revenues, the fiscal condition of central cities will improve at the expense of suburban areas. Since these taxes account for only 14 percent of locally generated revenues, this impact on fiscal condition is modest.

Population

Freedom of residential choice is a cornerstone of the Section 8 Existing program. Recipients can choose their residential locations: individuals, not dwellings, are eligible for assistance.[11] As indicated earlier, mobility induced by a program of housing assistance payments is probably modest. Both the demand and supply experiments of EHAP reported that normal mobility patterns, not housing allowances, are the key determinant of population shifts among communities. There is no reason to believe there will be noticeable population shifts away from central cities to suburban areas as a result of the program.

In this section, we turn to the effectiveness of freedom of choice for minorities. In an early evaluation of Section 8, among black households that moved, 50 percent went to neighborhoods with a lower percentage of black residents (U.S. Department of Housing and Urban Development, 1978, p. 23). Of the remainder, 21 percent moved to neighborhoods with the same percentage of blacks, and 29 percent moved to areas with a higher percentage. The effects of the demand-side housing program on residential locations was also studied in the EHAP (Vidal, 1978). The experiment analyzed the movement of black

---

[11] The principle of freedom of choice was compromised under the Loan Management program. Even though this program is no longer in effect, many Section 8 units are earmarked for HUD-held properties to be sold to private interests. Like the Loan Management program, this Property Disposition program restricts the freedom of choice.

TABLE 9: Percentage Distribution of HUD-Subsidized Families, by Income, for Various Programs

Income (dollars)	Group A[a]	LRPH[b]	Section 8[c]	Section 8 Existing
0–2,999	17.3	40.3	43.9	37.6
3,000–4,999	31.3	32.9	37.3	38.0
5,000–7,999	40.1	16.9	16.6	20.0
8,000–9,999	8.6	4.4	1.9	3.3
over 10, 000	2.7	5.5	0.3	1.1
Total	100.0	100.0	100.0	100.0

Source: HUD memo, from Paul Burke to Joseph Burke, dated May 4, 1977. Data for Section 8 Existing are based on Table 2.

Note: The table is based on an estimate of the number of units that would be available for occupancy in September 1978 and the distribution of HUD-subsidized families, by income and family size, in 1976.

[a] Includes Rent Supplements, Sections 202 and 221(b).
[b] Low Rent Public Housing.
[c] Includes Section 8 Existing, Substantial Rehabilitation, and New Construction programs.

households among types of neighborhoods: black (with more than 50 percent black households); mixed neighborhoods (with more than 15 percent, but less than 50 percent black households); white neighborhoods with black enclaves (fewer than 15 percent black households, but with black or mixed census tracts); and white neighborhoods (less than 15 percent black).

Concentration of the black population in every type of neighborhood, except white, fell as a result of black mobility. In the experiment, black movers increased the number of black households residing in white neighborhoods from 7 to 10 percent—a 43 percent increase. None of these changes are caused by the program: experimental and control households were equally likely to move to neighborhoods with fewer blacks as a proportion of the population. Section 8 Existing does not appear to generate any noticeable population shifts among geographical areas.

EVALUATION OF ALTERNATIVES

The Section 8 Existing program serves low income communities and people well. Although it is not as well targeted to central cities as are some other HUD programs—46 percent of Section 8 Existing units are in central cities, whereas 72 percent of Low Rent Public Housing and 53 percent of three other programs are located in this part of metropolitan areas—Section 8 is better targeted to low income people than other programs.[12] Table 9 shows the percentage distribution of HUD-subsidized families by income. Only the

[12] The three programs are Rent Supplements, Section 202, and Section 221(b).

Low Rent Public Housing program is as well-targeted to low income families, but it suffers disadvantages that do not accompany the Section 8 Existing program: it inhibits freedom of choice and requires public sector administration of a large housing stock. Compared to the current alternatives, Section 8 is a well-conceived program.

In 1979 the Section 8 Existing program is expected to add an additional 123,000 units. This will bring the total to 778,363 reservations. The number of units of Section 8 Existing reserved for Loan Management and Property Disposition, programs that tie assistance to units rather than families, fell to 14,000 in 1979 from 37,172 in the previous year. A new set-aside program, the Moderate Rehabilitation program that is earmarked for units which can be rehabilitated for less than $5,000, was begun in Fiscal 1979. The Moderate Rehabilitation program accounts for 39,000, almost 32 percent of the most recent Section 8 Existing allocation. Since this program will almost inevitably be concentrated in areas with a relatively poor housing stock, it may further concentrate units in central cities.

In terms of spatial allocation, Section 8 has one weakness—the program does not adequately serve the geographic areas with the most substandard housing. In this respect, central cities, the Northeast, and North Central regions receive allocations in proportion to their share of substandard housing. The South receives too few units and the West receives far more than can be justified on the basis of housing need. This gain comes at the expense of nonmetropolitan areas. This is a direct result of the requirement that limits nonmetropolitan allocations to between 20 and 25 percent of the total.

REFERENCES

Abt Associates, Inc. *Housing Allowance Demand Experiment. Fourth Annual Report.* Cambridge, Mass., December 1977.

Drury, Margaret; Lee, Olsen; Springer, Michael; and Yap, Lorene. *Early Experience in the Section 8 Existing Housing Program. Draft Report.* Washington, D.C.: Urban Institute, August 1978.

Friedman, Joseph, and Weinberg, Daniel. *Draft Report on the Demand for Rental Housing: Evidence From a Percent of Rent Housing Allowance.* Cambridge, Mass.: Abt Associates, September 1978.

Khadduri, Jill. "The Rent Reduction Credit Feature of the Section 8 Existing Housing Program." Unpublished. Washington, D.C.: Division of Housing Research, U.S. Department of Housing and Urban Development, June 1978.

MacMillan, Jean. *Draft Report on Mobility in the Housing Allowance Demand Experiment.* Cambridge, Mass.: Abt Associates, June 1978.

Mendelsohn, Robert. "Empirical Evidence Improvements," *Journal of Urban Economics,* no. 4 (October 1977): 459–68.

Rand Corporation. *Fourth Annual Report of the Housing Assistance Supply Experiment.* Santa Monica: Rand Corporation, May 1978.

Struyk, Raymond J., et al. *Housing Policies for the Urban Poor.* Washington, D.C.: Urban Institute, 1978.

U.S. Department of Commerce, Bureau of the Census. *Construction Reports.* "Residential Alterations and Repair," Series C50-77-5, Annual 1977. Washington, D.C.: U.S. Government Printing Office, 1978*a*.

————. *Current Housing Reports, Series H-150-76 Financial Characteristics of the Housing Inventory for the United States and Regions, Annual Housing Survey: 1976, Part C.* Washington, D.C.: U.S. Government Printing Office, 1978*b*.

U.S. Department of Housing and Urban Development. *1976 HUD Statistical Yearbook.* Washington, D.C.: U.S. Government Printing Office, 1978.

————. *Housing in the Seventies.* Washington, D.C.: U.S. Government Printing Office, 1974.

————. *Lower Income Housing Assistance Program (Section 8),* Office of Policy Development and Research. Washington, D.C.: U.S. Government Printing Office, February 1978.

U.S. House of Representatives, Survey and Investigations Staff. *A Report to the Committee on Appropriations on the Section 8 Housing Assistance Payments Program,* February 1978. Unpublished.

Vernez, Georges, et al. *Regional Cycles and Employment Effects of Public Works Investments.* Santa Monica: Rand Corporation, January 1977.

Vidal, Avis. *Draft Report on the Search Behavior of Black Households in Pittsburgh.* Cambridge, Mass.: Abt Associates, July 1978.

Yap, Lorene, Greenston, Peter, and Sadacca, Robert. *Early Experience in the Section 8 Existing Housing Program: Technical Supplement. Draft Report.* Washington, D.C.: Urban Institute, August 1978.

————. "Social and Economic Characteristics of the Metropolitan and Nonmetropolitan Population: 1977 and 1970," *Current Population Reports.* Special Studies P-23, no. 75. Washington, D.C.: U.S. Government Printing Office, 1977.

CHAPTER ELEVEN

The Urban Impact of National
Health Insurance

CHARLES ANDERSON

INTRODUCTION

Current national efforts to construct a viable federal health care policy have promoted a triad of interrelated goals. Summarily, a feasible policy emphasizes cost constraint, efficiency, and equity in the production and delivery of medical services. Second, an efficient policy motivates a strong coordination of federal, state, and local policies in matters of national health concerns. And finally, a comprehensive form of national health insurance assures reasonable access to medical care for all as a matter of right (Krizay and Wilson, 1976, pp. 1–10; Keintz, 1976, pp. 1–11).

The urbanist is concerned with the potential impacts of emerging national health care policy on metropolitan areas in two respects. In a positive sense, a central question focuses on the likely economic or fiscal impacts of federal health care policy on urban units and areas. Economic or fiscal impact refers to local changes in the economic opportunities or relative economic situations and behavior of urban units as a consequence of the introduction of federal health care programs on a national scale. Urban units refers to households, firms, medical care providers, and municipal units situated in metropolitan space.

Normatively, a central question focuses on the likely welfare outcomes of policy effects on metropolitan areas. That is, to what extent will the welfare objectives of federal health care policy be realized in urban municipalities and, in general, will the benefits of health care programs exceed the various costs imposed on urban units as a whole?

This paper narrowly concentrates on one aspect of the preceding problem: an urban impact analysis or statement of national health insurance. In this endeavor, three bills will be considered—the Kennedy-Corman bill, the Burleson-McIntyre bill, and the Long-Ribicoff bill. Their consideration provides broad indicators of the types of urban impacts that may accompany an implementation of national health care policy given that national health insurance is a major policy instrument. Although their ends are similar, the policy parameters proposed by each bill to achieve program goals vary enough to warrant comment. The possible implementation of any of these measures implies significantly different fiscal consequences for urban areas.

First, this paper specifies the general components of a national health insurance program and discusses their relevance to urban impact analysis. Then it assesses the likely effects of the Kennedy-Corman, Burleson-McIntyre, and Long-Ribicoff programs on urban areas. And finally, these analyses are evaluated from points of public interest.

ELEMENTS OF A NATIONAL HEALTH INSURANCE PROGRAM

A socially feasible national health insurance program addresses two basic problems. It must reasonably reduce cost barriers to medical care for beneficiaries, and it must prescribe socially optimal limits of the use of medical facilities and services under certain levels of government health care expenditures (Krizay and Wilson, Chapter 10). In this respect, a national health insurance program consists of three components: benefit provisions, program financing means, and cost and efficiency guidelines.

Benefit provisions

Benefit provisions derive from social judgments regarding the mix of services to be subsidized and the proportion of the population to receive subsidized services.

Several testable hypotheses follow for urban areas given the introduction of a national health insurance program. First, benefit levels will be highest in metropolitan areas whose demographic and socioeconomic characteristics and health care needs closely match the values of benefit parameters. Secondly, the utilization of service subsidized by a national health insurance program will tend to increase across metropolitan areas. Subsidized households will demand higher levels of services due to lower prices. Also, providers will tend to increase the supply of subsidized services as a result of their increased "profitability." Hence, in effect, program services will be redistributed towards beneficiary groups.

And finally one expects that the expenditures of urban governments on subsidized services will sharply decrease given high levels of outside fiscal relief in the provision of services. To comment further, urban governments will respond to the reduced fiscal burden of providing services in two distinct ways. Clearly, a substitution effect is likely to occur with the introduction of national health insurance. Urban governments will offer, relative to other public goods, larger quantities of subsidized services since they are relatively less expensive to offer. Second, an income effect is apt to be associated with an introduction of national health insurance. Assuming that public goods are normal goods, urban expenditures on all public services will increase (Henderson and Quandt, 1971, Chapter 1).

Program financing

The financial means of meeting program costs must be specified in any national health insurance proposal. For households, the suggested instruments are deductibles and coinsurance rates, insurance premiums, wage taxes, and income tax surcharges. Deductibles and coinsurance rates serve to constrain consumer demand and defer increases in the costs of medical care. Premiums, wage taxes, and income tax surcharges serve to pool funds for meeting the costs of care.

For firms, the suggested instruments for raising funds are payroll taxes and employer contributions to health insurance premiums. These also serve to pool funds for meeting the cost of care. Financing patterns have two decisive effects at national levels. First, they determine how income will be redistributed from the population at risk to beneficiary groups. And second, they determine how funds will be distributed from healthy to ill individuals.

Cost and efficiency guidelines

Cost and efficiency guidelines serve to constrain costs and promote efficiency in the production and delivery of medical services. Several general means of constraining costs are proposed by various national health insurance proposals. A direct means of cost restraint is the regulation of provider charges or expenditures. Limits are placed on levels and increases in provider charges or expenditures according to program formulas. A second means of constraining costs is through the regulation of hospital investment or borrowing activities. Cost levels over the long term may be constrained by requiring that investment funds or types of borrowing activities be subject to approval by an outside agency. A third means of constraining costs is to require sanction for the provision of new services. A related policy would allow providers to discontinue services which are no longer financially viable or of great value to the larger community.

In contrast, efficiency guidelines encourage the development of innovative organizational and productive techniques which promise increased efficiency in the provision of services. Currently, a number of national health insurance programs advocate the subsidization of health maintenance organizations and paramedical manpower programs.

AN ASSESSMENT OF NATIONAL HEALTH INSURANCE PROPOSALS

In this section, the structures of three proposed bills for national insurance are presented along the lines described in the preceding section. These are the Health Security proposal or the Kennedy-Corman bill, the Health Insurance Association of America proposal or the Burleson-McIntyre bill, and the Long-Ribicoff bill. These bills were selected because of their wide variances in benefit provisions, financing means, and cost and efficiency guidelines. The likely impacts of these programs on urban areas also will be related. This task is a difficult one. In spite of the popularity of the notion of national health insurance, most policy discussions, with reference to any specific proposal, have been directed towards the national implications of universal or voluntary coverage. Even at this, expenditures and cost studies pertaining to national health insurance proposals are difficult to come by and even more difficult to evaluate.

The criteria used to evaluate the impact of national health insurance on urban areas are as follows. Program effects on households are assessed by considering the fiscal situation of persons before and after the introduction of the proposals mentioned above. Benefits are measured by per capita national health expenditures. There is no claim here that this measure fully captures the size or distribution of gross benefits to consumers as a result of introducing national health insurance. If anything, this measure grossly understates the value of national health insurance to beneficiary groups; it ignores the consumer surpluses associated with both the lower prices of services and the reduced levels of risk occasioned by greater coverage of health services.

Changes in the composition of costs paid by persons for health services are measured by per capita out-of-pocket expenditures, per capita employee contributions to health insurance premiums, and per capita expenditures associated with individual insurance policies. Changes in federal, state, and local tax expenditures on health care, which are also a cost to consumers for the provision of health care, are measured by per capita federal tax expenditures and per capita state and local health expenditures. The contributions of firms to the financing of medical care under a national health are measured by per capita employer tax contributions. Per capita employer contributions to health insurance premiums are also used as an indicator of financing.

Finally, national health insurance reduces the fiscal burdens of State and local governments regarding health expenditures. These reductions are measured by per capita State and local expenditures before and after the introduction of national health insurance.

These statistics provide, at best, a gross indication of how urban areas will be affected by national health insurance once population and utilization parameters are introduced. More accurate measures necessarily await the development of further studies. The derivation of the above statistics rests heavily on a national health insurance cost study that is currently being conducted by the Department of Health, Education, and Welfare (HEW). The most complete estimates for program expenditures are those for the year 1980. Consequently, these estimates will be used.

The health security proposal

Eligibility and benefit provisions. With the exception of military personnel, their families, and some veterans eligible for Veterans Administration services, all residents of the United States would be covered for medical care benefits under the Kennedy-Corman bill. Coverage includes aliens admitted as permanent residents or for permanent employment. The range of services provided by the bill is quite extensive. Virtually no limits are placed on inpatient institutional and personal services. Personal services include physician, home health, and dental services. The bill also provides for prescription drugs and prosthetic devices (Waldman, 1976).

Program financing. Half of the program would be financed by payroll taxes and the other half by federal general revenues. The payroll taxes would be levied on 150 percent of the earnings base under Social Security as follows: 1 percent for employees, 3.5 percent for employers, and 2.5 percent for self-employment and unearned income. The taxes would apply to all earned and unearned income including that of State and local government employees (Waldman, 1976).

Cost and efficiency guidelines. The bill proposes comprehensive measures to regulate cost increases and to promote efficiency in the production and delivery of services. Provider charges would be regulated through annual budget assignments for inpatient facilities and the setting of fees, capitation rates, and salaries for physicians and other specialists. Investment and capital accumulation would be monitored through enforcement of existing certificate-of-need laws. These procedures are administered at state and local levels (Waldman, 1976). And, program costs would be contained by allocating federal health funds to states and local areas by area budget formulas. The formulas are equity measures since they allow for the medical needs of state populations by densities and other characteristics. They include cost provisions in that only a fixed number of dollars are to be disbursed from the federal budget.

Lastly, one purpose of the bill is to promote efficiency in the production and delivery of medical care. This effort encompasses:

1. subsidizing new but promising forms of medical care organization and delivery techniques;
2. requiring continuing professional education for physicians and other specialists;
3. the establishment of provider participation standards; and
4. subsidizing the development of new types of health care personnel.

A global intent of the bill is to serve as a planning catalyst for the supply and distribution of medical manpower and facilities and the organization of health services. The administration of the bill will be coordinated with state and local planning agencies.

Potential urban impacts of the health security program. The salient characteristics of the Kennedy-Corman bill are: no deductibles or coinsurance payments are required of consumers, the assumption of municipal health expenditure burdens by the Federal government, and the use of the payroll tax to finance the proposal. The effects of these measures on urban areas are considered in turn.

Consumer benefits. The sharp reduction in the price of medical care implies strong increases in demands for medical care among households. Changes in the fiscal situation of individuals are given in Table 1. Under the Kennedy-Corman program, per capita national health expenditures would increase by 11.2 percent, out-of-pocket expenses would decrease sharply by approximately 46 percent. Federal taxes, in contrast, would increase by 219 percent, and state and local taxes would decrease by 52 percent.

Medical care providers. Expenditures on medical care are projected to be $180.2 billion in the year 1980 in the absence of a national health insurance program. The Kennedy-Corman bill would increase this amount to $200.2 billion, or by 11 percent. This does not mean that separate categories of medical care would be equally financed under the Kennedy-Corman program, as indicated by Table 2. Overall, increases in the demand for services imply an expansion of medical facilities and manpower in urban areas. Estimated expenditure elasticities suggest that the increase will be greatest for long-term and psychiatric care followed by home health care, skilled nursing services, and routine and preventive services.

Municipal expenditures. In the year 1980, approximately $17.3 billion would be spent by State and local governments in the absence of the Kennedy-Corman bill. Under the Health Security Proposal, the amount spent by State and local governments would decrease by approximately $9 billion. This reduction implies, on the basis of population distribution, a savings of $7 billion for metropolitan governments. This level of fiscal relief will induce urban areas to provide greater quantities of medical services. It will also allow urban governments to expand other programs of high social priority. These increased expenditures also imply expanded employment in the public sector (American Hospital Association, 1978, p. 7).

TABLE 1: Estimated Per Capita Costs of Proposed Health Security Program, 1980

	Per Capita Expenditures		
	Without Program	*With Program*	*Change (%)*
Health expenditures	$780	$867	11.2
Out-of-pocket	245	133	−45.7
Individual policies	33	4	−87.9
Employee contributions	48	2	−95.8
Federal taxes	207	661	219.3
State and local taxes	75	36	−52.0

Source: U.S. Department of Health, Education and Welfare cost study, Contract No. HEW-OS-74-138.

TABLE 2: Estimated Expenditures Covered by Proposed Health Security
Program for Selected Services, 1980

	Expenditures (millions of dollars)	
	Without Program	With Program
Inpatient services		
General hospital care	$48,680	$53,962
Psychiatric/long-term care	8,580	2,535
Skilled nursing facilities	16,270	885
Outpatient services		
General hospital	8,880	8,882
Mental health	3,300	3,298
Home health	770	771
Physicians	34,750	32,484
Dentists	10,920	4,396

Source: U.S. Department of Health, Education and Welfare cost study, Contract No. HEW-OS-74-138.

Firms. The use of a payroll tax to finance medical services has two obvious effects. First, it will tend to increase commodity prices and, second, unemployment levels. The extent of these impacts are, of course, unknown.

Surely, there are off-setting factors. Increase in medical care may be indirectly related to productivity levels. Second, the expansion of employment in the medical care and public sector may strongly offset unemployment increases in other parts of the urban economy. Again, the extent to which these processes will occur is a matter of conjecture.

Health Insurance Association of America proposal

Eligibility and benefits. The Burleson-McIntyre plan would make coverage available to the entire population. It would establish three voluntary health insurance programs for each of three population groups: wage and salary earners, self-employed individuals, and the poor or needy. The personal services provided by the program are quite generous and include home health, mental health, and dental services. For institutional services, no limits are placed on inpatient hospital care; care within skilled nursing facilities is limited to 180 days. Prescription drugs, prosthetic devices, and other medical supplies and equipment are also provided. Program benefits are not provided at zero prices to consumers. Except for low-income persons, there would be an annual deductible of $100 per person and a 20 percent coinsurance rate for services provided. Cost-sharing for a family is limited to $1,000 per year (Waldman, 1976).

Financing. All health insurance programs would be administered through private insurance carriers and supervised by the State and Federal governments. The types of plans and their financing are as follows. Employee health care plans would, through the use of a tax mechanism, encourage employers to provide qualified health insurance plans with specified benefits for employees and their dependents. Private insurance carriers would collect the premiums and process the claims for benefits. Premiums would be paid by the employer and employees and the plan would be supervised by state insurance departments. The Federal government would determine the status of a plan under tax laws.

Insurance plans for self-employed individuals would provide income tax incentives to encourage the purchase of individual policies providing specified health insurance benefits. Premiums would be paid by the policyholder, and the State and Federal governments would have supervisory responsibilities similar to those under the employee plan. State health care plans are designed to provide the standard benefits for the needy and certain others. It would be administered by private insurance carriers in each state, and financed by premiums payments from covered persons and contributions from state and federal general revenues. Needy individuals would pay premiums determined by a sliding income scale adjusted by family size (Waldman, 1976).

Cost and efficiency guidelines. Payments to health care institutions would be based on prospectively approved rates after budgets submitted to state-cost commissions had been reviewed. Charges would be required to be reasonably related to the cost of the efficient production of services.

Physicians, dentists, and other noninstitutional providers would also be paid on the basis of reasonable charges after taking into account the customary charges of the practitioner and the prevailing charges in the area. Payment could not exceed the seventy-fifth percentile of the distribution of actual charges in the previous year. The plan contains a number of provisions that would ensure the availability of medical resources. One provision subsidizes development of comprehensive ambulatory health care centers, particularly in densely populated areas lacking such facilities. Loans to students in a wide range of health and allied professions would be increased. Grants would be provided to professionals agreeing to serve in areas of critical need and to health training schools that emphasize staffing ambulatory health care centers (Waldman, 1976).

Potential urban impacts of the Health Insurance Association of America proposal. The salient characteristic of the Burleson-McIntyre bill is that it provides health coverage almost solely through the private sector. Since it is a voluntary program, it competes with other forms of health insurance offered in the market. Thus, consumers are offered a wider range of policies. Further, the bill subsidizes the poor by reducing the price of medical services and insurance costs. And, last, it restrains increases in the costs of medical care by requiring consumers to directly share the costs of services.

Consumer benefits. The Burleson-McIntyre bill is apt to affect consumers in two respects. First, a larger number of poor will elect to purchase health insurance. Correspondingly, their demand for medical care will increase. Second, the program promises a uniform coverage of medical services for the proportion of the population that enroll in the program. This may also lead to higher demands for medical services. The fiscal situation of the average consumer under the program is depicted in Table 3.

Per capita health expenditures under the Burleson-McIntyre program would increase by 5 percent; out-of-pocket expenditures would decrease by approximately 17 percent. Federal taxes earmarked for health care would increase by 13 percent on a per capita basis, and per capita state and local taxes for health expenditures would decrease by approximately 1 percent.

Municipal expenditures. Under the Burleson-McIntyre program, state and local expenditures in the year 1980 would be reduced from $17.3 billion to $17.0 billion, a saving of $.3 billion. This implies, on the basis of population distribution, a savings of $219 million for metropolitan governments.

Firms. Under the Burleson-McIntyre bill, firms would not have to assume a major burden in the financing of medical care for employees. Rather, if a firm offers policies which provide specified services and contribute to employee insurance premiums, then employer contributions are deductible as tax credits. To qualify for tax privileges, however, the policy offerings of employers must be approved by federal tax authorities.

The Long-Ribicoff bill

Eligibility and benefits. The Long-Ribicoff proposal, the Catastrophic Health Insurance and Medical Assistance Reform Act, would establish two new Federal health insurance programs. One, the Catastrophic Health Insurance Program, would finance medical care for the entire population. Its corollary, the Federal Medical Assistance Program, would replace the Medicaid program and provide care for the needy. Second, the proposal would provide for the establishment of certified health insurance policies to provide basic

TABLE 3: Estimated Per Capita Costs of Health Insurance of America Proposal, 1980

	Per Capita Expenditures		
	Without Program	*With Program*	*Change (%)*
Health expenditures	$780	$819	5.0
Out-of-pocket	245	202	−17.2
Individual policies	33	24	−27.2
Employee contributions	48	57	18.8
Federal taxes	207	234	13.0
State and local taxes	75	74	− 1.3

Source: U.S. Department of Health, Education and Welfare cost study, Contract No. HEW-OS-74-138.

hospital and medical services that complement the catastrophic health insurance benefits.

Benefits provided by the Catastrophic Health Insurance Program cover a comprehensive range of inpatient and outpatient services. But under the program hospital benefits would begin only after 60 days of inpatient care. Payments would be made for the full reasonable cost of care. For physician services, benefits would begin only after a family had accumulated more than $2,000 in such services over a continuous period of 15 months. Full and reasonable payments for services would continue until a family had incurred less than $500 of physician charges in a 90-day period.

The Medical Assistance plan covers roughly the same services as the Catastrophic Health Insurance Program. In contrast, inpatient hospital services are provided up to 60 days and only nominal cost-sharing is required for any services. Long-term care is an exception. A special copayment requirement would apply to individuals after they have spent 60 continuous days in a long-term care facility (Waldman, 1976).

Financing. The Catastrophic Health Insurance Program would be financed by a 1-percent payroll tax on self-employed persons and employers, including Federal, State, and local governments. The wage base for the tax would be the same as under Social Security. All those subject to the tax could elect to establish a private plan furnishing the same or greater benefits and take the average cost of catastrophic health insurance benefits in their state as a credit towards the payroll tax (Waldman, 1976). The Medical Assistance plan would be financed by federal and state general revenues. The contributions of each would be determined by matching formulas.

Cost and efficiency guidelines. The only cost guidelines for these programs are those provided by the Medicare program. Reimbursement to providers would be made on the basis of reasonable cost or charges as determined under the Medicare program. Physicians who accept assignments or benefits for any services would have to agree to accept the reasonable charge as payment in full (Waldman, 1976).

Potential urban impacts of the Long-Ribicoff proposal. The distinguishing characteristic of the Long-Ribicoff bill is its reliance on employer payroll taxes and federal and state general revenues to finance catastrophic health coverage. Since consumers above poverty levels must finance the first 60 days of hospital care or the intial $2,000 of physician charges through supplemental health insurance, the impact of the program on federal and state budgets is not as marked as in other proposals.

Consumer benefits. The impact of the Long-Ribicoff bill on consumers is shown in Table 4. Per capita health expenditures under the Long-Ribicoff bill would increase by 4.4 percent or $34 per person. Out-of-pocket payments for health expenditures would decrease by 6.1 percent. Federal taxes under the program would increase 26.6 percent per capita, and state and local taxes would decrease by 10.7 percent per capita.

TABLE 4: Estimated Per Capita Health Costs under Long-Ribicoff Proposal, 1980

	Per Capita Expenditures		
	Without Program	*With Program*	*Change (%)*
Health expenditures	$780	$814	4.4
Out-of-pocket	245	230	− 6.1
Individual policies	33	32	− 3.0
Employee contributions	48	47	− 2.0
Federal taxes	207	262	26.6
State and local taxes	75	67	−10.7

Source: U.S. Department of Health, Education and Welfare cost study, Contract No. HEW-OS-74-138.

Not explicit in Table 4 is the strong subsidization of the socially disadvantaged and elderly. Federal and state contributions to the Federal Medical Assistance program would equal $24.5 billion if the Long-Ribicoff plan were implemented. This is an increase of $8.3 billion over the expected 1980 level of Medicaid expenditures.

Municipal expenditures. Under the Long-Ribicoff plan, state and local expenditures would decrease from $17.3 billion to $15.4 billion, a savings to State and local governments of $1.9 billion. The metropolitan share of savings would equal $1.4 billion if state and local funds were distributed by metropolitan/total population ratios.

Employer contributions. Employer contributions would increase by 3.8 percent or $1.2 billion under the Long-Ribicoff proposal. The bill would allow, however, a 50-percent tax credit against the 1-percent payroll tax imposed on firms.

CONCLUSIONS

This paper has suggested that national health insurance will affect urban economies in several distinct respects. First, national health insurance will induce large increases in demand for medical care as a consequence of lower medical care prices for beneficiaries and increased insurance coverage for the population as a whole. Certainly, the policies discussed here are not atypical in this respect. Second, the medical care sector of urban economies, as measured by employment, capital growth, and output, will expand. Although the greater part of expansion will be demand-based, growth will also be related to the subsidization of innovative organizations, delivery techniques, and medical manpower-training programs. Last, urban governments will be largely relieved of the burden of financing medical services subsidized by national health insurance. Although the provision of subsidized services by urban municipal hospitals and clinics may substantially increase, associated increases in the expenditures of urban governments on these services may be fairly small.

The welfare outcomes of national health insurance with respect to urban areas have only been alluded to in this paper. Most studies concerning the benefits and cost aspects of national health insurance attempt to rank policies in terms of the scope of program benefits and the costs borne by various income classes.

With respect to benefits, the Health Security proposal ranks as one of the plans with the most equitable approach to the structure of benefits, by providing universal eligibility and coverage, together with no cost-sharing requirements (Keintz, 1976, Chapter 11). The Health Insurance Association of America plan ranks second. The benefits provided by the plan are approximately comparable to those of the Kennedy-Corman bill, but deductible and coinsurance requirements may discourage a number of poor individuals from enrolling in the program. Second, poor health risks would be excluded from employee plans and required to pay a premium that reflected their high expected expenditures (Davis, 1975, p. 105). The Long-Ribicoff bill would be a substantial improvement over the current Medicaid program. Since the plan is a federal one with uniform benefits administered by the Social Security Administration, the extreme variations in benefits that now exist under the Medicaid program should be greatly reduced. Furthermore, by covering all low-income individuals, whether working or on welfare, many of the disparities in access to medical care between those on welfare and other poor people would be eliminated. For families above the poverty line and in the absence of insurance to allay the sizable deductible of the catastrophic plan, many families could still incur severe financial burdens in paying for the first 60 days of hospital care or the first $2,000 of medical bills (Davis, 1975, p. 88).

In terms of cost distribution, the Health Security proposal requires half of the total program costs to be financed from progressive sources, that is, from federal general revenues, but half also from regressive payroll taxes. Evidence suggests that the overall distributional cost effects could be at least slightly progressive. The Burleson-McIntyre bill is primarily financed by premiums, with federal and state general revenues financing a plan for the low-income and medically indigent groups. The premium cost structure is proportional since the premium payment is based on a fixed percentage of income. Federal contributions would vary from 70 to 90 percent; the State contribution would depend on per capita income. The Medicare payroll tax would remain in effect. The Long-Ribicoff bill primarily relies on regressive sources of financing, with the exception of federal general revenue contributions to a medical assistance plan for the poor. A regressive payroll tax would be used to fund a program for catastrophic coverage. The payroll tax would remain in effect for the Medicare hospital insurance plan. State general revenue contributions, a regressive source, would be dependent on current State Medicaid expenditure levels (Keintz, 1976, Chapter 11).

REFERENCES

American Hospital Association. *Comparative Statistics on Health Facilities and Population: Metropolitan and Non-Metropolitan Areas.* Chicago: American Hospital Association, 1978.

Davis, Karen. *National Health Insurance.* Washington, D.C.: Brookings Institution, 1975.

Gordon Trapnell Associates. *A Comparison of the Costs of Major National Health Insurance Proposals.* HEW Contract No. HEW-OS-74-138. Washington, D.C.: U.S. Government Printing Office, 1977.

Henderson, James, and Quandt, Richard E. *Microeconomic Theory.* New York: McGraw-Hill, 1971.

Keintz, Rita M. *National Health Insurance and Income Distribution.* Lexington, Mass.: D.C. Heath, 1976.

Krizay, John, and Wilson, Andrew. *The Patient As Consumer.* Lexington, Mass.: D.C. Heath, 1976.

Waldman, Saul. *National Health Insurance Proposals.* HEW Publication No. SSA-76-11920. Washington, D.C.: U.S. Government Printing Office, 1976.

CHAPTER TWELVE

The Urban Impacts of Federal Manpower and Wage Policies

GEORGE TOLLEY AND RONALD KRUMM

INTRODUCTION

President Carter's National Urban Policy Message of 1978 affirmed in unmistakable terms that providing more opportunities for the urban unemployed should be given a top priority in formulating national urban policy. The message also pointed out the need to bring the Federal government's diverse programs to bear in a consistent manner on urban problems. The need is particularly great to assess the effects of manpower and wage programs on the distressed urban parts of the economy, inasmuch as these policies have grown up largely independent of urban policy.

Manpower and wage policies have been evolving, and promise to change further as new approaches are discussed. This paper is concerned with the analysis needed to integrate these policies with urban policy. The economic effects of manpower and wage policies are discussed and a framework is developed for estimating the short-run and long-run effects of existing and proposed policies on different geographic parts of the United States economy. A detailed method is illustrated for one important set of policies.

In the second part of this paper, four major elements of manpower and wage policies are identified, each having distinctive urban and regional effects and each calling for its own estimation approaches. The third part systematizes the ways in which the four types of policies can be expected to affect regions and cities. This systemization provides a framework for estimating urban and regional impacts. The state of knowledge regarding the parts of the framework is discussed, as are the analytic and empirical needs required to apply the framework operationally.

The fourth part turns in detail to wage subsidies, which have, in significant ways, become an integral part of national policy and are being discussed as an approach that might be expanded. Estimates are presented of effects on unemployment, by state, that two types of expanded wage subsidy programs would have over an intermediate period of one to three years. Models for refinement of the estimates are developed. Finally, approaches are suggested for estimating longer-term effects, involving skill composition of the labor force and industry location decisions, which could be of vital importance to the future of distressed parts of the economy.

DELINEATION OF PROGRAM TYPES

A review

The federal role in manpower and wage programs has taken a variety of forms, some focusing on countercyclical employment measures, others pertaining more specifically to low-skill, low-wage persons, with the method of implementing such programs sometimes based on Federal grants to State and local governments (with the choice of application often open to some local discretion), and others are characterized by direct federal administration. The implications of the different means of administering programs and the different intentions of the programs can have very different regional impacts.

Work relief programs undertaken in the 1930s as a reaction to the severe economic downturn of the decade extended into the early 1940s. A major concern was to provide employment in construction activities, but the scale and focus of operations differed substantially among programs.

The Employment Act of 1946, mandating the Federal government to take steps to promote employment opportunities for persons able and willing to work, has served as a philosophical guide, legitimizing diverse efforts to reduce unemployment since 1946. Among other developments over the years, unemployment insurance has been extended and meshed with state systems, and federal minimum wage coverage has been extended along with substantial raises in the minimum wage.

Recent experience with federal manpower programs started in the 1960s with concern over employment of lower-skill workers. As exemplified by the Manpower Development and Training Act (MDTA), Job Opportunities in the Business Sector (JOBS), and other programs, a characteristic of federal involvement has been the attempt to provide more fully for meaningful productive opportunities for low-skill, chronically disemployed persons. These efforts have evolved into a complex and multifaceted set of programs which are now carried out under the Comprehensive Employment and Training Act of 1973 (CETA).

A principal focus of the programs contained in CETA is with the urban ills of current national concern. The precise content of the programs is left to the discretion of local sponsors who receive the funds.

Title I of CETA establishes comprehensive manpower programs providing for recruitment, orientation, counseling, testing, placement, classroom instruction, institutional and on-the-job training, allowances for persons in training, supportive services, and transitional public service jobs.

Title II provides for transitional and public employment programs in areas having an unemployment rate of 6.5 percent or higher. Title III provides for special manpower programs for Indians, migrants and other target groups including youth, offenders and ex-offenders, older workers, persons of limited English-speaking ability, and those with disabilities.

Title IV contains a continuation of the Jobs Corps program, previously part of the Economic Opportunity Act of 1964. Title V establishes a National Commission for Manpower Policy to serve as an advisory group dealing with manpower problems. Title VI, established by the Emergency Jobs and Un-employment Assistance Act of 1974, sets up a program of temporary public service employment for those who are unemployed during periods of high unemployment, and is especially applicable to those who are not eligible for relief under any state or federal unemployment compensation law.

All prime sponsors are eligible for Title I funds. To be eligible for funds under II, the primary sponsor must contain within its jurisdiction an "area of substantial unemployment"—any area of sufficient size and scope to sustain a public service employment program which has an unemployment rate of 6.5 percent or higher for three consecutive months.

Title II is aimed at countering cyclical unemployment and Title I is mostly concerned with training and training support services. The public service employment components (Titles I, II, and IV) and work experience part (Title I) of CETA restrict employment of participants to public or private nonprofit enterprises. The private sector can participate in on-the-job training programs under Title I although payments for such activities can be made only for costs in excess of those normally borne by the employer. This policy differs greatly from programs to be discussed below involving direct wage subsidies for persons employed in the private sector.

Participation in CETA programs is very much concentrated in Title I programs although the share of Title II and VI participation has grown, probably due to the higher unemployment rates observed in recent years.

More recently, the Humphrey-Hawkins bill has increased the likelihood of emphasis on public employment. In addition, interest has risen noticeably in the possibility of more widespread use of wage subsidies of various sorts in the private sector as a means of expanding employment, most of which focuses on subsidies for targeted groups. Experience with such policies in the United States has been obtained through the Work Incentive Program (WIN) tax credit which applied to the wages of persons receiving welfare and enrolled in the work incentive program, and the more generalized welfare recipient employment incentive credit (1975), both being early experiments with such devices. As discussed in Hammermesh (1978, p. 9), "the WIN credit, a nationwide categorical subsidy, applied to workers eligible for the work-incentive program and required that they be retained for two years. It provided a 20-percent tax credit up to a limit of $1,000 on each employee's annual wages, with the rate falling to 10 percent after a firm's credits for the year reached $25,000. The 1975 welfare credit also provides a 20 percent credit but has a retention period of only ninety days and a 10 percent rate after the firm's credits reach $50,000."

These tax credits for employment of disadvantaged groups allow for more flexible training and job experience than public service employment, providing greater possibilities of retaining or obtaining new employment in the private sector after the programs' completion. However, the limited length of participation in the programs is very important. While the two-year retention under the WIN credit plan may be of sufficient duration to enable a participating worker to acquire relevant skills that could enable him to stay on the job or obtain meaningful employment in other parts of the private sector after the programs' completion, the 90-day retention under the 1975 welfare credit extension reduces these chances.

In addition to these specific experiences with wage subsidies, proposals have been seriously discussed for various more-widespread programs. Discussions have taken place in and out of government about the possibility of a tax credit for additions to employment above an historical base. Analogies have been drawn between the rationales for the investment tax credit and for additions to new employment. Direct wage subsidy programs have been discussed that would take a variety of forms such as being mandated as a given dollar amount per hour for labor or as a percentage amount, and as applying to all labor earning less than a given amount or targeted very specifically to workers with special characteristics, such as sporadic work histories.

Four types of policies

From the above review of the historical development and content of federal manpower and wage programs four basic types of policies emerge:
—manpower training policies
—unemployment insurance
—public employment
—wage policies.
CETA contains elements of manpower training programs and public employment policies. Unemployment insurance and wage subsidy policies, such as the WIN tax credit system, are separate programs.

The following section develops a framework to guide the preparation of Urban Impact Statements (UIS) for the four types of policies.

OVERVIEW OF PROGRAM EFFECTS

General framework

The prime objective of an urban impact statement to be used for urban policy must be to identify and quantify those effects which could have an important bearing on the well-being and functioning of cities. Among the considerable problems that confront this task are the identification of goal variables, obtaining an analytical understanding of the processes by which goals may be affected, and attempting to estimate effects on goals in a situation where the knowledge and accuracy surrounding estimates are subject to uncertainty. Table 1 presents a suggested outline for UIS on manpower and wage policies which will now be discussed.

Primary or direct impacts

A starting point, with which urban impact analysis should be consistent and from which much aid can be obtained, is the estimation of overall program effects undertaken without any particular regard for spatial impacts. The overall effects are of concern in the general course of formulating and evaluating policies apart from any requirement to produce an urban impact statement. Thus, manpower and wage policies are undertaken to increase earning power through enhancing skills, to make income transfers through unemployment insurance, and to increase employment through public employment and wage policies. Because the policies are most often targeted to problem groups, they have important income distributional as well as output effects. A vast effort and expertise have been concerned with these effects. The urban impact analyst can sift extant estimates carefully, and, hopefully, will face a minimal need for making new estimates of overall effects.

Urban impact analysis should thus not be undertaken independently of the overall effects, but rather should start with the best possible estimates of them. It should then proceed, first, to subdivide the overall effects spatially within the United States economy and, second, estimate various induced effects on private and local economies which are not the primary concern of the policies as originally conceived.

Fungibility. A requirement for accurate estimation of the overall effects is

TABLE 1: Outline for Statement on Urban Impacts of Manpower and Wage Policies

A. Primary or Direct Impacts
B. Fungibility
C. Short-Run Impacts by Location
   1. Geographical Distribution of Primary Impacts
   2. Local Employment and Income Multipliers
D. Permanent Impacts by Location
   1. Duration of Short-Run Impacts
   2. Career Aftereffects and the Urban Labor Force
   3. Effects of Migration on Skill Levels and Income Composition
   4. Amount of Industry Attracted to Cities
   5. Tax Revenue Elasticities
   6. Quantification of Fiscal Surpluses Generated

that they be true net effects and not wholly or partly effects that would have occurred in the absence of the policy. The problem of ascertaining net effects is particularly severe for many federal programs affecting cities, because of the possibilities of substituting federal aid for local expenditures that would otherwise have been devoted to the functions aided.

Evidence of substitution of federal funds for state and local resources for particular projects was widely noted in policies during the depression of the 1930s. Table 2 presents comparisons of Federal and local government expenditures on construction activities during this period, illustrating the magnitudes involved and the decline in state and local expenditures relative to increases in federal expenditure in this area. More recent experience along these lines with regard to public employment and manpower training programs has been examined by Johnson (1978) and Johnson and Tomola (1977) suggesting potential expenditure substitutions in conjunction with current programs.

Short-run locational impacts. The direct locational impacts are sometimes mandated by formulas, as when funds are legislatively allocated to areas for narrowly defined purposes. In other cases, estimating the locational distribution of impacts even in the short run may pose major analytical problems. Local discretion, as in the case of CETA, may make it difficult to predict which of several quite different types of measures local communities will opt for. Even for federally administered programs, eligibility and participation

TABLE 2: Fiscal Substitution Effects of Public Construction Projects

Year	Federal* Sources	State and Local* Sources	Ratio of State and Local to Federal Expenditures
1930	$ 307	$2,469	8.04
1931	422	2,156	5.11
1932	460	1,334	2.90
1933	647	707	1.09
1934	1,380	794	0.58
1935	1,234	616	0.50
1936	2,335	881	0.38
1937	2,043	845	0.41
1938	2,085	1,103	0.53
1939	2,206	1,314	0.60

Source: Kesselman, J. R. "Work Relief Programs in the Great Depression," in *Creating Jobs: Public Employment Programs and Wage Subsidies,* edited by J. L. Palmer (Washington, D.C.: Brookings Institution, 1978).

* Dollar amounts in millions.

rates for targeted programs can be particularly difficult to foresee on an area basis.

A part of the shorter-run impacts may be local multiplier effects which require estimation of spending and employment induced in an area because of the primary increases in employment and income. This will require techniques going beyond those used in estimating direct impacts, and will depend critically on the degree of unemployment and slackness of nonlabor resources as those vary by area.

Locational effects induced in the longer run. The most important urban effects of many policies may occur because the policies alter the conditions determining the growth and development of cities. It is the very purpose of urban policies to alter these conditions. The fact that these longer-run effects are difficult to estimate means that they must be faced as best they can, and that their possible effects should be discussed without implying in an urban impact statement that the exact magnitudes are known. In spite of the difficulties, much progress can be made in gaining and communicating an understanding of the general order of magnitudes of the effects. The large effects that a variety of policies have on city sizes has recently been studied by Tolley, Graves, and Gardner (1979).

With regard to the goals of reducing unemployment and poverty, as well as promoting job growth and raising average or median incomes, three related longer-run urban effects of manpower and wage policies should be the focus of concerted attention, as follows.

First, formal training and job experience have career pattern effects of long-lasting significance, particularly when they affect those entering the labor force, by leading to an earlier date of first job and by affecting the skill level at which job entry takes place. As is well known, the future height and slope of a person's earnings profile over time is affected importantly by the entry point. Recent empirical work by Lazaer (1976) suggests that being out of the work force for one year reduces the stock of human capital (future earning power) on average by about $.25 per hour. For a young person this is most important—approximately one-third of his overall compensation is in the form of job training, with the present value of this unemployment experience worth approximately $5,000 to him.

To some extent, the effect on the earnings profile will show up in careful present-value analyses of benefits of programs. Recent empirical analysis of the effects of training programs on earnings after program completion (as, for example, Ashenfelter, 1974, 1977, and Kiefer, 1977) suggests increases in earnings for participants relative to what they would have been otherwise but such analysis needs to be extended to more fully examine benefits in terms of career pattern aftereffects. However, present-value analysis gives only the efficiency effects from the national point of view. The future earnings have distributional consequences desired for the persons involved over and above the efficiency effects. Moreover, the growth in the skill of a city's labor force over time may increase its viability, tax base, and attractiveness to industry, relieving symptoms of social distress, one of urban policy's purposes. Career aftereffects of job training and employment programs thus have special significance for urban policy, and should have more attention paid to them than they have received to date in analyses of the job-training and employment programs.

Second, while short-run impact analysis may be able to assume that all job effects are felt in changes in employment by people living in an area, longer-run analysis should not make this assumption. For persons of some ages and skill levels, whether they live in an area is largely dependent on whether jobs are available. This is particularly true of higher-income persons. A desideratum in urban policy is to keep and attract diverse people to cities in distress. Lower-skill workers and older workers tend to be less mobile, though not completely so, as attested to by myriad migration studies. Migration response coefficients can be used to gain insights to the extent to which migration or unemployment change in response to programs affecting employment. Table 3 provides an illustration, showing estimates made for a study pertaining to higher-skilled workers in Wisconsin.

Third, if the skill characteristics of the labor force of a city are upgraded or if the wages that must be paid are lowered through wage subsidies, the city will be more attractive to industry. Increasingly the emphasis in formulating urban policy has turned toward fostering jobs and development. Often the policy tools in this area are directed toward credit and nonhuman factors of production. Yet the magnitude of payrolls as a cost component is testimony to the overriding importance of labor among all factors of production. The industry location consequences of urban policies, and of manpower and wage policies in particular, appear to be among the most important and least understood effects. There is a need in the analysis of urban policies both for basic studies and for bolder attempts to utilize such information as is available on industry location.

Turning from concerns with jobs and their income consequences, another set of impacts has to do with effects on local government finances and services. These are increasingly matters to be given serious consideration, with the recent experiences of urban fiscal strain. Quantitative estimates can be made of the effects of programs on city revenues and expenditures. Researchers' recent formal inquiries into the nature of these effects (for example, Auten and Robb, 1976, and Bahl and Greytak, 1976) need to be more fully developed, especially in conjunction with the fiscal characteristics of federal unemployment and manpower programs. Apart from the fungibility issue, which directly affects local governments, tax revenue elasticities with respect to property value, sales, and income can be used to estimate changes in revenues due to ; n increase in jobs. Induced effects, such as those on industry location, have both tax revenue and cost implications, because industry and population

TABLE 3: Effects of a Change in Jobs on Migration and Unemployment in Wisconsin

Age in 1980	Percentage Distribution of a Change in Total Jobs	Migration Response Coefficient	Per 100 Jobs Lost in the Area	
			Outmigrants	Remaining in Area without Work
Males				
14–15	1.22	1.00	1.22	0.00
16–17	2.91	1.00	2.91	0.00
18–19	4.36	1.00	4.36	0.00
20–24	11.72	1.00	11.72	0.00
25–29	15.27	1.00	15.27	0.00
30–34	11.76	1.00	11.76	0.00
35–39	10.04	1.00	10.04	0.00
40–44	8.59	0.95	8.16	0.43
45–54	16.53	0.90	14.88	1.65
55–64	13.28	0.75	9.96	3.32
65+	4.32	0.33	1.43	2.89
Total	100.00		91.71	8.29
Females				
14–15	0.83	1.00	0.83	0.00
16–17	3.17	1.00	3.17	0.00
18–19	6.58	1.00	6.58	0.00
20–24	16.82	1.00	16.82	0.00
25–29	12.14	1.00	12.14	0.00
30–34	10.05	1.00	10.05	0.00
35–39	8.59	0.66	5.67	2.92
40–44	8.17	0.66	5.39	2.78
45–54	16.36	0.70	11.45	4.91
55–64	13.21	0.71	9.38	3.83
65+	4.08	0.30	1.22	2.86
Total	100.00		82.70	17.30

Source: Tolley, Upton, and Hastings, *Electric Energy Availability and Regional Growth* (Cambridge: Ballinger, 1977).

bring demand for services that must be met from any increased tax revenues before a fiscal surplus will be available for other uses. A reduction in the welfare rolls will reduce the city's payment for its share of welfare costs.

Implications

It would appear that preparing meaningful urban impact statements will require an eclectic approach to analysis and estimation in each of the subjects outlined of direct effects, fungibility, short-run locational impacts and the long-run impacts on incomes, jobs, and local governments in different locations. Two of the greater challenges will be to include all of these subjects and to present results in a reasoned and understandable way in the face of the difficulties inherent in precisely estimating some of the more important effects.

The way in which the steps outlined in this discussion will be carried out can be expected to vary greatly from program to program, as illustrated in the following discussion on wage subsidy programs.

FRAMEWORK FOR ANALYSIS OF WAGE SUBSIDY PROGRAMS

National model

Wage subsidies have been offered as remedies for a variety of problems as discussed by Kesselman, Williamson, and Berndt (1977), and others. In estimating effects of wage subsidies, a number of factors need to be considered, including differences among workers, differences in wage subsidy provisions, such as whether the subsidy applies to all workers or to targeted groups and whether the subsidy is specified in absolute or percentage terms, and, most importantly for the present, subject differences in labor market conditions, including regional wage differentials. This section attempts to develop more adequate means than heretofore available for estimating the effects of wage subsidy policies.

A simple case. Consider first a wage subsidy for a group of homogeneous workers who would be employed in any case. Figure 1 illustrates the market for such labor, abstracting from interindustry and interregional differences in the labor supply and demand relationships which will be dealt with more fully below. Under market clearing conditions the wage of this particular type of labor is p_e and the quantity employed is q_e. Implementation of a wage subsidy in the amount of s induces an increase in the quantity of labor employed to q_s with all laborers receiving p_1 and employers paying only p_0. Letting β be the elasticity of demand for labor and γ the elasticity of supply, the percentage increase in labor employed (relative to equilibrium) due to a wage subsidy of s is

$$\frac{s/p_e}{\frac{1}{\gamma} + \frac{1}{\beta}} \tag{1}$$

The costs to the government in terms of funding this wage subsidy relative to the equilibrium wage bill is $s \cdot q/p_e \cdot q_e$ which, in terms of the parameters of the model is

$$s/p_e \left[1 + (s/p_e) / \left(\frac{1}{\gamma} + \frac{1}{\beta} \right) \right]. \tag{2}$$

The extent to which this subsidy is received by workers depends on the relative demand and supply elasticities with

$$p_1/p_e = 1 + (s/p_e\beta) / \left(\frac{1}{\gamma} + \frac{1}{\beta}\right) \tag{3}$$

representing the gain to each worker in terms of increased wages. As seen from Figure 1 the portion of the wage bill paid by employers decreases with the total amount increasing or decreasing depending upon the value of β.

A wage subsidy applied to some workers induces an expansion of economic activity, with the increased number of workers and the higher wage leading to increases in demands for goods and services, and thereby increases employment opportunities. These multiplier effects lead to an expansion of labor demand (and increased wages) to which the subsidy need not apply, thus leading to smaller costs of the program relative to employment gains than is suggested by the above computations. However, in the above example the subsidy is applied to all workers with the multiplier contained in the labor demand function.

FIGURE 1: Effect of Wage Subsidy on Demand and Supply of Labor

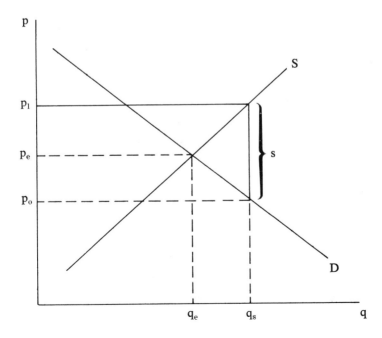

Empirical estimates of the elasticity of demand for labor (as recently summarized by Hammermesh, 1976) suggest that the demand for labor is quite sensitive to wage changes so that these employment increases could be substantial. As seen from Equation 1, large values of either γ or β will serve to increase the employment impacts of the wage subsidy and higher values of p_e serve to lessen the impact.

Although the employment impacts depend symmetrically on values of γ and β, increased income going to workers does not. For any given elasticity of labor supply, increases in the elasticity of demand lead to larger increases in wages received by workers. On the other hand, for any given elasticity of demand, increases in γ may lead to dramatic decreases in the wage increase associated with the wage subsidy. Under this general wage subsidy program, increased income of workers includes increased wages received by existing workers as well as the payments to new workers. The extent to which income of already employed workers increases depends heavily on the elasticity of labor supply, decreasing as γ increases. Targeting the wage subsidy to only newly employed workers will, in this case, decrease the costs of the program while not altering the net employment and wage impacts.

Structural unemployment. The above framework considers the impacts of a uniform wage subsidy for employment and earnings of homogeneous workers. A more likely situation is that a wage subsidy program will attempt to improve employment opportunities in the presence of structural unemployment. Such a case is depicted in Figure 2 where p_M represents the existing non-market clearing wage with associated employment of q_M. At p_M there is a pool of unemployed workers of $q_0 - q_M$ who are willing to work at p_M but cannot find employment.

If p_e, the market clearing wage, were known, a general wage subsidy of $p_M - p_e$ would bring about equilibrium employment of q_e. Under such a situation the costs of the program would be $q_e \cdot (p_M - p_e)$, where the benefits would accrue only to those newly employed by the program (since until q_0 is reached there will be no increase in the wage for this type of laborer). Under these conditions the percentage increase in employment is given by

$$\frac{s/p_M}{\dfrac{1}{\beta}} \qquad (4)$$

which is similar to the expression in Equation A-1, except that labor supply here is perfectly elastic at p_M.

The benefits accruing to newly employed workers as a fraction of the previous wage bill in this case is given by $(q - q_M)/q_M$. On the other hand, the costs of funding this subsidy as a percent of the previous wage bill is

FIGURE 2: Wage Subsidy with Structural Unemployment

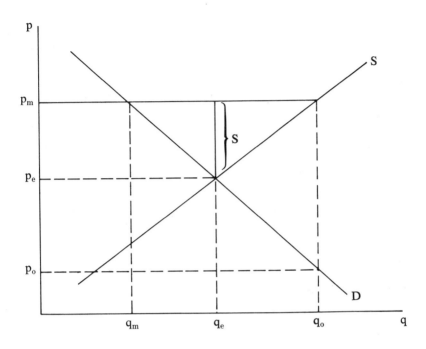

$$s/p_M\left[1 + (s/p_M)/\left(\frac{1}{\beta}\right)\right], \tag{5}$$

with larger elasticities of demand leading to larger employment benefits relative to program costs.

An important concern for policy-makers is the cost of such a program relative to the labor employment and earning impacts induced by it. Comparison of the effects of a general wage subsidy applied to a market in equilibrium with that just described above suggests a variety of differences in effects. First, previously employed workers receive no additional pay benefits when there is structural unemployment in the system and the net employment effects are larger because of the pool of unemployed laborers willing to work at the existing wage. In this sense, a larger "bang for the buck" is obtained when such a wage subsidy policy is introduced during periods of high unemployment because of inflexibility of market wages to their equilibrium value.

Recent experience with wage subsidies, such as with the WIN tax credit scheme, limited the subsidy to targeted groups among those not employed.

In terms of the current framework, under structural unemployment conditions as illustrated in Figure 2, such programs (ignoring the differential credits associated with credit ceilings) would not alter the net employment effects of such subsidies, except to the extent that employers might substitute toward unemployed workers, possibly laying off similarly skilled workers. This attempt to take advantage of the government wage subsidy is discouraged by the ceilings contained in those programs. Targeting thereby serves to limit the costs of the program but does not seriously affect the resulting employment increases.

Moreover, targeted wage subsidies serve to decrease the cost of newly employed workers, thus allowing for potential skill accumulation by these targeted groups that is useful for their continued employment and income growth as well as in their current job opportunities. To the extent that wage subsidies lower the overall costs of labor, previously employed labor may be better able to take advantage of on-the-job-training programs and achieve future gains as well. In order to remain employed in the face of wage constraints, as considered above, some workers may sacrifice current opportunities for skill improvement with wage subsidies targeted more toward skill level groups and less toward only those currently unemployed. This leads to less future unemployment problems for these groups as a whole. Indirect effects of wage subsidy programs on already employed workers need to be examined and potentially large opportunities for skill accumulation applied to these groups as well.

Differences in skills among workers. The above discussion of the impacts of wage subsidies makes the traditional assumption that labor inputs in an affected skill group are homogeneous. However, it is likely that those unemployed possess fewer skills than those employed.

Consider the case where workers differ in the amounts of skill they possess so that each worker has a marginal productivity to an employer that depends not on mere employment but on the effective skill possessed, with workers having small amounts of skill being paid less than those with higher amounts of the relevant skill. The schedules for supply and demand for labor considered above apply to only one very specific skill category, which is a subset of a whole continuum of labor skill demand and supply schedules.

In contrast to the above homogeneous labor demand and supply framework, recognizing differences in labor skills under conditions of structural wage rigidities implies that lower-skill workers suffer the brunt of unemployment and more completely identifies those who make up the pool of unemployed. Further, recognizing skill differences allows more complete identification of workers who may be termed disadvantaged (at the very bottom of the skill distribution) and those who are temporarily unemployed (for example, during general economic downturns) who can be re-employed when conditions improve. A model which distinguishes between skill levels among workers suggests that the lowest productivity workers within a skill group are those that are not employed due to structural wage constraints. The effects of a wage subsidy in such a case will differ from those discussed in the above sections, because of the productivity differences among workers.

Consider the case of a fixed rate wage subsidy for all workers when the government pays the employer s dollars for each manhour of employment. The demand for skill services shifts to the right as s increases, leading to increased employment of workers with low skills, although the very lowest skill workers remain unemployed. In terms of the homogeneous labor market framework developed earlier, the unemployed ($q_0 - q_M$) will be hired more rapidly the greater their skill level, with those remaining unemployed being the most disadvantaged workers. This framework allows for identification of those unemployables suffering from a structural wage constraint who will be most likely to be hired, given a wage subsidy. The result is those with higher skills will be first to be accepted into the program.

Regional impacts

The above section developed a framework for analyzing the effects of a wage subsidy on employment and earnings in the context of a single market—the national economy. A national uniform wage subsidy may induce differential impacts among regions due to differences in characteristics of regional economies not only with respect to mix of industries, labor types, and unemployment conditions, but also because of quite substantial variation in nominal wages and prices among areas. The framework developed for the nation allowed workers to be employed or unemployed; a framework for regional analysis must also consider migration of jobs and people among areas. Job opportunities in a particular region may play an important role in explaining movements of people in the United States and differences in the cost of labor may play a very important role in determining industrial location. Building on the considerations described above, a framework is developed below to estimate differential impacts of a national wage subsidy program among regions.

Regional differences in nominal wages and prices. Comparison of regional wages and prices reveals substantial variation in nominal values, many of which persist over time. In terms of the impacts of a national wage subsidy, which is based on uniform application of a nominal subsidy or nominal tax credit limit (as in the WIN tax credit program), particularly large disparities in regional incentives to participate may result. However, a wage subsidy as a percentage of the wage will not induce differential relative employment impacts among regions in the absence of significant differences in industry demand elasticities. In such a case, the relative wage to employees in all areas is decreased by the same percentage amount leading to the same percentage increase in employment, although the magnitude of employment increases will differ depending on the level of employment to which the percentage increase applies.

Previous experience with wage subsidy programs has been based on percentage tax credits, such as 20 percent for the WIN program, which would not in themselves alter incentives among regions, but, in conjunction with credit limits (whether absolute or associated with stepwise decreases in credits), alter the overall incentives of producers to participate. The WIN tax credit program discussed earlier provides a tax credit of 20 percent of a worker's annual wages up to a limit of $1,000 per employee. In terms of the nonmarket clearing model presented earlier, this amounts to a subsidy that differs not only with respect to the skills of a worker but also in regard to the local nominal wage level. For example, considering employment of a worker for a year who earns $10,000, this amounts to a subsidy of 10 percent of his earnings; for a lower-skill worker who would earn $5,000 per year, this is a 20 percent subsidy. This system does increase the relative incentives for using the lower-skill workers, although two workers with the same skills located in different areas are affected differently, with those in high nominal-wage regions being subsidized less than those in low nominal-wage regions.

These considerations, in conjunction with structural unemployment, serve to make those very low-skill workers in high nominal-wage areas less likely to be employed under such a program while favoring lower-skill employment opportunities in low-wage areas.

Regional and skill impacts. The impacts of a wage subsidy in the presence of structural unemployment will be not to employ those workers at the very lowest end of the skill distribution, but rather those nearer the cutoff point determined by the wage constraint. Moreover, this problem will be exacerbated in higher-wage areas where a substantial portion of the most disadvantaged and low-skill workers live.

Since the wage subsidy is more effective in low-wage areas, being a larger real wage subsidy, there is an incentive for industry to move to these areas in order to take greater advantage of the reduced labor costs. However, to the extent that wage subsidy programs are not permanent policies, the necessity to make long-lived plants and equipment commitments might reduce the probability of such moves. On the other hand, because the price of a unit of skill is reduced more in the low-wage areas as opposed to higher-wage regions, there will be an incentive for those previously employed in low-wage areas to move to higher-wage regions, thereby tending to offset some of the employment impacts. And those previously not employed might tend to move to low-wage regions where the probability of finding employment has increased relatively more. A more complete analysis is needed to determine the potential magnitudes of such flows.

Employment impacts: empirical results

The above sections outlined potentially important differential employment and earnings effects among regions of a variety of federal wage subsidy programs. A more complete examination of the magnitudes of these differences is needed in order to determine the extent to which disparities in effects among regions may lead to migration of industry and people, and the further impacts of these flows on regional development and urban problems.

An important impact of a general wage subsidy is that it enhances the employment opportunities of those unemployed workers that, in the absence of wage rigidities, would be most productive. Increases in the wage subsidy increase the extent to which employment opportunities are increased for lower-skill workers.

Models, allowing for nonhomogeneity of workers and regional wage and unemployment differences along the lines developed above, appear essential for estimating who is employed and where, as a result of a wage subsidy. This section presents empirical applications applying labor demand elasticities for refined demographic worker categories from Graves, Krumm, and Tolley (1977), based on extensions of work by Mincer (1976), and takes account of variations in nominal wages among states, to determine the likely employment effects of wage subsidy programs targeted to unemployed workers. The estimates are derived from estimates of impacts of changing the minimum wage and are consistent with other labor demand elasticity estimates reviewed in Hammermesh (1976), although no attempt was made to determine if the elasticities themselves were subject to regional variation.

Table 4 presents estimates of the one-to-three-year percentage employment effects for various demographic groups in each state due to a national uniform nominal wage subsidy of $.50. Based upon estimates of the elasticity of demand for labor over this period of time, the percentage impacts differ substantially among states and demographic category. These estimates take into account medium-run local-employment multiplier impacts due to induced job creation resulting from the direct employment of workers under a wage subsidy program, although they most probably do not capture much of the very longer-run impacts on migration of industry and people to areas with enhanced job opportunities.

The greatest percentage impacts are observed in low-nominal-wage areas, such as Arkansas, Florida, Georgia, Maine, Mississippi, New Hampshire, New Mexico, North Carolina, and South Carolina while high-nominal-wage states, such as Alaska, Michigan, and Washington, are less affected.

The effects differ dramatically among demographic groups. As expected, the employment impacts are greatest not for the very lowest skill groups, but rather for those who are more skilled yet unemployed and hence more likely to be employed due to such a subsidy program. On the other hand, the effects on older, more skilled groups is smaller mostly because there is not a large pool of unemployed in these categories. In addition, as discussed in previous sections, it is possible that the wage subsidy induces substitution away from these more skilled, already employed workers (because they are not subsidized by the program) thereby reducing the net employment increases in such worker categories.

TABLE 4: Percentage Change in Employment due to a Uniform National Wage Subsidy of $.50

State	Male Teenagers (Ages 16–19)		Female Teenagers (Ages 16–19)		Young Males (Ages 20–24)		
	White	Non-white	White	Non-white	White	Non-white	Other
Alabama	8.80	8.10	7.23	5.63	5.34	10.83	.227
Alaska	5.04	4.64	4.14	3.23	3.06	6.21	
Arizona	7.50	6.90	6.16	4.80	4.55	9.23	.195
Arkansas	10.13	9.32	8.32	6.48	6.15	12.46	.263
California	6.98	6.42	5.73	4.47	4.24	8.59	.183
Colorado	7.38	6.79	6.06	4.72	4.48	9.08	.190
Connecticut	7.61	7.00	6.25	4.87	4.62	9.36	.199
Delaware	7.17	6.60	5.89	4.59	4.35	8.83	.179
D.C.	6.59	6.06	5.41	4.22	4.00	8.11	.184
Florida	9.00	8.28	7.39	5.76	5.46	11.08	.238
Georgia	9.37	8.62	7.70	6.00	5.69	11.53	.242
Hawaii	7.89	7.24	6.46	5.04	4.78	9.69	.198
Idaho	7.70	7.09	6.33	4.93	4.68	9.48	.199
Illinois	6.73	6.20	5.53	4.31	4.09	8.29	
Indiana	6.63	6.09	5.44	4.24	4.02	8.15	.178
Iowa	6.73	6.20	5.53	4.31	4.09	8.29	.175
Kansas	6.80	6.26	5.59	4.35	4.13	8.37	.203
Kentucky	6.80	6.26	5.59	4.35	4.13	8.37	.203
Louisiana	7.56	6.96	6.21	4.84	4.59	9.30	.193
Maine	9.54	8.78	7.84	6.11	5.79	11.74	.250
Maryland	7.23	6.65	5.94	4.63	4.39	9.69	.188
Massachusetts	8.13	7.49	6.68	5.21	4.94	10.01	.214
Michigan	5.91	5.44	4.86	4.56	4.33	8.77	.184
Minnesota	7.13	6.56	5.86	4.56	4.33	8.77	.184
Mississippi	10.24	9.43	8.41	6.56	6.22	12.60	.263
Missouri	7.65	7.04	6.29	4.90	4.65	9.42	.199
Montana	6.83	6.29	5.61	4.37	4.15	8.41	.178
Nebraska	8.06	7.42	6.62	5.16	4.89	9.92	.203
Nevada	6.91	6.36	5.68	4.42	4.20	8.51	.183
New Hampshire	9.20	8.47	7.56	5.89	5.59	11.33	.249
New Jersey	7.37	6.79	4.64	4.72	4.48	9.08	.193
New Mexico	9.32	8.58	7.66	5.97	5.66	11.47	.256
New York	6.99	6.43	5.74	4.48	4.24	8.61	.192
North Carolina	9.83	9.04	8.07	6.30	5.97	12.09	.270
North Dakota	7.77	7.15	6.38	4.72	4.72	9.56	.213
Ohio	6.12	5.63	5.03	3.92	3.72	7.53	.168
Oklahoma	7.74	7.12	6.35	4.95	4.70	9.52	.213
Oregon	6.23	5.73	5.11	3.98	3.78	7.66	.171
Pennsylvania	6.95	6.40	5.71	4.45	4.22	8.56	.191

TABLE 4 (continued)

State	Male Teenagers (Ages 16–19)		Female Teenagers (Ages 16–19)		Young Males (Ages 20–24)		
	White	Non-white	White	Non-white	White	Non-white	Other
Rhode Island	8.98	8.26	7.37	5.75	5.45	11.05	.247
South Carolina	9.62	8.85	7.90	6.16	5.84	11.84	.264
South Dakota	8.23	7.57	6.76	5.27	4.99	10.12	.226
Tennessee	8.85	8.14	7.27	5.66	5.39	10.89	.243
Texas	7.50	6.90	6.16	4.80	4.55	9.23	.209
Utah	8.76	8.06	7.20	5.61	5.32	10.78	.241
Vermont	8.45	7.78	6.95	5.41	5.13	10.41	.232
Virginia	8.70	8.00	7.14	5.50	5.28	10.70	.239
Washington	5.90	5.43	4.85	3.78	3.58	7.26	.162
West Virginia	6.94	6.39	5.70	4.44	4.21	8.54	.191
Wisconsin	6.50	5.99	5.34	4.16	3.95	8.00	.179
Wyoming	6.89	6.34	5.66	4.41	4.18	8.47	.189

While the percentage-employment effects of a wage subsidy are seen to vary greatly among regions and worker categories, a relevant concern is determining the overall impacts of reduced unemployment, generated by the total new employment, on the urban ills and fiscal strain of local and State governments. Based on the results presented in Table 4, estimates of the total employment resulting from such a wage subsidy program are presented in Table 5. As illustrated, there is substantial variation among states in increased employment, suggesting potentially large overall disparate impacts of wage subsidies on regional growth potential and the lessening of urban ills associated with large numbers of unemployed, disadvantaged persons. While many of the southern, low nominal-wage states experience larger percentage increases in employment, a great bulk of the increase in number employed is concentrated in northern states where many cities, currently facing extreme problems with unemployed workers and the associated fiscal strain, are located.

The above results may be compared with those expected from implementing a wage subsidy which is specified in percentage rather than absolute terms. Table 6 presents estimates of the employment increases under a program that subsidizes employers by an amount equivalent to $.50 at the national level, being higher in high-wage states and lower in low-wage states by the ratio of the national to state average wages. For such a policy the percentage increases in employment for any demographic group is the same for each state and is equal to that for the national average associated with the estimates in Table 4. Comparisons of the results in Tables 5 and 6 illustrate

TABLE 5: Increase in Employment due to a Uniform National Wage Subsidy of $.50

State	Male Teenagers (Ages 16–19) White	Male Teenagers (Ages 16–19) Non-white	Female Teenagers (Ages 16–19) White	Female Teenagers (Ages 16–19) Non-white	Young Males (Ages 20–24) White	Young Males (Ages 20–24) Non-white
Alabama	3,049	873	1,089	253	3,588	1,894
Alaska	127	13	71	13	131	35
Arizona	1,977	90	863	42	1,810	246
Arkansas	2,082	321	816	113	2,412	722
California	17,666	1,343	8,170	748	18,744	3,829
Colorado	2,558	66	1,232	37	2,349	155
Connecticut	3,408	162	4,258	95	3,148	450
Delaware	494	57	239	29	517	149
D.C.	100	367	80	240	215	1,253
Florida	7,290	1,079	3,263	570	6,613	2,422
Georgia	4,989	1,529	2,141	634	5,574	3,479
Hawaii	242	448	134	265	314	1,110
Idaho	975	20	418	5	776	18
Illinois	10,433	854	5,871	559	9,952	2,645
Indiana	5,505	266	2,447	157	5,466	655
Iowa	3,476	38	1,684	22	2,890	87
Kansas	2,542	87	1,170	52	2,231	201
Kentucky	2,680	158	1,102	76	3,109	359
Louisiana	2,417	759	921	258	2,950	1,982
Maine	1,306	4	663	3	1,365	9
Maryland	3,434	591	1,716	303	3,620	1,586
Massachusetts	7,466	176	4,527	131	6,805	466
Michigan	8,016	640	4,058	352	7,385	1,814
Minnesota	4,944	60	2,960	39	4,126	124
Mississippi	1,896	763	730	267	2,230	1,794
Missouri	4,850	374	2,315	222	4,735	818
Montana	678	24	316	10	615	39
Nebraska	2,143	55	1,082	30	1,861	110
Nevada	438	28	204	15	459	83
New Hampshire	1,111	6	593	3	1,079	8
New Jersey	6,106	517	2,790	353	6,385	1,484
New Mexico	1,170	35	512	23	1,154	159
New York	13,308	1,188	7,860	846	15,703	4,079
North Carolina	6,123	1,579	2,538	631	6,560	3,355
North Dakota	665	6	355	6	607	1,213
Ohio	9,564	677	4,537	399	9,791	1,606
Oklahoma	2,735	206	1,154	109	2,624	448
Oregon	1,869	43	94	23	1,832	107
Pennsylvania	10,706	738	5,544	423	10,697	1,820
Rhode Island	1,322	26	741	23	1,228	62

TABLE 5 (continued)

State	Male Teenagers (Ages 16–19)		Female Teenagers (Ages 16–19)		Young Males (Ages 20–24)	
	White	Non-white	White	Non-white	White	Non-white
South Carolina	2,765	1,049	1,140	404	2,871	2,318
South Dakota	919	29	450	13	736	38
Tennessee	3,786	554	1,651	232	4,738	1,430
Texas	11,024	1,169	4,512	543	11,849	2,985
Utah	1,687	25	817	13	1,582	64
Vermont	595	2	315	0	589	4
Virginia	4,302	810	1,957	329	4,859	2,041
Washington	2,781	105	1,333	48	2,731	218
West Virginia	1,270	36	491	14	1,585	70
Wisconsin	5,082	129	2,598	60	4,377	321
Wyoming	358	6	157	1	319	9
Total	196,429	20,180	96,679	10,036	199,886	52,373

that this type of subsidy increases employment more in high-wage states and less in low-wage states than the uniform subsidy, sometimes by a substantial degree. Total employment generated under the wage subsidy corrected for regional variations in nominal wages is slightly larger due to the concentration of employment of these demographic groups in higher nominal-wage states.

Under either the nominal or percentage wage subsidy, the average $.50 per hour subsidy applied to 2,000 hours of work per year implies an annual government cost of $1,000 for each worker under the program. For the groups shown in Tables 4 and 6, the government cost would come to somewhat over $.5 billion yearly.

In light of the tendency for across-the-board wage subsidy programs to create job opportunities for workers who are just at the margin of employability to a greater extent than those with lower skills whose productivity is far below the market wage, further consideration of a spectrum of wage subsidies based on current skill levels is needed. Possibly a wage subsidy program, with flexibility in payment based on worker skill, in conjunction with training and placement programs to increase the usable skills of the very disadvantaged, could serve to decrease transitional as well as permanent unemployment among currently disadvantaged groups more effectively than either based independent of the other.

The uniform nominal-wage subsidy policy not only increases employment by a greater percentage in low nominal-wage areas but also extends employment opportunities more fully to lower-skill workers in these areas as compared to high-wage areas. On the other hand, a wage subsidy specified in percentage terms increases the extent to which very low-skill workers' em-

TABLE 6: Employment Changes Associated with a Wage Subsidy of $.50 at the National Level, Adjusted to Compensate for Differences in Nominal Wages among States

State	Male Teenagers (Ages 16–19) White	Non-white	Female Teenagers (Ages 16–19) White	Non-white	Young Males (Ages 20–24) White	Non-white
Alabama	2,774	793	990	229	3,267	1,724
Alaska	202	21	113	20	207	55
Arizona	2,111	95	921	44	1,933	253
Arkansas	1,645	253	644	89	1,907	571
California	20,268	1,541	9,379	857	21,494	4,393
Colorado	2,775	71	1,337	39	2,549	168
Connecticut	3,586	170	1,973	99	3,312	473
Delaware	552	63	267	32	577	167
D.C.	122	446	97	291	261	1,522
Florida	6,286	960	2,904	507	5,889	2,154
Georgia	4,263	1,307	1,829	541	4,762	2,974
Hawaii	245	456	136	269	319	1,128
Idaho	1,013	20	434	4	805	18
Illinois	12,413	1,015	6,983	663	11,830	3,146
Indiana	6,649	322	2,958	189	6,612	804
Iowa	4,136	45	2,003	26	3,435	103
Kansas	2,992	102	1,376	61	2,625	237
Kentucky	3,156	186	1,296	10	3,659	422
Louisiana	2,560	804	975	273	3,124	2,100
Maine	1,096	3	556	2	1,146	7
Maryland	3,803	654	1,900	335	4,008	1,628
Massachusetts	7,354	169	4,458	128	6,698	458
Michigan	10,861	867	5,492	477	10,001	2,455
Minnesota	5,553	67	3,322	43	4,632	139
Mississippi	1,419	596	571	208	1,742	1,403
Missouri	5,077	391	2,420	231	4,550	855
Montana	794	28	370	11	720	46
Nebraska	2,129	54	1,074	29	1,850	109
Nevada	508	33	236	17	531	95
New Hampshire	967	5	516	2	938	7
New Jersey	6,635	561	3,954	383	6,929	1,610
New Mexico	1,005	30	440	19	991	136
New York	15,254	1,361	9,007	968	18,006	4,669
North Carolina	4,907	1,286	2,069	513	5,343	2,735
North Dakota	685	6	366	6	625	12
Ohio	12,514	886	5,932	522	12,797	2,102
Oklahoma	2,829	213	1,195	112	2,714	463
Oregon	2,402	55	1,204	29	2,356	138
Pennsylvania	12,335	849	6,386	487	12,323	2,095

TABLE 6 (continued)

State	Male Teenagers (Ages 16–19)		Female Teenagers (Ages 16–19)		Young Males (Ages 20–24)	
	White	Non-white	White	Non-white	White	Non-white
Rhode Island	1,179	23	661	20	1,095	55
South Carolina	2,301	873	948	336	2,390	1,929
South Dakota	894	28	438	11	717	36
Tennessee	3,425	501	1,493	210	4,289	1,794
Texas	11,770	1,248	4,818	579	12,661	3,187
Utah	1,542	23	746	12	1,466	58
Vermont	546	1	298	0	558	3
Virginia	3,959	746	1,802	303	4,474	1,879
Washington	3,774	141	1,807	64	3,708	295
West Virginia	1,465	41	566	16	1,831	80
Wisconsin	6,261	158	3,200	73	5,387	395
Wyoming	415	6	182	1	371	11
Total	213,397	20,575	105,042	10,390	216,414	53,296

ployment opportunities are increased in high nominal-wage areas and moderates these effects in low nominal-wage areas. The percentage subsidy is thus likely to contribute more to alleviating urban ills and fiscal strain in many of the large cities, usually those having relatively higher nominal-wage levels. Explicit estimates would be useful and could be made of the effects of these policies on welfare and other transfers to unemployed and disadvantaged workers. The results would differ among states and within states, especially with respect to urban and rural areas. More refined empirical examination of the skill levels of workers making up the demographic categories used above is needed in order to complete such an investigation.

Longer-term impacts

The results presented above do not consider incentives for workers to migrate to areas with higher probabilities of employment and for industries to relocate to places where the real wage subsidy is high. With either a nominal or a percentage wage subsidy, incentives for migration of workers will be affected by the extent to which unemployment is reduced in one area relative to others, with the nominal-wage subsidy more heavily favoring migration of workers to low-wage areas. The extent to which unemployment differs among regions before the wage subsidy is introduced in conjunction with the amount of new job creation will determine the extent to which probabilities of finding employment will change among regions. Migration of workers could tend to equilibrate some of the initial regional disparities in reducing unemployment, with workers moving to regions where the initial impact of the wage subsidy is to reduce unemployment substantially. It should be possible to examine more completely which workers are employed and which workers have the highest incentives to move in reaction to changing regional job opportunities induced by a wage subsidy.

Potentially more important, the wage subsidy acts to reduce the cost of labor for industries, with these impacts differing substantially among regions inducing firms to move to relatively lower-cost areas, which, in this case, is in low-nominal-wage areas. Relatively low-wage industries will find the relative costs of production between regions changing more than high-wage industries will result in a higher incentive for these firms to relocate. This latter impact will also be important for a wage subsidy policy that weights the wage credit according to regional average wage differences because of intrastate differences in average wages among industries.

The magnitudes associated with these longer-term movements of industries depend on the long-run elasticity of demand for labor. Previous studies suggest that, under a wide range of conditions, estimates of the long-run elasticity of national labor demand are near unity. Moreover, estimates of national labor demand elasticities do not measure the full extent to which demand in a particular region is sensitive to a change in its labor costs relative to other parts of the country. It is well known that many industries are quite footloose with even small changes in relative labor costs among regions leading to potentially large flows of jobs to favorable areas even though the national demand for labor changes little. There is no other way to explain the continual very large geographical shifts in industry location observed in the United States economy.

Although many other factors may well be partly responsible for the great changes observed in the location of industry, the significance of labor inputs in production suggests potentially large effects of changes in relative wages among regions on these location decisions. National estimates of demand elasticities do not take into account regional disparities in prices which serve to establish the location of economic activity. While overall demand for labor may not increase dramatically, given an overall reduction in wages, this does not mean that the location of labor demand will not be very sensitive to changes in relative wage differences among regions, with the magnitude of flows of industries to areas most benefited by a wage subsidy program larger than that suggested using national labor demand elasticity measures. A simple example illustrates this point.

Let production be characterized by $q = AN^\alpha K^\beta$ where N is effective labor input and K is capital. Under profit-maximizing conditions, with the product price taken as given, the long-run wage elasticity of demand for labor is $1/[1 - \alpha/(1 - \beta)]$. With reasonable values of $\alpha = .7$ and $\beta = .2$ (with production exhibiting decreasing returns to scale) the elasticity of labor demand with respect to its wage is 4.5. While industry capital labor ratios differ, the overwhelming importance of labor in the production process suggests that long-run elasticities in the neighborhood of 3 to 5 are reasonable. Changes in relative costs of lab or among regions, that might be induced by wage subsidies, could thereby induce extensive shifts of production toward those low-wage areas while substantially decreasing economic activity in higher-wage regions. It would be fruitful to examine more systematically the sensitivity of production location to variations in input costs among regions in order that the magnitudes of these longer-run impacts can be determined.

The longer-run impacts over and above those considered in Tables 4 through 6 are all in the direction of accentuating the estimated regional impacts. The results of this chapter are thus sufficient to indicate that making the employment of lower-skilled workers more attractive through a wage subsidy would have profound favorable effects on employment in northern cities.

REFERENCES

Ashenfelter, Orley. "The Effect of Manpower Training on Earnings." *Research in Labor Economics*, Supplement 1, 1977.
―――. "The Effect of Manpower Training on Earnings: Preliminary Results." *Proceedings of the 27th Annual Meeting of the Individual Relations Research Association*, 1974.
Auten, G. E., and Robb, E. H. "A General Model for State Tax Revenue Analysis." *National Tax Journal* 29, no. 4 (December 1976): 422–35.
Bahl, R. W., and Greytak, D. "The Response of City Government Revenues to Changes in Employment Structure." *Land Economics* 52, no. 4 (1976).
Graves, P. E., Krumm, R. J., and Tolley, G. S. "The Effects of Minimum Wages on the U.S. Economy." *Urban Economics Report*. Chicago: University of Chicago, 1977.
Hammermesh, D. S. "Econometric Studies of Labor Demand and Their Application to Policy Analysis." *Journal of Human Resources* 6 (Fall 1976): 507–25.
―――. "Subsidies for Jobs in the Private Sector." *Creating Jobs: Public Employment Programs and Wage Subsidies*, edited by J. L. Palmer. Washington, D.C.: Brookings Institution, 1978.
Johnson, George. "The Labor Market Displacement Effects in the Analysis of the Net Impact of Manpower Training Programs." *Research in Labor Economics* 7 (1978).
―――, and Tomola, James. "The Fiscal Substitution Effect of Alternative Approaches to Public Service Employment Policy." *Journal of Human Resources* 67, no. 3 (1977): 3–26.
Kesselman, J. R. "Work Relief Programs in the Great Depression." In *Creating Jobs: Public Employment Programs and Wage Subsidies*, edited by J. L. Palmer. Washington, D.C.: Brookings Institution, 1978.
―――, Williamson, S. H., and Berndt, E. R. "Tax Credits for Employment Rather than Investment." *American Economic Review* 67 (June 1977): 339–49.

Kiefer, N. M. "The Economic Benefits from Manpower Training." *Research in Labor Economics*, Supplement 1, 1977.

————. "Federally Subsidized Occupational Training and the Employment and Earnings of Male Trainees." Unpublished paper, University of Chicago, 1977.

Lazaer, E. "Age, Experience, and Wage Growth." *American Economic Review* 66, no. 4 (1976): 548–58.

Mincer, J. "Unemployment Effects of Minimum Wages." *Journal of Political Economy* 84 (August 1976): 87–104.

Tolley, G., Upton, C., and Hastings, V. *Electrical Energy Availability and Regional Growth*. Cambridge, Mass.: Ballinger, 1977.

————, Graves, P., and Gardner, J. *Urban Growth Policy in a Market Economy*. New York: Academic Press, 1979.

PART IV

Urban Impact Analysis 2: Urban-Related Programs

CHAPTER THIRTEEN

Urban Impacts of Self-Help Neighborhood Development

EDWARD GREENBERG, CHARLES L. LEVEN, AND JAMES T. LITTLE

INTRODUCTION

In his Urban Message of March 27, 1978, the President called for an analysis of the urban impacts of new federal initiatives, essentially to identify unintended and uncontemplated impacts on our cities. On the other hand, stating that the urban impacts of a new policy initiative should be identified prior to its approval does not tell us what impacts are important, or how they are to be identified. This chapter is an example of what an operating urban impact statement should be.

In formulating an urban impact statement, such things as environmental or employment impact analyses serve as examples of the variety of impact statements already required by law. In these cases, however, the problem of impact analysis is different: environmenal impact statements generally call for the effect on the environment of a specific facility, such as a dam or reservoir in a particular location; employment impact statements are often concerned with the expected job loss from the closing of a particular military installation. So far as urban impacts are concerned, however, a *general* initiative that is being proposed for the Nation or some class of agents in it, rather than a specific action in a particular place, will be examined.

We should also note that approach taken does not deal directly with the question of whether the proposed initiative should be carried out; it is not a cost-benefit analysis. By the same token, this chapter is not meant to recommend definitively the particular way in which the initiative should be carried out, but it does discuss the conditions under which favorable or unfavorable urban impacts might be expected.

There are four ways in which a self-help program could be carried out. To some extent these could involve initiatives aimed directly at individual neighborhood residents (NIND) and these will be discussed as one of the four possible patterns for organizing a self-help effort. Much more likely is that they will be carried out by some sort of neighborhood organization (NORG). The organizational details and specific range of powers of such groups cover a wide range, but for the most part, they seem to be of three general types.

The simplest kind of NORG is one which engages almost exclusively in planning, coordinating, and lobbying. Such a coordinating NORG (COORD-NORG) exists for the purpose of increasing the neighborhood's share of community-wide programs and/or insuring that funds spent in its neighborhood are used in ways consistent with the neighborhood's objectives.

A more substantial form of NORG is one which not only plans and lobbies, but also operates services and/or facilities, typically with grants or under contract from a private or government body. The most typical kind of contracting NORG (CONTRNORG) is one which operates services which supplement or parallel those of local government; such things as neighborhood health clinics, after-school enrichment programs, or vocational counseling and job referral. A stronger form of CONTRNORG is a neighborhood organization which takes over the operation of a neighborhood public service on behalf of, and substituting for, the service normally provided by municipal government.

In its most developed form, the NORG would not only plan and provide services, but would also own and operate residential and other property such as stores, service establishments, and even manufacturing enterprises. Actual ownership might be by the NORG or by the tenants, employees, or customers of the property or establishment. In any event, even if not cooperatively owned, it would be operated for the cooperative benefit of a particular group or of the neighborhood as a whole. Thus, the third kind of NORG to be considered will be the cooperative NORG (COOPNORG).

THE NATURE OF URBAN IMPACTS

By "urban impacts" we mean something other than the benefits of the program. For example, the major direct benefits of a neighborhood self-help initiative might lie in the increased feelings of potency or efficacy that neighborhood residents could enjoy by virtue of achieving a sense of control over at least part of their lives. These benefits might accrue whether or not any substantial impacts, positive or negative, on the larger dimensions of urban area performance were manifest. It is the impact on these larger more generalized aspects of urban performance that are analyzed here.

The relevant urban impacts likely to be indicated by Office of Management and Budget (OMB) directives can be classified under four headings:

- Impacts on housing and neighborhood condition.
  These include changes in the stock (construction or demolition), changes in the quality of existing housing units (reinvestment or maintenance), and various neighborhood characteristics other than housing which would directly impinge

on residential quality. There is special concern with the impacts on housing and residential quality available to the disadvantaged and minority (DM) components of the population.

• Impacts on income and employment.

Many public programs directly effect incomes through wage or transfer payments, especially to DM components. These payments, moreover, would affect other incomes indirectly through respending and multiplier relationships. Here, too, we are especially interested in income and employment impacts on the DM population.

• Impacts on population and residential assignment.

First, these include any impact on total population and its composition in any impacted areas. Second, they include the distribution of population or residential assignments among individual jurisdictions and neghborhoods, including the assignment of particular cohorts, like DM groups. Third, they include three other more subtle dimensions of the resultant assignment: (1) What would be the impact on *displacement*, especially displacement of DM groups? (2) Would DM groups, whether displaced or not, have a wider or narrower range of *choice* of neighborhoods and living arrangements as a result of a policy initiative? (3) What would be the impact on the degree of *integration* by race and/or socioeconomic class?

• Impacts on local fiscal condition.

Almost any federal policy initiative will have an impact on local fiscal condition simply due to the associated expenditure of federal funds at the local level. Expenditures of local governments might be decreased (lower welfare outlays as DM groups are brought into the labor force) or increased (need for more security services as population increases); expenditure requirements might also be reallocated between the central city and the suburbs. Similarly, tax revenues might increase (higher employment and/or sales taxes as economic development occurs) or decrease (displacement of local tax effort from federal initiative), or be redistributed among jurisdictions.

URBAN IMPACTS OF SELF-HELP BY NEIGHBORHOOD INDIVIDUALS (NIND)

It is unlikely, in our view, that a NIND effort could be very effective. Its biggest limitation probably lies in the difficulty of providing satisfactory incentives for nonhomeowner residents to exert self-help efforts. Under a CETA effort, tenant residents of a neighborhood could be employed to fix up housing units or other facilities in their neighborhood with the wages received being sufficient incentive for their participation. But the fact that they were working in their own neighborhood would be relatively incidental to the effort, and the impacts would be essentially the same as with any initiative directed at increasing employment among DM groups.

Providing the incentives for tenants to engage in a *self-help* effort (that is, where at least part of the return to the participant is in the form of the improvement to his or her neighborhood and surroundings) would be difficult.

Successful tenant efforts at improving their housing, for example, would result in increased rents, partly offsetting the benefits of their efforts at best, displacing them from the neighborhood at worst.

Real improvements in nonhousing components of the neighborhood also are likely to result in increased rents. Even efforts aimed at improving their income-earning ability as opposed to their neighborhood condition (for example, operation of day-care centers) is likely to produce higher site-rents for the neighborhoods affected. This could be avoided, of course, by extending the initiative to all DM groups regardless of neighborhood, but then we would no longer have a *neighborhood* self-help effort.

In principle, homeowners would find it much easier to capture the benefits of their efforts, but the opportunities for their effective participation might be severely limited. In general, homeowners would find self-help efforts outside their own home fairly unattractive. True, a group of them might be encouraged to clean up an empty lot on their block; except for these kinds of fairly trivial examples, however, they probably would find the return to their time much higher in fixing up their own home than in fixing up the neighborhood. The frequently encountered high quality of individual apartment interiors in very distressed public housing projects is an example of this kind of rational response.

Encouraging them to fix up their own home would seem to be fairly easy, and a variety of instruments for stimulating that effect are available. The simplest is to subsidize the nonlabor efforts, an extension of the "I'll buy the paint, if you paint the flat" technique commonly invoked by landlords. Limitations on a paint-up/fix-up campaign seem severe, however. First of all, only about 20 to 30 percent of housing units in poverty neighborhoods are owner-occupied and probably at least half of these are occupied by nonpoverty families. And of those owned by DM groups, a large share are probably owned by elderly and disabled (both of whom are heavily represented in poverty areas), so that perhaps as few as 5 percent of the housing units in target neighborhoods might respond to this kind of initiative, especially if confined to improvements within the scope of the skills possessed by eligible residents.

More extensive home improvements might be attempted, done by professional as well as owner labor. Inducement could come via reduced interest rates or, more effectively, insured credit, but that would call for the use of the owners' efforts as part of the process. An example would be to allow the owner to furnish part of the required labor effort in lieu of a downpayment ("sweat equity"). But, here again, we are limited to the DM homeowner in targeted areas whose income is low enough to qualify, whose health is good enough to provide substantial labor, and whose present employment commitments are limited enough to allow substantial time for a self-help effort.

An initiative directed at neighborhood organizations (NORG) as opposed to individuals probably should allow for subsidized raw materials or credit to DM homeowners wanting to fix up their own properties, simply as a matter of equity. By themselves, however, NIND efforts would have trivial urban impacts (though it is hard to imagine that they would be negative) and so they will not be considered further.

URBAN IMPACTS OF SELF-HELP BY NEIGHBORHOOD
ORGANIZATIONS (Norgs) IN TARGETED NEIGHBORHOODS

In this section, the discussion concerns the likely impacts of self-help efforts through NORGs, and is confined, for the most part, to those impacts that would occur in the participating *targeted neighborhoods* and to the nature of impacts without respect to the funds available or to the areal scope of NORGs. In a later section, the impacts on neighborhoods other than those targeted is considered in more detail, as well as the sensitivity of impacts to the size and scope of NORG efforts.

The discussion of impacts on targeted neighborhoods will be organized into four subsections corresponding to the four classes of urban impacts indicated above. In each section, the various kinds of NORGs—COORDNORG, CONTRNORG, and COOPNORG—will be discussed, as appropriate to the impact being considered.

Impacts on housing and neighborhood condition
Basic to any belief that a NORG could result in overall improved housing conditions is the belief that it could improve the attractiveness of investment in housing in the DM neighborhoods that would be targeted. Presumably NORGs would have no federal resources at their disposal other than what might be needed to support their administrative overhead so that, whatever resources—private or public—they attract to their neighborhood must result generally in a reduction in resources available in other neighborhoods.

The fact that the resource allocation is a zero-sum game does not imply that re-allocation in the direction of neighborhoods with sponsored NORGs will not produce net benefits. Indeed, one of the most powerful arguments in favor of a self-help initiative is that the NORG may be in a good position to identify the neighborhood's needs and redevelopment potential. The NORG also can serve as coordinating agent for resources drawn from diverse sources and thereby increase the effectiveness with which they are used. However, the available evidence from the Model Cities program is mixed; in some cases neighborhood control led to less, rather than more, effective resource utilization.

Impacts on housing improvement funds from the private sector could be significantly positive to the extent that a NORG increases the profitability of residential investment in its area. By virtue of its existence and the formulation of an overall neighborhood plan, it could reduce lender uncertainty. This effect could be substantially strengthened to the extent that the NORG identifies particularly promising rehabilitation projects which qualify for any federal credit set-asides for lenders making special efforts to finance inner-city investments. Perhaps even more important, a NORG could increase the ability of residents in its neighborhood to pay for housing services by alerting them to their eligibility for Section 8 rent-subsidy assistance and by assisting property owners in their area to have their buildings qualified for Section 8 tenancy. As is argued later, this rent subsidy may be critical if the benefits of the housing improvement are to accrue to lower income residents.

A basic issue for housing impacts is the extent of need for the modest upgrading that would seem most appropriate to a NORG-type effort vs. substantial rehabilitation and/or replacement of capital. Even a COOPNORG would hardly engage in anything close to new-project construction. Also, it is the structurally more modest kinds of rehabilitation that could most easily generate the employment impacts discussed later.

Data from the National Housing Survey indicate a significant role for rehabilitation which could use low-skilled resident labor fairly intensively. Roughly speaking, about 10 percent of all rental units in 13 sample cities have open cracks or holes in the interior walls with something in excess of 5 percent having broken plaster or peeling paint.* Furthermore, significant numbers of units occupied by black-headed households exhibit these same structural deficiencies as well as defective floors and leaking roofs, which could also be remedied using neighborhood labor.

Of structural deficiencies which require substantial capital investment for correction, heating systems would appear to be the most widespread problem for rental units. The overall breakdown rate varies across cities with a low of 2.2 percent of rental units in Columbus to a high of 17.2 percent in Newark.

The relatively high incidence of such breakdowns poses two problems for any rehabilitation program. First, it is unlikely that the repair or replacement of these systems can employ neighborhood labor—volunteer or otherwise—to any significant extent. Second, it requires substantial capital investment. Experience with self-help cooperative housing in New York indicates that, even where it is very selectively applied and economically successful, only very modest renovation is possible out of tenants' own funds. This further underscores the need for integrating housing rehabilitation with a program which increases tenants' ability to pay.

There is good reason to expect that the success of the program may depend on the ability of the NORG to undertake not only light rehabilitation, but also to make some substantial capital improvements. While it might be less true for single-family units, it is the case that major improvements were needed in the multifamily homesteading sponsored by U-HAB in New York. More-

* Details are to be found in Appendix.

over, even in these cases substandard "sweat equity" labor had been supplied by prior tenants in substantial amounts, both for previously abandoned-building and for "as-is" sales to existing tenants.

NORGs might also act to improve neighborhood conditions other than in residential structures. Outside regular municipal service systems results likely would be modest, but could be positive. Data from the *National Housing Survey* show that a high percentage of all households including black-headed households found neighborhood conditions undesirable or services inadequate. Perhaps the most striking feature of these data is the relatively small number of households which found schools inadequate. This is important because the adequacy of schools is effectively beyond the control of the NORG (probably even a CONTRNORG), a high level of dissatisfaction might severely limit the effectiveness of the NORG's efforts. However, other neighborhood conditions and services which elicited a significantly higher negative response can be affected by a self-help program. Litter, for example, is clearly a problem and neighborhood cleanup efforts are frequently one of the first projects undertaken by NORGs. NORGs which do not get beyond this stage frequently sink into a sea of disillusionment. But coupled with a strong housing program, with antilitter activities following rather than leading, the neighborhood improvement impacts could be significant. Abandoned and deteriorating housing, which also loom as important concerns, are directly addressed by the housing improvement efforts.

Supplementing or reorganizing regular municipal services would be very difficult for a NORG, though conceivably a CONTRNORG could undertake such a role, essentially as an agent or sub-contractor of the city government. Individual subdivisions within suburban municipal jurisdictions frequently undertake such a role; for the most part these have been middle- or upper-middle class phenomena. Perhaps these kinds of activities could be stimulated in DM neighborhoods, though likely some "give-back" of their *pro rata* share of municipal funds for particular purposes would be required. Positive impacts from these activities are thus possible, but they are likely to be modest. The main problem is the likely reluctance of city agencies to surrender part of their budget, and hence control over jobs, to a neighborhood group during the current period of generally falling municipal employment. Also, the public services that are seen as most unsatisfactory in the *National Housing Surveys* are not especially suitable to self-help employment efforts by neighborhood residents themselves (police protection) or amenable to solution at the neighborhood level (public transportation).

A final area of housing and neighborhood condition in which NORGs might make an impact is in private business services. However, so far as service availability is concerned, here too the prospects are probably modest. This is concluded despite the fact that large numbers of all, including very large numbers of black-headed, families report dissatisfaction with shopping. But, even in middle-class neighborhoods with constant population, neighborhood commercial business has declined sharply relative to the number of households. In inner-city areas where property values have been rising sharply (northwest Washington east of 14th Street, for example), commercial redevelopment has lagged far behind. It may be that some large retail chains have closed down inner-city outlets largely out of irrational fear or unrealistic expectations as to the profitability of serving entrapped residents. Aside from overcoming this kind of bias, however, a NORG is not likely to have much effect on making more business service available in its neighborhood.

These kinds of business opportunities could be exploited even by a COORDNORG, simply by reducing uncertainties for a private investor. They might be exploited even more effectively by a COOPNORG depending on the COOPNORG's ability to achieve lower operating costs through greater cooperation of neighborhood residents, since it is not sensible for a COOPNORG to provide a business service that was not otherwise profitable. Perhaps the COOPNORG would have more success in utilizing hard-to-discipline, low-skilled workers, often with low motivation and poor health, than did the Model Cities agencies, but on the basis of past experience, large successes are unlikely.

Impacts on income and employment

Conceivably, rental returns to DM property owners and business operators in targeted neighborhoods would be affected by a self-help initiative, but only to a minor extent. Also, increased demand for workers in occupations that pay above the minimum wage also would be small compared with the size of the metropolitan labor market. Accordingly, the positive income and employment impacts would be confined to increased employment prospects for DM segments of the population.

Without a major thrust of a COOPNORG to get into such major employment-creating activities as manufacturing, and in view of the rather limited employment impacts in business service establishments or public service takeovers, the main direct employment impact would come from the improvement in the housing stock and associated neighborhood space.

However, there is also an indirect employment impact via the multiplier effect. Each new job created via the self-help program will increase income in the urban areas to the extent that wages exceed the transfer payments (unemployment compensation and welfare) previously received by the newly employed worker. This additional income will in turn create additional opportunities. The magnitude of the multiplier effect depends on the size of the urban area; in the New York standard metropolitan statistical area (SMSA), for example, each dollar of income generated directly by the program will generate an additional $2.50 to $3.00 through the multiplier effect. In a small urban area, such as Madison, Wisconsin, an additional $0.75 approximately would be generated. It must be stressed, however, that this does not imply that one additional job in New York will create more additional employment than an additional job in Madison, but rather that more of the jobs which are created will be in New York because of its large and diversified economic base. None of these multiplier effects will occur, however, unless the sponsored NORG is able to create new jobs through rehabilitation and neighborhood improvement programs. An important question then is how such programs would affect employment in general and DM groups in particular.

It is quite possible that the labor used for rehabilitation and repair would be hired from the general labor force of the city and surrounding areas. In this case, one can expect little or no impact on the employment patterns of neighborhood residents or even of DM groups. We will assume, therefore, that the NORG makes special attempts to utilize DM workers from the neighborhood. We recognize that some short-run efficiency may be lost in pursuing this policy. However, since the distribution of employment and income is itself an object of policy, it is important to understand whether utilization of neighborhood DM residents is feasible.

A major factor in the impact on employment is the labor force characteristics of the DM part of the population. We focus particularly on the unemployed, the part-year employed, and nonparticipants in the labor force. Hiring a full-time employed person for the program is not likely to have significant short-term or long-term effects since the jobs will probably not lead to a major increase in income or skills. (Supporting data for the following discussion may be found in the Appendix.)

The unemployed. As is well known, poor people and people living in poverty areas tend to suffer greater unemployment rates than the general population. Unemployment rates in urban poverty areas are high, both absolutely and relative to the rest of the metro area. Poverty-area workers are relatively concentrated in occupations which could be utilized in the rehabilitation, repair, and neighborhood improvement jobs that would be undertaken. For 1970, the higher unemployment rates among experienced workers were found in the categories of nonfarm laborers, operatives, and service workers (other than private household). Indeed, these three categories accounted for 50 percent of the unemployed in 1970. Considering the high incidence of these occupations in poverty areas and their low-paying nature, it is reasonable to believe that even more than 50 percent of the unemployed in poverty areas are in these kinds of occupations.

Although teenage unemployment rates are extremely high, they do not represent the majority of the unemployed in poverty areas. The "Urban Employment Survey" revealed that in New York poverty areas, for example, teenagers accounted for less than one-third of the jobseekers. The fact that the unemployed include a large proportion of men and women over 20 is favorable for the employment impacts of a self-help initiative.

Part-year employed. In addition to the unemployment rate at a particular point in time, poverty-area residents are much more likely to experience some unemployment during the course of a year than are other workers. Data gathered for the "Urban Employment Survey," which covered poverty areas in six major United States cities, indicated that from a quarter to a third of the workers experienced a spell of unemployment during the year, about twice the rate for the country as a whole. Another aspect of part-year employment is the part-time job. There is some tendency, according to the "Urban Employment Survey," for employed persons in poverty areas to be more likely to have part-time jobs than the national average, though this incidence was not constant across the six cities included in the study. Although most of those working part-time did so voluntarily, a somewhat greater proportion of workers in poverty areas than in the rest of the nation worked part-time for such economic reasons as slack work, material shortages, and repairs to plant and equipment.

The nonparticipants. As will be discussed later, some of the unique features of self-help programs may be exploited to draw many people not now participating into the labor force. The difference in participation rates of poverty areas as compared with nonpoverty areas is extremely large in most age and sex categories. Thus, the phenomenon of lower participation rates is not due to the age or sex distribution itself, but rather to DM status. Of particular interest for our purposes is that lower participation rates persist for male family heads in the 25 to 64 age bracket, a group which we would expect to be working, or at least looking for work.

Perhaps the most striking difference between poverty and nonpoverty areas is the difference between participation rates of female family heads between the ages of 25 and 64. We find that in poverty areas 49 percent of this group are in the labor force, while 73 percent are members of the labor force in nonpoverty areas. A possible explanation is that the female family heads, aged 25 to 64, in poverty areas have more children to care for than those in nonpoverty areas. A NORG which is sensitive to the problems of caring for children may be able to arrange flexible hours and provide day-care facilities to enable increased participation. Moreover, since the work will take place in the neighborhood, travel time will be reduced.

The experience of nonparticipants residing in New York City poverty areas indicates that 12 percent of the 25- to 65-year-old men were neither working nor looking for work. "Ill health or disability" as the reason for nonparticipation is given very often by poverty area residents. In connection with a self-help program, it is noted that 40 percent of nonparticipants reporting health problems "wanted or might want a job." About half of these would require special arrangements, such as rest periods, light work, part-time work, and care of physicians. It might be more feasible for such special needs to be accommodated by a NORG than by a commercial employer. Health problems figure prominently as a reason for nonparticipation in poverty areas because the occupational patterns there are heavily skewed to work which requires physical strength and stamina. Accordingly, a NORG which is sensitive to these issues may be able to structure work tasks so that the disabled can engage in useful work.

Another aspect of labor supply deserves a brief mention. In "Work Attitudes of Disadvantaged Black Men," an attempt was made to examine nonparticipation as a function of attitudinal variables. Such factors as discrimination, preferences for black coworkers or supervisors, and discontent with norms of bureaucracy and authority, were found to be on the minds of many of the men who had never worked. It may be possible for a NORG in a black area to be sensitive to such issues.

If special attention is paid to recruiting from the ranks of the unemployed and from nonparticipants who would like to work, employment can be increased, at least in the short run. Of course, there may be some sacrifice in efficiency from the use of such workers. It may also be more expensive to recruit from these groups, and they may require special services. Nevertheless, the data suggest that employment and income of neighborhood residents can be increased, at least for the period during which the improvements are being made.

A rough idea of labor supply and demand for repairs and rehabilitation may be obtained from the following computation. Atlanta, Chicago, and Detroit had 391,200 units needing repair of cracked walls or to be painted in 1970. Reaching this total involves substantial double counting, but underestimates the number of units requiring rehabilitation. Thus, a figure of 235,000 units (60 percent of the total) is an order-of-magnitude estimate of the number of units in poverty areas which would be susceptible to the kind of light- or medium-level rehabilitation that would be appropriate to a self-help initiative.

Assuming that it costs $10,000 to rehabilitate a unit, that three-quarters of the cost would be for labor, and that one-half of the labor would come from relatively unskilled neighborhood residents, a demand for about $881 million of labor services of neighborhood residents could be generated. Assuming a five-year rehabilitation effort and a wage rate modestly above the minimum wage (say $6,000 per year at present levels), this adds up to about 30,000 potential jobs per year for neighborhood residents compared to over 500,000 residents who were unemployed or out of the labor force in the poverty areas of these cities in 1970.

Longer-run gains in income and employment (after rehabilitation is completed) are less certain. The main source would appear to be in the training, the experience, and the changes in attitudes toward work which occur as a result of participating in the program. If the self-help initiative is linked with vocational training, and with CETA or the youth employment program, workers can increase their human capital and therefore their permanent income. Beyond these effects, however, it is difficult to see why there should be any longer-run effects, with the possible but not likely exception that new business will be attracted into areas which are able to arrange flexible working hours and work tasks.

Impacts on population and residential assignment

As indicated earlier, although impacts on housing and neighborhood condition and on income and employment might be very weak, in no case was it seen as plausible that they would be negative. Impacts on population and residential assignment are likely to be more controversial, displaying both positive and negative dimensions.

Impact on total metropolitan population is likely to be fairly trivial in extent. The resultant neighborhood improvement, if successful, would make at least some neighborhoods more attractive to DM groups and might be expected to hold them in large metropolitan areas to a greater extent. There are two reasons for believing that such impacts would be weak. First, recent experience indicates that higher welfare payments do not seem directly to attract DM groups to large cities, though they may hold them there longer. Many of the DM in-migrants to New York, for example, do not apply for welfare benefits until many months after their arrival. And if welfare is a weaker magnet than was thought, improved neighborhood conditions are not likely to be very strong either at the metropolitan level. Second, even if they were an attraction, they presumably would be being developed in poverty areas of most large SMSA's at the same time, thus offsetting a substantial part of the drawing power of any particular SMSA.

Impacts on the population *within* a given metropolitan area are quite another matter, however. This is a critical issue, since the extent to which the benefits of the housing and neighborhood improvement fall to original neighborhood residents depends on their willingness and ability to remain in the neighborhood. If the housing and neighborhood improvement aspects of the program is successful, housing price increases are to be expected for two closely related reasons. First, as we have argued earlier, landlords' gross revenues must increase if they are to have an incentive (or the ability) to undertake property improvements. And second, rents will rise as a consequence of the increased attractiveness of the housing and the neighborhood. In the absence of a rent subsidy which increases the ability to pay of lower income residents (or an operating subsidy to a COOPNORG), this price increase will inevitably lead to displacement. Thus, the ability of the NORG to coordinate Section 8 and the housing improvement program is crucial insofar as direct impacts on the DM population are concerned.

Increased use of Section 8 in DM neighborhoods raises an important policy issue. The issue is whether or not special efforts should be made to qualify Section 8 housing for such households *in their original neighborhoods*. To a considerable extent, Section 8 has been used as a way of providing housing opportunities for DM groups in middle class and/or white neighborhoods.

It seems unlikely that Section 8 can be used simultaneously as a way of providing improved housing opportunities for DM groups in their "own" neighborhoods and as a way of securing housing for the same groups in nonpoverty areas.

Note that qualifying "everything" of sufficient quality for Section 8 is not a way out. Indeed, present law (and there seems no proposal to the contrary on the horizon) permits, but does not require, the landlord of any standard quality housing to make it available to Section 8 tenants, and Section 8 does not guarantee a market rate of return on the property. Although at present Section 8 qualification probably assures occupancy at fair-market rentals, it assures that occupancy only to the end of the lease of the occupying family, which at present is limited to three years. Accordingly, for the availability of Section 8 tenants to increase a landlord's willingness to bring his property up to standard condition, there must be some assurance that his qualification for Section 8 continues much longer than the original three-year lease and that a substantial aggregate excess of Section 8 units not be made available in the housing market as a whole. Thus using Section 8 as the device to protect the DM population from displacement as their original neighborhood improves is likely to come at the expense of the range of choice open to them in other neighborhoods. Restriction of location choice would operate even in the absence of barriers to movement or limitations on entry to new neighborhoods. It lies simply in the economic reality of requirements for aggregate balance in the Section 8 market over all neighborhoods. One is somewhat reluctant to define this impact unambiguously as either negative or positive. If an objective of DM groups is a desire to live as a minority in nonpoverty areas, their objective will be frustrated. On the other hand, if their objective is to live in standard housing with decent neighborhood conditions, regardless of the DM composition of their neighborhood, they may be better off with a strong NORG initiative.

We are tempted to conclude that the latter, more optimistic, view may be closer to reflecting reality. For one thing, we note that the strongest resistance to assisted relocation of inner-city DM residents to the suburbs through Section 8 has come from existing NORGs in inner-city neighborhoods, at least in the experimental relocation programs in the Chicago area. This resistance may reflect the self-serving objectives of some NORG officials, but we also note the painfully slow rate at which interested landlords and willing migrants are being paired up—not more than a few dozen families a month in 1978.

While the pulls on displacement are all in the direction of providing more protection, and the pulls on choice all in the direction of limiting it, pulls on the resulting degree of socioeconomic class integration, at least in targeted neighborhoods, would be in both directions. On the one hand, to the extent that NORG efforts produce significant improvements in housing and neighborhood condition, its neighborhood would become more attractive to the middle class. On the other hand, insulating the initial residents from displacement would limit the opportunities for in-migration of the middle class, at least short of new-project development specifically aimed at middle class occupants. Despite the fact that the neighborhood could emerge as a satisfactory and low-cost alternative for the middle class, increases in socioeconomic integration in targeted neighborhoods would be nominal. Perhaps most important is the apparent unattractiveness to the middle class of lower class neighborhoods regardless of physical condition. In fact, strong middle class appeal could be expected to develop only where it was anticipated that the area would become predominantly middle class. Without displacement, this could only occur in neighborhoods with very substantial developable open space and where the management of the NORGs would not be concerned about losing control to middle class in-migrants; these conditions are not likely to occur in many places.

Impact on local fiscal condition

These impacts are likely either trivial or offsetting. The one possible exception is the impact on local fiscal condition stemming from changes in income and employment. Increased employment, especially of those previously nonparticipants in the labor force, would both increase taxes (wage taxes and/or increased sales taxes through greater spending) and reduce expenditure (welfare and public assistance costs). On the other hand, as indicated earlier, it is doubtful that more than modest employment impacts could be realized, and even then they would probably be fairly short run, for five years or so.

Property tax yields from targeted neighborhoods could increase substantially, since property values would rise substantially if expected improvements in housing and neighborhood conditions were realized. Part of this increase, however, might be offset by tax concessions to the NORG, especially a COOPNORG. In many areas, there would be nothing to prevent a COOP-NORG from acting as a private redeveloper. In Missouri, for example, under the Section 353 urban redevelopment program, a COOPNORG could secure a blighted-area designation, control over eminent domain powers, and abatement of improvements from increased property taxation completely for 15 years and partially for another 10 years. A COOPNORG would have more limited abilities to borrow from private lenders than would a private developer, but its tax abatement possibilities would be the same. In any event, tax abatement possibilities notwithstanding (and they would seem not to be an essential feature of rehabilitation under Section 8), at least in the long run property tax yields in targeted areas would rise. As will be indicated later on, however, much of this is likely to be offset by declines in other neighborhoods, though the offsetting declines might be outside the central city jurisdiction and the offsets might not be complete.

Except for impacts on wage and property taxes and somewhat indirectly on sales taxes, there is no reason to expect any other impacts on locally generated revenues. Also, there is no reason to expect any particular direct impact on grants-in-aid or revenue-sharing payments from State and Federal governments, except for the limited funds granted by the Federal government for operating expenses of the NORGs.

Noticeable impacts on the expenditure side probably would be confined to reductions in welfare and public assistance due to increased employment, but these impacts would be modest and mostly temporary. So far as other expenditures are concerned, there may be pressures for increases as a consequence of the demands by NORGs for complementary program support from local government and/or discrimination in public service delivery away from DM neighborhoods in reaction to increasing fiscal stringency. Overall, however, impacts on local expenditures likely would be small, as would net impact on total local fiscal position.

IMPACT OF NORGs ON NONTARGETED NEIGHBORHOODS

The impact of a NORG initiative on nontargeted neighborhoods would depend on geographic coverage and scale of NORG efforts. These will be discussed more fully in the next two sections, but for the most part, effects in nontargeted neighborhoods are likely to be modest in scope and confined mostly to other central city neighborhoods.

If successful, the self-help program will shift housing demand toward target neighborhoods. Since NORG efforts are unlikely to affect total metropolitan population, the shift in housing demand toward the self-help neighborhoods must necessarily affect other neighborhoods within the metropolitan system. But, given the likely scope and scale of effort, the overall impact on the overall housing market and population distribution is likely to be small. It is difficult to pinpoint exactly which neighborhoods will be affected in terms of a central city–suburban dichotomy, but the impacts of the program should be highly localized to neighborhoods which are spatially adjacent to the target neighborhood or those which occupy a similar position in the overall ranking of housing and neighborhood quality. The impact will be at a maximum in neighborhoods which are close both spatially and in quality. Hence, the magnitude of central city and suburban impacts will depend on the location of target neighborhoods. It might be expected that a majority of the NORG efforts would be in central city neighborhoods; however, in many metropolitan areas there are significant numbers of older suburban neighborhoods which could benefit from the program.

First, the impacts of the NORG initiative on neighborhoods similar to targeted neighborhoods will be considered. Impacts on the rehabilitation of housing units can be broken down into two parts: the "removal" of low-quality units and the addition of higher quality units. Even simple rehabilitation can be thought of as the removal of a substandard unit and the addition of a standard one. Removal of low-quality units reduces their supply and will result in a price increase. It will also result in increased demand pressure both at slightly higher levels and lower quality levels, causing price increases at these quality levels if the rehabilitated housing had been occupied. If it had been abandoned, these effects will not occur, and the program will produce a pure supply increase.

The addition of higher quality units will result in lower prices for units of that quality and for units of slightly higher and slightly lower quality. Hence the net effect of the rehabilitation program will be a lowering of prices for units of about the same quality as the new quality level and an increase in prices of units of about the same quality as before rehabilitation.

Improvement in neighborhood services would have similar price effects: price increases in low service-quality neighborhoods and price reductions in higher service-quality neighborhoods. Independent of any rental subsidies under the Section 8 program (and the self-help program must be evaluated in this way since the Section 8 subsidies would exist independently of the self-help program), the price impacts of housing rehabilitation and improvement in neighborhood services under the self-help initiative would work to the disadvantage of those households who consume *lower* quality housing. The price effects are simply another aspect of the displacement problem which often accompanies substantial upgrading of a neighborhood. Not only are lower income households priced out of rehabilitated neighborhoods, but also their moving puts upward pressure on prices in neighborhoods to which they move.

On the other hand, a rent subsidy program, such as Section 8, will create demand pressures at those quality levels to which the subsidy applies. It could be argued, therefore, that self-help rehabilitation programs would be useful in offsetting these price increases, at least for housing at the quality level with which the initiative is concerned. However, it must also be recognized that a subsidy-induced price increase will induce a supply response from the market. One aspect of this supply response is a reduction in the rate of flow of units from the standard quality level in the program to lower quality levels; this would occur as part of the normal filtering process. This will ultimately lead to *increased* prices at lower quality levels.

The strength of the price effects clearly depends on the number of units and the quality distribution of affected units that are upgraded in any metropolitan area housing market. If the total number of units is small, or if they are distributed over a fairly wide range in the quality spectrum, the price effects are likely to be negligible. If, on the other hand, a significant number of units in the same quality spectrum are affected, the price effects could be substantial.

The impacts of NORG programs on geographically adjacent neighborhoods are somewhat more difficult to predict. It is clear that deteriorating housing and low service levels have a negative impact, not only in the neighborhood in which they occur, but also in adjacent neighborhoods. Similarly, improvements which result from the NORG initiative would have a positive impact on adjacent neighborhoods. Finally, a successful NORG may be highly visible in adjacent neighborhoods and serve as a model for similar efforts.

However, the most important impacts in adjacent neighborhoods are likely to result from market effects. This results from the fact that metropolitan-area housing markets are to some extent localized. Thus, the demand and supply shifts induced by self-help or neighborhood improvement will tend to be concentrated in the localized market. For example, a program which reduces the supply of lower quality housing could generate a significant increase in the price of housing for lower income households. This, in turn, could set socioeconomic change downward in another neighborhood. Thus the self-help initiative could, through its very success, create another problem neighborhood. On the other hand, the program might, through its success, stabilize or reverse the negative expectations which generally underlie the neighborhood change process as a whole. Since the widely held expectation of socioeconomic change can, by itself, produce the expected result as an outcome, the reversing of the expectations could have a positive impact.

But even here, the effect must be evaluated with care. It is through the neighborhood change process that low-cost, although moderate quality, units are provided to the low income market. Once having entered the low income market, these units typically are depreciated fairly quickly. In fact, it can be argued that depreciation is too rapid and the poor must move too frequently. Nevertheless, given their low incomes, these are the only circumstances under which units of even moderate quality would be available to them. Therefore, if the neighborhood change process were significantly slowed, the continued supply of moderate quality units to the low income market would abate, with the result that prices would rise as would the average quality of housing occupied by such households, though only if they could meet the higher costs.

Impacts on income and employment in nontargeted neighborhoods would be small and mainly offsetting. DM populations in nontargeted neighborhoods would tend to get some jobs from a NORG initiative—more jobs to the extent that the NORG-generated labor needs were focused on DM groups in general and fewer to the extent they were focused on target neighborhoods. In any case, the sum of increased demand for DM participants would be unaffected by the division between targeted and nontargeted areas. Proximity to work and easier access to information about it would suggest a preponderance of effect in targeted neighborhoods. This probably would be reinforced by the special efforts required to bring the "hard to employ" into the program since NORGs may be expected to concentrate their efforts almost solely on neighborhood residents.

The impact on the demand for non-DM labor, which mainly would reside outside targeted areas, is uncertain. On the one hand, the NORG-sponsored rehabilitation and neighborhood improvement efforts would create additional demand for skilled labor services complementary to the unskilled DM labor used. On the other hand, to the extent that NORG-sponsored efforts were exempted from Davis-Bacon requirements to pay "prevailing wages" for construction labor (if they were not exempted, their prospects for absorbing large amounts of DM labor would be seriously reduced), some DM labor might substitute for more skilled labor. In any event, given the offsetting nature of these impacts, we conclude that the net impact on income and employment in nontargeted areas would be minimal.

The impacts on population in nontargeted areas are implicit in the earlier discussion of impacts on housing supply and demand and prices in nontargeted areas. For example, if residents of targeted neighborhoods were effectively protected from displacement, residents of nontargeted DM neighborhoods would also be less susceptible to displacement, and residents of non-DM neighborhoods less likely to experience socioeconomic downgrading of their neighborhoods. On the other hand, if a NORG initiative produced displacement by virtue of its success, displacement or flight in nontargeted areas would be induced as the process of neighborhood filtering speeded up.

Practically speaking, a NORG initiative would not worsen the ability of DM groups in targeted neighborhoods to choose other locations, but it would likely result in increased choices to stay in their original areas. To the extent that that was true, it would also be neutral with respect to the choice-set available to residents of nontargeted neighborhoods, but would tend to reduce the number of families opting for interneighborhood moves. Finally, to the extent that the NORG initiative successfully insulated DM groups in targeted neighborhoods from displacement by the middle class, it would result in less movement of DM groups into middle-class neighborhoods. In that sense it would not promote socioeconomic integration at the neighborhood level and would tend to slow down interneighborhood movement for all groups and the neighborhood succession process for most neighborhoods. Thus it might lead to less socioeconomic neighborhood integration than is arithmetically possible with an equi-proportional assignment of housing quality and family types among neighborhoods. However, if we allow for responses in the supply of housing types and the demand for locating in different neighborhoods as part of the dynamic adjustment process, whether a successful NORG initiative would produce less socioeconomic integration in final equilibrium has to be regarded as an open question.

As far as local fiscal condition is concerned, the impact on nontargeted areas substantially would offset those in targeted areas. If employment taxes generated in nontargeted neighborhoods rose because of employment of DM groups there, this would be offset by lower employment taxes generated by employing residents of targeted neighborhoods. The total reduction in welfare or public assistance costs generated by a NORG initiative also would be substantially independent of its neighborhood distribution.

By far the most important fiscal impact on nontargeted neighborhoods would be on their property tax base. To the extent that the property tax base consists of site rents, any increase in property tax yields in targeted neighborhoods would be partially offset by decreased tax collections in other neighborhoods. Moreover, since, as was argued above, most of the affected nontargeted neighborhoods probably would be geographically nearby, any substantial interjurisdictional transfer of property tax base is unlikely. Some net increase in property tax yields is possible, of course, to the extent that the property tax base consists of reproducible capital in addition to site value. Thus assuming that targeted neighborhoods were concentrated in the inner city, one should expect some increase in the central city's property tax receipts, but the net increase would be far smaller than the increase in tax yields from targeted neighborhoods only.

EFFECT OF GEOGRAPHIC SCOPE ON URBAN IMPACTS

Presumably the scale of neighborhood at which NORGs are likely to be organized is similar to that of existing organizations, many of which came out of the Model Cities experience; they typically operate over a half dozen or so Census tracts. It is important to note that impacts could be quite sensitive to the real scale at which NORGs were created.

Larger scale NORGs would have the advantage of internalizing impacts in nontargeted neighborhoods, might offer some administrative scale economies (but these are likely to be small), and might achieve superior bargaining power with municipal agencies. Smaller scale NORGs, on the other hand, would seem much more effective in meeting particular residential needs and focusing on DM groups especially, thus making real self-help participation much more likely. Perhaps the appropriate balance could be struck by encouraging NORGs to form at the geographic scale that the residents themselves think of as their "neighborhood." In that regard, however, Anthony Downs believes that that scale can vary greatly from city to city, from as many as a few hundred thousand down to as few as 10- or 15-thousand population.

Another and more subtle consideration involved in the question of the most appropriate geographic scope for a NORG is the emerging role of the neighborhood as a decision-making unit in the mature or declining metropolitan area. This can be most easily understood by considering the notion that the mature metropolis is likely to consist of a number of residential/employment nodes, each somewhat denser than most of present suburbia, but less dense than present inner cities. They would be quite scattered in space to enhance living-working at a fairly small and secure scale, but also integrated into a regional transport network for periodic but fairly infrequent access to specialized consumption and services. In this type of metropolis, there would be a metropolitanwide interest only in facilities for fairly specialized functions (such as airports, medical centers, universities, stadiums) and much of the land use in the regional system would be nonurban. In essence, metropolitan regions are merging into substantial segments of, and in some cases entire, states.

This suggests that budgeting for specialized functions might gravitate to the state level, and for routine functions to individual communities so that scale diseconomies can be avoided and idiosyncratic needs of residents met. The problem here, however, is that, while most suburbs have satisfactory scale, most central cities are too large to fit into this emerging metropolitan/regional system optimally. What this suggests is the emergence of the central city neighborhood as a quasi-suburb. This would reinforce the political viability of the metropolitan/regional system; it would also conflict with the political strength of the central city government. Sensitive and important political issues are involved—the vested political interests of "city hall" and the ambitions of DM groups for capturing those interests. Without pretending to predict or assess the desirability of various possible outcomes on this score, it seems apparent that fostering NORGs at this time may speed up the evolution of such organizations into legitimate government units.

Another aspect of geographic scope is whether NORGs blanket, or only selectively target on, DM neighborhoods. If they are very selectively targeted, possibilities for adverse compensating effects on nontargeted poverty and/or DM neighborhoods are substantial. Such negative spillover effects could be avoided if NORGs were organized over very broad geographic scope, but, as indicated above, that would limit their program effectiveness as well as political cohesiveness. The other alternative is simply to have a large number of NORG organizations; that possibility depends mainly on the scale of resources available.

EFFECT OF PROGRAM SCALE ON URBAN IMPACTS

It is obvious that the effectiveness of self-help initiatives is related to the amount of resources devoted to their stimulation and support. A particularly troublesome feature of this obvious relationship is that it is unlikely to be a directly proportional one.

In the extreme case of an effective NORG in only one of many DM inner-city neighborhoods, the impacts could be substantially disruptive. This is not because of any probable failure of the self-help initiative in the targeted neighborhood; quite the contrary, it is likely that without competition it would be very successful in attracting federal program and municipal resources disproportionately to its area. But it would also likely draw to it the most effective leadership and the most productive and most easily employable of the DM population throughout the city. This could leave other DM neighborhoods still more deprived in the same way that the selectivity of rural-urban migration in the 1950s left many rural counties sociologically and economically deprived.

To prevent these negative impacts on nontargeted neighborhoods and thereby enhance the overall effectiveness of the initiative, NORGs should be made available and encouraged in almost all DM neighborhoods within a metropolitan area simultaneously. If total resources are limited, this suggests that favorable impacts would substantially be enhanced by the support of NORG initiatives more or less exhaustively in a small number of metropolitan areas, rather than selectively in a large number, based on the view that substantial inter-SMSA migration is not likely to be stimulated by differential development of self-help initiatives among SMSAs.

In this regard, one notes that the figure indicated in the President's Urban Policy Message, $15 million a year, is disturbingly small, and not simply because more is better than less. It is disturbing because it will lead to difficult allocation decisions on which political pressure will be exerted for a decision that would be counter-productive to achieving the most substantial positive impacts with the available resources. Assuming a modal neighborhood of about 50,000 population, a paid staff of about ten people would be needed for an effective NORG, even of only a COORDNORG variety. A mix of professionals, subprofessionals, and some unskilled workers might result in an average salary of about $15,000 a year, or a wage bill of $150,000. With overhead for space rental, supplies, and other items, and a minimal resource commitment to secure cooperation of volunteers, at least a $300,000 annual budget for a typical COORDNORG would be required; a CONTRNORG or COOPNORG would probably require greater minimum commitment. Moreover, while some local resources might be available for NORG support (some local matching might even be a program requirement), in the present era of local fiscal stringency it seems unrealistic to think of more than a third of the cost being borne locally.

What this all adds up to is that $15 million of federal funds at $200,000 per NORG could not support more than about 75 NORGs *nationally*. Effective blanketing of DM areas in an SMSA might call for from five to 20 NORGs, with more being required in the larger, more troubled SMSAs. Thus, at the announced funding level, only about eight or 10, or maybe 15, SMSAs could participate in a neighborhood self-help initiative that was organized to secure maximum positive urban impacts. On political grounds, it is doubtful that such an allocation could prevail; much more likely is that 50 or 75 areas would get one, or maybe two, NORGs each with chances for substantial positive impact being largely dissipated. Indeed, as remarked above, one cannot rule out the possibility of a significant negative impact in that event.

In conclusion, this paper was produced on the basis of a modest effort, drawing much more on an accumulated knowledge of past and on-going urban research than on a special study organized especially for this assessment. Based on past research experience it is doubtful that these findings would be materially altered with a much longer and more detailed study. We certainly would develop greater confidence that our understanding was correct with more study, but we probably would not reduce by much the annoying ambiguities which necessarily still linger in our understanding.

It also might be argued that other experts could have been found whose judgment of the urban impacts of a self-help initiative would differ from ours; we have no doubt this is the case. But it is unlikely that those differences would disappear or even be much reduced by each of us doing a major

APPENDIX. SUPPORTING DATA

TABLE 1: Housing Conditions, All Households
(thousands of units reporting conditions)

| | | | Interior Walls | | | |
| | Owner-Occupied | Renter-Occupied | Open Cracks | | Peeling Paint | |
SMSA	(O-O)	(R-O)	(O-O)	(R-O)	(O-O)	(R-O)
Atlanta	295.3	210.8	6.8	19.8	5.7	15.2
Chicago	1,269.6	1,013.1	27.6	98.0	14.3	63.6
Cincinnati	276.4	169.2	6.6	17.1	6.5	12.5
Columbus	184.3	123.5	4.9	11.3	4.8	7.7
Detroit	970.3	366.3	25.5	42.0	31.6	41.1
Hartford	131.2	87.3	2.0	7.1	1.4	3.4
New Orleans	186.2	171.4	5.2	22.6	3.9	13.3
Newark	322.3	260.9	8.1	36.4	5.7	31.0
Paterson-Clifton-Passaic	270.5	161.2	6.4	14.9	5.6	12.1
Philadelphia	1,030.3	494.4	43.3	69.4	33.2	45.0
Rochester	188.0	94.4	4.2	8.0	4.1	5.4
San Diego	304.5	233.7	4.8	13.8	3.4	11.2
Washington, D.C.	471.0	501.9	17.0	62.2	14.1	46.7

research study, given the very general nature of the initiatives that are to be assessed and the wide variety of particular actions possible within them. Thus, simple analysis or complicated research-study notwithstanding, it appears that ultimately the administrator or legislator who decides on the initiative must also decide which of the possibly conflicting assessments of its urban impacts is most cogent and compelling.

Defect. Stairs *(R-O)*	*Roof Leak*		*Fuse Blowout*		*Heat Breakdown*	
	(O-O)	*(R-O)*	*(O-O)*	*(R-O)*	*(O-O)*	*(R-O)*
9.1	11.7	16.5	35.8	19.8	13.9	10.0
67.0	60.7	63.5	185.7	124.1	68.5	89.5
10.3	10.7	13.2	43.4	19.4	18.0	11.1
2.3	6.6	8.4	24.4	13.4	11.5	8.2
22.2	43.2	22.1	132.1	45.2	63.8	24.3
6.7	3.0	5.3	18.7	9.2	6.1	6.5
4.9	9.1	13.6	31.7	26.4	7.0	7.6
26.3	16.8	23.8	31.0	23.5	28.9	45.0
8.9	10.0	10.9	29.3	15.6	17.9	20.1
15.0	50.6	51.1	131.4	47.4	71.5	58.3
3.1	6.7	5.6	25.4	10.5	12.7	9.2
4.2	12.3	13.4	34.7	22.1	11.4	7.6
19.5	17.8	35.0	75.9	57.9	27.2	59.3

Source: Annual Housing Survey, 1974 (Washington, D.C., Detroit, and Newark), 1975 (all others).

TABLE 2: Housing Conditions, All Households
(percent of units reporting condition)

SMSA	Percent Owner-Occupied With:					Percent Renter-Occupied With:					
	Open Cracks	Peel- ing Paint	Roof Leak	Fuse Blow- out	Heat Break- down	Open Cracks	Peel- ing Paint	Roof Leak	Fuse Blow- out	Heat Break- down	Defect. Stairs
Atlanta	2.3	1.9	4.0	12.1	4.7	9.4	7.2	5.6	9.4	4.7	4.3
Chicago	2.2	1.1	4.8	14.6	5.4	9.7	6.3	6.0	12.2	8.8	6.6
Cincinnati	2.4	2.4	3.9	15.7	6.5	10.1	7.4	6.3	11.5	6.6	6.1
Columbus	2.7	2.7	3.6	13.2	6.2	9.1	6.2	5.3	10.9	2.2	6.6
Detroit	2.6	3.3	4.5	13.6	6.6	11.5	11.2	6.0	12.3	6.6	6.0
Hartford	1.5	1.1	2.3	14.3	4.7	5.4	2.6	4.0	7.0	5.0	5.1
Newark	2.5	1.8	5.2	9.6	9.0	14.0	11.9	9.1	9.0	17.2	10.0
New Orleans	2.8	2.1	4.9	17.0	3.8	13.2	7.8	5.3	15.4	4.4	2.9
Paterson-Clifton- Passaic	2.4	2.1	3.7	10.8	6.6	9.2	7.5	6.2	9.6	12.5	5.5
Philadelphia	4.2	3.2	4.9	12.8	6.9	14.0	9.1	10.3	9.6	11.8	3.0
Rochester	2.2	2.2	3.6	13.5	6.8	8.5	5.7	5.3	11.1	9.7	3.3
San Diego	1.6	1.1	4.0	11.4	3.7	5.9	4.8	5.3	9.5	3.3	1.8
Washington, D.C.	3.6	3.0	3.8	16.1	5.8	12.4	9.3	7.0	11.5	11.8	3.9

Source: Table 1.

TABLE 3: Housing Conditions, Families Headed by Blacks
(number of units reporting condition)

SMSA	Open Cracks or Holes	Broken Plaster/ Peeling Paint	Holes in Floor	Plumbing Breakdown	Heating Breakdown	Poor Structure	Roof Leak
Atlanta	11,100	8,100	3,900	2,400	3,500	8,000	6,300
Chicago	45,300	22,600	14,500	7,700	33,700	34,800	20,000
Cincinnati	27,100	4,300	2,800	600	3,800	3,700	4,300
Columbus	2,500	1,300	1,000	900	1,800	1,900	1,200
Detroit	23,400	23,800	6,500	4,800	10,500	n.a.	8,600
Hartford	800	300	200	100	1,500	1,100	600
Newark	19,300	15,700	7,800	4,100	6,700	n.a.	11,200
New Orleans	14,400	8,100	7,500	2,600	3,300	7,300	6,900
Paterson-Clifton-Passaic	3,500	2,900	1,100	800	1,600	2,800	1,200
Philadelphia	32,000	17,400	12,700	5,900	21,300	19,800	12,900
Rochester	1,600	1,500	600	700	2,300	2,100	1,300
San Diego	1,300	400	200	700	800	900	1,400
Washington, D.C.	33,200	24,000	12,100	83,000	31,200	n.a.	18,200

Source: Annual Housing Survey, 1974 (Washington, D.C., Detroit, and Newark), 1975 (all others).

TABLE 4: Neighborhood Conditions, All Families
(percent of families reporting conditions)

| SMSA | Undesirable Neighborhood Characteristics | | | Inadequate Services | | |
	Litter	Aban-don. Housing	Deter. Housing	Schools	Street Lights	Shop-ping
Atlanta	17.3	8.6	9.3	4.2	24.4	10.8
Chicago	15.0	8.7	9.6	3.7	n.a.	12.1
Cincinnati	18.6	8.1	11.5	3.9	22.2	11.0
Columbus	19.9	7.1	12.0	3.5	40.9	9.2
Detroit	15.5	11.4	10.2	5.6	22.4	13.7
Hartford	14.1	6.9	10.8	4.0	16.0	11.7
Newark	13.5	7.6	8.6	5.4	13.9	12.6
New Orleans	22.6	10.0	12.6	6.1	11.8	8.6
Paterson-Clifton-Passaic	12.2	6.7	9.3	3.7	21.9	13.4
Philadelphia	18.7	14.5	11.1	4.0	20.3	14.1
Rochester	14.2	7.8	10.3	2.2	33.3	11.7
San Diego	12.9	1.9	9.7	5.8	29.8	12.8
Washington, D.C.	14.6	5.0	6.2	5.3	14.2	12.1

Source: Compiled from Annual Housing Survey.

TABLE 5: Neighborhood Conditions, Families Headed by Blacks
(% of families headed by blacks reporting)

| SMSA | | Undesirable Neighborhood Characteristics | | Inadequate Services | | |
	Litter	Aban-don. Housing	Deter. Housing	Schools	Street Lights	Shop-ping
Atlanta	23.8	15.9	13.6	3.3	17.1	24.3
Chicago	29.8	28.9	20.6	8.4	10.8	22.2
Cincinnati	33.7	26.9	26.1	5.5	14.4	22.8
Columbus	35.7	17.7	20.3	6.9	33.7	17.7
Detroit	33.1	33.4	19.7	10.2	19.5	24.6
Hartford	28.9	21.4	26.6	11.6	13.3	26.6
Newark	31.4	27.9	22.8	9.4	17.9	22.9
New Orleans	34.4	16.5	20.0	4.5	16.6	12.4
Paterson-Clifton-Passaic	34.2	27.1	28.6	5.6	14.7	19.5
Philadelphia	30.7	43.4	23.1	6.3	16.9	23.6
Rochester	31.8	28.6	29.7	6.3	19.8	14.6
San Diego	23.8	6.6	12.9	8.1	39.0	24.3
Washington, D.C.	25.2	13.0	12.2	6.3	12.8	24.0

Source: Annual Housing Survey, 1974 (Washington, D.C., Detroit, and Newark), 1975 (all others).

TABLE 6: Unemployment Rates, First Quarter, 1978

| | Total U.S. | | Metropolitan Areas | |
	Poverty Areas	Nonpoverty Areas	Poverty Areas	Nonpoverty Areas
Total population	23.3	17.2	32.3	17.1
Both sexes, 16+ yrs.	9.4	6.3	13.0	6.2
Males, 20+ yrs.	7.4	5.0	11.0	4.9
Females, 20+ yrs.	9.0	5.7	11.4	5.6
White	16.1	15.6	20.8	15.2
Both sexes, 16+ yrs.	6.8	5.9	8.8	5.7
Males, 20+ yrs.	5.5	4.7	7.2	4.6
Females, 20+ yrs.	6.7	4.7	8.5	5.2
Black	41.2	38.1	44.1	38.2
Both sexes, 16+ yrs.	15.8	11.1	17.8	11.0
Males, 20+ yrs.	13.0	8.7	15.9	8.8
Females, 20+ yrs.	13.8	9.2	14.3	9.1

Source: Employment and Earnings.

TABLE 7: Occupational Distribution of Employed Persons, 1970

	Percent of Employed Persons in:	
	Poverty Areas	Remainder of City
Professional, technical, and kindred	8	17
Managers and administrators	3	8
Sales workers	4	8
Clerical and kindred	18	24
Craftsmen and kindred	11	12
Operatives	18	11
Transport	6	4
Laborers	8	4
Service workers	20	11
Private household	4	1

Source: U.S. Census Special Study, "Low Income Areas in Large Cities."

TABLE 8: Labor Force Participation Rates, First Quarter, 1978

	Total U.S.		Metropolitan Areas	
	Poverty Areas	Nonpoverty Areas	Poverty Areas	Nonpoverty Areas
Total population	55.0%	63.7%	53.5%	64.2%
White	56.0	63.4	54.3	63.8
Black	52.6	67.1	52.5	67.4

Source: Employment and Earnings.

TABLE 9: Labor Force Participation Rates, 1970

	Poverty Areas	Nonpoverty Areas
Males, by age and status		
16–24	59%	67%
25–64	83	93
Family head, 25–64	88	95
Females, by age and status		
16–24	43	54
25–64	48	53
Family head, 25–64	49	73
Wife of head, 25–64	42	44
With own children under 6 yrs.	34	32
With own children 6–17 yrs.	42	45

Source: U.S. Census Special Study, "Low Income Areas in Large Cities."

TABLE 10: Status of Nonparticipants in the Labor Force Age 25 and Over, New York City and U.S., 1968

	NYC Poverty Areas		U.S.	
	Ages 25–44	Ages 45–54	Ages 25–44	Ages 45–54
Male				
In labor force	90%	84%	97%	95%
Not in labor force	10	16	3	5
In school	1	0	0	0
Ill health or disability	7	14	1	3
Other reasons	2	2	2	2
Female				
In labor force	48	55	46	54
Not in labor force	52	45	54	46
Ill health or disability	10	19	2	4
Family responsibilities	36	22	50	41
Other reasons	5	1	1	1

Source: Bureau of Labor Statistics (1971).

REFERENCES

Ahlbrandt, Roger S., and Brophy, Paul C. *Neighborhood Revitalization.* Lexington: Lexington Books, D.C. Heath, 1975.

Davies, J. Clarence III. *Neighborhood Groups and Urban Renewal.* New York: Columbia University Press, 1966.

Feasibility of Large-scale Expansion of Sponsored Mutual Self-Help Housing Programs in the United States, The. Cambridge, Mass.: Organization for Social and Technical Innovation, June 1970.

First Year: A Status Report to the Community on the Bronx Neighborhood Stabilization Program. Neighborhood Stabilization Program. New York: New York City Commission on Human Rights, 1977.

Kolodny, Robert. *Self-Help in the Inner City: A Study of Lower Income Cooperative Conversion in New York.* New York: United Neighborhood Houses of New York, 1973.

Leven, Charles L. "Regional Income and Product Accounts: Construction and Application." In *Design of Regional Accounts,* edited by W. Hochwald. Baltimore: Johns Hopkins Press, 1961.

———, ed. *The Mature Metropolis.* Lexington: Lexington Books, D.C. Heath, 1978.

———; Little, J. T.; Nourse, H. O.; and Read, R. B. *Neighborhood Change.* New York: Praeger, 1976.

Little, J. T. "Residential Preferences, Neighborhood Filtering, and Neighborhood Change." *Journal of Urban Economics* 3 (January 1976).

McNulty, Robert H., and Kliment, Stephan A., eds. *Neighborhood Conservation:*

A Handbook of Methods and Techniques. Washington, D.C.: Witney Library of Design, 1976.

Neighborhood Decentralization Newsletter. "Neighborhood Planning with Residents: Approaches of Six Local Planning Departments." Washington, D.C.: Center for Governmental Studies, 1976.

New Partnership to Conserve America's Communities, A. The President's Urban and Regional Policy Group Report. Washington, D.C.: U.S. Department of Housing and Urban Development, March 1978.

Niebanck, Paul L., and Pope, John B. *Residential Rehabilitation: The Pitfalls of Non-Profit Sponsorship.* Philadelphia: Graphic Printing Associates, 1968.

Rodgers, J. L. *Citizen Committees: A Guide to Their Use in Local Government.* Cambridge, Mass.: Ballinger, 1977.

Second Annual Report and Proposal for Funding for U-HAB; the Urban Homesteading Assistance Board. New York: Cathedral of St. John the Divine, January 1976.

Steggert, Frank X. *Community Action Groups and City Governments.* Cambridge, Mass.: Ballinger, 1975.

U.S. Department of Labor, U.S. Bureau of Labor Statistics. "Work Attitudes of Disadvantaged Black Men." Washington, D.C.: U.S. Department of Labor, Report 401, U.S. Government Printing Office, 1972.

———— "Working Age Nonparticipants." Regional Reports No. 22. Washington, D.C.: U.S. Department of Labor, June 1971.

CHAPTER FOURTEEN

The Urban Impacts of HUD's Urban Development Action Grant Program, or, Where's the Action in Action Grants?

SUSAN S. JACOBS AND ELIZABETH A. ROISTACHER

INTRODUCTION: UDAG AS AN ECONOMIC DEVELOPMENT PROGRAM

One of the few new urban initiatives implemented under the Carter administration is the Urban Development Action Grant program (UDAG). It was approved by the Congress as part of the Housing and Community Development Act of 1977, six months before the president's Urban Policy Statement of March 27, 1978. The U.S. Department of Housing and Urban Development (HUD) is authorized to spend up to $400 million per year in fiscal years 1978, 1979, and 1980 in "severely distressed cities and urban counties to help alleviate physical and economic deterioration . . . in areas with population outmigration or a stagnating or declining tax base."[1] The objective of UDAG is to stimulate the private sector to create employment and to improve the fiscal viability of distressed local economies. While the program is predominantly metropolitan in focus, twenty-five percent of the funds are allocated by law to small cities—those with populations below 50,000 which are not central cities of Standard Metropolitan Statistical Areas

The authors wish to thank Dan Robinson and Sarah Underwood for their valuable assistance in the preparation of this paper.

[1] Housing and Community Development Act of 1977, §§ 110, 119, 42 U.S.C. §§ 5304, 5318 (1977).

(SMSAs). As of October 1978, HUD had completed its first year's awards—241 Action Grants[2] to 214 cities.

The explicit urban focus of the Action Grant program sets this urban impact analysis apart from many others in this volume. For most of the programs under discussion here, the urban impacts are not central to the program or policy objective. Indeed the whole focus on urban impact analysis is a result of the realization that past federal policy has had adverse, unintended impacts on urban areas. If a program does not have as its central objective assistance to or support of urban economies, then an Urban Impact Statement is, at worst, lip-service to an urban constituency; optimistically, an input into the cost-benefit calculus of the particular program; or, at best, a cause for modification of the policy to blunt its undesirable urban impacts. For example, the modification of the investment tax credit to include rehabilitated structures was at least partly the result of urban advocates' claims that subsidies to new investment would speed up disinvestment in distressed cities.

However, because urban impacts are a primary objective of UDAG, urban impact analysis overlaps with program evaluation. An urban impact analysis of a program with an urban mission must take into account not just the spatial allocation of funds, but also examine whether primary program objectives are being satisfied. As such, our Urban Impact Statement will include an analysis not only of the spatial distribution of Action Grants and their induced effects, but also whether funded projects are efficient and equitable mechanisms for achieving the economic development objectives of the program.

While UDAG is a small program compared to many of the programs and policies examined in this volume, it is indicative of a number of current trends in federal policy toward cities and other local jurisdictions—in particular, targeting to distressed places through a reliance on discretionary funding and capital subsidies to promote private investment. It is these characteristics which shape the urban impacts of the Action Grant program. Before turning to the actual urban impact analysis of UDAG, we first focus on the significance of targeting and capital subsidies and the assumptions inherent in such an approach to urban economic development. As part of an overall view of urban economic development, we first focus on these two characteristics in turn, and then proceed with an actual Urban Impact Analysis of UDAG.

Targeting urban economic development

As the entitlement programs of the 1970s (e.g., General Revenue Sharing and Community Development Block Grants [CDBG]) have not been adequate

---

[2] By October 1978, there had been three quarterly funding rounds for metropolitan jurisdictions and two for small cities. The data compiled for this paper are based on these rounds. (It is anticipated that there will be four metro rounds and small-cities rounds in subsequent fiscal years.)

in addressing the needs of "distressed" localities,[3] the Carter administration's approach has been to introduce greater targeting of funds through discretionary categorical assistance programs such as Action Grants. UDAG is targeted to distressed cities through its eligibility criteria which include changes in population and employment, poverty and income measures, unemployment, and age of housing. The parameters of the eligibility factors result in the program's having a northern tier, central city bias, as is discussed in detail later in this paper.

Before *urban* economic development became a familiar term, the development literature focused on "underdeveloped" countries. In the early 1960s the Federal government became engaged in regional economic development; with the establishment of the Economic Development Administration (EDA) within the Department of Commerce, the focus was on Appalachia.[4] Then, in the late 1960s, as a result of the urban turmoil of that period, discussions of urban economic development were often limited to ghetto development, with an analogy drawn between the urban ghetto and the underdeveloped colony.[5]

Currently, urban economic development in its policy context means something different. It focuses less on distressed *parts* of the cities than it does on entire distressed or declining cities, and the concern is with fiscal base as well as economic base. This new view was partly a result of the downturn in the economy in the first half of the 1970s which brought the message to Washington policy-makers that entire cities and regions were facing economic decline and that many cities, with New York City in the vanguard, were verging on "fiscal crisis." Consequently, federal participation in urban problems now required serving a constituency represented by mayors and governors rather than by a subset of vocal residents within a city.

A targeted economic development program such as UDAG is tantamount to a policy of geographic income redistribution, or at least a slowing down of market forces to prevent a continuing redistribution away from distressed places. The decision to target aid to distressed jurisdictions implicitly assumes the resolution of a fundamental development issue: Should declining cities be saved? From the point of view of the individual jurisdiction, such a question is unthinkable. But from the Federal government's point of view, this question should be answered in terms of equity and efficiency criteria, espe-

---

[3] For example, the general revenue sharing formula distributes aid in part on the basis of per capita income. However, a restriction that no city may receive more than 145 percent of the median allocation in its state prevents the formula from distributing the specified amount of funds to distressed cities (*see* Nathan and Adams, 1977, p. 103).
[4] EDA is now attempting to convert its experience in economic development into helping it expand its role in urban economic development policy. (*See* Hausner, 1979). One new EDA effort to support urban economic development is its Title 9 program.
[5] *See,* for instance, Harrison (1974*a*) and Tabb (1970).

cially when the resources to help competing demanders for federal aid are so scarce.[6] Once we decide to save declining cities, several policy alternatives remain. Should we attempt to contribute to all distressed cities by spreading the limited resources relatively thin, or direct federal aid toward the most distressed cities, or focus attention on cities in the early stages of decline in the hope of capturing the greatest "bang per buck"?

Implicit in the law establishing the UDAG program is the decision to assist all eligible cities, giving priority to the most distressed among them. From an efficiency standpoint, though, the question still remains: Why should we save distressed cities? In rather cold economic terms, a declining city may be viewed as an aging piece of capital which may have outlived its viable economic life. For example, the old mill towns of New England died, as did the ghost towns of the western frontier. As long as towns or cities no longer have a viable economic function and as long as the residents are able to relocate, then the death of a city does not present any kind of social or economic problem. However, if there are externalities which either speed up or induce city decline, then government intervention to remove these externalities or promote positive externalities can be consistent with economic efficiency from the vantage point of the Federal government looking at the system of cities as a whole. That is, the prisoner's dilemma (Davis and Whinston, 1961) usually applied to neighborhood externalities, may be applied to an entire city: no single investor finds it worthwhile to invest in a distressed place, but society as a whole—and in some instances the individual investors—would be better off if all investors did.

City externalities may involve interdependencies between public and private investment decisions as well as among private investors, as suggested by the prisoner's dilemma. A prime example is a deteriorating and/or obsolete public infrastructure which induces individual firms to relocate; the exodus of firms and households reduces the tax base and leads to further deterioration of infrastructure, thus speeding up or inducing departure of households and firms.

For private firms, the externality phenomena include a "demonstration effect" in which unrelated firms are induced to invest because they see that another firm or firms has done so. In addition, the potential to enjoy agglomeration economies may induce firms to locate near the original investor.

The interdependencies among private investors may take rather subtle forms. Consider a not-so-obvious scenario: as firms leave declining cities they may leave behind a skilled labor force. (Take as case in point the closing of the steel plants in Youngstown, Ohio.) This labor force represents an agglomeration economy which has the potential for attracting other firms; but no single firm would find the declining city attractive because, although the

---

[6] The scarcity of resources is, of course, the result of overall budgetary priorities, among which urban and social problems seem to have a relatively low rank.

labor force is there, the supply of other inputs may not be adequate. If a large number of firms were to relocate to that place, however, suppliers may grow up around them. The alternative is a dispersal of that labor force to a large number of cities across the country resulting in an elimination of any external agglomeration economies of labor supply.

It is sometimes argued that the reason declining cities should be saved is because the investment already in place has current economic value. However, if there were no externalities, then the private market decisions would make it clear in just which cities the marginal return from investment is highest. Hence, this existing capital argument is valid only if there is an externality present.

In the absence of efficiency or externality arguments to aid declining cities, it is often suggested that the appropriate governmental policy would be to speed up the transition of decline in one area and growth in another area by assisting the relocation of households and firms who have difficulty relocating. However, relocation of households to growing cities may not be efficient. In particular there may not be jobs available in growing areas for unskilled workers. The presence of "pockets of poverty" even within growing cities is testimony to the problem.

Given the arguments in support of targeting, it is not surprising that the concept has received broad popular support.[7] However, the ability to implement targeted federal programs is constrained by the broad political representation in the Congress. It is inevitable that targeting is subject to a balancing of diverse interests and often substantial dilution as programs go through the legislative process. A recent attempt in the Congress to modify UDAG to include growing cities with pockets of poverty is characteristic of this problem.[8]

As targeted urban economic development programs are designed to increase both efficiency and equity in the system of cities, such programs induce a reallocation of resources among places and people. While there is a continuing controversy between place-oriented and people-oriented policies (*see* Edel in this volume as well as Simms and Roistacher, 1979), in the final analysis a program must be evaluated in terms of its impact on households even if it is targeted geographically. This holds regardless of whether the objective is increased efficiency or equity.

With respect to UDAG, the law and regulations indicate who the program beneficiaries ostensibly should be. Not only are poverty population and unemployment included in the eligibility criteria, but the law and the regulations

---

[7] The "jobs to people" strategy is one of the recommendations in the Final Report of the White House Conference on Balanced Natural Growth and Economic Development (1978). It should be noted that UDAG was already on the books well before this conference took place.

[8] Senator John Tower of Texas led an unsuccessful attempt to amend UDAG to expand eligibility to growing cities with "pockets of poverty." *See* "Senate Votes HUD Bill, Rejects Hill Veto Effort," *Washington Post*, July 21, 1978, A4.

both specify that the impact of Action Grants on the problems of low income and minority households be taken into account in choosing among applicants. However, as the key program objectives are building up economic and fiscal bases, as discussed below, it may be difficult to satisfy these goals and simultaneously meet the housing and employment needs of the poor and unskilled. (Chinitz, 1979, discusses this problem of conflicting policy objectives.)

Capital subsidies

Coupled with targeted discretionary aid to distressed cities is another characteristic of UDAG which has evolved through federal urban policy: a reliance on the private market through the use of capital subsidies. UDAG is designed to provide local jurisdictions with "up-front" money to help them capture and "leverage" private investment when it is "live" or ready to be committed, hence the term *Action Grant.* Consistent with the action orientation are the regulations that each UDAG application include legally binding letters of commitment from private participants and that, in metropolitan cities, funds may not be used for planning purposes. This emphasis on the private market has led to somewhat pejorative comparisons between UDAG and urban renewal. A key distinction, however, between UDAG and urban renewal is that UDAG requires private participation from the inception of a project in order to obtain the capital grant itself.

This private participation is part of a clearly observable policy continuum. In the first half of the 1970s, the Federal government had become involved in direct employment creation, most notably through the Comprehensive Employment and Training Act (CETA) (1973). As Daniel Hamermesh (1978) has noted, disenchantment with CETA and the shift in the economy toward significant cyclical as well as structural unemployment aroused interest in the use of wage subsidies (*see* Tolley and Krumm in this volume) to private employers. Examples of this are the Work Incentive (WIN) tax credit attached to the Revenue Act of 1971 and the current employment tax credit. At the current stage of the continuum is the use of a capital subsidy to the private market which is hoped to have an indirect job creation effect. UDAG is an example of this indirect approach.

Pragmatically speaking, a capital subsidy (as compared to an ongoing labor subsidy) is a one-time commitment which reduces the long-term burden on the Federal government. Moreover, since a capital subsidy is "up front" and is a one-time injection, it may be viewed by private firms as a more certain commitment by the government than an operating subsidy. Because operating subsidies would require ongoing commitments in the face of changing budget priorities and administrations, firms may discount their value. It could further be argued that any jobs created by capital subsidies for the private sector would indeed be permanent jobs. An additional argument levied in support of this approach is that private sector jobs would have psychological benefits for the workers who would feel less like recipients of relief and more like mainstream participants in the economy (Chinitz and Jacobs, 1977). However, the issue of capital subsidies versus labor subsidies as a means of increasing employment poses a number of important empirical questions. These involve the degree to which capital subsidies stimulate the *level* and *location* of investment and how successful such an indirect approach is in stimulating *employment.*

As for the level of investment, we can assume that there is some effect on private market investment through a capital subsidy, although the extent of that effect will vary with each project undertaken through the Action Grant program. The greater is the investment sensitivity to a given change in its rate of return, the greater will be the potential social benefits in terms of employment and fiscal effects. Although there is an empirical literature on investment elasticities, these estimates are at too high a level of aggregation to provide much insight for an urban impact analysis of UDAG.[9] Investment sensitivity of specific firms, industries, and locations is likely to vary substantially from aggregate estimates.

The growing literature on the location decisions of firms, however, is a useful starting point for examining the extent to which capital subsidies in distressed cities are likely to have an impact on the location of investment. The work of Schmenner (1978) and of Harrison and Kanter (1978) give us some insights. First, these authors have found that location decisions are made primarily when a firm is at a point of plant expansion or when it is implementing a change in production technique requiring new facilities. This would suggest that capital subsidies are an appropriate mechanism for influencing firm relocation decisions (for instance, land clearance and infrastructure assistance of UDAG). However, Schmenner has also found that firms have a preference for on-site expansion, again suggesting that capital subsidies for specific projects as allowed under UDAG will help central cities retain businesses.

Harrison and Kanter (1978), however, have noted that local tax subsidies do not do much to influence the location of firms except perhaps the smaller, more competitive ones. Their analysis suggests that larger-scale, more technological firms are not sensitive to local tax subsidies. If their findings hold for one-shot capital subsidies as well, then it may be difficult (that is, costly) to use Action Grants to leverage investments from large firms. Of course, further practical experience is necessary before this hypothesis can be tested empirically. In any case, while UDAG's capital subsidies are potentially powerful development tools, the Harrison-Kanter results indicate that the tax abatements that localities often give in conjunction with or independent of UDAG are a questionable policy which may rob the local municipal fisc of badly needed revenues.

The concern with capital subsidies as an indirect mechanism to stimulate

---

[9] For instance, *see* Aaron, Russet, and Single (1972).

employment involves both the level and the composition of the employment effect. Since UDAG and other economic development programs are concerned not only with building up the tax base but also with reducing unemployment and providing jobs for minorities and workers with lower skills, the potential for a capital subsidy to accomplish this objective is examined below.

The basic controversy over job creation through the use of a capital subsidy to encourage investment is whether or not the "output effect" dominates the "substitution effect." A capital subsidy lowers the relative price of capital, and thus shifts the production function away from labor inputs; this is the substitution effect. However, if the capital subsidy brings about additional investment which might not otherwise have taken place, expansion of total production may result in employment of more labor and more capital; this is the output effect. The impact on labor, however, could be a reduced demand for unskilled labor and an increased demand for skilled labor. Moreover, the existence of a capital subsidy may influence the rate of change of firms from a technology which is relatively labor intensive to a new technology which is relatively capital intensive. Industries which are growing and have a chance for success are unlikely to hire substantial numbers of low-skilled workers at steady (nonseasonal) jobs from which they may move upward on occupational or income ladders. This is suggested by the research of Harrison and Hill (1979). Given the existence of a dual labor market (*see* Doeringer and Piore, 1971), it is not realistic to expect capital subsidies to be powerful mechanisms for creating jobs for low-skilled and minority workers. The dual labor market hypothesis also suggests that to the extent that capital subsidies do create jobs for low-skilled workers, these jobs are not likely to provide upward mobility; while it is possible to start as a dishwasher and end up as a chef, this is not a likely outcome.

These two issues in economic development—targeting and capital versus labor subsidies—highlight important aspects of the urban impact analysis of UDAG that follows.

THE URBAN IMPACTS OF UDAG

In its simplest form an urban impact analysis examines the geographic distribution of federal funds as well as the distribution of the indirect effects of federal spending or federal policy on central cities, suburbs, and nonmetropolitan areas. This urban impact analysis of the UDAG program is based on the funding decisions made during the program's first year of operation. No projects are as yet completed, and only a few are actually under construction. This analysis, therefore, is akin to those required as part of the agency's budget submission by Office of Management and Budget (OMB) Circular A-116: it is projective. However, it does go one step further, identifying the actual commitments made to central cities, suburbs, and nonmetropolitan areas.

Although there are some data on the extent of private commitments which provide some information on the distribution of leveraging, we are not able to determine whether or not the private investment was truly induced by the Action Grant. Assuming that we can make this determination, we are still faced with the problem of sorting out the geographic or spatial distribution of indirect or multiplier effects of the private spending.

Evaluating net spatial impacts: the substitution enigma

The decision to redirect funds to distressed cities results in a spatial reallocation of resources. A capital subsidy in the form of an Action Grant is designed to induce net investment (or prevent disinvestment) in a given jurisdiction. However, this may not be net investment for the nation as a whole if public dollars supplant private dollars. Nevertheless, even in this instance, the subsidy may satisfy program objectives by altering the location of economic activity. However, one must be careful in sorting out these net effects. In particular, the following collection of spatial or locational substitutions must not be ignored: on-site displacement; intrajurisdictional substitution; intrametropolitan substitution; and intermetropolitan substitution.

In the case of *on-site substitution*, a single firm may replace its own plant or equipment; or alternatively one firm may replace another firm, which may or may not be in the same industry. In the three other cases, the substitution may be firm A relocating or firm A replacing firm B which is in the same industry or which serves the same market.

The impact of *intrajurisdictional substitution* (including on-site displacement) depends upon whether the replaced activity has different employment and fiscal effects, resulting from different types of workers and suppliers as well as from the location of these workers or suppliers. A local jurisdiction could face either increases or losses of economic activity and fiscal revenues depending upon the precise nature of the replacement. Relocation within the local economy may, in addition, have serious local political consequences as trade-offs are made among the neighborhoods that are the beneficiaries or bearers of costs, and on-site changes may stir up political controversies within a neighborhood.

Development subsidies which result in *intrametropolitan substitution* by keeping a firm from moving out of the central city to a suburban location, or by inducing a firm to move from the suburbs to the central city, might be considered undesirable on efficiency grounds (assuming no externalities). Clearly, the same inefficiency arguments can be made for subsidies which encourage *intermetropolitan substitution*. However, the objectives of economic development programs may be served despite some loss of efficiency through the resultant employment effects and fiscal effects.

The fiscal gains to a central city from retention or addition of firms is a consequence of the way in which local political boundaries are drawn. While it can be argued that the efficient solution would involve certain local fiscal reforms such as tax base sharing or metropolitan government, the serious political obstacles to such reform suggest that we cannot rely on this sort of relief. Fiscal gains, however, may be relatively inconsequential, since a good deal of the fiscal effects may still accrue to other jurisdictions because employees may reside outside the local jurisdiction and because suppliers and even company headquarters may also be outside the central city—and possibly outside the metropolitan area.

A policy of encouraging firms to choose central city locations is aimed at creating job access as well. Evidence of the labor market problems of low income and minority households by Kain (1968) has indicated that suburban transportation networks do not work well for inner city residents, so that the notion of a metropolitan area as a single labor market does not hold for these residents. Keeping firms in central cities may serve development goals by retaining jobs for these labor force participants; and relocation of firms to the central city may bolster job opportunities. This would be an alternative to suburbanization of such households. The research of Harrison (1974b), however, suggests that this result may not be realistic. Suburbanization of minority households seems to have had little impact on income and unemployment patterns for these households, suggesting that discrimination rather than location is responsible for their labor market difficulties—a problem that UDAG does not profess to solve.

The regulations for UDAG are consistent with the notion that UDAG should not support intermetropolitan "beggar-thy-neighbor" substitution. On the other hand, intrametropolitan relocation is considered acceptable, as indicated below:

> No assistance will be provided for projects intended to facilitate the relocation of industrial or commercial plants or facilities from one area to another, unless the Secretary finds that such relocation does not significantly and adversely affect the unemployment or economic base of the area from which such industrial or commercial plant or facility is to be relocated. However, moves within a metropolitan area shall not be subject to this provision.[10]

The thrust of the statement is consistent with a philosophy that for intrametropolitan relocation, employment or fiscal gains may outweigh efficiency arguments. For intermetropolitan relocation, the regulations allow for firms to be relocated from nondistressed areas to distressed areas at the discretion of the secretary of HUD and his/her staff. This suggests that the Action Grant will be awarded if it is deemed that sizable gains accrue to the new jurisdiction at the expense of insignificant losses to the original jurisdiction.

It is worth adding that, in terms of economic efficiency, there is little dif-

[10] 43 Federal Register, January 10, 1978, p. 1606.

ference between inducing a firm to stay in one area and inducing a firm to relocate to another area (assuming moving is costless). In practice, however, relocations will be more politically controversial than will grants which induce a firm to stay.

For both relocation and expansion, our subsequent analysis of actual activity under UDAG examines leveraging ratios between private dollars and public dollars. However, because of the numerous possibilities for substitution, these ratios may overstate the impacts of the program. At worst, neither the location nor the volume of private investment will have been altered and UDAG dollars will be superfluous. At best, the UDAG dollar will have altered the location and/or level of private economic activity in a manner consistent with increasing efficiency and equity among and within jurisdictions.

As important as these substitutions may be, neither currently available data on UDAG nor existing empirical evidence allow us to examine these effects in the analysis which follows.

Limitations of the data and the analysis

In this analysis, data provided by HUD on private commitment and on employment is utilized. The employment figures have been provided by applicant cities themselves. In some cases they have been adjusted by HUD Area Office reviewers on the basis of other information about the area's industrial structure, the type of development project proposed, and anticipated industry impacts. Even so, these data may be upwardly biased, since it is clearly in the interest of a competing local jurisdiction to show strong anticipated employment effects for its project. Of course, the implementation of a project may have even greater direct employment effects than originally estimated as well as smaller ones. Despite the uncertainty of these initial employment estimates, it is useful to examine them because they may provide at least relative magnitudes of the direct employment effects of various types of potential and their employment impacts.

Once we go beyond the simple distribution of Action Grants, private commitments, and direct employment estimates by type of jurisdiction, our analysis will change from quantitative to qualitative. We will discuss the fiscal impacts of UDAG projects, the types of employment which might be generated, and the problem of multipliers and flows within local economies and across jurisdictions. The focus is on two specific types of projects, shopping centers and hotels, which are consistent with the new view of cities as consumption (rather than production) centers. These types of projects were selected because they received so many awards in the early rounds and have since been the subject of extensive debate with regard to their development potential and their employment impacts.

Our object is not only to specify the urban impacts but to spotlight some of the deficiencies in current methodology and empirical techniques as well.

General urban impacts

The strategy of the Action Grant program is to provide a vehicle for eligible distressed communities to leverage significant private investment; that is, to attract private funds which otherwise would not be forthcoming.

The eligibility and selection criteria, the construction activity, and, finally, the long-term operation of the projects all influence the character of the urban impacts.

By law, UDAG funds are targeted to distressed cities through generally stated eligibility criteria: age and condition of housing, including residential abandonment; average income; population outmigration; and stagnating or declining tax base. The final regulations promulgated by HUD, however, determine exactly how distress shall be defined for eligibility purposes. It is important to address the regulations because amending them is one of the most expedient ways to change the urban impacts accruing to different jurisdictions.

Given eligibility, the law specifies that the primary selection criterion for funding metropolitan cities must be the comparative degree of physical and economic distress as defined by three factors, to which the regulations assign relative weights and numerical values as follows: the percentage of the total housing stock built prior to 1940 (.5), the percentage of the total current population "in poverty" in 1970 (.3), and the degree to which the population growth rate lags behind that of all metropolitan cities (.2).

HUD has called the sum of these the "impaction index."[11] Several factors in addition to the UDAG impaction index are utilized as selection criteria. These include: (1) the UDAG "distress index,"[12] equally weighting per capita income, unemployment, and job lag/decline; (2) other measures of distress "as the Secretary may determine to be relevant"; (3) the city's demonstrated performance in carrying out housing and community development programs; (4) the impact of the program on low and moderate income persons and minorities, including employment, housing, and training opportunities; (5) the nature and extent of financial participation by private entities; (6) the financial assistance made available by the state; (7) the financial participation by other federal or local sources; and (8) the impact of the project on the deterioration of the community.

The relative importance attached to each of these criteria, which are partly determined by program administrators, affects the allocation of funds to different types of cities. For example, projects in distressed suburbs and the largest central cities received no financial assistance from their states. Increasing the importance of state assistance in the selection criteria, therefore, would make it more difficult for these cities to obtain Action Grants.

---

[11] This should not be confused with the discussion of impaction in Bunce and Glickman in this volume.

[12] The UDAG distress index is discussed in more detail in Jacobs, forthcoming.

Once construction has begun, the recipient jurisdiction will experience the direct effects of UDAG projects. They are the expansion and improvement of the stocks of commercial and industrial buildings and housing in distressed jurisdictions as a group; the provision of construction jobs in the short run; and jobs in commercial, industrial, and housing maintenance sectors in the long run. Local fiscal relief should occur through increased local revenues from the expanded tax base as long as these increased revenues exceed increased costs.

Indirect effects include the additional output, employment, and earnings in supplying industries generated by the construction and operation of UDAG projects, as well as the externality effects of economic development projects described earlier. For a given project, these indirect effects will vary substantially among cities. Larger, more diversified jurisdictions will retain many more of the indirect effects created by supply linkages. The potential for "bandwagon effects" generated by a single economic development project depends as well on other forces affecting the city's economic climate.

These general impacts are applicable to central cities as well as cities in suburban and nonmetropolitan areas. In the next section, the distribution of UDAG funds to types of jurisdictions is discussed and their urban impacts more fully explored.

Distribution[13]

Although the legislation specifies that 75 percent of the UDAG funds be allocated to large suburbs and central cities through the metropolitan funds, and 25 percent to small suburbs and nonmetropolitan cities through the small city set-aside, there is no further specification of allocations among central cities, suburbs, and nonmetropolitan areas.

In Fiscal 1978, 66 percent of all central cities in the United States were eligible for the UDAG program, as were a smaller percentage of all suburbs and nonmetropolitan areas. Eleven urban counties were eligible, although none applied for Action Grants.

As Table 1 shows, central cities received 75 percent, suburbs 12.5 percent, and nonmetropolitan areas 12.5 percent of all UDAG funds. However, the combination of private, federal, state, and local funds attracted by UDAG funds to different types of jurisdictions resulted in 71 percent of the total dollars committed to projects flowing to central cities, 13 percent to suburbs, and 16 percent to nonmetropolitan areas.

State and local contributions to UDAG projects vary by type of jurisdiction. Table 2 shows that approximately $171.8 million was contributed by State and local governments toward UDAG projects in central cities. These funds were used in 31 percent of the central cities receiving UDAG awards.

---

[13] The distribution of UDAG funds by region and by degree of distress of recipient cities is discussed in detail in Jacobs, forthcoming.

TABLE 1: Percent of Each Source of Funds, by Type of Jurisdiction (Decisions through October 1978)

Source	Central Cities	Suburbs	Nonmetro-politan Areas	Total
UDAG funds	75.0%	12.5%	12.5%	100.0%
Private funds	68.0	14.0	18.0	100.0
Local funds	90.0	5.0	5.0	100.0
State funds	83.0	1.0	16.0	100.0
Other federal funds	90.0	4.0	6.0	100.0
Total funds	71.0	13.0	16.0	100.0

Source: HUD News.

State and local contributions were smaller for suburbs and nonmetropolitan areas; approximately 16 percent of suburban and 16 percent of nonmetropolitan cities receiving UDAG grants received state or local funding as well, totaling $9.7 million in suburbs and $11.1 million in nonmetropolitan areas.

UDAG is a program which directs funds more heavily to the North than to the South. This is largely attributable to the regional location of eligible cities—distressed cities are found predominantly in the Northeast and North Central regions. Forty-two percent of UDAG funds were allocated to the Northeast, 30 percent to the North Central, and 28 percent to the South and West combined.

TABLE 2: Funding Sources of UDAG Projects, by Type of Jurisdiction (Decisions through October 1978)

Source	Central Cities $ Millions	Central Cities No. Cities	Suburbs $ Millions	Suburbs No. Cities	Nonmetropolitan Areas $ Millions	Nonmetropolitan Areas No. Cities
UDAG funds	366.9	91	60.6	37	60.5	78
Private funds	1,954.1	89	406.2	37	500.8	78
Local funds	162.4	29	9.5	6	9.1	12
State funds	9.4	6	0.1	1	2.0	4
Other federal funds	80.0	22	3.2	3	5.7	3
Total funds	2,572.7	91	479.7	37	578.1	78

Leveraging Ratios ($)	Central Cities	Suburbs	Nonmetropolitan Areas
Private/UDAG	5.32	6.7	8.27
UDAG/local	2.26	6.4	6.7
Total/local	14.85	49.32	62.49

Leveraging

The comparative financial advantage that UDAG provides for central cities, suburbs, and nonmetropolitan areas in attracting private funds may be examined by focusing on the private funds flowing to each group of jurisdictions and the cost (in terms of UDAG dollars) of attracting these funds. Central cities were able to attract 68 percent of the private commitments, compared to suburbs (14 percent), and nonmetropolitan areas (18 percent), as shown in Table 1. Although central cities were awarded the largest share of UDAG dollars and attracted the largest share of private dollars, on average, central cities as a group were able to leverage the fewest (5.32) private dollars per dollar of UDAG grant. This is not surprising as it reflects the fact that central cities as a group are losing their share of industrial and residential growth in the private market and are often perceived as riskier areas for investment.

The leveraging of funds from all sources by local government expenditures may also be measured. Although central cities committed 90 percent of all local funds flowing to UDAG projects, Table 2 shows that they leveraged 14.85 dollars from all over sources for every dollar of local funds. This compares to 49.3 dollars and 62.5 dollars for suburbs and nonmetropolitan areas, respectively. An intriguing comparison is the leveraging ratios of UDAG to local funds across types of jurisdictions; how much in local funds did it take to attract UDAG funds? Again, central cities had the most difficult task. They were able to leverage only 2.26 UDAG dollars for each local dollar, while suburbs and nonmetropolitan areas were able to leverage 6.4 and 6.7 UDAG dollars, respectively.

The jurisdictional breakdown of leveraging ratio differences described above may reflect the nature of the economic activities funded in each type of jurisdiction. Therefore, a further breakdown of these spatial leveraging ratios by type of project may be enlightening. Table 3 shows leveraging ratios for projects classified by type of economic activity.[14] Central cities find it easier to leverage private dollars for commercial ventures and hotels than do other jurisdictions, and suburbs, to attract residential development. Among industrial projects, suburban projects leveraged, on average, the most private dollars per UDAG dollar (6.35), although nonmetropolitan areas leveraged the largest total amount of private funds per UDAG dollar (13.01). Nonmetropolitan areas leveraged the fewest dollars vis-à-vis other types of places for commercial and residential uses. Since the majority of nonmetropolitan projects are industrial, this may account for the high overall leveraging ratio attributed to nonmetropolitan areas (Table 2). The differences in leveraging ratios among types of jurisdictions reflect the relative attractiveness of central cities and suburbs for alternative uses that is observed in the private market;

---

[14] This classification is based on sectors of the economy, rather than the commercial/industrial/neighborhood classification of UDAG projects made by the Action Grant staff.

TABLE 3: Total and Average Leveraging Ratios of Private Funds to UDAG Funds by Type of Activity (Decisions through October 1978)

	Commercial[a]		Residential		Industrial		Hotel	
	Total Leveraging Ratio	Project Average Leveraging Ratio	Total Leveraging Ratio	Project Average Leveraging Ratio	Total Leveraging Ratio	Project Average Leveraging Ratio	Total Leveraging Ratio	Project Average Leveraging Ratio
Central cities	5.81	5.85	4.09	5.27	4.56	5.31	5.93	6.41
Suburbs	5.29	5.30	16.75	8.06	7.18	6.35	3.50	3.50
Nonmetropolitan areas	3.77	4.80	3.68	3.80	13.01	5.82	3.55	3.72

Source: HUD News.

Notes: Total leveraging ratios indicate the total number of dollars leveraged by activity for each jurisdiction type. Project average leveraging ratios represent an average of the leveraging ratios for each project by activity and jurisdiction. For example, central cities leveraged 4.09 private dollars for each UDAG dollar for residential activity. The residential projects in central cities leveraged, on average, 5.27 private dollars for each UDAG dollar. The fact that the average leveraging ratio among projects exceeds the leveraging ratio for total dollars indicates that there are a few projects with high leveraging ratios and a larger number of projects with lower leveraging ratios. These averages reflect leveraging ratios for single activity projects only. Funds for mixed use projects were not allocated by use in the available HUD data base.

[a] Does not include hotels.

central cities are more likely to attract commercial and hotel uses, and suburbs are more likely to attract the relatively land intensive residential and industrial uses. That is, it takes more UDAG dollars to leverage a given amount of private dollars in these latter categories in central cities than in suburbs.

It is important here to step aside and consider the difference between the interpretation of these findings for a program evaluation and an Urban Impact Statement. If this were a program evaluation, the leveraging ratios might serve as guidance for directing funds to places which succeed in attracting the most private funds with a UDAG dollar, that is, nonmetropolitan areas. Alternatively, projects of different categories may be directed to places in which they attract the greatest "bang per buck": commercial and hotel projects to central cities, residential projects to suburbs, and industrial projects to nonmetropolitan areas. (As discussed earlier, the attraction of private funds is a program objective specified in the law.) However, from an urban impact standpoint, we must raise the following questions: Do we want to reinforce the pattern of housing construction in the suburbs? Commercial jobs in central cities? Industrial expansion in nonmetropolitan areas? On one hand we do, if this reallocation draws firms from nondistressed jurisdictions of the same type. On the other hand, we do not, if this accelerates the exodus of low-skilled jobs from central cities. Reinforcing the private market pattern may exacerbate the general scenario of low-skilled and blue-collar jobs leaving central cities, residential expansion continuing in the suburbs, and central city commercial activity providing new jobs, but for suburban commuters. Some of these employment effects are taken up in the next section.

Employment and income effects

The activities funded by UDAG generate direct and indirect jobs through multiplier effects during both the construction period and the actual operation of the projects. The direct employment effects for a given jurisdiction are comparatively easy to estimate.

Jobs created in the construction sector are predominantly blue collar, and the national average wage in the construction sector is significantly above the national average wage for all industries as a whole ($14,765 versus $9,431).[15] Minority participation in the construction industry is higher than for the economy as a whole—17.5 percent as compared to 16.5 percent (U.S. Equal Employment Opportunity Commission, 1977), although it varies by region.

Turning to the direct permanent employment, Table 4 presents adjusted job estimates taken from UDAG applications themselves. These are gross estimates of jobs created (implying that firms either expanded or are new to the area) and saved (implying that firms had been planning to relocate). Since the UDAG data base does not contain quantifiable information on projected output, sales volume, or square footage of all funded projects, it is difficult

[15] *See* Council of Economic Advisers (1979; Table B-36, p. 225).

TABLE 4: Total Expenditures and Direct Jobs by Use for UDAG Projects (Decisions through October 1978)

| | Central Cities | | | | | Suburbs | |
| | Project Funds, All Sources ($ Millions) | % | Jobs | | | Project Funds, All Sources ($ Millions) | % |
			New	Saved	Sum as % of Total		
Commercial	$786.2	31%	13,078	13,215	30%	$83.4	17%
Residential	235.1	9	2,030	464	1	13.4	3
Industrial	418.0	16	10,249	15,199	28	277.2	58
Hotel	250.6	10	6,883	3,257	11	18.0	4
Total[a]	2,572.7	100	51,614	39,140	100	479.7	100

to make estimates of job creation from these or other economic variables. As discussed earlier, although these estimates have not been reexamined in this study, their information on relative shares is valuable and should not be ignored.

In the suburban and nonmetropolitan categories, more jobs are created in the industrial sector than in any other sector of the economy. Commercial activity dominates in the central city. At least 30 percent of the central city jobs created are in commercial activity (including retail), 28 percent are in the industrial sector, 11 percent are in hotels, and 1 percent is in residential activity. These four uses represent 70 percent of the total projected employment in central cities. Central cities are also the site of 83 percent of the hotel jobs. In suburbs, at least 38 percent of the jobs are in industrial and 30 percent in commercial activities. The employment pattern in nonmetropolitan areas is dominated by industrial activity, which generates at least 63 percent of the jobs.

Table 4 also shows that of the total number of direct jobs attributed to UDAG projects for each jurisdictional category, central cities had the highest share of their UDAG jobs as saved jobs; thirty-nine thousand jobs saved out of a total of ninety thousand central city jobs. Within central cities, industrial projects and commercial projects accounted for approximately thirty-nine percent and thirty-four percent, respectively, of all retained jobs. The number of jobs saved in central cities was significantly greater than the 5.5 thousand of those retained in suburban and nonmetropolitan areas combined. This evidence suggests that UDAG projects may provide central cities with the best advantage in retaining economic activity that might otherwise relocate to

Suburbs			Nonmetropolitan Areas				
Jobs			Project Funds, All		Jobs		
New	Saved	Sum as % of Total	Sources ($ Mil- lions)	%	New	Saved	Sum as % of Total
6,584	429	38%	$66.0	11%	2,009	239	15%
20	4	1	27.0	5	230	0	2
8,088	736	30	362.3	63	7,220	2,112	63
1,600	0	7	22.6	4	412	0	3
20,441	2,630	100	578.1	100	11,967	2,927	100

Note: Job estimates are from applications and *HUD News.*
ª Includes commercial, residential, industrial, and hotel projects, as well as mixed use projects for which employment estimates were not available by separate categories.

other areas and supports Schmenner's finding that industrial firms prefer plant expansion over relocation.

Further comparisons between industrial and commercial projects show that there may be a trade-off between the potential for a UDAG dollar to attract private funds and to create jobs. Although job creation is a key goal of the Action Grant project, the leveraging of private funds is an important economic development goal unto itself because the new private investment attracted by the Action Grant may stimulate additional private investment in the future. Turning to central cities, industrial projects leveraged fewer private dollars per UDAG dollar than did commercial projects (Table 3). More UDAG dollars, however, were necessary to create a commercial job ($4,047) than an industrial job ($2,790). In suburbs this pattern is also evident. Among the three major sectors, commercial projects had the lowest leveraging ratio (Table 3), but cost the least in UDAG dollars to provide jobs ($1,864 per job).

To the contrary, in nonmetropolitan areas industrial projects leveraged the greatest number of private dollars per UDAG dollar, but also used the fewest UDAG dollars to create a job. Clearly, the possibility of a trade-off between achieving two valuable objectives of the program (at least for some jurisdictions) calls for further investigation, especially if one of these factors becomes a more important selection criterion in the future.

The various economic sectors and types of industries funded by UDAG will generate jobs in different occupational categories. Because residential projects, manufacturing plants, office buildings, hotels, and retail shopping centers were awarded a substantial amount of UDAG funds, the occupational characteristics of employment in these industries will be briefly discussed below. Because actual data for occupational distributions of UDAG project employment are not available, national estimates of occupational distributions for these broad industrial categories (U.S. Equal Employment Opportunity Commission, 1977) and of average wages are used in the discussion that follows.

Although $50.3 million of UDAG funds were committed to *residential* projects, the residential sector provides relatively few permanent jobs after the actual construction period. Housing services are generated for residents with the use of a relatively small number of labor inputs compared to other types of economic activity; the production of housing services depends mainly on the housing units themselves.

Of the 43.6 thousand jobs created through the industrial projects, most, if not all, will be in *manufacturing*. A substantial amount of employment in manufacturing is composed of craftworker and operative jobs. Professional and managerial jobs are the next most frequent occupation, although the construction of branch plants whose corporate headquarters are located elsewhere are likely to result in fewer professional and managerial laborers employed at the UDAG site than the national average may suggest. Manufacturing industry wages average $11,492 nationally, and although this may be a high estimate, it substantially exceeds the wage levels in other UDAG project categories.

Office buildings, funded through commercial projects, predominantly contain economic activities categorized as finance, insurance, and real estate, and the service sector. Employment in these sectors is largely white collar. Managerial, professional, and clerical occupations represent a large share of the employment. The national average wage for these industries is $8,320.

Employment in the *hotel* industry primarily consists of low-skilled, low-wage, and nonsupervisory service jobs. Jobs are seasonal, and turnover in service jobs of over 100 percent per year is not unusual. In 1967, overall employment of blacks in the hotel industry was about 32 percent (Koziara and Koziara, 1968). This is significantly higher than for the labor force as a whole. Black employment in the housekeeping and food preparation categories was relatively high: 61 percent and 42 percent respectively. National chains tended to employ blacks in a larger percentage of job categories than did regional chains or independently owned hotels. There is speculation that new immigrants to the United States currently compete effectively with low-skilled minorities for central city hotel jobs, possibly reducing the share of these jobs held by minorities.

Many commercial and mixed-use projects contain shopping centers. *Retail shopping centers* employ fewer laborers per square foot of gross leasable area than do traditional retail stores. Downtown malls, with a larger number of small stores, are likely to employ more people per square foot than suburban malls in which large stores predominate. Approximately 40 percent of employment in retail shopping centers is part-time. Women are employed to a much greater extent than in the labor force as a whole, and minority employment is about the same as for the labor force as a whole. Shopping centers, especially those with "fast-food" stores, employ a greater than average percentage of youth than does the economy as a whole. The occupational distribution of retail trade in general is heavily weighted toward low-skilled, low-wage sales jobs. This occupational distribution is further skewed for shopping malls; as chain stores comprise more than sixty percent of stores in shopping centers, the complementary management and professional employment is usually located at the national headquarters of the chains and not at local branches. Thus, the $6,188 national average wage for retail employees is a high estimate for wages earned at UDAG projects.

Earnings from direct employment accruing to a jurisdiction depend on the number of jobs created in each economic sector and on the commuting of workers to jobs across jurisdictional boundaries as well. On the average, suburban workers holding central city jobs exceed central city workers holding suburban jobs. Thus, the suburban share of earnings may exceed the suburban share of jobs. Profits are most likely to be retained locally in industries which are dominated by small firms that are owned and operated by local residents. Of course, owners may live in other jurisdictions. Local firms owned by national companies will generate their profits elsewhere—possibly outside distressed cities as a group. This may be most important for UDAG projects that include shopping centers which rent a large share of their space to national chains.

In addition to direct employment, jobs are also created indirectly by UDAG projects in supplying industries, and may be estimated using multipliers. From the 1967 national input-output model, gross output multipliers have been calibrated for various sectors of the economy. Coupling these multipliers with employment-to-output ratios and adjusting their product for inflation and labor productivity, one can roughly approximate the jobs created indirectly by UDAG projects. The multipliers, however, are not available for separate jurisdictions. Leakages from the jurisdiction's economy should exceed those characteristic of regional multiplier effects, because supplying industries are likely to be located in neighboring jurisdictions within the region. As in the case of direct employment, these leakages may be exacerbated if employees working in the jurisdiction spend their consumption dollars elsewhere.

In addition to employment effects, fiscal effects are requested for urban impact analysis by OMB Circular A-116, and would also be part of the focus of a program evaluation.

Fiscal effects

One of the primary goals of economic development activity is to improve the fiscal condition of the host jurisdiction in the long run. In the absence of local tax abatements, UDAG projects will produce higher property tax revenues through direct site improvements. Additional property tax revenues from neighboring sites will become available to the extent that UDAG projects create a bandwagon effect in complementary investment. If, however, property values decline elsewhere in the local jurisdiction due to the physical or market activity substitution described above, then net tax revenues will be lower.

The total fiscal effects on jurisdictions depends upon the local fiscal structure—the nature of sales, income, and business, and property taxes. Just as there are multiplier effects in jobs and income there are multiplied fiscal effects from these effects. But as indirect job creation and direct and indirect income generation are subject to crossjurisdictional leakages, potential fiscal gains might be diluted.

The types of jobs created themselves have varying fiscal effects. If we can compute the net fiscal value of a job on an annual basis (the yield per employee by industry in property taxes, corporate income taxes, personal income taxes, and sales taxes), we can calculate the maximum amount it is rational to spend to create that job (federally, as well as locally).[16]

The short-run direct cost to localities for obtaining UDAG-funded projects differs by type of jurisdiction. As the leveraging ratios of Table 2 show, it was clearly more costly for central city local governments to attract economic development activities. Central city local governments spent $162 million to attract UDAG projects, while suburban local governments spent $9.5 million, and nonmetropolitan local governments spent $9.1 million. Not only did central cities spend more, but they also received less. Central cities were able only to leverage 14.85 dollars from private, state, UDAG, and other federal sources, per dollar of local spending. Suburbs were able to leverage 49.32 dollars, and nonmetropolitan areas, 63.49 dollars per dollar of local spending.

Such expenditures may still be most worthwhile for the central city (or other locality) to incur if the intial investment made by the city is more than paid back by the fiscal effects generated directly and indirectly by the program.

Although not requested explicitly in the OMB Circular, UDAG's effects on neighborhoods is assessed below.

Neighborhood effects

One of the primary goals of the UDAG program is neighborhood revitalization. By law, the Secretary must allocate UDAG funds "in a manner which achieves a reasonable balance among programs that are designed primarily to (1) restore seriously deteriorated neighborhoods, (2) to reclaim for industrial purposes underutilized real property, and (3) to renew commercial employment centers." In order to achieve this goal of neighborhood revitaliza-

---

[16] In a detailed study for New York City, Bahl, Campbell, and Greytak (1977) found that the most fiscally productive jobs are in the Wholesale and Retail and Finance, Insurance and Real Estate sectors. These results, however, should not be generalized to all localities, as local tax structures vary.

tion and restoration, two issues must be explored. First, does neighborhood revitalization mean directly improving the physical place called "the neighborhood," or the economic situation of the residents of the neighborhood (possibly enabling them to relocate outside the neighborhood, if they so choose)?

If one accepts the "place" concept of neighborhood, then does neighborhood revitalization mean improving the level of economic activity in a (residential) neighborhood, or improving the housing stock there? If one accepts the "people" concept of neighborhood, then activities fostering neighborhood revitalization may involve a neighborhood's residents although the activities are physically located outside the neighborhood.

In order to administer the program to effectively execute the legislative allocation for neighborhoods, the Action Grant staff has formulated a working definition of neighborhood projects. A project is classified "neighborhood" if:

1. the project is predominantly residential, even if it is located in the central business district;
2. the project is predominantly commercial or industrial and is *not* located in the central business district or in an industrial park; or
3. the project is predominantly commercial or industrial, is located in a central business district or industrial park, but has targeted the jobs created to residents of a neighborhood.

This broad definition encompasses both the "place" and "people" concepts of neighborhood described above. In practice, however, most of the projects satisfy the "place" criteria (1) or (2).

Although some HUD programs, such as CDBG, require the designation of recipient neighborhoods by the eligible jurisdictions, there are no restrictions regarding the types of neighborhoods which may be the site of UDAG projects within the eligible cities.

In the three rounds of metropolitan funds, 18 percent, 41 percent, and 37 percent of the Action Grants were sequentially awarded to neighborhood projects. The increase may be attributed to the increase in the number of applications submitted for neighborhood projects that were strong enough to meet the funding criteria, and to vehement reaction of proneighborhood pressure groups after UDAG's first round of decisions in which a large number of hotels received Action Grants.

This concern with neighborhood-nonneighborhood activity again stems from the people versus places dilemma: is neighborhood thought of as a place or a community of people. Viewed as the place concept, hotels and neighborhood revitalization projects represent a trade-off; funds allocated for downtown hotels could have been used for projects located in residential neighborhoods. Moreover, if these downtown investments generate additional private investment demand for downtown locations, private funds for investments in neighborhoods may provide employment for low income, low-skilled, and possibly unemployed residents of low income neighborhoods, and may indirectly improve neighborhoods by helping the employment and financial situation of their residents.

When neighborhoods are the physical site of UDAG activity, it is hoped that they will experience improved neighborhood conditions in proportion to their improved housing and/or neighborhood business. If the scale of activity is large enough, the UDAG project may spur additional private investment in the area. In turn, this may lead to the inevitable problem of displacement. If UDAG activities drive up rents for businesses and residents, low income individuals and low-profit small businesses may be financially unable to remain in the neighborhood. Although the neighborhood may be revitalized, the original residents and business owners may be driven to other neighborhoods, possibly even less desirable than their first location. This phenomenon may be mitigated to the extent that UDAG provides funds for the rehabilitation of privately owned housing and reduced rate mortgages to current neighborhood residents. The incorporation of SBA loans and Section 8 housing assistance would also abate the financial hardships that are likely to cause displacement. To some extent, the UDAG program does ease the burden on the directly displaced property owner and tenant by requiring cities to pay relocation costs commensurate with the Uniform Relocation Act of 1970.

The displacement problems which may arise from retail projects is a good example. A substantial amount of UDAG funds has been allocated for retail trade both in neighborhoods and in central business districts. Activities requiring totally new construction range from large enclosed malls in central business districts to smaller, strip shopping centers in neighborhoods. Those requiring rehabilitation and new additions range from rehabilitating neighborhood shopping areas to building parking garages and enclosed pedestrian walkways to enable existing downtown retail centers to compete with suburban, climate-controlled shopping malls.

The construction of new shopping centers poses several displacement problems which affect both the recipient neighborhoods as well as nonrecipient neighborhoods. First, there may be on-site displacement. In order to obtain financing for the construction of a large, regional shopping mall, a developer must demonstrate to the lender that his project will be profitable. Most lenders financing a development project require that, for at least 50 percent of the gross leasable area of the center, legally binding commitments are made by firms which themselves have AAA credit ratings. Stores other than national chains are unlikely to possess such a rating. Thus, space for displaced business may be at a premium. In addition, the mall stores constructed may be larger in square footage than would be profitable for some types of small businesses displaced.

UDAG money used for parking garages and pedestrian walkways is likely to cause less displacement than would the construction of a new mall on an existing retail site. Only those firms occupying the site of the parking garage would be displaced. To the extent that the retail area is made more attractive, however, rents may be bid up in the remaining buildings, and marginal firms may be indirectly displaced in the same fashion.

Downtown shopping centers may pose yet another displacement problem. Although the intent of revitalizing downtown retail areas is to recapture some of the market from suburban shopping malls, the effect may be to draw shoppers from other intown neighborhood retail areas, leaving these areas less profitable. Empirical evidence is necessary to determine the conditions under which this may be true. If the shopping activity does shift, there may be little net change in the volume of business for the city as a whole, but there may be significant net transfer of ownership (and profits) from small local owners to national chains, the closing of smaller neighborhood stores, and an indirect, adverse effect on neighborhood revitalization. However, even if neighborhood stores do lose their share of the city's retail trade, downtown shopping centers do provide employment opportunities for workers from all accessible neighborhoods.

SUMMARY AND CONCLUSIONS

The evidence available after one year of commitments to projects indicates that the UDAG program favors central cities over suburbs and nonmetropolitan areas, the Northeast and North Central Regions over the South and West, and the more distressed over the less distressed cities. This targeting is not coincidental, but results from the eligibility and selection criteria defined by the law and written into the regulations which explicitly direct funds to distressed cities. These findings, of course, relate to direct expenditures, and the net fiscal, employment, and income effects may differ as a result of leakages across jurisdictional and regional boundaries.

Since the purpose of UDAG is to enable funded jurisdictions to leverage private investment, leveraging ratios have been explored in this paper. We found that among jurisdictions, central cities were least able to leverage private funds with UDAG dollars, private funds with local dollars, and UDAG funds with local dollars.

Two key criticisms of UDAG, and of economic development programs in general, are that they are "beggar-thy-neighbor" policies and that they would have taken place without UDAG (or other government funds). It is worth emphasizing that these criticisms cannot be true simultaneously for any one project.

Under what conditions, however, is either one of the criticisms true for any particular project? In the absence of the externalities which lead to the prisoner's dilemma, the beggar-thy-neighbor phenomenon is an explicit trade-off made by the Federal government (of which it may or may not be aware). But do we know exactly under what conditions a jurisdiction has received funds that would have gone to its neighbor? And from which neighbor?

The beggar-thy-neighbor phenomenon is, in certain circumstances, consistent with the objectives of UDAG. In contrast, UDAG grants which do not alter the location or expansion decisions of private firms violate any reasonable objectives of government spending, UDAG or otherwise! To some extent, the existing literature and further research on firm location decisions should provide information for local and federal decision-makers to identify likely cases of pure transfers to the private sector. Identification of this phenomenon will depend heavily on knowledge of the specifics on the projects and the locality in question. This information should be more readily available at the HUD Area Office level than at the HUD Central Office level.

Attracting industry to any site within a local economy may be sufficient to generate additional economic activity in the SMSA as a whole. From the efficiency standpoint, the firm should choose its preferred location within the local economy, be it in the central city, the suburbs, or nonmetropolitan places. Goals, however, go beyond efficiency alone. In the absence of local fiscal reform in the short run and in the presence of the hypothesized locational mismatch of jobs and low-skilled workers (due to transportation costs and restrictive residential zoning) we are willing to trade off economic efficiency. UDAG funds are directed to distressed central cities to simultaneously attack the fiscal and job problems of those cities. Alas, due to the potentials for central city employees to be suburban residents and supply links to be located in the suburbs, the net result of UDAG's efforts may not a fiscal and job gain for central city residents.

Although UDAG succeeds in targeting funds to central cities and other distressed places, it is not a panacea for all urban problems. Consider the three explicit objectives of job creation, fiscal stability, and unemployment reduction. Some might find it advantageous to utilize UDAG to provide locational incentives directed toward distressed SMSAs rather than toward distressed cities per se, and construct a package of other complementary policies which would better achieve some of these goals than could UDAG do itself.

For example, the fiscal impact of any economic development program is still confined by the structural problems which may exacerbate local fiscal distress. These problems may be best addressed by broad reforms, such as tax base sharing or the shifting of fiscal responsibility to higher levels of government (*see* Chinitz, 1979). In addition, although new jobs will be created, high unemployment rates in distressed cities may not be significantly reduced by economic development programs in general and UDAG in particular. Job creation in industries which are most viable in the central cities may not have a substantial impact on job creation for the unskilled or raising the income levels of low income workers. Tying UDAG projects more directly to other federal programs, such as CETA, may better serve this objective.

The hope for the success of this or any urban policy in the future depends heavily on the availability of more information and practical research results on some of the issues that have been addressed in this paper to guide policy-makers before the fact, rather than by trial and error.

REFERENCES

Aaron, Henry; Russett, Frank; and Single, Neil. "Tax Reform and the Composition of Investment." *National Tax Journal*, March 1972.
Bahl, Roy W.; Campbell, Alan K.; and Greytak, David. *Taxes, Expenditure and the Economic Base: A Case Study of New York City*. New York: Praeger Publishers, 1977.
Chinitz, Benjamin. "Toward a National Urban Policy." In *Central City Economic Development*, edited by Benjamin Chinitz. Cambridge, Mass.: Abt Books, 1979.
————, and Jacobs, Susan. "Central City Economic Development: The Post War Experience." Presented at the North American Regional Science Association Meetings, November 11–13, 1977.
Council of Economic Advisers, *Economic Report of the President*. Washington, D.C.: U.S. Government Printing Office, 1979.
Davis, Otto A., and Whinston, Andrew B. "The Economics of Urban Renewal." *Law and Contemporary Problems* 26, no. 1 (Winter 1961).
Doeringer, Peter B., and Piore, Michael J. *Internal Labor Markets and Manpower Analysis*. Lexington, Mass.: D. C. Heath, 1971.
Hamermesh, Daniel. "Subsidies for Jobs in the Private Sector." In *Creating Jobs: Public Employment Programs and Wage Subsidies*, edited by J. L. Palmer. Washington, D.C.: Brookings Institution, 1978.
Harrison, Bennett. "Ghetto Economic Development." *Journal of Economic Literature* 12 (1974a): 1–37.
————. *Urban Economic Development*. Washington, D.C.: Urban Institute, 1974b.
————, and Hill, Edward. "The Changing Structure of Jobs in Older and Younger Cities." In *Central City Economic Development*, edited by Benjamin Chinitz. Cambridge, Mass.: Abt Books, 1979.
————, and Kanter, Sandra. "The Political Economy of States' Job-Creation Business Incentives." *AIP Journal*, October 1978.
Hausner, Victor A. "EDA's Urban Economic Development Initiatives." In *Central City Economic Development*, edited by Benjamin Chinitz. Cambridge, Mass: Abt Books, 1979.
Housing and Community Development Act of 1977. § 110, 119, 42 U.S.C. § 5304, 5318. 1977.
Jacobs, Susan S. "The Urban Impacts of the Urban Development Action Grant." In *The Urban Impacts of the HUD Budget*, edited by Norman J. Glickman and Susan S. Jacobs. Forthcoming.
Kain, John F. "The Distribution and Movement of Jobs and Industry." In *The Metropolitar Enigma*, edited by James Q. Wilson. Cambridge: Harvard University Press, 1968.
Koziara, Edward C., and Koziara, Karen S. *The Negro in the Hotel Industry*.

Wharton School Industrial Research Unit, Report no. 4. Philadelphia: University of Pennsylvania, 1968.

McHugh, Richard, and Puryear, David. "Tax Credits for Urban Revitalization." In *The Federal Response to the Fiscal Crisis in American Cities*, edited by K. Hubbell. Cambridge, Mass.: Ballinger, forthcoming.

Nathan, Richard P.; Adams, Charles, Jr.; and Associates. *Monitoring Revenue Sharing: The Second Round*. Washington, D.C.: Brookings Institution, 1977.

Nelson, Kathryn P., and Park, Clifford H. "Decentralization of Employment during the 1969–1972 Business Cycle: The National and Regional Record." Washington, D.C.: U.S. Department of Housing and Urban Development, June 1975.

Roistacher, Elizabeth A., and Simms, Margaret C. "Recession and the Cities: Metropolitan Structure and Unemployment over the Business Cycle." Paper presented at the American Economic Association meetings, August 31, 1978.

Schmenner, Roger W. *The Manufacturing Location Decision: Evidence from Cincinnati and New England*. Cambridge: Harvard Business School, 1978.

Simms, Margaret C., and Roistacher, Elizabeth A. "The Rocky Road to an Urban Policy." Unpublished. January 1979.

Sternlieb, George; Roistacher, Elizabeth; and Hughes, James. *Tax Subsidies and Housing Investment: A Fiscal Impact Analysis*. Center for Urban Policy Research. New Brunswick: Rutgers University, 1976.

Sundquist, James L. *Dispersing Population: What America Can Learn from Europe*. Washington, D.C.: Brookings Institution, 1975.

Tabb, William K. *The Political Economy of the Black Ghetto*. New York: Norton, 1970.

Uniform Relocation Assistance and Real Property Acquisition Policies Act of 1970, as amended. 42 U.S.C. § 4601 *et seq.* 1976.

U.S. Department of Commerce, Bureau of Economic Analysis, "The Input-Output Structure of the U.S. Economy—1967," *Survey of Current Business*, February 1974.

U.S. Department of Commerce, Bureau of Economic Analysis. *Industry-Specific Gross Output Multipliers for the BEA Economic Areas*, January 1977.

U.S. Department of Housing and Urban Development. Community Development Block Grants, 24 C.F.R. Part 570, Subpart G. 1978.

U.S. Equal Employment Opportunity Commission, *Equal Employment Report, 1975*. 052-015-00031-6. Washington, D.C.: U.S. Government Printing Office, 1977.

Vaughan, Roger J. *The Urban Impacts of Federal Policies*. Vol. 2, *Economic Development*. Santa Monica: Rand Corporation, 1977.

The White House Conference on Balanced National Growth and Economic Development—Final Report. Washington, D.C.: U.S. Government Printing Office, July 1978.

CHAPTER FIFTEEN

The Urban Impact of Air Pollution and Its Control

EDWIN S. MILLS AND HYUN-SIK KIM

INTRODUCTION

The subject of this paper is the impact on urban areas of air pollution and governments' attempts to abate air-polluting discharges.

During the 1960s, more was known about water than air pollution. One reason was simply better data on discharges. A second factor, probably both cause and effect, was the earlier concern of federal legislation with water rather than with air pollution. A third consideration, again both cause and effect, was that scholars had devoted more attention to water than to air pollution.

The situation has changed dramatically during the 1970s. Much better data have become available concerning airborne discharges and ambient air quality. It is by now much easier to obtain an accurate picture of the quality of the air over Philadelphia than of the water in the Philadelphia estuary. Equally important, high-quality research papers and books have appeared in large quantities during the 1970s on the subject of air pollution.

Presumably, the basic reason for the early lead of water-quality research over air-quality research was a deep and natural concern with drinking water. Even during the 1960s, it was thought that the largest benefits of water-pollution abatement were in the form of improved recreational opportunities. Nevertheless, concern with drinking-water quality had for decades inspired research and monitoring on water quality, with the result that an "at best" tolerable data base was available for water pollution studies even during the 1960s. Until the health effects of self-pollution from smoking became known in the 1960s, few people worried much about health effects of air pollution.

But there is a fundamental reason why more is known about air than water pollution: it is a much simpler subject in every way. First, only a few substances appear to be discharged into the air in substantial quantities. Particulates, sulfur oxides, hydrocarbons, carbon monoxide, and nitrous oxides constitute the vast bulk of airborne discharges. Heat and carbon dioxide would also be added to some people's lists of important air pollutants. Even with the additions, it is a short list. Including organic wastes, heavy metals, and chemicals, among others, the list of potentially harmful waterborne discharges is much longer. Second, water moves in special and predictable ways over the earth's surface. The result is that water bodies can be and are classified by use. Drinking-water sources must be of high quality, whereas, at the other extreme, shipping channels can be of low quality. But all of the air close to the earth's surface is breathed and people are harmed if any of it is sufficiently polluted. We can be and are much more selective about the ways we use water than about the ways we use air. The possibility of greater selectivity with respect to water use considerably increases the complexity of government policy-making regarding water pollution in comparison with air pollution. Third, control technologies are fewer and simpler with air than with water pollutants. There is no analog relating air to the large-scale government collection and processing of organic wastes which is so important in preventing water pollution. Governments have major financing and management responsibilities regarding water pollution, but not regarding air pollution. Finally, even monitoring appears to be easier with air than with water pollution. One would not have made that statement a few years ago. But recent concern with heavy metals and carcinogenic chemicals in drinking water seriously stretches the capacity to monitor such substances. No comparable problems exist with air pollution, so far as is known.

Most air pollution and most monitoring stations are urban. Monitoring stations have been concentrated in urban locations because the air is more polluted there than in rural areas and because that is where people live and breathe. Although people also mostly drink their water in urban areas, most of it is extracted from the environment in rural areas. Equally important, much water-based recreation takes place in rural areas, because the water is cleaner there and because people prefer to recreate in bucolic surroundings. Thus, air pollution is naturally much more of an urban subject than is water pollution. Reflecting that fact, almost all economic studies of benefits, costs, and government strategy alternatives are explicitly or implicitly placed in an urban context. Thus, a review of literature on air pollution is by and large a review of literature on urban air pollution.

Several logical distinctions should be made in a paper on the urban impacts of air pollution. First is the distinction between the impact of air pollution and the impact of air pollution abatement. The two are asymmetrical in that abatement requires government programs whose effects depend on detailed characteristics of the programs adopted. Second, one should distinguish between the nature of the impact of abatement costs and the impact of abatement benefits. Third, impact on whom or what? One might consider impact on the structure of an urban area, for example, on its density. Or, one might consider impact on the welfare of urban residents. In considering welfare impacts, one might want to distinguish people geographically, by central city, suburban residence or income level. Finally, one might distinguish between the impact on things and the impact on people. Logically, one might want to distinguish the impact on animals, but in this case, the assumption is that an abatement program that is optimum for people is adequate for animals. Of course, impact on property is important only insofar as it affects people.

HISTORICAL BACKGROUND

The Clean Air Act, which was passed in 1963, has been amended many times. Automobile emissions were first controlled by a 1965 amendment; the 1967 amendments mandated that ambient air-quality goals be set in air-quality regions throughout the country. Most important was the 1970 amendment which basically set in place our present air-pollution-control program. The Environmental Protection Agency (EPA) was directed to set ambient air-quality standards and to ensure that total emissions were consistent with them within a short time. New stationary sources were required to use the "best adequately demonstrated control technology." Extremely stringent emissions standards were set in the legislation for mobile sources. During the 1970s, amendments have mainly set back dates by which certain ambient and discharge standards had to be met.

The basic administrative mechanism set by the 1970 amendment was the issuance of discharge permits to stationary sources in quantities that would ensure that the ambient standards were met. The mechanism for motor vehicles established in 1970 appears to be quite different, but is not. The law specifies permitted discharge quantities (in grams per mile during a specified test), instead of leaving precise discharge quantities to administrative discretion. But in fact the discharge standards for motor vehicles can be viewed as analogous to discharge permits, but with permitted discharges being set in the legislation. Why the asymmetry between the procedure for controlling discharges from stationary and mobile sources should exist is a good question. But the difference is of greater interest to the student of legislative vs. executive branch warfare than it is to students of urban and environmental problems.

Two characteristics of the United States approach to air- (and, indeed, water-) pollution control determine the course of subsequent events. First is the emphasis on inputs instead of on outputs. Inputs in pollution control programs are capital, labor, energy, etc. used to reduce discharges. Outputs are the resulting discharge abatement. The law explicitly mandates that the EPA judge emission-control efforts from new stationary sources by inputs employed instead of by the resulting outputs of polluting substances. Although the law sets output standards for motor vehicles, EPA has inevitably been drawn heavily into the business of approving particular input combinations.

The result has been crucial and catastrophic to the entire notion of the separation between government and the business sector. Instead of telling businesses what pollutants they may discharge (or, better yet, what penalties they must pay as a function of discharge quantities) and permitting businesses to choose the input combination to meet the output requirement in the business's best interest, government has intruded itself into the details of business decision-making. Government officials are now partners in almost every important business decision, including plant and product design, plant location, and emission-control technology. The result has been to make the United States pollution-control program hopelessly complex and to impair the ability of United States business to respond to market conditions.

Second is the legal mandate to set emission standards on the basis of available technology instead of on the basis of benefits and cost abatement. Both the law and the legislative history display contempt not only for the economics of benefit-cost analysis but also for the entire notion of national problem solving. It is clear that technology enables (or can be improved by research and development so as to enable) society to do many things that are not worth doing. We could certainly run a 100-mile-per-hour passenger train from New York to San Francisco or dig a highway tunnel under the Rockies from Denver to Salt Lake City. With some design and development effort, we could build a tower ten times as high as the Eiffel. But none of these things is worth doing. Common sense as well as economic theory compels us to justify expenditures of scarce resources by examining their resulting benefits.

Of course, common sense sneaks into the environmental program because EPA employs intelligent people, because the courts require it, and because of political pressures by businesses and unions not to impose absurdly high costs on business. But the law discourages it.

The two basic criticisms just made pertain generally to the pollution-control program, but not especially to its urban impacts. They are included as background to the subsequent discussion because basic program characteristics pervade its applications in urban areas and the foregoing evaluation colors all the comments that follow.

URBAN IMPACTS OF AIR POLLUTION

There are by now at least a baker's dozen of high-quality empirical studies of air pollution damages (or benefits of abatement), all of them concentrating on urban data. Following are some simple theoretical considerations and a review of several sets of empirical studies.

Theoretical analysis

The key issue is how to measure benefits of pollution abatement. In fact, except for some arcane niceties, the subject is hardly controversial among economists anymore. Basically, benefits are measured by willingness to pay for a cleaner environment, which is well approximated by consumer surplus, that is, the area under the demand curve for air of various qualities. Since there is no market on which air is sold, the demand or willingness-to-pay curve must be estimated by a variety of tricks. The two basic tricks consist of property-value and wage-level studies and, in the case of water pollution, of travel-cost studies. Execution of these tricks is certainly still controversial but the underlying theory is not. The only legitimately controversial issue is how much weight can safely be placed on the assumption of consumer rationality. That is a difficult question, but some approaches place less stress on the assumption than others.

The above refers to efficiency or resource-allocation aspects of environmental problems. Equity or distributional aspects are another matter. There is a surprisingly strong literature on equity aspects, almost all contributions to which conclude that air pollution, and its abatement, have slightly regressive distributional implications. For an elementary discussion of all the welfare aspects of pollution problems, see Mills (1978).

Subsidiary welfare questions have to do with effects of air pollution on the sizes and structures of urban areas, as follows.

If one assumes that air-polluting discharges are concentrated near urban centers because of concentrations there of both stationary and mobile sources, then effects of air pollution on the structure of an urban area are obvious. Polluting discharges cause the urban area to be both more dispersed and of lower average density than it would be in their absence. When the urban area's capital stock is in equilibrium, it is found that residences have dispersed to avoid, at least partially, the low-quality air concentrated near the urban center. To put the matter more formally, the normal locational trade-off in urban models between decreased housing costs and higher commuting costs as one moves away from the center is changed. If air pollution is taken into account, not only do housing prices fall but air quality rises as one moves away from the center. The result is greater residential dispersal with air pollution in the model than without it.

The foregoing analysis is qualitatively unchallenged. But it is doubtful that the effect is substantial. Air quality does not improve greatly as one moves away from many urban centers, and the increase in willingness to pay greater residential costs as one moves away from the center is unlikely to 'be large.

The second urban theoretical issue has to do with the effect of air pollution on the size distribution of urban areas. Once again, the analysis is easy. Air quality deteriorates as the urban area's population increases. Each combination of wage rates, air quality, and perhaps other amenity variables, attracts a given labor force to the urban area. The wage rate reflects labor's marginal product, but if air quality deteriorates as the urban area's population increases, it follows that the marginal contribution to pollution of an additional worker exceeds the average. If people base their location decisions on the average air quality, too many people are attracted to the urban area relative to the number that represents efficient spatial resource allocation. If the divergence between marginal and average contribution to air pollution increases with the population of the urban area, then large urban areas are too big relative to small urban areas.

Some people use the foregoing argument as a justification for government controls on population of large urban areas. There are two things wrong with the inference. First, the effect is not large. Air quality is not much worse in large United States urban areas than in middle-sized urban areas. Second, and much more important, air pollution does not depend just on the population of an urban area. It also depends on how resources are allocated: on combustion systems in factories, homes, and thermal electric plants; on modes and emission controls of transportation; and on spatial properties of the urban area. Institution of an optimum set of air pollution controls might even cause an increase in the urban area's population. The cost of the controls would increase the cost of doing business in the urban area and would tend to reduce the population, but the air quality would improve and that would tend to increase the population. The net effect is unclear from the qualitative argument. But a moment's careful thought indicates that reducing the population of the New York, Chicago, or Los Angeles metropolitan areas is a clumsy way to improve air quality in these places. A system of permits or effluent fees would be much better. The result might be a modest change in population, but that effect would be incidental. The best qualitative analysis of this issue appears in Henderson (1977).

Property-value and wage-rate studies

Property-value studies were the first serious empirical studies of air pollution damages. The first high-quality property-value study was by Ridker (1967). Early studies regressed market values of residential properties on physical characteristics of properties, on neighborhood characteristics, on ambient air quality measures, and on other amenity measures. The theoretical foundation of such attempts at benefit measurement was greatly improved by a study by Rosen (1974). He showed that such hedonic-price equations are reduced-form equations and that demand or willingness to pay for clean-air equations requires additional assumptions and calculations. Recent contributions have benefited from Rosen's analysis and also from better formulations of housing-demand equations. The latter formulations are necessitated by the fact that properties affected by air pollution are normally developed. Observations are thus total property values and it is necessary to separate variations in property values caused by air pollution from those by the differences in physical characteristics of structures.

The best available property-value study is that by Harrison and Rubinfeld (1978). Their dependent variable was values of owner-occupied houses in the Boston metropolitan area. Independent variables included physical characteristics of dwellings, local-government-tax and service-provision variables, accessibility variables, neighborhood amenities, and nitrous-oxide levels used as a proxy for highly correlated air pollution variables. Having estimated the property-value equation, they differentiated it to obtain marginal willingness to pay for reduced NO_x levels. That gave them the dependent variable in a willingness-to-pay equation in which willingness to pay was regressed on the NO_x concentration and on income. Using the estimated willingness-to-pay equation, they are able to calculate the benefits from given reduction in NO_x levels. They calculate the annual benefits to be obtained from the motor vehicle emission controls mandated by the 1970 Clean Air Act amendment to be $83 per household, in 1970 prices.[1] Multiplying by the 65 million households in the country, the implied national benefit estimate is about $5.4 billion per year, remarkably close to national motor vehicle emission-control benefits estimated by quite different techniques.

Land a given distance from an urban center is supplied perfectly inelastically. It is thus reasonable to assume that damaging effects of air pollution are capitalized into land values and provide a basis for benefit estimation. Labor, in contrast, is the most mobile contributing element, and it is striking that the assumption of perfectly mobile labor also provides a basis for benefit estimation. Assume that family utility depends on income and amenities, including air pollution. Then, the labor force adjusts itself among urban areas so that wage rates compensate for air pollution levels. Thus, regressing wage rates by urban area on air pollution levels, and on nuisance variables, provides a measure of utility lost from air pollution. The best studies of this type are by Tobin and Nordhaus (1973), Kelley (1977), and Hoch (1976). Unfortunately, such studies have not proceeded far enough to permit benefit estimates of air pollution abatement that can be compared with other estimates. But the technique is promising.

Health-effect studies

There are by now hundreds of scientific studies of the health effects of air pollution. Property-value and wage-rate studies are estimates of demand equations. Their validity depends on people's perceptions of the damages done by polluted air. Health-effect studies are analogous to estimates of production functions. Their validity depends only on knowledge by the researcher of the technological relationships between mortality and morbidity, on the one hand, and air pollutants and other variables, on the other. Those who doubt that people can accurately perceive effects of air pollution on themselves and on their property should pay more attention to health-effect studies than to property-value and wage-rate studies.

There are three kinds of health-effect studies. First is laboratory experiments, usually on small mammals but sometimes on humans. Typically, ani-

---

[1] The annual benefit estimate is for 1990, allowing time for the stock of cars to be replaced by those fully subject to the most stringent emission standards.

mals are subjected to severe dosages of pollutants and mortality and morbidity effects are recorded. Usefulness of the studies depends on the ability
to extrapolate effects from the high experimental dosages to the low dosages
to which humans are typically exposed, and to extrapolate from animals to
humans. Both extrapolations entail judgment and guesswork. A recent survey
of such studies was performed by the National Academy of Sciences (Vol. 2,
1974). Experimental studies make clear that pollutants found in the atmosphere affect mortality and morbidity. They also cast doubt on the notion of
thresholds below which ambient concentrations have no adverse health effects.
There may be a threshold for a young healthy person, but exposed populations vary by age and health to an extent that the threshold notion is dubious.
Congress was unwise to instruct EPA to base ambient standards on thresholds
instead of on benefits and costs of abatement.

The second kind of health-effect studies concerns catastrophic pollution
episodes, such as have been recorded in London, New York, and elsewhere.
In the right weather conditions, inversions have been accompanied by extremely high ambient sulfur-oxide levels and large numbers of excess deaths
and illnesses have been recorded. Such episodes have been studied in detail
as described in Lave and Seskin (1977). But the best contemporary opinion
is that most air pollution damage is chronic, and episodic studies miss chronic
effects. There appears not to have been a severe air pollution episode in any
urban area in the industrialized world for more than a decade. It is presumably the consequence of emission-control programs.

The third kind of health-effect studies are epidemiological. Urban area-wide
mortality or morbidity rates, or those associated with pollution-related dis-
eases, are regressed on characteristics of the population likely to affect mortality and morbidity and on air pollution levels. Population characteristics
typically included are age distribution, racial mix, income level, and occupational mix. By far the best such study is in recent Lave and Seskin (1977).
They estimate that a 50 percent reduction in ambient concentrations of sulfur
oxides and particulates from their 1970 levels in the average metropolitan
area in their sample would add about 0.8 years to life expectancy of a child at
birth. This is a dramatic finding which appears to be insensitive to equation
specification. It suggests substantial benefits from abatement of the pollutants
included. Lave and Seskin were unable to find evidence of health effects of
motor vehicle pollutants: carbon monoxide, hydrocarbons, and nitrous oxides.

Such epidemiological estimates are crude because mortality and morbidity
rates by metropolitan area are aggregated over large numbers of people whose
characteristics are not known in detail. Detailed information is not available
on time of residence in the metropolitan area, on location of residence and
work place, on the history of air pollution, on health status, and so forth. Nor
is there a good theory as to the variables that should appear in mortality and
morbidity equations, or as to their functional form.

There are problems with every conceivable approach to the study of damages from air pollution. It is a subtle and complex phenomenon, and no single study or approach can possibly provide definitive answers. But no one can deny that recent studies have been much more careful and have employed much better data than earlier studies. The cumulative effect of such studies is to make an objective observer believe that air pollution levels in the United States around 1970 almost certainly imposed substantial damages on people.

National pollution abatement benefit studies

The property-value, wage-rate, and epidemiological studies reviewed above provide a basis for estimation of total benefits of air pollution abatement. Various government and private studies have made such estimates. The following analysis is restricted to those judged best and most up-to-date.

Based on their mortality regressions, Lave and Seskin (1977) calculate that abatement mandated by the 1970 amendments for stationary sources would result in $16.1 billion of health benefits in 1979 in 1973 dollars. The best estimate of damages to property from stationary source emissions is by Waddell (1974). He estimates that damages to materials were $1.1 billion, and damages to residential structures and soiling of household effects were $5.4 billion. These are 1970 estimates and refer to total damages from air pollution. They should not be added to the Lave and Seskin benefit estimates because of the differences in years and price levels, and because Waddell's estimates are of total damages, whereas Lave and Seskin's are of benefits from abatement mandated by the 1970 amendment. Nevertheless, these and other studies imply that 1979 benefits of the abatements mandated in 1970 can hardly be less than $20 billion in 1972 dollars. EPA (Council on Environmental Quality, 1974) has estimated that the 1979 costs of meeting standards mandated by the 1970 amendments for stationary sources will be about $10 billion in 1973 dollars. Thus, it appears that benefits are of the order of twice the costs for the 1979 stationary source abatement program mandated by law. Dollar figures must be raised from those above by about 50 percent to place them in 1978 prices. Thus, total benefits might be $30 billion and total costs $15 billion. Of course, marginal benefits and marginal costs are the variables that should be looked at for policy purposes. But these calculations suggest that the government program is not far off target for stationary sources.

Mobile sources are another matter. The National Academy of Sciences (NAS) (Vol. 4, 1974) estimated that annual benefits from the emissions controls mandated in 1970 might reach $5 billion in 1973 prices by 1985. The estimate is probably generous. Annual costs were estimated to be about $8 billion. As pointed out above, the $5-billion benefit estimate is consistent with the more recent Harrison and Rubinfeld study. Again, dollar figures must be increased about 50 percent to put them in 1978 prices. There seems no doubt that the 1970 amendment mandated excessively stringent controls on mobile emissions. In fact, the stringent controls mandated in 1970 have been postponed several times and may never come into effect. The NAS studies were available to Congress when the most recent changes in the law were made and may have had some effect.

All the foregoing benefit estimates are subject to substantial error, and those for motor vehicles may be biased upward. But the implications of these figures are unlikely to be contradicted by subsequent findings. First, it seems clear that the government has cracked down too much on motor vehicles relative to stationary sources. Marginal abatement costs must have been several times as high for motor vehicles as for stationary sources during the first half of the 1970s. Second, the original 1976 emission standards set for motor vehicles in the 1970 amendment were undoubtedly too stringent. Evidence of health effects of motor vehicle emissions is much poorer than of health effects from sulfur oxides and particulates, which come almost entirely from stationary sources. The automobile was the whipping boy of American society during the first half of the 1970s. Third, it appears that standards set for stationary sources have been at about the right level.

But the final conclusion of this section is the one with which the paper started. The worst thing about the United States pollution-control program is not the standards that have been set. Instead, it is the administrative characteristics of the program—its cumbersomeness, intrusion into business decision-making, its lack of flexibility, and the rigidity it imposes on emitters. For a detailed analysis of the automobile emission-control program, see the paper by Mills and White in Friedlaender (1978), an exceptional analysis of the program for control of emissions from stationary sources.

URBAN IMPACTS OF AIR POLLUTION ABATEMENT

Air pollution has probably been as well analyzed as any social problem. We know quite a bit about benefits and costs of abatement, about the effects of alternative government pollution abatement, and about the history of the program actually adopted. We know that ambient concentrations of particulates, sulfur oxides, and carbon monoxide have declined substantially since about 1970, and that urban residents must have received substantial benefits from the improvements. We know a great deal about the deficiencies of the national programs that have been put in place since 1970. But there has been almost no analysis of the impacts on urban structure or on the sizes of urban areas of the programs that have been adopted. This section concludes the paper with some speculations on the subject.

First, one should not expect significant results from current programs on either the size distribution of urban areas or on the structure of urban areas. The motor vehicle emission-control program which, as was stated in the previous section, is more stringent than the program of controls for stationary sources, nevertheless imposes less than $0.02 per mile on the cost of automobile driving. The total time-and-vehicle cost of commuting trips is probably about $0.30 per mile, so air pollution controls increase driving costs by only about six percent. Secondly, it is unlikely that current emission-control programs have had or will have measurable effects on the size distribution of urban areas. The largest metropolitan areas have grown relatively slowly for at least a decade, and probably will continue to do so, but that has little to do with emission controls. The costs in question are too small and hardly vary from one urban area to another. Thus, the speculations in this section will concentrate on the effects on the structure in urban areas; specifically, with the effects of pollution-control programs on dispersion of jobs and residents from central cities to suburbs. That subject is properly a matter of great social concern. Urban areas have been decentralizing in the United States and elsewhere for at least a century and United States metropolitan areas are by now highly decentralized. No changes in pollution-control programs, or any other programs, will reverse that historic trend. Forces promoting suburbanization are too powerful. But the details of emission control programs might affect the speed and extent of forces promoting suburbanization.

Since pollution promotes suburbanization, it seems logical that its abatement should curtail suburbanization. The case seems most obvious for mobile sources. The motor vehicle emissions-control program can be viewed as a tax of about $0.02 per vehicle mile on driving. It is of course uniform between central city and suburban driving. The effect of such a tax must be to decrease the amount of driving which, in the long run, must make urban areas somewhat more compact. Thus, it should slow the process of suburbanization. In addition, motor vehicle emission controls should improve central city air quality relative to that in the suburbs, and that too should slow suburbanization.

The only problem in achieving the above is the threat of direct controls on motor vehicle travel in central cities. Two provisions of the 1970 amendment have not been implemented. One instructs EPA to encourage states to inspect emissions controls on motor vehicles at annual safety inspections. Only New Jersey has fully implemented this provision, and only a few states have implemented it in any degree. Mills and White in Friedlaender (1978) claim that lack of annual emissions inspections is a grave defect of the present program. The other unimplemented provision directs EPA to force states to adopt direct controls on driving in places where emission-control standards cannot be met. The law envisages such things as parking or driving bans in congested parts of cities, parking permits that are valid only part of the time in order to encourage car-pooling, and so forth. Such draconian measures are certainly undesirable. They are utterly inflexible and much more costly than annual inspections at set emission standards that would achieve the same air quality. But if they are implemented, their main effect will be to drive businesses out of central cities to suburbs.

Of course, public transit systems are subsidized sufficiently to offset the effects of driving controls on central cities. But emissions controls have had almost no effect in reversing the trend away from public transit use and toward automobile use in urban areas. The required subsidy would be large and cost-ineffective relative to annual emissions inspections.

Stationary sources are somewhat harder to deal with. Standards imposed on new sources presumably are the same in central city and suburb, so no greater costs are imposed on central city producers than on suburban producers. Thus, on the cost side, there should be little effect on suburbanization of employment. Perhaps, uniform emission standards on central city and suburban stationary sources will improve central city air quality relative to that in suburbs, and thus attract residents to central cities. But the density of manufacturing employment is by now nearly uniform between central city and suburb in many metropolitan areas. It is thus unlikely that controls on new stationary sources will have much locational effect.

Old sources are more doubtful. Although there appears to be no public evidence, it seems likely that EPA is somewhat less tough on old sources in central cities than in suburbs. If so, it should slow down the migration of manufacturing from central cities to suburbs.

The majority of central city jobs are now in service industries. It is hard to imagine that stationary source emission controls have any locational effect on service industries. Their only emissions are from fossil fuel combustion for space heating and there are almost no controls on such activities. What controls there are probably apply about equally to suburban office buildings.

REFERENCES

Council on Environmental Quality. *Environmental Quality 1974.* Washington, D.C.: U.S. Government Printing Office, 1974.

Friedlaender, Ann, ed. *Approaches to Controlling Air Pollution.* Cambridge: MIT Press, 1978.

Harrison, David, and Rubinfeld, Daniel. "Housing Values and the Willingness to Pay for Clean Air." *Journal of Environmental Economics and Management 5* (1978): 81–102.

Henderson, J. V. *Economic Theory and the Cities.* New York: Academic Press, 1977.

Hoch, Irving. "City Size Effects, Trends and Policies." *Science* 193 (September 1976): 856–63.

Kelley, Kevin. "Urban Disamenities and the Measure of Economic Welfare." *Journal of Urban Economics* 4 (October 1977): 379–88.

Lave, Lester, and Seskin, Eugene. *Air Pollution and Human Health.* Baltimore: Johns Hopkins University Press for Resources for the Future, 1977.

Mills, Edwin. *Economics of Environmental Quality.* New York: W. W. Norton & Co., 1978.

National Academy of Sciences. *Air Quality and Automobile Emission Control*, Vols. 1–4. Washington, D.C.: U.S. Senate, Committee on Public Works, 1974.

Ridker, Ronald. *Economic Costs of Air Pollution.* New York: Praeger, 1967.

Rosen, Sherwin. "Hedonic Prices and Implicit Markets," *Journal of Political Economy* 82 (January 1974): 34–55.

Smith, Barton. "Measuring the Value of Urban Amenities." *Journal of Urban Economics* 5 (July 1978): 370–87.

Tobin, James, and Nordhaus, William. "Is Growth Obsolete?" In *Measurement of Economic and Social Performance*, edited by Milton Moss. New York: Columbia University Press for National Bureau of Economic Research, 1973.

Waddell, T. E. *The Economic Damages of Air Pollution.* EPA-600/5-74-012. Washington, D.C.: U.S. Government Printing Office, 1974.

CHAPTER SIXTEEN

Urban (Metropolitan) Impacts of Highway Systems

STEPHEN H. PUTMAN

INTRODUCTION

One of the most clearly visible public investments of this century is the nationwide network of highways built with federal, state, and local funds in the twenty-five years between 1950 and 1975. The construction of this system has been accompanied by massive shifts in location, both interurban and intraurban, of population and employment. It is true, as is the case in social science generally, that it is virtually impossible to prove the existence of a causal relationship here. There is, nevertheless, a good deal of empirical support for the hypothesis that changes in transportation systems result in changes in the location of employment and population. The problem lies in properly specifying the mechanism(s) by which these locational changes are brought about. Computer simulation models embodying such mechanisms, and which seem to possess a high degree of descriptive validity, have recently been developed. One set of such models was used to perform a series of analyses of the urban impacts of highway systems. The results of these analyses, along with a discussion of their implications, are presented in this paper.

The history of transportation planning and its attempts to form links to land-use planning are briefly recounted in the next section of this paper in order to set a context of legislative concern for urban transportation planning, including analysis of the urban impacts of transportation system developments. This is followed by a discussion of what is currently understood (or at least believed) about the relationships between transportation and land use, and the levels of detail at which these relationships may be fruitfully examined. The next two sections of the paper describe the examination, by use of an integrated transportation and land use simulation model package, of a number of typical policy questions. These results demonstrate current capabilities for the analysis of urban impacts of highway systems. The final section of the paper discusses the substantive and methodological implications of the previous sections' analyses.

TRANSPORTATION AND LAND-USE PLANNING POLICY

Transportation planning in the United States can trace its origins to the early 1930s when rapidly growing numbers of automobiles began exceeding the limited capacities of the country's highway system. The obvious need for some form of systematic data collection and analysis, along with more comprehensive highway planning, resulted in the congressional proposal of an arrangement between the Bureau of Public Roads and the various state highway departments. Further, the Federal-Aid Highway Act of 1934 authorized the expenditure of up to 1.5 percent of each state's highway construction fund apportionment on surveys, plans, engineering, and economic analysis of future highway construction projects. (*See* Weiner, 1976, for a concise review of the history of urban transportation planning; much of the material in this section is abstracted from the Weiner paper.)

By 1940 all of the states were participating in this program, in the form of the statewide highway-planning surveys. Not long after, in the Federal-Aid Highway Act of 1944, a system of highways, designated the "National System of Interstate and Defense Highways," was recommended. However, it was not until 1956 that any significant work on the system was begun.

The same 1944 Highway Act authorized the expenditure of funds on urban extensions of the Federal-Aid Primary and Secondary highway systems. The home-interview, origin-destination survey was developed to meet the planning needs of these new urban extensions. The emergence of electronic data-processing technology, along with the planners' increased awareness of the existence of relationships between transportation and land use, led to the first major attempts at computerized highway planning analysis in the early 1950s.

Section 701 of the Housing Act of 1954 authorized the provision of federal planning assistance to state, metropolitan, regional, and city agencies. This planning was to be regionwide in scope, and within a comprehensive planning framework. The Housing Act of 1961 further provided assistance for comprehensive planning of both urban transportation needs and urban development. Soon after, the Federal-Aid Highway Act of 1962 encouraged multimodal transportation planning and coordinated highway and other mode planning. The first real effort to provide federal assistance for urban mass transportation followed, two years later, in the Urban Mass Transportation Act of 1964.

The year 1965 saw the passage of the Housing and Urban Development Act of 1965 and the creation of the Department of Housing and Urban Development (HUD). This was followed, in 1966, by the creation of the Department of Transportation (DOT), including the Federal Highway Administration (FHWA). There was, however, no clear statement as to the separate responsibilities for urban transportation planning until an agreement between the two departments in 1968, which also created the Urban Mass Transit Administration (UMTA). By the early 1970s, both FHWA and UMTA were working on joint regulations to guide urban transportation planning. These efforts resulted in a set of regulations being issued in 1975.

During the period of development of these acts, agencies, and regulations, there were parallel and interacting developments in urban land use and transportation theory and practice. By the late 1960s an FHWA-sponsored comprehensive package of computer programs for transportation network analysis was in routine use by most of the transportation planning (highway) agencies in the United States. Also in the late 1960s, UMTA was sponsoring the development and dissemination of a package of computer programs for transit planning. In the early 1970s the two packages were combined. Since then the combined package, known as Urban Transportation Planning System (UTPS), has become the most widely used set of transportation planning and analysis programs in the United States.

Land use, or activity location models, saw rather irregular use and development during this same decade, from the early 1960s to the early 1970s. An initial burst of enthusiasm for urban land-use model development in the early 1960s gave way to disappointment and disillusionment by the late 1960s. The premature attempts at model application, with inadequate theory and techniques to support them, yielded more failures than successes during this period. The inescapable complexity of urban spatial phenomena resulted, by the early 1970s, in a re-emergence of interests in urban spatial models in the United States. By the late 1970s, this interest had resulted in a whole set of reliable and operational land-use models which were suitable for integration with the UTPS. One set of these models was used to perform the simulation analyses described later in this paper. Before they are described in this paper, some of the problems and assumptions of these techniques are discussed.

TRANSPORTATION-LOCATION SIMULATION:
PROBLEMS AND ASSUMPTIONS

Any science may be said to follow phased sequences; first of discovery then of explanation (Homans, 1964). Discovery consists of hypothesizing and testing the existence of relationships. This involves the development of explicit definitions of variables and specification of relationships. Successful discoveries are then followed by attempted explanations of why the particular relationships function in the ways that have been discovered. An explanation of a finding or discovery is a demonstration that the particular phenomenon discovered follows as a logical conclusion from a specific set of general propositions under specified conditions.

Urban transportation and location-simulation models are based on several well-documented discoveries (or findings) plus a number of hypothesized but unproved explanations. In fact it may be said that the field of urban simulation (and perhaps urban economics generally) is just now entering the explanation phase of its first major discovery-explanation cycle.

The phenomena considered in urban transportation and location simulation are a subset of observed transportation-associated phenomena. It is helpful to consider the following partitioning scheme. First, some of these phenomena have a spatial dimension, for example, a transport linkage between points *A* and *B*, or the location of population in zone *J*. Other transport-related phenomena, however, have no spatial dimension, for example, investment multiplier effects of capital equipment expenditures. The analyses described below are concerned only with phenomena having a spatial dimension.

Another dimension along which transportation-associated phenomena may be compared is that of geographic scale. One may consider nationwide effects, or regional or local effects. Analyses may be conducted at an interurban or an intraurban level of detail. While there are important, observable, transport-related phenomena at the interurban level, they are not included for analysis here (*see* Putman, 1975, for an example of an interurban model). The geographic scale of the analyses described here is intraurban, with urban taken to mean metropolitan.

The models whose outputs are described here have been shown to possess a high degree of descriptive validity, subject to certain constraints regarding level of detail of analysis units, and subject to certain assumptions concerning the stability of the system being analyzed. These assumptions cover spatial, sectoral, and temporal dimensions. The spatial constraints call for analysis of more or less complete metropolitan areas geographically defined so as to minimize spatial interaction across the boundaries of the region. Within these metropolitan regions the area will be divided into thirty to three hundred subareas, depending jointly on the overall size of the region and on data availability. Within each of these subareas the activities will be disaggregated into from two to ten types of population and employment, with two to six associated classes of land use. The transportation system connecting the metropolitan region's subareas will be described in terms of from a few hundred to several thousand links and nodes, again depending upon the numbers of subareas. Finally, the models are usually run recursively in five- or ten-year time increments over a total range of twenty or more years.

The underlying descriptive hypothesis of these models is that the spatial distributions of activities are related to "costs" of spatial interaction and measures of relative attractiveness of the subareas in a region. Equations have been developed which explicitly represent this hypothesis and whose parameters may be estimated from appropriate data sets. Models of this type, describing residential location, have been successfully estimated for a rather wide variety of cities with a considerable degree of success (Putman and

Ducca, 1978). Similar work is currently in progress for other portions of the urban activities-transportation system. Analyses making use of these techniques assume that the underlying equation structure will continue to describe the system throughout the forecast or analysis period. They further assume that future values of variables will not exceed the range for which the equation structure is valid, and that the behavior of the system will not shift out of the range of the equations' parameters. These assumptions, which are a prerequisite for virtually all quantitative forecasting and analysis techniques, are sure to be violated to some degree. The only recourse is through sensitivity analysis of the model systems' response to such possible violations of assumptions, thus allowing sensible use and interpretation of the techniques and their results.

In the next section of this paper three illustrative analyses are briefly described. These will serve to illustrate some of the interactions between the urban (metropolitan) highway system and the spatial distribution of activities in the metropolitan region. These analyses serve as a prelude to a more extensive series described in the penultimate section of the paper.

PRELIMINARY METROPOLITAN
TRANSPORTATION-LOCATION ANALYSES

Over the past eight years there have been a series of DOT- and National Science Foundation (NSF)-sponsored research projects which have focused on transportation-location (land use) interactions. These projects have yielded both methodological and substantive outputs (*see* Putman, 1973, 1974, 1976). This section of the paper describes the results of a preliminary set of analyses of the San Francisco Bay region. These analyses were performed with an early form of an integrated set of transportation-location (land use) models called the Integrated Transportation and Land Use Model Package (ITLUP). The results clearly demonstrate, even allowing for some margin of error in the model specifications, the degree to which transportation and location phenomena are related. Thus these results set the stage for those presented in the next section of the paper, which were produced by a more sophisticated recent version of the integrated package, including the Disaggregated Residential Allocation Model (DRAM), known as DRAM-ITLUP.

In the initial ITLUP project three basic types of policy input were analyzed and tested:

1. a change in location of specific basic employment increments;
2. an imposition of land use controls in certain areas; and
3. specific improvements in the transportation network facilities.

In these analyses, the BASE run used exogenous basic employment forecasts which lead to rapid urbanization of the eastern part of Alameda County. (*See* Figure 1.) As this area was indeed experiencing problems of rapid growth,

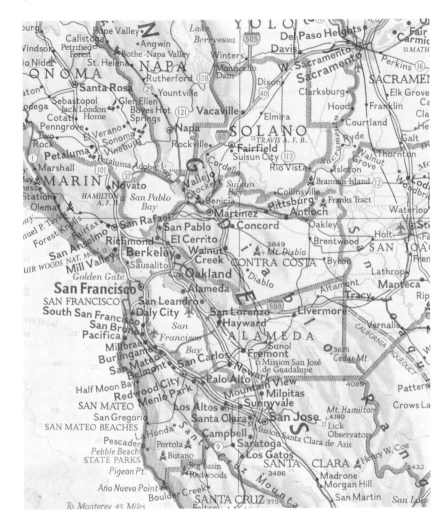

FIGURE 1: The 9-County San Francisco Region, Showing Place Names
© 1966. Courtesy of the National Geographic Society.

the first tests of the sensitivity of the model to policy input examined the behavior of this area in response to different patterns of industrial development. It was felt that in practice it would be difficult to alter the location of existing industry, but that new development would be more susceptible to policy measures. With this in mind, the forecast 1980 distribution of basic industry increments was examined. Most of these increments fell in the northwest corner of the county, with small increments scattered elsewhere. The policy input thus took the form of restricting all the basic employment increases to the present heavily urbanized areas of Berkeley and Oakland in the northwest corner of Alameda County. In this way employment would be directed away from easy access to the less developed areas of the county, and so could be expected to lead to less urbanization in those areas. In addition, local transport congestion might be created, leading to longer journey times and more centralization in the county.

A full run of ITLUP was done to examine the effects of the basic employment redistribution in Alameda County as described above. Bearing in mind that the total basic employment in Alameda County was unchanged by this policy, and that the 1965–80 change represented a little less than 30 percent of the 1980 total, the effects on the distribution of population seemed to be quite significant. The general tendency was for population to move out of Alameda, and to a lesser extent, Contra Costa and Santa Clara, into the counties to the north of the region. Of these, Sonoma and Solano showed the greatest increases, followed by Marin and Napa. San Mateo and San Francisco showed only very small changes.

It would appear that the "natural" area for workers in northern Alameda to live is in the northern counties, as that section of Alameda, and closer sections of Contra Costa, are already developed. The concentration of additional population in Sonoma and Solano suggests that commuters find most land available by using the Richmond–San Rafael and the Carquinez bridges, both of which connect Contra Costa to the northern counties. A more detailed examination of the zonal totals for this run (the actual forecasts are made for 291 zones and then aggregated to the county level) confirmed the overall impression given by the county totals. In Contra Costa one zone, close to major roads running north and east, and containing substantial developable land, showed an increase in population, while the other zones in the county that showed noticeable changes (i.e., greater than 10 percent) all showed decreases. In Marin, Napa, and Sonoma, the major changes were found in zones at the southern ends of the counties close to the Bay. Almost all zones in Solano showed large changes in resident population, the exceptions were zones that were already well built-up. In contradistinction, Santa Clara, San Mateo, and San Francisco showed little change on a zone-by-zone basis. The broad arrow on Figure 2 represents the policy-determined movement of basic employment while the county level shifts in population are shown as percentages below each county name.

Finally, and showing some of the highway-associated impacts, the zonal changes in Contra Costa and Alameda were concentrated in the inland sections of the counties. One consequence of this development results from the fact that the main access routes from northern Alameda County into these areas are through built-up areas and thus are likely to be increasingly congested. The routes from the south, while not such high-capacity roads, are less likely to carry traffic and are therefore less likely to be congested. There were significant increases in congestion in both Napa and Alameda counties as a result of this policy. The trips (predominantly work trips) from Marin,

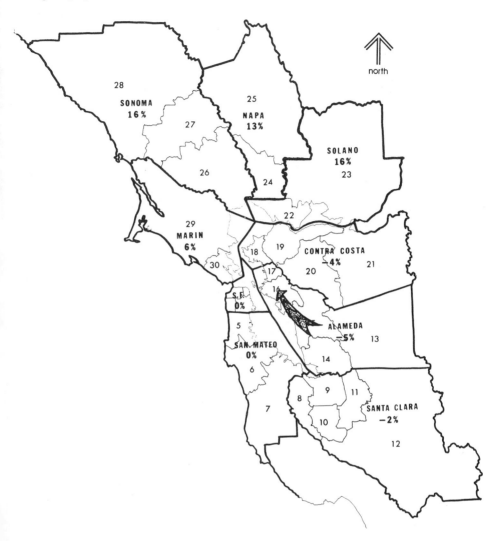

FIGURE 2: Policy 1: County Population Changes

Sonoma, Napa, and Solano were all somewhat less in the policy run, corresponding to the northward shift of the employment locations to which many of the residents of these counties commute. The trips from San Mateo, Santa Clara, and Alameda are, as one would expect, somewhat longer.

The second full round of policy test runs was an attempt to assess the effect of a specific highway network change by installing high-speed, high-capacity links (shown on Figure 3) between Oakland (northern Alameda County) and Livermore Valley (central Alameda County), and between Livermore and an area just northwest of San Jose (northern Santa Clara County). Note that

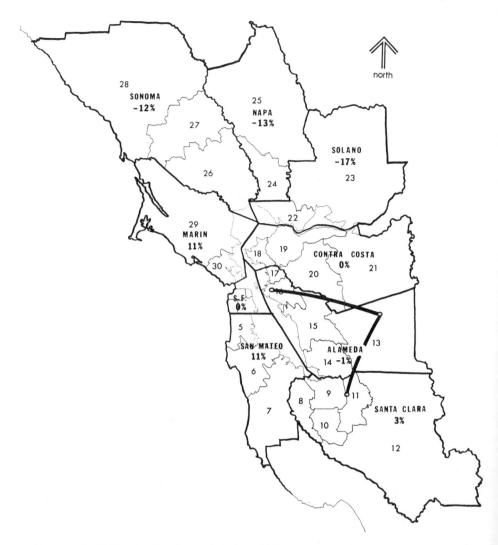

FIGURE 3: Policy 2: County Population Changes

the basic employment relocation used in Policy Run 1 was not used here. Again, comparison is made with the BASE run. First, as might be expected, the three most northern counties lost population, some of which moved into the southern counties of Santa Clara and San Mateo. Somewhat unexpected results came in Alameda, which showed little change in total population, and in Marin, which showed a large increase. The behavior of Alameda may be attributed to the redistribution of population between zones within the county, which will be investigated below. Marin is more difficult to explain. It is possible that Marin and the other northern counties are almost equally accessible, with Marin sufficiently "closer in" that it only requires small changes in the network to tip the balance. This notion appears to be confirmed by the more detailed analysis given below. The bold lines on Figure 3 indicate the new network links while the county level shifts in population are shown as percentages below each county zone name.

At the zonal level, in Santa Clara County, the zones to the east and south of the county showed gains. The largest increases were in zones near the end of the new highway links. This is to be expected, since these are the areas rendered more accessible by the network changes. San Mateo County showed mixed changes at the zonal level. The largest change was an increase in a large, relatively undeveloped zone at the end of the Dumbarton Bridge and thus more likely to benefit from the new highway links. Large increases took place at the extreme northern end of the county, adjacent to San Francisco, while large negative changes occurred at the extreme south and west. Zones in Sonoma, Napa, and Solano showed fairly uniform decreases in almost all zones. Marin, however, showed uniform increases, though the largest was in the zone adjacent to the end of the bridge to Berkeley and Oakland.

Contra Costa showed, for the most part, only small changes. The northern zones followed Solano, and showed decreases. The southern and inland zones followed the inland areas of Alameda and also showed decreases. However, a zone in Contra Costa, which is relatively near one end of the new highway link, increased, along with another zone in Alameda, also near the end of the new link, which showed significant increases. The zones in Alameda showed mixed behavior. As could be expected, zones near the end of the superhighway showed a substantial increase in population. This balanced the loss in population in zones which the new highway bypasses in the Livermore Valley. In part, this is a positive result, since it suggests that such a limited-access highway might inhibit urban sprawl in the area it crosses but to which it does not give access.

Overall, it appears that the regional effect of the new highway links was to shift the concentration of employment and population of the region towards the south. At the same time the southern end of Marin County had a significant influx of new residents, with San Mateo and Santa Clara taking the rest of the shift. Those residents remaining in the northern half of the region found themselves making much longer work trips. Even the work trips of residents in Santa Clara and Alameda increased, as they probably made use of the new road to commute to the Berkeley-Oakland area in northeastern Alameda and Contra Costa counties.

The response of the region to land-use control was tested by rerunning the BASE run with land-use controls, imposed by defining additional land in certain zones as being unavailable for development. The county level shifts in population are shown on Figure 4 as percentages below each county zone name, and the areas in which stringent land-use controls were applied is shown shaded.

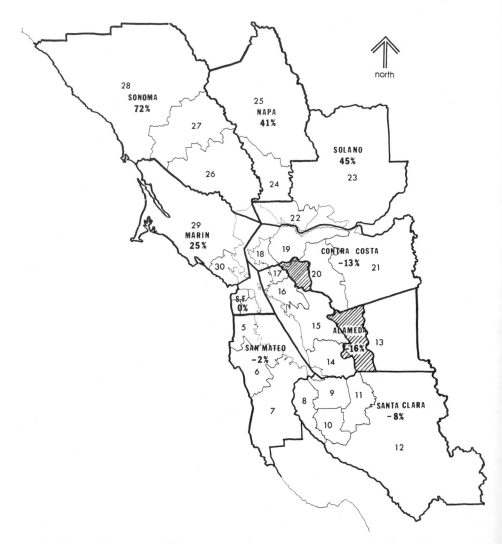

Figure 4: Policy 3: County Population Changes

As can be seen on the map, the effect of these controls is to reduce population growth in the counties (Contra Costa and Alameda) where the controls
were applied. Note that this is a reduction from the "no-controls" BASE run
but there is still substantial absolute growth in these counties over the period
1965 to 1980. The counties to the south and southeast (San Mateo and Santa
Clara) also showed a relative decline in population. This presumably was due
to declines in local-serving employment in Contra Costa and Alameda to
which employees residing in San Mateo and Santa Clara formerly commuted.

Further, indirectly induced declines in population and local-serving employment took place throughout these four counties.

True to the notion that if a growing region is squeezed in one place it bulges out in another, there was substantial relative growth in the four northern counties: Marin, Sonoma, Napa, and Solano. This growth, for the most part, represents residential location of employees of San Francisco and Contra Costa (Berkeley, Oakland, and others) who may have been unable to find residential space in Contra Costa and Alameda. Again, indirect effects via the local-serving employment tend to amplify the situation. The results at the zonal level are exactly what would be expected from the county level results. It is, however, worth noting that virtually all the significant zonal changes took place on the urban fringe. This suggests that if appropriate policies were to be developed and implemented there would be a fair chance of having some effect on the shape of the future development of a region.

We summarize the implications of these few policy tests by noting that in a growing metropolitan region, the actual regional growth rate may be determined by factors over which the regional policy-maker has little or no control. This is even more true for the local policy-maker in subareas of the region. The regional policy-maker finds himself in a paradoxical position to the extent that the overall growth of the region is significant and beyond his control. A policy which seems perfectly reasonable for one part of the region may have serious, undesirable consequences in another part. A salient feature of these policy test runs is the appearance of this regional interrelatedness in the simulation results. In each of these policy runs, a change in one portion of the region appears to produce significant changes in other parts of the region.

To summarize these policy test results:

POLICY RUN 1. A policy to inhibit the spatial dispersion of basic employment in Alameda County by prohibiting new location in the south central and eastern parts of the county did reduce residential and local-serving employment sprawl in both Alameda and Contra Costa counties. In the absence of a comprehensive regional land-use control policy, however, the desirable results in Alameda and Contra Costa were offset by the generation of considerable sprawl in Marin, Sonoma, Napa, and Solano counties.

POLICY RUN 2. A policy to centralize impending development in eastern Alameda County by the introduction of a high-speed, very limited-access highway did not seem to produce the desired results. There was a decline in population and local-serving employment in the area where it was to be centralized. The new highway seems to have been utilized for longer distance commuting and to have resulted in a general southerly shift in the location of the region's employment and population. This seems to have had a substantial effect only in Marin County, the southeastern portion of which witnessed a substantial influx of new residential, and local-serving employment development.

POLICY RUN 3. An attempt to limit development in western Contra Costa County and central Alameda County by the imposition of stringent land-use controls was generally successful in those counties. Again, the lack of a regionwide policy allowed the development which was controlled in those counties to re-emerge in the northern counties of Marin, Sonoma, Napa, and Solano.

Before continuing, it should again be noted that these tests were in no way representative of any real policy intentions known to the authors. They are presented here as examples of the use of the model package and, to a limited extent, as a demonstration of the types of phenomena which are likely to occur in reality. The clear lesson to be learned from these preliminary tests is that identifying the specific impacts of one policy (land-use controls) on another (new highway construction) may well be an exercise in frustration. These actions yield a whole array of impacts both directly and via second- and third-order interactions with other parts of the urban system.

In the next section of this paper we examine several additional sets of policy simulations. These were done with a somewhat updated version of the integrated transportation-location package called DRAM-ITLUP. The same data sets for San Francisco were used, but the analyses of results were conducted at a more detailed 30-zone level after it was discovered that county level analysis obscured some of the results.

FURTHER METROPOLITAN
TRANSPORTATION-LOCATION ANALYSES

The first of this new series of policy tests was really more of a sensitivity test done for the purpose of establishing a range of forecast responses against which to evaluate subsequent model runs. The six runs examined here analyze the spatial distribution consequences of changes in the rate of growth of the region's population and non-basic employment. The importance of using an integrated transportation-location simulation package is clearly demonstrated in this set of runs.

Consider first that the underlying hypothesis of virtually all urban location models is: the probability of residential location in a particular area is directly proportional to a measure of that area's "attractiveness" to the residential locator and inversely proportional to the generalized "cost" of travel between the area and the locator's workplace. The resulting probability estimates for all locators in all zones are transformed into a vector of proportions (or shares) which each area will have of the total population (of each locating group) in the region. Thus for virtually all operational simulation models of urban location, a regionwide population increase of say 5 percent will result in an across-the-board increase of 5 percent in each zone's population (subject in some cases to exogenously imposed constraints on density, and other considerations).

This, at first glance, is not an unreasonable result yet it is nevertheless true that in periods of regional growth or decline some subareas of regions seem to grow or decline faster (or slower) than others. One reason, perhaps a major one, for this differentiated response is the region's transport system. As the transport system will become congested at some places and not at others, differential subarea growth or decline will begin to appear. Only an integrated transportation-location simulation package can begin to represent this phenomenon and thus produce the rather interesting results described below.

For these analyses the same San Francisco data base is used that was used in the previously described set. The results, however, are presented here at a 30-zone level of detail, rather than the nine-county level used above. The six simulation runs involved plus 5 percent, 10 percent, and 15 percent growth rates for the first three and minus 5 percent, 10 percent, and 15 percent growth rates for the second three. The principal basis for comparison was the spatial distribution of total households. It is not a trivial matter in simulation analyses to decide which variable outputs provide a clear and succinct description of the model results; for several reasons total households are used here. Each of these "policy" run outputs is compared to a "BASE" run which involved an unaltered forecast of the region's spatial distribution of activities produced by a full run of the model package.

In each of the six runs roughly one-half to three-quarters of the 30 zones differed from the BASE run by the roughly same percentage as did the regional totals. The one-quarter to one-half of the zones that varied at significantly different rates were of considerable interest. Some zones increased much more than regionwide increases and decreased much more than regionwide decreases. These might be termed volatile or highly responsive zones. Other zones increased significantly less than the regionwide increases and decreased significantly less than the regionwide decreases. These might be termed stable or unresponsive zones.

A third group of zones differed from the regionwide average only when there was a regionwide increase in growth rates. For example, some increased more than average and some increased less than average, with both types decreasing at approximately the average rate. Finally, a fourth group differed from the regionwide average only when there was a regionwide decrease in growth; again either greater or lesser than average decreases with a regionwide decrease, but approximately average increases with a regionwide increase. Figure 5 shows the numbers of the zones discussed below.

Three out of 30 zones show rather volatile responses to changes in regional growth rates. These zones, Zones 4, 19, and 25, grow much faster than the regional average (when compared to the BASE, or control, run) for all six test runs of the models. It is not clear from initial comparisons why these three zones should be the region's most volatile. Zone 4 is an area which is relatively less developed than the other zones at the north end of the San Francisco peninsula. Zone 19 is a relatively undeveloped zone separated by a

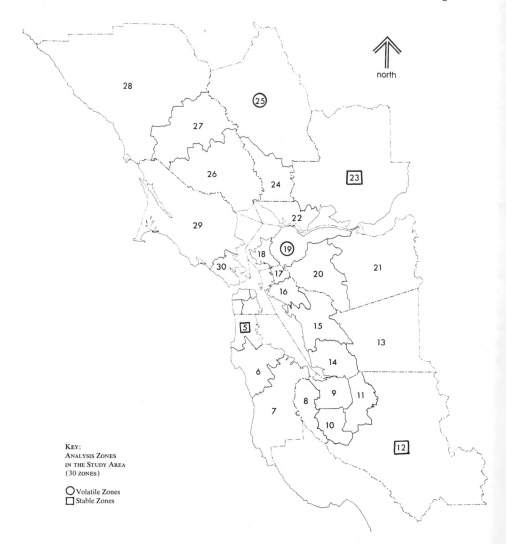

FIGURE 5: Zonal Response to Changes in Regional Growth Rates

mountain range from the rather heavily developed Berkeley-Oakland area, while Zone 25 includes the predominantly rural Napa Valley which appears to decline in the BASE run. None of these zones show exceptional changes in highway congestion measures or average trip-length measures. Hopefully, more detailed analyses at the 291-zone level may give clues to their behavior.

The three most stable zones, growing slower than average with increased regional growth rates and declining less than average with decreased regional growth rates, are Zones 5, 12, and 23. Again, it is not clear why these three zones should be the most stable ones in the region, as superficially they too have nothing in common. Perhaps, however, it is worth noting that on average the three volatile zones show a highway congestion index which is significantly less than the average for the three most stable zones. The difference is roughly that the stable zones have a 17 percent greater congestion index than the volatile zones. Further, the average trip length (for trips originating) is roughly 12 percent shorter for the stable zones as compared to the volatile zones. These results are suggestive but not definitive.

Turning next to the zones which differ only with regionwide growth increases, Zones 2, 6, and 26 grow faster than average while Zones 3, 17, and 24 grow less than average. These zones, too, are apparently dissimilar. Again, however, the congestion index for the slow-grow zones is 38 percent greater than the congestion index for the fast-grow zones (again, on average for each group). The average trip length for the slow-grow zones is roughly 13 percent shorter (again, on average) than the trip lengths for the fast-grow zones.

Finally, for regionwide growth decreases, Zones 18 and 16 decrease faster than average, while Zones 8 and 29 decrease slower than average. Here again we find the congestion measure for the fast-decline zones being 54 percent greater than the slow-decline zones. The trip lengths (on average) are 3 percent shorter for the fast-decline zones than for the slow-decline zones. This represents a slight anomaly in the emerging pattern, but this may be explained by the substantial difference in congestion levels.

Corroborative evidence may be found in observing the effects on Zone 30 of the several regionwide growth rate increases. With a 5 percent increase in the regionwide growth rates, Zone 30 exhibits a 19 percent increase in total households, almost four times the region average (compared to the BASE run). A 10 percent increase in regionwide growth rates results in a 12 percent increase in Zone 30, and the 15 percent regionwide increase yields an 18 percent increase in Zone 30. Thus we see a dramatic growth in the zone for a small change in the region's growth but only slightly above average increases in the zone when there are larger regionwide increases. A quick check of the congestion index sheds light on this behavior. While the volatile zones, Zones 4, 19, and 25, show only small increases (usually less than 2 percent) in congestion for each different change in the zones' growth, Zone 30 shows virtually no change at the 5 percent regionwide increase, but an 11 percent congestion increase with the 10 percent regionwide ·growth increase. This congestion increase (probably due in large part to the Golden Gate Bridge connecting Zone 30 in Marin County to the San Francisco peninsula) apparently has the effect of retarding the zone's future growth.

To summarize these results, it appears at this level of analysis, that the level of highway congestion (an index created by calculating the average volume/capacity ratios on the highway load links in the zone) is consistently associated with the zone's growth or decline responses. The greater the zone's congestion index, the more sluggish its response to regionwide growth and the more pronounced its response to regionwide decline. Further, an additional measure of trip lengths (an index created by calculating the weighted average trip length of all trips originating in a zone) shows longer trip lengths to be associated with less congested zones and thus with more vigorous responses to regionwide growth and more modest responses to regionwide decline. One inference which may be drawn from this is that in zones with less congestion it is easier for residents to consider employment over a wider geographic area (or employees in a less congested zone may consider residence over a wider geographic area) and thus be more responsive to growth opportunities. As a final point, it should be noted that, in general, longer trip lengths are associated with regionwide growth increases and shorter trip lengths are associated with regionwide growth decreases. All-in-all there are clear impacts of the highway system on spatial patterns in response to changes in regional growth rates.

The second set of test runs in this group was intended to examine the spatial distribution consequences of regionwide changes in transportation cost (note that as above, only highway travel is included in these runs). Four full runs of the model package were made, examining plus 5 percent and 10 percent regionwide changes and minus 5 percent and 10 percent regionwide changes in transportation cost. No attempt was made here to transform these percentage changes into dollar terms, as the data available for use in this study were not adequate for that purpose. The general question of dollar cost of travel and "generalized" cost of travel should receive further investigation in any case.

Many relatively knowledgeable persons are of the opinion that in the face of significant transport cost increases metropolitan regions will witness a recentralization of activities towards the region's "central business district." More careful analysis of the dynamics of urban spatial patterns suggests that such "global" recentralization of metropolitan areas is unlikely. What is more likely than "global" recentralization, is centralization around existing concentrations of activities throughout the region, resulting in a pattern of "subnucleation," or a dispersed set of more concentrated urban centers and subcenters.

The comparison of growth by zone resulting from a 10 percent transport cost increase shows ten zones growing faster than in the BASE run. These zones, Zones 1, 2, 3, 8, 9, 16, 17, 18, 21, and 28, contain obvious existing clusters of employment and population. Thus these zones are "existing centers of activity" and it is to them that previously dispersed development recentralizes. The zones which lost population in this run were suburban in character, thus confirming the "recentralization around existing clusters" hypothesis. These results, obviously, are of considerable importance to long-range metropolitan planning and offer further evidence of the pervasive impacts of highways (that is, transportation cost) on metropolitan spatial patterns.

The opposite phenomenon appears to result from a transportation cost decrease. A 10 percent reduction in transport cost resulted in relative growth (as compared to the BASE run) in "suburban" zones and relative decline in the more densely occupied areas. Analysis of the two sets of tests shows that the zones which grow with transport cost increases are, with but few exceptions, the zones which decline with transport cost decreases. A particularly interesting example is Zone 28 in Sonoma County. This is a predominantly rural area, with the city of Santa Rosa located in the center of the zone. Santa Rosa in no way resembles the central business district (CBD) for the San Francisco region. With transport cost decreases, Santa Rosa declines (relatively) due to spread growth. With transport cost increases, Santa Rosa grows due to centralization around existing concentrations of population and employment. Subnucleation seems quite apparent here. The zones which grow with a regionwide transport cost increase are shown on Figure 6, and the zones which grow with a regionwide cost decrease are shown on Figure 7.

The final two sets of simulation analyses to be discussed in this paper are grouped together by virtue of their both being more "micro" changes in the region's transportation (highway) system. The first set of runs examined the consequences of increased parking charges for trips terminating in the San Francisco CBD, that is, Zones 1, 2, and 3. It should be noted that this results in increased travel costs for residents of these zones, or employees who work in these zones. The results of these cost increases were a significant decline in Zone 1 residents and lesser declines in Zones 2 and 3 residents. These were accompanied by increased numbers of residents in Zones 4, 5, 6, and 30. Effectively then, residents were forced out of the CBD to the immediately adjacent zones to the north and to the south of the CBD.

The magnitude of these residential shifts was not sufficiently great to produce noticeable changes in the congestion indices for any of the zones involved. The effect on average trip lengths was, however, quite significant. Before the imposition of the parking charges the average trip lengths for the three declining zones (Zones 1, 2, and 3) were virtually identical to the average trip lengths for the four increasing zones (Zones 4, 5, 6, and 30). After the imposition of the downtown parking charges the average trip lengths for Zones 1, 2, and 3 (taken together) increased by 15 percent over the BASE run. Thus the average trip lengths of residents of the newly-increased zones become 33 percent greater than the trip lengths of the residents of the newly diminished zones. Once again the interrelatedness of the components of the urban system are shown to lead to unanticipated effects of policy actions.

The second of these last two sets of simulation tests involved manipulating the tolls on the Golden Gate Bridge between Zones 2 and 30, and on the San Francisco–Oakland Bay Bridge between Zones 1 and 17 (and very nearly 16 because the actual connection falls virtually on the boundary between Zones 16 and 17). As it was difficult to make an accurate conversion from change in bridge toll (in dollars) to change in travel time (in minutes, which is the actual zone-to-zone impedance metric used in the analyses) it is not

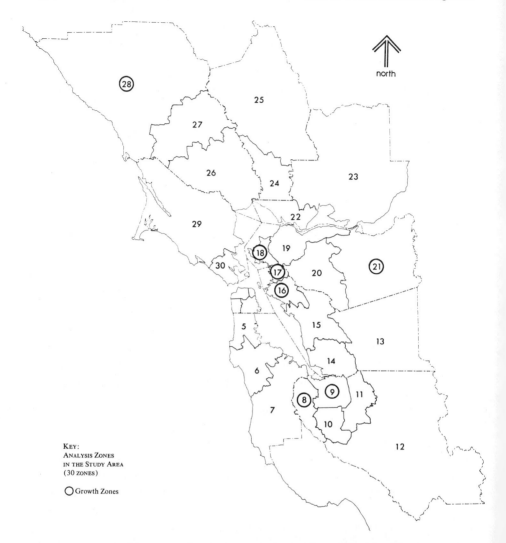

FIGURE 6: Zones Showing Growth with Regionwide Increase in Transport Cost

possible to state reliably what the likely percentage changes in zonal populations are. The directions of change and relative magnitudes, however, clearly show the tendencies of the likely results.

With an increase in bridge tolls there is significant (relative) growth in total resident households (compared to the BASE run) in Zones 1, 2, 3, 4, 5, and 25. There is a corresponding decline in Zones 15, 17, 26, 29, and 30. This is essentially due to a reduction in commuting to San Francisco from suburban zones, plus a reduction of decline in the declining Zone 25, due to

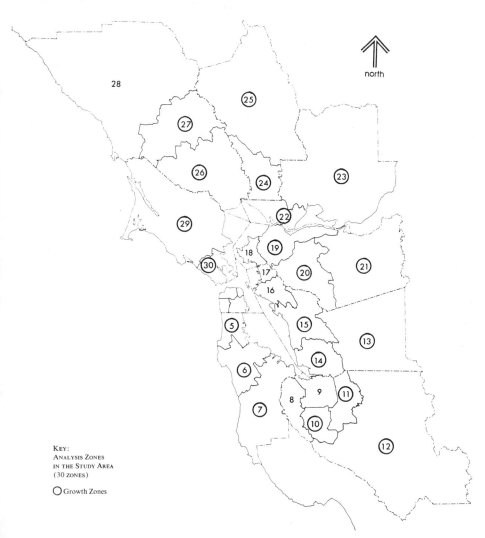

28

FIGURE 7: Zones Showing Growth with Regionwide Decrease in Transport Cost

its population not migrating to suburbs closer to San Francisco, as these suburbs are no longer as highly accessible to San Francisco.

The results due to a decrease in bridge tolls are almost the mirror image of the above. There are relative population declines in Zones 1, 2, 3, 4, and 5, and relative population growth in Zones 15, 16, 18, 22, 29, and 30. The clear tendency with this simulated improvement in accessibility to the San Francisco CBD is for suburbanization of population who can now more easily commute from suburban areas to the CBD.

In concluding this section of the paper it should be stressed that there appear to be two types of effect of the transportation (highway) system which need to be considered in urban impact analyses. First, specific alterations in the transportation system will, of course, be associated with specific rearrangements of spatial patterns. Second, and often overlooked, the existing transportation system will be associated with regionwide spatial impacts that may be as great or greater than the results of the specific system modifications. In the last section of the paper these points are discussed, along with several others, with regard to their implications for analyzing the urban (metropolitan) impacts of highway systems.

CONCLUSIONS

It must first be emphasized that analyses of the urban impacts of highways are really analyses of the interrelationships between transportation and location in metropolitan areas. The purpose of describing the various simulation experiments presented here is to illustrate the complexity of these interrelationships. They operate both directly and indirectly, and in both directions between transportation and location.

The complexity of these interrelationships suggests that it is probably counterproductive to expend much energy trying to resolve the "which came first" type of question. It is more than likely that "growth" accompanying transportation innovations would have taken place without those innovations. It is also likely that it would have been expressed according to somewhat different spatial and temporal patterns. Similarly it is quite clear that new transportation facilities are often constructed in the face of insufficient visible demand to justify their costs.

The question of "equilibrium" is sometimes raised in this general context. This question is probably more misleading than helpful. It seems quite clear that no metropolitan area is ever likely to achieve equilibrium. Rather, at any instant the whole system of transportation facilities and activity locations may be considered to be at the start of a unique path to a possible equilibrium. However, the exogenous shocks to the system, along with endogenous shocks to the system, along with endogenous variations in behavior, shifting parameters, and so on, all operate to deflect the system from this path. This circumstance granted, it becomes reasonable to consider analysis in terms of stable cross-sections tracked along some forecast time path. This is precisely how existing transportation-location models operate, as it will probably be impossible, in the near future, to develop practical techniques for simulation and analysis of dynamic systems of this order of complexity.

What then are the implications for urban impact analyses? From the substantive viewpoint there are several. First, the notion of interrelatedness must never be overlooked. One of the clearest statements to be drawn from the analyses presented above is that there are sets of impacts on the spatial patterns of activities that are only likely to be observed via integrated analyses. Some of these impacts are at least as important as the direct impacts traditionally examined. Highways, for example, have impacts at the time of construction but, equally important, as a system they have impacts in terms of how the subareas of a metropolitan region respond to exogenous changes (for example, changes in growth rates).

From the standpoint of method the same clear need emerges. Integrated analyses of transportation and location are essential. Additionally, it is clear that certain factors omitted from the sample analyses presented above must eventually be included. While this author is of the opinion that mass transit systems do not yield substantial spatial location impacts, their inclusion in the above analyses would certainly have changed some of the results to some degree. Similarly it is to be noted that basic employment location was exogenous to the above described analysis. This omission has already been remedied and the importance of this factor in transportation-location analyses is currently being examined.

Another consideration concerns the specified level of detail of the analyses. Those done here were done at a census tract aggregate level of geographic detail and for only a half-dozen activity sectors. For regionwide analysis this seems quite appropriate. For neighborhood analysis other techniques are necessary which could work within the context (forecast envelope) of the regionwide analysis. Thus we conclude that urban impact statements of highway systems must be done (a) at a regionwide level with integrated transportation-location analysis techniques, and (b) at a neighborhood level, where necessary, within the context of the regionwide analysis. To do otherwise is to risk overlooking potentially critical effects on the areas involved.

REFERENCES

Homans, George C. *The Nature of Social Science*. New York: Harcourt, Brace & World, 1964.
Putman, Stephen H. "The Interrelationships of Transportation Development and Land Development." Urban Planning Division, Federal Highway Administration. Washington, D.C.: U.S. Department of Transportation, 1973.
————. "Preliminary Results from an Integrated Transportation and Land Use Models Package." *Transportation* 3 (1974): 193–224.
————. *An Empirical Model of Regional Growth*. Philadelphia: Regional Science Research Institute, 1975.
————. "Further Results From the Integrated Transportation and Land Use Model Package (ITLUP)." *Transportation Planning and Technology* 3 (1976): 165–73.
————, and Ducca, Frederick. "Calibrating Urban Residential Models 2: Empirical Results." *Environment and Planning A* 10 (1978): 1001–14.
Weiner, Edward. "Evolution of Urban Transportation Planning." Office of Transportation Systems Analysis and Information. Washington, D.C.: U.S. Department of Transportation, 1976.

CHAPTER SEVENTEEN

Impact of Federal Rail Transit Investment Programs on Urban Spatial Structure

DAVID E. BOYCE

INTRODUCTION

The Federal government is currently investing in urban mass transportation improvements at the rate of about $2 billion annually. About three-fourths of this investment is being made in rail transit facilities in 11 large metropolitan areas. Seven areas have extensive rail transit systems which are being modernized and extended at present, and new rail transit systems are being built in four areas.

What differences will this federal capital assistance program make in the existing and new rail transit cities in the coming decades? Will these cities offer better living and working environments, as well as commuting facilities, than the nonrail cities? How will their futures as rail transit cities differ from what would have transpired without these investments? What policies and programs at the local, state, and federal level are needed to reap the full benefits of these investments?

In a recent federal policy statement on rail transit (U.S. Department of Transportation, 1978), some of the above questions are addressed. In stating the rationale for federal support of rail transit, the policy states:

Rail transit can be a supportive tool of urban revitalization. When properly coordinated with land use planning and real estate development, rail investment can help rejuvenate declining core areas, increase the city's tax base, create a more attractive investment climate and promote a more efficient, livable urban environ-

The author wishes to thank R. Abrams and B. Green of the Urban Mass Transportation Administration for providing information on the rail transit capital assistance program, R. Mudge of the Congressional Budget Office for providing a number of useful tables, and Brian Day for his detailed comments and criticisms of an earlier draft of this paper.

398

ment. For older urban centers rail transit can thus be part of a strategy to arrest center city decline and stimulate economic recovery.

After noting the strong role of rail transit systems in shaping the pattern of urban development in the past, the policy continues:

While today rail facilities are less effective in shaping land use, because automobiles have given people much greater freedom to live and work where they choose, evidence shows that when supported by appropriate zoning policies and development incentives, rail transit can still exert a strong shaping influence on the pattern of urban growth. To the extent that it can foster higher density, clustered development, rail transit can be a means to more efficient forms of urban settlement.

The urban impact analysis requirement of the U.S. Office of Management and Budget (OMB) will result in the preparation and submission of policy statements addressing many of the above issues prior to the approval and implementation of new programs. Its intent is to help federal agencies understand the wider implications of their own programs for urban areas, and to stimulate them to formulate better programs than might have otherwise been the case.

The purpose of this paper is to examine the federal rail transit capital-assistance program with respect to the urban impact analysis requirement. The paper attempts to interpret the requirement and to provide an analysis of the dimensions and issues that should be addressed in an urban impact analysis of the rail transit program.

The paper begins with a set of definitions pertaining to *rail transit*. Too often studies of rail transit impacts have been careless in defining the technical characteristics of the modes being studied. Next, the federal rail transit capital-assistance program is reviewed in a historical sense. Like most large-scale public investment programs, the recent history of rail transit investment is not simple. A few metropolitan areas began investing in rail transit systems before the federal program began. The rules have changed as the federal program developed, in response to increasing pressures for funding and shifting objectives of local areas. The brief review in this paper does not attempt to describe this history in detail, but only to provide a general context for the analysis which follows.

The findings of rail transit impact studies conducted to date for the U.S. Department of Transportation are also briefly reviewed. These studies provide one basis for estimating the general impacts of the federal program. They are also suggestive of what actions should be taken by local areas to assure that new rail systems achieve their desired impacts.

Finally, the dimensions and basic issues of an urban impact analysis of the federal rail transit program are examined. This examination focuses on the impacts of rail transit on *urban spatial structure*, which includes not only the traditional concerns with land use and development but also the location of urban activities (such as households, firms) within those physical land uses. This discussion leads to a brief consideration of some research problems which need to be solved to improve planners' capabilities to evaluate alternative transit systems with respect to their effect on urban structure and growth.

DEFINITIONS AND TERMINOLOGY

Terminology concerning rail transit is not well standardized in the United States, and is often confusing to individuals not specializing in transit technology. For the purposes of the paper, a common terminology is adopted; these terms are defined in this section.

A transportation mode is defined by three sets of components: vehicles, fixed facilities, and operating and system characteristics. To a substantial extent, each rail mode can be defined in terms of a combination of these three components. Modes are not discretely defined, but may be regarded as nearly continuous variations in component characteristics.

In this paper, three rail modes are discussed: light rail, rail rapid transit, and commuter rail. A fourth mode, streetcar, is defined in this section in order to differentiate it from light rail. The characteristics of each of these modes are shown in Table 1, which is based on a descriptive analysis by Vuchic, Day, and Stanger (1975). As shown in the table, streetcar is characterized by operation of individual vehicles at grade in mixed traffic at relatively low speeds and fairly high frequencies. This mode was very common in the United States until the 1930s when it was largely replaced by the motorbus.

Light rail is characterized by operation of streetcar-type vehicles, often in short trains, on exclusive or semi-exclusive, at-grade or grade-separated rights-of-way. Their speeds are substantially higher, and a higher frequency of service is typically offered, than for a streetcar. A few light rail lines and systems exist in the United States (Boston, Philadelphia, and San Francisco), and many systems are found in Europe. Recently, there has been a revived interest in this mode in the United States, largely because of its lower cost, greater flexibility, and ease of implementation, as compared with rapid transit.

Rail rapid transit is characterized by operation of heavier, high platform cars, usually in trains, on exclusive, grade-separated facilities with stations. Service is generally frequent and at regular intervals. In the United States, rail rapid transit systems presently operate in seven metropolitan areas (New York, Chicago, Philadelphia, Boston, Cleveland, Washington, D.C., and San Francisco-Oakland). These systems include examples of both urban and regional rapid transit. Urban systems have lower speeds, shorter station spacings, and tend to serve higher-density central city areas; regional systems have higher speeds, longer station spacings, and tend to connect lower-density suburban areas with the region's principal business district.

The two submodes utilize similar equipment and fixed facilities, and have the same basic operating philosophy. The quality of service offered, however, in terms of speed and station access, is quite different. The older United States systems, especially in New York, Chicago, Boston, and Philadelphia, are examples of urban rapid transit. Extensions to these systems, such as the Philadelphia-Lindenwold Line linking southern New Jersey to Philadelphia's Central Business District (CBD), and the Boston South Shore Line, are examples of regional type extensions to urban rapid transit systems. The Bay Area Rapid Transit System (BART) is a rather pure example of a regional rapid transit system. The Washington, D.C., Metro Rail System, when completed, will be a regional system with an extensive inner city distribution system.

All rail modes are electrically powered except for commuter rail, which may use electric or diesel-powered heavy rail cars operating over facilities which are often shared with other rail services (intercity passenger and freight). Service is typically at irregular intervals and less frequent than rapid transit, with the primary service being offered in peak commuting periods. Commuter rail, therefore, is a less-intensive, lower-cost mode than regional transit.

Rail transit systems usually require the support of access and egress modes, usually auto and feeder bus for access, and bus, "people movers" (such as moving walkways and horizontal elevators) or light rail for egress. The presence of these access modes and their degree of integration with the rail mode often determine the success of the system and the extent and nature of its impact on an urban area.

Vuchic, Day, and Stanger (1975) stress that the four rail modes form a "family of rail modes," meaning that a range of service attributes can be achieved by selecting the most appropriate combination of vehicle, fixed facilities, and operating and system characteristics. Each local set of circumstances and objectives has a most efficient combination of rail mode service characteristics best suited to its needs. No one mode, therefore, should be regarded as the best or most suitable for all situations.

Moreover, the system characteristics do overlap, as noted in the above discussion. Thus, two or more rail modes might be appropriate choices for a given local condition, each having a different set of costs, performance characteristics, and long-term impacts. Unfortunately, once a given mode is implemented, converting it to another mode in response to changing conditions may be difficult, mainly for institutional reasons. From a technical viewpoint, conversion from light rail to rapid transit, or commuter rail to light rail, can be readily accomplished. Some systems have been designed providing for such future conversions. Labor union agreements, operating rights of freight services and competing bus services, subsidy agreements, and other institutional factors often impede such conversions.

TABLE 1: Technical and System Attributes of Urban Rail Modes

	Streetcar	Light Rail	Rapid Transit	Commuter Rail
Vehicle characteristics				
Minimum operational unit	1	1	1–3	1–3
Maximum train composition	3	2–4	6–10	6–10
Vehicle length (m)	14–20	20–33	15–23	20–26
Vehicle capacity (seats per vehicle)	16–60	16–80	36–84	80–125
Vehicle capacity (riders per vehicle)	80–150	80–200	100–250	100–300
Fixed facility characteristics				
Exclusive right-of-way (%)	<40	40–90	100	90–100
Way control	visual	visual/signal	signal	signal
Fare collection	on vehicle	on vehicle or at station	at station	at station or on vehicle
Power supply	overhead	overhead or third rail	third rail or overhead	overhead or third rail
Platform height	low	low or high	high	low or high
Access control	uncontrolled	fully controlled	fully controlled	uncontrolled or controlled

Operational and system characteristics

Maximum speed (km/hr)	60–70	60–125	90–130	90–160
Mean operating speed (km/hr)	10–25	20–45	20–70	30–70
Maximum frequency:				
Peak (joint section/hr)	140	40–120	20–40	6–30
Offpeak (single line/hr)	5–12	5–12	5–12	1–4
Capacity (riders)	10,000	3,000–18,000	6,000–30,000	10,000–40,000
Reliability	poor	good	excellent	good
Network area and coverage	dispersed; good area coverage	good CBD coverage; branching common	primarily radial; good CBD coverage	radial; limited CBD coverage
Station spacing (km)	0.2–0.5	0.4–1.0	0.5–3.0	1.0–5.0
Mean trip length	short to medium	medium to long	medium to long	long
Relationship to other modes	feeder line for regional system	park-and-ride, bus feeder; egress mode for regional system	park-and-ride, bus feeder; bus, light rail egress	park-and-ride, bus feeder; bus, light rail egress

Source: Based on Vuchic et al. (1975).
Notes: Figures shown are typical ranges for existing systems. 1 km = 0.6 miles. 1 m = 3.3 feet.

FEDERAL RAIL TRANSIT CAPITAL GRANT PROGRAMS

Federal efforts to aid state and local governments with urban public transportation, and rail transit specifically, began with the passage of the Urban Mass Transportation Act of 1964. Responsibility for implementation of the Act, as amended, is vested in the Urban Mass Transportation Administration (UMTA) of the U.S. Department of Transportation (DOT). In this section the capital grant programs administered by UMTA are described in a general way, and the funding levels are indicated.

Historical information on funding is not readily available except at the project approval level. Project funding categories do not correspond easily to functional classifications that would be desirable for an analysis of this type. Some of the tables presented below are compiled from a list of project approvals compiled by Abrams (1977). More complete information is available on rail modernization programs from analyses conducted by UMTA (1978).

This review of the federal capital grant programs begins at the most general level and proceeds to more detailed categories. Table 2 shows federal commitments to urban mass transportation by fiscal year for a 16-year period. The amounts shown are evidently expenditures as opposed to approvals. The first three columns pertain to programs administered by UMTA and its predecessors. Capital grants include grants under Section 3 of the Urban Mass Transportation Act as well as Interstate Transfer Grants and Urban Systems funds. Initially, these grants were awarded on a ⅔ federal, ⅓ state and local matching basis, to cover the project cost, net of passenger revenues. Subsequently, the matching ratio was changed to ⅘ federal, ⅕ state and local.

The fourth column of Table 2 shows commitments to the Washington Metropolitan Area Transit Authority (WMATA) for construction and operation of the Washington Metro rail system. Funding for WMATA is a matter of separate legislation. Commitments through fiscal 1977 exceeded 11 billion dollars, with 80 percent of the expenditures occurring during the past five years.

The capital grant program supports bus purchases, rail modernization and extension projects, and construction of new rail transit systems. In recent years, about 30 percent of capital grant funds was allocated to the purchase of buses, with the remainder for rail transit. That sum was split about evenly between new rail systems and the modernization and extension of existing rail systems, according to analyses by the Congressional Budget Office (CBO) (1977); *see* Table 3.

Operating assistance grants are made on a formula basis under Section 5 of the amended Act; these grants include some funds for bus purchases, which are included in the first row of Table 3. According to CBO (1977), UMTA's past practice has been to fund nearly all bus proposals. Major rail system proposals have been closely scrutinized, although only one (Denver) was rejected outright.

TABLE 2: Federal Commitments to Urban Mass Transportation, by Fiscal Year, 1962–1977

(millions of dollars)

Fiscal Year	Capital Grants	Operating Grants	R & D, Pl. Adm.[a]	WMATA[b]	Total
1977	1,737	588	120	128	2,577
1976[c]	1,954	434	132	127	2,623
1975	1,287	143	96	127	1,652
1974	966	NA	114	165	1,245
1973	826	NA	152	179	1,157
1972	510	NA	94	188	792
1971	284	NA	57	180	521
1970	133	NA	27	163	324
1969	148	NA	25	6	180
1968	122	NA	10	3	135
1967	121	NA	12	3	136
1966	106	NA	9	3	119
1965	51	NA	9	<1	61
1964	NA	NA	12	<1	13
1963	NA	NA	20	3	23
1962	NA	NA	<1	1	1
Total	8,245	1,165	890	1,277	11,559

Source: Congressional Budget Office.
Note: NA = not applicable or not available.
[a] Primarily research, development, demonstration, planning and training grants, and administration.
[b] Washington Metropolitan Area Transit Authority.
[c] Includes transition quarter (July 1, 1976–September 30, 1976).

Rail modernization grants have been made to eight urban areas, but only four (New York, Chicago, Boston, and Philadelphia) received over 90 percent of the funds through 1977. Rail extensions are major additions to systems in the traditional rapid transit and commuter rail cities—New York, Chicago, Boston, Philadelphia, and Cleveland. As shown in Table 3, rail extensions have only been considered a separate category in recent years.

New rail systems have been approved and funded by UMTA in Atlanta, Baltimore, Miami, and Buffalo. The first three are full-scale rapid transit systems; Buffalo will use light rail vehicles to operate a rapid transit-type service. These new systems will join other new systems or lines completed since 1969 in San Francisco-Oakland (BART), Washington, D.C. (METRO), and Philadelphia (Lindenwold Line). Urban regions have an option of building transit facilities and noninterstate highways in place of "nonessential" urban interstate segments; this represents another source of rail transit funds, the so-called Interstate Transfer Funds. In fact, however, no funds are actually

Table 3: Distribution of UMTA Capital Grants by Purpose and Fiscal Year
(millions of dollars)

Purpose	1975	1976[a]	1977	1978[b]
Bus and paratransit	442	431	480	470
Rail modernization	513[c]	588[c]	384	320
Rail extensions	—[c]	—[c]	137	210
New rail systems	251	359	288	475
Total capital grants	*1,208*	*1,378*	*1,289*	*1,475*
Interstate transfer grants for transit[d]	66	553	406	645
Total capital grants	*1,272*	*1,931*	*1,695*	*1,920*

Source: Congressional Budget Office.
[a] Includes Transition Quarter (July 1, 1976–September 30, 1976).
[b] Estimate.
[c] Rail modernization data for 1975 and 1976 include rail extension grants.
[d] Interstate transfer grants are used primarily for new rail systems and rail extensions.

transferred from transit to the Highway Trust Fund and a separate appropriation is required.

Table 4 shows funding of projects by year, purpose, and mode. This table was derived from the list of projects compiled by Abrams (1977, 1978). Because each project was placed in only one category, there may be some misclassification, especially by mode. Table 4 indicates that rail modernization projects were divided about equally between rapid transit and commuter rail, whereas rail extension and new systems have been primarily rapid transit.

Table 5 shows funding of projects by modes and urban area. Cities with rail systems prior to 1960 received 60 percent of the funds, whereas the new rail systems cities received 40 percent. Four cities with existing rail systems (Philadelphia, Pittsburgh, Cleveland, and Detroit) received less than 10 percent of total funds compared to 51 percent for New York, Chicago, and Boston. A preliminary commitment of about $600 million to Detroit made in late 1976 is not reflected in these totals. Also, the main project approvals to Miami are not shown here.

More detailed information is available on the expenditure of rail modernization grants by function than for rail extensions and new rail systems. Table 6 shows a breakdown of project funding by function and rail mode for the eight urban areas receiving such grants. Rapid transit and light rail make up about 60 percent of the total program. About 40 percent of these grants was expended on rolling stock and the remainder on fixed facilities. By and large, these improvements serve central cities and older inner suburbs. Commuter rail projects have expended a much greater proportion of their total allocation on rolling stock, partly because the fixed facilities are often jointly used by intercity rail freight and passenger services, and improvement costs are shared by those other users.

REVIEW OF IMPACT ANALYSES OF RAIL TRANSIT

Background and orientation

As programs to construct new rail transit facilities progressed in the 1960s in the San Francisco Bay area, Chicago, Philadelphia, and Boston, opportunities and interest developed in undertaking analyses of the impact of these systems on travel, land development, and related matters. The first specific expression of these interests was a workshop held by the Highway Research Board (1970) in early 1970, at Berkeley, California, to consider the design of an impact study for the BART System, then under construction.

Interest in such studies came from three sources. First, the academic research community began to recognize, often too late, that these new systems and extensions offered unusual opportunities for testing hypotheses on the response of households and developers to substantial changes in the transportation system. These interests were sparked in part by the failures of land use and transportation programs of the 1960s to develop models suitable for predicting the future land development that would result from alternate transportation systems; see Boyce, Day, and McDonald (1970) for a review of this experience. The orientation of these academic researchers was a mixture of urban economics, policy, and modeling. While most of the studies, proposed or performed, had eventual policy applications, there was a strong focus on testing models of urban structure, especially models of land value.

Second, some officials of federal agencies, especially in the U.S. Departments of Transportation and Housing and Urban Development, were convinced that lessons could be learned from this new generation of transit systems which would be valuable in planning subsequent systems in other areas. Their interests were naturally more policy oriented and pragmatic than those of the academic community. Third, metropolitan planning organizations in some of the areas realized that impact studies could both enhance their capabilities for long-range planning and provide additional funding for professional staff activities.

These joint interests led to modest funding of impact studies at two universities (Pennsylvania and California, Berkeley) and the establishment of programs within two metropolitan planning agencies (Bay Area Metropolitan Transportation Commission's BART Impact Program and Metropolitan Washington Council of Governments' METRO Impact Study). Subsequently, additional impact studies were discussed for Atlanta, Miami, and Baltimore, but evidently none has been funded. A study of the land use impacts of rail transit by Knight and Trygg (1977) was also funded by DOT.

In terms of urban development and policy, all of these impact studies were

TABLE 4: Distribution of UMTA Project Approvals by Fiscal Year, Purpose, and Rail Mode, 1965–1978

(millions of dollars)

Purpose/Mode	1965	1966	1967	1968	1969	1970	1971
Modernization							
Light rail	—	—	—	—	—	17.7	18.5
Rapid transit	16.7	35.4	—	39.2	3.8	—	29.4
Commuter rail	4.8	—	48.7	56.6	27.0	113.7	14.0
Total	21.5	35.4	48.7	95.8	30.8	131.4	61.9
Extensions							
Light rail	—	—	—	—	—	—	—
Rapid transit	12.3	4.5	62.9	52.0	67.9	—	—
Commuter rail	—	—	—	—	—	1.8	—
Total	12.3	4.5	62.9	52.0	67.9	1.8	—
New systems							
Light rail	—	—	—	—	—	—	—
Rapid transit	—	24.6	26.3	26.0	88.0	—	—
Commuter rail	—	—	—	—	—	—	—
Total	—	24.6	26.3	26.0	88.0	—	—
All projects							
Light rail	—	—	—	—	—	17.7	18.5
Rapid transit	29.0	64.5	89.2	117.2	159.7	—	29.4
Commuter rail	4.8	—	48.7	56.6	27.0	115.5	14.0
Total	33.8	64.5	137.9	173.8	186.7	133.2	61.9

Source: Abrams (1977, 1978).

[a] Includes Transition Quarter (July 1, 1976–September 30, 1976).

[b] October 1, 1977–May 31, 1978.

short-lived. The emphasis was on the short-term impacts of the new systems on travel, new development, environmental effects, and impacts of the construction activity itself. Even the longest study, the BART Impact Program, had only three to four years of evidence after the full operation of BART began to assess its influence on development and locational decisions.

Thus, long-term changes in regional structure, which would be most directly useful for urban policy and impact analysis of new programs, were not attempted in the analyses undertaken to date. Neither the study designers nor the funding agencies have been willing to make the commitment necessary (15 to 25 years) to monitor long-term impacts. Hopefully, census data and data collected by local agencies will be sufficient to enable retrospective analyses of these systems to be made at some future date.

1972	1973	1974	1975	1976[a]	1977	1978[b]	Total
69.5	78.7	12.0	0.3	—	58.4	9.3	264.4
227.9	68.1	160.1	94.8	238.1	199.9	17.0	1,130.4
104.8	42.4	231.2	35.0	153.7	138.1	30.9	1,000.9
402.2	189.2	403.3	130.1	391.8	396.4	57.2	2,395.7
—	—	—	—	—	7.1	—	7.1
43.1	370.6	148.1	5.0	21.0	113.2	—	900.6
—	29.1	55.0	25.7	—	87.6	85.0	284.2
43.1	399.7	203.1	30.7	21.0	207.9	85.0	1,191.9
—	—	—	—	8.0	—	—	8.0
1.0	1,009.3	63.0	—	418.1	428.0	149.4	2,233.7
—	—	—	—	—	—	—	—
1.0	1,009.3	63.0	—	426.1	428.0	149.4	2,241.7
69.5	78.7	12.0	0.3	8.0	65.5	9.3	279.5
272.0	1,448.0	371.2	99.8	677.2	741.1	166.4	4,264.7
104.8	71.5	286.2	60.7	153.7	225.7	115.9	1,285.1
446.3	1,598.2	669.4	160.8	838.9	1,032.3	291.6	5,829.3

Summary of findings—BART

This section provides a brief summary of the findings of the BART Impact Program with respect to urban development, locational decisions, and other variables related to urban land use and development. The summary is based on a series of working papers of the Land Use and Urban Development Project, one of six major projects comprising the BART Impact Program; see Dyett (1978). Webber (1976) has also presented a brief review of BART's overall impacts; his views are also reflected in the following summary.

System description. The BART system is a 71-mile regional rapid transit system which connects the central business districts of San Francisco and Oakland and several lesser centers with residential areas in three counties of the metropolitan region. Of the 34 stations, 23 are park-and-ride stations with

TABLE 5: Summary of UMTA Project Approvals by Urban Area and Mode, 1965–1978

(millions of dollars)

	Light Rail	Rapid Transit	Commuter Rail	Total	Total/%
Atlanta	—	799.9	—	799.9	14
Baltimore	—	348.8	—	348.8	6
Boston	92.4	488.9	132.7	714.0	12
Buffalo	8.0	—	—	8.0	<1
Chicago	—	342.2	228.1	570.3	10
Cleveland	—	65.0	—	65.0	1
Detroit	—	—	1.6	1.6	<1
Miami	—	34.3	—	34.3	1
New York	—	1,060.3	638.2	1,698.5	29
Philadelphia	6.2	117.3	270.7	394.2	7
Pittsburgh	18.1	—	2.0	20.1	<1
San Francisco	154.8	261.8	—	416.6	7
Washington, D.C.	—	746.1	11.9	758.0	13
Total	279.5	4,264.6	1,285.2	5,829.3	100

Source: Abrams (1977, 1978).

about 20,000 spaces. Fares ranged from $0.25 to $1.45 in 1978; patronage was about 150,000 one-way trips per day.

The BART System cost $1.6 billion, financed primarily from local funds. The entire system was operating in late 1974, but service was limited to weekdays for several years following its opening.

TABLE 6: Distribution of Rail Modernization Grants by Function and Mode, 1965–1977

Function	Light Rail $ (Millions)	%	Rapid Transit $ (Millions)	%	Commuter Rail $ (Millions)	%	Total $ (Millions)	%
Rolling stock	131	43	473	41	718	72	1,321	54
Way and structures	97	32	341	30	222	22	660	27
Stations and terminals	27	9	217	19	30	3	275	11
Yards and buildings	18	6	47	4	<1	—	66	3
Operational improvements	27	9	52	5	8	1	87	4
Other	<1	—	23	2	24	2	47	2
Total	301	100	1,154	100	1,001	100	2,455	100
% total rail	—	12	—	47	—	41	—	100

Source: UMTA (1978).

Overall effects. By 1978, the overall impact of BART on urban development in the Bay area was small, but not inconsequential. Both office and housing construction were influenced by BART, and the system was becoming a minor factor in location decisions of households and employers. BART was less influential on retail activities, both in the sense of retailer locations and retail sales.

Many development impacts projected in the early planning stages of BART had not been realized by 1978. High-density residential development had not been attracted to station areas. The reasons may include insufficient time for development to occur, lack of demand for residential and office space in station areas, and zoning changes near some stations designed to protect existing development.

Construction impacts. BART's consumption of land and buildings was not highly disruptive. Only about 1,000 acres of land was acquired, most of which were undeveloped or previously used for transportation purposes. About 3,000 households and 500 businesses were displaced by the 71-mile system.

No negative effects on new construction or maintenance of adjacent properties could be attributed to BART construction activities. The activities did, however, cause or contribute to the decline of retail sales in some areas.

Location decisions. BART and public transportation generally were found to be minor factors in most firms' locational choices. Although access to the labor force was considered by most locating firms, it was secondary to site availability and cost, and access to other firms.

BART was a factor in the location of a few government and commercial offices in station areas. At the regional level, no evidence was found that BART affected the centralization or decentralization of business districts. Retail and service firms located in station areas were found to have almost completely disregarded BART as a decision factor.

Desirability of job locations by workers was found to be related to BART's availability. A substantial number of persons who had recently changed jobs were found to have sought a job location with the intention of commuting by BART.

BART was becoming a common decision factor among households relocating within the Bay area. Compared to other decision factors, however, BART was fairly minor. About one-fifth of the movers surveyed expressed a willingness to pay more for a location near BART.

Development decisions. BART had not caused a redistribution in office space in the Bay area, either in suburban station areas or in the region's central business districts. The rapid transit system did, however, influence the specific sites of several major buildings wtihin the San Francisco CBD. Four other municipalities have experienced increased office construction near BART stations.

Although BART had become a factor in housing developers' decision processes, the total amount of new housing identified as being BART-related was small by 1978. No high-density developments had occurred in station areas. Demand for housing had increased in outlying areas previously perceived to be beyond a reasonable commuting distance to the CBDs.

Property prices and rents. BART's impact on property prices and rents has been small to negligible in station areas. BART may have raised areawide property prices and rents in certain highly desirable locations, and, therefore, may have had a marginal redistributive effect by allocating demand for higher-priced housing to these areas.

Speculation in real property has not occurred prominently in station areas; where it did occur, speculation was in small commercial and residential properties.

Regional effects. To the extent that they have occurred, BART's impacts have taken place primarily at the local rather than the regional level. BART did not appear to have altered the population or employment in its service area in relation to adjoining counties.

BART has not caused special impacts on minorities. It does not appear to have changed outmigration of whites from the central cities, nor to have affected minorities' migration to the suburbs. BART has improved minority household mobility, but has not substantially increased access of inner city residents to suburban employment opportunities.

Conclusions. By 1978, BART appears to have had more effect on location decisions of firms and households than on development decisions. This result suggests that many years are required for the physical restructuring of a built-up area to occur, especially in the absence of an active station development program including rezoning, assistance in land assembly, and other incentives.

Locational and development decisions are secondary, or indirect impacts, of a transportation system, even one as large as BART. While BART will undoubtedly be responsible for shifting the locus of some development and activity locations in the longer term, its primary impact will continue to be on travel. The greatest single impact in this regard is likely to be one of extending the area within which commuting to the CBDs occurs, thereby contributing further to lower urban densities and conversion of land to urban uses.

Summary of findings—Lindenwold

The analyses of the impact of the Lindenwold Line undertaken by a group at the University of Pennsylvania were much more limited than those of the BART Impact Program. This brief summary is based on papers by Boyce, Allen, and Tang (1976), Boyce and Kohlhase (1977), and Boyce and Rosen (1977), as well as several unpublished doctoral dissertations.

System description. The Philadelphia-Lindenwold Line is a 14-mile rail rapid transit line extending from the Philadelphia CBD through the Camden

CBD and into suburban Camden County. The residential area served had a population of about one-half million in 1970, and consisted mainly of single-family and medium density multiple-family housing. In 1976, the Line had 12 stations, including six suburban stations with over 9,000 parking spaces. Automobile was the primary access mode, fares ranged from $0.35 to $0.75, and patronage was about 42,000 one-way trips per day.

The Line cost $94 million and was financed by surplus bridge toll revenues and revenue bonds. The Line was an extension to an existing line from Philadelphia to Camden, which included tracks over a Delaware River bridge. From the time the Line opened in early 1969, service was offered 24-hours per day, seven days a week.

Overall effects. The overall impact of the Line on development and location decisions in the South Jersey area was modest, but significant. Commercial office and multiple-family apartment location was influenced by the Line. The Line became a factor in office and household locational decisions.

High-density residential development did not occur in station areas, partly because of opposition by residents of the communities. Garden apartment developments occurred within a one- to three-mile radius of suburban stations in those areas where land was available. Medium-rise suburban office buildings were built in several suburban station areas; some involved clearance of existing development.

Location decisions. In a survey of residents of garden-type apartments in the South Jersey area, access to the Lindenwold Line was rated as the most important of several factors considered in choosing an apartment by persons who used the Line to commute to work. Persons who did not use the Line, however, rated its importance very low. This survey indicates that a housing location convenient to the rapid transit line was a key requirement for persons using the Line for the journey-to-work.

A survey of commercial office location decisions indicated that access to the Line was an important factor considered in locational choices. This factor, however, was not as important as factors related to general environment and ease of access to the office location by automobile. The transit line was more important in these location decisions for business travel, including access to offices by clients, than for the journey-to-work by employees. These effects did not occur until four to six years after the Line was opened.

Property prices. Extensive statistical analyses of single-family residential land prices in the area served by the Lindenwold Line indicated that prices were significantly correlated with the travel savings accruing to the user, as well as with the usual housing attributes and locational variables. The contribution of user savings to the overall property value in the period after the Line began service was about $3,000 per dollar of daily savings. This estimate corresponds to an annual savings of $250 capitalized at 8 percent. The contribution of the savings variable to sales prices before the Line began operation was about $2,000 per dollar of daily savings. This amount may be regarded as an anticipated increase in property value, properly discounted to a point in time prior to operation.

These estimates were made with housing prices observed during the period, 1965–1973. Variables accounting for overall inflationary trends were also included in the analysis and were highly significant.

Statistical models formulated on a price gradient defined on transit stations were less successful in detecting price impacts. Thus, the functional form of the model was very important in detecting the property value impact of the Line.

Conclusions. The Lindenwold Line, like BART, had more of an impact on locational decisions than on development, although the evidence is relatively scanty. No major land developments have occurred related to the Line. Locational decisions of commercial offices and households do appear to have been positively affected. The Line facilitated outmigration of both offices and households from central city and inner suburban locations to more outlying locations. The Line also increased the rate of decline of business activity in Camden, a depressed inner city area.

Summary of finding—Knight and Trygg

The Office of the Secretary, DOT, funded a study by Knight and Trygg (1977), of DeLeuw, Cather and Company, of the implications of the recent experience with land development impacts of rail transit. The study reviewed light rail, rapid transit, commuter rail, and busways in the United States and Canada, as well as a limited review of the European experience. The principal findings of this study are briefly summarized below.

1. Recent rail transit investments have been important inducements to CBD development, but only if supported by other powerful factors such as land availability, demand for rental spaces, other public investments coordinated with the transit improvements, zoning and development incentives, and a positive public attitude toward private development. The timing of private development was found to be completely unpredictable, and typically more than five years. The authors recommended that policy on rail transit financing should not be based on a presumption of public revenues from early land use impacts being available to finance subsequent system expansion.
2. Rail transit investments have played a key role in land development in station areas outside the CBD, but only if joined with other favorable factors. These factors included support, or at least lack of opposition, from local residents; positive social, economic, and physical conditions; ease of access to the station; availability of developable land; and demand for office space or housing.
3. Recent experience provides no specific evidence that any rail transit investments have led to new urban economic or population growth. Although a major transit improvement project might be one element in a coordinated program to revitalize a declining urban area, transit's effects are too indirect for it to be the primary tool for achieving such a goal.

4. Local land use policies have often been crucial in determining rail transit's land development impacts. The transit improvement itself, however, has sometimes provided the rationale needed for acceptance of such policy changes. A more precise definition of local, land development policy objectives was recommended prior to consideration of rapid transit improvements.
5. A consistent set of factors was found to be involved in the generation of rail transit land development impacts, including attractiveness of site for development; availability of developable land; other new nearby land investments, both public and private; public commitment to specific transportation improvements; local land use and governmental policies; and demand for new development.

The study did not specifically consider impacts on location of urban activities or other urban spatial impacts other than land use and development.

IMPACTS OF UMTA's RAIL TRANSIT PROGRAM

This section of the paper has two objectives. The first is to provide a framework or outline for urban impact analyses of rail transit capital investment programs, especially as related to urban spatial structure. The second is to speculate about the impacts to date of the capital investments UMTA has made. Where appropriate, the speculative portion of the section addresses the three types of rail programs in which UMTA has engaged: modernizations, extensions, and new systems. Also, as appropriate, the conclusions on impact are specific with respect to rail modes.

The section begins with a discussion of the dimensions of the impacts which are likely to result from a rail transit program. Next, the basic impact issues arising from such investments are examined. Finally, research problems raised by the analysis are considered.

Dimensions of the impacts

Five dimensions of impacts identified by Glickman in the Editor's Introduction are germane to this analysis of rail transit: short-term versus long-term; location of activities versus land development; direct versus indirect; absolute versus differential; and scale or size of the impact. The following discussion indicates the orientation of this paper with respect to each of these dimensions.

Impact analyses of completed systems have found little evidence of anticipatory or short-term land development impacts. Typically a period of 2 to 5 years has passed before developers have begun to respond to changes in market conditions brought about by the system. At the same time, there is considerable evidence that public intervention in the development process and development planning can do much to stimulate developers and hasten their response to transit improvements. Considerable efforts of this type have been made regarding development of outlying stations of the Washington, D.C., Metro system. An extensive and highly aggressive station development program has been mounted by Dade County for the Miami system.

On balance, however, development impacts are more of a long-term than a short-term phenomenon. Existing development is unlikely to be affected except in unusual situations. The timing of new development may be affected slightly by transit investments, but in general land development tends to proceed independently of new rail transit system construction. Long-term research is needed to resolve more fully these issues related to the timing of transit-related development.

The timing of location of activities in existing as well as new structures is a different matter. Locational decisions probably begin to adjust to transit development well before service is inaugurated, especially in the case of longer-term commitments of firms and governments. Household location decisions tend to have a shorter time horizon, especially in the case of rentals. Even so, statistical evidence has been found of willingness to pay higher prices and rents that seem to be related to future transit service improvements; see Boyce, Allen, and Tang (1976) and Lerman et al. (1977).

These locational decisions are likely to produce very subtle and gradual changes in the communities in which they occur. Only in highly transient areas, such as apartments with high turnover, are highly visible changes likely. More typically, several years must pass before a substantial change can be detected. Even then, it may be confounded by other events such as changes in household size and energy shortages. In sum, locational shifts are more likely to occur in the short run than are development impacts, but the former are harder to detect.

The dichotomy between land development and location of activities has already been emphasized in the above discussion. Simply because the existing stock of housing and offices is large compared with new development, impacts will be slow to take place except in very rapid growth areas. Relocation of households and firms in the highly mobile United States economy offers much opportunity for locational impact.

Urban spatial impacts of transportation systems are indirect by definition. In contrast, travel requirements of households and firms are directly affected by such systems. To the extent that these requirements determine locational choices, then transit systems impact these choices indirectly. Other indirect impacts relate to opportunities for employment by various occupational, sex, and racial groupings in the population; availability of housing to the above groups; and the tax impact of the system upon households and employers paying for the system. All of these impacts tend to be unevenly distributed with respect to location.

For similar reasons, the impacts tend to be more differential than absolute in their effect on population and employer groups. Examples of differential impacts among subareas are also noted below.

A final dimension concerns the scale of the impacts. Transit system improvements and new systems tend to be relatively small in comparison with existing highway (automobile and bus) systems. The proportion of all work trips on rail transit systems for most large urban areas is relatively small, except for New York.

In summary, the dimensions of rail transit impact are long term, more related to activity location than land development, indirect, differential in character, and relatively small in scale or size. The next section attempts to address more specific types of impact within this overall framework.

Basic urban impact issues

In the following discussion, four basic issues related to the urban spatial impact of rail transit systems are examined: relationship of centers to market corridors; types of employment activities affected; types of households affected; and qualitative effects. Each of these issues is examined in turn with respect to UMTA's three types of rail investment.

Relationship of centers to corridors. Any transportation improvement in an existing urban area alters in some way the travel times and costs among locations. Because a rail transit improvement serves specific points, its impacts are often highly selective. In the case of improvements with extensive access and egress systems, however, these impacts are extended over larger areas, normally on the residential end of the trip.

Rail transit systems are typically radial. A concentrated area of origins or destinations is required in order to achieve the necessary frequency of operation to be competitive with bus and automobile modes. Such concentrations are not required, however, on both ends of the trip, as is commonly believed, if suitable access or egress modes are provided. Thus, rail transit systems can effectively serve extensive low-density residential areas if a substantial number of trips originating in such areas have a common destination. Although the term *corridor* is commonly used to describe such market areas, one must be careful not to interpret this term as meaning only a narrow strip of locations within walking distance of stations. The delineation of the corridor served, therefore, depends primarily on the access modes which can be effectively utilized in reaching transit stations.

As noted above, transit systems tend to reduce travel costs and times in a highly selective manner. The relative changes in times and costs are more important than the absolute changes, because it is the altered comparative advantage of one center over another which is important.

In general, experience indicates that the primary business district of the region benefits most from rail transit improvements. Secondary business districts can also benefit, but are perhaps more likely to lose in a relative sense. Outlying centers served by a rail transit line may also benefit relative to competing centers in their subregion, again depending upon the relative changes in travel costs and times. Which outlying centers emerge as the dominant ones depends on a variety of local as well as subregional conditions including land availability, local zoning and attitudes toward subcenter development, neighborhood quality, and the relative image or prestige of the area.

Within the context of the above generalities, consider the three types of UMTA capital grant programs. Rail modernization programs are primarily directed at rehabilitating existing systems; much of the expenditure to date has been for rolling stock. Such improvements tend to restore the dominance of the regional central business district relative to suburban employment subcenters. The resurgence in office employment of most major CBDs in the United States has probably been strengthened and possibly even increased by rail transit modernization programs.

At the same time, it seems likely that the office construction would have occurred somewhere in the region. Thus, CBD development occurs at the expense of the development of outlying centers and vice versa. Rail transit modernization programs, then, have undoubtedly had some impact in holding office employment in the center during a period of outmigration of office, retail sales, and service activities to subregional centers. Whether this impact is desirable or not is a matter of judgment and depends substantially on one's viewpoint. Renewed development of the CBD is an important element of any central city revitalization program, strengthening its tax base and providing employment opportunities for inner city residents. However, CBD renewal may increase commuting times, costs, energy consumption, and vehicle emissions for employees residing in suburban areas; require larger capital investment in transportation and other services; and tend to reduce opportunities for suburban employment of minority groups.

Rail extension programs have impacts somewhat similar to those of modernization programs. In addition, these programs strengthen further the importance of the regional CBD, probably at the expense of existing central city secondary centers. Moreover, they create opportunities for outlying centers at newly established stations. For example, an extension from an existing secondary center into an outlying area may transform the secondary center from a major terminal on the existing system to an intermediate stop on the extended system. The former terminal generally declines in importance relative to the primary CBD and the newly served outlying areas.

New rail systems have the potential of having the most profound impact on the relative status of existing and emerging centers. The location of stations in the regional CBD and the selection of route alignments and station locations can alter relative travel times and costs significantly. The opportunity to use transit investment as a means of implementing a multicenters plan is a logical application of these impacts, but can only be expected to occur if carried out in a highly coordinated manner. Implementation of a new system without the existence of a regional plan and without numerous other implementation programs is unlikely to achieve the degree of impact possible or otherwise anticipated.

In conclusion, rail transit investment, whether in new systems or in improvements of existing systems, can encourage private investment in the regional CBD, and can be one instrument in strengthening or creating a system of regional subcenters. The substantial experience accumulated to date, however, strongly indicates that constructing a rail transit system is neither a necessary nor sufficient condition for the development of a strong system of regional centers. If a system of centers, including a strong regional CBD, is considered to be an important regional development goal, then it should be implemented as such, and the required transit and highway systems to support that system should be constructed.

Impact on employment activities. Implicit in the above discussion of centers and subcenters is the notion that rail transit investment is selective with respect to the type of employment activities served. Commercial and governmental offices are the principal types of employment activities which can be located in compact areas, and, therefore, can be readily served by rail transit. Higher education, medical centers, and large sports facilities are other examples of activities than can benefit from rail transit service.

In contrast with the situation in the first half of the twentieth century, retail trade and many personal service activities are not candidates for location at rail transit stations. Retail trade is increasingly served by the automobile and bus. Efforts to combine subregional shopping and office centers with rail transit may be counterproductive, because it may result in more local congestion than would otherwise occur. Personal services, including banking, insurance, and real estate, are likely to be increasingly oriented to retail and residential locations, and thus may be unaffected by rail transit investment. Business services, including the legal profession; business financial services; and office machines and services are likely to continue to locate in areas with high access to business centers. Subregional office centers with high quality rail transit service throughout the day are likely locations for such business services.

Rail modernization programs have tended to impact positively on commercial and governmental office activities as well as some universities and medical centers. Major department stores in CBDs have typically continued to decline in spite of such improvements. Banks and other financial institutions serving the business community have also benefited.

Rail extensions have strengthened some centers, such as office locations, but led to the decline of some secondary centers. There is some evidence that stations on rail extensions are prime locations for business services, especially of smaller firms desiring locations outside the CBD.

New rail systems can introduce new locational considerations for offices, but are likely to have little impact on retail trade and personal services. CBD locational decisions of offices may shift slightly to take advantage of the convenience of rail transit service, and the labor market opportunities it provides. It seems unlikely that new rail systems have altered or will alter substantially the total amount of CBD activity, but they may tend to result in higher density development both within the CBD and outlying centers.

It is also useful to be explicit about what rail transit investment will not accomplish with regard to location of employment. Manufacturing employment location is almost totally unaffected. Although some central city manufacturing locations are served by rail transit stations, or by buses providing egress service, the overall impact is small. Land requirements of manufacturing operations continue to be the dominant factor in their locational calculus.

Employment which is mainly related to residential locations (such as education, medical offices, household and personal services, as well as the case of retail trade discussed above), is largely unaffected by rail transit. Thus, on balance, rail transit systems are highly selective in their impact on employment. Since the composition of employment among major categories varies substantially among metropolitan areas, the specific nature of impacts will also differ. Areas which specialize in commercial and governmental offices (New York, Washington, D.C., and subnational centers and some state capitals such as Chicago, Atlanta, San Francisco, Boston, Houston, and Denver) would appear to benefit from rail systems. Manufacturing centers such as Detroit, Cleveland, Pittsburgh, St. Louis, Milwaukee, and Los Angeles would appear to be less likely candidates. Each situation, however, should be evaluated on its own merits. Such sweeping generalizations are unlikely to be sound guides for national policy.

Impact on household location and activities. The impact of rail transit on households follows directly from its impact on industry. Persons employed in commercial and governmental offices, universities, medical centers, and business service firms are candidates for using rail transit. Such individuals and households are attracted to areas which have high quality access to rail transit stations. Such locations, however, are by no means limited to station areas. Residential areas within four to eight miles of park-and-ride stations or with feeder bus service are prime rail transit markets. Such areas over time may be expected to have a higher proportion of the white collar labor force including clerical, secretarial, and business service as well as professional and managerial occupations. Blue collar occupations, sales clerks, personal services, and medical-related professions are largely unaffected.

These residential locational preferences may tend to reinforce existing income and racial patterns of household location. Such effects, however, are relatively subtle and represent only one of several housing location criteria. Local neighborhood factors, quality of schools, prestige, and other attitudinal factors will continue to play a major role. Except in high turnover multiple-family structures, many years are required to establish significant changes in the character of mature residential areas.

An unsettled question of major importance concerns the extent to which rail transit enables households to choose locations farther from their employment locations, thereby increasing resources (energy, labor, taxes) expended on urban travel. Travel time and costs are generally regarded as constraints on choice of location, rather than locational objectives. To the extent that transit improvements reduce travel time, these constraints are relaxed, and households may consider more distant locations.

In the sense of maximizing household utility, a relaxation of travel-related constraints is desirable, since presumably a higher level of utility is achieved. From a societal viewpoint, however, longer work trips may increase energy consumption, reduce the central city tax base, lead to increased segregation, and cause other negative effects. Also, such relocations may result in lower densities with increased costs of public services. The extent to which such effects actually occur requires further investigation.

Certain types of rail transit (high frequency, regular service throughout the day and evening) provide additional benefits for nonwork-related activities of households. Access to cultural activities, major sporting events, and other recreational pursuits can be substantially improved by such systems. Such characteristics are likely to be secondary factors to place of work and local characteristics in a locational decision, but may be of increasing importance in the future.

Rail modernization programs tend to reinforce existing location patterns of the type described above in older residential neighborhoods, both inner city and suburban. In effect, such programs provide a benefit in return for premium housing prices that may have been paid at an earlier time. Such programs may be important in revitalization of declining central city neighborhoods, especially in traditional higher income, white collar neighborhoods.

Rail extension programs may be important in revitalizing older neighborhoods, or providing special character to developing residential areas. Those households able to utilize such systems prefer such areas resulting in some specialization that would otherwise not occur.

The impact of new rail systems on residential location patterns also tends to be more gradual since existing patterns reflect past commuting facilities and local characteristics. In time, new images and patterns do appear.

Qualitative effects. Are rail transit cities different from cities relying solely on automobile and bus transportation? To what extent are these differences attributable to rail transit? Clearly, one cannot imagine how New York, Chicago, or Philadelphia could function without their rail transit systems. But are there also qualitative differences in these places beyond the fact that they have different modes of travel?

Are cities that have functioned for years without rail transit (San Francisco and Washington, if their commuter rail lines are neglected) different now that they have rapid transit systems? How are they different? Do they have a degree of permanence, stability, and structure which they lacked before? Are they more cosmopolitan, and, if so, why?

For the visitor, Washington, D.C., and San Francisco are clearly different.

One uses METRO or BART for business travel instead of a taxi. The diligent transit patron might have used buses before rail transit became available, but this is much more difficult for the occasional traveler.

How do these systems affect the residents? Do they feel differently about their lifestyle than before? In the case of the South Jersey corridor served by the Lindenwold Line, a qualitative difference has evolved. Communities wtih stations along the Line have regional identities they did not possess before. Residents throughout the metropolitan area know that commuters in this corridor are served by a highly reliable, efficient, and modern rapid transit line, whereas others must rely on somewhat modernized versions of systems built prior to 1940. Developers and real estate agents include the Line in their advertising.

Could this same image have been obtained with a very high quality bus operation? The Shirley Busway in Virginia achieved some of the same qualitative results as Lindenwold, but with some differences in actual service; *see* Vuchic and Stanger (1973). Yet there is for most riders a positive qualitative difference in rail transit that is not captured by quantitative analysis. Perhaps the answer will be revealed in comparisons between Atlanta, Baltimore, Buffalo, Miami, and the San Francisco Bay area in the year 2000 and similar cities which did not invest in rapid transit. Perhaps Houston, Cincinnati, Toledo, New Orleans, and Seattle will provide interesting comparative cases. Such comparisons, while interesting, will hardly settle the issue. The question of whether actual or perceived differences were the result of rail transit or whether the construction of a rail transit system was one of the results of deeper differences in urban quality and vitality would remain.

Modeling issues

This discussion of the spatial impacts of rail transit would be incomplete without some reference to questions of modeling the impact of rail transit systems. Modeling and analysis conducted to date have largely been oriented to data analysis and hypothesis-testing related to sales prices, development, location criteria, and other revealed preferences and attitudes. Such efforts, while useful and worthwhile in terms of documenting what impacts did occur, are not very helpful in quantitatively predicting future impacts. What is needed is a modeling system which will capture the spatial/locational effects of the fairly subtle changes introduced by construction of a rail transit system.

Given the negative experiences of the 1960s with urban spatial models, several researchers including the author of this paper, counseled against using urban location and transportation models to study the effects of BART, Washing, D.C., METRO, and the Miami system. By and large, that advice was accepted, although the BART Impact Program did attempt to define and analyze the impact of a no-BART alternative. As of the date of this publication, no operational model yet exists which seems capable of capturing the subtle residential and employment locational effects of rail transit system.

It does appear to this observer, however, that a class of models is on the horizon which may have this capability, namely the multimodal network equilibrium models developed by Florian and Nguyen (1978) and Abdulaal and LeBlanc (1978) (*see* Boyce and Southworth [forthcoming] for a discussion of how these models can be extended to examine locational questions). These models have the property that travel times and costs are determined endogenously. Thus, they have the capability of examining the effect of the supply of transportation services on route choice, modal choice, destination choice, and ultimately choice of residential and job location. Recently, models of this class have been successfully used to predict modal choice, in an equilibrium sense that has not been possible heretofore; see Florian et al. (1978). Extensions to operational models in which destination and modal choices are simultaneously determined are fairly straightforward, although not necessarily easily implemented, as shown by Putman's efforts over the past 10 years (*see* Putman [1973], and subsequent reports, and the work of Kain and Ingram on the National Bureau for Economic Research [NBER] model).

Despite this note of optimism, a reasonable estimate of the time required to bring this approach to truly operational status appears to be on the order of 10 years. Thus, it seems reasonable to hope that by 1990, we may have achieved the modeling capability that Britton Harris, I. S. Lowry, and others set out to develop in the early 1960s.

CONCLUSIONS

New rail transit systems and improvements to existing systems require large-scale investments. The improved systems provide a specialized type of transportation without which several United States cities could not presently function. In other cities, new systems provide substantial improvements in both commuting and in residential and working environments.

Even so, the impacts of rail systems on urban travel, and, therefore, on households, firms, and government are selective. The principal groups affected are white collar office workers and some professionals. Manufacturing, retail sales, and personal service workers are not directly affected by these programs, either in terms of commuting or in the choice of firm and household locations.

This observation implies that some cities, especially subnational office and governmental centers, are more likely candidates for rail transit investment than manufacturing centers. But, it also means that within these cities, only certain groups benefit directly and that the overall impact of these investments may be relatively small.

Large urban areas are subject to powerful long-run demographic and economic forces. Seemingly abrupt changes in these trends have occurred in the past decade, especially with regard to migration, household size, and population growth. Whether the trend toward spatial decentralization and specialization of activity locations within urban areas will continue is not clear.

Rail transit programs alone, although large in an absolute sense, cannot be expected to counter these trends. If long-range metropolitan objectives which run counter to existing trends are to be achieved, ambitious programs need to be mounted and continued on a variety of fronts. In some cases, rail transit is one appropriate tool in this overall effort. In other cases, the same functions can probably be performed nearly as well and less expensively by highway-based transportation services including buses and paratransit.

During the remainder of the twentieth century, Americans will be making difficult choices concerning the allocation of increasingly scarce resources, especially energy, agricultural land, and air quality. Often these choices will result in constraints being placed on daily travel, housing, and the quality of the working environment. As these constraints become more binding, it will be the responsibility of public officials, with the advice of policy analysts and researchers, to identify the most effective strategies for location of urban activities, land development, and transportation. Whether rail transit has a major role to play in this more constrained future remains to be demonstrated.

REFERENCES

Abdulaal M., and LeBlanc, L. J. *Methods for Combining Modal Split and Equilibrium Assignment Models*. Technical Report OREM 78006. Dallas: Southern Methodist University, 1978.
Abrams, R. L. *U.S. Department of Transportation Rail Transit Capital Grant Approvals Through May 31, 1977*. Washington, D.C.: American Public Transit Association, 1977.
———. *U.S. Department of Transportation Rail Transit Grant Project Approvals, June 1, 1977 to May 31, 1978*. Washington, D.C.: American Public Transit Association, 1978.
Boyce, D. E.; Allen, W. B.; and Tang, F. "Impact of Rapid Transit on Residential-property Prices." *Space, Location and Regional Development*, edited by M. Chatterji. London: Pion, 1976.
———; Day, N. D.; and McDonald, C. *Metropolitan Plan Making*. RSRI Monograph Series, no. 4. Philadelphia: Regional Science Research Institute, 1970.
———, and Kohlhase, J. "Choice of Mode and Suburban Apartment Location During a Period of Gasoline Shortages and Price Increases." Final report (draft). Washington, D.C.: Federal Energy Administration, 1977.
———, and Rosen, H. "Locational Choice of Commercial and Governmental Offices in Suburban Rapid Transit Station Areas." Final report (draft). Washington, D.C.: Federal Energy Administration, 1977.
———, and Southworth, F. "Quasi-dynamic Urban Location Models with Endogenously Determined Travel Costs." In *Environment and Planning A, 11*, forthcoming.
Congressional Budget Office. *Urban Mass Transportation: Options for Federal Assistance*. Washington, D.C.: U.S. Congress, 1977.
Dyett, M.; Dornbusch, D.; Fajans, M.; Falcke, C.; Gussman, V.; and Merchant, J.

Land Use and Urban Development Impacts of BART: Final Report. DOT-BIP-FR-5-78. Washington, D.C.: U.S. Department of Transportation, 1978.

Florian, M., and Nguyen, S. "A Combined Trip Distribution Modal Split and Trip Assignment Model," *Transportation Research* 12 (1978): 241–46.

————; Chapleau, R.; Nguyen, S.; Achim, C.; James-Lefebvre, L.; Galarneau, S.; Lefebvre, J.; and Fisk, C. "Validation and Application of EMME: An Equilibrium Based Two-Mode Urban Transportation Planning Method." Centre de Recherche sur les Transports, Publication no. 103. Montreal: Université de Montreal, 1978.

Highway Research Board. *Impact of the Bay Area Rapid Transit System on the San Francisco Metropolitan Region.* Special Report 111. Washington, D.C.: Highway Research Board, 1970.

Knight, R. L., and Trygg, L. L. *Land Use Impacts of Rapid Transit: Implications of Recent Experience.* Final Report and Executive Summary. Washington, D.C.: U.S. Department of Transportation, 1977.

Lerman, S. R.; Damm, D.; Lam, E. L.; and Young, J. "The Effect of Washington Metro on Urban Property Values." Center for Transportation Studies Report no. 77-18. Cambridge: Massachusetts Institute of Technology, 1977.

Putman, S. H. *The Interrelationships of Transportation Development and Land Development.* Washington, D.C.: Federal Highway Administration, 1973.

U.S. Department of Transportation. "Policy Toward Rail Transit," *Federal Register* 43 (45) (March 7, 1978): 9428–30.

Urban Mass Transportation Administration. *The UMTA Rail Modernization Program.* Washington, D.C.: U.S. Department of Transportation, 1978.

Vuchic, V. R., and Stanger, R. M. "Lindenwold Line and Shirley Busway: A Comparison." In *Highway Research Record 459.* Washington, D.C.: Highway Research Board, 1973.

————; Day, F. B.; and Stanger, R. M. "Rail Transit—Characteristics, Innovations, and Trends." In *Transportation Research Record 552.* Washington, D.C.: Transportation Research Board, 1975.

Webber, M. M. *The BART Experience—What Have We Learned?* Institute of Urban and Regional Development Monograph no. 26. Berkeley: University of California, 1976.

CHAPTER EIGHTEEN

The 1968 Congressional FHA Amendments to the National Housing Act: Their Impact on Urban Areas

SUSAN M. WACHTER

INTRODUCTION

This paper analyzes the impact of the 1968 Congressional Federal Housing Administration (FHA) amendments on urban areas. The legislation's major impact on population, employment, and the fiscal condition in urban areas is likely to occur through changed neighborhood property values. Some provisions of the programs have a positive impact and others a negative impact on urban property values. Thus the overall impact of the programs on population, employment, and the fiscal condition in urban areas is unclear.

The paper is written as an example of a prospective urban impact statement. Data are not collected; rather the likely direction of the programs' impact is determined on the basis of empirical relationships that have already been tested. The purpose of doing such a study is to indicate the feasibility of providing economic analysis of the likely impact of major legislation on urban areas before the legislation is implemented. With this evidence, trade-offs between a program's goals and any negative urban impact can be evaluated. Alternative formulations which achieve a program's goals with less harm to urban areas can possibly be devised.

In examining the 1968 legislation it is shown that negative trade-offs do not have to exist. Aspects of the programs which have a negative urban impact are not essential to the legislation's intended goal of increased urban home-ownership. Indeed the very goal of the legislation is hurt by its negative urban impact.

The paper is organized as follows: The first section briefly describes the

The author wishes to thank Jack Guttentag, Norman Glickman, and John Weicher for helpful comments on an earlier draft.

content of the programs, the second section analyzes their impact on real urban property values, and the third and fourth sections examine the programs' impact on urban population, employment, fiscal condition, equity, and racial segregation. The final section suggests ways to reformulate the programs to eliminate the possible negative urban impact and achieve the programs' goal.

THE 1968 CONGRESSIONAL AMENDMENTS
TO THE NATIONAL HOUSING ACT

The Housing and Urban Development Act of 1968 amended the National Housing Act of 1934 by incorporating Sections 223(e), 235, and 237. The major goals of the original National Housing Act of 1934 were to restore borrower demand for and lender confidence in residential mortgages in response to the housing crisis of the Depression. The legislation established the Federal Housing Administration (FHA) which was authorized under Section 203 to insure relatively low down payment, long maturity mortgages on one-to-four family dwellings against default losses.

Congress initially mandated an actuarially sound insurance program with each mortgage to be "economically sound." In response, the FHA adopted neighborhood, property, and borrower standards that appraisers generally felt assured economic soundness. As a result, the FHA provided little insurance on properties in declining or racially changing areas or to low income borrowers.

Congress called into question the primacy of the principle of economic soundness in 1954. To help house low-income families (especially those displaced by federal urban programs instituted in the postwar years), Congress permitted homes to be financed with a $200 minimum down payment, under Section 221(d) (2), and waived the requirement of economic soundness for these loans. Congress only required compliance with local ordinances and with "conditions that the Secretary [of FHA, later of HUD] may prescribe to establish the acceptability of such property for mortgage insurance."

The legislation that directly presaged the changes of 1968 was passed in 1966, in response to the urban riots in the summer of 1965. Because riot-torn areas could not meet the normal requirement of economic soundness, Congress relaxed these standards under Section 203 (1), for low and moderate income families.

Although the 1968 changes are similar in intent to Sections 203 (1) and 221(d) (2), they go considerably further. Section 223(e) extends the authorization of Section 203 (1) so that liberalized underwriting standards can be applied in all declining urban areas. Specifically, under Section 223(e), the Secretary is authorized to insure properties

located in an older, declining urban area. . . . if the Secretary finds that (1) the area is reasonably viable, giving consideration to the need for providing adequate housing or group practice facilities for families of low and moderate income in such area, and (2) the property is an acceptable risk in view of such consideration.

A special Risk Insurance Fund was established in Section 238 to cover the claims on mortgages insured under this program.

Section 235 carries Section 221(d) (2) further (Section 221[d] [2] remains in force). The low down payment provision is included in Section 235; in addition, Congress authorized subsidies to lenders to lower the borrower's interest costs to a minimum of 1 percent. The relaxed property and neighborhood criteria of Section 221(d) (2) requiring compliance only with local ordinances and standards of acceptability were also to apply to underwriting under Section 235.

Section 237 allows the insurance of loans to a mortgagor who is a reasonable credit risk "if he were to receive budget, debt management and related counseling." However, funding for such counseling was not appropriated by Congress until 1972.

The implementation of these programs has varied over time and across geographical area. (*See* Table 1 for the yearly total of mortgages issued by program.) The most dramatic change in the implementation occurred in 1973 when the Section 235 program was suspended. The program was reactivated at considerably lower levels in 1975. The other programs also have declined in size over time though not as dramatically. The special programs represented almost half of all FHA-insured mortgages in 1971, the year of their peak use. In 1977, less than 15 percent of FHA-insured mortgages fell under these programs.

Cities across the country differ substantially in the use of these programs with no apparent regional pattern to this variation. (*See* Table 2 for program

TABLE 1: Number of Mortgages Issued, by Program, U.S., 1968–1977

	Section 203	*Section 221(d)(2)*	*Section 223(e)*	*Section 235*	*Section 237*
1968	371,256	40,748	—	—	—
1969	341,639	73,073	45,828	25,613	—
1970	274,020	78,984	27,694	105,229	909
1971	305,948	98,314	19,548	144,248	566
1972	216,153	76,693	14,057	119,247	562
1973	125,596	48,240	10,352	57,673	428
1974	142,007	34,275	8,211	13,962	346
1975	214,327	27,606	6,389	5,695	248
1976	219,211	25,318	6,223[a]	280	263
1977	272,496	34,330	8,511[b]	62	271

Source: Compiled from HUD-FHA, Management Information Division, Single Family Insured Branch, Statistic Volumes.

Note: Data are in numbers of mortgages issued under each section. Value issued is not available.

[a] Rev. 837.

[b] Rev. 7227.

TABLE 2: Number of Loans Issued under Each Section, by City, 1968–1977

	Total		Section 203		Section 221(d)(2)		Section 223(e)		Section 235		Section 237	
	No.	% Total	No.	% Total	No.	% Total	No.	% Total	No.	% Total	No.	% Total
Philadelphia	94,688	100	45,569	48.13	40,987	43.29	6,032	6.37	1,841	1.94	259	0.27
New York	94,543	100	79,283	83.86	6,551	6.93	8,058	8.52	651	0.69	—	—
Atlanta	40,798	100	31,607	77.47	4,828	11.83	1,461	3.58	2,775	6.80	127	0.31
Dallas	101,144	100	74,216	73.38	11,906	11.77	3,433	3.39	11,588	11.46	1	—
Los Angeles	128,243	100	66,253	51.66	53,091	41.40	3,479	2.71	5,419	4.23	1	—
Chicago	114,117	100	81,627	71.53	7,649	6.70	16,927	14.83	7,906	6.93	8	—
St. Louis	39,488	100	23,856	60.41	7,094	17.96	4,365	11.05	3,253	8.24	920	2.33
Minneapolis-St. Paul	54,424	100	49,731	91.21	1,231	2.26	1,171	2.33	2,274	4.17	17	0.03
Boston	17,514	100	14,437	82.43	554	3.16	2,010	11.48	513	2.93	—	—

Source: Compiled from HUD-FHA, Management Information Division, Single Family Insured Branch, Statistic Volumes.

use in selected cities.) However, there is a strong pattern to the geographical dispersion of loans under these programs within regions: these are urban rather than suburban or rural programs. Nearly 100 percent of Section 223(e) mortgages are in urban areas as intended. Approximately 80 percent of Section 235 loans are urban. Section 237 has been a relatively small program but again it is about 75 percent urban. Thus the changed underwriting procedures have had a direct impact on urban housing markets and through this, an indirect impact on urban-suburban migration patterns. The nature of the impact, direct and indirect, is examined in the following sections.

IMPACT OF SECTIONS 223(e), 235, AND 237
ON NEIGHBORHOOD PROPERTY VALUES

This section attempts to evaluate the impact of the 1968 legislation on urban neighborhood property values. Our concern is with change in real-site value caused by the 1968 programs as opposed to change caused by other factors. Given the role of other factors, has the impact of these programs been positive, negative, or zero? Because the programs' principal provisions are likely to affect site value in opposing directions, the answer is by no means clear. Aspects of the programs which are likely to have negative and positive effects are discussed separately and the overall impact by program is evaluated.

Sources of negative impact on neighborhood property values

This section links several provisions of the FHA legislation of 1968 and pre-existing FHA procedures to neighborhood property value decline. The first part discusses aspects of the legislation which increase the likelihood that borrowers will default and undermaintain their properties. The second analyzes incentives for lenders using FHA underwriting both to select risky loans and to foreclose quickly. The third examines lender incentives which lead defaulted FHA-insured properties to be abandoned. And the fourth links these aspects of the 1968 legislation and FHA procedures to declines in real urban property values through neighborhood effects.

Default and undermaintenance under provisions of the 1968 legislation. The 1968 legislation increases the availability of low down payment loans and extends FHA underwriting to previously ineligible borrowers and properties. These changes may increase the likelihood that borrowers will default and undermaintain their properties through the following mechanisms.

First, the high (mortgage) loan-to-(property) value ratio which results from a low down payment requirement increases the borrower's incentive to default. Even if a borrower-household has difficulty in maintaining its mortgage payments due to loss of job or illness, for example, default and foreclosure need not result. If the property can be sold for sufficiently more than the amount of the mortgage, the borrower-household may be able to recover some of its equity after paying for missed mortgage installments and still be compensated for the time and effort of selling. If so, choosing the route of default and foreclosure is irrational. With foreclosure the house is sold at a sheriff's sale which generally brings a lower price than a sale by the owner (especially if, as in many cases, the house is vacant and subject to vandalism before the final sale). A likely result is the loss of some or all of the owner's equity.[1] With a high loan-to-value mortgage, the borrower has limited equity in the property, perhaps an insufficient amount to cover missed mortgage payments. In this case, there is no gain to the borrower in selling versus default: in either event the equity will be lost.

Second, the availability of insured high loan-to-value mortgages affects the composition of borrowers. Borrowers who are capable of paying high down payments usually have the financial resources to deal with emergencies without defaulting. High loan-to-value loans, insured by the FHA, encourage lending to borrowers with lower financial reserves. Inasmuch as they do not have a source of inexpensive borrowing, they may be more likely to default than to borrow or sell assets.[2] In addition, the relaxing of borrower credit standards under Section 237 directly encourages lending to those who may lack the financial resources.

Third, the likelihood of physical deterioration in a property insured under these programs may be increased because while property standards have been lowered, interest subsidies and/or income limits have not been raised to take into account the greater maintenance expenditures required by less sound structures.[3]

Fourth, the increased availability of low down payment mortgages in declining areas may affect borrower housing-investment decisions. The borrower-household has the option of maintaining and investing in its house. In declining neighborhoods (such as those authorized for FHA insured lending by Section 223[e]), investments and maintenance expenditures may be less likely to be

[1] It should be noted that even though choosing default may be irrational, the borrower under FHA may have little choice because of the incentive to foreclose defaulted FHA mortgages quickly. This is discussed in the following section.

[2] The impact of high loan-to-value ratios on default rates may be large. Von Furstenberg (1971), indicates that default rates rise with the loan-to-value ratio on an increasing scale, the higher the ratio. For example, default rates increase by 16 percent when the loan-to-value ratio rises from 90 percent to 91 percent, they jump by 50 percent when it rises from 96 percent to 97 percent. Default rates are shown to quadruple (holding other variables such as income constant) as loan-to-value ratios go from 90 percent to 97 percent (the former is the ratio generally given on privately insured conventional loans, the latter on Section 223[e] loans).

[3] It is also true that structural defects, not known at the time of sale, once they are obvious, lower property value and wipe out borrower equity. Borrowers may have relied on FHA insurance as a sign of structural adequacy and paid higher prices than they otherwise would have. HUD now offers to compensate homeowners for repairs required by defects, that threaten occupant safety, if a proper FHA inspection could have disclosed the defects.

reflected in selling prices when a property is sold. An a result of the actual or expected decline homeowners may have less incentive and may be less likely to reinvest in their homes.

Fifth, the down payment requirement deals only with the loan-to-value ratio at the time of purchase. The ratio will rise during the course of the mortgage lending period if the value of the property falls faster than the value of the mortgage through amortization. The value of a property may fall over time due either to deterioration in the physical condition of the property or to deterioration in the value of surrounding property. Loan-to-value ratios are more likely to increase over time on loans collateralized by properties in poor condition and in declining areas, with the consequent impact on borrower default incentives discussed above.

In addition, the incentive to default deriving from a high loan-to-value ratio may also discourage property maintenance. The defaulting borrower has no incentive (and may lack the finances) to maintain or invest in a property whose sales price will go entirely to the mortgagee. As a result, the decision to default on the mortgage (due to the borrower's low equity) is likely to be accompanied by a decision not to maintain the property before foreclosure.

In sum, low down payment provisions together with changed underwriting criteria may increase the likelihood of default and property undermaintenance. In the following it is shown that the FHA-insured lender, especially because FHA mortgages are often discounted, has little or no incentive to keep the defaulted property from being foreclosed and the foreclosed property from being abandoned. The undermaintenance and deterioration of a property, especially its abandonment, can cause neighboring properties' land values to fall even when they are physically unchanged. Once land values decline the demand for housing services in the area is likely to fall, with the result that the surrounding properties are physically undermaintained. Thus the abandonment or undermaintenance of a property insured under these programs may, through neighborhood effects, cause an overall deterioration in neighborhood land and housing stock values.

Financing risky loans and foreclosure: FHA-insured lenders' incentives. This section explores the incentives for mortgage lenders using FHA underwriting to finance risky properties and borrowers and to foreclose as quickly as possible. These incentives are created by the setting of FHA interest rates below market rates, which results in points being charged to raise the effective interest rate.

To illustrate, assume an FHA rate fixed at 6 percent, with a market rate of 6.5 percent. Assuming the loan is repaid in 30 years, the lender attains an effective yield equal to the market rate of 6.5 percent by charging 5 points.[4] That is, on a mortgage of $15,000, the lender may give the borrower a check for only $14,250 while requiring the repayment of $15,000 (the $750 dif-

---

[4] For the method of calculating the effective yield, see Curley and Guttentag (1977).

ference is 5 percent of $15,000 or the 5 points). The borrower pays a contract interest rate of 6 percent on $15,000 while receiving $14,250. The 6 percent contract interest rate is not the effective yield on the loan. The effective yield depends on when the principal is repaid.

The sooner the loan is repaid, the greater is the return. To illustrate, with repayment in six months, $15,000 is made on a $14,250 investment for a greater than 10 percent annual rate of return *without* including interest payments. Thus there may be a financial incentive for lenders to seek prepayment of discounted FHA loans and the larger the discount the greater the incentive. Whether there is such an incentive depends on the legal, administrative, and financial costs involved in the foreclosure process, which vary by state and by lender.[5]

Prepayment of FHA loans can be encouraged in two ways. First, defaulted FHA loans can be foreclosed quickly. Second, those loans likely to default quickly can be actively selected. Given that points may not vary with the characteristics of the loan, there may be an incentive, in order to maximize the return on invested capital, to finance the worst loans acceptable to FHA. Because lenders only have a limited amount of funds that they invest in urban housing, lowering FHA's minimum lending standards may make it more difficult to get financing for urban areas where these standards are not met.

Property abandonment: FHA-insured lenders' incentives. Property abandonment may be more likely to result after default on an FHA-insured mortgage than after default on an uninsured mortgage. This can be attributed to the delay between default and resale and to the greater stake that the uninsured lender has in the mortgaged property during this period.

A delay is mandated by FHA regulation and by state law (the latter applies to both FHA and conventional loans). First, there is a period of forebearance (of 3 months under FHA regulation) during which the property cannot be sold.[6] In this period, there is clearly a lessened incentive for the defaulting household to maintain the property. Second, after the foreclosure sale has taken place, there is, in many states, a statutory redemption period when the defaulting household has an option to repurchase. In some states, the delay between default and resale may extend to two years.

---

[5] It has been estimated that, on the average, such costs are exceeded by the gains of early repayment when loans are made at 4 or more discount points. See Curley and Guttentag (1977). Since 1968, an increasing share of FHA-insured loans has become packaged in Government National Mortgage Association (GNMA) and Federal National Mortgage Association (FNMA) mortgage-backed securities. Mortgage bankers are unlikely to have an incentive to originate bad loans to be packaged in these instruments. There still may be an incentive for the servicers of these loans to foreclose quickly because of the high cost of servicing delinquent accounts. In addition, loan generation procedures may be set up (for example, which areas and brokers are well serviced and which are not) with the aim of generating risky loans, and these will affect the quality of all loans.

[6] A borrower now has a minimum of three months after default before foreclosure can take place, as a result of a recent FHA regulation. This eliminates the worst abuses and gives the borrower at least some time to find a buyer.

Conventional mortgagees have a stake in maintaining the value of their properties. The value of the property at the end of the redemption period determines whether the mortgagee will be repaid in full. Thus considerable resources in terms of time and money may be spent (depending on the value of the property) in preventing property value decline after a mortgage payment is missed.[7]

Under FHA regulations the lending institution is obligated to maintain a vacated property before it is conveyed to HUD.[8] However, in the past, there seems to have been limited enforcement of these regulations (Bradford et al., 1975, pp. 121–62), and it is not clear whether enforcement can be cost efficient.[9] After foreclosure or receipt of deed-in-lieu of foreclosure, the FHA-insured property is usually unoccupied until resale and there is a significant likelihood of vandalism. As a result properties mortgaged by defaulted FHA loans deteriorate further and contribute to the cycle of neighborhood decay that may or may not have initiated the default.

Overview of the negative impact. To the extent the low down payment mortgages financed under the programs replace conventional mortgages, seasoned mortgages (that have been substantially or wholly paid off) and Section 203 mortgages, and to the extent they replace mortgages on properties whose value is less likely to decline over time, higher loan-to-value ratios result, which

[7] Conversations with bankers attest to the use of various strategies: First, if it seems likely that the mortgagor will repay the loan and is maintaining the property, mortgage payments may be renegotiated to allow the mortgagor to continue in the property. Second, if this is not the case and foreclosure occurs, a temporary renter may be sought who will make sure the property is not vandalized for perhaps a nominal rent. Even though the property is occupied, conventional lenders may arrange for regular surveillance to make certain the property is maintained during the period before resale. Third, resale is arranged as expeditiously as possible through purchase money mortgages or other financing options. Fourth, in the conventional market where the risk of default is high, mortgagees may make use of the land installment contract because it allows for the simple and quick repossession of the property. (Under the land installment contract the seller retains title to the mortgage until the balance of the mortgage is paid. In this sense it differs from the other mortgages where title is delivered to the buyer at the time of the execution of the agreement.) A study by Frederick Flick (1977) indicates that in one city, Marquette, the new programs have largely substituted for this form of financing.

[8] HUD encourages the receipt of deed-in-lieu of foreclosure, when property title is clear. This eliminates the redemption period and shortens the time before resale. In addition, official HUD-FHA policy has been to encourage lenders to exercise forbearance when borrowers become delinquent. The HUD handbook states that "foreclosure is a last resort and shall not be initiated until all other servicing have been exhausted."

[9] According to the study, "Protecting and Disposing of Single Family Properties Acquired by the Department of Housing and Urban Development," *Report of the Comptroller General of the U.S.* (Washington, D.C.: U.S. Government Printing Office, 1976), HUD lost an average of $9,341 on each home that it acquired. To mitigate such losses, FHA has instituted some new procedures, but these procedures are not costless. First, FHA has increased the incentive to the lender to assign defaulting mortgages to FHA (which then negotiates a mortgage payment schedule with the delinquent borrower) rather than to foreclose them. The lender receives 100 percent of the mortgage in either

increase borrowers' incentives to undermaintain their properties and default. To the extent the mortgages replace conventional co-insured financing, and default does occur, there is increased likelihood of abandonment due to lenders' incentives, given FHA insurance.

Neighborhood effects then cause a decrease in land values of properties surrounding the undermaintained or abandoned property. Because of the decline in land values, investment in the neighboring properties is less likely to be reflected in the price of the properties when sold. As a result, surrounding properties are undermaintained and more likely to deteriorate over time. The area becomes a less attractive one for equity and conventional mortgage financing. In the long run, the net flow of mortgage money (FHA and conventional) to the neighborhood may decline. Thus, the abandonment or undermaintenance of a property insured under these programs may, through neighborhood effects, cause deterioration in neighborhood land and housing-stock values.

The legislation also has an impact in areas where properties are not insured under the programs. Because the funds that lenders invest in urban mortgages are somewhat limited by portfolio considerations, the funds that otherwise would be used to provide mortgages for other urban properties are diverted to financing mortgages under these programs. This is because the FHA encourages lending under these programs through interest subsidy and low down payment provisions and because lenders have an incentive (due to the FHA/market interest rate differential and to FHA insurance) to substitute risky loans for good ones. Thus, the FHA underwriting of properties in declining areas and in poor condition encourages borrowing on properties in

---

case. In case of default, the lender is reimbursed at two-thirds of foreclosure costs. However, many mortgages do not qualify, including mortgages that are defaulted due to borrower choice or that are not likely to be repaid in time due to continuing financial difficulties. This program is useful when dealing with a defaulting household that does not wish to lose its property (i.e., where the equity is not zero) and that is suffering a temporary financial problem. It complements the three-month foreclosure delay policy. However, the program cannot deal with borrowers who are unable to pay due to ongoing or severe financial difficulties or who are not motivated to repay due to their lack of equity in the property. (For the most part these are the circumstances behind mortgage defaults discussed above.) Second, the FHA is experimenting with a limited rental program which allows the mortgagor of an FHA-assigned mortgage to rent the property during the redemption period. This keeps the property occupied (if not maintained) but the administrative costs may be high. There is also a possible perverse influence on other borrowers' motivation to default once the procedure becomes known. (This is also true of renegotiating mortgage payments.) Third, the FHA now holds the mortgagee responsible on mortgages insured after January 1977, for damage due to failure to take "reasonable" action to preserve the property once it is vacant. However, this may have little impact on abandonment since, in general, FHA mortgagees currently follow the accepted procedures of merely boarding up and tending the grounds of vacant properties. What is needed is differential maintenance depending on the value of the property and costs of efficient upkeep. Enforcement of the use of flexible cost-efficient strategies is unlikely to be administratively feasible.

areas where incentives for maintenance and reinvestment do not exist, and, to some extent, the withdrawal of funds from areas and properties where such incentives do exist.

Sources of positive impact on neighborhood property value

The FHA legislation of 1968 is likely to have positive effects on neighborhood property values as well as the negative ones detailed above. The positive effects are the more obvious. Indeed they were the intended effects of the legislation. They derive from three sources: First, the programs increase the availability and lower the cost of financing housing in urban areas. This directly raises the demand for and increases the price of urban housing. Second, the programs lower the cost of owning relative to renting in urban areas. If homeownership increases there is likely to be an additional positive impact on urban property values deriving from the increased maintenance usually associated with homeownership. Third, if urban areas are redlined (that is, discriminated against by mortgage lenders), increased mortgage supply to these areas will raise property values.

Urban housing demand. Housing costs are directly and substantially affected by the cost of borrowing. Interest costs represent approximately half of the homeowners' housing costs. The 1968 legislation lowers the cost of credit through three routes. First, Section 235 subsidizes the borrower's interest costs so that, in the original legislation passed in 1968, they could be as low as 1 percent, or in the amended 1973 program, as low as 5 percent. Even the amended program may cut borrower's interest costs by one half.

Second, Sections 235 and 221(d)(2) lower the down payment requirement. A lower down payment means that the borrower-household can use less of its money to purchase the same quantity of housing and can earn an income on the rest. This effectively lowers housing costs. (Alternatively, the household-borrower can purchase more housing for the same down payment.) Third, the 1968 changes in underwriting criteria allow lending on properties and to borrowers that previously did not meet FHA's minimum standards. The financing that had been available, if any, to these properties and borrowers, was likely to be more expensive.

The lower cost of financing the purchase of an urban property increases the demand for such properties. The impact on quantity demanded is strengthened because the substantial lowering of costs and the liberalization of underwriting criteria bring in new borrowers.

Unless urban housing is in infinitely elastic supply, the result of the decreased financing costs and consequent increased housing demand is higher prices on all eligible urban housing. If the programs finance very small portions of urban housing, the aggregate impact on prices will be small. However, if the properties financed under the programs are concentrated in a few areas there is a local positive impact on urban property values.

The positive short-run impact on existing urban property values through increased mortgage supply then has an additional longer-run positive impact on the urban housing stock. With the possibility of a higher selling price, there is an incentive to maintain and invest in urban properties. Higher selling prices may come about through increased demand for eligible properties and, in the long run, through the increased maintenance and higher land values resulting from the neighborhood effects of the increased maintenance.

Urban homeownership. The legislative amendments of 1968 lower the costs of owning relative to renting in urban areas. Once again there are several provisions of the legislation that work in this direction. First, the interest subsidies of Section 235 directly lower the ongoing costs of homeownership. Second, the small down payment requirement of Section 235 (and Section 221[d] [2]) decreases the capital requirement which is often the effective bar to homeownership. Third, the adjustment of area, borrower, and property criteria extends FHA insurance of single-family mortgages to previously ineligible properties and borrowers. In sum, families who wished to purchase one-family homes and who were unable to do so in the past because of the cost or lack of financing now can do so.

The net effect of this aspect of the legislation is to increase the share of owner-occupied properties from what it otherwise would have been. There are several studies that show the positive impact of owner-occupancy on maintenance of properties (e.g., Sternlieb, 1973). To the degree the legislation increases owner-occupancy maintenance, property values are likely to be higher than otherwise. The extent of neighborhood advancement that results depends on the distribution as well as the size of the increase. Some degree of concentration of the increase in owner-occupied units may be necessary for maximum effect.

Mortgage supply to redlined areas. The programs, besides increasing the supply of mortgage money to urban areas, also channel mortgage flows away from some urban areas into others. As argued above the rechanneling may be to areas where the funds are less efficiently used, and that, for this reason as well as others, urban property values are lower than in the absence of the programs. However, if urban areas served by the programs were previously redlined, either because of discrimination or self-fulfilling-hypothesis effects,[10] the positive impact on property values discussed above will be strengthened. There may be demand for properties in these areas that is not met by mortgage suppliers. That is, if sufficient mortgage funds are supplied the rate of return may be more than adequate to cover opportunity costs, but nonetheless the supply of mortgage funds to these "redlined" areas is restricted. Supplying funds to specifically designated urban areas only solves these efficiency problems if the areas are redlined in the above sense. Furthermore, such designation may signal these areas as risky to conventional lenders (Taggart,

---

[10] For definitions of redlined areas and why the channeling of funds into these areas may result in higher rates of return, see Guttentag and Wachter, forthcoming.

1977). To extent that funds are specifically to go to declining areas, and to the extent that lenders have an incentive to invest in risky areas, the possibility that rechanneling in this way will have an additional positive impact may be small, but nonetheless it exists. If urban areas on the average have been redlined, the positive impact of increased mortgage flow to urban areas on urban neighborhood property values will be higher than otherwise.

Overview of the positive impact. The initial impact of the legislation on urban property value is likely to be positive: Since the programs reduce the costs and increase the availability of home financing in urban areas, the demand for urban properties is likely to increase. In the longer run, with increased housing demand, there is likely to be increased maintenance of the stock. Positive neighborhood effects ensue. As a result there is likely to be a positive impact on mortgage flows to urban areas. If funds are rechanneled to redlined areas there is an additional positive impact on mortgage supply and demand for one-family housing services. In the long run, the flow of mortgage money and demand for one-family homeownership are endogenous. If these programs have a net positive impact on urban property values, they also have a net positive impact on mortgage supply and one-family homeownership which in turn strengthens the positive impact of the programs. The following section evaluates the programs' net impact on urban property values.

Net impact

The net impact of the legislation is difficult to assess. It is true, as Table 3 indicates, that over the past decade, foreclosure rates associated with Sections 223(e), 235, and 237 (and Section 221d[] [2] as well) have been high, far higher than the Section 203 foreclosure rate (which is itself about five times higher than the rate on conventional loans).

However, we cannot conclude from this evidence that the high foreclosure rates on properties in these programs were the result of these programs and would not have occurred in their absence. The properties may have been foreclosed and abandoned in any case, without these programs. That is, although high abandonment rates and neighborhood decline are linked, causation goes in both directions. Urban neighborhood decline that occurred over this period due to other factors undoubtedly contributed to the high foreclosure rates in these predominantly urban programs. Indeed, the positive impact of these

TABLE 3: Defaulted Mortgages, by Section, Cumulative, U.S.
(% defaulted of total issued under each program)

Section 203	Section 221(d)(2)	Section 223(e)	Section 235	Section 237
4.34	16.25	22.09	18.98	19.15

Source: Compiled from HUD-FHA, Management Information Division, Single Family Insured Branch, Statistic Volumes.

programs on urban property values may have kept some properties from being abandoned that would have been otherwise. To assess the impact of these programs requires empirical estimation of a model of urban property value change.[11] Here the negative and positive effects that result from the various aspects of these programs are merely traced out. Their size is not estimated. Flow charts are used to summarize these linkages for Sections 223(e) and 235. The charts follow with a brief explanation of their contents.

Section 223(e). By design, Section 223(e) lowers neighborhood risk standards. As a result FHA mortgages are available in neighborhoods with declining property values that were previously unacceptable for FHA underwriting. The negative impact of this results from two kinds of substitution effects. First, there is a substitution in the form of financing used. The FHA-insured financing is likely to replace equity and land installment contract financing on one-family homes (if any) in declining areas. The higher loan-to-value ratio and insurance in FHA loans increase default and abandonment rates by the mechanisms described earlier in this paper. The concomitants of abandonment-land value decline and undermaintenance of nearby properties may lower property values in the declining areas and in neighboring, more stable areas.[12] Second, the opportunity to make FHA loans at a financial advantage in declining areas may limit loans in other more stable areas, with negative neighborhood effects resulting in these as well. The negative impact on property values deriving from these substitution effects occurs over the long run. The extent of the impact varies directly with the amount and dispersion of mortgage financing under the program. If the net impact of the program is negative, the program may still have an impact even at relatively low scale. That is, even few abandoned properties may have a significant negative impact on the value of the immediately surrounding properties.

Section 223(e) has additional effects in the opposing direction. The lowered neighborhood standards allow the FHA to underwrite lending on one-family homes in declining areas where such underwriting was previously prohibited. The increased availability of this form of financing lowers mortgage costs and raises demand. Property values increase with the increase in demand. As long as the program continues, this positive impact remains. In the longer run, the increased availability of financing for owner-occupied as

---

[11] Data collected on any one variable such as urban, one-family mortgages cannot indicate the success or failure of these programs. For example, the increase (or decrease) of urban, one-family mortgages does not imply the success (or failure) of the programs. Although they have increased (or decreased) they may have been even higher (or lower) in the absence of the programs. To evaluate the net impact of the program it is necessary to test a simultaneous-equations model of urban property value change with mortgage lending as one of the variables.

[12] In addition, the outmigration of low income residents, who attempt to escape the worsened conditions, lower property values in the areas to which they move. See Leven et al. (1976) for a discussion of the role of resident income change and other factors in the process of urban neighborhood filtration.

TABLE 4: Flowchart: Impact of Section 223(e) on Neighborhood Property
Values

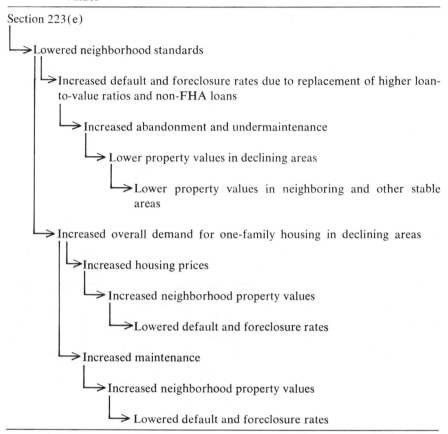

Section 223(e)

└→Lowered neighborhood standards

  └→Increased default and foreclosure rates due to replacement of higher loan-
    to-value ratios and non-FHA loans

    └→Increased abandonment and undermaintenance

      └→Lower property values in declining areas

        └→Lower property values in neighboring and other stable
          areas

  └→Increased overall demand for one-family housing in declining areas

    └→Increased housing prices

      └→Increased neighborhood property values

        └→Lowered default and foreclosure rates

    └→Increased maintenance

      └→Increased neighborhood property values

        └→Lowered default and foreclosure rates

opposed to rental residencies is likely to have an additional positive impact,
since owner-occupancy tends to be associated with greater maintenance. The
positive effects operate in the short and long run. The extent of their impact
varies directly with the amount of mortgage financing and inversely with the
dispersion of mortgage financing across urban neighborhoods.

The net short-run impact of the program is likely to be positive due to
the immediate impact on prices of the increased demand. The net long-run
impact (when the new equilibrium maintenance and reinvestment rates are
established) may be positive, negative, or zero. A zero impact occurs either
because the positive and negative effects counter each other or because the
overall impact of this program, either negative or positive, is outweighed by
other factors. The program may have to be sufficiently large-scale and/or
concentrated to have any positive impact at all. To demonstrate, assume that
the net impact of this program is positive. If there is a decline in demand for

TABLE 5: Flowchart: Impact of Section 235 on Neighborhood Property Values in Declining Areas

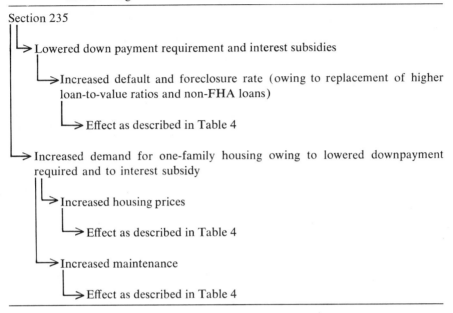

Section 235

→ Lowered down payment requirement and interest subsidies

→ Increased default and foreclosure rate (owing to replacement of higher loan-to-value ratios and non-FHA loans)

→ Effect as described in Table 4

→ Increased demand for one-family housing owing to lowered downpayment required and to interest subsidy

→ Increased housing prices

→ Effect as described in Table 4

→ Increased maintenance

→ Effect as described in Table 4

one-family housing in this area due to other factors that outweigh the increased demand resulting from this program, the neighborhood will decline in any case. In the long run, homeowners will choose not to reinvest and the percentage of owner-occupied residencies in the area will decline to what it would have been in the absence of the program.

Section 235. Section 235 is likely to have negative and positive effects similar to those of Section 223(e), as can be seen by referring to Table 5 which describes the impact of Section 235 in declining areas. Again the increased availability of these loans to lower income borrowers (because of the lower down payment requirements and interest subsidies available) encourages substitution of these loans for non-FHA and/or higher loan-to-value financing with increased risk of default, foreclosure, and abandonment. Again there is a negative rechanneling effect and a negative effect deriving from the lack of adjustment of required income level or interest subsidies to the higher maintenance expenditures required by physically deteriorated properties.

On the positive side, there is again an increased demand for owner-resident housing with the consequent short- and long-run positive effects on property values. The short-run net impact in declining areas is clearly positive due to the substantial interest subsidies involved.

Section 235 loans are made in stable as well as declining areas. In addition to the effects described, negative effects on property values in stable areas arise from the response of the current residents to the movement into the area of households of a lower socioeconomic and perhaps a different racial group.[13] However, because financing is now available to those who may have been previously excluded from owning houses in these areas (due to race or income level) the net short-run impact on housing demand and prices is unclear. It will vary with conditions of the housing market in question and in particular, with the extent of previous racial discrimination.

The long-run net impact of this program on property values in stable or declining areas may have been negative, positive, or zero depending on the size and distribution of financing under the program and the strength of exogenous forces.

Sections 221(d) (2) and 237. The above can be extended to provide brief analyses of the impact of Sections 221(d) (2) and 237, since these programs share elements of Section 235. The impact of Section 221(d) (2), an earlier program that remains in force, in both declining and stable areas, is likely to be similar to that of Section 235, since the program lacks only the interest rate subsidies of Section 235.

Section 237 provides FHA-insured financing for lower income families who would not be viewed as reasonable credit risks without debt management and related counseling. Because the program is likely to provide less expensive higher loan-to-value financing than was previously available to these borrowers, its impact again may duplicate that of Section 235. However, Congress anticipated that counseling would be provided under this program (as it has been, in recent years). Counseling may overcome negative implications for property maintenance and mortgage repayment due to lack of information on budget management and housing maintenance though obviously not those due purely to lack of income or the high loan-to-value ratio of the loan.

IMPACT ON POPULATION, EMPLOYMENT, AND FISCAL CONDITIONS IN URBAN AREAS

The net impact of sections 223(e), 235, and 237 on neighborhood property values determines the programs' net impact on the broader urban aggregates of population, employment, and fiscal condition. If the impact on urban neighborhood property values is positive (negative), the impact on the broader aggregates is positive (negative). As seen in Tables 6 and 7 the impact on the broader aggregates occurs through changes in the urban property tax base and through changes in the relative attractiveness of urban neighborhoods to middle class residents.

Assume, first, as illustrated in Table 6, a negative impact on property values.

---

[13] This effect does not have to be in this direction. Whether it is or not depends on the strength of residents' preferences for income homogeneous or heterogeneous neighborhoods. Leven et al. (1976) provides evidence of a negative effect on neighborhood property values of the inmigration of a lower income population.

TABLE 6: Flowchart: Impact of Neighborhood Property Value Decline on Urban Outmigration

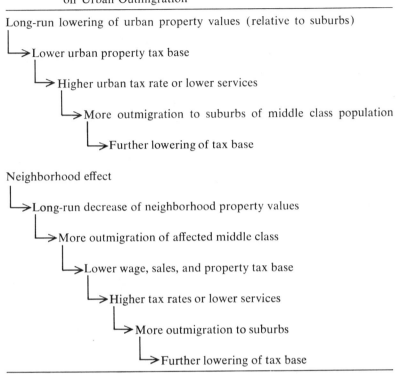

Long-run lowering of urban property values (relative to suburbs)

↳ Lower urban property tax base

↳ Higher urban tax rate or lower services

↳ More outmigration to suburbs of middle class population

↳ Further lowering of tax base

Neighborhood effect

↳ Long-run decrease of neighborhood property values

↳ More outmigration of affected middle class

↳ Lower wage, sales, and property tax base

↳ Higher tax rates or lower services

↳ More outmigration to suburbs

↳ Further lowering of tax base

This has a direct negative impact on the city's property tax base with negative consequences for tax rates and/or public services. To the extent that surrounding suburbs do not suffer from similar problems, they become relatively more attractive than when there are no programs. As a result, there is a negative impact on urban population and employment relative to that of the surrounding suburbs.

There is also a neighborhood effect that has a direct impact on urban-suburban migration patterns and an indirect effect on the property tax base. The threat of long-run property value decline along with property undermaintenance and abandonment in urban neighborhoods encourages the outflow of middle class homeowners.

As a result of the higher outmigration of the middle class, wage, sales, and property taxes are lower than otherwise. Thus once again property and other tax rates must be raised or services lowered more than in the absence of the programs. Depending on how this is done, further outmigration, employment loss, and suburban-urban fiscal disparities may result.

As Table 7 illustrates, a net positive impact on neighborhood property values reverses the impact of these programs on urban population, employ-

TABLE 7: Flowchart: Impact of Neighborhood Property Value Increase on Urban Outmigration

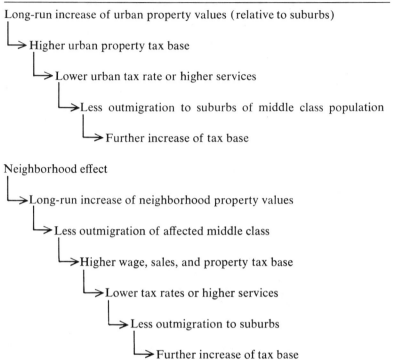

Long-run increase of urban property values (relative to suburbs)

 ↳ Higher urban property tax base

  ↳ Lower urban tax rate or higher services

   ↳ Less outmigration to suburbs of middle class population

    ↳ Further increase of tax base

Neighborhood effect

 ↳ Long-run increase of neighborhood property values

  ↳ Less outmigration of affected middle class

   ↳ Higher wage, sales, and property tax base

    ↳ Lower tax rates or higher services

     ↳ Less outmigration to suburbs

      ↳ Further increase of tax base

ment, and fiscal conditions. The positive impact on property values results in property tax revenues that are higher than otherwise and allow higher per capita public expenditures or lower tax rates than otherwise. This has a net positive impact on urban population and employment.

Similarly an increase in homeownership combined with an expected increase in property values encourages homeowners to reinvest in their urban properties and has a positive impact on urban population flow. This has secondary positive effects on the urban tax base and enables lower tax rates and/or increased public expenditures and decreased suburban-urban fiscal disparities than in the absence of the programs.

IMPACT ON EQUITY AND RACIAL SEGREGATION

This section considers the direct and indirect effects of the legislation on equity and segregation. Equity effects can be examined by considering the impact of the legislation on different income groups. Segregation effects are reflected by the dispersion of white and nonwhite within the city as indicated by the block-by-block ratios of white to nonwhite within the city and by the ratio of white to nonwhite in the city compared to the suburbs.

Equity impact

The legislation has direct and indirect equity effects. Direct equity effects occur through the impact on borrowers of funds insured under the programs. Indirect equity effects result from the programs' impact on nonparticipant urban property owners and renters. The direct benefits, that is, the lower cost housing financing now available, go, for the most part, to urban, lower middle class families, and not to the poor as designed. Even in the pre-1973 version of Section 235, the program which most served the poor, the average annual income of participating families was $7,000. Overall, the lower middle class participants in the programs gain. However, those who are encouraged to invest in properties whose value declines over time may lose their equity.

Besides home buyers, there was another group of beneficiaries: property sellers. These were typically urban, middle class homeowners and rental property investors who gained from higher buy-out prices. Of course any subsequent decline in property due to the programs does not affect their gain.

Whether urban property owners, who did not sell, on the average gain or lose depends on whether the programs have, on the average, a positive or negative impact on urban property values. If the effect is positive, urban land-owners (owners of homes and rental properties) gain. If negative, urban landowners lose.

The impact on renters is unclear. When property values and the property tax base change, public services and tax rates change as well. But these changes are reflected in land values and rents. The distributional effects deriving from this source depend on the renter's tastes and income level and on whether the renter was in equilibrium previously. To the extent renters were in equilibrium but no longer are, they lose. However, to the extent the programs have a differential impact on the availability of cities with the amenities a given renter desires (and is willing to pay for), the renter gains.

The legislation also has an impact on the availability of neighborhoods with given amenity levels within a city. The legislation is likely to lead to a wider dispersion of lower income families throughout the city's neighborhoods and therefore to fewer homogeneous neighborhoods. Again, this has a negative impact on renting families who were previously in equilibrium in their neighborhood. And again, because this legislation affects the supply of homogeneous (and heterogeneous) neighborhoods, it has distributional effects which depend on renters' neighborhood preferences.

Impact on racial segregation

The legislation's impact on racial segregation within the city derives from two sources. First, given the urban white and nonwhite population, the legislation affects the distribution of that population. This is because the legislation leads to a greater dispersion of lower income families throughout the urban area and lower income families are disproportionately nonwhite. This reduces racial segregation within the city. If there is racial discrimination in the selling of urban housing, nonwhites pay more for housing than whites. The higher prices that lower income nonwhite families now can afford due to the programs may allow an expansion of the racially integrated area and perhaps a significant breaking down of geographical racial barriers, if the lack of nonwhite demand at high enough prices helped to maintain the barriers. Thus the positive impact on integration is greater to the extent there was racial discrimination that can no longer be supported. The effect holds no matter what the net impact of the legislation on urban property values.

Second, the legislation may have an impact on the overall ratio of white to nonwhite within the city, through its impact on middle class outmigration to the suburbs. If property values decline over time, middle class residents' outmigration increases. The outmigration of the middle class, to the extent the middle class is disproportionately white, results in an increase in the segregation of nonwhite in central cities. Thus, if the programs have a negative impact on property values, there is a positive impact on the concentration of nonwhites in urban areas. If the impact is positive the programs, for this reason as well, contribute to decreased racial segregation in urban and metropolitan areas.

HOMEOWNERSHIP FOR THE URBAN POOR:
ARE THERE WORKABLE ALTERNATIVES?

According to the analysis presented here, the impact of the 1968 amendments on urban property values, tax base, and population may be negative or positive. The amendments were not primarily designed to aid urban areas. The major goal of the 1968 legislation was to increase lower income urban homeownership. Clearly the changes of 1968 increase the availability and decrease the cost of home financing in urban areas, but it is unclear whether this shift in the supply of mortgage funds results in an increase in one-family homes. As a consequence of the negative impact on neighborhood property values, homeownership may decrease. The provisions of the legislation that create negative neighborhood effects are primarily those that raise default, foreclosure, and abandonment rates and lower property maintenance. As the preceding indicates, when neither the mortgagor nor the mortgagee bears the financial consequences of property abandonment, they lack the incentive to prevent it. The high down payment limits the borrowers' loss and FHA insurance limits the lenders' losses from undermaintenance and abandonment.

How might a lower income urban homeownership program be constructed to avoid negative neighborhood effects? More stringent borrower, property, and area underwriting standards, along with increased borrower counseling, could be applied. Indeed, there is evidence that such program changes have already occurred.[14] An alternative policy approach would be higher down payment loans with interest subsidies and co-insurance. While such a program could be constructed, it is no panacea. Higher down payment loans in the absence of a wealth transfer, limit the programs' availability to lower income families. Another alternative is to simulate the market response to lending to low income families through subsidizing interest payments on land-installment mortgage contracts or rental payments while an equity account is built up. This allows the slow growth both of equity and homeownership skills. Under either of these programs, borrowers would have incentives to keep up property maintenance and mortgage payments.

Co-insurance gives lenders incentives to oversee maintenance of the property and to limit default and foreclosure. In addition, co-insurance provides lenders with an incentive to choose to fund those loans that have lower default risk. This last is two-edged. If co-insured the lender has an incentive to choose less risky loans and no incentive to undertake lending to low income borrowers whom the government wishes to aid. Thus the government's role would switch from assuring property maintenance and the adherence to minimum loan standards to assuring that subsidized loans went to the groups the programs were designed to aid (Guttentag, 1976).

There is no guarantee that this is a less costly task. Similarly, the reliance on interest subsidies rather than near-zero down payment mortgages both increases government expenditures through higher subsidy payments and decreases expenditures through lower insurance losses. The net effect on federal budgetary costs of either of these programs changes is, thus, uncertain. However, formulating the programs in this way lessens the danger of urban property value loss through neighborhood effects. The legislation is assured of advancing urban homeownership only if damaging neighborhood effects are limited.

REFERENCES

Bradford, Calvin P., et al. *The Role of Management Lending Practices in Older Neighborhoods: Institutional Lenders, Regulatory Agencies, and Their Community Impacts.* Evanston, Ill.: Center for Urban Affairs, Northwestern University, 1975.

Curley, Anthony J., and Guttentag, Jack M. "Value and Yield Risk on Outstanding Insured Residential Mortgages." *Journal of Finance* 32 (1977): 403–61.

———. "The Yield on Insured Residential Mortgages." *Explorations in Economic Research* 1 (1974): 114–61.

"Defaults on FHA-Insured Home Mortgages—Detroit, Michigan." Fifteenth Re-

---

[14] The author is currently conducting research on the differential impact of underwriting standards and loan-to-value ratios on defaults.

port of the Committee on Government Operations, U.S. House of Representatives. Washington, D.C.: U.S. Government Printing Office, 1972.

Flick, Frederick. "Analysis of the Role of FHA in Older Urban Areas in Response to the Marquette Park Complaint." Mimeographed. Washington, D.C.: Program Impact Evaluation Division, U.S. Department of Housing and Urban Development, June 7, 1977.

Furstenberg, George M. von. "Technical Studies of Mortgage Default Risk: An Analysis with FHA and VA Home Loans during the Decade 1957–1966." Pamphlet. Ithaca: Center for Urban Development Research, Cornell University, 1971.

Green, Jeffrey R., and Furstenberg, George M. von. "The Effects of Race and Age of Housing on Mortgage Delinquency Risk." In *Urban Studies*, edited by J. T. Hughes. vol. 12. Edinburgh: Longman Group, 1975.

Guttentag, Jack M. "Direct Federal Housing Loans Versus Interest Rate Subsidies." In *Housing in the Seventies Working Papers 2*. Washington, D.C.: U.S. Department of Housing and Urban Development, 1976.

———, and Wachter, Susan M. *Redlining and Public Policy*. Salomon Brothers Center for the Study of Financial Institutions Series in Finance and Economics. New York: New York University Graduate School of Business, forthcoming.

Leven, Charles L., et al. *Neighborhood Change: Lessons in the Dynamics of Urban Decay*. New York: Praeger, 1976.

Lowry, Ira S. *Housing Assistance for Low-Income Families: A Fresh Approach*. New York: Rand Institute, May 1971.

Stegman, M. A. *Housing Investment in the Inner City: The Dynamics of Decline*. Cambridge: MIT Press, 1972.

Sternlieb, George, and Burchell, Robert W. *Residential Abandonment: The Tenement Revisited*. Center for Urban Policy Research. New Brunswick: Rutgers University Press, 1973.

Taggert, Harriet Tee. "FHA Redlined Maps in Four Massachusetts Cities—Boston, Lynn, Springfield and Worcester—under the 223(e) Program." Mimeographed memorandum. Boston: Massachusetts Banking Department, May 16, 1977.

U.S. Department of Housing and Urban Development. *Consumers' Primer of Housing and Development*. Washington, D.C.: U.S. Government Printing Office, January 10, 1977.

PART V

Urban Impact Analysis 3: Tax Policies

CHAPTER NINETEEN

The Urban Impacts of the
Revenue Act of 1978

KATHY JEAN HAYES AND DAVID L. PURYEAR

INTRODUCTION

The federal tax system has had a profound impact on the process of economic growth and development in the United States. Not only has the tax system been an important macroeconomic tool in periods of recession and inflation, but it has substantially influenced the spatial pattern of household and business investment. The tax benefits of homeownership and the investment stimuli of tax credits and accelerated depreciation have speeded up the process of urban decentralization with adverse impacts on many central cities.

In recent years, however, modifications in the tax code have begun to erode some aspects of this de facto spatial bias, although others continue unabated. The Revenue Act of 1978, the most recent revision of the federal tax code, is no exception to this trend. By reducing the number of taxpayers who receive a tax subsidy for homeownership, it reduces the incentives for households to leave high-density, central city areas where the predominant form of housing is the multifamily rental unit.

The Revenue Act of 1978 is not so kind to inner cities, however, when it comes to corporate taxation. The Investment Tax Credit (ITC) is significantly liberalized and this stimulus to new investment is likely to benefit suburban and nonmetropolitan areas to a far greater extent than central cities.

The purpose of this paper is to examine certain spatial impacts of the Revenue Act of 1978. Specifically, the relative effects of the Act on central cities and suburbs are considered. Both personal and corporate tax changes are examined and some crude estimates of the potential central city impacts are presented. The following section briefly examines the historical pattern of

The authors wish to thank Philip Brewer for his helpful assistance in preparing this paper.

federal tax impacts on cities. Next the provisions of the Revenue Act of 1978 with significance for urban areas are described. Estimates of the central city impacts of the changes in the personal income tax are presented in the fourth section and the corporate income tax impacts are examined in section five. Finally, a brief summary concludes the paper.

FEDERAL TAXES AND CITIES

Personal income taxes and urban development

By far the most significant spatial impact of the federal tax system has arisen from the substantial subsidy it offers to homeownership. This subsidy arises from several sources. First, the definition of income for tax purposes does not include any imputed rental income earned by owner-occupiers. Second, mortgage interest payments are deductible from income if the taxpayer itemizes deductions. Third, state and local property taxes are also deductible if the taxpayer itemizes. These subsidies are substantial and rise with income. A number of studies have examined this subsidy and estimated its magnitude.

These studies have generally estimated each of the housing cost items, mortgage interest payments, property tax payments, imputed rental income, and maintenance and depreciation, as a proportion of house value. A variety of assumptions about housing costs are used in these studies. Two of the studies, Laidler (1969) and Sunley (1970), assume no differential between mortgage interest payments and imputed rents. Shelton (1968) assumes that the homeowner has equity equal to 50 percent of the market value of his home. He assumes an 8 percent rate of return on owner equity and a 6 percent mortgage interest rate. Aaron (1970) estimates net imputed rent under two alternative assumptions about rates of return on homeowner equity. Using sample data, he calculates mortgage interest costs and property tax deductions. In a more recent study for the U.S. Department of Housing and Urban Development, Tolley and Diamond (1977) assume the interest costs to be 6 percent a year on 90 percent of the capital cost. The rate of return on the equity portion, the remaining 10 percent, is assumed to be 12 percent.

Despite this variety of assumptions, estimates of the total annual rate of return on housing investment from these studies fall between 10 and 14 percent of housing unit value. Those housing cost items subsidized by the personal income tax are estimated to be from 65 to 88 percent of gross housing costs.

The tax subsidy is directly related to the marginal tax rate of the homeowner. As the marginal rate increases, the tax subsidy also increases. The estimates of these studies suggest that the tax subsidy ranges from 11 percent of gross housing costs for taxpayers in the 14 percent marginal bracket upwards to 55 percent for those homeowners in the 70 percent bracket.

The Tolley and Diamond study adjusts the subsidy estimates for the effect of standard deductions and exemptions. These have a dampening effect on the subsidy and reduce its range across income brackets, so that the tax subsidy is 12.6 percent in the lowest marginal tax bracket and 35.6 percent in the highest bracket.

Thus, the degree of subsidy provided by the federal tax treatment of homeownership is substantial. Coupled with the historic pattern of United States urban development, it accelerates metropolitan decentralization and thus constitutes a de facto bias against central cities, particularly older, high-density central cities. A large majority of owner-occupiers live in single-family, detached houses. These houses require a large amount of land per family, land that was most readily and inexpensively available at the urban fringe. Thus, the development pattern of recent decades has been one of low-density suburban communities. For those who could afford this housing, the federal tax code has been generous.

By raising the relative rate of return on housing investment, the federal tax system has accelerated the pace of urban decentralization. The relationship between these tax subsidies and the pattern of development in the residential sector is examined in Peterson (1977), who finds that the tax system is responsible for raising the single-family share of metropolitan housing construction significantly. Since the single-family, detached house accounted for more than 80 percent of owner-occupied homes in metropolitan areas in 1976 (*see* U.S. Bureau of the Census, Part A), this tax system through its subsidy to homeownership has contributed heavily to the decline in urban residential densities in recent decades. This decline in densities is more accurately described as a flattening of density gradients. It is well documented in Mills (1972).

For many central cities, this process of decentralization has created adjustment problems. The ability of these central cities to adapt to decline depends, in part, on the rate at which they must make their adjustments, and the tax system's role in accelerating the pace makes it harder for many cities to cope with their problems.

In sum, the personal income tax subsidizes homeownership which has the effect of accelerating the decentralization of population in urban areas. This causes a period of hardship for some cities and for the people left behind in them.

Business taxes and urban development

The principal urban impact of federal taxes on business arises from incentives for new investment. Just as encouraging homeownership is a desirable goal with some undesirable urban side effects, the use of tax policy to stimulate new investment in the economy can have undesired impacts.

A variety of tax and subsidy mechanisms has been used in recent years to influence the aggregate level of capital formation in the United States economy. For the most part, they have been employed to stimulate investment in periods of recession or to provide incentives for expansion of specific sectors of the economy. Whether these mechanisms have taken the form of tax credits, accelerated depreciation, or some other special tax treatment, their influence has depended on the impact of changing the relative price of capital in the private capital market. Investment impacts have been determined by the responsiveness of capital markets to these price changes.

The secondary impacts of these investment stimuli include traditional macroeconomic multiplier effects and derived demand for complementary factors, such as labor. The benefits of investment stimulus as a macroeconomic tool include its contribution to long-run productive capacity, which helps to avoid inflationary bottlenecks later on.

For all these reasons the use of capital subsidies as a macroeconomic tool has been generally accepted. Recently, however, attention has focused on allegations of uneven impacts of these incentives on central cities and suburbs (Bahl and Puryear, 1978, and McHugh and Puryear, forthcoming). For a number of reasons, central cities and other relatively densely populated urban areas are not likely to share proportionately in new investment stimulated by tax incentives. To some extent this anticity bias is inherent in any investment stimulus program. Changes in industrial technology, higher central city land costs, difficult transportation access, and an aging stock of buildings and infrastructure, all contribute to this situation.

On balance, the stimulative effects of tax incentives in central cities may outweigh their anticity bias, especially in the short run, but they are likely to further erode the position of central cities *relative* to suburbs and nonmetropolitan areas.

THE REVENUE ACT OF 1978

The Revenue Act of 1978 includes several changes which affect homeownership subsidies and business investment incentives. The Act cuts both personal and corporate taxes and affects cities in several ways. Reductions in personal income taxes are estimated to reduce liabilities by $13 billion in 1979, corporate tax cuts are expected to total $6.4 billion, changes in the treatment of capital gains will reduce liabilities by $2.9 billion, and liberalization of the Investment Tax Credit will reduce taxes by $13.5 billion. The total effect in calendar 1979 is a tax cut of $34.8 billion (U.S. Treasury, 1978). The major personal income tax features of this bill include reductions in rates, increases in the capital gains exclusion, a one-time $100,000 exclusion of capital gains on a principal residence for homeowners 55 years and older, and increases in the standard deduction and personal exemptions. Tax cuts for business include a reduction in corporate income tax rates and liberalization of the Investment Tax Credit (ITC).

Reduction in personal income tax rates. The new personal income tax schedule has wider brackets, with 15 instead of 25 marginal rates for married taxpayers (16 brackets for single taxpayers). In general, tax rates are reduced, although the changes in bracket definitions make simple comparisons impossible.

In addition to these changes in tax brackets and rates, the standard deduction is raised to $2,300 for single filers and heads of households, and $3,400 for joint filers. The Act also increases the personal exemption from $750 to $1,000 and allows the general tax credit to expire. The net result of all these personal income tax changes is an estimated reduction in tax liabilities of $13 billion in 1979.

Reduction in capital gains tax. The Revenue Act of 1978 increased the share of capital gains that may be excluded from taxable income from 50 percent to 60 percent. A second significant change in the treatment of capital gains is the exemption of the first $100,000 of capital gains from the sale of a principal residence by persons 55 years or older. This exemption is available on a one-time basis and replaces the current partial exemption for persons over 65. Capital gains on the sale of a principal residence by persons of any age can be *deferred* if the gain is reinvested in a principal residence within 18 months. This deferral is not affected by the new law. The estimated tax reduction from these capital gains tax changes is $2.9 billion.

Reduction in business tax rates. Corporate tax rates are reduced to 17 percent of the first $25,000 of taxable income, 20 percent of the next $25,000, 30 percent of the third $25,000, 40 percent of the fourth $25,000, and 46 percent of corporate income in excess of $100,000. These tax cuts are largest for firms in the $50,000 to $100,000 income range which were formerly in a 48 percent marginal bracket. They are expected to reduce corporate tax liabilities by about $6.4 billion.

Liberalization of the ITC. Three changes were made in the ITC by the Revenue Act of 1978. First, the credit, which was scheduled to decline to 7 percent in 1981, was made permanent at its current 10 percent level. Second, it may now be used to offset up to 90 percent of tax liabilities instead of only 50 percent. Finally, the ITC was extended to expenditures for the rehabilitation of structures for all types of businesses, provided the structures have been in use for at least 20 years. These changes are expected to reduce tax liabilities by $13.5 billion in 1979.

The following sections examine the urban impacts of these new tax provisions, particularly their relative impacts on central cities and suburbs.

PERSONAL INCOME TAX IMPACTS

As noted earlier, the principal urban impact of the personal income tax provisions of the federal tax code occurs through its influence on homeownership patterns. Thus, the first step in evaluating the urban impact of the Revenue Act of 1978 is to examine the differential tax treatment of owners and renters. This is done in several steps: First, tax liabilities have been calculated for prototypical owners and renters by income level. Second, central city and outside central city patterns of ownership have been examined. Third, composite central city and outside central city taxpayer liabilities have been calculated on the basis of the first two steps. This procedure has been carried out for three changes in the tax structures: the changes in tax brackets and rates, the increase in the capital gains exclusion, and, separately, for the $100,000 capital gains exclusion for taxpayers 55 years and older. The procedures and the results of these calculations are presented below.

Impacts of rate and capital gains changes. Using the 1978 tax return form and tax rates for 1979 (based on the Revenue Act of 1978 as reported in the October 14, 1978, *Congressional Record*, 1978), tax liabilities were calculated for owner-occupiers and renters at four income levels. Liabilities were calculated for both 1978 rates and in successive steps, the new provisions effective in 1979. These tax liabilities are presented in Table 1. The tax reductions are substantial at each income level and the differential between owners and renters is smaller at each income level under the new tax provisions.

Calculations were based on the assumption that a joint return was filed and four exemptions were claimed. Average property tax and mortgage interest deductions for each income level were calculated. It was assumed that renters used the standard deduction. Owner-occupiers of all but the lowest level benefited from itemizing their deductions. In calculating tax liabilities for the lowest income group of owners, the standard deduction was used. To

TABLE 1: Tax Liabilities of Renters and Owners, by Income Level

	Wage and Salary Income			
	$9,500	*$17,500*	*$22,500*	*$40,000*
Calendar 1978				
Renter	$ 365	$ 1,932	$ 3,157	$ 9,226
Owner-occupied	365	1,877	2,936	7,710
Revenue Act of 1978[a]				
Rate changes[b]				
Renter	0	1,080	2,076	7,065
Owner-occupied	0	1,071	1,948	5,919
60% capital gains exclusion				
Renter	314	1,855	3,061	8,890
Owner-occupied	314	1,800	2,861	7,398
Rate and capital gain changes				
Renter	0	1,018	1,999	6,900
Owner-occupied	0	1,009	1,871	5,653

Note: See text for assumptions and methodology.
[a] Effective 1979.
[b] Includes changes in personal exemption and standard deduction.

TABLE 2: Homeownership, by Income and Urban Location
(percent owner-occupied)

Location	*Income*				
	$0–9,999	*$10,000–19,999*	*$20,000–34,999*	*$35,000+*	*Total*
Central cities	35.5%	57.0%	75.9%	78.8%	52.0%
Outside central cities	53.9	70.7	86.4	92.3	71.0
U.S. total	49.6	69.1	84.4	88.6	64.7

Source: U.S. Bureau of the Census, *Annual Housing Survey, 1976.*

determine the new adjusted gross income associated with the 60 percent capital gains exclusion, an extra 10 percent of the average gain claimed in each income class (20 percent of the formerly taxable gain) was deducted from adjusted gross income.

Tax liabilities under the Revenue Act of 1978 (effective in calendar 1979) were initially calculated under the new rate structure, assuming no increases in capital gains exclusion. This reduced the renter-owner differential in tax liabilities at the highest two income levels by $93 and $370, a substantial narrowing of this gap. Next the increase in the capital gains exclusion was considered, assuming no change in the rate structure. The renter-owner tax liability differential at the two highest income levels is also reduced by this increase in capital gains exclusion, but only by $21 and $24 dollars. This is a substantially smaller reduction than that resulting from rate changes alone. Finally, tax liabilities were calculated for both the new rate structure and the 60 percent capital gains exclusion combined. This reduced the renter-owner differential by $93 and $269 at the two highest income levels, a substantial reduction, but a smaller one than in the case of the rate changes alone.

The next step in evaluating the spatial impacts of the Revenue Act of 1978 is to examine central city and outside central city patterns of homeownership. The *Annual Housing Survey* provides data on ownership by income class and location (*see* Table 2). These data show a clear difference in patterns of ownership by both income and location. Homeownership rises significantly with income in both central cities and suburbs. Only one-third of lower-income central city residents own their homes while more than three-fourths of high-income residents do. In the suburbs, the pattern is similar but the ownership shares are substantially higher at all incomes. In those outside central city areas, more than half of the lower-income residents own homes while more than 92 percent of high-income residents do.

The final step in examining this aspect of the urban impacts of the tax bill is to calculate a set of composite tax liabilities for central city and outside central city residents by income class. These composite tax amounts are obtained by multiplying the prototype tax liability from Table 1 by the share of owners and renters in each income class and location from Table 2. These crude estimates clearly overstate the change in tax liability for both owners and renters because they assume four exemptions and one tax return per household and income levels in Table 1, which are well above the average for the two lowest income classes in Table 2 (these two classes contain more than three-quarters of the households), and because all owners are assumed to itemize when many clearly do not find it profitable to do so. Nonetheless, the results provide a valid comparison of the relative impact of the new tax law on central cities and suburbs.

Table 3 presents the composite tax amounts for central cities and outside central city areas. These composite tax liabilities exhibit a consistent pattern of reduction in suburban-central city tax differentials as the result of the tax rate changes (and increased personal exemptions and higher standard deduction) in the Revenue Act of 1978. This decline in homeowner subsidies narrows the gap at all levels of income. The new capital gains exclusion is neutral with respect to ownership and, therefore, affects central cities and suburbs equally. When these two sets of changes are combined, the central city effect is beneficial.

TABLE 3: Composite Tax Liabilities, by Income and Urban Location

	Wage and Salary Income			
	$9,500	$17,500	$22,500	$40,000
Calendar 1978				
Central city	$ 347	$ 1,901	$ 2,989	$ 8,030
Outside central city	347	1,888	2,966	7,827
Difference	0	13	23	203
Revenue Act of 1978[a]				
Rate changes[b]				
Central city	0	1,075	1,978	6,161
Outside central city	0	1,070	1,965	6,007
Difference	0	5	13	154
60% capital gains exclusion				
Central city	314	1,824	2,909	7,714
Outside central city	314	1,810	2,888	7,513
Difference	0	14	21	201
Rate and capital gain changes				
Central city	0	1,012	1,902	5,917
Outside central city	0	1,009	1,883	5,749
Difference	0	3	19	168

Note: See text for assumptions and methodology.
[a] Effective 1979.
[b] Includes changes in personal exemption and standard deduction.

TABLE 4: Effect of Over-55 Residential Gains Exclusion on Tax Liabilities

	Wage and Salary Income			
	$9,500	$17,500	$22,500	$40,000
Calendar 1978				
Ages 55–64	$2,374	$ 4,672	$ 6,677	$17,954
Ages 65+	680	2,211	3,717	12,140
Revenue Act of 1978[a]				
Over-55 exclusion only	680	2,211	3,074	8,275
All provisions combined[b]	476	1,436	2,383	6,615

Note: See text for assumptions and methodology.

[a] Effective 1979.

[b] Includes changes in tax rates, personal exemption, standard deduction, regular capital gains exclusion, and over-55 residential gains exclusion.

Special capital gains exclusion for persons 55 and over

The Revenue Act of 1978 allows a one-time $100,000 exclusion of capital gains on the sale of one's principal residence for taxpayers 55 and older. Under the previous law, an individual 65 or older could exclude from gross income the entire gain realized on the sale of his principal residence if the adjusted sales price were $35,000 or less. For sales prices greater than $35,000, a partial exemption existed. Tax liabilities for four income levels were calculated under the old and new laws concerning this one-time exclusion. Assumptions about house values were made on the basis of data from the *Annual Housing Survey*. Because the new law includes those taxpayers 55 to 64 years old, two sets of tax liabilities were calculated. For those 55 to 64 years old, tax liabilities fell considerably because the gain from the sale of a residence would previously have been taxed at the regular (50 percent) capital gains rate (*see* Table 4). Under the Revenue Act of 1978, the gain was assumed to be less than $100,000 at all income levels and, therefore, was completely excluded from adjusted gross income calculations. For those 65 and over the change in the capital gains exclusion did not affect the tax liabilities of the two lowest income levels. It was assumed that they could sell their home for less than the $35,000 adjusted sales price.

The number of taxpayers likely to use the new exclusion was calculated from data on recent movers presented in the *Annual Housing Survey*. This source provides the number of movers by age, by previous and current ownership status, and by location. The number of households eligible for this exemption which move in any year is a very small fraction of the total number of urban households. About 11 percent of metropolitan households are headed by persons over 55 and of these, about 3.3 percent move from owning to renting in any one year. Another 5.0 percent of this age group moves from one owned house to another. Both of these groups are eligible for the exemption although some of those who continue to own their principal residence will elect to defer their gains and avoid using the one-time exemption. In any case, both of these groups combined constitute only 0.9 percent of metropolitan households, so this tax provision of the Revenue Act of 1978 will not have a significant effect on overall central city and suburban tax burdens. This provision could trigger some new real estate activity for the purpose of avoiding capital gains taxation, but the level of this activity is not likely to be large enough to significantly affect relative central city and suburban tax burdens.

Despite this modest overall impact, it is worth looking at the probable central city and suburban changes which result from this one-time exclusion. It is assumed that all eligible movers claim the exclusion and no moves are induced by it. Capital gains from the sale of a principal residence are estimated by deflating current house values for each income level by the Consumer Price Index for the average length of ownership status of households with heads over 55, calculated from *Annual Housing Survey* data. These assumptions and calculations allow the use of *Annual Housing Survey* data on movers to estimate aggregate tax liabilities of eligible movers for central cities and for suburbs.

This procedure is imprecise but it clearly illustrates the substantially larger aggregate tax reduction which accrues to outside central city areas as the result of the over 55 capital gains exclusion. The aggregate reductions for central cities are smaller than for outside central cities at all but the highest income level (*see* Table 5). This high-income anomaly reflects the disproportionately large number of central city households in this age group who sell their homes. When the four income classes are aggregated, the suburbs receive about 57.5 percent of the tax benefits available to eligible movers 55 and older. In contrast, only 54.5 percent of the population over 65 lives in the suburbs. This pattern holds true for the over 55 exclusion by itself and for all the personal income tax provisions of the new Act combined. In other words, this exclusion is sufficiently valuable for the eligible movers that its pro-suburban bias outweighs the pro-central city impact of the changes in tax rates for this group of taxpayers. Fortunately for central cities, this tax benefit is limited to a small fraction of the population and does not outweigh the beneficial effects of the rate changes when all taxpayers are considered.

These results for the personal income tax changes of the Revenue Act of 1978 demonstrate a mixed pattern in terms of their central city impact. The reduction in tax rates helps central cities but the changes in capital gains treatment, both the increase in the allowable exclusion and the special exclusion for taxpayers 55 and older, benefit suburban areas more than central cities. The combined effects, however, are clearly in the favor of the central city because the rate changes have a considerably larger impact than the capital gains changes. Thus, the personal income tax provisions of the Revenue Act of 1978 are beneficial to central cities both in absolute terms and also relative to suburban areas.

TABLE 5: Aggregate Tax Liabilities of Movers Eligible for the Over-55 Exclusion, by Income and Urban Location
(millions)

	Income[a]				
	$9,500	$17,500	$22,500	$40,000	Total
Calendar 1978					
Central city	65	238	253	215	711
Outside central city	71	369	511	109	1,060
Revenue Act of 1978[b]					
Over-55 exclusion only					
Central city	38	135	125	115	413
Outside central city	35	214	261	66	576
Reduction due to over-55 exclusion only					
Central city	27	103	128	100	358
Outside central city	36	155	250	43	484
All provisions combined[c]					
Central city	26	87	98	92	303
Outside central city	25	139	202	53	419
Reduction due to all provisions					
Central city	39	151	155	123	468
Outside central city	46	230	309	56	641

Note: See text and notes for assumptions and methodology.

[a] Individual liabilities are based on this level of wage and salary income; aggregate is based on number of eligible households by income groups: $0–9,999; $10,000–19,999; $20,000–34,999; $35,000 and over.

[b] Effective 1979.

[c] Includes changes in tax rates, personal exemption, standard deduction, regular capital gains exclusion, and over-55 residential gains exclusion.

BUSINESS TAX IMPACTS

Two business tax provisions of the Revenue Act of 1978 are likely to affect urban areas. First, the corporate income tax rate structure has been changed to increase the number of brackets and to reduce the marginal rates in each bracket. Second, the investment tax credit has been liberalized. The urban impacts of these business tax provisions are more difficult to determine than those of the personal income tax changes, for at least two reasons: the impacts are often less direct and, therefore, more difficult to trace, and data availability is an even more serious problem. Despite these constraints, it is worth a brief examination of the potential urban impacts of these provisions.

Corporate tax rate reductions. The largest reductions in corporate tax rates occur in the $50,000–$100,000 income range. Only if there are systematic differences between central cities and suburbs in the income size of firms will this provision have a significant differential direct impact. The evidence on this point is inconclusive and data which would provide a clear answer do not exist. Indirect impacts via the incidence of corporate income taxes are even less clear.

Data from the U.S. Internal Revenue Service (1973) indicate that the wholesale and retail trade sector has the largest number of firms in this income range, with the manufacturing and finance, insurance, and real estate sectors having the next largest numbers. Employment in wholesale and retail trade, however, is distributed between central cities and suburbs in almost exactly the some proportion as total employment (U.S. Bureau of the Census, 1977 and 1970), while employment in manufacturing is slightly more suburbanized and the finance, insurance, and real estate sector is slightly less suburbanized than total employment. Even if there were a clear pattern of central city or suburban specialization in sectors with a large number of firms in the $50,000–$100,000 income range, there are no data on the income-size distribution of firms in a given industry between central cities and suburbs. Thus, the urban impacts of the corporate income tax rate reduction are indeterminate.

A second difficulty in interpreting these rate reductions stems from their uncertain incidence pattern. The literature on the incidence of the corporate income tax, including empirical analyses such as Cragg, Harberger, and Mieszkowski (75: 811–21) and Krzyzaniak and Musgrave (1963), is not at all conclusive about who bears its burden. The results of Krzyzaniak and Musgrave (1963) suggest that the corporate profits tax in manufacturing is shifted by more than 100 percent. Cragg, Harberger, and Mieszkowski (75: 811–21) added a cyclical variable and a dummy variable for mobilization and war years, and the estimate of shifting dropped to 60 percent, although the tax coefficient is not statistically different from zero.

Investment Tax Credit (ITC). The three changes in the ITC included in the Revenue Act of 1978 were a permanent extension of the 10 percent rate, an increase from 50 percent to 90 percent in the share of tax liabilities which the ITC could be used to offset, and the inclusion of expenditures for rehabilitation of structures in use for at least 20 years as investments eligible for the credit.

The impacts of these liberalizations of the ITC merely reinforce its existing spatial bias in favor of new activity in suburban or nonmetropolitan areas. This spatial bias arises in large part because the older central city areas are at a comparative disadvantage in attracting new investment in the first place, especially manufacturing investment. By stimulating new investment, the ITC accelerates the process of shutting down older factories which are more likely to be located in central cities and rebuilding elsewhere.

Central cities are at a disadvantage in attracting new industry for several reasons. Although the ITC applies to equipment, but not structures (except for the new rehabilitation provision), new equipment in old buildings may be less efficient than new equipment in new buildings, particularly if the new equipment embodies significant technological change. Since older central cities tend to have an older inventory of industrial structures, this sort of limit on flexibility is more likely to occur there. The most obvious result of this would be a disproportionately small share of new investment in older buildings and, therefore, a smaller share in older cities. It is worth noting that this reasoning suggests that the aggregate impact of the rehabilitation credit will be small. Since it is the only aspect of the ITC changes with potential for improving the relative position of central cities, the overall impact of all three ITC changes will almost certainly work to the disadvantage of central cities.

One indication of the extent to which the ITC will be used by firms in central cities and other areas is the use of the ITC by industry type. Except for employment in the service sector, which is highly concentrated in central cities, usage of the ITC varies inversely with the concentration of employment in central cities. Table 6 compares the ITC as a percentage of corporate income tax liabilities with the central city share of metropolitan employment. The construction and manufacturing sectors with average ITC claims of 9 percent and 6 percent, respectively, of tax liabilities have below average shares of central city employment. The wholesale and retail trade sector and the finance, insurance, and real estate sector, with average ITC claims of only 4 and 3 percent, respectively, have central city employment shares that are average or above average.

The only conclusions it is possible to draw in the case of these three liberalizations of the ITC are that they almost certainly work to the disadvantage of central cities but that the severity of their impact is unclear.

CONCLUSIONS

This paper has examined the urban impacts of the Revenue Act of 1978. On balance, the personal income tax changes improve the relative position of

TABLE 6: Investment Tax Credit and Central City Employment, by Major Industry Type

Major Industry Type	ITC as % of Tax Liability	Central City Share of Employment
Services	11%	46%
Construction	9	35
Manufacturing	6	38
Wholesale and retail trade	4	40
Finance, insurance, and real estate	3	44

Sources: Internal Revenue Service, *Corporation Income Tax Returns, Statistics of Income, 1973* and U.S. Bureau of the Census, *Social and Economic Characteristics of the Metropolitan and Non-Metropolitan Population, 1977 and 1970.*

central cities, because the rate changes outweigh the capital gains changes. The business tax changes are likely to hurt the relative position of central cities, however, as the indeterminate impacts of the corporate tax rate changes will probably be more than offset by the changes in the ITC. Central cities will fare worse than suburban areas under the ITC changes because the relatively greater suburban stimulus of the credit at 10 percent and the increase in the share of tax liabilities which can be offset by the credit will combine to outweigh the effects of extending the credit to rehabilitation expenditures on buildings in use for 20 years or more. Unfortunately, the absence of 19 quantitative estimates of the relative impacts of these components makes it impossible to assess their net impact, but the following comments are worth noting.

Because the personal income tax changes are beneficial to central cities and the business tax changes are not, the overall effect of the Act on central cities is uncertain. It is instructive, however, to consider it in the context of the alternatives available for achieving the primary goals of the tax cut: general stimulus of aggregate demand in the national economy and special stimulus of business investment. Beneficial urban impacts are only one of many federal program goals and only a secondary goal of the tax system. Thus, it is appropriate to ask if there are ways to achieve the primary goals of the program with better or worse urban side effects. Viewed in this context, the new tax bill looks far more favorable to central cities.

There are a variety of ways to use tax cuts for economic stimulus, not all of which are beneficial to central cities. Larger personal exemptions or proportional tax credits, for example, could provide tax cuts without significant reductions in homeowner subsidies. The Revenue Act of 1978, however, continues the last decade's trend toward increasing the share of taxpayers using the standard deduction rather than itemizing. This alone reduces the owner-renter bias of the tax system and, indeed, the aggregate impact of homeowner subsidies is smaller now than it was a decade ago. In a period of inflation, it would be quite easy for the tax code to move in the opposite direction and increase the fraction of taxpayers who itemize, but the Revenue Act of 1978 reduces this fraction and thereby decreases the tax code's spatial bias.

The spatial bias of the ITC, however, is largely inherent in any investment stimulus policy and, when the national economy needs such a stimulus, the ITC is a relatively efficient means of providing it. Therefore, the more important urban impact may well be the central city boost provided by the personal income tax changes, because these were in a sense discretionary. In other words, virtually any means of achieving the microeconomic goal of investment stimulus would have undesirable impacts on central cities, but several forms of personal income tax cuts could have been less beneficial to central cities. Where the negative central city impact was avoidable, the Revenue Act of 1978 successfully avoided it.

REFERENCES

Aaron, Henry. "Income Taxes and Housing." *American Economic Review* 60 (December 1970): 789–806.

Bahl, Roy W., and Puryear, David. *The President's Tax Program.* Methods of Urban Impact Analysis no. 1. Washington, D.C.: Office of Policy Development and Research, U.S. Department of Housing and Urban Development, 1978.

Cragg, J. G.; Harberger, Arnold C.; and Mieszkowski, P. "Empirical Evidence on the Incidence of the Corporate Income Tax." *Journal of Political Economy* 75 (December 1967): 811–21.

Hall, C. A., Jr. "Direct Shifting of the Corporation Income Tax in Manufacturing." *Papers and Proceedings of the American Economic Association* 54 (May 1964): 258–71.

Harberger, Arnold C. "The Incidence of the Corporate Income Tax." *Journal of Political Economy* 70 (June 1962): 215–40.

Krzyzaniak, M., and Musgrave, R. A. *The Shifting of the Corporation Income Tax.* Baltimore: Johns Hopkins Press, 1963.

Laidler, David. "Income Tax Incentives for Owner Occupied Housing." In *The Taxation of Income from Capital*, edited by Arnold C. Harberger and Martin J. Bailey. Washington, D.C.: Brookings Institution, 1969.

McHugh, Richard, and Puryear, David. "Tax Credits for Urban Revitalization." In *The Federal Response to the Fiscal Crisis in Cities*, edited by Kenneth Hubbell. Cambridge, Mass.: Ballinger, forthcoming.

Mieszkowski, Peter. "Tax Incidence Theory: The Effects of Taxes on the Distribution of Income." *Journal of Economic Literature* 7 (December 1969): 1103–24.

Mills, Edwin. *Studies in the Structure of the Urban Economy.* Baltimore: Johns Hopkins Press, 1972.

Muth, Richard. *Cities and Housing.* Chicago: University of Chicago Press, 1969.

Peterson, George E. "Federal Tax Policy and Urban Development." Testimony before the Subcommittee on the City of the Committee on Banking, Finance, and Urban Affairs, U.S. House of Representatives, 95th Cong., 1st sess., 1977.

Shelton, John P. "The Cost of Renting Versus Owning a Home." *Land Economics* 44 (February 1968): 63–68.

Slitor, Richard E. *Tax Effects on Urban Growth in Three Cities.* WN-8424-NSF. Santa Monica: Rand Institute, October 1973.

Sunley, Emil M. "Tax Advantages of Homeownership Versus Renting: A Cause of Suburban Migration?" *Proceedings of the Sixty-Third Annual Conference on Taxation*, pp. 386–87. Columbus, Ohio: National Tax Association, 1970.

Tolley, George S., and Diamond, Douglas B. *Homeownership, Rental Housing and Tax Incentives.* Report to the U.S. Department of Housing and Urban Development, February 1977. Submitted as part of the Appendix to *Federal Tax Policy and Urban Development.* Hearings before a Subcommittee of the House Committee on Banking, Finance, and Urban Affairs, House of Representatives, 95th Cong., 1st Sess., 1977.

U.S. Congress. House Conference Report on H.R. 13511, Revenue Act of 1978. 95th Cong., 2nd Sess., October 14, 1978. *Congressional Record*, No. 168, Part III.

U.S. Department of Commerce. Bureau of the Census. *Current Housing Reports,* Series H-150-76. Annual Housing Survey, Part A. Washington, D.C.: U.S. Government Printing Office, 1978.

————. *Current Housing Reports,* Series H-150-76. Annual Housing Survey, Part C. Washington, D.C.: U.S. Government Printing Office, 1978.

————. *Social and Economic Characteristics of the Metropolitan and Non Metropolitan Population, 1977 and 1970.* Washington, D.C.: U.S. Government Printing Office, 1978.

U.S. Internal Revenue Service. *Corporation Income Tax Returns, Statistics of Income, 1973.* Washington, D.C.: U.S. Government Printing Office, 1976.

————. *Individual Income Tax Returns, Statistics of Income, 1975.* Washington, D.C.: U.S. Government Printing Office, 1978.

U.S. Treasury Department, Office of Tax Analysis. *Revenue Effects of H.R. 13511.* Mimeographed; October 26, 1978.

CHAPTER TWENTY

Federal Policy and State and Local Fiscal Conditions

ROGER J. VAUGHAN

INTRODUCTION

The debate on what the Federal government can do to help fiscally distressed State and local governments has focused almost entirely on direct grants. Yet, as we have become uncomfortably aware during the last few years, federal impacts on local fiscal conditions extend beyond the design and volume of grants. This paper explores three ways in which federal policies could be modified to improve local fiscal conditions:

1. State and local governments would be allowed to offer taxable bonds with interest cost subsidies provided by the U.S. Treasury;
2. the state portion of revenue sharing would be used to subsidize state property tax circuit breakers, in the form of a closed-end matching grant; and
3. federal incentives would be offered to reduce interstate tax competition to attract business.

These three measures will be discussed within the framework of Urban Impact Analyses as described in Executive Circular A-116 as if these were new initiatives. They have been chosen because they require little or no additional net federal expenditure and have received some consideration in the ongoing urban policy debate. The summary also identifies the data needed for a more thorough analysis.

The author is grateful for comments on an earlier draft from Professor James Little of Washington University.

ALLOWING A TAXABLE STATE AND LOCAL BOND[1]

The exemption of state and local bond interest payments from federal income tax was intended to reduce the cost of borrowing to State and local governments. Purchasers of bonds require lower interest payments since they pay no federal taxes—a taxpayer in the 50 percent marginal tax bracket would be satisfied with a rate of interest about half that paid on taxable corporate bonds. Galper and Peterson (1973) found that about 70 percent of household tax-exempt bonds were held by households with marginal tax rates above 50 percent. From the viewpoint of the local public sector, the "tax expenditure" approach has some advantages. First, it is open-ended—the more bonds that are floated, the greater the implicit federal subsidy. Second, the policy is an automatic entitlement—no congressional approval is required so no budget cutting fever will cut off the subsidy. However, tax expenditures also have several disadvantages. Local governments must now expand capital expenditures to make up for maintenance and repair projects deferred by the 1973–75 recession and the painful rebuilding of local portfolios. At the same time, there is considerable public pressure to reduce expenditure at all levels of government. This is an appropriate time to reconsider the merits of the tax-exempt bond.

Problems

The first problem is that only a part of the tax receipts foregone by the Treasury actually goes to reduce public borrowing costs. The remainder is a subsidy to high-income bondholders. Estimates place the personal subsidy at between 25 percent and 30 percent of foregone revenues. Morris (1976) estimates that the tax exemption of bond interest cost the Treasury $4.8 billion in 1976, of which only $3.5 billion effectively reduced state and local borrowing costs. Intramarginal bondholders enjoyed a subsidy of $1.3 billion. Total state and local interest payments in that year were approximately $10.5 billion.

A second problem is that the market for tax-free bonds has been narrowing while public issues have been competing, increasingly, with pollution-control bonds. For example, commercial banks made 90 percent of net purchases of tax free bonds in 1968, but only 10 percent in 1975 (Table 1). Other tax shelters have become more attractive during periods of rising inflation. The lowering of the maximum federal income tax rate on personal income in 1976 may have reduced the number of household buyers. Pollution-control bonds, granted tax-exempt status in 1969, grew from only $100 mil-

---

[1] This section has benefited by access to "Federal Action to Improve Access to Credit Markets by Urban Governments: A Bond Guarantee Proposal," unpublished paper prepared by the Office of Policy Development and Research, U.S. Department of Housing and Urban Development, September 16, 1977. *See also* Galper and Peterson (1973) and Shaul (1977).

TABLE 1: The Municipal Bond Market, 1960–1976

| Year | Total Outstanding State and Local Government Securities (Par Value) (billions of dollars) | NET PURCHASES | | | | | |
| | | Commercial Banks | | Households | | Nonlife Insurance Companies | |
		Billions of Dollars	% Total Purchases	Billions of Dollars	% Total Purchases	Billions of Dollars	% Total Purchases
1960	70.8	0.6	11	3.5	66	0.8	15
1961	75.8	2.8	55	1.2	24	1.0	20
1962	81.2	5.7	106	−1.0	—	0.8	15
1963	86.9	3.9	68	1.0	18	0.7	12
1964	92.9	3.6	60	2.6	43	0.4	7
1965	100.3	5.2	71	1.7	23	0.4	5
1966	106.0	2.3	41	3.6	64	1.3	23
1967	113.7	9.1	117	−2.2	—	1.4	18
1968	123.2	8.6	90	−0.8	—	1.0	10
1969	133.1	0.2	2	9.6	97	1.2	12
1970	144.5	10.7	96	−0.8	—	1.4	12
1971	161.9	12.6	72	−0.2	—	3.9	22
1972	177.3	7.2	47	2.1	14	4.8	31
1973	193.6	5.7	35	7.3	45	3.6	22
1974	213.2	5.5	28	11.1	57	2.4	12
1975	230.5	1.7	10	8.7	50	1.7	10
1976	247.7	2.9	17	6.4	37	3.6	21

Sources: Board of Governors, Federal Reserve System, Flow of Funds Accounts, various years; U.S. Treasury, Treasury Bulletin, various years; U.S. Bureau of the Census, Governmental Finances, various years.

FIGURE 1: The Ratio of A and Aaa Municipal Tax-Free Bond Yields to Aa Corporate Yields (new issues)

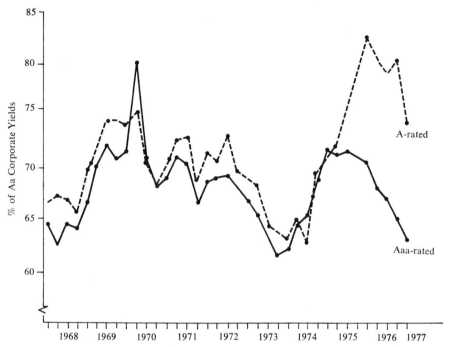

Source: Gray, in U.S. Congress (1977).

lion in 1971 to $2.2 billion in 1975, a year when State and local governments issued $31.6 billion in long-term debt. The tax-exempt market contains some 120,000 issues put out by 20,000 local authorities.

Third, the interest on state and local bonds is much more volatile than on taxable issues. This volatility results from the selling of municipal bonds by banks during periods when alternatives become much more attractive. The price falls and yields rise to induce other investors to absorb these sales. For example, the average yield on Aa municipals rose from 62 percent of the yield on Aa corporate bonds in January 1968 to 73 percent in June of 1970. A similar shift occurred between 1973 and 1975 (Figure 1).[2] A period when inflationary expectations rise leads to more rapid increases in public borrowing costs than private borrowing costs. The fluctuations are even more pronounced for those municipalities that do not enjoy Aa rating.[3] The fiscal

[2] See *Treasury Bulletin*, U.S. Department of Treasury, Washington, D.C., various months.

[3] In December 1978, Cleveland bonds with a Ca rating yielded a tax-exempt 12 percent, while U.S. Treasury bonds yielded a taxable 8.2 percent.

crises in New York, Cleveland, Yonkers, Newark, and other cities have served to increase the volatility of bond-interest payments.

The initiative[4]

State and local governments would be allowed to offer taxable bonds with a given percent of the annual interest cost refunded by the U.S. Treasury.

The urban impacts of taxable bonds

The impacts depend upon the level of the subsidy and whether the taxable bond is an option or mandatory. Given the prevailing atmosphere of fiscal restraint, it is reasonable to anticipate that a subsidy rate of 33 to 35 percent is politically feasible since this would involve little net increase in Treasury outlays and yet would provide State and local governments with substantial benefits. Under the optional strategy, benefits are greater when the market for tax-exempt bond is tight, and relatively small when the market is easy. It is therefore difficult to pinpoint the aggregate annual benefit. A report to the House Ways and Means Committee in 1976 estimated that a 35 percent subsidy would save State and local governments about $1.0 billion a year, and cost the Treasury only $140 million in the long run. It takes several years for benefits of this level to be enjoyed since it takes time for tax-exempt bonds to be replaced with taxable bonds by interested borrowing authorities. The short-run benefits would be smaller but qualitatively similar to the long-run benefits examined below.

Under the strategy that would abolish tax exemption, the maximum benefits that State and local governments could receive at no net expense to the Treasury is obviously the $1.5 billion subsidy currently received by intra-marginal investors. For the calculations of benefits we shall assume that approximately $1 billion in benefits would be provided under the optional strategy, at negligible cost to the Treasury.

The shift into the taxable market will have a small effect on interest rates—an increase of between 0.01 and 0.03 percentage points on corporate rates (*Fortune*, 1973). How are the benefits of this $1 billion reduction distributed? Table 2 shows benefits per capita and per $1000 of personal income by state, and is based on the simplifying assumption that benefits are distributed among states according to their share of total state and local debt. States are grouped according to their fiscal "blood pressure" as calculated by the Advisory Commission for Intergovernmental Relations. It is apparent that benefits tend to

[4] There have been several initiatives of the sort outlined below. Using a large econometric model, *Fortune* (1973) simulated the impacts of taxable bonds with different levels of subsidy. In June 1976, Treasury advocated removing the exemption and granting of a 30 percent subsidy. The House Ways and Means Committee approved a bill that offered a 35 percent subsidy (the Municipal Taxable Bond Alternative Act of 1976, H.R. 12774). Earlier Senator Proxmire had introduced a bill with a 33 percent subsidy (S. 3215, 1972). Senator McGovern endorsed a 50-percent subsidy during his presidential campaign in 1972.

TABLE 2: Benefits of a $1 Billion Reduction in State and Local Borrowing Costs, by Fiscal "Blood Pressure" of States

State, by "Blood Pressure"[a]	*Benefits* Per Cap.	Per $1,000 Pers. Inc.	State, by "Blood Pressure"[a]	*Benefits* Per Cap.	Per $1,000 Pers. Inc.
High and Falling			*High and Rising*		
Wisconsin	$3.3	$ .54	New York	$10.0	$1.41
Arizona	4.8	.84	Vermont	4.9	.91
New Mexico	2.9	.55	Massachusetts	6.1	.92
Louisiana	4.9	.94	California	3.7	.53
Wyoming	4.5	.70	Hawaii	7.9	1.13
Montana	2.7	.48	Minnesota	5.0	.81
Oregon	6.7	1.09	Maine	3.7	.70
Washington	8.9	1.33	Nevada	4.4	.64
Mississippi	3.1	.69	Maryland	6.0	.88
Unweighted av.	*4.6*	*.79*	Rhode Island	4.6	.74
			West Virginia	4.0	.76
Low and Falling			Michigan	4.0	.59
South Dakota	2.0	.40	New Jersey	4.7	.64
Iowa	1.9	.31	Illinois	4.1	.55
Colorado	3.3	.51	Delaware	7.7	1.09
Utah	2.1	.41	Pennsylvania	5.5	.85
North Dakota	2.5	.43	*Unweighted av.*	*5.4*	*.82*
Indiana	2.0	.33			
Idaho	1.3	.24			
Kansas	3.8	.59	*Low and Rising*		
North Carolina	1.9	.35	Kentucky	4.8	.89
Nebraska	7.8	1.30	Connecticut	6.4	.86
South Carolina	3.1	.61	Alaska	21.9	2.24
Texas	4.0	.66	Georgia	3.2	.59
Oklahoma	3.1	.55	New Hampshire	3.3	.57
Florida	3.7	.62	Dist. of Columbia	14.3	1.74
Tennessee	4.3	.82	Virginia	3.3	.52
Alabama	3.3	.65	Missouri	2.5	.42
Arkansas	2.1	.44	Ohio	3.2	.51
Unweighted av.	*3.1*	*.54*	*Unweighted av.*	*7.0*	*.93*

Sources: ACIR (1977); U.S. Bureau of the Census (1978).

Note: The assumption is made that benefits from the $1 billion savings are distributed in proportion to the states' share of total state and local indebtedness.

[a] States are listed in descending order of fiscal "blood pressure" within each category.

be greatest in the fiscally distressed states which tend to be located in the Northeast (Table 3).

The targeting is not precise, however. Among the "low blood pressure" areas receiving high benefits are Alaska, Nebraska, and the District of Co-

TABLE 3: Benefits of a $1 Billion Reduction in Borrowing Costs, by Region

	Benefits	
	Per Capita	*Per $1,000 Pers. Inc.*
New England	$4.8	$0.78
Middle Atlantic	6.7	0.97
East North Central	3.3	0.50
West North Central	3.6	0.61
South Atlantic	5.2	0.80
East South Central	3.9	0.76
West South Central	3.5	0.65
Mountain	3.3	0.55
Pacific	9.8	1.26

Source: Derived from Table 2.

lumbia. California and the New England states receive little assistance among the "high and rising" states.

Actually, the benefits will be more effectively targeted toward fiscal distress than Table 2 suggests. The taxable option will be exercised more readily by those distressed states and cities in the Northeast whose relatively low bond rating has either squeezed them out of the bond market, or has left them paying very high rates. The proportional federal subsidy would mean that their subsidy per $1 million of bonds issued would be much higher than elsewhere.[5] The broader market for taxable bonds will also lead to a reduction in the net interest rate they would have paid had they stayed in the tax-exempt market, and reduce fluctuations. Table 4 shows the municipal bond ratings and current average yield for a selection of cities that score high and low on the Nathan urban conditions index, as well as per capita indebtedness. Those cities that score highly on the urban conditions index tend to have less favorable bond ratings. The correspondence is not perfect, however.

It is difficult to trace the distribution of benefits below this rather aggregated level. Some of the savings will be passed on in terms of tax reductions, while some will be used to expand capital borrowing. Since the cost of the program is borne almost entirely by high-tax-bracket households, the net effect of the program will be to redistribute income toward less well-off households, although the benefits to the poor will be negligible.[6]

---

[5] If the subsidy were accompanied by a federal guarantee then this additional targeting would be reduced since the bonds would carry no risk premium implicit in their rates.

[6] Local government response to revenue sharing funds suggest that a gain in resources leads to increases in education expenditure at the state level, but no increases in public safety and tax stabilization at the local level (Vernez et al., forthcoming).

TABLE 4: Urban Conditions, Bond Rating, Yield, and Per Capita Indebtedness, for Selected Cities

City	Urban Conditions Index	Bond Rating (General Obligation) (Dec. 1978)	Average Annual Yield (Dec. 1978)	Per Capita Indebtedness (FY 1975)
St. Louis	351	A	6.60	304
Newark	321	Baa	7.00	422
Buffalo	292	Baa	7.00	710
Cleveland	291	A	6.60	596
Boston	257	Baa	7.00	846
Unweighted av.	302		6.84	576
Baltimore	226	A	6.60	643
Philadelphia	216	Baa	7.00	700
Detroit	201	Baa	7.00	550
Chicago	201	Aa	6.41	411
Atlanta	118	Aa	6.41	1,237
Unweighted av.	192		6.68	708
Denver	106	Aa	6.41	719
Los Angeles	74	Aaa	6.05	837
Dallas	39	Aaa	6.05	586
Houston	37	Aaa	6.05	494
Phoenix	20	Aa	6.41	497
Unweighted av.	55		6.19	626
15-city av.	183		6.57	637

Sources: Dommel et al. (1978); U.S. Bureau of the Census (1978); *Moody's Bond Record* (January 1979).

The program has several desirable outcomes: it helps fiscally distressed cities, encourages increased public borrowing at a time when lack of capital spending is viewed by some as nearing a crisis, is paid for by the relatively affluent, and will tend, in aggregate, to shift spending toward the less affluent. What are its main disadvantages? The major disadvantage is, that by reducing the local cost differentials associated with different bond ratings, some of the incentive for prudent fiscal management is reduced. This is unlikely to be a serious problem, since the incentive is not so much the increased interest rates as it is the inability to enter the bond market on any terms. Second, the shifting of public borrowing into direct competition with private industry may tend to displace some private investment. In view of the fluidity of international capital flows the supply of loanable funds is highly elastic and so displacement is unlikely to be a major problem. Second, because the subsidy, unlike the tax exemption, would be "a direct, visible, and growing cost for the Federal government, some have argued that Congress would try to gain control over this substantial expenditure" (Shaul, 1977, p. 13). Politically, it would be difficult for Congress to curtail the subsidy. A final potential problem is that the narrowing of the tax-exempt market may create problems for those remaining in it—pollution control authorities, industrial development authorities, and high-grade State and local governments. This seems unlikely since the market will contain a broad range of issues.

FEDERAL SUBSIDIZATION OF STATE CIRCUIT BREAKERS FROM STATE PORTION OF GENERAL REVENUE SHARING

While the previous initiative has been debated often in the last decade, the initiative discussed in this section is new. It is intended to deal with the problems of taxpayer revolt against property taxes and the failure of revenue sharing—particularly that portion going to State governments—to lead to substantial redistribution of resources toward either poor jurisdictions or poor households.

The problem

Within the polar views held by those who would concentrate almost all fiscal functions in Washington, and extreme states' rightists, the growth of the state and local sector has created a dilemma. Local authority over expenditure, at least in some categories, is applauded, while the regressive structure of state and local taxes is regretted (Table 5, column 7). General Revenue Sharing was viewed as a partial solution. Revenue collected through the relatively progressive federal tax structure is turned over to State and local governments, with no strings attached, and with some consideration given to local needs and resources. The program now distributes over $6 billion annually, with about one third going to State governments and the remainder going to counties, municipalities, and special districts.

Opposition to the state portion has grown. Fiscally strapped local governments point to state surpluses and to the non-redistributive structure of state disbursements. President Carter is known to oppose extending the state allocation. Table 5 (column 8) shows a redistributive index of state expenditures (computed by ACIR). States vary widely, and many have little or no redistributive impact. Even states that have implemented intrastate revenue sharing programs have little redistributive impact (Table 6).[7] If redistribution at the household level were examined, states would score even lower. There is little evidence that state General Revenue Sharing funds trickle down to benefit the poor. The inequity of the present local taxing and expenditure structure has been recognized in the landmark court decisions concerning school finance. Because of court decisions in other states following *Serrano v. Priest* in California, state aid to education will be increased and reliance on the local property tax reduced.

---

[7] Individually, states resist too much redistribution in their expenditures and progressivity in their tax structures in fear of driving away high-income households.

TABLE 5: Summary of State Fiscal Condition, Revenue Sharing Receipts, and Circuit Breakers

State	Property Tax $ Per Capita 1975	Sharing Receipts FY 1977 $ Per Capita	Sharing Receipts FY 1977 $ Millions	Property Tax Limitations on Rate[a]	Property Tax Limitations on Levy[a]	State/Local Tax Redistribution Index	Expenditure Redistribution Index	Circuit Breakers, 1977 Total Program Cost ($ millions)	Circuit Breakers, 1977 Number Beneficiaries	Circuit Breakers, 1977 Cost Per Beneficiary ($)
Alabama	22	9.67	35.7	CMS	M	78	111	—	—	—
Alaska	79	10.89	4.4	M	M	—	250	—	—	—
Arizona	106	11.26	25.9	M	CM	89	122	n.a.	n.a.	n.a.
Arkansas	35	10.85	23.3	CMS		106	47	0.7	8,916	75.76
California	202	10.61	232.4	CMS	CM	123	78	85.0	440,000	193.18
Colorado	97	9.22	24.2		CMS	88	89	11.0	58,875	187.00
Connecticut	199	9.09	28.3			62	50	24.7	101,574	243.70
Delaware	53	11.95	7.0	C		104	181	—	—	—
D. C.	102	0	0			—	—	—	—	—
Florida	82	7.94	67.1	CMS		53	106	0.6	6,000	100.00
Georgia	72	9.16	46.3	CMS		103	100	—	—	—
Hawaii	86	11.25	10.1			—	205	4.2	n.a.	n.a.
Idaho	51	9.55	8.2	CMS		115	92	4.0	17,323	231.00
Illinois	117	9.96	112.0	CMS		71	111	100.0	405,000	250.00
Indiana	88	8.62	46.0	CMS	CMS	71	69	0.8	28,665	29.45
Iowa	87	9.48	27.3	CMS	CM	79	97	9.6	83,200	114.56
Kansas	83	8.49	19.7	CMS	CMS	81	78	8.8	62,955	140.17
Kentucky	37	10.81	37.4	CMS		86	97	—	—	—
Louisiana	32	11.96	46.9	CMS		78	142	—	—	—
Maine	104	12.63	13.6			80	125	4.3	20,786	209.10
Maryland	126	11.82	48.9			91	69	20.8	83,863	248.12
Massachusetts	229	11.78	68.1			83	133	—	—	—
Michigan	130	10.00	91.3	CM		99	139	275.6	1,234,800	223.18
Minnesota	103	11.85	47.1	MS	CM	98	125	134.2	857,277	156.54

State								
Mississippi	38	14.02	33.5	CMS	68	122	—	—	—
Missouri	76	8.64	41.5	<u>CMS</u>	85	72	7.0	56,260	124.57
Montana	95	10.65	8.1	CMS	96	117	—	—	—
Nebraska	91	8.95	14.0	CMS	82	42	—	—	—
Nevada	133	8.43	5.3	<u>CMS</u>	56	83	1.4	10,560	127.84
New Hampshire	163	8.54	7.3		62	36	—	—	—
New Jersey	216	9.37	68.7		67	61	—	—	—
New Mexico	34	12.09	14.4	CMS	103	158	1.5	40,000	37.50
New York	181	16.38	293.7	CMS	142	144	n.a.	n.a.	n.a.
North Carolina	48	10.92	60.3	CM	98	119	—	—	—
North Dakota	54	9.38	6.1	CMS	109	75	1.2	9,964	120.20
Ohio	86	8.28	88.6	<u>CMS</u>	89	69	44.6	329,462	135.42
Oklahoma	41	8.58	24.1	<u>CMS</u>	106	69	0.4	4,159	85.93
Oregon	128	9.99	23.8	<u>CMS</u>	126	58	74.1	502,575	147.52
Pennsylvania	62	9.81	115.6	CMS	77	117	58.9	413,974	142.32
Rhode Island	150	13.12	12.3		84	131	0.01	249	51.92
South Carolina	42	11.81	34.0	S	109	50	—	—	—
South Dakota	80	10.78	7.4	CMS	59	58	1.5	15,095	98.51
Tennessee	52	9.47	40.7		56	83	—	—	—
Texas	68	8.61	110.6	CMS	57	86	—	—	—
Utah	65	9.80	12.4	<u>CMS</u>	90	103	0.9	10,000	95.00
Vermont	137	12.87	6.2		106	106	7.7	36,516	210.05
Virginia	83	8.63	44.3		95	72	—	—	—
Washington	123	11.22	41.1	<u>CM</u>	51	111	—	—	—
West Virginia	39	12.54	23.3	<u>CMS</u>	91	94	0.02	1,265	13.94
Wisconsin	115	11.55	53.7	CMS	99	133	48.1	234,201	205.55
Wyoming	66	8.70	3.5	CMS	57	61	—	—	—

Sources: ACIR, *Family Tax Burdens* . . . (1978); U.S. Bureau of the Census (November 1978); *State Government News* (1978).

Notes: The entry n.a. means data are not available. Absence of a program is indicated by a dash.

[a] Key to codes: C—the limitation applies to counties; M—the limitation applies to municipalities; S—the limitation applies to school districts; <u>underline</u>—the limitation is by constitutional amendment.

TABLE 6: State Programs of Revenue Sharing with Local Governments
($25 Million or More), 1973

State	Revenue Source	Allocation Factors	Amount Shared (millions)	Relative Degree of Equalization
Arizona	General sales tax	Counties: origin basis Municipalities: population	$ 83.8	Negligible
California	Motor vehicle licenses	Population	245.0	Negative
	Cigarette taxes	Sales tax collections and population of cities	74.3	Negative
Florida	Miscellaneous excise taxes	Population, sales tax collections, and (inversely) property tax capacity	171.3	Slight
Illinois	Personal and corporate income taxes	Population	95.0	Slight
Louisiana	Tobacco taxes	Population	26.0	Negative
	General funds	Population and number of homesteads	86.0	Negligible
Michigan	General sales tax	Population	116.0	Negligible
	Personal income tax	Population and relative tax effort	82.0	Negligible
	Intangibles tax	Population and relative tax effort	27.5	Slight
Minnesota	General sales tax	Population	100.7	Negligible
New Jersey	General sales tax	Population	25.0	Negligible
New York	Personal income tax	Population, personal income, real property full value	450.8	Slight
North Carolina	Intangible property tax	Population, origin, property tax rates	25.6	Negligible
Ohio	Miscellaneous taxes	Population, municipal valuation, "need"	117.7	Negligible
Tennessee	General sales tax	Population	27.5	Negligible
Wisconsin	Miscellaneous taxes	Population, property tax rates, value of utility property	265.4	Negligible

Source: ACIR (1974), pp. 79–81; interpretation by Rafuse, 1974.

Any increase in state redistributive activity has been made more remote by the scrutiny of taxpayers angered by spiralling property taxes. Property tax rates or levies are limited at either the state, county, or municipal level in 39 states, in differing ways (Table 5, columns 5 and 6).[8] The property tax is without a doubt the least popular of all taxes.[9] The weight of the evidence suggests that local assessment practices coupled with the basic incidence of the tax unite to make it regressive, inequitable, and unpopular in most areas. This perception, coupled with rapidly rising property values, has caused 30 states and the District of Columbia to introduce circuit breakers (*see* Table 5, columns 9, 10, and 11).[10] This is a form of tax relief in which benefits depend on both household income and the amount of property taxes paid. It may take two forms (ACIR, 1978):

Under the *threshold approach*, an "acceptable" tax burden is defined as some fixed percentage of household income (different percentages may be set for different income levels), and any tax above this portion of income is "excessive" and qualifies for relief. Under the *sliding scale approach*, no threshold is defined. Rather a fixed percentage of property tax . . . is rebated for each eligible taxpayer within a given income class; the rebate percentage declines as income rises.

Wisconsin was the first state to adopt a circuit breaker in 1964. By 1970, six states had circuit breakers, and by 1978, 29 states and the District of Columbia had adopted some form of circuit breaker. Most non-circuit-breaker states have below average property tax rates, except Massachusetts, New Jersey, Nebraska, and New Hampshire. In 1977 more than 5 million households received benefits totalling nearly $1 billion—an average of nearly $184 per household (Table 5). Both homeowners and renters are covered in 24 of the states.[11] Benefits vary among states, from $250 per beneficiary in Illinois, to $14 in West Virginia. In some cases, the rebate is either in cash, a credit against state income tax due, or a reduction in property tax payments.

The initiative

To encourage greater redistribution of resources among households by State governments and to mollify opposition to the property tax without increasing federal obligations, the state portion of General Revenue Sharing ($2.3 billion) would be set aside as a closed-ended matching fund to subsidize

---

[8] For a recent description of fiscal limitations, see National Governors' Association (1978).

[9] See the results of the Gallup Poll, reported in "The Big Tax Revolt," *Newsweek*, June 19, 1978.

[10] This discussion has benefited from an unpublished manuscript, *Property Tax Relief*, by Steven Gold, to be published by the Urban Institute, Washington, D.C.

[11] For renters, it is assumed that some proportion of the rent represents property taxes passed on to tenants by landlords. This ranges from 6 percent in New Mexico to 30 percent in Illinois, and averages around 20 percent.

state-financed property tax circuit breakers. Only that portion of such circuit breakers that assisted households with incomes below an upper limit would be eligible. Programs would also have to extend participation to renters as well as homeowners to be eligible for federal matching grants. Thus if eligible state programs made $4.4 billion in payments or foregone revenues on other taxes, 50 percent of states' costs would be reimbursed. At $6.6 billion in state expenditure, 33 percent of costs would be reimbursed.

The urban impacts of federal circuit-breaker subsidies

The urban impact of the initiative depends upon the type of circuit-breaker programs that are eligible for federal matching funds. The purpose of a circuit breaker is redistributive, and, therefore, designing must ensure that the greatest benefits flow to those in greatest need and none to those not in need. To ensure that the program operates effectively, key issues are eligibility and the distribution of benefits among the eligible.

Three of the most common characteristics used to define eligibility are income (in all but four states), age, and occupancy. Upper income limits range from $3,750 for single homeowners in New Mexico, to $20,000 for elderly homeowners in the District of Columbia. Some upper limit seems reasonable. Some programs are limited to the elderly because many elderly are poor and because they tend to be relatively immobile and live on fixed incomes, so that they cannot easily adapt to soaring local property taxes. However, this may make the program relatively regressive. The federal subsidy would only be available for that share of the state-run program that went to households below an upper limit—perhaps between $12,000 and $15,000.

Treatment of renters is a difficult problem. Under most programs that include renters, homeowners receive more generous benefits (ACIR, 1973). Most programs that extend benefits to renters assume that about 20 percent of rent represents property taxes. The highest is Illinois at 30 percent, and the lowest is 6 percent in New Mexico. There is also a problem in that incomes in the two groups are not directly comparable. A household that owns its own home is "better off" in some sense than a household of comparable money income that rents because of the value of the housing services it enjoys. Whether this should be taken into account depends upon whether the circuit breaker is used primarily as property relief or as an income supplement. As an income supplement, a circuit breaker can never perform as well as a cash transfer, but may be more politically expedient and administratively simple. Overall, the circuit breaker works well in targeting benefits to those who need them.

To minimize the problem of interjurisdictional movement by households seeking maximum benefits, responsibility for financing a circuit breaker should rest with the State government, not with local jurisdictions. The program redistributes resources toward jurisdictions with relatively high concentrations of low income households.

Even within the design parameters outlined above, the cost of circuit breakers depends upon the percent of the "excess" property tax that a household receives in a rebate. This is defined by two factors: the percent of income that tax payments cannot exceed for threshold type programs; and the design of the sliding scale. In 1970, the ACIR (1973) estimated that if 7 percent were the household level, a nationwide program would cost $2 billion and reach 13.5 million households. A 5 percent threshold would cost $4.3 billion, reaching 21 million households, and a 4 percent threshold $6.1 billion reaching half of all households. If costs have risen proportionately with property tax payments—surely a conservative estimate—costs today would be more than double.

It is difficult to assess, with any degree of accuracy, the distribution of the benefits because state participation would be voluntary. Present programs would have to be modified in several states to make them eligible. Net benefits will be greatest in those jurisdictions with a high incidence of poverty, high property tax rates, and low per capita receipts of state revenue sharing funds. Like the previous initiative, the full benefits of this would be delayed some years, as states adopted new or modified existing programs to take full advantage of the federal subsidy. Table 5, column 2 shows residential property tax collections per capita by state. High taxing states include California, Connecticut, Massachusetts, New Hampshire, New York, and Rhode Island. These also tend to be relatively rich but with large concentrations of urban poor. New York and Rhode Island enjoy high per capita state revenue sharing payments (Table 5, column 3), and would therefore gain smaller net benefits than the other states. California's Constitutional Amendment 13A has reduced, at least temporarily, the benefits that state would enjoy from the program and it would probably be a net loser. Other almost certain net losers from the program would include Alabama, Arkansas, Mississippi, and West Virginia, even if they were to implement circuit breakers. Property taxes in these states tend to be so low that eligible refunds will not equal current state revenue sharing payments.

Within states, there are not sufficient data to estimate how benefits would be distributed between city and suburbs. While central cities have greater concentrations of the poor, they have lower valued housing and, often, lower property tax rates. In general, the initiative would tend to provide greater per capita benefits for cities than suburbs, depending upon the fraction of rent ascribed to property taxes. The benefits would be effectively targeted toward poorer jurisdictions, and allowing them to raise local taxes without imposing extreme hardship upon the local poor and lower middle income groups. It would, therefore, strengthen the fiscal position of those jurisdictions with a relatively weak fiscal base. It would also weaken property tax limitation movements and perhaps avoid too many repetitions of the clumsy efforts made in California.

The program does target effectively on distressed cities. Table 7 shows 15 cities grouped according to their urban conditions index, showing the per capita residential property tax and percent of the population below the poverty level—the two main determinants of the relative benefits under a circuit-breaker program. The final column shows a crude index of the likely relative benefits under a circuit breaker—calculated as the product of their tax payments and poverty rates indexed to the average of all 15 cities. Among the

TABLE 7: Urban Conditions Index, Per Capita Residential Property Tax, Percent Poverty, and Benefit Index, for Selected Cities

City	Urban Conditions Index[a]	Per Capita Residential Property Tax (1976)	Percent Poverty (1970)	Index of Per Capita Benefit from Circuit Breaker (15-city av = 100)[b]
St. Louis	351	228	33.6	148
Newark	321	493	22.1	211
Buffalo	292	307	14.8	88
Cleveland	291	286	17.0	94
Boston	257	483	15.3	143
Unweighted av.	302	359	20.6	137
Baltimore	226	196	18.0	68
Philadelphia	216	237	20.8	95
Detroit	201	352	14.7	96
Chicago	201	319	14.3	88
Atlanta	118	256	19.8	98
Unweighted av.	192	272	17.5	89
Denver	106	284	11.5	63
Los Angeles	74	419	11.2	91
Dallas	39	247	13.3	64
Houston	37	286	13.9	77
Phoenix	20	218	11.6	49
Unweighted av.	55	290	12.3	69
15-city av.	183	307	16.8	100

Sources: Dommel et al. (1978); The Tax Foundation, *Monthly Tax Features* (August 1978).

[a] For definition, *see* Dommel et al. (1978).

[b] Calculated as follows:

$$\frac{\text{Per capita residential property tax}}{\text{Mean for all 15 cities } (= \$307)} \times \frac{\text{Percent poverty}}{\text{Mean for all 15 cities } (= 16.8)}$$

severely distressed cities, Buffalo scores well below 100, because of its relatively low poverty rate.

There are two provisions of a circuit-breaker program that could influence its urban impact. These are:

Provision	*Impact*
Adjustable upper income limit depending upon cost of living	Would favor large cities and cities in the Northeast
Changing the percent of rent attributed to property tax	The higher the percentage, the more favorable to central cities

The major objection to the program is that it replaces general fiscal assistance to State governments with assistance to the poor. There are several responses to this. First, the steadily accumulating state-government surpluses have probably provided sufficient padding so that the withdrawal of $2.2 billion in states' revenue sharing would not be disastrous. Second, states are expanding circuit breakers without federal assistance, from barely $100 million five years ago to over $1 billion today. Tax-cut fever will probably spur their adoption over the next two or three years, making the program subsidy welcome. Finally, the program reflects a widely held view that the problem of the poor is a national problem, and should not be left to a state's or city's residents, but should be addressed at the federal level.

Perhaps the major drawback of the initiative is that it may perpetuate the concentration of the poor in central cities, and would encourage low income households to vote for expensive social programs since they would not have to bear the consequences in terms of a higher tax burden. We cannot predict the strength of these affects. Already, the Federal government shoulders a major part of the costs of subsidies to the poor, and so the connection between local redistributive programs and tax burden has been reduced. Also, the taxpayer revolt may well have coalesced the middle class property owner into a block of sufficient strength to oppose any attempt to increase local taxes. Finally, many states already have circuit breakers, and so the initiative would merely assist those areas in meeting the burdens they already face.

LIMITING INTERSTATE TAX COMPETITION FOR BUSINESS

The slow growth of employment during the 1970s, which has been experienced with particular severity in the Northeast, has led to competition among states for industry. The fight between Ohio and Pennsylvania over Volkswagen is a well publicized example. The competition is escalating.

The problem

The competition for industry has led fiscally distressed states and municipalities to forego much needed tax revenues in development programs that have been singularly ineffective. Tax reform has been delayed, and the state and local tax burden has shifted from businesses to households, which has led to outmigration from high-taxing states of high income households.

There are no accurate data on the total cost by state in foregone revenues, but some data suggest the magnitude of these programs. Harrison and Kanter (1976) estimate that the ten incentive programs offered by Massachusetts are costing the state about $100 million annually. By 1980, Michigan's incentives will cost $50 million in state revenues and $30 million in local taxes. Local governments have entered the competition. In just one year, New York City exempted $461 million in properties from $44 million in taxes. St. Louis has exempted nearly $1 billion in residential, commercial, and manufacturing real estate—nearly half the tax base.

Figure 2 shows how widespread the competition has become. It also illustrates that, far from being a war between the Sunbelt and the Snowbelt, the rivalry is usually between adjacent states. After all, most of the firms that left New York went no farther than Connecticut, New Jersey, or Pennsylvania (Rubin et al., 1978). Many of the most fiscally distressed states and localities have foregone taxes in the vain hope of expanding their tax base in the long run. Table 8 lists the tax incentive programs offered by states. Some appreciation of the escalation of tax competition can be gauged from the rate of increase in the number of states offering incentives (Table 9).

There is no evidence that these fiscal bribes have had any impact on local growth.[12] Weinstein (1977, p. 75) summarizes:

Taken as a whole, these incentives probably represent a serious misallocation of resources. In the main, the government is subsidizing firms for performing activities they would have undertaken in any case. Furthermore, when one considers that any incentive designed to reduce a company's state or local tax bill will increase that firm's federal tax liability—the superfluity of tax incentives becomes even more apparent. The result is a form of reverse revenue sharing in the amount of 48 cents on the dollar.

There is no evidence that local taxes strongly influence either interstate growth differences or location decisions. In fact, business relocation is not, in itself, a major component of interstate growth differences. Using a sample of firms from Dun and Bradstreet data, Jusenius and Ledebur (1978) concluded:

Between 1969 and 1974, 879 firms in the Dun and Bradstreet sample migrated out of the North, accounting for only 0.58 percent of the total lost to the region. Moreover, 280 firms migrated into the region. Thus, the net loss of firms through migration was 599, or 0.4 percent of the total firm loss.

Firm closings were much more important. Factors such as the quality and quantity of available labor, transportation facilities, and energy prices are

---

[12] The literature is enormous and almost unanimous. See Bird (1966); Bridges (1965); Due (1961); Harrison and Kanter (1976); Morgan and Hackbart (1976); Mulkey and Dillman (1976); Weinstein (1977); and Williams (1967).

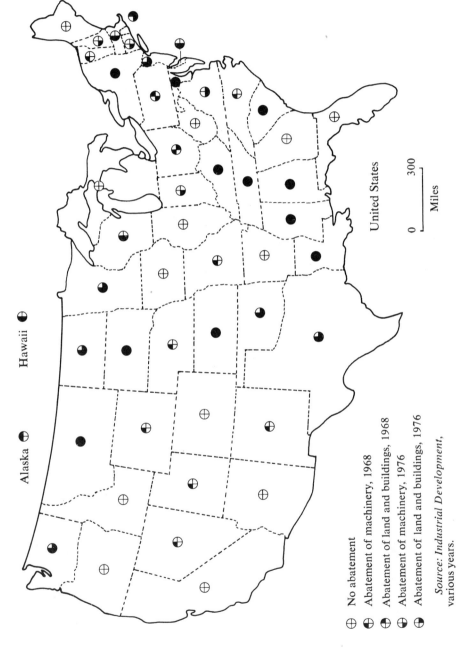

FIGURE 2: Tax Abatement Measures by State, 1968–1976

Alaska ⊕ Hawaii ⊕

United States

0   300

Miles

⊕ No abatement
⊕ Abatement of machinery, 1968
⊕ Abatement of land and buildings, 1968
⊕ Abatement of machinery, 1976
⊕ Abatement of land and buildings, 1976

Source: Industrial Development,
various years.

TABLE 8: Tax Incentive Programs Offered by States

Tax Exemptions on Land and Capital Improvements

Full Exemption	Partial Exemption	
Alabama	Kansas	Rhode Island
Mississippi	Kentucky	Tennessee
Montana	Louisiana	Texas
New Jersey	Maryland	Virginia
Ohio	Michigan	
Oklahoma	Minnesota	
South Carolina	New York	
South Dakota	North Dakota	
Washington	Oregon	

Tax Exemptions on Equipment and Machinery

Full Exemption		Partial Exemption
Alabama	New Hampshire	Connecticut
Delaware	Oklahoma	Kansas
Hawaii	South Carolina	Kentucky
Indiana	South Dakota	New Jersey
Louisiana	Washington	New York
Maryland	Wisconsin	North Dakota
Massachusetts		Pennsylvania
Michigan		Rhode Island
Minnesota		Tennessee
Mississippi		Texas
Montana		Virginia

Ad Valorem or Sales Tax Exemption—Plant, Machinery, or Equipment	Tax Credits to Expand Employment	Investment Tax Credits
Alabama	Massachusetts	Massachusetts
Georgia	New York	New York
Mississippi	North Dakota	Rhode Island
North Dakota		West Virginia

Sources: Cornia et al. (1978); Namson and Kanter (1976).

much more important than local taxes. Even local bureaucratic red tape may play a bigger role than actual tax levels (Vaughan, 1977).

Tax competition among states for business has shifted the tax burden from businesses to individuals. In 1948, personal income taxes provided 7.4 percent of states' revenues, and corporate income taxes 8.7 percent. In 1977, while personal income taxes had swollen to 16.4 percent of states' revenues, corporate income taxes had actually fallen to 5.8 percent. And yet there is growing evidence that interstate tax differences in personal taxes—income and

TABLE 9: Number of States Employing State and Local Tax Incentives for Industry

Type of Exemption	1966	1970	1978
Corporate income tax exemption	11	21	21
Excise tax exemption	5	9	10
Tax exemption or moratorium on equipment	15	21	28
Inventory tax exemption on goods in transit	32	39	41
Tax exemption on raw materials used in mfg.	32	39	44
Sales/use tax exemption on new equipment	16	26	33
Accelerated depreciation on industrial equipment	9	14	25
Tax exemption or moratorium on land and improvements	10	17	23

Source: ACIR, *Regional Growth Differences* (1978).

residential property—may influence local development much more strongly than business tax differences. They influence both the locational decisions of households—the more affluent shun high-taxing locales—and also wage demands—high taxes lead to high wages.

Finally, Due (1961, p. 171) argued that, more harmful than high taxes themselves was the *belief* that taxes were influential:

The endless propaganda on the subject and strategy-inspired announcements of business firms when tax changes are being considered lead many legislators to exaggerate the influences of the taxes beyond any effect which they may have. The result is a potential danger of state cutthroat competition, and more seriously in fact, a major obstacle to reform of tax structures. In terror of "driving business out," legislatures become unwilling to adjust taxes to levels necessary to meet the desires of the community for services, and to bring the tax structures in line with popularly accepted ideas of equity in taxation.

These words sound depressingly prophetic.

While tax exemptions may be a zero sum game, states and localities fear to withdraw from the competition, fearing that they will lose jobs and also votes from voters feeling local development policies are insufficiently aggressive.

The initiative

How can the Federal government assist in de-escalating this harmful competition? Constitutional issues prevent outright prohibition. However, it would be possible to use the power of the federal grant programs to dissuade states and localities from offering special exemptions. A few measures that could be implemented relatively easily include:

1. Overall Economic Development Plans prepared by states and municipalities that offer special incentives could be rejected by the Economic Development

Administration on the grounds that they did not present a balanced development plan by not treating all companies equally. This would make the areas ineligible for Title II loan guarantees;
2. the Department of Housing and Urban Development could reject community development plans on the same grounds, and hold up Community Development Block Grants and Urban Development Action Grants funds;
3. a penalty clause could be written into General Revenue Sharing funds, so that for each dollar of taxes foregone through an exemption or abatement program that did not apply uniformly to all firms in a given class, a given amount of revenue sharing funds would be sacrificed; and
4. the corporation income tax code could be rewritten to include provisions that add a federal tax penalty to firms granted special local exemptions.

The urban impacts of tax incentive limitation

The impacts of an initiative of this sort are extremely difficult to assess. First, how effective would the measures be in reducing state and local tax expenditures? Second, will State and local governments simply substitute direct expenditures on infrastructure and business services in order to attract businesses? And third, how will the reduction in tax expenditures affect development patterns?

We really cannot predict how effective the initiative will be in reducing tax competition. Success depends upon how broadly the anti–tax exemption bias is applied, and how much effort is devoted to enforcing the provisions. Experience with hastily implemented countercyclical programs suggests that local governments can avoid regulations if they are ill-defined and little effort is spent on enforcement (Vernez and Vaughan, 1978). On the other hand, threat of withdrawal of education grants has been used, with some success, to encourage integration of schools and the provision of special school services. Without a careful review of the relationship between federal enforcement activity and state and local behavior, and also more detail on how the program would be enforced, it is difficult to predict the outcome. A priori, it is probable that the initiative will tend to reduce the use of firm specific special incentives by states and lead to a greater emphasis on tax changes that influence the business climate to all local firms, not just newcomers. This would probably be favorable to local development in those states that have concentrated their incentives on new large companies. This shift will probably make the local revenue structure more elastic with respect to local growth in income and employment and that may strengthen those fiscally distressed states that have provided many special incentives. However, this may mean that revenues are more volatile in the face of a national recession and thus are not an unmixed blessing.

States are likely to switch some of their resources toward across-the-board tax cuts and toward infrastructure development in order to attract industry. Some of the tax cuts may even be directed at personal rather than business taxes, in response to taxpayer unrest.

How effective this switch is depends upon the efficiency of the state and local development effort. One possible benefit of the reduced reliance on tax incentives would be that states and cities may reexamine their development efforts and try and compensate for real local weaknesses—inadequate manpower training services, cumbersome red tape, or problems of site assembly. Addressing these problems would help all local firms including small firms which are the engine of local growth but which rarely benefit from the "personalized" development programs that center around tax incentives.

Finally, it is doubtful that the reduced use of firm specific tax incentives will place any area at a disadvantage. The evidence suggests that little growth or decline can be blamed on high local taxes.[13] There is little harm that is likely to result from this initiative and the possibility of some local benefit. To the extent that the aggregate level of local taxes is raised, the Treasury will forego some receipts.

SUMMARY

The three initiatives discussed in this paper could lead to greater fiscal strength for the state and local sector and for those states and localities that are laboring under fiscal strains in particular. The characteristics and impacts of the program are summarized in Table 10 below. There are sufficient data available to predict that the first two initiatives are likely to provide fiscal assistance to State and local governments at negligible cost to the Federal government. There are insufficient data to analyze the spatial impacts of the final initiative, although there are some a priori reasons for believing that the initiative may help states and jurisdictions and may encourage more efficient local development efforts. However, data on local tax expenditures are necessary to analyze this effort. At present, only California systematically prepares an annual review of state and local tax expenditures (Ch. 1762 of the Statutes of 1971). Other states should follow suit.

---

[13] New York may be the one exception to this. First, personal taxes are far out of line with any other state, and business taxes are somewhat higher for some industries and for long-lived investments. Second, Connecticut and New Jersey are within easy commuting distance of New York City and have maintained low tax rates.

TABLE 10: Summary of Impacts of Initiatives to Strengthen State/Local Fiscal Conditions

	Initiative 1: Optional taxable state/local bond with 35% of interest costs	Initiative 2: Use state portion of revenue sharing as a closed-end matching subsidy for state-financed property tax circuit breakers	Initiative 3: Penalize interstate tax incentives for regional development
Cost of program borne by:	Upper income households.	All federal taxpayers.	Large relocating, new or expanding firms, in the future.
Size and distribution of benefits	In the long run, about $1 billion in reduced debt finance costs. Greater per capita benefits for states and localities with the greatest per capita indebtedness and those with relatively unfavorable bond rating.	Poor households (homeowners and renters). Poor and high-taxing jurisdictions. Jurisdictions receiving low per capita allocations from state expenditure.	Unknown. Will be felt in those states making the largest tax expenditures.
Regional benefits	Favors Middle Atlantic and North Central regions.	No real regional pattern.	Probably concentrated in Northeastern states and cities.
City/suburb benefits	Will probably help central cities and older suburban cities.	Probably favors central cities because of their concentration of poor.	Unknown.

Household distribution of benefits	Households will benefit from general state/local tax cut and from increased capital costs. Overall, the program is redistributive, from rich to all households. Little benefit to the poor.	Effectively targeted on poor.	Unknown.
Sensitivity to alternative designs	If accompanied by a guarantee, interest rates in distressed cities will fall, reducing the Treasury subsidy but reducing local costs even more.	Income threshold adjusted by local cost of living would favor large and Northeastern cities. Raising fraction of rent ascribed to property taxes favors central cities.	Unknown.
Data needs	Data already available.	Full analysis must await 1980 census. Estimates of tax payments and income distribution of renters and homeowners in cities, suburbs, and nonmetropolitan areas needed.	Data on state/local tax expenditures under development tax incentive programs needed.

REFERENCES

Advisory Commission on Intergovernmental Relations. *Family Tax Burdens Compared Among States and Among Cities*. Washington, D.C.: U.S. Government Printing Office, 1978.
————. *Federal-State-Local Finances: Significant Features of Fiscal Federalism*. Report M-79. Washington, D.C.: U.S. Government Printing Office, 1974.
————. *Financing Schools and Property Tax Relief—A State Responsibility*. Report A-40. Washington, D.C.: U.S. Government Printing Office, January 1973.
————. *Measuring the Fiscal "Blood Pressure" of the States—1964–1975*. Report M-111. Washington, D.C.: U.S. Government Printing Office, February 1977.
————. *Regional Growth Differences*. Washington, D.C.: unpublished staff computations.
————. *Significant Features of Fiscal Federalism, 1976–1977*, vol. 2. Washington, D.C.: U.S. Government Printing Office, 1977.
Bird, Richard M. "Tax-Subsidy Policies for Regional Development." *National Tax Journal* 19 (1966): 113–24.
Bridges, Benjamin. "State and Local Inducements for Industry, Parts 1 and 2." *National Tax Journal* 18 (1965): 1–14, 175–92.
Dommel, Paul R., et al. *Decentralizing Community Development*. Report to the U.S. Department of Housing and Urban Development. Washington, D.C.: Brookings Institution, January 1978.
Due, John F. "Studies of State-Local Tax Influences on Location of Industry." *National Tax Journal* 14 (1961): 163–73.
Forbes, Ronald W., and Petersen, John E. *Building a Broader Market*. New York: Twentieth Century Fund, 1976.
Fortune, Peter. "The Impact of Taxable Municipal Bonds—Policy Simulations with a Large Econometric Model." *National Tax Journal* 26 (1973): 29–42.
Galper, Harvey, and Peterson, George E. "The Equity Effects of Taxable Municipal Bond Subsidy." *National Tax Journal* 26 (1973): 612–21.
Gary, Cornia; Testa, William A.; and Stocker, Frederick D. *Local Fiscal Incentives and Economic Development*. Columbus: Academy for Contemporary Problems, June 1978.
Gray, Jean M. "Testimony before the Joint Economic Committee, U.S. Congress." In *Financing Municipal Needs*, U.S. Congress. Washington, D.C.: U.S. Government Printing Office, July 1977.
Harrison, Bennett, and Kanter, Sandra. "The Great State Robbery." *Working Papers for a New Society* 4 (Spring 1976): 54–66.
Jusenius, Carol L., and Ledebur, Larry C. "Documenting the 'Decline' of the North," *Economic Development Research Report*, Economic Development Administration, U.S. Department of Commerce, Washington, D.C., June 1978.
Kimball, Ralph C. "Commercial Banks, Tax Avoidance, and the Market for State and Local Debt Since 1970." *New England Economic Review*, February 1977, pp. 3–21.
Morgan, William E., and Hackbart, Merlin M. "An Analysis of State and Local Tax Exemption Programs." *Southern Economic Journal* 41 (1974): 200–205.
Morris, Frank. "The Taxable Bond Option." *National Tax Journal* 29 (September 1976): 353–58.

Mulkey, David, and Dillman, B. L. "Location and the Effects of State and Local Development Subsidies." *Growth and Change* 7 (1976): 37–43.

National Governors' Association. *Tax and Expenditure Limitations.* Washington, D.C., December 1978.

Rafuse, Robert W. "The New York State Personal Income Tax: Essays in Fiscal Analysis." Prepared for the New York State Temporary State Commission on State and Local Finances, December 1974.

Rubin, Marilyn, et al. *Industrial Migration.* New York: Office of Economic Development, March 1978.

Shannon, John. "After Jarvis: Tough Questions for Fiscal Policy Makers." *Intergovernmental Perspective* 24 (Summer 1978): 8–12.

Shaul, Marnie. *The Taxable Bond Option for Municipal Bonds.* Columbus: Academy for Contemporary Problems, 1977.

Tax Foundation, The. *Monthly Tax Features,* August 1978.

"Tax Wealth in Fifty States." *State Government News,* July 1978.

U.S. Bureau of Census, U.S. Department of Commerce. *County and City Data Book 1977.* Washington, D.C.: U.S. Government Printing Office, 1978.

———. *Governmental Finances, 1976–1977.* Washington, D.C.: U.S. Government Printing Office, November 1978.

Vaughan, Roger J. *The Urban Impacts of Federal Policies.* Economic Development, vol. 2. R-2028-KF/RC. Santa Monica: Rand Corporation, 1977.

Vernez, Georges, and Vaughan, Roger. *Assessment of the Countercyclical Use of Public Works and Public Service Employment Programs.* R-2214-EDA. Santa Monica: Rand Corporation, 1978.

Vernez, Georges, et al. *Federal Activities in Urban Economic Development.* Santa Monica: Rand Corporation, forthcoming.

Weinstein, Bernard L. "Tax Incentives for Growth." *Society* 14 (1977): 73–75.

Williams, William V. "A Measure of the Impact of State and Local Taxes on Industrial Location." *Journal of Regional Science* 27 (Summer 1967): 49–59.

CHAPTER TWENTY-ONE

Urban, Regional, and Labor Supply Effects of a Reduction in Federal Individual Income Tax Rates

MARTIN HOLMER

INTRODUCTION

This chapter has two objectives. First, it presents an outline of a general method for estimating the economic impact of shifts in federal budget policy using a computer simulation model. The development of this economic simulation model will eventually permit estimation of the economic effects—disaggregated by geographical region and social class—of changes in federal expenditure and tax policies. Second, it presents estimates generated by the current version of the simulation model of the economic effects by region and class of the Kemp-Roth tax reduction bill.

The first section of the chapter outlines the eventual structure of the economic simulation model, and then describes the current version of the model. The next section presents national estimates of Kemp-Roth induced changes in labor supply, earnings, federal income taxes, and disposable income by income class under alternative labor supply response assumptions. These economic effects are examined by geographical region in the third section. The final section of the chapter reports estimates of changes in consumption, production, and labor demand caused by the tax reduction for 23 regional groups of states.

STRUCTURE OF THE ECONOMIC SIMULATION MODEL

The Office of Income Security Policy, Department of Health, Education, and Welfare (HEW), is currently engaged in the development of a computer simulation model that generates disaggregated estimates of the economic effects of the federal budget. When the development work is completed, the economic simulation model will be able to estimate the effects of changes in numerous types of federal budget policy on economic activity by region and industrial sector, and on the distribution of income in each state and in a few cases for metropolitan areas within states. The development of this simulation capability will lead to a model that consists of a microsimulation model of household labor supply and consumption behavior, and a highly disaggregated macrosimulation model of business production and labor demand behavior. These two submodels are linked together by modules that simulate the processes by which markets for commodities and markets for labor adjust to eliminate disequilibrium. In this economic simulation model, government policy changes or autonomous changes in household or business behavior induce a sequence of endogenous changes in household and business behavior that constitute the circular flow of the Keynesian multiplier process. The major elements of this sequence are represented in the schematic diagram labeled Figure 1.

FIGURE 1: Structure of the Economic Simulation Model

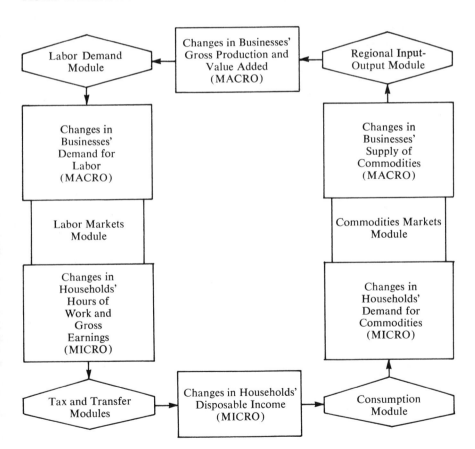

A $1-million increase in Federal government aircraft purchases in California, for example, would generate the following sequence of effects. In the macrosimulation model, production would increase in many industries and regions to supply the California aircraft industry with the intermediate goods necessary to produce the extra million dollar's worth of airplanes. This increase in production would generate extra demand for labor in different occupations, industries, and regions. The resulting disequilibrium in labor markets would be eliminated by increases in hours worked, entry into the labor force, or changes in occupation by certain individuals included in the sample survey used in the household microsimulation model. Households experiencing an increase in gross earnings would experience increases in taxes and possibly reductions in transfer benefits that result in a somewhat smaller increase in disposable income. This increase in disposable income would then generate some increase in spending on a variety of consumption goods as well as an increase in saving. This increase in the aggregate demand for commodities then generates in the economic simulation model another round of increases in production, employment, income, and consumption. The increase in consumption in each successive round grows smaller, of course, because part of the increase in the value of production goes to property income instead of earnings, part of the higher earnings is taxed away by governments, and part of the increase in disposable income is saved. The cumulative effect of these rounds produces an estimate of the original federal expenditure's effect on production that is disaggregated by region and industry, and estimates of employment, income, and consumption effects that are disaggregated to the individual and household level. This amount of disaggregation is required to make statements concerning the effect of policy changes on the distribution of income and on the spatial distribution of economic activity.

The microsimulation model of household behavior would consist of tax and transfer modules, a consumption module, and a sample survey of the United States population. The tax and transfer modules would simulate federal payroll, federal individual income, and state individual income taxes, and several welfare, social insurance, and federal pension programs in each state. The sample survey is the *Survey of Income and Education* (SIE), which contains calendar year 1975 information on residential location, transfer receipt, hours of work, occupation, and earnings for 200,000 nuclear families living in approximately 150,000 households. These tax and transfer modules and the SIE form the core of HEW's present microsimulation model, which is described in Betson, Greenberg, and Kasten (forthcoming). The model has the capability of estimating individuals' labor supply responses to changes in disposable income and net wage rate caused by alterations in tax or transfer policy, and of predicting the extent to which individuals will seek out public service jobs with certain characteristics. The SIE sample, which was drawn as a supplement to the March 1976 *Current Population Survey*, is large enough to generate for almost all variables of interest individual state estimates that are reliable at conventional levels of statistical significance. The consumption module would consist of a set of consumption functions that relate family disposable income, and possibly information on the age, sex, and place of residence of family members, to family saving and consumption in 56 different commodity groups. The parameters of these consumption functions would be estimated using cross-sectional data from the 1971–72 *Survey of Consumer Expenditures.*

The macrosimulation model of business behavior would consist of a regional input-output module and a labor demand module. Changes in businesses' supply of commodities for final use generates changes in the production of intermediate goods in various industries and regions. These interregional and interindustry linkages among business firms would be characterized in the regional input-output module by the United States Multiregional Input-Output Model developed by Polenske (1975). This model divides business firms into 78 industrial sectors in each of the 50 states and the District of Columbia, and includes estimates of technical production coefficients in each region and interregional commodity trade flows for 1963. It would be desirable, of course, to update both the technical coefficients and the estimates of trade flows. The resulting changes in gross production—that is, both goods for final use and intermediate goods—in each regional industry would then be translated by the labor demand module into changes in the demand for labor in each of 114 occupations. Updating the 1963 labor-output ratios for each regional industry found in Rodgers (1972) would permit estimates of the change in total labor demand in each regional industry. This total change in each regional industry would then be allocated among occupations in proportion to the occupational distribution of employment in the national industry as estimated using 1970 Census data and a methodology described in Bureau of Labor Statistics (1969).

These macrosimulation and microsimulation models would be linked together by simulation modules of the commodities markets and of the labor markets, in which imbalances in supply and demand are eliminated by adjustments in quantities supplied. In the commodities markets module, changes in the demand for commodities by individual households would be aggregated into regional industry totals and combined with any autonomous change in commodity demand generated by a government policy change, a shift in business investment, or an alteration in export demand. The resulting total changes in commodity demands create disequilibria in regional industry markets that are eliminated by the business firms in each regional industry adjusting their output to the new level of demand without any change in commodity prices.

In a similar fashion the labor markets module would translate the change in labor demand in each occupation in a regional industry into changes in annual hours worked and possibly in the occupation or industrial location of jobs held by individual household members in that region. This translation of changes in the demand for labor into changes in supply would take place without any changes in wage rates. This feature of the economic simulation model is logically consistent with the commodities markets adjustment process normally assumed in input-output analysis and specified in the commodities markets module discussed above. It is also consistent with the Keynesian view that short-run adjustments in labor markets are accomplished by quantity, not price, changes. Eventually it will be possible to specify alternative labor markets adjustment processes, and therefore, to determine the sensitivity of the economic simulation model's estimates to changes in assumptions about how labor markets react to disequilibrium.

It would be desirable to include eventually in these two markets' adjustment modules some recognition of the fact that large imbalances in supply and demand may not be able to be eliminated completely by changes in quantities supplied to the markets. In the commodities markets, capital capacity constraints may create situations in which supply cannot be increased further, and therefore, in the short run commodity prices are bid up and in the long run investment expenditures by firms in these industries presumably increase so that the capacity constraint is eventually eliminated. In the labor markets, limitations on the ability of supply to increase may cause wage rates to rise in the short run and migration of labor or capital in the long run. Incorporating in some fashion these aspects of the commodities and labor markets adjustment processes would increase significantly the accuracy of the economic simulation model's estimates of the effects of policy changes that bring sectors of the economy close to "full employment."

The circular flow of income simulated in this model, and represented in Figure 1, would be affected by government expenditure and tax policies in several different ways. Changes in government hiring and compensation policies would alter the demand for labor and gross earnings, respectively, and therefore, initiate a sequence of adjustments beginning in the labor markets module. Shifts in government procurement policies would change the demand for commodities and start a series of adjustments that begin in the commodities markets module. Government tax and transfer policies would have two different types of effect. Even when these policies are unchanged, they would determine in the tax and transfer modules how much of a household's increase (decrease) in gross income is lost (regained) in higher (lower) taxes and lower (higher) transfers, and how much remains as an increase (decrease) in disposable income. In addition to their role in shaping the circular flow of income, changes in tax or transfer policy would also initiate a sequence of changes in the economic simulation model. In principle, both Federal government and State and local government budget policies, as well as intergovernmental grants-in-aid, could be incorporated into the model, thus creating the capability of estimating the economic effects, disaggregated by geographical region and social class, of changes in expenditure or tax policies at any level of government.

At the writing of this paper the development of the economic simulation model described above has not been completed. The analysis of the Kemp-Roth tax reduction bill reported below was produced using the partially developed model, and hence, includes only partial estimates of its economic effects. Before presenting these somewhat incomplete results, the current structure of the simulation model is described.

In the current version of the simulation model, the tax and transfer modules are as described above. In addition to simulating the federal payroll, federal income, and state income tax laws, and numerous welfare, social insurance, and federal pension programs in each state, the modules have the ability to estimate for adults in each family included in the SIE sample changes in labor supply that are caused by tax or transfer policy-induced changes in net wage rates and family disposable income. This capability will be discussed in greater detail in the next section of the paper, where estimates of the Kemp-Roth bill's labor supply effects are presented. The present versions of most of the tax and transfer modules, as well as the capability of estimating labor supply responses, were developed by Betson, Greenberg, and Kasten (forthcoming). In a forthcoming work, the author has added rudimentary modules for several additional transfer and pension programs.

The other component of the household microsimulation model, the consumption module, exists only in aggregate form. First, changes in the disposable income of individual families in the SIE sample are aggregated into regional totals for each of seven family-income classes. The six boundaries of these income classes, expressed in 1971–72 dollars, are $2,000, $3,000, $4,000, $5,000, $6,000, and $12,000. Second, the change in total consumption for each regional income class is estimated using the national, class-specific marginal propensities to consume reported by Friend and Schor (1970). And third, the increase in total consumption for each regional income class is allocated among 56 consumption categories using national, class-specific marginal budget shares estimated from data collected in the 1971–72 *Consumer Expenditure Survey*. This version of the consumption module, which is similar to the one specified by Golladay and Haveman (1977), except that more recent data are used to estimate the budget shares, was developed by Hollenbeck and Wilson under contract to HEW.

The commodities market module combines changes in households' consumption with changes in commodity demand created by shifts in government procurement policy. Within each region, changes in demand for the 56 consumption categories are translated into changes in demand for commodities produced by the 78 industrial sectors identified in the regional input-output module. Specification of the regional and industrial composition of changes in Federal government, military, and civilian procurement, and State and local government education and noneducation procurement, is discussed in Holmer (forthcoming). The total change in commodity demand within each regional industry is assumed to elicit an equal change in commodity supply from the business firms in that regional industry.

These shifts in commodity supplies generate a complex series of production and labor demand changes in the business macrosimulation model. The pattern of the changes in gross production is determined by the nature of the interindustry and interregional trading patterns represented in the regional input-output module. Currently this module consists of a version of the United States Multiregional Input-Output Model—originally developed by Polenske (1975)—that has been collapsed from 51 regions (the 50 states and D.C.) to 23 regions. This condensed version of the model was originally developed by Golladay and Haveman (1977), and has been modified slightly by Holmer (forthcoming). The model's 1963 technical production and interregional trade coefficients have not been updated in the current module.

The changes in gross production generated by the regional input-output module are translated in the labor demand module into changes in businesses' demand for labor in 114 occupations in each regional industry. The current version of this module—developed by Golladay and Haveman (1977)—is as described above, with the total employment-output ratios updated to 1973 by extrapolating their 1947–63 growth.

The current version of the simulation model does not include a labor markets module that translates changes in labor demand into changes in hours of work and gross earnings for individuals included in the SIE sample. This means, among other things, that the present version cannot produce estimates that include the Keynesian multiplier effects of some policy-induced or autonomous change in commodity demand. It also means that it is impossible to combine estimates of the distributional effects of changes in labor demand with estimates of the direct distributional effects of a change in tax or transfer policy generated by the household microsimulation model. To do so would lose all the demographic detail present in the latter estimates. The lack of a labor markets module also implies that the effects of changes in government hiring policy cannot be simulated, although it is possible to simulate the effects of changes in government compensation policy since they affect the gross earnings of individual government workers who can be identified in the SIE sample.

ALTERNATIVE ESTIMATES OF THE NATIONAL LABOR SUPPLY EFFECTS OF THE KEMP-ROTH BILL

Although the Kemp-Roth bill was voted down in the House of Representatives during 1978, it was introduced again in 1979 as the Tax Reduction and Spending Limitation Act. It symbolizes the tax-limitation movement at the Federal level, as California's Proposition 13 represents the movement at the State and local government levels. The new bill is much like the old; its central feature is a provision that reduces federal individual income tax rates by one-third, in stages, over a three-year period. It also calls for matching expenditure reductions, but nowhere specifies the expenditures to be reduced or the procedure by which the spending cuts will be accomplished if the bill becomes law. The original version of the bill did not provide for expenditure reductions. On the contrary, many of its supporters argued that the reduction in tax rates would enhance work incentives so much that the resulting increase in hours of work and gross earnings would produce a rise in tax revenues large enough to nearly offset—more than offset, some argued—the original one-third reduction in tax revenues. Assessing the plausibility of this claim is the purpose of this section of the paper. The following two sections present estimates of the urban disposable income effects and the regional economic effects of the Kemp-Roth bill.

Estimates of the effects of the Kemp-Roth bill presented in this paper are based on a comparison of the historical situation in the United States during 1975 and a hypothetical situation in which the one-third tax reduction had been fully implemented in 1975. The characteristics of the historical situation are derived both from information contained in the SIE sample and from simulation estimates based on that sample. For the purposes of this discussion, the prime example of simulated information in the pre-Kemp-Roth situation is each family's federal income tax liability. The characteristics of the hypothetical situation are based on estimates generated by the present version of the economic simulation model described above. The one-third tax reduction induces in the model changes in labor supply, which combined together, cause changes in disposable income that, in turn, generate increases in consumption, production, and labor demand.

Before presenting estimates of the Kemp-Roth-induced changes in labor supply, gross earnings, federal income taxes, and disposable income, the method used to estimate individual labor supply responses in the simulation model is discussed. A net wage rate for each adult in a family is computed for the pre-Kemp-Roth (Wb) and post-Kemp-Roth situation (Wa). The net wage rate takes into account not only the cumulative marginal tax rate imposed by the federal income, federal payroll, and state income taxes, but also the cumulative marginal-benefit-reduction rate imposed by the transfer programs from which the individual receives benefits. A family disposable income is also computed for each adult in the pre-Kemp-Roth situation (Ib) and in the post-Kemp-Roth situation (Ia). And finally, a pre-Kemp-Roth gross family income excluding public assistance transfer payments (Yb) is computed for each individual. Estimates of the change in hours of labor supplied (Ha-Hb) for each individual are generated by an equation that has the following general form:

$$(Ha\text{-}Hb) = C(1)*[Wa\text{-}Wb] + C(2)*[(1/Wa) - (1/Wb)] + C(3)*[(Ia\text{-}Ib)/1000] + C(4)*[(Ia\text{-}Ib)/(Yb + 1000)].$$

The values of the four coefficients for each of three types of individuals under alternative specifications of the labor supply response equation are shown in Table 1.

TABLE 1: Alternative Labor Supply Response (LSR) Assumptions Used
to Estimate the Labor Supply Effects of the Kemp-Roth Bill

	Coefficients of the LSR Equations			
	C(1)	C(2)	C(3)	C(4)
Nonlinear LSR				
Husbands	0	−166.1	− 15.0	−162.4
Wives	0	−168.1	−225.5	346.1
Female heads	0	−118.1	− 51.7	−130.9
Linear LSR				
Husbands	83.2	0	− 34.4	0
Wives	168.0	0	−142.9	0
Female heads	125.8	0	−101.1	0
Pro-Kemp-Roth LSR				
Husbands	83.2	0	0	0
Wives	168.0	0	0	0
Female heads	125.8	0	0	0
No LSR				
All three groups	0	0	0	0

The coefficients for the nonlinear and linear specifications are estimated econometrically using pre- and post-experimental data on individuals enrolled in the Denver and Seattle Income Maintenance Experiments. While these data are superior to cross-sectional data because they permit direct observation of labor supply responses generated by experimentally induced changes in net wage rates and disposable incomes, they have two weaknesses that are pertinent to this analysis of the Kemp-Roth bill. The first problem with these data is caused by the fact that single individuals were enrolled in the experiments only if they lived in a household with a married couple. The sample of single individuals, therefore, is very small and almost certainly unrepresentative. Instead of using the coefficients estimated with these experimental data, the labor supply response equation uses the husband coefficients for single males and the female head-of-family coefficients for single females. Labor supply equations estimated with cross-sectional data for different demographic groups suggest that this procedure may understate somewhat the responsiveness of single individuals' labor supply to changes in tax and transfer policy.

The second problem with the Seattle and Denver data stems from the fact that high income families were censored from the sample. As a result, only one percent of the families enrolled in the experiments during 1970 and 1971 had incomes above $15,000, while at the same time 22 percent of all families in the United States had incomes above that level. The sample is also thin in the $12,000- to $15,000-income range since there are less than half the number of families in that range as would be found in a randomly drawn sample of the same total size. This means that the labor supply coefficients for individuals in families with 1975 incomes over $18,000—about 17 percent of all families—are extrapolated from coefficients estimated with data on families with incomes below that level. This makes the selection of a labor supply response equation particularly critical since families with incomes over $18,000 paid about two-thirds of federal income taxes in 1975.

The alternative labor supply response equations specified in Table 1 exhibit different net wage effects and disposable income effects. In the nonlinear equation the magnitude of the net wage effect—measured in elasticity terms—is relatively small for high income individuals and relatively large for individuals with low incomes. The magnitude of the disposable income effect increases as family income rises. In the linear equation, on the other hand, the magnitude of both the net wage and disposable income effects rises as income increases. The third labor supply response equation in Table 1, labeled "Pro-Kemp-Roth," is simply the linear equation with the labor supply-reducing disposable income effect set equal to zero. This is the type of labor supply response implicitly assumed by those who argue that the Kemp-Roth bill will increase substantially the total number of hours worked. It would be difficult to specify an equation more favorable to the Kemp-Roth labor supply argument since the linear equation's net wage effect produces an increase in hours that is large (relative to the decrease in hours caused by the linear equation's disposable income effect) and that increases in magnitude for higher income families, from whom the bulk of income taxes are collected. The pro-Kemp-Roth equation assumes that the increase in disposable income generated by the Kemp-Roth tax reduction causes no reduction in hours worked. The final equation in Table 1 assumes no labor supply response to changes in tax and transfer policy; it is included for purposes of comparison only.

National estimates based on these four labor supply response equations are presented in Table 2. The table shows the estimated change in labor supply, gross earnings, federal income taxes, and disposable income for three income classes. Both the nonlinear and linear equations generate reductions in total labor supply, while the pro-Kemp-Roth equation predictably yields an increase in total labor supply. The differences in labor supply response between the three income classes are also predictable given the ways in which the elasticities of the net wage and disposable income effects vary across income classes. The reason a decline in labor supply leads to a rise in gross earnings in the simulation based on the linear equation is that the total decline is composed of a decrease in wives' hours that is slightly larger in absolute value than the increase in husbands' hours of labor supply. Since the average hourly wage of the husbands who increase their hours is substantially above that of the wives who decrease their hours, total earnings actually increase by small amounts in each of the three income classes. The increase in earnings generated by the linear and pro-Kemp-Roth equations imply that Federal income tax revenues drop by less than the one-third cut shown for the simulation done

TABLE 2: Estimates of Kemp-Roth-Induced Changes in Labor Supply, Earnings, Federal Income Taxes, and Disposable Income, by Income Class under Alternative Labor Supply Response (LSR) Assumptions

	1975 Level	Kemp-Roth-Induced Absolute & Percentage Changes Assuming:			
		Pro-Kemp-Roth LSR	Linear LSR	No LSR	Nonlinear LSR
Labor Supply (million work-yrs) [a]					
All families	87.7	+ 2.0 (+ 2.3%)	− 0.3 (− 0.3%)	0.0 (0.0%)	− 1.9 (− 2.2%)
under $6,000 income [b]	14.9	+ 0.1 (+ 0.7%)	0.0 (0.0%)	0.0 (0.0%)	− 0.1 (− 0.7%)
$6,000 to $18,000 income	44.7	+ 0.8 (+ 1.8%)	+ 0.1 (+ 0.2%)	0.0 (0.0%)	− 0.4 (− 0.9%)
over $18,000 income	28.1	+ 1.1 (+ 3.9%)	− 0.4 (− 1.4%)	0.0 (0.0%)	− 1.4 (− 5.0%)
Earnings ($ billions)					
All families	834.0	+39.1 (+ 4.7%)	+10.2 (+ 1.2%)	0.0 (0.0%)	−24.9 (− 3.0%)
under $6,000 income	52.5	+ 1.0 (+ 1.9%)	+ 0.4 (+ 0.8%)	0.0 (0.0%)	− 0.1 (− 0.2%)
$6,000 to $18,000 income	367.0	+ 8.4 (+ 2.3%)	+ 2.3 (+ 0.6%)	0.0 (0.0%)	− 4.1 (− 1.1%)
over $18,000 income	414.5	+29.7 (+ 7.2%)	+ 7.5 (+ 1.8%)	0.0 (0.0%)	−20.7 (− 5.0%)
Federal Income Taxes ($ billions)					
All families	121.0	−30.4 (−25.1%)	−36.7 (−30.3%)	−40.3 (−33.3%)	−45.5 (−37.6%)
under $6,000 income	1.7	− 0.4 (−23.5%)	− 0.4 (−23.5%)	− 0.6 (−33.3%)	− 0.5 (−29.4%)
$6,000 to $18,000 income	38.1	−11.3 (−29.7%)	−12.2 (−32.0%)	−12.4 (−33.3%)	−13.0 (−34.1%)
over $18,000 income	81.2	−18.7 (−23.0%)	−24.1 (−29.7%)	−27.3 (−33.3%)	−32.0 (−39.4%)
Disposable Income ($ billions)					
All families	858.8	+64.8 (+ 7.5%)	+44.6 (+ 5.2%)	+40.3 (+ 4.7%)	+21.8 (+ 2.5%)
under $6,000 income	77.3	+ 0.4 (+ 0.5%)	+ 0.4 (+ 0.5%)	+ 0.6 (+ 0.8%)	0.0 (0.0%)
$6,000 to $18,000 income	355.5	+18.7 (+ 5.3%)	+13.4 (+ 3.8%)	+12.4 (+ 3.5%)	+ 7.6 (+ 2.1%)
over $18,000 income	426.0	+45.7 (+10.7%)	+30.8 (+ 7.2%)	+27.3 (+ 6.4%)	+14.2 (+ 3.3%)

Source: Estimates generated by the household microsimulation model, using a 10 percent SIE sample.

[a] A work-year equals 2,000 hours of employment.

[b] Income classes are defined using pre-Kemp-Roth gross family income excluding public assistance transfers (*Yb*). The 97.2 million families in the U.S. are distributed as follows: 39.9 million in the lower income class, 40.1 in the middle class, and 17.2 in the upper class.

with the assumption of no labor supply response. But even under the extreme pro-Kemp-Roth labor supply response assumption, the increase in earnings is so modest that it generates new tax revenue equal to only about one-fourth of the original $40.3 billion tax reduction. This is quite far from the situation predicted by some Kemp-Roth advocates. Under the linear labor supply response assumption the tax reduction is about 30 percent, while the labor supply reductions under the nonlinear response assumption, combined with the one-third reduction in tax rates, yield a cut in tax revenues of almost 38 percent. Under all four labor supply response assumptions the increase in disposable income is concentrated heavily in the upper income class with 65 to 70 percent of the total increase accruing to families with 1975 gross incomes above $18,000.

ESTIMATES OF THE URBAN DISPOSABLE INCOME EFFECTS OF THE KEMP-ROTH BILL

The purpose of this section is to examine the feasibility of using the economic simulation model discussed above to estimate the urban effects of a federal policy change, in this case the Kemp-Roth tax reduction bill. The extent to which it is possible to present accurate estimates of a policy change's urban effects depends not only on the geographical detail present in the SIE data for each family, but also on the number of families sampled in particular geographical regions.

The SIE data contain three variables that provide information concerning a family's place of residence. The first variable identifies the state in which the family resides. The second locates a family's place of residence in a central city within an urban (that is, standard metropolitan statistical) area, in a suburb within an urban area, or in a nonmetropolitan area. And the third variable indicates whether or not a family lives in each one of the 98 largest urban areas. This type of geographical information offers two ways of presenting estimates that go beyond the geographical detail of state estimates. One way would be to estimate a policy change's effects by central city, suburb, and nonmetropolitan areas perhaps for different groups of states. The other way would be to estimate a policy change's effects for particular urban areas, and perhaps even for subareas within each urban area.

The first way of approaching urban impact analysis is not feasible with the SIE. The Bureau of the Census has censored the information contained in the central city-suburban-nonmetropolitan variable for 60 percent of the families included in the SIE sample. Tabulations of the sample indicate that substantial numbers of families who live in each of these three types of residential locations have been assigned an unclassified value for this variable. This has been done to ensure that the provisions of the Privacy Act are being enforced and that the confidentiality of survey information gathered from individuals is maintained.

This leaves the second way of presenting estimates of the urban effects of federal policy changes. Even though several urban areas have been deleted from the list, the 90 identified urban areas include virtually all major population centers in the United States. So while it is technically possible to present estimates for each of the 90 urban areas, the issue of the statistical reliability of these estimates remains to be discussed.

The discussion of the accuracy of estimates produced by the simulation model does not account for the potentially major errors caused by inadequate information in the SIE data for a family and, by imprecision, in the model's simulation of government policy or household and business behavior. The discussion here focuses only on the error in the estimate introduced by the fact that the estimate is generated from a sample survey (rather than a complete census) of the population. Estimates can usually be classified as one of two types: the average value of some quantity or the fraction of a population with a certain characteristic. The first type of estimate is formed by computing the mean of the values of the variable for families in the sample. The values of the variable are distributed in the population according to some continuous probability distribution that may be normal or may be some other distribution. The second type of estimate is formed by computing the mean, or relative frequency, of the characteristic in the sample. The occurrence of the characteristic in the population is distributed according to the binomial distribution. In either case the estimate—the sample mean—is itself a random variable with a mean and variance that can be computed if both the sample size and the distribution of the variable or characteristic in the population are known. The ratio of the estimate's standard deviation and mean is called the estimate's coefficient of variation. A 5 percent coefficient of variation means that the 95 percent confidence interval around the estimate has a radius of 10 percent of the estimate; a 10 percent coefficient of variation implies a 95 percent confidence interval, the boundaries of which are the estimate plus or minus 20 percent of the estimate.

On the other hand, given the distribution of the variable or characteristic in the population, it is possible to calculate the random sample size required to generate an estimate with a desired coefficient of variation. The SIE sample size required to produce an estimate of desired statistical reliability is larger than the corresponding random sample size because the SIE is a stratified cluster sample rather than a random sample. Although it varies somewhat across states, the resulting sample design effect reduces the effective size of the SIE sample by about one-third. This means that the SIE sample size required to produce an estimate with a given coefficient of variation is approximately 150 percent of the size of the required random sample. Table 3 presents both random and SIE sample sizes necessary to produce estimates with 5 and 10 percent coefficients of variation for a variable that is normally distributed in the population and for a characteristic that occurs in the population with a binomial distribution.

TABLE 3: Random and SIE Sample Sizes Required for Estimates with a Given Coefficient of Variation Based on Normal and Binomial Distributions

	Coefficient of Var. = 0.05		*Coefficient of Var. = 0.10*	
	Random Sample	*SIE Sample*	*Random Sample*	*SIE Sample*
Normal dist. with mean m & standard deviation s				
s/m = 0.5	100	150	25	37.5
s/m = 1.0	400	600	100	150
s/m = 2.0	1,600	2,400	400	600
s/m = 4.0	6,400	9,600	1,600	2,400
Binomial dist. with parameter p				
p = 0.50	400	600	100	150
p = 0.25	1,200	1,800	300	450
p = 0.10	3,600	5,400	900	1,350
p = 0.05	7,600	11,400	1,900	2,850

Note: In the normal case, $n = (1/(cv*cv))*(s/m)*(s/m)$; in the binomial, $n = (1/(cv*cv))*((1 - p)/p)$; and the SIE sample design effect is assumed to be 1.50.

Table 4 shows the number of urban areas identified in the SIE data that have samples of certain sizes. A comparison of Tables 3 and 4 indicates that simulations based on the SIE sample cannot produce statistically reliable estimates of all policy change effects for even the largest urban areas. Accurate estimates for a significant number of urban areas are possible only in cases where the estimate is the average value of a variable that occurs in the population with a relatively low-variance normal distribution. Unfortunately, these cases are rare since most economic variables are distributed in the population

TABLE 4: Number of Identified Urban Areas with SIE Samples of a Given Size

SIE Sample Size (no. families)	*No. Urban Areas*	*SIE Sample Size (no. families)*	*No. Urban Areas*
200 or more (+)	69	1,800+	11
400+	42	2,000+	7
600+	29	2,200+	4
800+	26	2,400+	2
1,000+	21	2,600+	2
1,200+	15	2,800+	2
1,400+	14	3,000+	1
1,600+	11	3,200+	0

Source: HEW tabulation of the SIE sample.

with disperse, asymmetrical distributions. In these cases the required SIE sample size is presumably somewhere between those shown in Table 3 for the normal and binomial distributions.

Proceeding on the admittedly somewhat speculative assumption that 1,400 families are necessary to generate a statistically reliable estimate of the change in disposable income induced by the Kemp-Roth bill, Table 5 presents such estimates for the entire United States and 14 urban areas. These estimates indicate that the disposable income effect of the Kemp-Roth bill is fairly even across the 14 areas. This is not a particularly surprising conclusion since the policy change being simulated is geographically neutral. The percentage increase in disposable income in these urban areas is slightly above the national average, presumably because these areas have a relative abundance of high income, high tax liability families.

ESTIMATES OF THE REGIONAL ECONOMIC
EFFECTS OF THE KEMP-ROTH BILL

This final section of the paper presents estimates of the changes in consumption, production, and labor demand generated by the Kemp-Roth tax reduc-

TABLE 5: Urban and National Estimates of the Absolute and Percentage Change in Disposable Income Induced by the Kemp-Roth Bill

Urban Area	Change in Disposable Income, 1975	
	$ Billions	%
Entire U.S.	45.9	5.3
Baltimore	0.5	5.7
Boston	0.7	5.6
Chicago	1.9	5.9
Denver	0.4	5.9
Detroit	1.2	6.4
Honolulu	0.2	5.8
Los Angeles	2.1	6.6
Minneapolis-St. Paul	0.5	5.6
New York City	2.1	5.7
Philadelphia	1.3	6.9
Portland, Oregon	0.2	5.3
Salt Lake City	0.1	5.4
Seattle	0.5	6.9
Washington, D.C.	1.2	6.8

Source: Estimates generated by the household microsimulation model using the entire SIE sample and the linear labor supply response equation.

TABLE 6: Estimates of the Regional Shares of the Changes in Disposable Income, Consumption, Production, and Labor Demand Induced by the Kemp-Roth Bill

| Region | Region's Percentage Share of National Changes in: | | | | Change in Labor Demand (% of 1975 em-ployment) |
	Dispos-able Income	Consump-tion	Produc-tion	Labor Demand	
1. New England[a]	5.9	5.9	5.3	5.4	3.3[d]
2. New York	9.8	9.8	7.5	6.9	3.1[d]
3. Pennsylvania, New Jersey	9.7	9.6	7.3	7.7	3.1[d]
4. Michigan, Ohio	9.3	9.3	7.0	6.9	2.8[d]
5. Illinois, Indiana	8.3	8.2	6.4	6.3	2.9[d]
6. Minnesota, Wisconsin	3.6	3.7	3.9	3.9	3.3[d]
7. Iowa, Missouri	3.1	3.1	3.6	3.7	3.6[d]
8. Plains States[b]	2.2	2.3	3.1	3.2	4.5
9. Delaware, D.C., Maryland	3.3	3.2	3.8	3.8	5.2
10. Virginia, West Virginia	3.0	3.1	3.6	3.8	4.4
11. North Carolina	1.8	1.9	2.8	3.1	4.2
12. South Carolina	0.8	0.9	2.2	2.6	7.6
13. Georgia	1.7	1.7	4.2	2.1	3.4[d]
14. Florida	3.3	3.3	3.5	4.0	4.0
15. Kentucky, Tennessee	2.5	2.6	3.2	3.3	3.4[d]
16. Alabama	1.0	1.1	2.3	2.3	5.5
17. Mississippi	0.7	0.7	2.0	2.8	10.3
18. Arkansas, Oklahoma	1.7	1.7	2.7	3.0	5.1
19. Louisiana	1.3	1.3	2.4	2.5	5.7
20. Texas	5.3	5.4	4.7	5.1	3.2[d]
21 Mountain States[c]	4.9	4.9	4.8	5.1	4.0
22. Hawaii, Oregon, Washington	3.5	3.5	4.3	3.9	4.5
23. California	13.1	12.8	9.3	8.5	3.1[d]

Source: Estimates generated by simulation model using the linear labor supply response and the entire SIE sample.

[a] Connecticut, Maine, Massachusetts, New Hampshire, Rhode Island, and Vermont.
[b] Kansas, Nebraska, North Dakota, and South Dakota.
[c] Alaska, Arizona, Colorado, Idaho, Montana, Nevada, New Mexico, Utah, and Wyoming.
[d] Regions below the national average of 3.7 percent.

tion bill. The estimates are based on the linear labor supply response assumption and the current version of the economic simulation model described above. As mentioned earlier, these estimates do not incorporate any Keynesian multiplier effects and are not comparable with the estimates derived from the household microsimulation model because the changes in labor demand have not been allocated by a labor markets module to individuals in the SIE sample. Despite these limitations the estimates provide some interesting information.

Table 6 shows for each of the 23 regions its fraction of the national increase in disposable income ($45.9 billion), consumption ($29.5 billion), production (measured in value added terms, and therefore, equal to the increase in consumption), and labor demand (3.10 million work-years). These estimates reveal a regional pattern of increase in labor demand that favors many, but not all, Southern states over Midwestern and Northeastern states. While this is somewhat surprising given that the tax policy change being simulated is geographically neutral, an inspection of the table confirms that the Midwestern and Northeastern states' share of the national increase in labor demand is significantly less than their share of the national increases in disposable income and consumption. There are at least two possible explanations of this phenomenon: the Northeastern and Midwestern states may be more specialized in capital-goods (rather than consumption) industries, and the industries located in these areas may be less labor intensive than the dominant industries in other regions. The figures in Table 7 lend some plausibility to the second explanation (particularly in the case of the apparel industry which is concentrated in a number of Southern states), but analysis of additional simulations will be necessary before a convincing explanation of this phenomenon can be offered.

REFERENCES

Betson, David; Greenberg, David; and Kasten, Richard. "A Micro-Simulation Model for Analyzing Alternative Welfare Reform Proposals: An Application to the Program for Better Jobs and Income." In *Microeconomic Simulation Models for the Analysis of Public Policy*, edited by Robert Haveman and Kevin Hollenbeck. New York: Academic Press, forthcoming.

Bureau of Labor Statistics. "The National Industry-Occupation Matrix and Other Data." *Tomorrow's Manpower Needs*. Vol. 4. Bulletin No. 1606. Washington, D.C.: U.S. Government Printing Office, 1969.

Friend, Irwin, and Schor, Stanley. "Who Saves?" In *Proceedings of the Conference on Consumption and Saving*, vol. 2, edited by Irwin Friend and Robert Jones. Philadelphia: University of Pennsylvania Press, 1970.

Golladay, Frederick L., and Haveman, Robert H. *The Economic Impacts of Tax-Transfer Policy: Regional and Distributional Effects*. New York: Academic Press, 1977.

Holmer, Martin. "Regional Economic Effects of the Federal Budget." In *Proceed-

ings of the Committee on Urban Public Economics Conference on Inter-Regional Growth in the American Economy, edited by William Wheaton. Washington, D.C.: Urban Institute, forthcoming.

Polenske, Karen R. *The United States Multiregional Input-Output Model*. Lexington, Mass.: Lexington Books, D. C. Heath, 1975.

Rodgers, John M. *State Estimates of Outputs, Employment, and Payrolls, 1947, 1958, 1963*. Lexington, Mass.: Lexington Books, D. C. Heath, 1972.

TABLE 7: National Estimates, by Industrial Sector, of the Changes in Consumption and Labor Demand Induced by the Kemp-Roth Bill

Industrial Sector	Change in Consumption		Change in Labor Demand	
	$ Billions	% Total	Million Work-Years	% Total
Agriculture, forestry, fisheries	0.2	1	0.09	3
Mining	a	b	0.03	1
Construction	0.3	1	0.03	1
Manufacturing	10.5	35	0.98	32
Food & related products	(2.7)	(9)	(0.08)	(3)
Apparel	(1.2)	(4)	(0.14)	(5)
Motor vehicles & equipment	(2.4)	(8)	(0.10)	(3)
Other manufacturing	(4.2)	(14)	(0.66)	(21)
Transportation, communication, elec., gas & sanitary serv.	1.6	6	0.16	5
Wholesale & retail trade	5.6	19	0.60	19
Finance, insurance, real estate	5.9	20	0.51	17
Services	5.4	18	0.66	21
Government enterprises	a	b	0.04	1
All sectors	29.5	100	3.10	100

Source: Estimates generated by simulation model using the linear labor supply response and the entire SIE sample.

[a] Less than $0.05 billion.

[b] Less than 0.5 percent.

PART VI

Urban Impact Analysis 4: Intergovernmental Relations

The Spatial Dimensions of the Community Development Block Grant Program: Targeting and Urban Impacts

HAROLD L. BUNCE AND NORMAN J. GLICKMAN

INTRODUCTION

This paper concerns the Community Development Block Grant (CDBG) program, a major program of the Department of Housing and Urban Development (HUD), that is directly targeted on cities, particularly those jurisdictions showing signs of social and economic distress. CDBG's structure reflects a philosophy, fostered in the Nixon administration, which placed funding responsibility at the federal level, with revenues distributed "without strings" to localities who were free in turn to spend these monies as local needs dictated. General revenue sharing, as discussed by Dommel in this volume, is one example of this sort of program. CDBG represents "urban revenue sharing," because it targets HUD funds to cities for general purposes involving urban development by formula, and without strong guidance as to the way jurisdictions spend their CDBG grants.

First, the program's historic background. The passage of the Housing and Community Development Act of 1974 marked a new era in relations between the Federal government and local government units. The Community Development Block Grant program, established by Title I of the Act, consolidated separate HUD programs for urban renewal, model cities, rehabilitation of deteriorated structures, neighborhood improvements, open space, historic preservation, and water and sewer facilities into a single, broad-purposed CDBG program. The new program simplified local application and federal review requirements and gave local elected officials, rather than special-purpose agencies, the primary responsibility for determining community development needs, establishing priorities, and allocating resources. Given their CDBG allocations, local officials were allowed considerable latitude as to the uses of the grants according to local needs, but within certain limits. Eligible activities included those funded by the former categorical programs. In Fiscal 1977, for instance, funds were spent on the following major categories: redevelopment related activities (22.1 percent), code enforcement (1.6 percent), water and sewer facilities (2.9 percent), "other public works" (29.0 percent), open space and neighborhood facilities (7.6 percent), housing rehabilitation (20.3 percent), service-related facilities and equipment (5.7 percent), and public services (10.7 percent).

Moreover, the 1974 Act listed several national objectives and also stipulated that activities financed with CDBG funds *must benefit principally families with low or moderate income*, or aid in the prevention or elimination of slums and blight, or meet other urgent community development needs. In this important sense, CDBG was targeted on cities and people in need.

The issue of the proper allocation of CDBG funds among cities has been one of the most important and controversial ones facing the CDBG program. Under the old categorical system displaced by CDBG, funds were distributed to applicants on a competitive, case-by-case basis. The 1974 Act *established a formula based on population, poverty, and housing overcrowding* for distributing community development funds among jurisdictions. However, in 1977, Congress replaced the 1974 single formula with a dual formula system proposed by the Carter administration, which included the 1974 formula and added a *second formula* based on *age of housing, poverty, and below average population growth.*[1]

The major purpose of this paper is to examine the extent to which the current dual formula, and three alternative formulas, target funds according to overall community development *need*[2] and the components of need (such as poverty need, age of city, and population decline need). The focus is on the funding redistributions that accompany changes in spatial targeting according to need that will vary with formula designations.

The targeting and redistribution analysis is both relevant and timely because the Carter administration has repeatedly emphasized that federal assistance to cities should be distributed according to city needs. Congress will begin reauthorization hearings on the CDBG program in the spring of 1980, and one of the most important topics concerns possible formula changes and the intercity funding redistributions (gains and losses) that will result. In fact, continued congressional interest in CDBG formula issues was indicated in 1977 when Congress mandated that HUD study the equity of current dual

---

[1] The 1977 authorization legislation also included $3.5 billion for Fiscal 1978, $3.65 billion for Fiscal 1979, and $3.8 billion for Fiscal 1980. The $3.5 billion for 1978 represents a $.95 billion increase over the initial $2.55 billion authorization in Fiscal 1975.

[2] For a full discussion of the conceptualization and measurement of need, *see* first part of next section.

formula and alternative formulas (*see* Bunce and Goldberg [1979] for that analysis).

Another purpose of this paper is to provide estimates of the urban impacts of the CDBG program on employment, earnings, housing units, and neighborhood condition. Although the analysis attempted here is somewhat preliminary, it can serve as a starting point for more sophisticated efforts at measuring the urban impacts of CDBG expenditures.

Before presenting the targeting analysis (in the third section of this paper), the dual formula system and the distribution of CDBG funds among types of recipients and regions are described. In the fourth section, measurements of the direct and indirect urban impacts of CDBG are presented, and in the final section we offer some conclusions.

THE ALLOCATION PROCESS

Description of the dual formula

The process of allocating CDBG funds is a multistep procedure. First, after deducting 3 percent for a special Secretary's fund, HUD allocates approximately four-fifths of the remaining funds to Standard Metropolitan Statistical Areas (SMSAs) and one-fifth to non-SMSAs. Within SMSAs, formula grants go to *entitlement* communities. These include *metropolitan* cities, which are central cities or any city with at least 50,000 population, and *urban counties*, which are counties with populations of more than 200,000 that have the authority to perform community development functions. The balance of the SMSA allocation is distributed on a discretionary basis to the smaller, non-entitlement cities and counties within metropolitan areas. Similarly, non-SMSA communities receive funds on a project or discretionary basis from the non-SMSA allocation.

In Fiscal 1978, there were 559 metropolitan cities of which 381 were central cities of SMSAs. The dual formula amount for each metropolitan city is the greater of the amounts computed under the 1974 formula and the 1977 formula. These two formulas and their variables are defined in Table 1. The 1974 formula is based on poverty (weighted .50), population (.25), and overcrowded housing (.25). On the other hand, the 1977 formula is based on poverty (.30), pre-1940 housing (.50), and growth lag (.20). Much of the analysis in this and later sections shows the ramifications of the formula change.

Studies of the 1974 formula and distribution among types of recipients

Prior to the 1977 Congressional reconsideration of the Housing and Community Development Act, HUD and the Brookings Institution made extensive studies of the 1974 formula arrangements. The HUD study (Bunce, 1976) found the 1974 formula to be highly responsive to the poverty dimension of community development (CD) need, but unresponsive to non-poverty

TABLE 1: Dual Formula Used to Allocate Community Development Block Grants

The basic dual formula amount for a metropolitan city or urban county is the greater of the amounts computed under the following equations:[1]

(1) 1974 Formula

$$\left(.25 \, \frac{POP_j}{POP_{SMSA}} + .50 \, \frac{POV_j}{POV_{SMSA}} + .25 \, \frac{OCRWD_j}{OCRWD_{SMSA}} \right) \times G_{SMSA}$$

(2) 1977 Formula

$$\left(.20 \, \frac{GLAG_j}{GLAG_{MC}} + .30 \, \frac{POV_j}{POV_{SMSA}} + .50 \, \frac{AGE_j}{AGE_{SMSA}} \right) \times G_{SMSA}$$

where

j–indicates the metropolitan city or urban county

SMSA–indicates that the variable is defined for all SMSAs

MC–indicates that the variable is defined for all metropolitan cities

G_{SMSA}–total dollar allocation to all SMSAs[2]

POP–total resident population, July 1975

POV[3]–extent of poverty (number of persons whose income is below the poverty level)

OCRWD[3]–overcrowded housing (number of housing units with 1.01 or more persons per room)

AGE[3]–age of housing (number of existing year-round housing units constructed in 1939 or earlier)

GLAG–extent of growth lag (the difference between [1] the population a city or urban county would have had if its population growth rate between 1960 and the date of the most recent population count had been equal to the growth rate of all metropolitan cities during the same period; and [2] the current population of the city or urban county. If the city grew at a higher than average rate, it receives a zero on this variable.)

[1] Additional funds to pay for giving entitlement recipients the choice between two formula amounts come from the SMSA balance (discretionary) account. The balance is computed as a residual by subtracting the amount going to entitlement recipients from the total SMSA appropriation. SMSA balances are, however, ensured a minimum total amount. The dual formula is also used to distribute the SMSA balance and non-SMSA funds among state areas; the only change is that total population replaces growth lag.

[2] A pro rata reduction of all amounts is applied to ensure that the amount allocated does not exceed the amount appropriated and available for distribution.

[3] Except for geographical updating, the counts for POV, OCRWD, and AGE will not change until publication of the 1980 Census results (expected in 1982).

dimensions such as age, decline, and density. Finally, the study showed that cities losing population exhibited far higher levels of CD need and fiscal strain than fast-growing cities. The Brookings study (Nathan et al., 1977) emphasized the impact that the phase-out of hold-harmless entitlements would have on the nation's older cities.[3] Compared to the displaced categorical programs, full funding under the 1974 formula would have reduced funding most heavily in the larger and older cities, especially those located in the Northeast and North Central regions. Both studies judged that the major flaw of the 1974 formula was its unresponsiveness to the severe physical, social, and fiscal problems of older, deteriorating metropolitan cities. The main purpose of the new dual formula was to redirect funds back to the older, declining cities.

To focus on these formula changes, we have included data in Table 2 dollar allocations by type of recipient (e.g., central city, urban county) and by region for the 1974 and current dual formula as well as for the displaced categorical programs. Column 1 presents per capita dollar averages for the dual formula projected to Fiscal 1980. In that year, central cities will receive an average per capita grant of $30.48, compared to $18.22 for large (over 50,000 population) noncentral cities, $13.37 for urban counties, $5.83 for small communities in SMSA balances, and $11.74 for small communities in non-SMSAs.

To see how the dual formula changed the shares among the types of SMSA recipients, refer to columns 2, 3, and 4 of Table 2. Compared to full funding (projected 1980) under the 1974 formula, full funding under the dual formula increased the central city share from 42.4 percent to 55.5 percent, or about 14 percentage points less than the 69 percent share received by central cities under the displaced categorical programs. The discretionary share for small communities in the SMSA balance decreased from a potential of 21 percent under full funding with the 1974 formula to less than 7 percent under full funding with the dual formula. To summarize, the change to the dual formula redirected CDBG funds toward central cities (although they still have a smaller share than under the categorical programs as shown in column 4 of Table 2) at the expense of small communities in SMSA balances. The urban county and non-SMSA shares remain approximately the same.

The regional patterns under the dual formula also differ from those under the 1974 formula. As shown in Table 2, the share going to metropolitan cities in the Northeast and North Central regions increases by 13.1 percentage points

[3] Under the present law, the "hold-harmless" provisions represent the primary method of achieving a smooth transition between the displaced categorical programs and the new block grant approach. Basically, the hold-harmless funds are the amounts cities received during Fiscal 1968–72 under the categorical programs. During the first three years of CDBG (1975, 1976, and 1977), those cities which had been receiving a higher level of funding under the displaced categorical programs continued to receive this higher level (were held-harmless). For each of these cities, during the three-year period 1978, 1979, and 1980, the excess of hold-harmless over the dual formula amount is being phased out by thirds. According to the present law, all cities will be receiving their full formula amounts in Fiscal 1980. The analysis in this paper is based on full formula (i.e., projected 1980) amounts.

Table 2: Distribution of CDBG Allocations by Type of Recipient and by Region, Projected to 1980

	(1) Per Capita $ under Dual Formula[a]	*Percentage Shares*		
		(2) Dual Formula[a]	*(3)* 1974 Formula[a]	*(4)* Displaced Categorical Programs[b]
SMSA	$19.10	81.3%	80.0%	87.5%
Metropolitan Cities (559)	28.36	62.5	48.0	74.0
City Type				
Central Cities (381)	30.48	55.5	42.4	69.6
Noncentral Cities over 50,000 population (178)	18.22	7.0	5.6	4.4
Region[c]				
Northeast	34.22	19.0	11.8	24.9
North Central	31.17	16.9	11.0	17.5
South	25.57	14.7	14.4	20.1
West	20.06	9.4	8.7	11.4
Remainder of SMSA	9.12	18.8	32.0	13.5
Urban counties (entitled)[d]	13.37	12.0	11.0	
SMSA bal. (discretionary)	5.83	6.8	21.0	
NON-SMSA (discretionary)	11.74	18.7[e]	20.0	12.5
U.S.	17.51	100.0	100.0	100.0

[a] These are full formula (i.e., no hold-harmless) amounts based on a projected 1980 appropriation of $3.8 billion.

[b] Allocations under the displaced categorical programs were estimated using hold-harmless averages. Basically, hold-harmless averages are the annual average amounts received during 1968–1972 under the displaced categorical programs.

[c] Because 8 cities in Puerto Rico are excluded, the regional percentages will not sum to the total percentage for all metropolitan cities.

[d] Data was not available for breakdown of hold-harmless between urban counties and the SMSA balance.

[e] The non-SMSA account falls below 20 percent because the SMSA balance account includes a minimum set-aside which is not divided on a 80–20 basis between the SMSA and non-SMSA accounts.

from 22.8 (11.8 + 11.0) percent under the 1974 formula to 35.9 (19.0 + 16.9) percent under the dual formula. This reflects the higher proportion of cities in the northern regions with older housing and low population growth; both factors are represented in the dual formula. The share allocated to metropolitan cities in the South and West increases by only one percentage point from 23.1 percent to 24.1 percent.

TABLE 3: Ten Most Needy and Ten Least Needy Cities on Three Dimensions of Community Development Need
(population over 250,000)

Dimension	Most Needy	Score[a]	Least Needy	Score
(1) Age and decline	Pittsburgh	1.63	San Antonio	−1.19
	Minneapolis	1.59	Tucson	−1.22
	Buffalo	1.59	Phoenix	−1.22
	Rochester	1.38	Jacksonville	−1.40
	Cleveland	1.27	Albuquerque	−1.43
	St. Louis	1.19	Houston	−1.52
	St. Paul	1.18	Austin	−1.67
	Boston	1.11	El Paso	−1.68
	Akron	1.01	San Jose	−1.74
	Philadelphia	1.01	Honolulu	−2.08
(2) Density	Washington	2.44	Toledo	−0.73
	Newark	2.42	Akron	−0.75
	New York	1.57	Wichita	−0.79
	Honolulu	1.32	St. Paul	−0.80
	Detroit	1.30	Minneapolis	−0.80
	Miami	1.22	Portland	−0.88
	Baltimore	1.06	Jacksonville	−0.90
	Atlanta	1.01	Nashville	−0.91
	Oakland	.85	Oklahoma City	−0.93
	Chicago	.77	Tulsa	−0.94
(3) Poverty	New Orleans	2.76	Omaha	−0.39
	San Antonio	2.29	Milwaukee	−0.39
	El Paso	2.22	San Diego	−0.41
	Birmingham	1.72	Wichita	−0.43
	Memphis	1.70	San Francisco	−0.51
	Newark	1.68	Portland	−0.58
	St. Louis	1.06	Minneapolis	−0.74
	Miami	1.05	San Jose	−0.80
	Jacksonville	0.96	Long Beach	−0.89
	Atlanta	0.93	Seattle	−1.12

[a] On each factor, the average score for the population of the 483 cities included in the analysis equals zero.

TARGETING UNDER CDBG

A needs index

During the past five years, particularly with the advent of government allocations based on "objective needs," social scientists and policy-makers have suggested ways of measuring and ranking the needs of local government units. In this paper, an index of community development need is used that was recently developed at HUD by Bunce and Goldberg (1979) to test alternative funding formulas. Bunce and Goldberg defined community development need in terms of the overall objective of the CDBG legislation. This objective is to assist the development of viable urban communities by providing decent housing, a suitable living environment, and expanded economic opportunities, principally for low and moderate income persons. Given this objective, twenty variables were selected as indicators of community development need. These variables consisted of direct indicators of community development need, socioeconomic variables associated with urban blight and substandard housing, and measures of economic and population loss.[4]

Because an analysis with so many variables would have been cumbersome as well as difficult to interpret, the statistical method of *factor analysis* was used to reduce the need indicators to a smaller set of factors; each factor was defined by a different group of variables that were highly correlated and which together were composed of indicators of particular dimensions of need for community development assistance. The 20 CD need indicators were reduced to three factors (or dimensions) of community development need: *age and decline, density,* and *poverty.*[5]

1. *Age and decline:* change in population (negative), pre-1939 housing, change in retail sales (negative), and change in employment (negative). A negative designation means that a lower value (for example, a minus 10 percent change in population) indicates higher need.
2. *Density:* violent crimes, population density, renter households, change in percent Negro (1960–70), nonwhite population, unemployment, and female-headed families.
3. *Poverty:* poor persons under 18, poor persons, nonwhite population overcrowded housing, houses without plumbing, female-headed families, and persons without high school education.

For each of the three dimensions of need, the factor analysis provides an index for each city that can be used to measure relative per capita need among cities. For instance, factor analysis transforms a city's percentages on several

[4] The twenty indicators of community development need used in the Bunce and Goldberg study were: poverty, children in poverty, overcrowded housing, housing with inadequate plumbing, persons without a high school education, nonwhite persons, unemployment, families with a female head, crime, density, renter-occupied housing, change in percentage Negro (1960–70), persons over 65, pre-1939 housing units, new housing units, change in population (1960–75 and 1970–75), change in retail sales (1967–72), change in retail establishments (1963–72), and change in private employment (1967–72). (The last six variables are inverse indicators of need.) Each variable was expressed in either percentage or per capita terms in order to characterize the "average" person in a city with respect to the variable being considered. The need variables measure *relative* differences in per capita need among the metropolitan cities. The large majority of entitlement cities (483, or 95 percent of the entitlement city population) was used in the needs analysis. *See* Chapters 3 and 4 and Appendix F of Bunce and Goldberg (1979) for a more detailed discussion of the above variables, including justifications for the variables in terms of the objectives of the CDBG legislation; an analysis using Annual Housing Survey data that shows how particular variables are associated with housing and neighborhood problems; and an examination of problems with the variables, such as out-of-date poverty counts, inability to adjust for boundary changes when computing the trend variables, and unreliable data sources.

[5] The following list shows the variables that were most highly associated with each factor.

TABLE 4: Average Factor Scores by Region, 483 Metropolitan Cities

	Age and Decline	Density	Poverty
Northeast	+0.79	+0.51	−0.12
North Central	+0.42	−0.26	−0.32
South	−0.58	−0.28	+0.84
West	−0.62	+0.09	−0.54

poverty-related variables into a single composite score that indicates the city's position relative to other metropolitan cities on the poverty dimension. Cities with high proportions of poverty and housing overcrowding receive a high score on the poverty dimension of community development need. In general, a city receives a high score on a particular factor (dimension) if it has a high percentage for most of the variables that define that factor. New Orleans, for example, has a high score on the poverty dimension (2.76), Pittsburgh on the age and decline dimension (1.63), and Newark on the density dimension (2.42), as shown in Table 3. For each dimension, the average score for the population of the 483 cities is zero. Positive scores indicate above-average per capita need for the factor being considered; negative scores indicate below-average per capita need.

Table 4 shows the average factor scores by region. As shown by the average scores in the first row of Table 4, urban problems associated with aged housing and economic and population decline are concentrated in the Northeastern and North Central cities. The negative scores for the South and West on the age and decline dimension reflect, of course, the relatively high rate of population and economic growth and the relatively low percentage of pre-1939 housing in these two regions. Such classic examples of declining cities as Pittsburgh, Buffalo, Cleveland, and St. Louis all fall into the neediest category on this dimension, and the growth cities of Houston, Phoenix, and San Jose into the least needy category (Table 3).

Above-average scores on the density dimension of need are concentrated in the Northeast and West; below-average scores are concentrated in the Southern and North Central regions.[6] The average poverty score for the 147

---

[6] The most significant aspect of the density dimension was (not surprisingly) its concentration in large cities. For example, consider the following average scores by population size:

	Less than 100,000	100,000– 250,000	Greater than 250,000
Age and Decline	−.09	−.15	+.09
Density	−.64	−.43	+.44
Poverty	−.31	−.08	+.17

The average scores on the density dimension exhibit the sharpest response to population size.

Southern cities (+.84) was much higher than the average for any of the other regions. In fact, 80 of the 96 cities in the first quintile of the poverty index were in the South. In contrast, Western and North Central cities accounted for 80 of 96 cities in the fifth, or least needy, quintile on this factor.

In order to test and summarize alternative formulas by an index of need, scores on the three dimensions of need were combined into a single measure of relative community development need. In the remainder of the paper when the term *need* is used, reference is to the following index developed by Bunce and Goldberg (1979):[7]

$$\text{need} = .40 \text{ (poverty)} + .35 \text{ (age and decline)} + .25 \text{ (density)} \quad (1)$$

The index scores for the cities over 250,000 population that result from this weighting are given in Table 5.[8]

Targeting according to need

The next step was to test which formula was most adaptive to CD need. To do this we employed regression analysis. If one regresses per capita CDBG grants on the index of need, as in equation (2), it is possible to simply interpret the statistics thus derived:

$$\text{Per Capita CDBG \$} = a + b \text{ *need*} \quad (2)$$

The slope coefficient (b) from the regression of per capita dollars on need indicates the rate at which per capita amounts change with changes in need scores; it is therefore a direct measure of the extent to which a formula tar-

---

[7] Although Bunce and Goldberg made no attempt to provide a detailed justification for each weight, the weights were not entirely arbitrary. The weight assigned to each dimension was based primarily on a perception of the relevance of the group of variables defining that dimension to the purposes and goals of the CDBG legislation. For example, given the legislative emphasis on directing funds to areas with high concentration of low income persons, the poverty dimension received the highest weight. *See* Bunce and Goldberg (1979; Chapter 3) for further discussion of this issue. Also *see* Appendix J of the study for a test of the needs index using direct measures (e.g., housing abandonment) of housing and neighborhood problems for a small sample of large cities, and U.S. Bureau of the Census (1977) for a test of the needs model using the distress rankings of suburbs in the Detroit SMSA obtained from a panel of knowledgeable individuals.

[8] Examination of the need scores by region shows that the highest level of per capita need exists in the Northeast, with an average need score of +.35, compared to +.06 for the South, —.04 for the North Central regions, and —.41 for the West. Approximately 64 percent of the Northeastern cities are in the top two quintiles of need, as against 54 percent for the South, 25 percent for the North Central cities, and only 15 percent for the West. Approximately 40 percent of the Western cities were concentrated in the lowest need quintile, compared to 5 percent of the Northeastern cities, 10 percent of the Southern cities, and 26 percent of the North Central cities. Of course, changing the weights in the definition of need would change the average need scores by region. For instance, if the weight of the poverty dimension had been increased in defining total need, the average score for the South would have risen at the expense of the scores for the three other regions.

TABLE 5: Need Scores and Need Rankings, Cities with Populations over 250,000

Rank	City	Need Score[a]	Rank	City	Need Score[a]
1	Newark	1.448	30	Kansas City	0.042
2	New Orleans	1.166	31	Los Angeles	0.017
3	St. Louis	1.022	32	Denver	−0.030
4	Cleveland	0.782	33	Fort Worth	−0.117
5	Birmingham	0.777	34	St. Paul	−0.134
6	Baltimore	0.764	35	Sacramento	−0.142
7	Washington	0.663	36	Portland	−0.160
8	Detroit	0.626	37	Columbus	−0.165
9	Atlanta	0.590	38	Toledo	−0.168
10	Boston	0.556	39	Baton Rouge	−0.178
11	Cincinnati	0.543	40	Long Beach	−0.202
12	Oakland	0.524	41	Seattle	−0.221
13	Chicago	0.521	42	Oklahoma City	−0.242
14	Buffalo	0.513	43	Dallas	−0.249
15	New York	0.507	44	Charlotte	−0.260
16	Philadelphia	0.495	45	Jacksonville	−0.331
17	Louisville	0.485	46	Houston	−0.356
18	Pittsburgh	0.484	47	Wichita	−0.363
19	San Antonio	0.467	48	Albuquerque	−0.365
20	Miami	0.459	49	Omaha	−0.389
21	Norfolk	0.341	50	Austin	−0.399
22	El Paso	0.322	51	Tucson	−0.435
23	Memphis	0.316	52	Honolulu	−0.476
24	Rochester	0.299	53	San Diego	−0.510
25	San Francisco	0.219	54	Tulsa	−0.517
26	Tampa	0.155	55	Nashville-Davidson	−0.556
27	Milwaukee	0.060	56	Phoenix	−0.564
28	Minneapolis	0.059	57	Indianapolis	−0.567
29	Akron	0.048	58	San Jose	−0.892

[a] The average need score for the population of the 483 metropolitan cities included in the needs analysis is zero. Large cities as a group are somewhat needier than average.

gets funds to needy cities.[9] The regression results for the dual formula are presented in column 2 of Table 6. For comparison, the regression results for the 1974 single formula, which the dual formula replaced, have been included in column 1 of Table 6.

[9] The regression statistic, r^2, which measures the degree to which need scores explain variations in the formula's allocations also has an interesting interpretation in this needs framework. It measures the consistency with which a formula responds to need, that is, a high r^2 statistic indicates that cities with similar levels of need receive similar levels of per capita allocations. A low r^2 value indicates the reverse. It is possible for a formula to exhibit a high level of targeting, as measured by a high regression slope, but be very

TABLE 6: Simple Regression of Per Capita Formula Amounts under the Various Formulas on the Total Need, 483 Metropolitan Cities

	1974 Formula[a]	*Dual Formula*	*IMPAC-TION*[b] *1*	*IMPAC-TION*[b] *2*	*IMPAC-TION*[b] *3*
Regression co-efficient for need ($)[c]	11.51	17.87	22.59	21.33	22.57
Intercept ($)[d]	28.88	28.88	29.76	29.51	28.76
Coefficient of determination (r^2)	0.77	0.67	0.74	0.72	0.76

[a] All formulas assume full-formula funding projected to 1980, that is, they assume that there are no hold-harmless allocations.

[b] See text for the definition of the impaction formulas.

[c] The statistics reported in this table resulted from regressions of the following form: Per capita $ = a + b$ NEED, where a is the intercept and b is a measure of slope, or the change in per capita dollars associated with a unit change in NEED. See Bunce and Goldberg (1979) and the text for definition of NEED.

[d] Since the average score for NEED is zero, the intercept equals the average per capita amount for the allocations being considered.

The results in column 2 show that under the dual formula, per capita allocations increased by $17.87 for each unit increase in the per capita need index. This response to need is $6.36 more than the $11.51 response under the 1974 single formula. A substantial difference thus exists in the extent to which the dual and the 1974 formula target funds according to overall city need: the dual formula is much more responsive to need than the single formula. That is, the dual formula tends to target funds to needy cities while the 1974 formula is likely to "spread" CDBG funds among the metropolitan cities.

It is possible, however, to further increase the targeting of CDBG funds according to city need. Practically any degree of targeting can be obtained by substituting variables, manipulating variable weights, and limiting or capping "impaction ratios" (defined below). Of course, increasing the targeting of funds to need always results in redistributions of funds among the entitlement communities (central cities, suburban cities over 50,000, and urban counties). In essence, the targeting question reduces to how much the most needy cities and the least needy cities should receive. Before examining this

unsystematic in its response to need, as measured by a low r^2 value. An example of this was the distribution of funds under the displaced categorical programs. Categorical funds were distributed, on average, to needy cities, but cities with similar levels of need were often allocated very different per capita amounts. For an analysis of the categorical programs, *see* Bunce (1979).

issue of gainers and losers in more detail, the concept of *impaction*, which is the basis for the three alternative formulas given in Table 6, must be discussed.

Impaction

"Impaction" was the central focus of the recent formula study by HUD mandated by Congress. As a funding concept, impaction recognizes the *intensity* of a city's need in the allocation of federal funds. The intensity of need for a city on a particular need variable is measured in terms of the city's proportion or percentage of that need variable. For example, in impaction formulas, one or more of the variables (such as number of poor persons, number of pre-1939 housing units) are multiplied by ratios which reflect the proportions of the variables (percentage of population which is poor, percentage of the housing stock which is old, etc.) in the community in question, relative to the average for the same variable(s) in all entitlement communities. Consider the following example: a city has a poverty percentage of 16 percent and the average for all entitlement communities is 12 percent. The poverty impaction ratio for this city would therefore equal 1.33 (16 divided by 12). Under a poverty impaction formula, this city's poverty count would be multiplied by 1.33.

When the ratio of one variable is applied to the value of another, impaction formulas can express the interaction as well as the intensity of need variables. Under an impaction formula that includes the interaction between percent poverty and pre-1939 housing and overcrowding housing, the pre-1939 and overcrowded housing data for the city in the above example would be multiplied by 1.33.

Additionally the impaction ratio can be limited ("capped") to moderate the redistribution of funds. For instance, in the above example the poverty impaction ratio could be allowed to vary from .75 to 1.50.

The statistics for three impaction formulas have been included in Table 6.[10] Impactions 1 and 2 are the same as the current dual formula except that a poverty impaction ratio has been used to adjust the pre-1939 and overcrowded housing counts in the manner described above. The difference between Impactions 1 and 2 is that the poverty impaction ratio varies from 0 and 2.0 under Impaction 1, but only from .75 to 1.50 under Impaction 2. This means that Impaction 2 does not reward (penalize) cities with high (low) percentages of poverty to the extent that Impaction 1 does. Impaction 2 will therefore have a smaller targeting effect than Impaction 1. Impaction 3 is the same as Impaction 2 except that total population, a nonneed variable, is replaced by poverty in the 1974 formula, thus increasing the weight of the poverty factor in that formula to .75. Therefore, Impaction 2 will also have a smaller targeting effect than Impaction 3. The impaction for-

---

[10] For additional analysis of these and other impaction formulas, *see* Chapter 5 of Bunce and Goldberg (1979).

mulas were chosen to illustrate how different degrees of targeting can be obtained and to show how changes in targeting result in changes in the number and magnitude of funding redistributions.

Redistribution of CDBG funds under different formulas

As shown in Table 6, each of the impaction formulas exhibits a higher per capita response to need than the current dual formula. For example, under Impaction 1 (column 3 of Table 6), per capita dollars increase by $22.59 for each unit increase in the needs index; this represents a $4.72 greater response to need than that exhibited by the current dual formula. Information on the dollar redistributions under these formulas for the 15 most needy cities and for the 15 least needy cities is provided in Table 7 for cities of over 250,000 population and in Table 8 for cities under 250,000 population. The percent change figures given in these tables illustrate how the targeting question reduces to gains for needy cities and losses for less needy cities. Under Impaction 1, Newark—the most needy large city—experiences a 28.5 percent gain, relative to the current dual formula, and San Jose—the least needy large city—suffers a 11.3 percent loss. The cities that tend to suffer the largest percent losses from an increase in targeting are the relatively high income suburban cities that rely on the total population variable in the 1974 formula. For example, Arlington Heights, a rich suburban city in the Chicago SMSA, suffers a 58.3 percent loss under Impaction 3, which replaces the population variable with an increase in the weight of the poverty variable to .75.

To show the relationship that exists between responsiveness to need (the targeting question) and number of cities that experience large losses, consider Impactions 1 and 2. Recall that Impaction 1 is the same as Impaction 2 except that its upper and lower caps on the impacting variable (percent poverty) have a wider range. This greater intensity shows up in the needs analysis as a larger response to need for Impaction 1 ($22.59 compared to $21.23 for Impaction 2). However, as shown in Table 9, 93 cities suffer losses greater than 20 percent under Impaction 1, which is 73 more than the 20 large losers under Impaction 2.

The direct relationship between targeting and the number of cities losing funds is illustrated even more dramatically by comparing Impactions 2 and 3. Impaction 3 exhibits a greater response to need than Impaction 2, but results in 136 cities losing over 20 percent, compared to only 20 cities under Impaction 2 (Table 9).[11] The relatively large number of losers under Impaction 3 arises because of the large number of small, suburban cities that rely heavily

---

[11] If it were felt that no community should suffer more than a 10 percent loss because of formula changes, then $91.3 million ($36.4 million for cities and $54.9 for urban counties) would have to be found if Impaction 3 was considered (Table 9). This is not much considering that $607 million was added to entitlement communities from 1976 to 1978. It is also worth noting that funding to nonneedy urban counties will have increased from $209 million in 1976 to $420 million by 1980.

TABLE 7: Percent Changes in Per Capita Allocations for the 15 Most Needy and 15 Least Needy Cities with Populations Greater than 250,000

	NEED Score	Per Capita $ under Dual	Percent Change from Current Dual Formula		
			IMPAC-TION 1	IMPAC-TION 2	IMPAC-TION 3
15 Most needy large cities					
Newark, N.J.	1.48	$ 50	28.5%	13.3%	14.3%
New Orleans, La.	1.16	41	26.8	10.9	11.9
St. Louis, Mo.	1.02	70	19.1	12.1	13.0
Cleveland, Ohio	0.78	63	11.6	11.4	12.4
Birmingham, Ala.	0.77	45	18.5	7.8	8.8
Baltimore, Md.	0.76	38	17.5	15.0	16.0
Washington, D.C.	0.66	33	10.8	10.7	11.6
Detroit, Mich	0.62	49	4.5	4.4	5.3
Atlanta, Ga.	0.59	34	13.2	7.6	8.8
Boston, Mass.	0.55	41	11.1	11.0	11.9
Cincinnati, Ohio	0.54	48	12.4	12.3	13.3
Oakland, Calif.	0.52	40	11.7	11.5	12.5
Chicago, Ill.	0.52	43	5.4	5.3	6.2
Buffalo, N.Y.	0.51	60	6.7	6.6	7.5
New York, N.Y.	0.50	35	8.1	8.0	8.9
15 Least needy large cities					
Charlotte, N.C.	−0.26	$ 19	− 1.6%	− 1.6%	3.2%
Jacksonville, Fla.	−0.33	21	4.3	4.1	13.6
Houston, Tex.	−0.35	20	0.5	0.4	4.6
Wichita, Kan.	−0.36	18	− 6.5	− 6.6	− 4.5
Albuquerque, N.M.	−0.36	18	− 0.3	− 0.5	2.7
Omaha, Neb.	−0.38	16	− 7.7	− 7.8	− 9.9
Austin, Tex.	−0.39	20	3.0	2.9	8.5
Tucson, Ariz.	−0.43	19	0.3	0.1	3.3
Honolulu, Ha.	−0.47	19	−16.8	−15.6	−22.1
San Diego, Calif.	−0.51	16	− 5.8	− 5.9	− 7.7
Tulsa, Okla.	−0.51	17	− 4.1	− 4.2	− 1.3
Nashville, Tenn.	−0.55	19	− 1.8	− 1.9	3.3
Phoenix, Ariz.	−0.56	17	− 4.9	− 5.0	− 6.0
Indianapolis, Ind.	−0.56	17	− 9.6	− 9.7	−11.9
San Jose, Calif.	−0.89	13	−11.3	−10.7	−21.8

TABLE 8: Percent Changes in Per Capita Allocations for the 15 Most Needy and 15 Least Needy Cities with Populations Less than 250,000

| | NEED Score | Per Capita $ under Dual | Percent Change from Current Dual Formula | | |
			IMPAC-TION 1	IMPAC-TION 2	IMPAC-TION 3
15 Most needy small cities					
San Benito, Tex.	2.33	$51.90	17.2%	6.0%	31.8%
East St. Louis, Ill.	2.17	68.88	18.2	6.6	7.5
Pharr, Tex.	2.17	49.93	20.1	7.5	31.3
Laredo, Tex.	2.00	48.96	20.1	7.5	31.1
Brownsville, Tex.	1.93	43.99	20.0	7.5	29.6
Harlingen, Tex.	1.66	40.00	16.9	6.0	28.2
Edinburg, Tex.	1.38	42.65	21.1	8.1	29.2
Augusta, Ga.	1.33	57.13	20.2	7.6	8.5
McAllen, Tex.	1.26	38.27	19.1	7.1	27.5
Camden, N.J.	1.22	58.17	21.6	11.6	12.5
Chester, Pa.	1.16	56.67	18.2	11.2	12.1
Charleston, S.C.	1.10	39.03	26.3	10.6	11.6
Wilmington, Del.	1.09	54.73	25.4	13.3	14.3
Asbury Park, N.J.	1.05	58.81	31.9	13.5	14.3
Atlantic City, N.J.	1.03	66.27	28.8	13.4	14.4
15 Least needy small cities					
Concord, Calif.	−1.33	$10.18	−18.4	−10.5	−35.4
Mesquite, Tex.	−1.33	11.63	−24.4	−13.1	−35.0
Scottsdale, Ariz.	−1.34	10.16	−16.4	−10.0	−33.9
Aurora, Colo.	−1.34	8.86	−14.5	− 9.4	−41.1
Huntington Beach, Calif.	−1.37	9.64	−16.1	−10.0	−36.9
Farmington Hills, Mich.	−1.38	9.27	−21.1	−10.8	−42.0
Bloomington, Ill.	−1.40	10.49	−31.8	−13.6	−42.7
Garland, Tex.	−1.45	9.68	−23.4	−12.0	−42.9
Arlington Heights, Ill.	−1.46	7.23	−21.3	− 9.7	−58.3
Arlington, Tex.	−1.47	10.27	−17.2	−10.5	−34.7
Southfield, Mich.	−1.48	8.15	−17.4	− 9.2	−46.5
Overland Park, Kans.	−1.50	7.54	−17.3	− 8.8	−51.9
Bellevue, Wash.	−1.51	7.83	−13.9	− 8.0	−46.1
Mount Prospect, Ill.	−1.51	7.77	−23.2	−10.4	−54.2
Troy City, Mich.	−1.53	8.08	−18.6	− 9.9	−49.1

TABLE 9: Large Losses and Gains under Formula Alternatives, Projected FY 1980 Allocations

	Losses in Excess of 10% [a]			Losses in Excess of 20% [a]			Gains in Excess of 20% [a]		
Formula	Cities	Urban Counties	Total	Cities	Urban Counties	Total	Cities	Urban Counties	Total
Impaction 1	29.8 (217)	29.8 (63)	59.6 (280)	9.3 (93)	7.3 (19)	16.6 (112)	4.7 (17)	0	4.7 (17)
Impaction 2	13.6 (190)	8.8 (49)	22.4 (239)	0.6 (20)	0.6 (5)	1.2 (25)	— (2)	0	— (2)
Impaction 3	36.4 (241)	54.9 (67)	91.3 (308)	12.8 (136)	24.8 (55)	37.6 (191)	9.7 (36)	0	9.7 (36)

[a] The first figure represents millions of dollars of aggregate excess loss or excess gain, and the second figure (in parentheses) represents the number of communities. For reference, 559 cities are expected to receive a total of $2,308.7 million under the present dual in 1980 and 81 urban counties are expected to receive a total of $442.0 million.

TABLE 10: Distribution of 1980 Formula Alternatives between Cities and Urban Counties

Formula	City Total	Central Cities	Noncentral Cities[a]	Urban Counties
Dual	2,308.7	2,051.8	256.9	442.0
Impaction 1	2,373.7	2,149.6	224.1	377.6
Impaction 2	2,353.2	2,118.2	235.0	397.5
Impaction 3	2,398.7	2,175.3	223.4	352.0

Note: Figures are in millions of dollars.

[a] Some of the "suburban" cities in this category are, in fact, highly distressed and gain from most of the alternatives.

on the total population variable for their funding under the current dual formula.[12]

In aggregative terms, central cities gain under the alternative formulas at the expense of noncentral cities and urban counties (Table 10). The projected 1980 amount to be allocated to noncentral cities would decrease from $256.9 million under the current dual formula to $235.1 million under Impaction 2, while the decrease for urban counties would be even larger, from $433.0 to $397.5 million. Dropping total population from the formula particularly affects the allocation to noncentral cities and urban counties. For example, under Impaction 3 the allocations to these two groups of recipients fall to $223.4 million and $352.0 million, decreases of 13 and 19 percent, respectively. The urban impacts of these redistributions are discussed in the next section of this paper.

The aggregate redistributions among regions are not as great as those among central cities, noncentral cities, and urban counties. Under the three impaction formulas, the South does quite well because of the increased role of poverty (Table 11). For example, the allocation to the South would increase from $650.7 million to $697.0 million under Impaction 3, an increase of 7 percent. On the other hand, the West and North Central regions, which contain many high income suburbs and urban counties, would suffer losses of 6.8 and 4.5 percent, respectively. The allocation to the Northeast would remain approximately the same. It should be emphasized, however, that the regional figures cover the full range of winners and losers—for example, in the case of the North Central region, from (needy) Detroit, a big gainer, to (less needy) Livonia, Michigan, a big loser.

To summarize, the redistributions of funds that result from an increase in

[12] Because they also rely heavily on total population for their funding, 55 of the 81 urban counties suffer losses of over 20 percent under Impaction 3. As a group, urban counties are relatively nonneedy. For instance, they exhibit a 6.3 percent rate of poverty, a 6.3 percent rate of overcrowding housing, and a 23.1 percent rate of pre-1939 housing. These percentages compare with 13.7, 7.9, and 44.1, respectively, for metropolitan cities.

TABLE 11: Regional Distribution of 1980 Formula Alternatives

	Entitlement Communities by Census Region[a]			
Formula	*Northeast*	*North Central*	*South*	*West*
Dual	848.0	710.4	650.7	476.2
Impaction 1	845.4	687.1	692.3	451.9
Impaction 2	855.2	697.9	673.8	455.8
Impaction 3	847.0	677.9	697.0	443.6

Note: Figures are in millions of dollars.

[a] Puerto Rico is not included, reducing the number of entitlement communities to 551 entitlement cities and 81 urban counties. The impaction alternatives benefit Puerto Rican cities.

targeting according to need are from high income suburbs and urban counties to more needy central cities located in all regions. That is, the results reported here indicate that an increase in targeting does not place the South against the Northeast, but instead, places needy central cities against less needy suburbs and urban counties.

Formula response to the different types of need

The above targeting discussion has focused on the per capita response of formulas to a single index of community development need. An equally important question is the response of the current dual formula and alternative formulas to the separate types of community development need, such as poverty, age, and decline. In fact, a major controversy in the CDBG program involves the relative importance of low income and poverty needs compared to city age and decline needs. Full funding under the 1974 formula (that is, after ending hold-harmless) would have directed CDBG funds to the low income cities in the South at the expense of the declining and aged cities in the Northeast and North Central regions. For instance, the 1974 formula exhibited a $6.59 per capita response to poverty need but only a $1.81 response to age and decline need (Table 12). In 1977, HUD argued that an age variable, supplemented by a growth-lag variable, was needed to guarantee more funding to cities experiencing the most severe physical and economic problems. The dual formula that resulted from this controversy increased the per capita response to age and decline need to $9.68, but decreased the response to poverty need to $4.90.

Impactions 1, 2, and 3, all of which emphasize poverty, redirect CDBG funding toward poverty need. For example, under Impaction 1, the per capita response to poverty is $7.49, which is not only greater than the response to poverty under the current dual formula, but is also greater than that under the 1974 formula. It is also important to point out that, because of their greater overall targeting, the responses under the impaction formulas to age

TABLE 12: Multiple Regression of Per Capita Formula Amounts on Per Capita Need Scores, 483 Metropolitan Cities

Regression Slopes for Dimensions of CD Need ($)[a]	(1) 1974 Formula[b]	(2) Dual Formula	(3) Impaction 1[c]	tion 2 (4) Impac-	(5) Impaction 3
(1) Age and decline[d]	1.81	9.68	10.43	10.38	10.48
(2) Density[d]	2.81	3.22	4.54	4.43	4.26
(3) Poverty[d]	6.59	4.90	7.49	6.44	7.61
Intercept ($)	28.88	28.88	29.76	29.51	29.96
Coefficient of multiple determination (R^2)	0.92	0.77	0.78	0.78	0.81

Note: All formula amounts are projected 1980 allocations.

[a] The multiple regression slope measures the rate of change of per capita amounts associated with a one-unit change in the index, for constant values of the other two indexes.

[b] To compare the distributional consequences of the 1974 formula and the dual formula, it was assumed that they allocated the same total dollar amount to the 483 cities. This is reflected by the two equal constant terms ($28.88) representing average per capita amounts under the two formulas.

[c] See text for the definition of the impaction formulas.

[d] Age and Decline, Density, and Poverty are factor scores, each with an average value of zero. For further discussion, see Chapter 3 of Bunce and Goldberg (1979) and the text.

and decline need do not decrease below that of the current dual formula. For instance, under Impaction 1, the per capita response to the age and decline index equals $10.43, which compares with a $9.69 response under the current dual formula (Table 12). To summarize, under the impaction formulas, it is possible to redirect CDBG funding toward poverty need without reducing the response to age and decline need.

THE URBAN IMPACTS OF CDBG

What are the principal urban impacts of CDBG program? Much of the program's influences are on community development efforts[13] and may be best estimated at a micro scale (e.g., community social structure, decisions to rehabilitate) which are often best done in qualitative terms. However, we indicate below some aggregative notions of urban impact in terms of dollars spent, jobs created, income earned, and housing units rehabilitated. Following the methodology developed in Glickman and Jacobs (1979), these variables are estimated for different types of cities and regions for projected Fiscal 1980 grant levels. Also these impacts are compared among the dual and the three impaction formulas and some of the impacts on neighborhood condition are discussed.

[13] The subject of a four-year CDBG evaluation currently underway at the University of Pennsylvania for the Department of Housing and Urban Development.

Methodology

A brief methodology note will introduce the results described below. Beginning with the value of *direct CDBG expenditures* given by the formulas, we calculate, via a set of national input-output multipliers, *total expenditures* in each set of cities which are generated by CDBG spending. Given the ratio of expenditures to employment by major industry affected by CDBG, we calculate expected *employment* (direct and indirect) which the program will likely generate. Given average wage levels in those industries, we convert employment change to increments in *earnings*.[14] Finally, given an estimate of the proportion of CDBG funds going to housing rehabilitation (20.3 percent in Fiscal 1977), we estimate the number of *housing units rehabilitated*.

Urban impacts by city type and region

Tables 13 and 14 show the projected impacts for the variables noted above for the different formulas already discussed. Table 13 gives a breakdown by city type. For the dual formula, central cities will receive $2,051.8 million in 1980, generating $4,042.0 million in total spending when multiplier effects are considered. This, in turn, will mean 172.9 thousand jobs with employee earnings of $2,298.0 million. Finally, slightly less than 70,000 houses[15] will be rehabilitated.[16] On the other hand, the roughly $949 million in direct spending going to the suburbs will create about 80 thousand jobs and $1,063 million in earnings. Parallel figures are given for nonmetropolitan areas.

The distribution of funds between central cities and suburban jurisdictions would change, given alternative formulas. As one can see from Table 13, central cities gain at the expense of suburbs under the impaction formulas, particularly with Impaction 3. This is highlighted in Table 13, where comparisons between the dual and the three impaction formulas are also made. For instance, under Impaction 3, there would be an additional $123.5 million in direct CDBG grants to central cities than under the dual formula. This, in turn, implies about $266 million more in total activity generated (through the multiplier), 17,500 more jobs, $243 million extra earnings, and 4,200 additional rehabilitated housing units. Table 13 thus shows the substantial intrametropolitan differences that could occur under different formulas.

Turning to the regional analysis in Table 14, the possible formula changes appear not to make large differences among the four large regions. Under the dual formula, for instance, total (direct plus indirect) expenditures for the

[14] This ignores nonwage components of the income accounts. Glickman and Jacobs (1978) estimate this for the Section 312 Program for construction firms.

[15] Assuming an average unit rehabilitation cost of $6,000, a figure provided by HUD rehabilitation officials.

[16] This is probably an underestimate because it ignores neighborhood effects which might lead to further private or local government-sponsored housing rehabilitation due partly to the rehab work done via CDBG. These effects are very difficult to measure, however, and thus an approximate lower bound is given.

TABLE 13: Spatial Impacts for Central Cities, Suburbs, and Nonmetropolitan Areas for Alternative Formulas (Projected Fiscal 1980)

	Direct CDBG Expenditures[a]		Total Gross Expenditures Generated[a]	
	Amount	Central Cities' Gains over Dual	Amount	Central Cities' Gains over Dual
Dual				
Central cities	2,051.8	—	4,042.0	—
Suburbs	948.9	—	1,869.3	—
Nonmetropolitan areas	688.7	—	1,356.7	—
Impaction 1				
Central cities	2,149.6	+ 97.8	4,234.7	+192.7
Suburbs	851.7		1,677.8	
Nonmetropolitan areas[c]	688.7		1,356.7	
Impaction 2				
Central cities	2,118.2	+ 66.4	4,172.9	+130.9
Suburbs	882.7		1,738.9	
Nonmetropolitan areas[c]	668.7		1,356.7	
Impaction 3				
Central cities	2,175.3	+123.5	4,285.3	+243.3
Suburbs	825.4		1,626.0	
Nonmetropolitan areas[c]	668.7		1,356.7	

Northeast are projected to be $1,670.6 million in Fiscal 1980. This varies little from the other formulas: the smallest level of total expenditures was $1,664.8 under Impaction 1, and the largest was $1,684.7 under Impaction 2. The differences are only about 1 percent in each direction. Given our discussion of Table 13, what is clear is that there is a redistribution *within* the large regions from suburban to central city jurisdictions, but little reallocation *among* regions.

Neighborhood condition

In Fiscal 1977, 76 percent of CDBG funds were allocated for activities in residential areas. HUD analysis indicates that the predominant focus of the CDBG program appears to be on low- and moderate-income homeowner families in neighborhoods that are in the early-to-moderate stages of decline. According to HUD (1978), the percentage of funds benefiting low and moderate income families was 64 percent in Fiscal 1975, 67 percent in Fiscal 1976, and 61 percent in Fiscal 1977. In Fiscal 1976, the pattern of spending

Employment[b]		Earnings[a]		Housing Units Rehabilitated[b]	
Amount	Central Cities' Gains over Dual	Amount	Central Cities' Gains over Dual	Amount	Central Cities' Gains over Dual
172.9	—	2,298.0	—	69.4	—
79.9	—	1,062.8	—	32.2	—
58.0	—	771.3	—	23.3	—
180.9	+ 8.0	2,407.6	+109.6	72.7	+3.3
71.7		953.9		28.9	
58.0		771.3		23.3	
178.3	+ 5.4	2,372.4	+ 74.4	71.7	+2.3
74.3		988.6		29.9	
58.0		771.3		23.3	
183.1	+10.2	2,436.3	+138.3	73.6	+4.2
69.5		924.4		28.0	
58.0		771.3		23.3	

[a] Amounts are in millions.
[b] Amounts are in thousands.
[c] It was assumed that nonmetropolitan areas' allocations would not change from DUAL under the IMPACTION formulas.

in residential neighborhoods was: renewal-related activities (25.8 percent), water and sewer (3.4 percent), "other" public works (21.4 percent), code enforcement (1.7 percent), rehabilitation (23.2 percent), service-related facilities (5.4 percent), and public services (11.3 percent).

Comprehensive data on the neighborhood impacts of CDBG are not readily available for a complete analysis of the program's impact. It is for that reason that HUD has recently begun a four-year study (to be carried out at the University of Pennsylvania) to study CDBG's major neighborhood-related impacts.

Many types of effects are likely to be felt, however. These include:

Rehabilitation impact. The effects of the availability of municipal rehabilitation grants and loans on the likelihood that a property owner will decide to rehabilitate, and on the magnitude and nature of expenditures. The length of time the rehabilitated units remain in improved condition relative to their condition if they had not been rehabilitated should be determined.

Impacts of redevelopment. The extent of differences in pre- and post-rede-

TABLE 14: Spatial Impacts for Large Regions for Alternative Formulas
(Projected Fiscal 1980)

	Direct CDBG Expenditures[a]		Total Gross Expenditures Generated[a]	
	Amount	Region's Gain over Dual	Amount	Region's Gain over Dual
Dual				
Northeast	848.0	—	1,670.6	—
North Central	710.4	—	1,399.5	—
South	650.7	—	1,281.9	—
West	476.2	—	938.1	—
Impaction 1				
Northeast	845.1	− 2.9	1,664.8	− 5.7
North Central	687.7	−22.7	1,354.8	−44.7
South	692.3	+41.6	1,363.8	+81.9
West	451.9	−24.3	890.2	−47.9
Impaction 2				
Northeast	855.2	+ 7.2	1,684.7	+14.1
North Central	697.9	−12.5	1,374.9	−24.6
South	673.8	+23.1	1,327.4	+45.5
West	455.2	−21.0	896.7	−41.4
Impaction 3				
Northeast	847.0	− 1.0	1,668.6	− 2.0
North Central	677.9	−32.5	1,335.5	−64.0
South	697.0	+46.3	1,373.1	+91.2
West	443.6	−32.6	873.9	−64.2

velopment property values and land uses. This will give an estimate of the benefits of land clearance.

Relocation associated with rehabilitation and redevelopment. The amount of household displacement costs to those displaced, for voluntary rehabilitation, for rehabilitation required in code enforcement programs, and for site clearance programs is unclear and must be understood.

Benefits of CDBG-financed public services. Utilization data and service area data should be used to measure the distribution of benefits by type of recipients (e.g., by race, age, income class).

Indirect impacts. Spillover effects which enhance or magnify direct effects will be studied in addition to questions related to the direct impacts of re-

Employment[b]		Earnings[a]		Housing Units Rehabilitated[b]	
Amount	Region's Gain over Dual	Amount	Region's Gain over Dual	Amount	Region's Gain over Dual
71.4	—	948.8	—	28.7	—
59.8	—	795.6	—	24.0	—
54.8	—	728.8	—	22.0	—
40.1	—	533.3	—	16.0	—
71.1	−0.3	946.5	− 2.3	28.6	−0.1
57.9	−1.9	770.2	−25.4	23.2	−0.8
58.3	+3.5	775.4	+46.6	22.8	+0.8
38.0	−2.1	506.1	−27.2	15.4	−0.6
72.0	+0.6	957.8	+ 9.0	28.9	+0.2
58.7	−1.1	781.6	−14.0	23.6	−0.4
56.7	+1.9	754.7	+25.9	22.8	+0.8
38.3	−1.8	509.8	−23.5	15.4	−0.6
71.3	−0.1	948.6	− 0.2	28.7	0.0
57.1	−2.7	759.2	−36.4	22.9	−1.1
58.7	+3.9	780.6	+51.8	23.6	+1.6
37.3	−2.8	496.8	−36.5	15.0	−1.0

[a] Amounts are in millions.
[b] Amounts are in thousands.
[c] It was assumed that nonmetropolitan areas' allocations would not change from DUAL under the IMPACTION formulas.

habilitation, redevelopment, and public service enhancement. An attempt to measure private responses to CDBG activity is important here. These indirect impacts are the changes or consequences of CDBG that are separated by time or distance from the observed community development activity because of lags and linkages that exist in the urban environment. This analysis should include impacts throughout the city, and it includes impacts on residents, owners, producers of housing, and financial institutions. Specific interests include the level and extent of induced investment (rehabilitation, redevelopment, and maintenance) and the practices of lending and financial institutions must be studied.

Coordinated neighborhood strategies. We need to understand the joint impacts of simultaneously pursuing a number of program strategies within neighborhoods.

Impacts on perceptions and attitudes. The effects of CDBG on attitudes and perceptions is crucial to know because the economic health of a neighborhood depends on a multitude of decisions that are affected by expectations. Especially important are the perceptions and attitudes of residents (decisions about whether to stay in a neighborhood), of producers (decisions to redevelop or rehabilitate), and of financial institutions (decisions to lend or insure).

Citizen involvement. The role of citizen participation in CDBG activity has to be examined since there is a presumption in the legislation and implementation of the CDBG program that citizen involvement is important to the success of urban neighborhood revitalization. Therefore, one issue is to what extent can citizen groups play valuable roles in developing support for community development projects as they are introduced in a neighborhood?

Hopefully, the results of the HUD evaluation study should provide answers to some of these questions and information on who ultimately benefits from the local government community development program, and on the long-run effects of alternative community development activities on neighborhood development.

CONCLUSION

Three main conclusions about the spatial impact of CDBG can be drawn from the results reported in this paper. First, the dual formula passed in 1977 exhibits a much higher level of targeting according to need than the single formula that it replaced. The dual formula is particularly responsive to community development need as measured by city age and city decline.

Second, alternative formulas, such as impaction formulas, can be designed that would further increase the response of CDBG funding to city need. Funding redistributions under these more targeted formulas can be characterized as shifting funds from less needy suburban cities and urban counties to more needy central cities, rather than from one region to another.[17]

Third, the bulk of the urban impacts accrue to central cities at present and will continue under the dual formula, despite the phase-out of hold-harmless. For 1980 over $7.3 billion in total gross expenditures will be generated by CDBG allocations (56 percent of it in central cities) and over 300,000 jobs will be created, directly or indirectly, under the dual formula. The amount of central cities' urban impact comes both from the increase in the size of the program through 1980, and also with possible formula changes, especially if Impaction 3 is adopted.

---

[17] This assumes that the amount allocated to SMSA balances and non-SMSAs would not change under the impaction formulas.

REFERENCES

Bunce, Harold. *An Evaluation of the Community Development Block Grant Formula*. Washington, D.C.: U.S. Department of Housing and Urban Development, 1976.

————. "The Community Development Block Grant Formula: An Evaluation." *Urban Affairs Quarterly* 14 (1979): 443–64.

————, and Goldberg, Robert. *City Need and Community Development Funding*. Washington, D.C.: U.S. Department of Housing and Urban Development, 1979.

Glickman, N. J., and Jacobs, S. S. "The Urban Impacts of HUD's Section 312 Program." *Urban Impacts Analysis Series 4*. Washington, D.C.: U.S. Department of Housing and Urban Development, 1978.

————, eds. *The Urban Impacts of the Budget of the Department of Housing and Urban Development*. Washington, D.C.: U.S. Department of Housing and Urban Development, 1979.

Nathan, Richard; Dommel, P.; Liebschutz, S. F.; Morris, M.; and Associates. *Block Grants for Community Development*. Washington, D.C.: U.S. Department of Housing and Urban Development, 1977.

U.S. Bureau of Census, Center for Census Use Studies. *Suburban Classification Project*. Washington, D.C.: U.S. Department of Commerce, 1977.

U.S. Department of Housing and Urban Development. *Community Development Block Grant Program: Third Annual Report*. Washington, D.C.: U.S. Department of Housing and Urban Development, 1978.

CHAPTER TWENTY-THREE

Distributional Impacts of General Revenue Sharing

PAUL R. DOMMEL

INTRODUCTION

General revenue sharing was enacted in 1972, establishing a five-year program to provide $30.2 billion in fiscal support to 39,000 units of State and local government. The program was extended in 1976, providing an additional $25.6 billion in funds for another three and three-quarter years. The current legislation is due to expire on September 30, 1980. The funds are provided with few strings attached, giving recipient governments wide latitude in how they spend the money.

Throughout the pre- and postenactment history of revenue sharing a number of issues have emerged involving the formula distribution system, who benefits from the program, civil rights compliance, citizen participation in revenue sharing decision-making, and the general question of political accountability. This paper focuses on the formula, or distributional impacts of revenue sharing, particularly as they affect urban areas. Before proceeding to the distributional impacts, it would be useful to review briefly the history of the program.[1]

The background

Revenue sharing legislation was first proposed in Congress in the 1950s, but it gained little attention until 1964 when the idea was refloated by Walter W. Heller, chairman of President Johnson's Council of Economic Advisers. The Heller proposal appeared to gain some initial support from the President, but was ultimately rejected by him because of opposition from organized labor, some key members of Congress, and the bureaucracy. The revenue sharing

The author would like to acknowledge the helpful comments of his colleague Richard P. Nathan .

[1] For a legislative history of the revenue sharing legislation, *see* Thompson, 1973; Dommel, 1974; and Nathan et al., 1975.

idea was unsuccessfully advanced by congressional Republicans because of opposition from the administration and, perhaps more importantly, because Chairman Wilbur Mills of the House Ways and Means Committee did not like the idea and would not even hold hearings on it.

Throughout the mid-1960s, therefore, revenue sharing was politically alive but legislatively dormant. Its prospects increased greatly with the election of Richard M. Nixon who made revenue sharing the cornerstone of the New Federalism, which in intergovernmental policy espoused increased decentralization of decision-making from the Federal to the State and local governments.

This presidential support, backed by a large coalition of organizations representing State and local officials, gave new legislative momentum to revenue sharing. The first obstacle to topple was Chairman Mills, who changed his mind and agreed to hold hearings, thus allowing revenue sharing to gain a foothold in the legislative process. The second major obstacle to crumble was the opposition of many congressional liberals who did not trust giving unconditional federal funds to State and local officials whom they believed were not sufficiently responsive to the needs of lower income groups. Also, to these liberals, revenue sharing would ultimately divert money from programs aimed at these groups to pay the cost of revenue sharing. Assurances from the administration that revenue sharing would be an add-on and not a substitution program, plus the lobbying by the state and local organizations, put heavy pressure on congressional liberals to go along. It was also an election year which brought its own form of pressure to bear. In the end it was the congressional liberals, the principal opponents of revenue sharing, who made it legislatively possible.

The legislation was signed into law by President Nixon on October 20, 1972, in a well-publicized ceremony on the steps of Independence Hall in Philadelphia.

The ink on the law was hardly dry and the first checks had not yet arrived on the desks of the governors and local executives when the President, just re-elected, stated his intention to eliminate some of the programs of Lyndon Johnson's Great Society. Within days of his election Nixon stated: "What we have to realize is that many of the solutions of the 1960s were massive failures. They threw money at the problems and for the most part they have failed and we are going to shuck off those programs and trim down those programs that have proved simply to be failures" (*New York Times*, November 10, 1977, p. 20). Thus the substitution issue was reopened, raising concern among state and local officials and confirming the suspicions of those congressional liberals who had reluctantly voted for the program.

When the legislation came up for renewal in 1976 it had the backing of President Ford but again faced a wary Congress. The criticisms focused on the weaknesses of the civil rights safeguards of the legislation, the issue of growing local dependency on federal aid, and the resurrected liberal concern that the lower income groups were being shortchanged. Prospects for the legislation were complicated by the fact that jurisdiction over the legislation had been shifted from the House Ways and Means Committee to the less friendly Government Operations Committee, headed by Congressman Jack Brooks of Texas, who had voted against the program in 1972.[2]

The Ford extension proposal called for only slight program changes in the areas of citizen participation and strengthened civil rights safeguards. He warned against "tinkering with the formula" and proposed only a small modification in the distribution system which would have the effect of providing more funds to some particularly distressed central cities.[3]

Some House Subcommittee members, led by liberal Congressman Robert F. Drinan of Massachusetts, sought to require the earmarking of specified shares of a recipient's allocation for programs benefiting lower income groups. That effort failed but the House Subcommittee did write much tighter civil rights and auditing provisions. The full committee rewrote some parts of the subcommittee proposal but on the House floor the subcommittee bill was the version adopted. The Senate made some changes, but in the end the final compromise bill signed by Ford on October 13, 1976, was a status quo outcome for the distributional provisions.

The future of revenue sharing is uncertain. Unlike his two predecessors, President Carter has reservations about revenue sharing, particularly the inclusion of the states in the programs. Presidential backing has been important to legislative successes of the program, but one thing is clear. Regardless of the diverse causes and bases of dissatisfaction with general revenue sharing, once the money starts to flow—and it has been flowing for seven years—it is extremely difficult to turn off, particularly when all governments get something.

DISTRIBUTIONAL IMPACTS

An important issue in intergovernmental aid policy, currently, is the extent to which federal funds target assistance to the neediest jurisdictions, however they may be defined. While this is not the only criterion for evaluating federal aid, it is the focal point of this analysis.

The extent of targeting or its opposite, spreading, of an intergovernmental aid program is determined by the two major components of any allocation system: (1) eligibility—who may participate in the program; and (2) resource distribution—the amount of funds those eligible will receive.[4] In for-

---

[2] For a legislative history of the renewal of revenue sharing, *see* Nathan and Adams, 1977, pp. 1–24.

[3] Ford's proposal was to change the ceiling that limited entitlements of individual cities and townships to 145 percent of the average amount of shared revenue per capita paid to municipal and township governments in any particular state. Ford recommended raising the ceiling by six percentage points per year over five years to 175 percent.

[4] For a fuller discussion, *see* Domniel, 1975, p. 61.

mulating intergovernmental aid policies the operative political imperative is to gain enough political support for adoption and funding of the policy. Therefore, the initial problem is one of adopting sufficiently broad eligibility standards to insure support. On the other hand, a policy with a maximum targeting objective must seek to limit eligibility on the basis of need. The eligibility standards are therefore of major importance to the final targeting-spreading outcome.

The second major component is the distribution formula itself. The principal points on a distribution continuum are: (1) at one extreme, the richer a jurisdiction is, the more it gets; (2) in the middle, per capita distributions; and (3) at the other extreme, the needier a jurisdiction is, the more it gets. In more practical terms, the policy choice tends to range between points 2 and 3.

Combining the eligibility and formula components of an allocation system, the greatest spreading would occur with universal eligibility and per capita distributions; a more targeted outcome would be distributions to a limited number of distressed jurisdictions with the actual allocations further scaled to need among the limited number of those eligible.

Within this two-part framework, where does general revenue sharing stand in terms of targeting or spreading?

The coalition-building process leading to enactment of general revenue sharing resulted in entitlements to all states and all units of general purpose local government, nearly 39,000 recipients. Once the coalition was built, at no point in the formulation or adoption of the program was serious consideration subsequently given to limiting the eligibility on the basis of any need factors. The targeting capability of general revenue sharing was thus constrained at the outset, putting the burden of any consequent distributional targeting on the formula elements themselves. While this analysis focuses on the distributions rather than the formula itself, some understanding of the general revenue sharing allocation system and its complexity is necessary.

The amount of shared funds received by an individual jurisdiction is determined by a complex series of calculations allocating funds among several levels of government.[5] Four major and a number of adjustment steps are involved in the process. First, the amount of funds available nationally, currently $6.85 billion annually, is allocated among the fifty state *areas* plus the District of Columbia. Second, the amount allocated to individual state areas is divided between the State government (one-third) and local governments (two-thirds). Third, the local share is divided among the county *areas* within each state. Finally, each eligible local government's share of the county area allocation is calculated. Various statutory constraints, involving "ceilings and floors," require that the last three steps be repeated several times before the allocations of individual governments are final.

The allocation of funds to individual state areas is based on the higher

---

[5] For a full discussion of the formula operation *see* Nathan et al., 1975, Chapters 3–5.

of two alternative formulas. This two-formula approach, which dates from the program's inception in 1972, was adopted when House and Senate conferees were unable to resolve a conflict between different formulas passed separately by them. The Senate formula is based on population, general tax effort, and relative per capita income. The House formula is a more complex, five-factor formula based on population, urbanized population, per capita income, general tax effort, and income tax revenue. Once allocations are determined for all state areas under each formula, each state is allocated the higher of the two amounts with appropriate prorationing downward if the total allocation exceeds the available appropriation. After the state area allocations are made, the State and local government distributions are calculated.

Generally, the Senate formula tends to favor smaller states with low per capita incomes and relatively small urban populations; the House formula generally favors the larger, more urbanized states with higher relative incomes and more progressive revenue systems.

These formula factors reflect the political ambivalence of targeting distributions on need factors. The formula system finally agreed upon avoided any single definition of need. As a general fiscal support grant, the formula sought to structure in factors of need (population, urbanized population, and income), fiscal capacity (relative per capita income), and tax effort. In the process, the final formulas came to include some data elements that work at cross-purposes with each other; for example, the advantage given to states with large urban populations and high tax effort is partially offset by their higher per capita incomes. On the other hand, states with low per capita incomes tend to have their advantage from that factor diluted by the fact that these states also tend to have a lower tax effort.

To sum up, the combination of universal eligibility and some formula elements with offsetting effects *diminishes* the targeting impact of general revenue sharing. The word "diminishes" is emphasized because, despite these factors, the general revenue sharing allocation system does reasonably well in differentiating among some types of jurisdictions on the basis of various need factors, as discussed in the analysis below.

Analytical points

Before proceeding several analytical points must be made. First, the complexity of examining the distributional impacts of general revenue sharing is increased by the fact that distributions are made to layers of governments occupying the same physical space. Most municipalities have an overlying county government which in turn has an overlying State government, each of the three levels receiving an allocation. Certain assumptions might be made about how the overlying governments spend their revenue sharing money in ways that benefit the underlying units of government. For example, an assumption might be made that a municipality benefits from the allocation to the overlying county government in direct proportion to its share of the county's population; that is, if a municipality has one-third of the county's population, it receives one-third of the benefits of the county's revenue sharing allocation. The targeting analysis that follows is based on the direct distributions to the areas or types of jurisdictions being analyzed and makes no assumptions about the impact or benefits of allocations to overlying governments.

By confining the analysis to direct allocations, the targeting capability of the allocation system itself is examined; that is, the analysis is of the relationship between the need variables of a given jurisdiction and its own allocation. The distribution of allocations to overlying governments and how these allocations may benefit their subunits is important, however, to a broader conceptualization of the total impacts of the program in urban areas. It is reasonable to assume that some of the benefits from a county government's allocation go to underlying units of government, although there are some cities such as St. Louis and Baltimore which have no overlying county. Such benefits can take the form of direct county expenditure of revenue sharing funds in a city or a city's share of the benefits when the county uses its money for tax stabilization or reduction. However, the proportion of benefits derived by the subunits is a complex measurement problem with the likelihood of considerable variations among jurisdictions.

To illustrate, hypothetically and simplistically: a county might use its entire payment to subsidize public transportation for the elderly. The proportion of benefits impacting upon the central city is not a function of the distribution of the population between the city and the rest of the county, but rather the distribution of the elderly and the layout of the transportation network itself. It may well be that such benefits disproportionately favor the central city, which frequently has a higher proportion of elderly than the county area outside of the city. Another example of the complexity of the problem, pointed out in the Brookings Institution monitoring study of revenue sharing, occurs when a county uses its allocation for tax stabilization or reduction.[6] In such cases, a central city's share of the benefits is determined by its share of the total county tax base (generally speaking, the property tax base) compared to its share of the county population. If its share of the tax base is smaller than its share of the county population, then its residents will receive less benefit from the tax relief. The reverse might also be the case. Overlying the problem of sorting out impacts for revenue sharing is the fungibility of the money; revenue sharing funds in most cases are mixed with other funds

---

[6] For an analysis using both a direct and prorationing approach, *see* Nathan et al., 1975, Chapter 5. For a presentation of findings on the use of overlying county funds in underlying central cities, *see* Nathan and Adams, 1977, pp. 88–100.

in the budgetary process and the ability to determine the precise use of the revenue sharing funds is very limited.

To summarize this point: targeting of impacts in the broad sense discussed above is not a function of the allocation system; it is a function of other variables which might include the distribution of population, the distribution of functional responsibilities, the distribution of taxable property, the extent of unincorporated territory in the county, and the more elusive variable of the distribution of political clout.

A second analytical point: the analysis is presented in two major parts. The first section examines the distributional patterns among the states and a sample of 2,361 municipalities. Following this spatial analysis, the distributional patterns among the sample of municipalities are examined relative to several need indicators. The indicators used are population change, the level of poverty, and an urban conditions index.

Third, the spatial analysis that follows is two-dimensional. The distributions are examined at a single point in time, in this case the ninth entitlement period (EP 9) covering the one-year period from October 1977 through September 1978. This focuses the current distributional patterns among recipients. Examination is also made of the changes in distributional patterns that have occurred since the beginning of the program, as the result of regular updating of the formula elements. The baseline data are from the first entitlement period (EP 1), which covered the six months from January through June 1972. To make the data comparable the allocations for the first entitlement period were doubled to extend them for a full year. Where the analysis is made in terms of trends in allocation shares, the first entitlement period allocations were multiplied by a factor of 1.29 to account for the difference in appropriation levels ($5.3 billion for the first entitlement period; $6.85 billion for the ninth entitlement period).

Spatial analysis

The focus of this paper is on the impacts of general revenue sharing on local governments. However, because of the four-step process of allocating funds by levels of government, allocation amounts to individual cities are influenced at the outset by the state area allocation. It is therefore necessary to present an overview of the distribution of revenue sharing money among the states.

Regional-state distributions. Generally, on a per capita basis the allocation system favors the Middle Atlantic, New England, Pacific, and East South Central census divisions.[7] In both entitlement periods, one (EP 1) and nine

---

[7] Regional divisions used by the U.S. Bureau of the Census are: *New England*—Maine, New Hampshire, Vermont, Massachusetts, Rhode Island, Connecticut; *Middle Atlantic*—New York, New Jersey, Pennsylvania; *East North Central*—Ohio, Indiana, Illinois, Michigan, Wisconsin; *West North Central*—Minnesota, Iowa, Missouri, North Dakota, South Dakota, Nebraska, Kansas; *South Atlantic*—Delaware, Maryland, the District of Co-

(EP 9), these regions had per capita allocations above the national averages of $26.08 and $31.77, respectively (Table 1, columns 2 and 5). The Middle Atlantic and New England regions also had the highest percentage growth in per capita allocations between the two periods (column 8). Per capita grants increased by 28.4 percent betwen EP 1 and EP 9 in the Middle Atlantic division and 27.8 percent in New England, compared with an average per capita increase of 21.8 percent for the nation. Three other regions—Pacific, Mountain, and East North Central—also had per capita increases above the national level.

The least advantaged region is the West North Central, which was below the per capita mean in both entitlement periods and increased at only about half of the national rate. As a result of the slow allocation growth, its per capita ranking among the nine census divisions dropped from fifth in EP 1 to ninth in EP 9. The East South Central region also increased at a low rate, 14.7 percent, dropping that region from first to fourth place between the two periods.

The data also show that the per capita range between regions increased between the two periods, the high-to-low range for EP 1 being $4.65, growing to $7.05 for EP 9.

The regional pattern of advantages and disadvantages does not apply, however, to each state within a region. For example, in New England, Massachusetts increased its per capita allocation by 31.6 percent, nearly ten percentage points above the national level, and Maine was below the national average with an increase of only 19.4 percent. The greatest increase was in Alaska, over 100 percent (from $21.83 to $46.51), while North Dakota had a per capita decline of nearly 35 percent (from $35.86 to $23.56). The range of per capita allocations among the states increased from $19.62 (Ohio $20.08 and Mississippi $39.90) in EP 1 to $22.95 (North Dakota $23.56 and Alaska $46.51) in EP 9, showing that among state areas the allocation system is becoming less distributive and more differentiating in its distributional pattern. What is the basis of the increasing differentiation among state areas?

One study concluded that variations among state area allocations are primarily accounted for by population, tax effort, and relative income—in that order of importance (Ross et al., 1975, p. 120). The study found that a 1 percent difference in population, on the average, makes a difference in the total allocation of nearly 1 percent. Analyzed on a per capita basis, controlling for population size, it found that a 1 percent difference in tax effort

---

lumbia, Virginia, West Virginia, North Carolina, South Carolina, Georgia, Florida; *East South Central*—Kentucky, Tennessee, Alabama, Mississippi; *West South Central*—Arkansas, Louisiana, Oklahoma, Texas; *Mountain*—Montana, Idaho, Wyoming, Colorado, New Mexico, Arizona, Utah, Nevada; *Pacific*—Washington, Oregon, California, Alaska, Hawaii.

TABLE 1: Total and Per Capita Allocations and Allocation Shares in Entitlement Periods 1 and 9, by Region and State Areas

	EP 1			EP 9			Changes (%), EP 1–9	
	Allocations ($ millions) (1)	$ Per Capita (2)	Share (%) (3)	Allocations ($ millions) (4)	$ Per Capita (5)	Share (%) (6)	Allocation (7)	Per Capita (8)
New England	*319.8*	*26.99*	*6.0*[a]	*421.4*	*34.49*	*6.2*[a]	*31.8*	*27.8*
Connecticut	67.2	22.17	1.3	84.8	27.20	1.2	26.2	22.7
Maine	32.0	32.18	0.6	41.1	38.43	0.6	28.4	19.4
Massachusetts	165.1	29.03	3.1	222.0	38.22	3.2	34.5	31.6
New Hampshire	16.6	22.49	0.3	22.9	27.81	0.3	38.0	23.7
Rhode Island	24.2	25.44	0.5	29.8	32.20	0.4	23.1	26.6
Vermont	14.7	33.07	0.3	20.8	43.75	0.3	41.5	32.3
Middle Atlantic	*1,033.7*	*27.78*	*19.5*	*1,330.2*	*35.68*	*19.4*	*28.7*	*28.4*
New Jersey	166.6	23.24	3.1	215.0	29.31	3.1	29.1	26.1
New York	589.2	32.29	11.1	770.1	42.58	11.2	30.8	31.9
Pennsylvania	277.9	23.55	5.2	345.1	29.09	5.0	24.2	23.5
East North Central	*959.2*	*23.82*	*18.1*	*1,205.9*	*29.46*	*17.6*	*25.7*	*23.7*
Illinois	274.0	24.66	5.2	346.5	30.86	5.1	26.5	25.1
Indiana	113.7	21.89	2.1	145.4	27.43	2.1	27.9	25.3
Michigan	224.4	25.27	4.2	281.3	30.90	4.1	25.3	22.3
Ohio	213.9	20.08	4.0	274.4	25.67	4.0	28.3	27.8
Wisconsin	133.2	30.16	2.5	158.3	34.35	2.3	18.8	13.9

West North Central	*417.8*	*25.59*	*7.9*	*481.2*	*28.63*	*7.0*	*15.2*	*11.9*
Iowa	75.5	26.71	1.4	79.8	27.80	1.2	5.6	4.1
Kansas	52.4	23.22	1.0	58.9	25.48	0.8	12.4	9.3
Minnesota	106.4	27.96	2.0	136.0	34.29	2.0	27.8	22.6
Missouri	98.3	21.00	1.8	129.3	27.05	1.9	31.5	28.8
Nebraska	38.9	26.16	0.7	41.5	26.73	0.6	6.6	2.2
North Dakota	22.2	35.86	0.4	15.1	23.56	0.2	−32.0	−34.3
South Dakota	24.1	36.19	0.4	20.6	30.01	0.3	−14.5	−17.0
South Atlantic	*741.3*	*24.16*	*14.0*	*968.7*	*29.35*	*14.1*	*30.7*	*21.5*
Delaware	16.1	29.31	0.3	21.2	36.47	0.3	31.7	24.4
Florida	146.6	21.60	2.8	201.7	23.95	2.9	37.6	10.9
Georgia	105.9	23.88	2.0	145.6	29.29	2.1	37.5	22.6
Maryland	106.4	27.30	2.0	136.0	32.81	2.0	27.8	20.2
North Carolina	136.0	26.79	2.6	166.9	30.52	2.4	22.7	13.9
South Carolina	72.1	27.83	1.4	90.2	31.68	1.3	25.1	13.8
Virginia	106.3	22.86	2.0	139.5	27.73	2.0	31.2	21.3
West Virginia	51.9	29.77	1.0	67.6	37.10	1.0	30.2	24.6
East South Central	*364.6*	*28.47*	*6.9*	*446.1*	*32.65*	*6.5*	*22.4*	*14.7*
Alabama	90.5	26.30	1.7	110.6	30.17	1.6	22.2	14.7
Kentucky	86.9	26.99	1.6	113.7	33.16	1.7	30.8	22.9
Mississippi	88.4	39.90	1.7	99.1	42.12	1.4	12.1	5.0
Tennessee	98.8	25.18	1.9	122.7	29.11	1.8	24.2	15.6
West South Central	*483.7*	*25.03*	*9.1*	*641.4*	*30.25*	*9.6*	*32.6*	*20.9*
Arkansas	54.5	28.36	1.0	66.0	31.31	1.0	21.1	10.4
Louisiana	122.5	33.63	2.3	154.9	40.34	2.3	26.4	20.0
Oklahoma	58.9	23.02	1.1	78.4	28.33	1.4	33.1	23.1
Texas	247.8	22.14	4.7	342.1	27.40	5.0	38.0	23.7

TABLE 1 (continued)

	EP 1			EP 9			Changes (%), EP 1–9	
	Allocations ($ millions) (1)	$ Per Capita (2)	Share (%) (3)	Allocations ($ millions) (4)	$ Per Capita (5)	Share (%) (6)	Allocation (7)	Per Capita (8)
Mountain	*231.7*	*24.96*	*4.4*	*311.7*	*31.70*	*4.6*	*34.5*	*27.0*
Arizona	50.3	28.32	0.9	73.6	32.44	1.1	46.3	14.5
Colorado	54.5	24.67	1.0	75.2	29.10	1.1	38.0	18.0
Idaho	21.3	29.85	0.4	23.8	28.66	0.3	11.7	− 4.0
Montana	20.5	29.50	0.4	23.7	31.43	0.3	15.6	6.5
Nevada	11.5	23.56	0.2	17.1	27.96	0.3	48.7	18.7
New Mexico	33.0	32.42	0.6	47.3	40.53	0.7	43.3	25.0
Utah	30.6	28.86	0.6	38.9	31.66	0.6	27.1	9.7
Wyoming	10.0	29.97	0.2	12.1	31.21	0.2	21.0	4.1
Pacific	*721.5*	*27.18*	*13.6*	*985.3*	*34.29*	*14.4*	*36.6*	*26.2*
Alaska	6.6	21.83	0.1	17.8	46.51	0.3	170.0	113.1
California	560.2	28.05	10.6	758.8	35.26	11.1	35.5	25.7
Hawaii	23.7	30.79	0.4	33.9	38.17	0.5	43.0	24.0
Oregon	53.0	25.35	1.0	74.3	31.90	1.1	40.2	25.8
Washington	78.0	22.85	1.5	100.5	28.72	1.5	28.8	25.7
United States	*5,300*	*26.08*	*99.5*[b]	*6,850*	*31.77*	*99.5*[b]	*29.2*	*21.8*

Sources: State allocation data for EP 1 from Nathan et al. (1975), Table 4-2, pp. 70–71; EP 9 state data from Office of Revenue Sharing, U.S. Department of the Treasury (1978), Table 1, p. 2.
[a] Owing to rounding of state figures, total regional shares do not necessarily equal sums of state shares.
[b] Excluding the District of Columbia.

TABLE 2: Per Capita Allocations, Tax Effort Factor, and Per Capita Income for Entitlement Period 9 (Unweighted Means), by Region

	Per Capita Allocations	*Tax Effort (%), 1974–75*	*Per Capita Income, 1974*
New England	$34.60	12.63	$4,424
Middle Atlantic	33.60	13.32	4,863
East North Central	29.84	11.56	4,669
West North Central	27.84	11.29	4,570
South Atlantic	31.20	11.00	4,354
East South Central	33.64	10.61	3,564
West South Central	31.85	10.66	3,773
Mountain	31.62	12.19	4,402
Pacific	36.11	13.09	5,183
U.S.	31.95	11.81	4,435

Sources: Per capita allocations calculated from data provided by the Office of Revenue Sharing, U.S. Department of the Treasury. Tax effort and per capita data calculated from Office of Revenue Sharing, Department of the Treasury (1977), p. 439.

Note: The tax effort data have been converted from decimal form to percentages.

yields an average per capita difference of .9 percent in a state's allocation; a 1 percent difference in relative income results in an average difference of only .5 percent.

This can be generally seen in Table 2, showing regionally the per capita allocations, tax effort, and per capita income for EP 9.[8] The data are un-weighted means, averaging the per capita allocations and formula factors of the states within a region. By using the unweighted mean for per capita allocations, the national mean increases slightly from $31.77 per capita to $31.95.

As noted earlier, there were four census divisions with above-average per capita allocations in EP 9—Middle Atlantic, New England, Pacific, and East South Central. As seen in the table, three of these regions had tax effort factors above the national mean, positively effecting their allocations. Of the four above-average divisions, only the East South Central division had a tax effort factor below the mean, but it was aided by a per capita income level that was the lowest among all nine regions. The only division with an above-average tax effort factor that did not have an above-average per capita allocation was the Mountain division, which was only slightly below the national allocation average. New England, which had the second highest unweighted per capita average in EP 9, was above the tax effort mean and slightly below the per capita income mean, thus being advantaged by both of these factors.

[8] Calculated from Office of Revenue Sharing, July 1977, p. 439.

The importance of the tax effort factor is particularly notable for the Pacific division, which had the highest per capita allocation; its very high per capita income of $5,183 was offset by a high tax effort level which was the second highest among the divisions.

The importance of the tax effort factor can also be seen in terms of individual state allocations, as illustrated by Alaska, which made the greatest per capita gain between the two entitlement periods, and North Dakota, which had the greatest loss. Alaska's tax effort increased from 10.43 percent to 12.34 percent, an increase of nearly 20 percent at a time when the national average declined by 1 percent. North Dakota had a very large decline in tax effort, declining from 14.19 percent in EP 1 to 10.73 percent in EP 9. Largely because of this decline its per capita allocation went from $35.86 in EP 1 when it ranked second among the states to $23.56 in EP 9 when it ranked last.

The significance of the tax effort factor is likely to be seen in California as the result of Proposition 13, limiting the local property tax levy. The state area tax effort factor is based on total state and local tax collections, which will decline sharply as a result of Proposition 13. For EP 9 California's tax effort factor was 14.49 percent, exceeded only by New York (16.77 percent) and New Hampshire (15.31 percent). California's high tax effort factor largely accounted for its having the twelfth highest per capita allocation (35.26) in EP 9. The state's high tax effort offset the negative allocation effect of a very high per capita income, $5,114, the sixth highest in the nation. When the full effect of Proposition 13 becomes factored into the distribution calculations, the state may be caught between the negative effects of significantly lower tax effort factor and a higher per capita income.

Analysis of per capita allocations is important to understanding the distributional advantages and disadvantages of the current allocation system, but there is another perspective that must be examined—a recipient's share of the funds. The per capita trend is influenced to some extent by the population changes themselves; for example, holding everything but population constant, a growing jurisdiction will show a per capita decline whereas a declining jurisdiction would show a per capita increase. Examination of shares and the trend in the distribution of shares partially takes into account the important effects of population in the overall allocation formula. To illustrate, between EP 1 and EP 9, Rhode Island had a 2.5 percent population decline; Rhode Island *increased* its per capita allocation by 26.6 percent (national average was 21.8 percent), in part reflecting the declining population; however, Rhode Island's share of general revenue sharing funds *decreased* from .5 to .4 percent of total funds at least in part because of the population loss (Table 1, columns 3 and 6). Between the two entitlement periods the national funding level increased by 29.2 percent; therefore, a state's share increased only if its allocation amount grew by a greater percentage. Of the nine census divisions, five increased at a rate above the national level while four fell below. As shown in Table 1, column 7, the gainers were New England (31.8 percent), South Atlantic (30.7 percent), West South Central (32.6 percent), Mountain (34.5 percent), and Pacific (36.6 percent). In terms of shares, therefore, with the exception of New England, the trend is toward the southern and western regions, a different pattern from that of the analysis based on per capita distributions. The only two census divisions to show both per capita and share increases were the New England and Pacific areas. The Middle Atlantic and East South Central divisions, which showed above average per capita increases, showed slight declines in shares.

Again, however, an individual state may show a different pattern from its census division. For example, within the Middle Atlantic area, New York state showed an increase in its share, going from 11.1 to 11.2 percent; Pennsylvania's share declined from 5.2 to 5.0 percent; New Jersey's share remained the same at 3.1 percent. While these changes are small they indicate the long-term shift in the distributional pattern of general revenue sharing allocations. It should be noted, however, that the shifts in shares are not solely the result of population change. New York, like Rhode Island, also lost population between 1970 and 1976 (—.1 percent), but New York had the highest tax effort factor of any state, which positively and strongly affects its allocation.

It might be argued that the more crucial long-term indicator is the trend in shares, rather than the per capita trends. General revenue sharing is a general support grant which recipients have tended to integrate into their regular budgets.

If a state's total share of revenue sharing declines, the State government's own one-third share automatically declines proportionately, thus eroding its revenue position. Further, the decline of the state area share filters down to some communities within that state. (The number of communities adversely affected by the declining state area share is dependent upon the relative changes of the formula factors among the local jurisdictions within the state.) In terms of the national allocation system and a recipient's own revenue position, the adverse fiscal effects of a jurisdiction's decline in shares can be offset only by compensating increases in the total amount of money distributed. (The same fiscal impact occurs when the rate of inflation exceeds the amount of additional money provided for the program. This differs from the effects of changing shares, however, since the effects of inflation are felt equally across all jurisdictions.)

Local distributions. Local governments receiving general revenue sharing funds include counties, municipalities, and townships. In addition to the influence of the state area share on local allocations collectively, the amount of funds going to an individual local government is influenced by the amount going to overlying county areas. This county area amount will vary depending upon the distribution of the formula elements among all county areas in the state. This analysis is confined to municipal allocations. It does not take into

TABLE 3: Allocations by Type of Government, Entitlement Periods 1 and 9

	EP 1		EP 9		
	Allocations ($ millions)	% of Total	Allocations ($ millions)	% of Total	$ Per Capita
States	1,774	33.5	2,293	33.6	10.76
Counties	1,347	25.4	1,715	25.1	9.04
Municipalities	1,913	36.1	2,450	35.9	17.99
Townships	261	4.9	354	5.2	7.32
Indian tribes	6	0.1	9	0.1	23.37

Sources: EP 1 data from Nathan et al. (1975), p. 6; EP 9 data from Office of Revenue Sharing, U.S. Department of the Treasury (1978), p. 7.

account the interrelated allocation patterns of county areas or county and township governments, which compete with municipalities for the county area funds.

As shown in Table 3, municipalities received the largest share of funds relative to other types of jurisdictions, including the states. The table also shows, however, that the municipalities' share decreased slightly between EP 1 and EP 9, from 36.1 to 35.9 percent of total allocations. With the exception of the Indian tribes, municipalities also received the highest per capita grants in EP 9.

Table 4 shows that the larger the municipality, the higher its per capita grant. While the larger municipalities are advantaged in terms of per capita allocations, the amount of general revenue sharing funds for cities over 50,000 population declined between EP 1 and EP 9. In the first entitlement period, cities over 50,000 collectively received 23.6 percent of total allocations, declining to 23.1 percent in the ninth entitlement period. At the same time municipalities between 2,500 and 50,000 population collectively increased their share from 10.8 to 11.2 percent. The smallest municipalities, under 2,500 population, had a decline from 1.8 to 1.6 percent.[9] In summary, the municipal share of total allocations has been declining at a slow rate; among all municipalities there has been a small shift away from the larger cities to smaller ones.

The analysis now turns to the distribution pattern among a sample of 2,361 municipalities and New England townships. The sample accounted for 41.6 percent of all local government allocations in EP 1 and 42.2 percent in EP 9. Of the total sample, 1,923 are small communities with populations under 50,000. Because of population changes the number of large cities (over 50,000

[9] Calculated from Nathan et al., 1975, tables 5–10, p. 130, and Office of Revenue Sharing, 1978, p. 7.

TABLE 4: Per Capita Distributions to Municipalities in Entitlement Period 9, by Size

Population	Per Capita Allocation
100,000 and up	$23.87
50,000–99,999	15.37
20,000–49,999	14.47
2,000–19,999	13.62
0– 1,999	10.68
All municipalities	17.99

Source: Office of Revenue Sharing, U.S. Department of the Treasury (1978), p. 8.

population) varies between the two entitlement periods—434 in EP 1 and 440 in EP 9. Populations are based on 1975 census data. The subset of 1,923 small communities is a random stratified sample drawn by the Department of Housing and Urban Development as part of a study on the development needs of small cities (Dommel and Jaffe, forthcoming). The large cities are from the Brookings Institution data base.

Of the small communities, 1,131 are nonmetropolitan municipalities and 792 are metropolitan. With the addition of the large cities, the total number of metropolitan communities is 1,230. The sample is distributed among population categories and metropolitan/nonmetropolitan areas, as shown in Table 5. The sample represents 10.6 percent of the total universe of municipalities and New England townships. Representation by population category ranges from 5.8 of the smallest category to 100.0 percent of the largest category.

As shown in Table 6, among the four types of communities the formula gives the greatest per capita distributional advantage to central cities, $17.96 in EP 1 and $23.50 in EP 9; small nonmetropolitan jurisdictions rank second, with $14.70 in EP 1 and $18.26 in EP 9. Both the large and small suburban municipalities collectively received per capita allocations that were about half that of the central cities.

In terms of shares, the central cities declined slightly between the two entitlement periods, going from 21.3 to 21.2 percent of the total allocation; the large suburban cities of the sample increased their shares from 2.2 to 2.5 percent; small metropolitan municipalities increased from 1.5 to 1.7 percent; and the nonmetropolitan communities had the same shares, 2.8 percent.

This overall pattern of distributions among the sample municipalities results from the same relative importance of the factors noted earlier for the state area distributions. Holding all state factors and local population constant, one study calculated that in the *intra*state distributions, a 1 percent difference in tax effort yields a difference in per capita allocations to a recipient

TABLE 5: Sample Communities by Population Category, Metropolitan/
Nonmetropolitan Status, and Percent of Universe

Population Size Category	Total Sample	Number Metro.	Number Nonmetro.	Total as % of Universe[a]
Small	*1,923*	*792*	*1,131*	*10.6*
Less than 2,500	649	224	425	5.0
2,500– 9,999	523	202	321	15.2
10,000–24,999	458	213	245	37.8
25,000–49,999	293	153	140	57.0
Large				
50,000 and over	*438*	*438*	*0*	*100.0*
Total	*2,361*	*1,230*	*1,131*	*12.8*

Source: Computed from sample.
[a] Based on the universe of municipalities and New England townships as defined in the 1977 Census of Governments, Vol. 1, No. 1, *Governmental Organization.*

of .6 percent, whereas a 1 percent difference in relative income yields an allocation difference of only .4 percent (Ross et al., 1975, pp. 120–21). Thus, as in the case of the state area allocation system, the local government distributions are influenced by population size, tax effort, and income—in that order.

The relative influence of the tax effort and per capita income factors in the pattern of per capita allocations among types of municipalities can be seen in Tables 7 and 8. The formula advantage of central cities comes in large part from their tax effort level, which is well above that of the other jurisdiction types, particularly the small municipalities (Table 7). Relative to the large and small suburban municipalities, the central cities also gain from the per capita income factor (Table 8). For the nonmetropolitan municipalities the income level is the factor that moves them close to the central cities' allocation level. The average per capita income in 1975 for the sample nonmetropolitan communities was only $4,085, well below any of the other categories.

At the regional level, there are some noteworthy differences from the national pattern. In New England the per capita differences among the types of jurisdictions are much narrower, with the suburban jurisdictions receiving per capita allocations well above the national level (Table 6). In two of the three southern regions, the small nonmetropolitan communities have per capita allocations nearly equal to that of the central cities. The most significant deviation from the national pattern, however, is in the Pacific division, where the nonmetropolitan per capita allocation exceeds that of the central cities (Table 6).

Central cities. Given the urban focus of this volume, particular attention

TABLE 6: Per Capita Allocations to Sample of 2,361 Municipalities, by Region and Type of Municipality

	Central Cities			Suburban Cities			Small Metro.			Small Nonmetro.		
	N	EP 1	EP 9	N	EP 1	EP 9	N	EP 1	EP 9	N	EP 1	EP 9
Northeast	56	$23.00	$32.09	59	$ 9.11	$11.89	220	$10.90	$14.87	179	$17.09	$20.84
New England	28	21.24	26.60	17	15.79	22.03	71	14.41	20.35	109	18.27	23.84
Middle Atlantic	28	23.41	33.42	42	7.18	8.73	149	7.95	10.15	70	15.46	16.59
North Central	67	16.24	21.51	42	8.63	11.78	280	7.52	10.23	428	12.24	15.21
East North Central	46	16.89	22.27	36	8.74	11.82	205	8.05	10.75	187	13.02	16.98
West North Central	21	14.19	19.15	6	8.11	11.58	75	5.50	8.31	241	11.31	13.10
South	88	17.37	21.05	13	11.76	13.48	190	10.04	12.65	385	16.82	20.72
South Atlantic	40	19.22	22.06	5	15.09	17.16	79	9.83	12.26	152	18.61	22.01
East South Central	14	18.80	23.10	1	25.73		38	11.46	13.52	96	18.08	22.09
West South Central	34	15.15	19.39	7	7.48	10.66	73	9.69	12.83	137	13.58	17.99
West	48	14.19	18.65	51	7.04	10.37	102	7.43	10.80	139	12.63	16.41
Mountain	15	16.62	18.80	6	7.02	10.08	23	10.36	13.39	81	11.25	13.58
Pacific	33	13.51	18.60	45	7.05	10.42	79	7.08	10.46	58	14.43	20.09
U.S.	259	17.96	23.50	165	8.59	11.54	792	8.98	12.15	1,131	14.70	18.26
Shares (%)		21.3	21.2		2.2	2.5		1.5	1.7		2.8	2.8

Source: Computed from allocation data provided by the Office of Revenue Sharing, U.S. Department of the Treasury.

TABLE 7: Average Tax Effort in Municipalities, 1976, by Region and Type of Community

	Central Cities	Suburban Cities	Small Metro.	Small Nonmetro.
U.S.	*2.79*	*2.28*	*1.67*	*1.61*
Northeast	*3.79*	*2.88*	*2.31*	*2.84*
New England	4.45	4.30	3.27	3.19
Middle Atlantic	3.13	2.20	1.85	2.27
North Central	*2.39*	*1.92*	*1.32*	*1.31*
East North Central	2.35	1.98	1.44	1.43
West North Central	2.46	1.56	.99	1.22
South	*2.60*	*2.01*	*1.33*	*1.46*
South Atlantic	2.92	2.61	1.64	1.72
East South Central	2.71		1.14	1.48
West South Central	2.20	1.61	1.12	1.17
West	*2.54*	*1.99*	*1.95*	*1.41*
Mountain	2.23	1.62	2.34	1.13
Pacific	2.69	2.04	1.83	1.82

Source: Computed from data provided by the Office of Revenue Sharing, U.S. Department of the Treasury.

Note: Tax effort is presented as a percentage of income paid in local taxes, excluding taxes for educational purposes.

$$\text{Tax effort} = \frac{\text{Adjusted (non-school) taxes}}{\text{Population} \times \text{Per capita income}} \times 100$$

is given to the allocations among central cities with populations above 50,000. For this group the sample is 100 percent of the category. The sample does not include the 119 central cities with populations below 50,000.

The general pattern is that the larger the central city, the higher its per capita allocation. This was the case in EP 9 and was generally true also in EP 1, although the 250,000 to 499,999 group had a lower per capita average than the size group below it (Table 9). Among the size groups, the per capita trend has been to further advantage the largest central cities, above 250,000, relative to those between 50,000 and 250,000. Nationally, the central city per capita increase was 30.8 percent between the two entitlement periods. Those below 250,000 had an average per capita increase of only 22 percent, those over 250,000 increased by an average of 35 percent. But it must be pointed out that the per capita increase of the cities in the over-500,000 population group was partially attributable to a population loss, the only size category of the sample in which there was an absolute population loss between 1970 and 1975.

When the analysis of population categories shifts to calculations of shares, the only group of central cities that increased its share was the 250,000 to

TABLE 8: Mean Per Capita Income in Municipalities, 1975, by Region and Type of Community

	Central Cities	Suburban Cities	Small Metro.	Small Nonmetro.
U.S.	$4,857	$5,702	$5,363	$4,085
Northeast	4,593	5,679	5,576	4,161
New England	4,666	5,976	5,395	4,170
Middle Atlantic	4,521	5,538	5,661	4,146
North Central	4,866	5,791	5,376	4,188
East North Central	4,793	5,862	5,448	4,219
West North Central	5,018	5,343	5,182	4,164
South	4,706	5,470	4,692	3,774
South Atlantic	4,875	5,806	5,332	4,020
East South Central	4,540		5,294	3,589
West South Central	4,578	5,246	4,428	3,637
West	5,227	5,722	5,634	4,530
Mountain	5,086	5,457	4,914	4,331
Pacific	5,296	5,760	5,841	4,816

Source: Computed from data provided by the Office of Revenue Sharing, U.S. Department of the Treasury.

499,999 category. The other three groups declined slightly in their allocation shares (Table 9).

Among regions, on a per capita basis the allocation system tends to favor most the large (over 50,000) central cities of the Northeast region (New England and Middle Atlantic divisions). In the first entitlement period the central cities of four of the nine census divisions had per capita allocations above the mean of $17.96 for central cities (Table 10). They were New England ($21.24), Middle Atlantic ($23.40), South Atlantic ($19.22), and East South Central ($18.79). In the ninth entitlement period only the New England ($26.60) and Middle Atlantic ($33.41) divisions were above the national central city mean of $23.50 per capita. The greatest relative per capita losers were the central cities of the South Atlantic and Mountain divisions, which had a slow rate of increase in per capita allocations of only about half that of the other regions. Although the influence of the state and county area allocations are involved, it should be noted that the per capita lag of the central cities of the Mountain division may have partially resulted from a large population increase. The central cities in that division had a population increase of 10.5 percent between 1970 and 1975, whereas the 259 central cities in the sample had an overall population drop of 1.6 percent.

In terms of shares the distributional advantage has been shifting to central cities in the Middle Atlantic, West South Central, and Pacific divisions, which

TABLE 9: Central City Allocations and Shares for Entitlement Periods 1 and 9, by Population Size

Population Size	N	Allocation EP 1 (thousands)	Per Capita EP 1	Share EP 1 (%)	Allocation EP 9 (thousands)	Per Capita EP 9	Share EP 9 (%)
50,000– 999,999	121	$ 125,614	$15.06	2.37	$152,210	$17.95	2.22
100,000–249,999	81	193,576	16.28	3.65	245,944	20.15	3.59
250,000–499,999	31	164,636	15.35	3.10	253,517	21.38	3.70
Over 500,000	26	643,332	20.24	12.13	799,075	27.39	11.66
U.S.	259	1,127,158	17.96	21.25	1,450,746	23.50	21.17

Source: Computed from data provided by the Office of Revenue Sharing, U.S. Department of the Treasury.

TABLE 10: Central City Per Capita Allocations and Shares for Entitlement Periods 1 and 9, by Region

	Per Capita EP 1	Share EP 1 (%)	Per Capita EP 9	Share EP 9 (%)
Northeast	*$23.00*	*7.28*	*$32.09*	*7.40*
New England	21.24	1.28	26.60	1.20
Middle Atlantic	23.40	6.00	33.41	6.20
North Central	*16.24*	*5.08*	*21.51*	*4.89*
East North Central	16.89	4.02	22.27	3.83
West North Central	14.19	1.06	19.15	1.06
South	*17.36*	*5.65*	*21.05*	*5.46*
South Atlantic	19.22	2.39	22.06	2.15
East South Central	18.79	1.11	23.11	1.06
West South Central	15.15	2.15	19.39	2.25
West	*14.19*	*3.24*	*18.65*	*3.42*
Mountain	16.62	0.82	18.81	0.80
Pacific	13.52	2.42	18.60	2.62
U.S.	*17.96*	*21.25*	*23.50*	*21.17*

Source: Computed from data provided by the Office of Revenue Sharing, U.S. Department of the Treasury.

increased their shares of the total allocations between the two entitlement periods. Central cities in the West North Central division had the same shares in both periods, while five divisions, including New England, showed a decline. The South Atlantic and Mountain divisions, which had a slow rate of per capita growth, also had declining shares.

REVENUE SHARING AND DISTRIBUTIONAL TARGETING

Targeting of federal aid has become a major issue in intergovernmental policy discussion and is an important part of President Carter's urban policy. What is not clear, however, is on *what* federal aid should target.

It is both an empirical and political question. The targeting issue emerged as a major controversy in 1977, prior to the issuance of the President's urban policy, when the Community Development Block Grant (CDBG) program came up for renewal. During congressional debate on the extension the central issue was the dual formula approach proposed by the Carter and the previous Ford administrations. The debate was over the question of whether community age or poverty was the best measure of community need. The choice between these two need factors had very important consequences for what areas of the country and what types of communities would have a formula advantage. The South and West do better with a poverty-oriented formula; the Northeast and Midwest benefit by a community age factor. The dual formula approach skirted the issue by seeking to target on both needs by allowing entitlement communities to choose that formula which gave the most money.[10] The final result of the dual formula allocation system was to substantially increase the share of CDBG funds giving to the Northeast and Midwest.

How well does general revenue sharing target funds, and on what does it target? The statement was made earlier in this paper that, generally speaking, revenue sharing does a reasonably good job at targeting aid despite the universal eligibility of all state and local governments. Also, it was explained that the variations among both the intra- and interstate allocations are primarily influenced by—in order of importance—population, tax effort, and relative income. Put another way, these are the factors, and the order, on which the formula targets. While there are other factors involved in the state area allocations—urbanized population and income tax revenues—they have less influence in the allocation patterns.

The targeting analysis of this paper focuses on other factors beyond those included in the formula itself. The factors examined are population change, poverty, and an urban conditions index composed of poverty, community age, housing factors, and population change. Other revenue sharing targeting analyses are also reviewed. The revenue sharing allocations analyzed are from EP 9.

Population change

An increase or decrease in population has been used as an important indicator of a community's fiscal distress or vigor (Peterson, 1976; Nathan and Dommel, 1977, pp. 285–88). This relationship was noted by George Peterson of the Urban Institute in a study of city financing problems resulting from population decline:

The dilemma confronted by the older cities is that few of the costs associated with urban growth are easily reversible into economies of diminution. Once a city's road, sewer, and water networks have been constructed to serve a given population, the cost of maintaining these networks does not decline significantly when population shrinks. On the contrary, as capital infrastructure ages, it becomes more costly to keep in repair (Peterson, 1976, p. 44)

. . . .

More importantly in terms of budget expense, a city's labor force tends to act as another fixed cost over-head item, whose cost must be spread over fewer tax-payers once net out-migration continues (ibid, p. 45).

Population growth tends to mean a growth in the middle income sector, bringing an expanded revenue base in the form of higher income levels and

---

[10] The original 1974 formula included the factors of population, overcrowded housing, and poverty (weighted twice); the second formula added in 1977 had the criteria pre-1940 housing (a proxy for community age, weighted twice), poverty, and population growth lag.

increased property values. A recent study, using the same sample as this analysis, showed that communities with increasing populations not only had more growth in the level of per capita income but also in the rate of increase (Dommel and Jaffe, forthcoming, pp. 31–34). A study of large cities showed a similar pattern for median housing values, growing cities having both a higher median housing value and a greater rate of increase in value (Nathan and Dommel, 1977, Table 9–1, p. 287).

Examination of the relationship between population change and per capita revenue sharing allocations shows little differentiation among growing or declining *small* communities, both metropolitan and nonmetropolitan (Table 11). In fact, among the small nonmetropolitan municipalities, those with the greatest population losses receive the lowest mean per capita revenue sharing allocations. Among the large cities, the general revenue sharing formula does favor those losing population. For the central cities, those losing population had an average allocation of $21.02 per capita compared with $17.71 per capita for municipalities gaining population. A similar pattern appears for the large suburban cities with losing jurisdictions having allocation averaging $13.17 per capita compared with $10.81 for growing jurisdictions.

These relationships between revenue sharing allocations and population change can also be seen through correlation analysis (Table 12). The coefficients show the differentiations by type of community. It should be noted that in no case does the coefficient go above —.2790 (central cities). Keeping in mind the low level of the coefficients, the general statement can be made that, overall, in terms of population change, general revenue sharing is more responsive to these changes among large municipalities (over 50,000) than among small ones.

Poverty

The data show that revenue sharing allocations are reasonably responsive to the level of poverty in the sample municipalities, with the mean per capita allocations increasing as the percentage of poverty increases in each type of community (Table 13). As in the case of population change, however, this responsiveness is greater among the large communities as can be seen in the correlation coefficients. As shown in Table 12, there is no significant correlation between per capita revenue sharing allocations and the extent of poverty among the small nonmetropolitan communities. The coefficient, still below the level of significance, increases to .2362 for small metropolitan communities. For the large suburban cities the coefficient is .4797, reasonably significant, dropping to .3423 for the central cities.

Urban conditions index

As part of its analysis of the CDBG formula, the Brookings Institution developed an urban conditions index to measure relative distress among the large entitlement jurisdictions (*see* Dommel et al., 1978). The variables in-

TABLE 11: Mean Per Capita Revenue Sharing Allocations in Entitlement Period 9, by Population Change (1970–1975) and Type of Community

	Central Cities		Suburban Cities		Small Metro.		Small Nonmetro.	
	N	Per Capita	N	Per Capita	N	Per Capita	N	Per Capita
Total	263	$19.50	177	$11.97	805	$11.05	1,138	$15.35
Decreases in population	142	21.02	87	13.17	243	11.89	386	15.72
Greater than 10%	13	23.47	8	18.48	38	14.31	59	12.36
10–5%	54	23.57	23	14.94	74	11.42	93	15.24
5–0%	75	18.77	56	11.69	131	11.46	234	16.75
Increases in population	121	17.71	90	10.81	562	10.68	752	15.17
0–10%	84	18.17	55	11.33	244	11.41	451	15.36
10–20%	27	15.98	15	11.19	142	10.77	185	15.19
20–30%	9	17.66	8	8.25	78	9.02	65	13.94
30–40%	1	26.58	4	9.33	28	11.85	26	14.05
40% and over	0		8	9.79	70	9.33	25	15.94

Source: Computed from data provided by the Office of Revenue Sharing, U.S. Department of the Treasury, and U.S. Department of Housing and Urban Development.

TABLE 12: Correlation Coefficients between Per Capita Allocations of Revenue Sharing and Population Change, Poverty, and Urban Conditions Index, by Type of Community

Variable	Total Sample	Central Cities	Suburban Cities	Small Metro.	Small Nonmetro.
Population change (1970–75)	−.0863	−.2790	−.2226	−.0569	−.0398
Poverty (1970)	.2118	.3423	.4797	.2362	.0627
Urban conditions index	.1262	.3399	.5255	.2229	.0071

Source: Computed from data provided by the Office of Revenue Sharing, Department of the Treasury, and the Department of Housing and Urban Development.

cluded in the index were percent poverty, as a socioeconomic indicator; percent of pre-1940 housing, as a proxy for community age; and population change between 1960–75, as a general measure of growth or decline. In a similar formula analysis of allocations among small communities, this index was expanded to include two housing factors—plumbing deficiencies and housing overcrowding—because of the relatively high incidence of these factors in small communities (Dommel and Jaffe, forthcoming, pp. 60–63). For the large-city analysis, community age was seen as the best indicator of physical development need; for small communities this was expanded into an age-housing factor, taking into consideration the broader range of physical development needs in the smaller municipalities. Because of data limitations, it was necessary also to change the time frame for the population change factor from 1960–75 for the large cities to 1970–75 for the small city analysis. The revised index showed that small nonmetropolitan communities are more distressed than either their metropolitan counterparts or large cities (ibid., p. 61). Regionally, small communities in the three southern and the West North Central regions appeared to be substantially more distressed than those in other regions (ibid., p. 64).

The revenue sharing allocation data show that, overall, communities above the index mean of 200, and thus more distressed, did better in EP 9 than the better-off communities below the index mean (Table 14). This was the case for each type of community. It should be noted, however, that the communities with the highest distress index (above 300) did less well than those with an index between the mean of 200 and the 300 level. One caution to be noted is that for the central and suburban cities, the number of cities above 300 is too small to draw any inferences.

Again, as in the case of both population change and the percentage of poverty the correlations are highest among the large cities (Table 12). Neither

568

TABLE 13: Mean Per Capita Revenue Sharing Allocations in Entitlement Period 9, by Percentage of Poverty (1970) and Type of Community

	Central Cities		Suburban Cities		Small Metro.		Small Nonmetro.	
	N	Per Capita	N	Per Capita	N	Per Capita	N	Per Capita
Total	263	$19.50	177	$11.97	805	$11.05	1,138	$15.35
Percent Poverty								
Less than 5	3	9.89	74	9.60	290	8.66	43	11.04
5– 9.9	52	16.71	77	12.18	262	10.77	217	14.02
10–14.9	124	18.82	20	17.55	119	13.15	306	15.55
15–19.9	52	22.29	4	17.13	59	15.74	183	16.18
Over 20	32	23.05	2	25.50	75	14.25	389	16.00

Source: Computed from data provided by the Office of Revenue Sharing, U.S. Department of the Treasury, and U.S. Department of Housing and Urban Development.

TABLE 14: Mean Per Capita Revenue Sharing Allocations in Entitlement Period 9, by Urban Conditions Index and Type of Community

	Central Cities		Suburban Cities		Small Metro.		Small Nonmetro.	
	N	Per Capita	N	Per Capita	N	Per Capita	N	Per Capita
Total	258	$19.49	154	$12.55	774	$11.22	1,120	$15.42
Urban conditions index								
100–200	207	18.28	150	12.22	673	10.60	639	14.81
200–300	48	24.60	3	23.97	64	16.04	288	16.59
300 and above	3	21.29	1	28.24	37	14.11	193	15.71

Source: Computed from data provided by the Office of Revenue Sharing, U.S. Department of the Treasury, and U.S. Department of Housing and Urban Development.

the nonmetropolitan communities (.0071) nor the small metropolitan communities (.2229) had significant coefficients. The highest correlation was found with the satellite cities (.5255), declining to .3399 for central cities.

When the three nonformula need measurements used above—population change, poverty, and the conditions index—are viewed overall, the conclusion suggested is that general revenue sharing does a better job at targeting funds among the larger municipalities than the smaller ones. This general conclusion about large cities is supported by other data.

In addition to the urban conditions index, several other indicators have been developed by the Brookings Institution to measure urban distress. One is a socioeconomic index which is used to measure both city-suburban disparities and relative intercity distress (*see* Nathan and Adams, 1976, pp. 47–61). Another measure, a composite economic activity indicator, examines changes in the level of value added by manufacturing, wholesale and retail sales, and service receipts between 1963 and 1972 (Nathan and Fossett, 1978). Both the socioeconomic index and the economic activity indicator were analyzed against a sample of large cities. Table 15 is based on 34 cities where the three measures—the urban conditions index, socioeconomic index, and economic activity indicator—could be matched.[11] In the table, the cities are grouped by quintiles rank ordered on the urban conditions index, the most distressed cities in the top quintile. It shows two principal things:

1) There tends to be a convergence of distress in the same cities; that is, if you rank high on one distress measure, you are likely to have a high ranking on another. An important exception to this is found among some southern cities. For example, New Orleans and Birmingham appear as distressed cities on the urban conditions and socioeconomic indexes but do better than the sample average for growing economic activity.
2) The average per capita revenue sharing allocation is highest in the top quintile (the most distressed cities) and becomes increasingly smaller as the level of distress decreases.

This same pattern of targeting among large cities has also been found in research using other need indicators.

The Treasury Department devised a fiscal strain measurement using changes in population, changes in per capita income, own source revenue compared to per capita income, long-term debt level compared to per capita income level, and full market property values during the decade of the 1970s.[12] The fiscal strain index was applied to the 48 largest cities, divided into categories of high (10 cities), moderate (28), and low strain (10). For EP 9, cities in the high strain category received an average per capita allocation of $33.92;

[11] The urban conditions index used in this analysis is the one developed for large cities only, using the factors of pre-1940 housing, poverty, and population change from 1960 to 1975.
[12] For the Treasury targeting analyses, *see* Office of Revenue Sharing, September 1978, pp. 12–31.

TABLE 15: Mean Urban Conditions Index, Intercity Socioeconomic Index, Economic Activities Indicator, and Per Capita General Revenue Sharing Allocations for 34 Cities for Entitlement Period 9 (rank-ordered in quintiles on the urban conditions index)

Quintile	Urban Conditions Index	Intercity Socio-economic Index	Economic Activity Indicator	Per Capita Allocations EP 9
I N = 7	383	64	213	$28.28
II N = 7	272	54	139	26.41
III N = 7	192	42	118	24.22
IV N = 7	116	41	71	19.51
V N = 6	49	41	57	16.20

Sources: For the urban conditions index, see Dommel et al. (1978), Appendix II; for the intercity socioeconomic index, see Nathan and Adams (1976), pp. 55–56; for the economic activity indicator, see Nathan and Fossett (unpublished).

moderate strain $25.20; and low strain $17.30. On the basis of fiscal strain as measured by the Treasury index, the revenue sharing formula has good targeting characteristics. It should also be noted that all of the 10 high strain cities of the Treasury fiscal index are well above the mean (more distressed) of the Brookings Institution urban conditions index, thus giving further evidence of the convergence-of-distress argument.

A second set of targeting data was developed by the Treasury Department for 162 large cities with populations above 100,000, comparing the targeting effectiveness of five federal programs—general revenue sharing, counter-cyclical revenue sharing (ARFA), the comprehensive employment and training program (CETA), the community development block grant (CDBG), and the local public works program (LPW). The summary of the findings presented below concerns only the revenue sharing data as related to the targeting of that program.

Population size was used as one indicator of need "because a government's need for services tends to increase directly with its population size" (Office of Revenue Sharing, 1978, pp. 12–31). It was concluded that general revenue sharing "followed a positive trend of allocating increased funds to the larger cities" (ibid., p. 21). It noted, however, that there were considerable variations in the per capita allocations among the eight largest cities with the distributions ranging from $15.32 per capita in Houston to $41.18 for New York

City. (The New York allocation accounted for 52 percent of the total allocation to the eight largest cities, thus tending to distort the group average.) These variations among the per capita allocations of the eight largest cities tend to follow the distress indexes showing Houston as a well-off city compared to Baltimore, which received $31.89 per capita.

The Treasury Department also took the population change categories of the 28 cities analyzed by George E. Peterson and found that the average per capita grant for declining cities was well above the average for all cities (excluding New York) (Office of Revenue Sharing, 1978, p. 22). The average per capita grant of the declining cities was $27.72 compared with $15.79 for growing cities and an average of $22.97 for the twenty-seven cities collectively.

A third set of findings for the 162 cities was based on analysis of the distress criteria for the urban development action grant program (UDAG) (Office of Revenue Sharing, 1978, pp. 24–25). The criteria include measures of per capita income, population growth, unemployment rate, employment growth, housing stock, and poverty level. The 162 cities were group according to how many of the six criteria they met. A city meeting all six criteria was included in the most distressed category. For general revenue sharing the average per capita allocations to the most distressed group were significantly higher than the average allocations to any of the other five groups. The allocations to the most distressed group averaged $31.20 per capita which was well above the $23.76 average per capita grant to the next category of distressed cities.

Summarizing the various findings of the targeting research among large cities, it can be concluded that among large cities the general revenue sharing formula is a reasonably good instrument for targeting on urban distress. At the same time, it must be recalled that targeting is less pronounced among smaller municipalities.

CONCLUSION

There would be little usefulness in framing the conclusions in terms of what might be done to improve the targeting of general revenue sharing. The political and legislative history provides little reason for optimism that either the eligibility list or the formula factors could be restructured to improve program targeting. Further, it is not evident that this would necessarily be desirable, given the nature of the program as a fiscal support grant. The analysis does, however, suggest another possibility.

There has been some discussion of, and the Carter administration has proposed, a program of supplemental fiscal assistance to needy cities. The Carter plan would target a relatively small amount of money ($250 million in fiscal 1980 and $150 million in fiscal 1981) on a limited number of distressed cities. One problem is the basis for distributing the funds. Once the crucial eligibility issue is resolved, the analysis of this paper suggests that using the existing revenue sharing formula as the allocation mechanism may have some merit. The formula does a reasonably good job of targeting among large cities (over 50,000), and this targeting impact would be further improved by applying it against a limited eligibility list.

To sum up, if the political problems of funding levels and eligibility can be resolved (and these are not small matters), we may not need to start from scratch on the formula itself.

REFERENCES

Dommel, Paul R. *The Politics of Revenue Sharing*. Bloomington: Indiana University Press, 1974.

————. "Urban Policy and Federal Aid: Redistributive Issues." In *Urban Problems and Public Policy*, ed. Robert L. Lineberry and Louis H. Masotti. Lexington, Mass.: Lexington Books, 1975.

————, and Jaffe, Jacob M. *Report on the Allocation of Community Development Funds to Small Cities*. Washington, D.C.: U.S. Department of Housing and Urban Development, forthcoming.

————; Nathan, Richard P.; et al. *Decentralizing Community Development*, Appendix 2. Washington, D.C.: U.S. Department of Housing and Urban Development, 1978.

Nathan, Richard P., and Adams, Charles F. *Revenue Sharing: The Second Round*. Washington, D.C.: Brookings Institution, 1977.

————. "Understanding Central City Hardships." *Political Science Quarterly* 91 (Spring 1978): 47–61.

Nathan, Richard P., and Dommel, Paul R. "The Cities." In *Setting National Priorities: The 1978 Budget*. Washington, D.C.: Brookings Institution, 1977.

Nathan, Richard P., et al. *Monitoring Revenue Sharing*. Washington, D.C.: Brookings Institution, 1975.

————, and Fossett. "Urban Conditions—Federal and State Roles." Paper read at the National Tax Association meeting, November 13, 1978, Philadelphia, Pennsylvania.

Peterson, George E. "Finances." In *The Urban Predicament*. Washington, D.C.: Urban Institute, 1976.

Ross, John P., et al. *General Revenue Sharing: Research Utilization Project*. Vol. 1: *Alternative Formula for General Revenue Sharing: Population-Based Measures of Need*. Washington, D.C.: National Science Foundation, July 1975.

Thompson, Richard E. *Revenue Sharing: A New Era in Federalism*. Washington, D.C.: Revenue Sharing Advisory Service, 1973.

U.S. Department of the Treasury, Office of Revenue Sharing. *Distributional Impact of General Revenue Sharing*. Washington, D.C.: U.S. Government Printing Office, September 1978.

————. *State and Local Data Elements: Entitlement Period 9*. Washington, D.C.: U.S. Government Printing Office, July 1977.

CHAPTER TWENTY-FOUR

The Urban Impact of the
Anti-Recession Fiscal Assistance Program

JOHN P. ROSS

INTRODUCTION

The Anti-Recession Fiscal Assistance (ARFA) program was a general purpose grant-in-aid program which distributed about $3.5 billion to State and local governments (and the territories) between July 1, 1976, and September 30, 1978. The distribution was based on a formula—the jurisdiction's general revenue sharing allocation times its excess unemployment rate—and all general purpose governments with the required rate of unemployment were eligible for aid. The program was unique among those being considered in this volume because it was not renewed for Fiscal 1979; however, it is included at a much reduced level in President Carter's 1980 budget. It is called "Targeted Fiscal Assistance," and $200 million has been requested for its continuation.

The purpose of this paper is to examine the urban impacts of the Anti-Recession Fiscal Assistance program. In particular, the paper analyzes the program in terms of the issues raised in Office of Management and Budget (OMB) Circular A-116, concentrating on the most straightforward of those issues as far as this program is concerned—the impact on the fiscal condition of large urban governments.

Three general conclusions regarding both urban impact statements as applied to general-purpose assistance and more specifically the urban impacts of ARFA can be drawn from this analysis. First, we lack a clear definition of the "fiscal condition" of a governmental jurisdiction. As a result, after over two years of research on Anti-Recession Fiscal Assistance the questions

The author wishes to thank Philip Brewer for his assistance in preparing this paper and Robert W. Rafuse, Jr., of Phoenix Associates, Inc., for providing helpful comments on an earlier draft.

asked in OMB Circular A-116 still cannot be satisfactorily answered. Obviously, a part of the problem is that most of the research was completed before Circular A-116 was issued and, therefore, was not specifically aimed at urban impact issues. A more significant obstacle, however, is that the present state of the art lacks at least a part of the analytical framework required to provide definitive answers to the issues raised by Circular A-116 as they apply to general purpose grants-in-aid.

For example, the fiscal condition of a place has at least three separate dimensions: social, economic, and financial. The social dimension concerns the condition of the residents of the place and the economic dimension involves the place's tax base and potential economic growth. The revenues, expenditures, and debt of the jurisdiction constitute the financial dimension of a place's fiscal condition.

Even with agreement on these three dimensions of fiscal condition, a quantitative definition remains illusive. There is no agreement on the way in which these dimensions should be measured. Nor is there an understanding of the way in which the dimensions should be combined to determine an overall estimate of fiscal condition. We are at this point not even sure of the impacts of federal aid on any one of these dimensions much less its impacts on the overall fiscal condition of the jurisdiction.[1]

The two purposes of this particular program—countercyclical stimulus for the national economy and support for fiscally stressed jurisdictions—also tend to cloud the impact issues by raising questions concerning the appropriate fiscal comparison. The relevant fiscal comparison for this kind of program concerns what would have happened to the national economy and to State and local governments had the aid not been forthcoming. This kind of comparison is difficult in the best of times. In a world of rapid inflation coupled with sharp declines in real gross national product (GNP) (as in the 1974–75 recession) this kind of comparison is next to impossible to make until we learn more about the relationships between the fiscal position of State and local governments and the swings of the national economy.

Second, we lack a general technical approach that can handle detailed impact issues involving new or expanded initiatives. Most important, the degree of substitution has not been satisfactorily estimated. ARFA aid was relatively well targeted to large jurisdictions experiencing high rates of unemployment; however, to say more than that, to actually estimate the impact of this program on the fiscal condition of urban governments has generally escaped the analytical ability of our present models. There is not even agreement on the most appropriate methodology nor the appropriate budget model for determining the impact of an aid program on the financial position of the jurisdiction receiving the money.

The principal stumbling block concerns the substitution issue, that is, the

[1] For a discussion of these issues *see* U.S. House of Representatives, 1978.

extent to which the net fiscal impact of ARFA was to reduce taxes or increase cash balances rather than increase State and local government spending. Removing that block requires being able to estimate the amount of the grant-in-aid money that was actually spent, the amount that was used to reduce taxes, and the amount that was held in cash balances. Estimates of the degree of substitution of ARFA for local own source revenues have been generated. The various estimates, however, are for different time periods and embody a considerable range of results—from only about 3 percent to about 64 percent substitution of grant-in-aid monies for own source expenditures.

In addition, because by its very nature and purpose general fiscal assistance aid cannot be easily traced through the budget allocation system, determining the impacts of ARFA on particular programs or particular groups of people has proved to be an elusive exercise. Even if we could derive reliable estimates of spending versus tax reductions versus increased cash balances, how that division affects the fiscal condition of a city is still unclear.

If the city increases its cash balances, it certainly improves its fiscal health. If the money is used to reduce taxes, that may also improve the fiscal condition of the city. What we do not know is how to compare the competing uses of these funds.

Finally, one of the most important urban impacts of this program is not even considered in OMB Circular A-116. That impact concerns withdrawal. For a program such as ARFA, a key consideration is an analysis of what happens when the program is abruptly terminated. The cost of abrupt termination may be quite significant and certainly must be considered in any attempt at quantifying the potential urban impacts of a general purpose fiscal assistance program. Even the threat of termination can change budget decision-making and, in turn, the potential fiscal impacts of the program.

These three general conclusions should not be interpreted as a condemnation of the requirement for an Urban Impact Statement. Rather, they confirm the need for that process by emphasizing how much we do not know about the impact of federal policy on urban places. They do imply, however, that with our present methodologies we cannot expect too much of these statements. They also point toward a need to refocus research priorities on the development of improved models for studying our system of fiscal federalism.

After providing a brief history of ARFA, this paper presents a discussion of the purposes of the program, pointing out basic inconsistencies in these purposes during periods of economic recovery. Next, the urban impacts of the program are examined emphasizing its fiscal impacts on large urban governments. Beginning with the least complicated of these issues, targeting, the discussion then moves to impacts on financial condition and, finally, to impacts on the economic condition of the place receiving the ARFA funds. The final section points to the kinds of research which must be undertaken before the questions asked in OMB Circular A-116 can be meaningfully answered.

The nature of the program dictates the spatial unit chosen for analysis—

the general-purpose jurisdiction receiving the aid. Attempts to disaggregate below the jurisdictional level require information which is not currently available. For that jurisdictional unit, two kinds of comparisons are discussed. The first involves that jurisdiction as compared against itself over time. In other words, what would have happened to the jurisdiction had the aid not been available. The second kind of comparison looks at the central city as opposed to its suburbs. The latter comparison is probably more relevant for policy purposes.

BACKGROUND

Express congressional interest in aid to State and local governments during periods of economic decline began in May and June of 1975 with hearings before the Subcommittee on Intergovernmental Relations of the Senate Committee on Government Operations on Senate Bill S-1359. The purpose of the bill was to "coordinate State and local budget-related actions with Federal Government efforts to stimulate economic recovery by establishing a system of emergency support grants to State and local governments" (U.S. Senate, 1975, p. 1). That bill became Title II of the Local Public Works Employment Act of 1976, which was vetoed by President Ford on February 13, 1976 on the grounds that it was too costly.

The original bill proposed a distribution formula based upon unemployment rates and tax effort. In order to gain additional support for passage, a new formula was incorporated into the legislation which based the allocations on the jurisdiction's excess unemployment rate times its general revenue sharing allocation. The result was that more money went to State and local governments with high unemployment rates and low tax efforts than had been the case under the original legislation.

The Public Works Employment Act was again passed by Congress and sent to the president. President Ford again vetoed the legislation as expected; however, this time there were sufficient votes to override the veto and the legislation became Public Law 94-369 on July 22, 1976.

The ARFA program

Title II of the Public Works Employment Act authorized $1.25 billion in Anti-Recession Fiscal Assistance aid to State and local governments. The program was to run for five calendar quarters beginning July 1, 1976 and ending September 30, 1977. Payments totaling $125 million, plus $62.5 million for each 0.5 percent by which the national unemployment rate for the preceding quarter exceeded 6 percent, were authorized for each quarter for State and local governments. No payments were to be made if the national unemployment rate was less than 6 percent. Every State or local general-purpose government was eligible for payment if its unemployment rate for the preceding quarter exceeded 4.5 percent.

In his Economic Recovery message of January 31, 1977, President Carter asked Congress to extend and modify the ARFA program as a part of his overall economic stimulus package. He asked that the program be authorized on a five-year basis and that it be made more sensitive to changes in the unemployment rate by making available $125 million plus $30 million for each one-tenth of one percent by which the national unemployment rate exceeded 6 percent.

The Senate quickly approved the extension; however, strong opposition developed in the Subcommittee on Intergovernmental Relations and Human Resources of the House Committee on Government Operations. (*See* "Dissenting Views," U.S. House, 1977). A number of objections were presented by the subcommittee; principal among them was opposition to the use of the unemployment rate as a measure of recession-induced fiscal distress. As a result of these objections, the subcommittee voted to kill the entire bill. The full House Committee on Government Operations voted to override the subcommittee report and authorized a one-year extension with a higher funding level.

The Intergovernmental Anti-Recession Act of 1977 (P.L. 95-30) extended the program for five quarters to September 30, 1978 and added $2.25 billion to the program. It also changed the formula to make it more sensitive to changes in the unemployment rate by making additional money available for every 0.1 percent by which the national unemployment rate exceeded 6 percent during the previous quarter.[2]

The Supplemental Fiscal Assistance program

Since the program was only extended for one year, hearings on renewal began again in May 1978 with the introduction of the Supplemental Fiscal Assistance program (U.S. Senate, 1978). That proposal requested $1,040 million for Fiscal 1979 and $1,000 million for Fiscal 1980 for supplemental fiscal assistance for local general-purpose governments. It changed the emphasis of the program from countercyclical assistance to fiscal relief and eliminated State governments from the list of eligible recipients. In addition, it introduced an extremely complex distribution formula which allowed local governments to receive the larger of the amounts generated by taking the general revenue sharing allocation of the jurisdiction times one of four factors: the relative local unemployment rate above 4.5 percent, the relative change in employment, the relative change in per capita income, or the relative change in population.

Local jurisdictions were divided between those contained within a Standard Metropolitan Statistical Area (SMSA) and those outside the boundaries of an SMSA. Governments within SMSAs were to compete with other

---

[2] For a detailed discussion of the history of this program *see* Advisory Commission on Intergovernmental Relations, forthcoming.

governments within SMSAs while non-SMSA governments competed with only other non-SMSA jurisdictions. Using per capita income as an example, for a government within an SMSA the relative growth in per capita income was to be calculated by subtracting the local rate of growth in per capita income for the jurisdiction from the rate of growth in per capita income for SMSA jurisdictions, and dividing the difference by the standard deviation weighted by population of all SMSA jurisdictions' rates of growth in per capita income.[3]

The new formula was supposed to provide a significant improvement in targeting, with 33 percent of the money going to the 48 largest cities (as opposed to about 20 percent under the original ARFA program). In addition, however, the proposed program actually increased the spread of the money, making approximately 2,000 more units of local government eligible—about 26,000 units would have qualified as opposed to only about 24,000 under ARFA.

Targeted Fiscal Assistance

The Supplemental Fiscal Assistance program was never brought to a vote on the floor of the House and as a result ARFA ended on September 30, 1978. Another proposed ARFA extension is contained in the president's 1980 budget. The new program is called Targeted Fiscal Assistance and an authorization of $200 million for Fiscal 1979 and $150 million for Fiscal 1980 is requested. Aside from the request for funds, no details on the new program are yet available. In addition a new countercyclical program is also discussed in the budget. No details are given and no funds are requested for this new program.

PURPOSES

The Anti-Recession Fiscal Assistance program had two major, though not necessarily consistent, purposes—countercyclical stimulus and fiscal support. As the program progressed through its various iterations, the purpose changed in emphasis from equal weight on both objectives to emphasis on only fiscal support with the suggestion that an entirely new and different program was needed for countercyclical purposes.

Senator Muskie provides the flavor of the original, two-pronged justification for ARFA as follows:

> The idea of emergency anti-recession budget assistance to State and local governments grew out of the concern of certain economists that during a recession, State and local governments experience a special budget squeeze and are often forced to make adjustments which run counter to Federal efforts to stimulate eco-

---

[3] Had this program passed, economists would have had a field day for the next few years figuring out how the formula worked. For a discussion of this formula *see* Ross, forthcoming.

nomic recovery. Such adjustments—which include tax increases, service cutbacks and reduced capital expenditures—become necessary because of revenue shortfalls due to the depressed local economy and a simultaneous increased demand for certain local services. In the past, such budget adjustments by State and local governments may not have been significant to the overall pace of economic recovery. But today, according to the theory of countercyclical assistance, State and local governments comprise a major sector of the U.S. economy, and thus the budget actions which they take can no longer be ignored in formulating national economic policy (Muskie, 1977, p. 1).

As a countercyclical fiscal policy tool, the purpose of the program is to make State and local governments fiscal agents of national stabilization policy. The grant-in-aid monies provided by ARFA were to be spent by the State and local governments, giving additional stimulus to the economy and in the process expanding employment and output. The principal advantage of this tool over other, more traditional fiscal policy measures—direct federal tax reductions or expenditure increases—was that it allowed geographic targeting of the stimulus. Given that different areas of the country are affected in varying degrees by a national recession, and that those variations in degree can be measured, then ARFA allowed the Federal government to target the aid to those areas most severely hurt by the recession.

The principal disadvantage of ARFA as a fiscal tool is that the newly created fiscal agents are at best difficult to control. To the extent that they spend all of their money in the correct time frame, there are relatively minor differences between the overall impact of this program and that of a direct federal spending increase except in terms of its geographic targeting.[4] As a matter of fact, if this aid proves to be at all stimulative of State and local government own source expenditures (an unlikely theoretical possibility) then even more employment and output could be generated. If, however, the money is used for purposes of tax reduction the multiplier would be less than that which could be expected from additional direct Federal government purchases of goods and services.

Finally, if the additional funds go to build cash balances—as a significant portion seems to have done—all else equal, there is very little impact on output and employment and the program as a countercyclical device will not be very successful. Because of the difficulties of controlling our new fiscal agents, the likely outcome of the program as an antirecession fiscal tool is problematic at best.

As a fiscal assistance grant-in-aid program, the purpose of ARFA was to provide additional money to those places most severely hurt by the recession.[5] How, or even if, the jurisdiction spent the money is not a major concern as

[4] The differences that do occur are the result of differences in purchase mix and differences in the multipliers of transfer payments versus direct payments.

[5] For a discussion of the way in which this type of grant-in-aid program could work *see* Greytak and Tussing, 1971, pp. 47–54.

long as some of the recession-induced fiscal pressure was removed from the jurisdiction. For analytical purposes, the major concerns are: that the jurisdiction actually did lose substantial revenue because of the recession and that the money was well targeted to places suffering the greatest loss.

During periods of economic decline, these two purposes blend nicely and provide a reasonable political rationale for the program. During periods of recovery and economic growth, the two purposes are no longer so well matched and can lead to problems of program design. If all areas across the country went into a recession at the level of fiscal health, if they all suffered the same revenue loss from the recession, and if they all recovered at the same rate, there would be no problem matching these two program goals. However, they do not. As a result, when, on national stabilization grounds, it is time to terminate the funds, some governments may still be suffering severe recession-induced fiscal distress. Moreover, some jurisdictions experiencing serious fiscal stress attributable to the long-run weakness or deterioration of their economies may not have realized very substantial gains from the general economic recovery. Taking the money away from such jurisdictions at that point could easily lead to a disruption of their financial stability (ACIR, 1978).

For this program the purposes are important when attempting to do an Urban Impact Statement for two general reasons. First, the two purposes taken together point to a basic weakness in the design of the overall program. That basic weakness leads in turn to some unexpected impacts of the program on urban areas during periods of withdrawal. Second, the purposes, when analyzed, allow us to look beyond the basic distributional patterns of the program and provide us with other objectives which also have to be examined.

URBAN IMPACTS

The principal urban impact of the Anti-Recession Fiscal Assistance program to be examined in this paper concerns the effects of the program on the fiscal condition of the recipient governments. That impact can be divided into three parts. The first concerns targeting. Did the money go to those governments suffering the greatest fiscal stress? The second deals with the actual impact of the money on the budgets of the recipient governments. How was the money used and how, if at all, did it reduce the fiscal stress of those governments? Not only is it important to understand the characteristics of the units of government which received the money, but it is also important to understand how those jurisdictions used what they received so that some link may be generated between the additional money and the kinds of public services and people which benefited from those additional dollars.

Finally, the economic impacts of the program are important. Did the program create new employment opportunities and, if so, what was the spatial distribution of those opportunities?

Targeting

ARFA was a formula grant with an individual jurisdiction's allocation dependent upon its general revenue sharing allocation times its excess unemployment above 4.5 percent. One-third of the money was set aside for State and two-thirds was for local governments. A jurisdiction which had an unemployment rate equal to or less than 4.5 percent for the previous quarter was not eligible for ARFA money.

For each quarter for which the national unemployment rate exceeded 6 percent, the national pot was equal to $125 million plus $30 million for each one-tenth of one percent by which the national rate exceeded 6 percent. If the national rate was less than 6 percent for the quarter prior to the allocation quarter, no money would be available for allocation.

Thus the dollar allocation going to an individual jurisdiction depended upon the national unemployment rate, the local jurisdiction's unemployment rate, and the general revenue sharing allocation for the local jurisdiction. At least on the surface, states competed with all other states for ARFA funds while local governments competed with all other local governments. However, that rather straightforward interpretation ignores the impact of the general revenue sharing allocation. For local jurisdictions, that allocation is dependent upon the population, tax effort, and relative income of the local jurisdiction as well as the population, tax effort, and relative income of like jurisdictions within the same county area as the jurisdiction under examination, the functional responsibilities of that class of jurisdictions, the county area in which the jurisdiction is contained, and the state area containing the jurisdiction. Finally, that allocation also depends upon the interaction of a set of three limits imposed on the allocations (Ross et al., 1975, pp. 154–67).

The point which must be recognized is that an individual jurisdiction's ARFA allocation was dependent upon the interaction of a number of factors. It was not a simple formula which depended primarily upon unemployment. Rather it depended upon the interaction of unemployment, population size, tax effort, relative income, functional responsibility, and geographic location. A change in any one of these factors changed the amount of money going to an individual jurisdiction. Over the long run such changes would be quite important. Determining the overall importance of each of these factors is no simple task and has as yet not been undertaken.

Who should get the money? Given the two distinctive purposes of the program, two answers are available to the question of who should get the money. As a countercyclical program, the money should be distributed to those jurisdictions which can spend it the most rapidly. Timing is the key to the effectiveness of this program as a countercyclical tool. To have the most impact on the national economy, the funds must be spent as rapidly as possible. Thus, the money should go to those jurisdictions with the greatest propensity to spend regardless of the jurisdiction's particular fiscal health.

A fiscal assistance program requires an entirely different targeting emphasis. As fiscal assistance the money should be targeted to those jurisdictions suffering the greatest financial stress. How rapidly the jurisdiction can spend the money is of only secondary importance. The fiscal characteristics of the recipient become the primary criteria.

To the extent that those jurisdictions suffering the greatest fiscal stress are likely to spend the money rapidly and to the extent that the level of unemployment is a good proxy for the recession-induced fiscal stress of the jurisdiction, these two purposes match nicely as allocation criteria. However, to the extent that these two characteristics diverge, these two criteria will not be compatible.

Little research has been done on the question of the characteristics of a jurisdiction's propensity to spend rapidly. A great deal of work has been done, however, on the validity of the level of unemployment as an indicator of cyclically induced fiscal stress. Most of the work points out that the unemployment level measures both the long-run (structural) unemployment conditions of the place as well as the short-run (cyclical) changes in those conditions. For the program to only reward those places suffering the greatest losses due to the recession, these studies argue that the allocation should be based upon the change in unemployment rather than the level of unemployment. That change, so the argument goes, is a better indicator of the cyclical effects of the recession than is the level by itself.[6]

The counterargument says that high absolute rates of unemployment are a good proxy for financial stress. Places with high absolute rates and small changes in those rates suffer more from a recession than places with low absolute rates coupled with large changes in unemployment. According to this argument, the latter places are in a much better position to weather a recession than are the former places. This argument has not as yet been resolved and more research on this point is needed before a new counter-cyclical program is passed.[7]

The relationship between the unemployment rate—either the level or the change—and the fiscal health of the community has received much less attention. There is simply an implicit assumption, probably correct, that the higher the level of unemployment the worse the fiscal health of the jurisdiction. This is a hypothesis which needs to be tested.

Who actually got the money? Almost all of the studies of ARFA conclude that it was well targeted to larger cities with high rates of unemployment.[8] About 40 percent of the total ARFA allocation went to municipalities. The 48 largest cities received almost 22 percent of total ARFA allocation (ACIR, 1978, p. 19).

---

[6] Comptroller General of the United States, November 29, 1977 and July 20, 1977, respectively.

[7] For the flavor of this debate *see* Rafuse, 1978, pp. 132–33, and Peterson, 1977, pp. 17–36.

[8] For an example *see* U.S. Department of Treasury, January 23, 1978.

TABLE 1: Characteristics and ARFA Allocations for the 48 Largest Cities

Region and SMSA	1975 Pop. (Thousands)	Nathan's Urban Cond. Index[a]	Total Allocations ($ Thousands)	Per Capita Allocations	ARFA as % of 1975-76 Budget
East					
Baltimore	851.7	224	19,985	$23.46	5.3%
Boston	636.7	257	13,816	21.69	2.6
Buffalo	407.2	292	9,084	22.32	6.9
Newark	339.6	321	15,716	46.22	10.7
New York	7,481.6	180	244,051	32.62	3.2
Philadelphia	1,815.8	216	44,983	24.77	5.5
Pittsburgh	458.7	260	9,453	20.59	10.7
Washington, D.C.	711.5	155	16,049	22.45	1.9
Midwest					
Chicago	3,099.4	201	40,077	12.93	5.0
Cincinnati	412.6	226	7,144	17.30	2.6
Cleveland	638.8	291	9,741	15.24	6.0
Columbus	535.6	90	2,739	5.11	2.5
Detroit	1,335.1	201	42,444	31.79	9.3
Indianapolis	714.9	71	2,936	4.11	1.8
Kansas City	472.5	121	4,099	8.67	2.2
Milwaukee	665.8	128	5,871	8.82	4.8
Minneapolis	378.1	174	1,861	4.92	1.9
Omaha	371.5	84	856	2.31	1.3
St. Paul	279.5	117	1,128	4.04	1.7
St. Louis	525.0	351	11,712	22.35	5.6
Toledo	367.7	101	2,527	6.87	3.4
South					
Atlanta	436.1	118	4,754	10.90	2.1
Birmingham	276.3	218	3,392	12.29	4.4
Dallas	812.8	39	30	0.04	0.0
El Paso	385.7	80	7,272	18.84	12.4
Ft. Worth	358.4	65	546	1.52	0.7
Houston	1,326.8	37	2,073	1.56	0.6
Jacksonville	535.0	61	2,504	4.46	1.8
Louisville	336.0	195	2,965	8.82	3.2
Memphis	661.3	75	2,364	3.58	1.8
Miami	365.1	106	7,091	19.37	9.6
Nashville	423.4	58	690	1.63	0.3
New Orleans	559.8	274	12,791	22.84	8.5
Norfolk	286.7	105	2,468	8.60	2.5
Oklahoma City	365.9	71	1,189	3.25	1.2
San Antonio	773.2	100	4,618	5.97	4.6
Tulsa	331.7	49	862	2.60	1.1

TABLE 1 (continued)

Region and SMSA	1975 Pop. (Thousands)	Nathan's Urban Cond. Index[a]	Total Allocations ($ Thousands)	Per Capita Allocations	ARFA as % of 1975–76 Budget
West					
Denver	484.5	106	5,469	11.28	2.3
Honolulu	705.4	32	7,792	23.83	4.3
Long Beach	335.6	68	2,144	6.39	1.7
Los Angeles	2,727.4	74	30,117	11.04	3.6
Oakland	330.7	176	6,837	20.68	6.3
Phoenix	664.7	20	3,718	5.59	2.9
Portland	356.7	142	5,890	16.44	6.4
San Diego	774.0	39	7,732	9.99	5.3
San Francisco	664.5	188	16,538	24.89	3.4
San Jose	555.7	11	2,905	5.23	2.4
Seattle	487.1	100	4,830	9.92	2.9

Source: Office of Policy Development and Research, U.S. Department of Housing and Urban Development, staff calculations based on U.S. Department of the Treasury, *Anti-Recession Payment Summary.*

[a] A complete description of Nathan's Urban Condition Index is included in Nathan, Dommel, and Fossett, Testimony Before the Joint Economic Committee, July 28, 1977.

Table 1 shows the characteristics and ARFA allocations for the 48 largest cities. The per capita allocations ranged from over $46 for Newark, a city often pointed to as suffering severe fiscal and economic stress, to Dallas with a per capita allocation of $0.04. As a percentage of their 1975–76 budgets, ARFA ranged from 12.4 percent for El Paso to less than 0.1 percent for Dallas.

Table 2 shows the per capita allocations for the central city and the suburbs for the 48 largest central cities. In general, central cities received more in per capita allocations than did their suburbs. For example, in the eastern cities the ratio of central city per capita allocation to suburban per capita allocation was from 54.7 for Washington, D.C., to 1.3 for Buffalo.

Other studies that have examined the distribution of ARFA funds agree that they are well targeted among large cities. For example, the Advisory Commission on Intergovernmental Relations (ACIR) found a simple correlation of 0.76 between ARFA and Nathan's Urban Conditions Index and a simple correlation of 0.84 between ARFA and unemployment rates for the 48 largest cities (ACIR, 1978, p. 27). In addition, the Congressional Budget Office found that ARFA was highly responsive to cities with high levels of social need, economic need, and fiscal need (U.S. House, 1978). This study was done for the 45 largest cities.

TABLE 2: ARFA Per Capita Allocation, Central City (CC) and Suburbs (OCC), 1975 Population

Region and SMSA	CC Per Capita Allocation ($)	OCC Per Capita Allocation ($)	Ratio CC to OCC Per Capita Allocations
East			
Baltimore	23.46	3.59	6.53
Boston	21.69	7.99	2.71
Buffalo	22.32	17.30	1.29
Newark	46.22	11.91	3.88
New York	32.62	3.62	9.01
Philadelphia	24.77	6.90	3.59
Pittsburgh	20.59	5.64	3.65
Washington, D.C.	22.45	0.41	54.76
Midwest			
Chicago	12.93	2.55	5.07
Cincinnati	17.30	6.47	2.67
Cleveland	15.24	2.87	5.31
Columbus	5.11	2.08	2.46
Detroit	31.79	10.01	3.18
Indianapolis	4.11	1.74	2.36
Kansas City	8.67	3.14	2.76
Milwaukee	8.82	4.07	2.17
Minneapolis- St. Paul	4.54	2.86	1.59
Omaha	2.31	3.69	0.63
St. Louis	22.35	4.64	4.82
Toledo	6.87	7.84	0.88
South			
Atlanta	10.90	7.48	1.46
Birmingham	12.29	6.12	2.01
Dallas-Ft. Worth	0.47	0.24	1.96
El Paso	18.84	61.28	0.31
Houston	1.56	1.41	1.11
Jacksonville	4.46	1.31	3.40
Louisville	8.82	1.60	5.51
Memphis	3.58	22.57	0.16
Miami	19.37	12.67	1.53
Nashville	1.63	2.52	0.65
New Orleans	22.84	2.77	8.25
Norfolk	8.60	8.23	1.04
Oklahoma City	3.25	2.49	1.31
San Antonio	5.97	14.61	0.41
Tulsa	2.60	4.05	0.64
West			
Denver	11.28	2.30	4.90
Honolulu	23.83	—	—

TABLE 2 (continued)

Region and SMSA	CC Per Capita Allocation ($)	OCC Per Capita Allocation ($)	Ratio CC to OCC Per Capita Allocations
Los Angeles- Long Beach	10.53	16.04	0.66
Phoenix	5.59	9.02	0.62
Portland	16.44	8.58	1.92
San Diego	9.99	22.14	0.45
San Francisco- Oakland	23.47	17.39	1.35
San Jose	5.23	8.02	0.65
Seattle	9.92	8.50	1.17

Source: Office of Policy Development and Research, U.S. Department of Housing and Urban Development, staff calculations based on U.S. Department of the Treasury, *Anti-Recession Payment Summary.*

Formula quirks. While all of the studies agree that ARFA was well targeted, it proved to be almost impossible for a city to predict its future ARFA allocations. The size of the total ARFA pot for each quarter varied with the national unemployment rate. In addition, the number of jurisdictions competing for that pot varied with the local unemployment rate. As a result, it was possible for a jurisdiction's unemployment rate to fall and its allocation to go up.

Figure 1 shows New York City's quarter-by-quarter allocations. For some quarters, New York City's unemployment rate went down and its allocation went up. For example, from quarter six to quarter seven, the unemployment rate fell by 0.2 percent and the allocation went up by $37 million.

What this quirk does is make financial planning very difficult. By increasing the degree of uncertainty, it encourages governments to hold their allocations in their cash balances rather than spend them. As will be shown in the next section, a lot of governments appear to have done just that. Rather than spend, they simply temporarily banked their ARFA funds.

Fiscal impact of ARFA

Questions of fiscal impact concern the ways in which the grant-in-aid program affect the financial health of the recipient government. The question itself is quite straightforward. The answer, however, appears to be quite complex and as yet we have not had much success in generating reliable estimates of fiscal impact.

Two problems pose the majority of the difficulties. The first concerns the question of substitution. When given additional grant-in-aid funds, a government may spend all the new money, plus what it had planned to spend of

FIGURE 1: New York City ARFA Allocation and Unemployment Rate

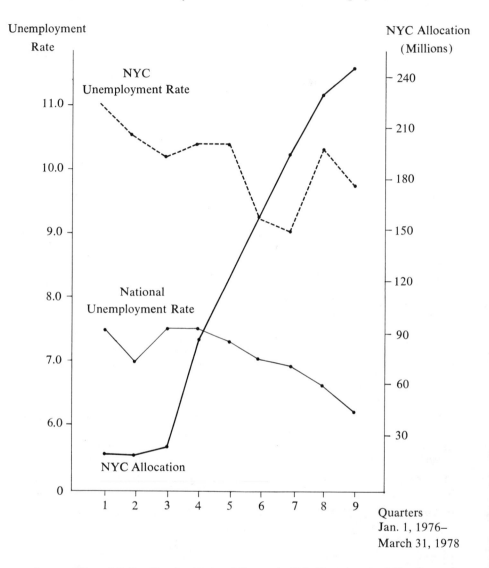

Source: Office of Policy Development and Research, U.S. Department of Housing and Urban Development, staff evaluation based on U.S. Department of the Treasury, *Anti-Recession Payment Summary*, various quarters.

its own money, plus in some cases even more of its own money. In this case, the grant stimulates own source spending of the recipient government. On the other hand, the recipient government may spend the grant money and at the same time reduce its own-source expenditures by an equal amount. In this latter case, the grant monies are substituted for own source expenditures. Total spending does not go up. The grant money is used for either tax reduction or increases in cash balances. The problem is that dollars can be traced through the budget process only with great difficulty; thus, it is very hard to estimate what the government would have done had it not received the additional grant-in-aid.

Even if the question of substitution could be solved, we are still faced with questions concerning how these decisions affected the fiscal health of the place. Since little is known about the relationship between the way in which a jurisdiction allocates its resources and its overall fiscal health, the assumption normally accepted is that a locality's decisions reflect the best possible judgment about what action is most needed. Thus, by assumption, whatever the locality does with its money is the most appropriate way to improve its fiscal health.

Three types of approaches are available for estimating the degree of substitution—case studies coupled with some kind of budget model either implicitly or explicitly stated, Nathan's monitoring technique, or an econometric model.[9] As indicated by the results of their extensive application to general revenue sharing none is completely satisfactory.

Both the case study method and the econometric model have been applied to ARFA. Table 3 shows the results. A study performed for the Office of Revenue Sharing used the case study approach on a sample of 50 jurisdictions, which included 26 cities. Eight of those cities were classified as "large-stressed," seven as "large-not stressed" and 11 as small. The results of this study indicate that roughly 75 percent of the money went into expenditures, 18 percent went into tax reduction, and 7 percent went into cash balances.[10] The Comptroller General Office's study also used the case study method with a sample of 21 city governments. (Comptroller General of the United States, 1978, p. 51). Their report indicates that almost all of the money went toward

---

[9] In general, in the case of a closed-end lump-sum transfer—the ARFA type of grant—the impact on expenditure depends upon the local government's propensity to spend versus its propensity to reduce taxes or increase cash balances. Given the nature of the grant, the expenditure impacts should be less than that of either an open-end matching grant or a closed-end categorical grant.

Using an econometric model Gramlich and Galper estimated that in general after one quarter, a $1.00 lump-sum transfer grant should increase surpluses by $0.96 with only a $0.04 increase in expenditures or reduction in taxes. In the longer run, that $1.00 increase in the lump-sum grant will increase expenditures between $0.25 and $0.43. *See* Gramlich and Galper, 1973, 1: 15–65.

[10] The findings cited in the text relate to the disposition projected to December 31, 1978 of the first six quarterly payments; that is, funds distributed between December 1976 (payments I and II) and October 1977 (payment IV). Peat, Marwick, Mitchell & Company et al., April 1978, pp. 111–25.

The extraordinary sensitivity of these estimates to the time period involved is suggested by the fact that this study estimates that, on December 31, 1977, 46 percent of the ARFA funds received by the 26 cities were still in cash balances. By June 30, 1978, this ratio is projected to have declined to 19 percent (ibid., pp. 111–12).

TABLE 3: Estimated Use of ARFA Funds by Cities
(percent)

	Off. of Revenue Sharing Study	*GAO Study*	*Gramlich*	
			Short-Run	*Long-Run*
Expenditures	75.0%	97.0%	3%	36%
Tax reduction	18.0	—	6	64
Cash balances	7.0	3.0	91	—

Sources: Office of Revenue Sharing study—Peat, Marwick, Mitchell & Company (1978); GAO study—Comptroller General of the U.S. (1978); Gramlich study—Gramlich (1979).

Note: Both the Office of Revenue Sharing study and the GAO study disaggregate expenditures by function. The disaggregations, however, are not comparable and therefore are not reported in this table.

increased expenditures. Finally, Gramlich used his econometric model to simulate the impacts of ARFA. His simulation found that in the long run, 36 percent of the money would be used for increased expenditures and 64 percent would go to tax reduction (Gramlich, 1979, p. 17).

The most interesting aspects of these estimates are their variation. The case study method in general yields much higher estimates of expenditure impacts than does the econometric model by a factor of two or three times. A part of the variation is a result of the different time frames covered by the studies and a part is due to different jurisdictions covered. More important, however, are the differences in the approaches. What these variations clearly point out is that additional work needs to be done in this entire area.

The next step—linking the changes in either increased expenditures or tax reduction to the fiscal health of the community—has not as yet even been attempted. Before a complete Urban Impact Statement can be written, this gap in our models must be filled.

Economic impact

Before beginning a discussion of what is known and unknown about the economic impact of the ARFA program, a brief discussion of the relevant comparison is important. The issue that must be raised is how to make the comparison. Is it to be made against other places receiving the money, against what would have happened had the program not been enacted, or some combination of the two? The point at issue is really the federal role in targeting grant-in-aid money. Is the Federal government attempting to equalize across places, as compared to what would have happened had the program not been enacted, or both? Given the dual purpose of this program, the answer is both across places and over time. Most of the research done to date, however, looks only at the across-place comparison and tends to ignore the over-time microeconomic implications of the program.

Three studies have been completed which attempt to estimate the aggregate employment impact of ARFA. Before the program was actually enacted, the Congressional Budget Office estimated that an ARFA type program funded at a level of $1.4 billion per year would increase employment by about 40,000 workers (U.S. Congressional Budget Office, 1977, Sec. II). This employment impact estimate was based on the assumption that between 50 and 60 percent of the money would represent increased direct spending by State and local governments and between 30 and 40 percent of the funds would go toward tax reduction. The remaining 10 percent was assumed to go into cash balances or reductions in debt.

Using the Data Resources Incorporated (DRI) macroeconomic forecasting model, the General Accounting Office in an early evaluation of ARFA, estimated that more than half of the ARFA funds would go to tax reductions or increases in cash balances. Well under half of the total allocations would actually find their way into increased expenditures. Based on these kinds of estimates, a continuing program funded at $3.25 billion per year could be expected to increase total job opportunities by 73,000 after eight quarters (Comptroller General of the United States, 1977, pp. 43–50).

Finally, a study sponsored by the Office of Revenue Sharing conducted a survey of 50 governments to determine the impact of ARFA on these jurisdictions. Based on their sample, they estimated that the maximum job-creation impact of the first six ARFA payments would occur in the first half of 1978 with between 54,000 and 66,000 jobs that would not otherwise have existed (Peat, Marwick, Mitchell & Co. et al., 1978, pp. v–20).

Two points need to be made about these estimates. First, the assumed program magnitude and procedures used are quite different. Second, the estimated number of jobs created depends upon the assumptions made about the appropriate employment multipliers and the percentage of the money actually spent versus the amount that goes to tax reduction and cash balances. The larger the estimated percentage spent, and the larger the employment multipliers, the greater the number of jobs created.

Fulfilling the mandate of OMB Circular A-116 requires that the number of jobs created be translated back into their spatial locations. At present, the technical models necessary to take this next step are simply not available. There is not enough information about the relationships between the national economy, local government expenditures, and the local labor market to make the next necessary connection. As a matter of fact what we do know tends to indicate that these relationships are not stable over time. The work that has been done in this area indicates that some places tend to lend a cycle while others tend to lag swings in the national economy. If the economic base of an area changes, it may lead the national economy in one recession and lag in another. Areas which enter recessions in already depressed conditions often do feel the recession to a much greater extent than those which are economically healthy going into the recession. They also tend to be much slower to recover, sometimes maintaining high rates of unemployment long after the national economy is showing strong signs of recovery. Thus, to take the next step requires the development of new analytical models which are capable of spatially fitting the macrojobs created back to labor market areas and ideally to jurisdictions within labor market areas. Such models are at present simply not available.

THE TERMINATION ISSUE

ARFA stopped as of September 30, 1978. The termination of this money raises an issue which is not contemplated in Circular A-116 concerning the urban impact of federal programs. That issue is what happens when the money is terminated. Present evidence available from the popular press indicates that the withdrawal of ARFA is causing severe financial disruptions for some of the cities already considered to be financially distressed. For future Urban Impact Statements, a major issue should concern the potential impact of withdrawing the grant-in-aid program, especially in programs with planned termination. In other words, the Urban Impact Statement needs to be broadened to include reductions as well as increases in federal programs.

CONCLUSION

The purpose of this paper has been to examine the urban impacts of ARFA. From this examination three general conclusions can be drawn. First, we lack a clear definition of "fiscal condition." As a result, research done on ARFA to date cannot answer all of the questions posed by a rigorous Urban Impact Statement. Second, ARFA was well targeted to large places with high rates of unemployment. Even though it was well targeted, estimates of its fiscal and economic impact are still very crude and require additional refinement. Finally, a complete Urban Impact Statement needs to include a discussion of the termination issue. The disruptions resulting from termination may be of sufficient magnitude to make the enactment of the entire program questionable. Programs with planned termination may elicit a different set of responses from state and local decision-makers and therefore a different set of urban impacts from those programs which are expected to continue. These kinds of issues must be included in a complete Urban Impact Statement.

REFERENCES

Advisory Commission on Intergovernmental Relations. *Countercyclical Aid and and Economic Stabilization.* A-69. Washington, D.C.: U.S. Government Printing Office, December 1978.
———. *State-Local Finances in Recession and Inflation.* vol. 2. Washington, D.C.: U.S. Government Printing Office, forthcoming.

Comptroller General of the United States. *Anti-Recession Assistance—An Evalua-tion.* Washington, D.C.: U.S. General Accounting Office, November 29, 1977.
————. *Anti-Recession Is Helping but Distribution Formula Needs Reassessment.* Washington, D.C.: U.S. General Accounting Office, July 20, 1977.
————. *Impact of Anti-Recession Assistance on Twenty-one City Governments.* Washington, D.C.: U.S. General Accounting Office, February 22, 1978.
Gramlich, Edward M. "State and Local Budget Surpluses and the Effect of Federal Macroeconomic Policies." In *State and Local Budget Surpluses and the Effect of Federal Macroeconomic Policies.* A study prepared for the use of the Sub-committee on Fiscal and Intergovernmental Policy of the Joint Economic Com-mittee. 95th Cong., 2d Sess. Washington, D.C.: U.S. Government Printing Office, 1979.
————, and Galper, Harvey. "State and Local Fiscal Behavior and Federal Grant Policy." In *Brookings Papers on Economic Activity*, vol. 1. Washington, D.C.: Brookings Institution, 1973.
Greytak, David, and Tussing, A. Dale. "Revenue Stabilizing Grants: A Proposal." *Proceeding of the Sixty-Fourth Annual Conference.* Columbus, Ohio: National Tax Association, 1971.
Muskie, Edward S. "Introduction and Summary." In *The Countercyclical Assist-ance Program: An Analysis of its Initial Impact.* Prepared by the Subcommittee on Intergovernmental Relations of the Committee on Governmental Affairs. U.S. Senate. 95th Cong., 1st Sess. Washington, D.C.: U.S. Government Printing Office, 1977.
Peat, Marwick, Mitchell & Company; Municipal Finance Officers Association; Phoenix Associates; and Harold A. Hovey. *An Analysis of the Antirecession Fis-cal Assistance Program.* Washington, D.C.: Office of Revenue Sharing, U.S. Department of the Treasury, April 1, 1978.
Peterson, George E. "Statement." In *Intergovernmental Antirecession Assistance Act of 1977: Hearings—March 1, 2, and 8, 1977.* Intergovernmental Relations and Human Resources Subcommittee, House Committee on Government Op-erations. U.S. House. 95th Cong., 1st Sess. Washington, D.C.: U.S. Government Printing Office, 1977.
Rafuse, Robert W. "The State-Local Sector and the Economy: Overall Perform-ance and Regional Disparities." In *State and Local Government Finance and Financial Management*, edited by John E. Petersen, Catherine Lavigne Spain, and Martharose F. Laffey. Washington, D.C.: Government Finance Research Center, August 1978.
Ross, John P.; Gustely, Richard; James, Judson; Watts, Ann; and Watts, Thomas. "Alternative Formulas for General Revenue Sharing: Population Based Meas-ures of Need." In *General Revenue Sharing: Research Utilization Project*, vol. 1. Washington, D.C.: National Science Foundation, July 1975.
————. "Countercyclical Revenue Sharing." In *A Federal Response to the Fiscal Crisis in American Cities*, edited by L. Kenneth Hubbell. New York: Ballinger, forthcoming.
U.S. Congressional Budget Office. *Short Run Measures to Stimulate the Economy.* Staff working paper. March 1977.
U.S. House of Representatives. *City Needs and the Responsiveness of Federal Grants Programs.* Subcommittee on the City of the Committee on Banking,

Finance and Urban Affairs.95th Cong., 2d Sess. Washington, D.C.: U.S. Government Printing Office, 1978.

————. *The Intergovernmental Anti-Recession Act of 1977*. House Report No. 95-275. 95th Cong., 1st Sess. Washington, D.C.: U.S. Government Printing Office, May 9, 1977.

U.S. Senate. *Hearings on S-1354*. Before Subcommittee on Intergovernmental Relations of the Committee on Government Operations. 94th Cong., 1st Sess. Washington, D.C.: U.S. Government Printing Office, May 6, 1975.

————. *Supplemental Fiscal Assistance Proposals Contained in the President's National Urban Policy Recommendations*. Hearings on S-2975 before the Subcommittee on Unemployment Compensation, Revenue Sharing, and Economic Problems of the Committee on Finance. 95th Cong., 2d Sess. Washington, D.C.: U.S. Government Printing Office, May 3, 1978.

U.S. Department of the Treasury, Office of State and Local Finance. *Report on the Fiscal Impact of the Economic Stimulus Package on 48 Large Urban Governments*. Washington, D.C.: Office of State and Local Finance, U.S. Department of the Treasury, January 3, 1978.

CHAPTER TWENTY-FIVE

Creeping Federalism: The Federal Impact on the Structure and Function of Local Government

ROBERT K. YIN

THE PREVALENCE OF BUREAUCRATIC IMPACTS

A friend of mine in Washington, D.C., spends most of his time following the latest urban legislation and regulations. He stays so current that I can usually learn from him the politics behind a certain action or even its presumed impact on specific cities and population groups. The interesting thing about my friend is that he is not a research person, nor is he a member of any federal agency or congressional staff. In fact, although he considers himself a member of the federal political community, his permanent home is not in Washington, D.C. His financial support comes from a consortium of local governments, and his full-time vocation is to serve as an informal representative of these local governments. He works, in other words, as a political lobbyist on behalf of these governments.

My friend's job is but one manifestation of a subtle change in local bureaucracy. Many city governments have begun to support their own D.C.-based representatives, often linked to an office of intergovernmental relations at home, in a manner that resembles the opening of a consulate or embassy. In fact, the intercourse between federal and local governments has become more intensive and formal, and reflects the increased business conducted between these two levels of government. My friend's job is a simple and direct example of a *bureaucratic impact of federal programs*. Thus, federal programs have become so large and prominent that their very implementation and administration may have an impact on local government operations.

Such federal influence over the structure of local bureaucracies is not an entirely new topic. Many studies of the antipoverty and model cities programs, for instance, concerned themselves with control and coordination at the local

level (Kramer, 1969, and Warren et al., 1974). This was especially true of
the model cities program, where the coordination of federal programs operating in the same target area was, at the outset, a major goal of the overall
program (Frieden and Kaplan, 1975). In addition, the major research studies
of both the antipoverty and model cities experiences did acknowledge the
tenuous nature of the new community organizations established by these programs (such as Community Action Plan [CAP] agencies, Community Development Agencies [CDAs], and their affiliates), as well as the obvious
conflicts that arose between these organizations and existing local government agencies. However, any conclusions about these bureaucratic impacts
were generally embedded within the context of more important ideological
issues, such as the disenfranchisement of the poor, the development of neighborhood capabilities, and the promotion of resident participation. Thus, lessons concerning the bureaucratic impacts themselves were not given special
attention beyond the context of antipoverty ideology and politics.

Today, in contrast, the impacts of federal programs on the structure and
function of local government have become so substantial that they may warrant attention in their own right (Pressman and Wildavsky, 1973; Haider,
1974; and Pressman, 1975). The very shape of city government may have
changed as a result of the requirements for administering federal programs—
an effect that occurs apart from the presumed substantive effects of these programs. Such bureaucratic impacts may result from:

1. The implementation of federal antidiscriminatory or other *regulations* involving the ways in which federally funded programs must be administered by
   local governments;
2. the administration of federally funded *nonurban programs* (e.g., defense installations) that may nevertheless impose new requirements on the operations
   of local governments and thereby create indirect bureaucratic impacts; and
3. the administration of federally funded *urban programs,* which usually bear directly on the structure and function of local government.

The major proposition of this paper is that these impacts have become
pervasive and substantial, and that local governments have become, in many
ways, captives of a creeping federalism whose institutional significance goes
far beyond the standard accounting of the size of the federal dollar. The purpose of the paper is to suggest that these bureaucratic impacts are only beginning to be understood, that they are hard to measure, and that much further
research is needed to develop improved assessment methods. But without
such methods, initiatives, such as Circular No. A-116 issued by the U.S.
Office of Management and Budget (OMB), which establish guidelines for
conducting urban impact analyses, will overlook the assessment of these
bureaucratic impacts.

The scope of the paper is limited by the very lack of information that is
needed to guide policy. Thus, the paper will only attempt to deal with the

bureaucratic impacts created by the third type of federal activity listed above—that is, the effects attributable to the administration of federally funded urban programs. This is not to suggest that the impacts of the other two types of programs have been unimportant. On the contrary, a recent Advisory Commission on Intergovernmental Regulations (ACIR) study found that there have been at least 33 regulations that are routinely attached to most federal programs administered through local governments. The regulations cover such issues as: environmental protection, citizen participation, residential location, wage rates, and affirmative action (ACIR, 1978b). These regulations cut across programs and do not even include the numerous program-specific regulations; however, the data required for a full impact assessment of these federal initiatives are lacking. Similarly, for federally funded nonurban programs, the direct local implications in at least one service area—education—have been openly recognized under the School Assistance in Federally Affected Areas program (P.L. 81-874 and P.L. 81-815). However, the bureaucratic impacts, created by the implementation process, need to be teased apart from the service impacts and again go beyond the scope of the present paper.

In dealing with the bureaucratic impacts of federally funded urban programs, this paper will draw from a variety of secondary sources. In addition, the paper includes information from a set of five case studies that specifically examined local bureaucratic effects created by federal programs (Yin et al., 1978). The case studies analyzed the local *administration* of 10 major federal aid programs to cities, including the general revenue sharing program, the community development block grants (CDBG) program, the U.S. Department of Housing and Urban Development (HUD) 701 Planning program, the Comprehensive Employment and Training (CETA) program, economic development grants, urban mass transportation programs, community services programs, the wastewater treatment construction grants program, and the small business loans program. Moreover, the case studies were designed to facilitate the development of aggregate conclusions *across* rather than *within* individual cities.[1] This meant that common topics were covered in each city, and that no attempt was made to develop a within-city view of the peculiar sources of economic and political change.

This cross-city approach has a potential methodological bias inasmuch as local agendas and the apparent unique circumstances of each city may be underappreciated. The response to this potential shortcoming, however, is that if aggregate patterns can be observed across cities in relation to some federal policy issue, one may claim that the relationship is significant, even though local factors may be needed to explain the full meaning of the rela-

---

[1] These two approaches may be likened to the differences in psychology between experimental and clinical methods. The former emphasizes the development of aggregate conclusions, even though an accurate clinical portrait of each individual person cannot be assembled in this manner; the latter provides the clinical portrait but can only rarely support general conclusions across individuals.

tionship.[2] It is the identification of these aggregate patterns that is most urgently needed in order to formulate federal urban policy, and thus it is to this aggregate level that we now turn.

THE FEDERALIZING OF LOCAL BUREAUCRACY

Traditionally, city governments have consisted of a narrow range of agencies whose main functions were to operate such municipal services as: police and fire protection; sanitation collection; parks and recreation facilities; and water, sewer, and other utilities. In addition, most city governments also had the routine range of staff services, including city planning, budgeting, personnel, and administration. The city budget usually contained both expense and capital items, but cities varied across the country regarding the specific organizational structure of each government—some were operated under strong mayors, most were completely separated from the school governance system, and so on.

The growth in the federal role in local affairs has changed this traditional picture. In large and small cities an increasing proportion of the municipal bureaucracy now consists of agencies that deal with federal programs in addition to traditional city services. One hypothesis is that a "counterpart bureaucracy" has emerged—that is, these local agencies are governed more by federal than local requirements and are therefore counterparts to specific federal programs. The counterpart local agencies appear to work in a similar manner from city to city, often serving as an integral part of the implementation apparatus of the federal programs. The characteristics of these counterpart agencies are described in a later section of this paper; first the reasons why these changes have occurred at all must be indicated.

Three types of federal awards

Urban analysts have noted for some time that federal programs may achieve different purposes, depending upon the type of award that is made to a local government. Three general types are possible:

1. General revenue sharing grants;
2. block grants; and
3. categorical grants.

---

[2] The within-city and cross-city approaches both produce different perspectives, both of which are nevertheless correct. From within the city, for instance, it may appear as if an innovative local staff has found a way of using federal funds to support a local priority; the initiative and agenda appear to be local, and little credit would be given to the federal influence. From across cities, these same matches of local projects with federal programs might be observed for a large proportion of the cities studied, hence leading to the opposite conclusion—that federal initiatives or agendas had instigated local changes. Both conclusions are correct, but the main point is that the presence (or absence) of cross-city patterns is the primary determinant in the formulation of federal urban policy.

Independent of the substance of a program, the type of award provides different degrees of discretionary control to local governments, and equity and other distributional issues may also be affected. Thus, one urban strategist has recommended that general revenue sharing awards may be most appropriately used to maintain the financial viability of city governments; block grants may be targeted to serve the needs of special and disadvantaged populations, but in a flexible manner; and categorical grants may be used to support specific innovations and special projects (Haar, 1975, p. 280; for a similar suggestion, *see* Frieden and Kaplan, 1975).

Apart from their strategic importance, the three types of awards also produce different bureaucratic effects at the local level. These are the effects that account, in large measure, for the emergence of the counterpart bureaucracy. Thus, each type of award can be said to have different bureaucratic implications.

General revenue sharing grants are funds that are distributed on a formula basis. Federal monies are allocated in Washington, and checks are simply disbursed from the U.S. Treasury to eligible general-purpose governments on a quarterly basis. When the checks arrive, the money is deposited in the local government's general cash account, and the money is used to support whatever local services are deemed of highest priority by city officials. General revenue sharing funds are thus administered with few federal restrictions, and the local government may not even be able to identify the specific activities that were supported by federal as opposed to local revenues. More important, the bureaucratic implication of a general revenue sharing program is that, at the local level, the administration of the program does not require any separate or new city agency; the local budget office generally deposits the U.S. Treasury checks as it would any other type of revenue.

A *block grant* is administered quite differently, although the initial step is similar to that of general revenue sharing: the distribution of funds among jurisdictions or eligible participants follows an entitlement, whether determined by a fixed formula or on allocations by a federal agency. However, and in contrast to general revenue sharing, after being informed of the approximate dollar amount of the allocation available, a local (or state) agency prepares an application in consultation with a federal office, such as a regional office or an area office. It is important to note that there is a *single* application from each jurisdiction, and this single application covers a *group* of projects or local activities that will be conducted. Moreover, the funds can only be used for a general type of activity, such as employment projects, and are therefore more restrictive than general revenue sharing grants.

If the application is approved (formal approval may or may not involve the headquarters federal office), a letter of credit is issued to the local government. Most important, in regard to bureaucratic impacts, the administration of a block grant program imposes a new bureaucratic burden (some would say "creates jobs") for the local government. A lead agency—sometimes called a prime sponsor—must be created at the local level to apply for the federal funds, coordinate the overall group of projects, and administer the projects. Thus, the prime sponsor, though staffed by local personnel and under local regulations, mainly operates according to demands imposed by federal requirements.

In contrast to these first two types of awards, the *categorical grant* program involves the submission of an application by a local agency or individual to a federal office. The federal office, whether in a region or in head-quarters, reviews the application, and if it is approved, funds are allocated from the U.S. Treasury to the successful applicant. The funds can only be used for the single project that was described in the application. Thus, cate-gorical awards may be spread widely among different local agencies; there may be no single local agency that receives more than one award or that coordinates several applications, awards, or projects.

Trends in federal aid patterns

A significant aspect of these three different types of awards is that their mixture has changed over the past decade. Until 1972, categorical grant pro-grams represented nearly all of the federal funds available to local govern-ments. Since then, however, the proportion of categorical funds has steadily declined, constituting about 75 percent of all federal funds to State and local governments in 1977 (*see* Table 1). In contrast, general revenue sharing funds now comprise about 15 percent of the total and block grants about 10 percent. This shift was a direct result of the politics of the Nixon administration, which emphasized the "decategorization" of grants and decentralization of control over programs (Haider, 1974, pp. 257–82), themes that first emerged in

TABLE 1: Percentage Distribution of Federal Aid Outlays, by Type, Selected Fiscal Years, 1968–77

Type	Fiscal Years			
	1968	*1972*	*1975*	*1977*
General revenue sharing[a]	2%	1%	14%	14%
Block grants[b]	—	1	11	10
Categorical grants	98	97	75	76
Total federal grants	100	100	100	100

Source: ACIR (1978a).

[a] Includes smaller amounts for Antirecession Financial Assistance, shared revenues, payments in lieu of taxes, and other small programs for which expenditures are unconstrained.

[b] Includes totals for block grants such as Partnership for Health, Safe Streets, Social Services, Comprehensive Employment and Training (CETA), and Community Development; a portion may be granted for specific projects under the discretionary allocation provided for by statute.

concrete form when President Nixon submitted several special revenue sharing bills to Congress in 1971 (the four major bills covered education, community development, manpower, and transportation).

The political significance of these bills, together with the legislation on general revenue sharing, is well known. The Nixon administration was attempting to shift the balance of control over federal resources from the Congress to general-purpose governments. In addition, the transition also meant that the federal role would be increasingly limited to an administrative one, with the delivery of actual services to be increasingly in the hands of state and local agencies (Nathan, 1975; and Warren, 1975). By the end of the Ford administration, six years after the submission of the first special revenue sharing bills, the change in federal strategy was still being implemented, with Ford's Fiscal 1978 budget (never implemented) containing renewed proposals for decategorizing grants programs in education and in health (*see* Office of Management and Budget, 1977). Although the strategy had not been extended to its fullest extent, however, the two administrations had created several large, noncategorical programs, authorized by such statutes as: the Omnibus Crime Control and Safe Streets Act of 1968; the State and Local Fiscal Assistance Act of 1972 (renewed in 1976, and responsible for general revenue sharing grants); the Comprehensive Employment and Training Act of 1973 (also renewed); the Housing and Community Development Act of 1974 (also renewed); and the 1974 amendments to the Social Security Act of 1935. Moreover, gradual administrative shifts in certain older programs, such as those operated by the U.S. Community Services Administration (CSA), in which antipoverty funds are allocated to special agencies at the local level, meant that other programs also began to be operated on a noncategorical basis.

At the same time that these shifts were occurring, the overall federal aid to local (and State) governments was also rising dramatically. The rise has been reflected in absolute terms, as well as relative, to local governments' own revenue base. One estimate is that, for State and local governments as a whole, federal aid has increased from about 15 percent of state and local revenues in 1960 to about 35 percent in 1977 (see Figure 1). For large cities, the proportions have been even greater and the rise even sharper. Thus, Table 2 shows that, for 15 large cities, the average percentage of federal aid was about 1 percent in 1957, about 5 percent in 1967, and estimated to be about 48 percent in 1978.

The point, in short, is that the type of awards shifted at the same time that the total amount of federal aid was rapidly increasing. In particular, the increase in block grant funds led to the formation of new or expanded local agencies to administer the programs. In addition, the amount of federal aid to every city government increased to such a significant proportion that other structural changes also occurred. These have given city governments a distinct federal flavor that is described in the following section.

FIGURE 1: Federal Grants-in-Aid as a Percentage of State-Local Receipts from Own Sources, 1960–1977

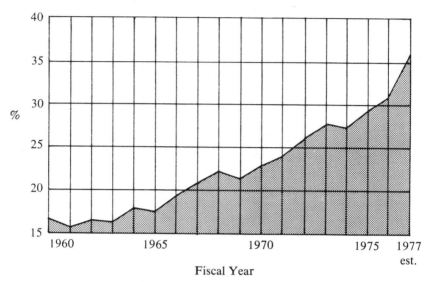

Fiscal Year

Source: ACIR (1978a).

THE FEDERAL IMPACT ON LOCAL BUREAUCRACY

As a result of these changes in federal policies, structural and functional changes have occurred at the local level. The extent of these changes is difficult to determine. Ideally, what is needed is a new survey of local governments that would assess the degree to which these changes have altered the composition of local government. However, at the present time, it is even hard to tell how many municipal employees are now supported, directly and indirectly, by federal funds of one sort or another. Moreover, the significant qualitative impacts—in terms of changed power and functional relationships within local government—would still not be easy to assess. Given the present availability of information, the best that can be done is to identify some of the salient trends, but the final determination regarding their importance must await a comprehensive data collection effort.

There have been at least two general ways in which local bureaucracies have changed in response to the increased federal role. First, new or expanded local agencies have emerged that specialize in administering federal aid programs rather than operating the traditional city services. These new agencies tend to follow bureaucratic rules that are a combination of federal and local regulations. Second, many city governments have established an intergovernmental office of one sort or another, to deal with the coordination of federal aid-gathering. These intergovernmental offices have generally been new to city

TABLE 2: Direct Federal Aid as a Percentage of Own-Source General Revenue, Selected Cities and Fiscal Years 1957–78

	Fiscal Years			
City	1957	1967	1976	1978 Est.
Detroit	1.3%	13.1%	50.2%	76.8%
Buffalo	1.3	2.1	55.6	75.9
Newark	0.2	1.7	11.4	64.2
Cleveland	2.0	8.3	22.8	60.3
Phoenix	1.1	10.6	35.0	58.7
St. Louis	0.6	1.0	23.6	56.1
Philadelphia	0.4	8.8	37.7	53.8
Baltimore	1.7	3.8	38.9	46.4
Chicago	1.4	10.9	19.2[b]	42.1
Atlanta	4.3	2.0	15.1	40.0
Los Angeles	0.7	0.7	19.3	39.8
Boston	[a]	10.0	31.5	30.2
Denver	0.6	1.2	21.2	25.9
Houston	0.2	3.1	19.4	23.8
Dallas	0	[a]	20.0	17.8
Unweighted average of 15 cities	1.1	5.2	28.1	47.5

Source: ACIR (1978b).
[a] Less than .05%.
[b] Percentage based on federal aid, excluding general revenue sharing. Funds withheld pending judicial determination.

government, and mainly represent the intention of the city to obtain as much federal aid as possible. To understand further these two bureaucratic developments, we turn to information collected from five specific cities and the patterns of administration for ten federal aid programs to cities (*see* Yin et al., 1978, for a more detailed description of the five-city study).

Administration of federal aid programs

Table 3 shows the agencies at the local level that are responsible for administering the major federal aid programs in Anaheim, Boston, New Orleans, Savannah, and Milwaukee. The table shows that, in many cases, a single agency is fulfilling a "prime sponsor" role—that is, a local agency is administering pools of awards within a single federal program. This generally means that: (1) there is a certain degree of coordination among projects by the local agency, if only through the use of a comprehensive plan that purports to cover all of the projects and their relative priorities, and (2) there may only be a single application from the local level to the pertinent federal office, covering all of the projects within the program.

Of the 10 federal aid programs that were examined, seven had a local

Table 3: "Prime Sponsors" Identified in Five Case Studies in Relation to Individual Federal Aid Programs

Federal Aid Program		Anaheim	Boston	New Orleans	Savannah	Milwaukee
	City					
General revenue sharing		City Manager's Office*	Office of the Mayor*	Office of the Mayor*	City Manager's Office*	Office of the Mayor*
CDBG		Community Development Department*	Office of Program Development*	Office of the Mayor*	Division of Community Planning & Development*	Community Development Agency*
HUD-701[1]		Four-city consortium*	Boston Redevelopment Authority*	City Planning Commission*	Ogeechee Council of Government	Department of City Development*
CETA-I		Orange County Manpower Commission	Employment and Economic Policy Administration*	Office of Manpower and Economic Development*	Savannah-Chatham Employment and Training Consortium*	Office of the County Executive
EDA-302		Orange County OEDP	Employment and Economic Policy Administration*	Office of Policy, Planning, and Analysis*	No awards	Department of City Development*
EDA-I, II, III, V, IX		No awards	No prime sponsor	No prime sponsor[2]	No prime sponsor	No prime sponsor
UMTA 3, 5, 9[3]		Southern California Association of Governments	Metropolitan Area Planning Council	Regional Planning Commission	Metropolitan Planning Commission	Regional Planning Commission

	Orange County Transit District	Massachusetts Bay Transit Authority	Louisiana State Department of Transportation and Development	Savannah Transit Authority	Milwaukee County Transit System
CSA	Orange County CD Council	Action for Boston Community Development	Total Community Action, Inc.	Economic Opportunity Authority	CR-SD Commission
EPA—wastewater treatment construction grants	Orange County Sanitation District	No prime sponsor	No prime sponsor	Engineering Division*	Milwaukee County Sewage Commission
SBA	No prime sponsor	No prime sponsor	No prime sponsor	No prime sponsor	No prime sponsor

Source: Yin et al. (1978).

* An agency of city government.
[1] Traditional process, prior to current absorption by CDBG program.
[2] A single office appears to generate all proposals, however.
[3] There may be a different prime sponsor for each title.

agency that served a prime sponsor function. Not all of these agencies were within local government itself; some were part of the relevant county government, and others were nonprofit entities that were not organizationally located within any unit of government. These local agencies, whether within or outside of city government, had four common features.

First, the local prime sponsors have generally been established (and abolished) in direct response to the initiation (or cessation) of the relevant federal program. As a further part of a dependent relationship between local agency operations and federal support, the counterpart local unit has usually been supported wholly by federal (or "soft") monies, and not by local revenues. To this extent, the counterpart agency has mainly been a creature of the Federal government. Where these counterpart agencies have gotten older, as in the case of local Community Services Agencies, their sources of funding might have become more diverse; for instance, most of the local CSA agencies now receive their support from a variety of federal programs, including those of CSA, the Department of Health, Education and Welfare (HEW), and the Law Enforcement Assistance Administration (LEAA). However, the funding still consists of "soft" monies.

Second, the local counterpart agency has played a substantial coordinating role with regard to the mixture of projects to be undertaken. Here, the key constraint has been the eligibility criteria of the federal program. Within these criteria, the local agencies have selected and designed their specific projects. However, after such criteria have been met, the local agency can set priorities among projects and develop a broader plan to insure that the array of projects is coherent from a local perspective.

Third, the local counterpart agency has usually had an ongoing relationship to the local federal office that administers the program. In the CDBG program, for instance, four of the five case study cities had established a local office or department to administer the CDBG program. The local HUD area office has provided technical or administrative assistance to this local office on a regular basis. Although the actual use of the grant money is determined by the local agency, there is continual fine tuning in the application-preparation process, regarding the exact amount of the city's allocation, the eligible projects, and any new changes in federal regulations. This vertical coordination between the local agency and the area office may actually result in the fostering of an informal alliance between the two offices, because it is in the interest of both to gain as large an allocation as possible and to see that the project plans are well documented and justified. Similar relationships have been established in the CETA program where, for instance, in Boston the state ETA representative and the head of the local prime sponsor (the Employment and Economic Policy Administration) meet at least once a week for regularly scheduled meetings throughout the year.

Fourth, unless the local prime sponsor has been the same organization for two or more federal aid programs (a situation that appears only to have occurred with Milwaukee's Department of City Development[3] and Boston's Employment and Economic Policy Administration—*see* Table 3), there may be little coordination *among* the local agencies administering the different federal programs. Thus, the counterpart local agencies appear to have developed stronger ties with their local federal offices than with other counterpart local agencies. In Anaheim, for instance, there was little communication between the local revenue sharing and CDBG offices, so that the selection of projects to be funded by one program did not account for projects being funded by the other, even though the two programs were capable, in theory, of supporting joint or otherwise similar projects.

The local prime sponsors have other features that can probably be discerned only after closer analysis on a case-by-case basis. For instance, turnover among federal programs—such as the transition from Model Cities to CDBG programs—may be followed by a parallel turnover among local prime sponsors; the new local prime sponsor may have the same staff (but different titles) as the old prime sponsor. Similarly, each local prime sponsor may implicitly represent an interest group within the local political spectrum. Thus, the administration of general revenue sharing funds often reflects the priorities of the municipal executives—mayors and city managers—whereas the local CDBG and CSA priorities may be more responsive to the demands of low income or minority groups within the city. Some of these implicit political relationships, which are usually difficult to identify from an external vantage point, can sometimes better account for the degree of cross-agency collaboration than can the apparent congruence among the federal mandates for the agencies' programs.

In summary, examination of these five cities demonstrated the emergence of one part of a "counterpart bureaucracy," consisting of local agencies that:

- Are mainly funded by "soft" monies
- Can coordinate the various projects within the pertinent federal program
- Establish close working relationships to the next echelon, e.g., a federal area or regional office—in the hierarchy within that program
- Tend to be isolated from the parallel structures (federal and local) established for other federal aid programs.

Coordination of federal aid-gathering

Many city governments, especially the larger ones, have had special staff people close to the mayor or city manager who have functioned as the chief executive's agency in the intergovernmental arena (Haider, 1974). At the present time, however, city governments have often gone beyond a full-time lobbyist and have created a full-scale intergovernmental office (e.g., an office

---

[3] Milwaukee's Department of City Development has been considered an unusual innovation because it combines traditional community development programs with economic development programs.

of "federal relations" or an office of "intergovernmental relations") to carry out these functions. In part, this expansion has been a reaction to the fragmented structure created by the proliferation of local prime sponsors. In part, the intergovernmental offices have also emerged because of the trend in federal aid to local governments, which has been shown to have risen rapidly over the past two decades. Whatever the combination of motives, these intergovernmental offices constitute a second aspect of the counterpart bureaucracy.

Intergovernmental offices were known to have been created in three of the five case studies: an Office of Intergovernmental Relations formed in 1977 in Anaheim, an Office of Federal Relations established in 1977 in Boston, and a division within the Office of Policy, Planning, and Analysis formed in 1973 in New Orleans. Of the remaining two cities, Milwaukee is also believed to have such an office, and only Savannah appears to lack one. In each case, the new entity has had the explicit purpose of generating and coordinating federal aid activities; it has usually been a close staff office of the municipal executive; it has been dominantly funded from local revenue sources; and it has not usually operated any programs of its own. To get a picture of the operations of these offices, let us examine one of them more closely.

The Office of Federal Relations (OFR) was created by the mayor in February 1977 to serve as the primary liaison between the city and all federal agencies.[4] The OFR's goals are geared toward generating more federal funding for Boston and advocating the city's best interests in Washington. First, the OFR coordinates the funding requests and proposals going from the city to Washington, in order to prevent duplication and to ensure that program requests build on one another. This function amounts to an internal A-95 review process. Second, the OFR searches for new sources of funds from federal agencies that may be matched to city projects. Third, the office reviews proposed changes in federal formulas to determine the impact on Boston; if an anticipated impact is adverse, OFR staff can try to influence the Congress to rewrite the formula. Fourth, in conjunction with a Washington-based city representative, the city has established relations with other organizations such as the Urban Consortium, the U.S. Conference of Mayors, the Council for Urban Development, and the National League of Cities. OFR cites as its accomplishments in the first year of operation the generation of an additional $66.4 million in federal funds, the successful lobbying on an EDA local public works formula to save Boston money, and the advancement of the *Boston Plan*.[5]

---

[4] This description of Boston's federally funded activities is based on an ongoing study of Peter Bateman, a Ph.D. candidate in the Department of Urban Studies and Planning, Massachusetts Institute of Technology, as well as the previously described case study.

[5] The Boston Plan is not so much a plan as it is a comprehensive strategy, developed by Mayor Kevin White, to initiate numerous local projects with at least partial support from federal sources.

Boston has also established a second office that may serve as a forerunner for other cities as well. Because of certain experiences, such as the threatened loss of certain CDBG funds due to a failure to comply with federal hiring regulations, the mayor established an Office of Federal Compliance (OFC) to complement the work of the OFR. The OFC currently has a staff of 14 people and is also funded from local revenues. It serves as the central point of information on federal regulations and has developed systems to ensure that city agencies comply in an efficient and uniform manner. All federal program reports, and equal employment opportunity, affirmative action, and fiscal regulations are handled by OFC, and the importance of its activities may be reflected by the fact that the office is still expanding.

In addition to the establishment of these intergovernmental offices in Boston and elsewhere, another mechanism that local governments have increasingly employed is the support of a city representative located in Washington, D.C. All of the case-study cities, except Savannah, had one or more persons permanently residing in Washington who acted as the city's emissary with the Congress, federal agencies, and national organizations. In some cases, city governments have also relied on their state agencies or representatives in Washington to keep informed on the availability of federal funds or changes in federal policies.

In summary, four of the five case studies show that city governments have created new organizational units to coordinate their federal aid-gathering activities. The city governments studied have developed a common local response to federal aid programs in the form of: (a) a federal relations coordinating office within the local government structure, and (b) a Washington-based representative; both have the primary purpose of obtaining the maximum amount of federal aid. Just as the initial opening of a consulate or embassy signifies more intensive relations between two foreign governments, the emergence of these offices suggests more intensive intergovernmental relations between federal and local governments in the future.

A longer view: cohorts of local organizations?

Although the prominent characteristics of the federal impact on local bureaucracy have only recently become evident, federal programs may actually have had a continuing impact on the structure and function of local governments. Table 4, for instance, arrays the major economic development organizations that have been operating in the five cities. These organizations are listed according to their basic type, their location within or outside of city government, and the year in which the organization was founded.

The most striking pattern is that similar types of organizations were created in all five cities in roughly the same sequence over time. In fact, there appear to be *cohorts of local organizations* across the cities. Among the older organizations, Table 4 indicates that, within city government, most cities have traditionally had a planning commission or an active city planning office (see

TABLE 4: Dominant Economic Development Organizations in Five Cities

City	City Government Agency			Non-City-Government Agency		
	Redevelopment or Renewal Agency	City Planning Agency	Other	Private	Nonprofit Economic Development Corporation	Regional Organization
Anaheim	Anaheim Redevelopment Agency[1] 1961; 15 No	Planning Dept. 19 ?; 50 No	Community Development Dept. 1971; ? CDBG	Anaheim Chamber of Commerce 1921; 12 No	Economic Development Corporation 1978; new No	
Boston	Boston Redevelopment Authority[1] 1957; 325 Urban renewal and housing HUD-701		Off. of Program Development 1976; 20 Model Cities; CDBG Employment and Economic Policy Administration[1] 1977; 80 CETA	Real Estate Board of Chamber of Commerce ?	Economic Development and Industrial Corporation[1] 1970; 20[2] No	Metropolitan Area Planning Council 1963; ? A-95
Milwaukee	Department of City Development[1] 1961; 500 Urban renewal and housing HUD-701 EDA-302		Community Development Agency 19 ?; 24 Model Cities; CDBG	Milwaukee Metropolitan Association of Commerce ?	Milwaukee Economic Development Corporation ?	Southeastern Wisconsin Regional Planning Commission 1960; 100 A-95 Community Relations-Social Development Commission 1963; 350 CSA

	Community Improvement Agency	City Planning Commission	Off. of Policy, Planning, and Analysis[1]	Economic Development Council (part of Chamber of Commerce)		Regional Planning Commission
New Orleans	1969; 73 Urban renewal and housing CDBG	1926; 40 HUD-701	1973; 30 EDA-302	1970; 11 No	—	1962; 40 A-95
Savannah	—	—	—	Savannah Area Chamber of Commerce 1806; 15 No	—	Savannah Port Authority[1] 1925; 7 No; Chatham-Savannah Metropolitan Planning Commission[1] 1955; 29 A-95

KEY:
Name of organization
Yr. created; full-time staff
Prime sponsor role

Source: Yin et al. (1978).
[1] Recipient of EDA grant.
[2] Staff are part of the mayor's Office of Economic Development.

the first two columns of Table 4). These agencies have been responsible for such older federal programs as HUD-701 planning. Outside of city government, the older organizations have typically been an active chamber of commerce.

Regional planning commissions, dealing with area-wide planning, and redevelopment agencies tend to be among the organizations formed during the 1950s and 1960s. A major supposition would be that the growth of both of these types of organizations was facilitated by changes in federal policy—the establishment of the A-95 requirement in the former case and the provision of federal urban renewal and housing funds in the latter. (In most cities, these two types of organizations perform these respective functions.)

Among the newer organizations within city government are the new prime sponsors previously described. In addition, newer types of organizations have been created outside of city government, with one example being the nonprofit, economic development corporation. Such a corporation has been formed mainly to promote industrial development and to collaborate with private sector institutions. This type of organization appears to be more attractive to private sector institutions, which may rightly feel that they can exercise greater influence over a nonprofit corporation than over an agency of local government. This issue was raised, for instance, in the formation of the economic development corporation in Anaheim; in that instance, the creation of an office of economic development within city government had been proposed as an alternative but was not considered desirable from the chamber of commerce's point of view. The separate organizational status appears to be important, even though most of the support for the nonprofit corporation, at least initially, will come from the local government. In some cases, however, the organization may also be empowered to raise funds by issuing its own revenue bonds (e.g., the Economic Development and Industrial Corporation in Boston).

The observation of these gradual changes over time—as represented by an apparent series of local organization cohorts across cities—suggests the potential long-term significance of the federal impact on local bureaucracy. Thus, although we may only now have become sensitive to the federal role because of the visibility of today's counterpart agencies, a gradual transition toward federalization of local government may have been occurring since the 1950s. It is this aspect of change in local bureaucracy that we have called "creeping federalism."

IMPLICATIONS FOR URBAN IMPACT ANALYSES

The preceding sections of this paper have tried to indicate the ways in which the structure and functions of local governments have been affected by federal programs. The main point is that federal urban aid programs have become so significant that their very implementation, often involving a substantial local agency role, has an urban impact that is independent of the substance of the aid program. This paper has argued that these impacts have been of an institutional nature that is difficult to assess, but that is quite observable on the basis of a recently conducted set of case studies in five cities. However, this paper has neglected other impacts that may have resulted from federal regulatory actions as well as nonurban programs that have nevertheless changed the ways in which local governments do business.

In spite of these observations, it may still be claimed that, although these bureaucratic changes appear significant from a case study perspective, they still do not warrant attention in any urban impact analyses because the effects may be minor from a broader, federal perspective. Let us therefore suggest, in a more speculative manner, three propositions concerning the importance of these local bureaucratic effects from the broader, federal perspective. These propositions are that: (1) the bureaucratic impacts affect all of the target variables covered by an urban impact analysis; (2) the impacts have important distributional variations geographically; and (3) the impacts relate directly to basic White House policy goals for urban development. To the extent that these propositions are correct, future urban impact analyses will have to address the bureaucratic impacts of federal programs.

Effect on major variables in urban impact analyses

Urban impact analysis is supposed to focus on the potential impacts of federal programs on five sets of variables: population, employment, income, fiscal capacity of local governments, and "other" variables such as neighborhood condition (*see* Glickman, Chapter 1 above). The first proposition to be advanced here is that *the implementation or bureaucratic effects can influence all of the target variables.*

Several steps would have to be taken to test this proposition. First, it would have to be shown that local government employment as a whole has become one of the largest economic sectors in many central cities. This could be illustrated through available data, but many of the effects are readily visible to the naked eye. The most dramatic of such effects, ironically, have taken place in state capitals across the country, which have generally been small or medium-sized cities that have grown rapidly during the last two or three decades. In many cases, the driving economic force for such growth appears to have been the growth in State and local government employment, especially in such service areas as social services, postsecondary education, and environmental programs. Second, data would be required to show the levels of city government employment that were attributable to federal programs, a proportion that is likely to be large, given that 48% of the revenues of 15 large cities was from federal sources in 1978. However, three different effects would have to be teased apart: local government employment resulting from the programmatic objectives of a federal initiative (e.g., CETA jobs); local government employment resulting from the implementation or bureaucratic impacts; and indirect effects concerning the extent to which federal programs had acted as a stimulant or substitute for the city government's own expenditures.[6] The validity of our main proposition, of course, would depend upon the proportion of employment attributable to the implementation or bureaucratic impacts.

Spatial or distributional effects

A major rationale underlying the conduct of urban impact analyses is not merely that the target variables may be affected, but that there may be significant distributional inequities regarding these variables. The distributional concerns have mainly focused on three geographic groupings (*see* Glickman in this volume): interregional distributions, intraregional distributions, and intrametropolitan distributions. A second proposition to be advanced here is that *the implementation or bureaucratic effects have had significant distributional effects for at least two of these levels (interregional and intrametropolitan).*

At the intrametropolitan level, the effects may even involve alterations in the relative power relationships among local units of government. Again, the major piece of missing data has to do with the proportion of local government employment attributable to the implementation of federal programs. However, if one assumes that this proportion is a constant function of the overall size of federal aid, it can be shown that, for the 10 major federally funded urban programs, the amount of aid administered by local governments varies at the intrametropolitan level. Thus, Table 5 shows that, for the five case-study cities, not all of the 10 programs were administered directly by city government. Some programs were administered by county governments and others by special taxing authorities or nonprofit organizations outside of city government; this proportion varied from metropolitan area to metropolitan area. Overall in Milwaukee, for instance, less than half of the funds flowed through the city government, whereas in Savannah, over three-quarters of the funds have been administered by city government agencies. In general, there may be a greater differentiation of units of governance in large cities, where special taxing authorities and the county government play a more important role vis-à-vis city government. Cross-sectionally, this means that federal programs may differentially influence the balance of governmental power at the local level; longitudinally, the trends may be equally important but have not been, to our knowledge, examined systematically. A potential

---

[6] One study has shown that federal aid to city governments from 1950 to 1970 served a stimulatory and not a substitutive role in relation to the city government's own expenditures (Lyons and Morgan, 1977). Although these effects may have been typical of the era before 1970, when the fiscal condition of city governments was better than it is now, to the extent that federal aid has enhanced the city employment base federal programs may have had a triple effect: the substantive programmatic effects, implementation effects, and the indirect enhancement of increased activity by city governments themselves.

TABLE 5: Proportion of 10 Federal Aid Programs Administered by Local Government, Fiscal 1977

(thousands of dollars)

City	(1) Total Amount Federal Funds	(2) Amount Administered by Local Govt.	(3) (2) as % of (1)
Anaheim	$ 11,107	$ 7,907	71.2
Boston	208,283	125,780	60.4
Milwaukee	69,560[a]	30,685	44.1
New Orleans	55,036	37,593	68.3
Savannah	14,440	11,331	78.5

Source: Yin et al. (1978).

[a] Does not include $55.4 million in revenue sharing funds to State of Wisconsin allocated directly to the public school system.

hypothesis is that, in these metropolitan areas, federal programs have helped to make county governments a more potent political force relative to city government.

At the regional level, there may also be distributional variations, although these probably carry more of an economic rather than institutional effect. The regional effects of federal programs have naturally been a sensitive issue for the last few years, with most of the concerns focusing on the apparent favoring of federal aid to "Sunbelt" over "Snowbelt" regions (Fainstein and Fainstein, 1976; and Perry and Watkins, 1977), as well as the compensatory changes that have been made in specific allocation formulas such as the CDBG entitlements (McFarland, 1978). Even if one is only limited to the effects of government *employment* (and disregards the distribution of program funds as a whole), these regional disparities remain. Federal employment, for instance, is unequally distributed between the Northeast and the "Sunbelt" regions (Morris, 1978). A major hypothesis would thus be that the implementation or bureaucratic effects on local governments also follow the same distributional patterns.

Effect on major policy goals

Because urban impact analyses are just now being initiated within the federal bureaucracy, there is currently a tendency to give too much attention to technical and methodological requirements, and it has been too easy to forget some of the larger policy issues that led to the impact analyses in the first place. Thus, it is useful to ask whether the implementation and bureaucratic impacts that have been identified can be related to some of the original policy goals that, for instance, appeared in the President's Urban Policy statement in 1978 (The White House, 1978). Here, a third proposition to be advanced is that *the implementation of bureaucratic effects extends to some of the major policy goals for urban development.*

The most important policy goal, of course, has been to alleviate conditions in distressed cities. A hypothesis that needs to be tested in the future is whether local government employment attributable to the implementation of federal programs has been more important for distressed cities than non-distressed cities. Furthermore, an argument can probably be made that local government employment is a relatively quick response mechanism for improving the economic conditions of a city-wide population. It may be easier to increase government employment with a minimal lead time, for instance, than to improve economic conditions through attempts to stimulate industrial relocation. Again, data are needed to show the precise degree to which distressed cities rely on employment related to the local administration of federal programs.

A second policy goal has been to increase the cooperation between the public and private sectors in dealing with urban problems. Progress toward this second goal is typically assessed in terms of the dollar value of joint projects or in terms of the dollar investments made by private firms in central cities. However, our observations of the local bureaucratic changes suggest that the amount of coordination can also be reflected in the extent to which joint organizational efforts are found. Thus, in economic development activities, the preceding section of this paper has already suggested that new, nonprofit economic development corporations have emerged in three of the five case-study cities. These new organizations were deliberately formed so that private interests could be integrated with those of the public sector. The potential importance of this type of collaboration is hinted at in a recent, unpublished study (Centaur, 1978), which showed that successfully implemented economic development projects in a nationwide sample were primarily associated with an integrated effort between the private sector (usually the Chamber of Commerce and its development arm) and the public sector (usually the city council or legislature). In contrast, no association was found between successfully implemented projects and either the presence of a strong local advocate for the project or the existence of other organizational arrangements. In short, the implementation and bureaucratic impacts may be the very point at which public-private cooperation is important and should be assessed.

Methodological implications for doing urban impact analyses

These three propositions, suggesting the possible importance of bureaucratic impacts on the target variables in urban impact analysis, on geographic distributions, and on major urban policy goals, begin to indicate some of the dilemmas facing the design of urban impact analyses. First, we have suggested that there are many quantitative impacts associated with the fact that the implementation and bureaucratic effects involve employment by city government, because such an activity is an important economic force in its own right. However, urban impact analyses, as presently designed, only permit the assessment of federal activities on a program-by-program basis, and this piecemeal approach is unlikely to uncover any aggregate employment effect. Second, the issues of intrametropolitan distributions and private-public cooperation suggest that the most important implementation and bureaucratic effects may be of a qualitative nature that is difficult to assess. What has been argued is that there may be major changes occurring in the structure and function of local governments, and that, from a broader historical and intergovernmental perspective, local power relationships have shifted and local governments are slowly becoming federalized. Local affairs may be increasingly being tuned to federal regulations and priorities rather than local diversity and agendas. If such a broad trend exists, it would have great significance for the state of the republic; yet, it is just this sort of impact that the urban impact analyses appear likely to ignore. Whether these two situations—the need to determine aggregate impacts across programs and the need to assess qualitative changes—can be rectified in the near future remains to be seen, in spite of the honorable intentions reflected in this volume of collected papers.

REFERENCES

Advisory Commission on Intergovernmental Relations. *The Intergovernmental Grant System: An Assessment and Proposed Policies.* Washington, D.C., 1978a.
———. "A Tilt toward Washington." *Intergovernmental Perspective* 4, no. 1 (Winter 1978b).
Centaur Management Consultants, Inc. Unpublished manuscript. Washington, D.C., 1978.
Fainstein, Susan S., and Fainstein, Norman I. "The Federally Inspired Fiscal Crisis." *Society*, May/June 1976, pp. 27–32.
Frieden, Bernard J., and Kaplan, Marshall. *The Politics of Neglect: Urban Aid from Model Cities to Revenue Sharing.* Cambridge: MIT Press, 1975.
Haar, Charles M. *Between the Idea and the Reality: A Study in the Origin, Fate, and Legacy of the Model Cities Program.* Boston: Little, Brown, 1975.
Haider, Donald H. *When Governments Come to Washington.* New York: The Free Press, 1974.
Kramer, Ralph M. *Participation of the Poor: Comparative Community Case Studies in the War on Poverty.* Englewood Cliffs: Prentice-Hall, 1969.
Lyons, William, and Morgan, David R. "The Impact of Intergovernmental Revenue on City Expenditures." *Journal of Politics* 39 (November 1977): 1088–97.
McFarland, M. Carter. *Federal Government and Urban Problems.* Boulder: Westview Press, 1978.
Morris, Richard S. *Bum Rap on America's Cities.* Englewood Cliffs: Prentice-Hall, 1978.
Nathan, Richard P. "Special Revenue Sharing." In *Restructuring the Federal System: Approaches to Accountability in Postcategorical Programs*, edited by Joseph D. Sneed and Steven A. Waldhorn. New York: Crane, Russak, 1975.

Perry, David C., and Watkins, Alfred J., eds. *The Rise of the Sunbelt Cities.* Beverly Hills: Sage Publications, 1977.

Pressman, Jeffrey L. *Federal Programs and City Politics.* Berkeley and Los Angeles: University of California Press, 1975.

————, and Wildavsky, Aaron. *Implementation.* Berkeley and Los Angeles: University of California Press, 1973.

U.S. Office of Management and Budget. *Issues '78.* Washington, D.C.: U.S. Government Publications Office, January 1977.

————, Circular No. A-116. Washington, D.C.: U.S. Government Publications Office, August 16, 1978.

Warren, Roland L. "Competing Objectives in Special Revenue Sharing." In *Restructuring the Federal System: Approaches to Accountability in Postcategorical Programs*, pp. 46–60, edited by Joseph D. Sneed and Steven A. Waldhorn. New York: Crane, Russak, 1975.

————, et al. *The Structure of Urban Reform.* Lexington: D. C. Heath, 1974.

White House, The. "New Partnership to Conserve America's Communities." Mimeographed report. Washington, D.C., March 1978.

Yin, Robert K. et al. "Federal Aid and Urban Economic Development: A Local Perspective," unpublished manuscript. Washington, D.C.: Rand Corporation, October 1978.

List of Contributors

Charles Anderson, Assistant Professor of Economics, Rutgers University.

Thomas J. Anton, Professor of Political Science and Public Policy, and Director, Ph.D. Program in Urban and Regional Planning, University of Michigan.

Kenneth P. Ballard, Regional Economist at the Bureau of Economic Analysis, U.S. Department of Commerce.

Roger Bolton, Professor of Economics, Williams College, and Research Associate, Harvard-MIT Joint Center for Urban Studies.

David E. Boyce, Professor of Transportation and Regional Science, University of Illinois at Urbana-Champaign.

Harold L. Bunce, Research Economist, Office of Policy Development and Research, U.S. Department of Housing and Urban Development.

Sheldon Danziger, Associate Professor of Social Work, University of Wisconsin-Madison, and Research Economist, Institute for Research on Poverty.

Paul R. Dommel, Senior Fellow, The Brookings Institution, Washington, D.C.

Matthew Edel, Associate Professor of Urban Studies, Queens College, City University of New York.

Norman J. Glickman, Visiting Scholar, Office of Policy Development and Research, U.S. Department of Housing and Urban Development, and Associate Professor, Departments of City and Regional Planning and Regional Science, University of Pennsylvania.

Edward Greenberg, Professor of Economics and Associate Director, Institute for Urban and Regional Studies, Washington University, St. Louis.

Robert Haveman, Professor of Economics, University of Wisconsin-Madison, and Fellow, Institute for Research on Poverty.

Kathy Jean Hayes, Visiting Scholar, U.S. Department of Housing and Urban Development.

John Helmer, Associate Professor of Sociology, George Washington University, and Chief, Urban Impact Analysis Office, Office of Management and Budget.

Martin Holmer, Office of Income Security Policy, Office of the Assistant Secretary for Planning and Evaluation, U.S. Department of Health, Education, and Welfare.

Susan S. Jacobs, Visiting Scholar, Office of Policy Development and Research, U.S. Department of Housing and Urban Development, and Assistant Professor, Department of Economics, Brooklyn College, City University of New York.

Hyun-Sik Kim, Ph.D. candidate, Princeton University.

Ronald Krumm, Ph.D. candidate, University of Chicago.

Charles L. Leven, Professor of Economics and Director, Institute for Urban and Regional Studies, Washington University, St. Louis.

James T. Little, Assistant Professor of Economics and Associate Director, Institute for Urban and Regional Studies, Washington University, St. Louis.

Ann R. Markusen, Assistant Professor, Department of City and Regional Planning, University of California, Berkeley.

Edwin S. Mills, Professor of Economics, Princeton University.

David L. Puryear, Director of the Division of Economic Development and Public Finance, U.S. Department of Housing and Urban Development.

Stephen H. Putman, Associate Professor, Department of City and Regional Planning, University of Pennsylvania.

David W. Rasmussen, Associate Professor of Economics, Florida State University.

Elizabeth A. Roistacher, Associate Professor, Department of Economics, Queens College, City University of New York.

John P. Ross, Economist, Office of Policy Development and Research, U.S. Department of Housing and Urban Development.

Lester M. Salamon, Deputy Associate Director for Organization Studies, Office of Management and Budget.

Eugene Smolensky, Professor of Economics, University of Wisconsin-Madison, and Fellow, Institute for Research on Poverty.

Karl Taeuber, Professor of Sociology, University of Wisconsin-Madison, and Fellow, Institute for Research on Poverty.

George Tolley, Professor of Economics and Director, Center for Urban Studies, University of Chicago.

Roger J. Vaughan, Economist, Department of Economics, Citibank, New York.

Georges Vernez, Deputy Commissioner, Human Resources Administration, New York City. This paper was written while the author was a Senior Social Scientist with the RAND Corporation.

Susan M. Wachter, Associate Professor of Finance, Wharton School, University of Pennsylvania.

Robert M. Wendling, Regional Economist at the Bureau of Economic Analysis of the U.S. Department of Commerce.

Robert K. Yin, Visiting Associate Professor of Urban Studies and Planning, Massachusetts Institute of Technology.

Library of Congress Cataloging in Publication Data

Main entry under title:
The Urban impacts of Federal policies.

(Johns Hopkins studies in urban affairs) Paper of a conference held in Washington,
D.C., Feb. 8–9, 1979, sponsored by the U.S. Dept. of Housing and Urban Develop-
ment's Office of Policy Development and Research and Johns Hopkins University's
Center for Metropolitan Planning and Research.   1. United States—Social policy
—Congresses.   2. Urban impact analysis—United States—Congresses.   I. Glick-
man, Norman J.   II. United States Dept. of Housing and Urban Development.
Office of Policy Development and Research.   III. Johns Hopkins University.
Center for Metropolitan Planning and Research.   IV. Series.
HN53 1979.   U7   353.9′292   79–2368
ISBN 0–0818–2292–0
ISBN 0–8018–2299–8 pbk.